Pigskin Pride

Celebrating a Century of Minnesota Football

by
Ross Bernstein

Nodin Press

"Pigskin Pride: Celebrating a Century of Minnesota Football"
by Ross Bernstein

(WWW.BERNSTEINBOOKS.COM)

Cover Painting by Tim Cortes

Published by Nodin Press,
(A division of Micawber's Inc.)
525 North Third Street
Minneapolis, MN 55401

Midwest Distribution by: The Bookmen (612) 341-3333

Printed in the USA by Printing Enterprises
Edited by Joel Rippel

ISBN 0-931714-87-7
Library of Congress Card Number: 00-107311

Photo Credits:
Minnesota Vikings: 22-67
Rick Kolodziej: 39, 45, 47, 48, 52, 54-58, 59-64, 66-67, 189
Vince Muzik: 65-66
University of Minnesota: 6, 11, 71, 74-117
Minnesota State High School League: 151-184
Minnesota State Football Coaches Assoc.:151-184
Pioneer Press: 28, 29, 31, 35, 55
Minnesota Historical Society: 4, 8-9, 69, 70
Northeast Minnesota Historical Center: 15
RB Collection: 7, 10-14, 21, 117,
John Gilbert: 16
University of Minnesota-Duluth: 138-140
St. Cloud State University: 146-48
Minnesota State University, Mankato: 148-50
Bemidji State University: 141-42
Southwest State University: 144
Augsburg College: 123-124
St. John's University: 17, 119-122, 136
University of St. Thomas: 18, 130-32
Hamline University: 134-35
Concordia College: 136
Gustavus Adolphus College: 127-29
St. Olaf College: 133-34
Carleton College: 126-27
Bethel College: 125
Jerry Seeman: 73
LeRoy Nieman: 73
Charles Schulz: 68

Acknowledgements:
I would really like to thank all of the people that were kind enough to help me in writing this book. In addition to the countless college
and university Sports Information Directors that I hounded throughout this project I would like to sincerely thank all of the men and
women that allowed me to interview them. In addition, I would particularly like to thank my publisher, and friend, Norton Stillman.

Tim Cortes	Ardie Eckhart	Tim Kennedy	Andy Johnson	Bob Nygaard	Mike Hemmesch
Paul Giel	Karen Zwach	Jim Martin	Mike Mohalis	Gene McGivern	Tony Nagurski
John Randle	Anne Abicht	Paul Allen	Howard Voigt	Dave Wright	Ralph Anderson
Bob Hagen	LeRoy Nieman	Edna Poehner	Ron Christian	Greg Peterson	Pro Football Hall of Fame
Dick Tressell	Ann Johnson	Corey Gasman	Chris Owens	Paul Allen	Steph Reck
Terry Turek	Tom Porter	Don Stoner	Chris Blisette	Ron Christian	Kelly Loft
Randy Johnson	John Sumner	Kurt Daniels	Tom Clark	Julie Nagel	Todd Rendahl
Tony Nagurski	Sarah Maxwell	Tim Trainor	John Griffin	Jim Cella	*H.J. Pieser*

For my wonderful wife Sara,
thank you for being such an amazing person.
I love you more than ever.

Cover Artwork by Tim Cortes

I would especially like to express my gratitude to Minnesota sports artist, Tim Cortes, for allowing me the privilege of showcasing his new gridiron masterpiece entitled: *"First-and-Ten Minnesota,"* on the cover of my new book. I couldn't be more pleased with the final product and simply can't thank him enough for all of his hard work. He is not only an amazing artist, he is also a wonderful friend.

One of the nation's premier photo realism artists, Cortes uses colored pencils as his preferred medium. Hundreds of his collectible lithographs have been sold throughout North America and his clients are a venerable who's-who of American sports. From Shaquille O'Neal to Mark McGwire and from Wayne Gretzky to Troy Aikman, Cortes has been commissioned to create countless commemorative works of art over the past decade.

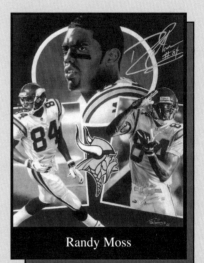

Randy Moss

His paintings have also been featured in numerous venues around the world, including: the US Hockey Hall of Fame, Franklin Mint, Kelly Russell Studios and Beckett's Magazine, as well as on trading cards, pro sports teams' game-day programs, and in various publications. Known for his impeccable detail, Cortes has dedicated his life to the pursuit of celebrating the life and times of many of the world's most famous athletes and the sporting events in which they play.

Cortes grew up in Duluth, where he later starred as a hockey goaltender at Duluth East High School. After a brief stint in the United States Hockey League, Cortes went on to play between the pipes for two seasons in the mid-1980s for the University of Minnesota's Golden Gophers. Cortes then decided to pursue his passion of art and sports full-time, and enrolled at the prestigious Minneapolis College of Art and Design.

Today Tim lives in Duluth with his wife Kathy and their two children. He continues to play senior hockey and also gives back by coaching both youth football and hockey.

Here are just a few of Cortes' works for you to enjoy. If you would like to purchase a signed, limited edition print of "First-and-Ten Minnesota," or any other of his hundreds of works of art, please check out his web-site or contact his new studio in Duluth, where you, too, can own a piece of sports history.

Tim Cortes Studio
Original Sports Art

Tim Cortes Studio
921 North 40th Avenue East
Duluth, MN 55804
(866) 525-2425 (toll free)

www.timcortesart.com

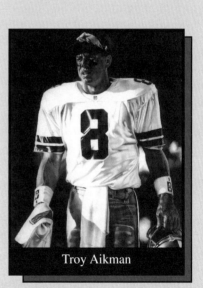

Troy Aikman

Patrick Roy

1998 Olympic Gold

Michael Jordan

Table of Contents

Foreword by Paul Giel

As a young boy, Paul Giel grew up playing football on the sandlots of Winona during the Great Depression. There, he would often try to emulate the smooth moves of his childhood hero, Gopher Halfback Bruce Smith. Paul's imagination was refueled every Saturday morning, when he religiously listened to his beloved Gophers on the radio. Soon he grew into an incredible prep athlete in his own right, starring in football, baseball and basketball at Winona High School. By 1950, not only was he one of the most celebrated prep football prospects in Minnesota history, he also had an opportunity to sign on with several major league baseball teams right out of high school as well. The kid was a natural, and luckily for us, he had decided long ago that he too was going to wear the maroon and gold.

Giel came in and literally took the Gopher sports world by storm. By the time he had finished his illustrious career in Minnesota, he had shattered most of Bruce Smith's records while single-handedly rewriting the record books. All in all, he rushed for 2,188 yards, caught 281 passes for 279 yards, and posted 417 return yards on both punts and kicks, for a total of 3,165 career all-purpose yards which also included 22 touchdowns — a number that still ranks eighth all-time as of the new millennium.

He was a throwback. Not only was he an unbelievable halfback, but he was also a tremendous quarterback, defensive back, punter, punt returner, kick returner, and sometimes even kicked. It is a wonder how he ever had time to come off the field to catch his breath!

So successful was Giel athletically, as well as academically, that in 1954 he was awarded the prestigious Big Ten Medal of Honor. In football he was a two-time All-American halfback, the first-ever two-time Big Ten MVP, and in 1953 was named as the Player of the Year. He even finished runner-up to Notre Dame's Johnny Lattner in the Heisman Trophy race that same year, in what remains the closest balloting ever recorded. In addition to all of that, he also starred on the baseball diamond, where, as a pitcher on Dick Siebert's Gopher Baseball teams, he also earned All-American honors.

His tenure as "Mr. Everything" at the U of M, however, was just a springboard for bigger and better things to come in the world of sports. He is truly a home-grown hero in more ways than one. Despite being drafted by the NFL's Chicago Bears, Giel opted to instead try his hand at professional baseball with the New York Giants. It would be the beginning of a marvelous six-year major league career, interrupted only by a two-year stint to serve his country in the military. He finished up his pitching career with his hometown Twins, back in 1961, before finally hanging up the spikes for good that same year.

From there he simply did it all, working first for the Vikings doing public relations and game management; followed by an eight year career as Sports Director of WCCO Radio, while also broadcasting prep, college and pro sports. In 1972 he was asked to come home, and serve as the University's Athletic Director, a position he would gladly accept and perform masterfully for more than 17 years in Gold Country. When that was up he even became a Vice President with the North Stars. Having seemingly covered every sport possible in the Land of 10,000 Lakes, in 1990 Paul settled down and took over as the Vice President of the Minneapolis Heart Institute Foundation, where, to date, he has helped raise nearly $10 million for heart health research and education. It was only fitting that a man with a heart as big as Paul's round out his illustrious career at such an appropriate place.

With an unbelievable resume like that, who better than to represent the past century of gridiron greats than our very own "Winona Phantom," Paul Giel.

"I first met Ross back in 1997, when he interviewed me for his book 'Fifty Years • Fifty Heroes.' While I was honored to be included in that unbelievable undertaking, about the history of all Minnesota sports, I was particularly humbled when he asked me to write the foreword for 'Pigskin Pride.' To be the spokesperson, so to speak, for the past 100 years of Minnesota football is quite an extraordinary responsibility. But I am excited about it, because I believe that Minnesota football, from top to bottom, is second to none."

"From Bernie Bierman's national championship teams of the 1930s and '40s to the days of Bud Grant and the four Superbowls, we have been blessed with a lot of tremendous talent to come through here over the years. Overall, I think the state-of-the-state of Minnesota football is strong, and is only going to get better. Denny Green is a solid coach with the Vikings, and they are only a few bounces away from getting deep into the post-season; the Gophers have definitely turned the corner and appear to be headed in the right direction under Coach Mason; and our high school programs continue to improve year in and year out."

"Sure, it's a tough time right now with the new stadium issues and what not going on, but overall, our major sports programs seem to be on the rise. It's competitive though, and I think that's good. I mean you've got the Gophers, Vikings, Twins, Timberwolves and now the Wild, all competing in a small market for only so many sports entertainment dollars. Not to mention the great outdoors — which could be considered by many to be the sixth major franchise to compete with. Minnesotans love to work hard and play hard, and one thing is for sure, if their team is not winning, they have a lot of other things to do with their time and money."

"As far as the prep game goes, overall, I think that the caliber of play in the youth and high school leagues is just unbelievable. To see how far they have come since I was a kid is really something. The coaching, the talent and the size of these kids truly boggles the mind. Bigger-faster-stronger is an understatement when you see young men who are six-feet-four, 225 pounds with 4.5 speed. That's just frightening! I'm just glad they weren't all that big when I was playing, or I never would've gotten as far as I did."

"I'm also glad to see that many of our kids today are getting the opportunity to play and learn at major Division I schools — because that's what it's really all about. Sure, it's not the same as the old glory days back in the 1930s and '40s, when the University's rosters were lined with all Minnesota kids, but as a state, we are contributing more and more onto the national scene. Coach Mason is doing a great job of recruiting, landing and developing more and more of the local and national blue-chippers, which is imperative to our program's success."

"In addition, I really like the fact that we have so many Division II and III schools here for kids to play at as well. We have a lot of pretty dog-gone good football players in this state and it's great to see so many kids who maybe don't have a shot at playing D-I, striving to go on and play at the next level after high school. The MIAC is a wonderful conference, and our D-II schools: Mankato, Duluth and St. Cloud, have great programs too. I recently went to a St. John's vs. St. Thomas game up in Collegeville, and I have to tell you, that was some darn good football! In addition to being entertaining, it was great to see those kids playing for the love of the game, knowing that none of them are receiving any scholarships."

"All in all though, with the exception of the youth game, football today is big business. And frankly, I don't miss the pressure of it all. But I can tell you this. Being a Gopher meant so very much to me that it is really hard to put into words. It had been a dream of mine since I was a kid and it was without question the wisest decision I ever made in my entire life. The opportunities that it afforded me both academically and athletically were immeasurable. It truly made me who I am today. To play for my home-state school, in front of so many wonderful fans who supported me so much through all those years was an honor I can't even begin to describe. Sometimes I have to pinch myself because it seems like a dream-come-true."

"It has been an amazing first century of football here in Minnesota, and as we head into the next millennium of gridiron action, I'm sure that it will only get better and better. We can all look forward to plenty of Prep Bowls, Rose Bowls, and Super Bowls... I just wish I could be around to see them all!"

Introduction

The epiphany behind "Pigskin Pride" was to celebrate the wonderful heritage of football that we, as Minnesotans, so dearly love and respect. Minnesota has an amazing football tradition, and I am honored and humbled to be able to bring so much of it to life for everyone to enjoy in my new book. When I first started writing this more than a year ago, I was immediately taken by just how much information there was about the sport of football in our state. This led to an interesting dilemma on just how I was going to disseminate it all. I mean there are literally hundreds, if not thousands of players, coaches, administrators, media personalities and others, who are deserving of being in a book such as this, and as a result, it was extremely difficult to put it all together. Knowing this, I have to issue a caveat of sorts to explain my rationale for how I chose to tackle a subject that is so passionate and yet so controversial with so many Minnesotans — the game, and lifestyle of football.

I have chosen to focus primarily on the historical side of the game for this book, and tried to chronicle as best as possible the true history of the game over the past 100 years. It was an arduous task, but one that was inspiring to complete. All in all, there were more than 400 sources that went into the project, not to mention an additional 50 interviews. Undoubtedly, and expectedly, whenever a book such as this is written, people usually get bent out of shape when they realize that so-and-so wasn't mentioned, or that he or she got more ink than so-and-so. I guess that is just the nature of the beast with stuff like this, and all I can say is that I tried to be arbitrary and objective in my research, and hopefully the vast majority of people that should be in here, are in here. For those who I have overlooked, or simply did not have the space to mention, I sincerely apologize. Believe me, it was a difficult process to have to eliminate so many wonderful biographies and funny stories because I simply did not have the real-estate to mention them. My main objective was to celebrate the positive aspects, such as the people, big games, history, and drama of football in the Gopher State, and hopefully I have succeeded in my mission.

Growing up in the southern Minnesota town of Fairmont, I loved to play and watch football. Fran Tarkenton, Ahmad Rashad and the rest of the Purple People Eaters were among my earliest childhood heroes, and I can still vividly remember getting to go up to Mankato with my dad and two brothers to watch the team practice during their Summer training camp. To see those guys up close and personal was a really special thing, and something that I have never forgotten.

I can also remember playing football in our backyard during the Summers and Falls, coming in only when it was simply too dark to see the ball. We grew up on Interlaken Golf Course, and would love sneaking out onto the fairways to play pick-up games at dusk on that beautiful, soft grass. I went on to follow in the footsteps of my two big brothers and played high school football for the Fairmont Cardinals. We had a great program down there, led by Tom Mahoney, who, at the time, was the state's all-time winningest coach.

As an offensive guard and a defensive end, I was fortunate enough to learn the game on both sides of the ball. I learned so much from the game, and still to this day, have a passion for it like no other. While I still enjoy playing competitive hockey, and can't get enough golf, I absolutely live and die for Sunday afternoons to watch the Purple.

Football has become that way for a lot of Minnesotans, who, these days are fortunate enough to be watching some pretty good Gopher games on Saturday, and even better Vikings games on Sunday. But for many, Friday nights are simply where it's at. While high school football isn't quite the same in Minnesota as it is in say, Texas, it is still a pretty big deal up here in the northwoods. I know that for those few, sacred Autumn Friday nights down in Fairmont, when teams like New Ulm, Blue Earth and Worthington came to town to do battle in Cardinal Park, I really never thought it could get any better than that. In small towns like where I grew up, the whole community came out to support us, and it was just incredible.

One thing I learned from those experiences though, was just how much Minnesotans love, respect and desire the game of football. It is such a part of our fabric of life here, and seems to touch nearly everyone in some way or another.

As we head into the new millennium, the future of football in the Land of 10,000 Lakes looks great. The Vikes are rock-solid under Denny Green; the Gophers have done a 180-degree turn in the right direction under Glen Mason; our small colleges, led by John Gagliardi up at St. John's, who is on the verge of becoming college football's all-time winningest coach, look better than ever; and our youth and high school kids keep improving and moving on up to the next levels, year in and year out. All in all, the state-of-the-state looks good, and is only getting better.

From the Duluth Eskimos to the Minneapolis Marines, and from the Golden Gophers to the St. Thomas Tommies, Minnesota has seen its fair share of gridiron heroes through the years. It has been a wonderful experience to learn about the first 100 years of Minnesota football, and it will surely be an amazing journey to see where we can aspire to in the next century.

So, sit back, relax, crack open a tall beverage, and get ready to read about some good ol' fashioned Minnesota football. Hopefully you will have half as much fun reading about and celebrating this amazing tradition as I did getting the opportunity to bring it all to life.

The 1987 Fairmont High School Juggernaut
(Yours truly playing iron-man football at a mean buck-seventy-five... Oh, those were the days!)

Football's roots in America go back a long, long way. We're talking ancient history here folks. That's right, evidence of games in which a ball was kicked and thrown as a sport has been found in both the writings of the ancient Greeks as well as in Biblical literature. The Greeks had even mastered a game called "harpaston," in which two opposing sides battled one another by passing, kicking or carrying a ball, across a designated line on the opposing side of a playing field.

The Chinese played a game called "Tsu chu" as early as 300 B.C., and the Japanese played a similar sport called "Kemari" around 100 A.D. In around 29 B.C., the Romans came up with a similar game, called "follis," which featured some 30 players per side vying to score by carrying or kicking a ball across a goal line. Later, during the Middle Ages, an Italian game called "calcio" emerged, which was a rugby-like game that was played on a square field. Through the ages almost every culture and ancient tribe has founded their own type of sporting amusement, and the roots to modern football are probably an amalgam of many of them. Irish antiquarians claim that some form of football had been played in their land for more than 2,000 years, while the Polynesians, Celts and Native Americans also made similar claims.

In around the year 1040 or so, a dead Dane may have also helped to promote the game. You see, at that time Britain was in and out of war with Denmark. One day, in a remote township, some kids dug up a buried soldier and began to kick the corpse's head around in an act of fun and rage. Soon other local townspeople joined in and the fun began. Once their feet got sore enough from kicking that poor sap's crusty melon, they decided to continue the game with a softer, leather ball.

Great Britain can claim the modern game of rugby, however, which was an off-shoot of English football, or soccer. By the 1400s football-like games were being played in a crude form throughout the United Kingdom, as a very rough and violent sport. In the mid-1600s the games of "hurling" and "camp-ball" emerged as a sort of combination between rugby and soccer, with a lot of running and very little kicking in order to score a goal on a goal-tender. These contests, by historical accounts, were barbaric to say the least.

By the 1800s football and rugby were in full swing throughout England and much of Europe. In 1871 the Rugby Football Union was formed, in an effort to bring uniform conformity to all of the individual schools as well as small communities which had added their own "house rules" to the game.

At this point, the rugby players became known as "handlers," while the soccer players became known as "dribblers." (Believe it or not, "soccer" is actually slang for the word "association.") Another innovation to the games came when the players decided to replace the round ball with an oval, leather one, encasing a crude blown-up or stuffed bladder, which was nicknamed as a "pigskin."

Soon the game was brought to North America via Canada, when the English settlers came across the pond to find work and religious freedom. Soccer and rugby quickly came down to the east coast, where it became quite popular at many of the Ivy League colleges during the mid-1800s.

In those days the playing areas were small and usually only kicking was permitted. The ball could not be carried and there was no forward passing allowed. The English rugby rules were gradually modified over the years, and have since developed into the modern American game of football. The Americanized version is a much more violent rendition of the British one, but that's just how we Yanks like it I suppose.

Football began to boom in popularity across the country by the late 1850s, and by the 1870s, it had found its way to Minnesota. By all accounts, Shattuck Academy, in Faribault, was the epicenter of the game in the Land of 10,000 Lakes. That's because there were many prep schoolers from the east coast who went there during this time, and with them they brought their new shiny leather pigskins. In fact, it was those same "Shad" cadets who introduced the game to the University of Minnesota during that same era. Believe it or not, back in the day, Shattuck used to whip the Gophers on a regular basis!

The game has since come a long way. It has remained a constant here in Minnesota, however, both on the collegiate level and also professionally, which is where our story begins.

The History of the Minneapolis Marines & Red Jackets

Minnesota's first taste of big-time pro football came back in 1921, when the Minneapolis Marines, a long-time semi-pro club which had played throughout the Twin Cities, joined the upstart American Professional Football Association. The APFA then folded in 1922 and reemerged as the National Football League, of which, the Marines, who were owned by local businessmen Johnny Dunn and Val Ness, became charter members of and played in for the next three seasons.

Prior to playing big-time pro football, however, the Marines were one of several outstanding local semi-pro clubs which had played competitively against teams from throughout the Midwest. While pro football was something relatively new in the 1910s and '20s, the high school and college game was thriving during this time, and young men from across the Land of 10,000 Lakes still wanted to continue to play the game after graduation.

The Minneapolis Park Board's Municipal Amateur Athletic Association served as a governing body to many of the independent semi-pro and amateur club teams that came and went during this era. Among them included: the "St. Paul Ideals," "East 26th Street Liberties," "Emerson's," "Deans," "Gedney Pickles," "Northern Pacific Apostles," "Hallie Q. Brown," "Fighting Margarets," "Camden Athletic Club," "Triangles," "Margaret Playground," "Junior Champs," "Minneapolis Park," "Chippewas," "Stillwater, Army-Navy's," "Duluth

The 1910 Senior League Champion "Laurels"

KC's (Knights of Columbus)," "Judeus" (a predominantly Jewish team) and "Phyllis Wheatley" (a predominantly Black team). In addition, there were also several all-star teams that would play local college and semi-pro teams, which included the "Minneapolis All-Stars," "Duluth All Stars" and the "Northland's" (sponsored by the Northland Oil Co.).

These teams, which often played for regional, mythical, city and even neighborhood championships, played throughout the Twin Cities at places such as Camden Park, Parade Stadium, Bottineau Field, Lexington Park and Nicollet Park. (Lexington and Nicollet Parks were also the home to the minor league St. Paul Saints and Minneapolis Millers baseball clubs.)

The Marines were the class of this group though, dominating regional play during the pre-W.W.I era. They used to battle teams from the strong Ohio and Illinois leagues, even laying claim to several "Northwest Championships." In 1917 the

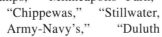

The 1935 "Phyllis Wheatley's" were one of Minnesota's first African American football teams.

Marines beat the Rock Island Independents, one of the marquis teams of the time, in front of more than 10,000 fans at Nicollet Park to win one of their most celebrated titles. The Independents got the last laugh though, when they lured many of Minneapolis' best players to come play for them that next season. Among the defectors were former Gopher All American Defensive End Bobby Marshall (one of the first African Americans to play pro ball), Quarterback "Rube" Ursella and Tackle Walt Buland. With the exodus, the team hit the skids.

Football was a different game back in the day. The players were two-way starters, the ball was bigger and harder to throw, the quarterback had to be one yard behind the center when the ball was snapped, and had to be five yards behind the line of scrimmage if he was going to attempt a pass. It was a smash-mouth style of play that featured big, bruising running backs and a lot of colorful characters. The men all worked, typically blue-collar jobs, and played just for the fun of it. Beer and pizza after the game was usually payment enough for most of the players.

In 1921 the Marines, led by Coach Rube Ursella, who had returned from playing in Rock Island, joined the first pro football league, the American Professional Football Association. The APFA was organized during a meeting that Fall held in Canton, Ohio by a bunch of pigskin pundits at the "Jordan and Hupmobile" car dealership. Fully 21 teams joined up for the league's inaugural season, paying the $75 franchise fee for admission.

Minneapolis, not quite ready for the jump to full-time big-league football, decided to play as many non-league sandlot games as they did league-sanctioned ones, in order to get some more seasoning. The team won all of its non-league games, beating the likes of the semi-pro Ideals and Emersons, but finished with just a 1-3 regular season record, good for just 13th place in the league

The 1919 St. Paul Ideals

Red Jackets' stars: Steponovich, Wilson, Haycraft and Lundeell

that year. They lost their opener, 20-0, to the Chicago Cardinals, but then played the mighty Packers brilliantly, losing just 7-6, in Green Bay, on a missed extra-point. They rebounded that next Sunday though, beating up on the Columbus Panhandles at home, 28-0. The team then lost its season finale to Rock Island, 14-3, to finish out the year. Several games were canceled due to inclemental weather, which contributed to the team's low number of games played.

In 1922 the APFA folded and was renamed as the NFL. The teams were then given the opportunity to acquire a new franchise, at which time the teams' owners, Johnny Dunn and Val Ness, promptly signed up. And with that, the NFL's "Minneapolis Marine Football and Athletic Club Incorporated," was officially born.

Coach Russell Tollefson was brought in to lead the troops for the 1922 campaign, but was only able to produce another paltry 1-3 record, good for just a 13th place finish. After getting blanked 17-0 and 3-0, by the Dayton Triangles and Chicago Cardinals, respectively, the Marines came back to beat a very good Oorang Indians squad, 13-6. Oorang, a team of Native Americans, was led by the legendary Hall of Fame Running Back, Jim Thorpe, who tallied on a short run in the loss. The team then rounded out their season with a very close 14-6 loss on November 12th to the Packers, in Green Bay.

In two seasons the club was undefeated at home, but winless on the road. That trend would continue in 1923 as well, when the Marines improved to post a 3-5-1 record under new player/coach, Harry Mehre. The team got off to a good start when they won the City Gridiron Championship by defeating the local Emerson's, 7-2, at Nicollet Park. The north side Emerson's rallied in the final moments of the game, but came up short on the one-yard line. Fullback Louis Pahl, who used to play for the St. Paul Ideals, scored the only touchdown of the game, after St. Olaf's Elnar Cleve and Eber Simpson caught key passes from Kaplan to get it to the five-yard line. From there the bruiser plowed in for what would prove to be the game-winner. Pahl and End Louis Mohs, both St. Thomas grads, proved to be the stars of the game, and celebrated by hoisting the championship trophy after the game.

The Marines opened their regular season with a pair of shut-out losses to both Green Bay, 12-0, and then to their in-state rivals, the Duluth Kelly's, 10-0. They rebounded in Game Three to blank Jim Thorpe and the Oorang Indians, 23-0, in front of a jam-packed Nicollet Park crowd. (One of the stars of the Oorang club was a Native American halfback from the White Earth Reservation named Jim Guyon, who would go on to be inducted into the Pro Football Hall of Fame.) Eber Sampson opened the scoring in the second quarter after Louis Pahl and Hamline's Sidney Kaplan had taken the ball to the three-yard line. Later in the quarter, Kaplan kicked a pretty 55-yard field goal, followed by Tackle Rudolph Tersch's 30-yard fumble recovery for a touchdown to make it 17-0. The Marines' final score came late in the fourth when Kaplan caught a long touchdown pass from Einar Irgens to seal the deal. The game was quite the spectacle for the Twin Cities crowd, which was entertained by a group of Native Americans from the White Earth Reservation who, in addition to cheering on Joe Guyon, performed a ceremonial pow-wow at half-time.

Nicollet Park

From there the Marines lost a couple of tough road games at both Chicago and Duluth by the identical scores of 9-0. They rebounded back in Week Six, however, beating a solid Racine Legion club, 13-6, at Nicollet Park. The street cars were running non-stop for this one, as the Marines kicked off to a full house. Racine, who had beaten the always-tough Packers and Bears that season, opened the scoring on a short touchdown run that capped a 65-yard scoring drive. Minneapolis then rallied back, first behind Louis Mohs, who leaped high into the air in the back of the goal line to catch Kaplan's 20-yard pass for a touchdown. Kaplan missed his drop kick though to keep it tied at six apiece. Then, behind Louie Pahl's punting, which kept Racine on the defensive in the second half, Minneapolis caught a break. That's when Harry Mehre intercepted a key pass and returned it all the way down to Racine's 35-yard line. From there Kaplan struck again, this time finding Elnar Cleve out of a swarm of bodies for the game-winning touchdown catch.

The Marines managed a respectable 6-6 tie out of Rock Island that next week at home, and then came right back and beat them 6-5 the week after at their house in Illinois. They rounded out their season with a 23-0 drubbing at the hands of Racine, but felt good about their much-improved season.

Leading the charge that year was Quarterback Sid Kaplan, who went 14 of 43 for 220 yards, threw a pair of touchdowns, rushed for 43 more and kicked several field goals. Halfback Dick Hudson led the team in rushing with 98 yards, while Fullback Louie Pahl added 79 yards and a pair of touchdowns as well. Louie Mohs was the team's leading receiver with five catches for 108 yards and a touchdown. In addition, Marine's Center Harry Mehre was selected to the 1923 All-Pro team.

The 1924 season was a forgettable one in Minneapolis, as the Marines posted a big donut by going 0-6, and finishing dead last in the league. So bad was their performance, that they didn't even score until their fourth game of the season, a 28-7 loss to the Milwaukee Badgers. For the year they were outscored by the pathetic margin of 108-14. The lone highlight was seeing Oscar Christianson earn All-Pro honors for his outstanding play at Defensive End. With the team's almost non-existent offense, Christianson was certainly out on the field enough on the defensive side of the ball that season to deserve it!

As a result, the franchise went inactive following the 1924 season. With the team's two seasons of on-the-field and box-office losses, team owners Val Ness and Johnny Dunn, who by then was serving as the NFL's Vice President, decided to stop the bleeding. They did, however, continue to maintain membership in the league by paying their annual fees and assessments. Then, in 1929, after taking a four-year leave of absence, the two decided to resurrect their dormant franchise as a new incarnation: the Minneapolis Red Jackets. This time they were determined to recruit more marquis college players, who

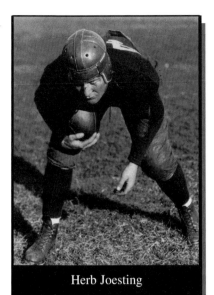

Herb Joesting

could get them over the hump. They started with a couple of great ones, in Gopher All-Americans Herb Joesting and George Gibson.

Incidentally, the Marines continued to play semi-pro ball, outside of the NFL during that four-year period from 1925-28, even winning the 1927 "Mythical Northwest Title" by beating the "Duluth All Stars" up at Athletic Park in the Zenith City.

Behind Fullback Herb Joesting, "the Owatonna

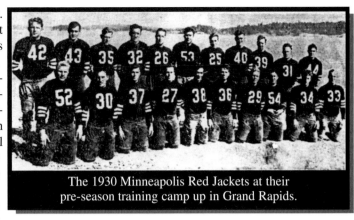

The 1930 Minneapolis Red Jackets at their pre-season training camp up in Grand Rapids.

Thunderbolt," who served as the team's player/coach, and his assistant coach, George Gibson, the team set out to prepare for the upcoming season by holding its preseason training camp up north at Clef Camp, near Grand Rapids on Lake Pokegama. After a successful two weeks of hell, the team came home and prepared to go to battle. The league had improved over the past couple of seasons, and they knew that the challenges ahead of them were not going to be easy.

"There is no comparison between professional football of the present day and our time," Joesting later recalled. "The game has come a long way. But we had a lot of good players in the old days. You couldn't make a team just on a college reputation. It was a tough league, no place for boys."

After winning a couple of preseason games, the Red Jackets opened their season at Madison, Wis., where they were beaten 19-6 by the Chicago Bears. They then lost to those same Bears that next Sunday, in Chicago, this time by the much closer margin of 7-6. They rebounded to take Game Three by beating the Chicago Cardinals, 14-7, thanks to Joesting's pair of short TD runs. But from there it got real ugly, as the team got outscored by more than a three-to-one margin of 185-48, and posted seven straight losses to the Packers (twice), Bears, Cardinals, Providence Steam Rollers, Frankford Yellow Jackets and Staten Island Stapletons.

When it was all said and done, the 1929 Red Jackets had unfortunately picked up right where the old Marines had left off, finishing in last place with at dismal 1-9 record. The lone bright spot saw Tight End Bob Lundell being named to the 1929 All-Pro team.

In 1930, George Gibson was promoted to player-coach, where he received a salary of $3,900. In addition, Gibson also moonlighted as an assistant coach at his alma mater, the University of Minnesota, where he was taking graduate courses in Geology. Determined to turn the franchise around, the team once again boarded a bus and headed up north to Grand Rapids to work out the kinks. After a solid camp, several new players joined the team, including Gophers Mally Nydahl, Kenny Haycraft, Wayne Kakela and southpaw kicker Art Pharmer. Another addition was Oran Pape, the "Iowa Flash" who had single-handedly beaten the Gophers in the closing minutes of the 1928 and 1929 contests.

"The owners commissioned me to get some top-notch players," said Gibson. "Nate Barrager — later all-pro several times at Green Bay, and Tony Steponovich and John Ward of USC were also signed up, giving us a terrific roster of players."

There were even several local players from some of the small colleges too. End Wilbur "Gloom" Lundell, one of Gustavus Adolphus' all-time stars, was there, as was Tackle Chief Franta and Guard Jack Corcoran, both of St. Thomas, and Halfback Vernie Miller of St. Mary's — who had led the country in scoring with 138 points in 1929. Former Hamline Tackle Wayne Kakela also joined the team that year, while continuing to coach at Hamline, and Macalester Tackle Sam Young and Carleton Halfback Henry Willegalle also made the squad.

"Our blocking back was on of the ruggedest men who ever pulled on a jersey — Augsburg's Jimmy Peterson," added Joesting. "Jimmy's the only man I ever saw meet Bronko Nagurski head-on and lift him into the air!".

The team kicked off the season by winning its first preseason game against the Northland Oil Co. of Spring Valley, in southern Minnesota. The "Northland's," which were a semi-pro all-star team, were led by the Glynn brothers, who had starred at Winona Teachers College.

From there the Jackets managed to tie the Chicago Cardinals in their home opener. Oran Pape thrilled the opening day crowd by galloping 78 yards to give his squad a 7-0 lead. But former Duluth Eskimos star Ernie Nevers got the equalizer late in the second, however, on a brilliant run around the end to make it 7-7.

In Game Two, Minneapolis hosted the mighty Chicago Bears, who were led by none other than Bronko Nagurski. Gibson enjoyed playing against his old Gopher roommate, "The Bronk," in this one, but the Bears, who got scores from both Nagurski and Red Grange, were too much to handle and won it easily, 20-0.

Lexington Park

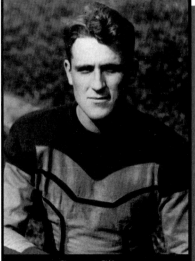

George Gibson

From there the team rebounded to beat the Portsmouth Spartans, 13-0, only to lose their next two to the Packers, 13-0 & 19-0, respectively. At that point the team, incredibly, announced that due to an economic hardship was going to be combining forces with the Frankford (Philadelphia) Yellow Jackets for the remainder of the season.

The combined squad, which played a double schedule, proved to be a logistical nightmare. Many of the players were cut, while others simply lost interest. After all, it was the beginning of the Great Depression, and people had more important things to worry about than football.

"The player limit was only 20," recalled Joesting, "and it was rugged after we combined with Frankford. A few times we played in Philadelphia on Saturday and hopped a train to play again Sunday. It's too bad we couldn't have carried on here," he added. "We had the start of a good team and it could have been built into something. But we didn't have the money. The Depression was on. It was a rugged way to make a living, but it was a job, and they were scarce in those days. And, hey it was fun."

As a result, the team lost its remaining four games in a big way to the Chicago Bears, Brooklyn Dodgers, Providence Steam Rollers and Portsmouth Spartans, by the ugly combined total of 106-7. While Gibson and Barrager were accorded All-Pro honors that season, the team's disappointing 1-7-1 record did not bode well. With that, Minneapolis regrettably suspended their operations for good following the season. Gibson was then hired by Frankford to serve as their player-coach for the upcoming 1931 season. But, after only eight games of poor play and horrid attendance, the Yellow Jackets, like the Red Jackets, went belly up.

"I tell everybody I was the only player-coach who worked for two teams that both went bankrupt in the same year," Gibson recalled jokingly.

Pro football was a different animal altogether 75 years ago. Large market teams, such as Chicago and New York, had big fan bases and survived to give the league some stability and credibility. There were also a few exceptions, like the Green Bay Packers — who had the insight to sell $5 shares of stock (which included season tickets) to their loyal fans, thus insuring themselves the financial fortitude to make it through the tough times. No fewer than 49 teams competed in the NFL at one time or another during the Roaring '20s, and all of them played a role in making the league what it is today. Eventually, college football and pro football made peace. While the college boys were happy playing on Saturdays, the pros, too, found a home on Sunday mornings. Minnesota would go without pro football for another 30 years, but the Gophers filled in nicely in the interim — winning six national championships to keep our local gridiron gurus happy and content.

The Minneapolis Marines and Red Jackets were a fun side-bar to Minnesota's rich gridiron history. And despite their paltry record, they played a big part in the evolution of pro football in America. They do hold one, albeit insignificant distinction, however, of being the only team to play before joining the NFL, after leaving the NFL, and then joining the league a second time. Hey, it's something! Who knows, had they not run into the Great Depression, they might still be here today instead of the Vikings? "Skol Red Jackets..." Nah!

Minneapolis Marines
Fullback Louis Pahl

MINNEAPOLIS MARINES & RED JACKETS ALL-TIME RECORD						
YR	WON	LOST	TIED	FIN	PF	PA
1921	1	3	0	13	37	41
1922	1	3	0	12	19	40
1923	3	5	1	13	48	51
1924	0	6	0	13	14	108
1925-28	— Team Suspended Operations —					
1929	1	9	0	11	48	185
1930	1	7	1	10	27	165
Totals	7	33	2	-	193	590

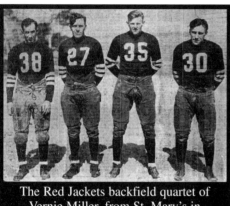

The Red Jackets backfield quartet of Vernie Miller, from St. Mary's in Winona, Mally Nydahl, Oran Pape and Art Pharmer.

THE 1930 MINNEAPOLIS RED JACKETS:

#	Player	Weight	Position q	School
10	John Ward	215	G	USC
25	Ken Haycraft	175	E	Minnesota
26	Wayne Kakela	220	T	Minnesota
27	Mally Nydahl	162	HB	Minnesota
29	Jimmie Peterson	185	HB	Augsburg
31	Harold Erickson	200	HB	Wash. & Jeff.
32	Herb (Chief) Franta	210	T	St. Thomas
33	Herb Joesting	192	FB	Minnesota
34	Tony Steponovich	185	E	USC
35	Oran Pape	179	HB	Iowa
36	John Corcoran	182	G	St. Louis
37	Leland Wilson	185	E	Cornell College
38	Vernie Miller	152	QB	St. Mary's
39	Ted Nemzek	205	T	Northwestern
40	Wilbur Lundell	205	E	Gustavus
42	Nate Barrager	210	C	USC
43	Sam Young	195	T	Macalester
44	George Gibson	200	G	Minnesota
53	Porky Seborg	189	QB	Kalamazoo
54	Art Pharmer	196	FB	Minnesota
55	Harold Truesdale	200	T	Hamline

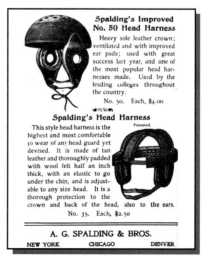

Northern Minnesota's first taste of professional football came back in 1923, when a team, known as the "Kelly-Duluth's," or "Kelly's" (because they were sponsored and outfitted by the local Kelly-Duluth Hardware Store), decided to field a team in a new alliance called the National Football League. The NFL at that time was a vagabond circuit originally started as the American Professional Football Association one year earlier in Canton, Ohio.

The league then was nothing like we know it as today. It was full of both shady promoters, who were out to make a few bucks by any means possible, and former college stars living vicariously through their past gridiron glory. At this stage of pro football's genesis, it was about as respectable as pro wrestling is today. Back then college football was all the rage, and this new "pro" thing was just a fad in most people's eyes.

The Kelly's, who, prior to joining the NFL, originally operated as an independent semi-pro club that played against local Iron Range teams, were one of 20 teams that had been awarded franchises by the new league. Seemingly anyone with a heartbeat and a football could join in at that point. In addition to large cities such as Chicago, New York, Philadelphia and Baltimore, other small town such as Kenosha, Wis., Hammond, Ind., Rock Island, Il., Pottsville, Pa., and Racine, Wis., also played in the upstart circuit, making for some interesting road-trips.

The team gained admission when four partners: Dan Williams, M.C. Gebert, Dewey Scanlon and Joey Sternaman, each ponied up $250 to pay the franchise's $1,000 admission fee. Gebert, the hardware store manager, handled the team's operations, Scanlon acted as the team's manager, and Sternaman served as the team's first official player/coach. In addition, a young local businessman by the name of Ole Haugsrud volunteered to be the club's secretary-treasurer.

With that, the group issued a cattle-call of sorts, offering open tryouts to any and all interested in suiting up. More than 100 former prepsters from throughout the Northland showed up, and after a few weeks of try-outs, the club had enough players to field its first squad. The players didn't receive a lot in the way of compensation back then — just a few bucks for beer and pretzels. Most all of the players held down regular blue-collar jobs during the week, and merely played for the love of the game on the weekends. The team played its home games in the West End of Duluth at Athletic Park, which was located next to the DM&IR ore docks, near where Wade Stadium sits today. Scheduling was tough back in the day, however, and teams barnstormed frequently in an attempt to secure games.

The Kelly's came out of the gates and won their first four games in their inaugural season, starting with the Akron Pros in Week One, 10-7. From there they downed the Minneapolis Marines (in the Twin Cities), 10-0, the Hammond Pros, 3-0, followed by the Marines again, 9-0, this time up in Duluth. But, from there the team lost its final three games on the road, first against the Milwaukee Badgers, 6-3, followed by the Chicago Cardinals, 10-0, and finally against the Green Bay Packers, 10-0, to finish up at 4-3 and out of the playoff hunt. All in all it was a good season though, as the team outscored its opponents by a 35-33 margin.

Ole Haugsrud

Ken Harris led the team in passing by completing a whopping nine of 28 passes for 171 yards, and no touchdowns. Bill Rooney led the squad in rushing with 31 yards, followed by Harris, who posted 25, and Wally Gilbert, had added 20 yards and a touchdown.

In addition, because rules and league protocols were hard to enforce, they were sometimes just made up on the fly — often-times making local "house rules" a part of the game. One of those protocols was eligibility for players who were out of the post-season being picked up late in the season by teams still in contention. As was the case after the Kelly's finished out their season, when the Bears signed their Quarterback, Joey Sternaman, as a "ringer" for their last four games.

Tired of losing money, Gebert dropped out that next year and Scanlon took over the coaching and managerial duties. The group then decided to do something pretty amazing — they let the players take over and operate the team on a cooperative basis. That's right, the players actually paid to play. They chipped in to help pay expenses, as much as $30 per player, and in turn hoped to share in the team's profits.

The Kelly's, under their new system, went on to finish the season in fourth place that year. They even beat the mighty Green Bay Packers at home in Week One, 6-3, thanks to a couple of Wally Gilbert field goals. Packers legend Earl "Curly" Lambeau apparently didn't find his club being beat by this rag-tag bunch very amusing, and as a result, refused to visit Duluth in 1925. From there the team downed Minneapolis, 3-0, on yet another Gilbert field goal, followed by a 32-0 blow-out win over the Kenosha Maroons. The Packers then got revenge that next week up in Green Bay, this time beating the Kel's, 13-0. Duluth finished strong though, beating the Rock Island Independents, 9-0, to post a much-improved 5-1 record. (Against Rock Island, Wally Gilbert boomed a punt from his own end-zone that finally came to rest at the Independent's two-yard line, prompting their star halfback, Jim Thorpe to say: "I thought I'd have to chase it to the Mississippi...") At season's end, Duluth Guard Doc Williams was honored by being selected to the 1924 All-Pro team.

By the start of the 1925 season, the NFL was in big financial trouble, and so were the Kelly's. Players were fed up with having to pay the travel expenses and what-not for cash-strapped opponents. Inclemental weather was wreaking havoc on their schedules, and the team — which didn't have a decent home field, literally had to bribe opponents to book games with them. As a result, the team played a shortened three-game schedule that year, ultimately losing all three to Kansas City, 3-0, Rock Island, 12-0, and Chicago, 10-6, to round out a very disappointing season. One of the stars of that year's team was former Gopher All American Defensive End, Bobby Marshall, who, at 45-years-old, became the team's

The Eskimo players even had their own personalized luggage

ERNIE NEVERS

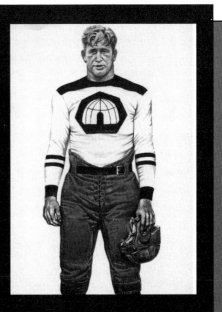

Ernie Nevers was one of the greatest football heroes our country has ever known. The speedy blonde-haired fullback could do it all. He ran, passed, kicked, punted, returned kicks and punts, called signals, and played a mean cornerback position on defense. He revolutionized the game, and even saved the once fledgling NFL from going broke way back in 1926, when he came home to play in one of the most storied football seasons of all time with the upstart Duluth Eskimos.

Born on June 11, 1903, in Willow River, Minn., Ernie later moved to Superior, Wis. It was at Superior Central High School where he blossomed into a three-sport star in football, baseball and basketball. At the age of 16 his folks moved to California, where Ernie graduated from Santa Rosa High School. After graduation he attended Stanford, and soon became a featured triple-threat fullback in Pop Warner's explosive double wing offense. The once timid teenager was now a house-hold name throughout America.

"As a youngster I was very shy," confessed Nevers. "I was scared to death of people. But football gave me an outlet for my emotions. You get the chance to go man-to-man and see if you can stand up against the best they can throw at you. On a football field I was just a different person."

Nevers, a two-time All-American selection, had been a headliner all through his collegiate career, but he reached superhuman status during the 1925 Rose Bowl against Notre Dame and the vaunted Four Horsemen. There, against the better wishes of his doctor, he played through one sprained and one broken ankle. With a pair of tin-snips and a hammer, Coach Warner concocted a crude artificial ankle brace out of sheet aluminum and rubber inner tubing, and taped it to Nevers' lower legs. Amazingly, Ernie played the entire 60 minutes, rushed for 114 yards on his two bum-hoofs, and even registering half of the team's tackles on defense. He played valiantly, but came up short though, as the Irish won, 27-10. That next year, against California, in his final college game, the workhorse handled the ball on every offensive play but three.

Pop Warner, who coached both Nevers and the legendary Jim Thorpe, was once asked who was the better player of the two. "Nevers," Warner quickly replied. "He could do everything Thorpe could do and he tried harder. No man ever gave more of himself than Ernie Nevers."

By the time the football season was over with during his senior year, Ernie was in big demand. So, with a semester of school remaining, he decided to turn pro. His first gig was for $25,000 to play in a series of all-star games against the New York Giants in Florida. Shortly thereafter, he signed a pro basketball deal for a Chicago team in a league that was a forerunner to the NBA. Then, that Spring he signed a $10,000 pro baseball contract as a pitcher with the St. Louis Browns. But after a year, he decided to get back to the gridiron and suit up for his old high school pal, Ole Haugsrud, and his upstart NFL Duluth Eskimos. There, he got a $15,000 contract plus 10% of the gate, to serve as the team's player/coach. Haugsrud even renamed his team as the "Ernie Nevers' Eskimos" in his honor. More importantly though, his presence, credibility and star-power single-handedly saved the NFL from going broke.

Ernie's two-year stint in Duluth was epic. In 1926 alone, the Eskimos played 29 games, 28 of them on the road, and traveled nearly 20,000 miles. Nevers played all but 29 of the total minutes for that season, with the 29 idle minutes coming after he ruptured his appendix. Nevers set five league marks for rushing, passing, and scoring that year, as the team barnstormed throughout the country. The Eskimos folded in 1928 and Ernie headed back to coach for a year under Pop Warner at Stanford. He came back in 1929 though, this time with the Chicago Cardinals.

Nevers played for the Cardinals from 1929-1931, also serving as player/coach for the latter two years. His most memorable moment in the Windy City came on Thanksgiving Day, 1929, when the Cards played the cross-town Bears, and their star running back, Red Grange, at Comiskey Park for the City Championship. Nevers came out, smashed over the Bear's goal-line six times, and kicked four extra points. The final score: Nevers 40, Bears 6. That's right, he scored all 40 points by himself! And, to prove it was no fluke, he scored all of his team's points again in a 19-0 win over Dayton that next Sunday.

"Ernie was probably the first of the triple-threat backs," said Grange. "He could run, kick, and pass. He was a star through and through. Guys like Nevers and Bronko Nagurski would have played the game for nothing."

In 1931, after suffering too many nagging injuries, the five-time All-NFL star hung up the cleats for good. He stayed on as a coach though, through the 1937 season, and again in 1939. His final numbers were awesome. In his five NFL seasons, he passed for 25 touchdowns, rushed for 38 touchdowns, kicked seven field goals, nailed 52 extra points, and tallied 301 career points. Not bad for just 54 games of work.

He made one final coaching stint in 1946, when he skippered the ill-starred Chicago Rockets in the All American Football League. He later moved to California, where among other business interests, he became the director of the California Clippers, Oakland's pro soccer team.

Once referred to as "America's all-time one-man team," Ernie Nevers was, in a word, amazing. He was to the NFL what Gale Sayers, Walter Payton and Emmitt Smith later exemplified. In 1963 Nevers was inducted as a charter member of the Pro Football Hall of Fame. Many years later Sports Illustrated called Nevers the "best college player of all time." He died on May 3, 1976, in San Rafael, Calif., at the age of 73, ironically, just six weeks after his old friend, Ole Haugsrud, had also passed on.

first African American player.

You see, back in the day, teams had to pay to play one-another. Their schedules were set up and prices were determined based on the draw each team predicted it would attract to the games. For instance, when the Kel's played a marquis team such as Rock Island, whose star was Olympian and future Hall of Famer Jim Thorpe, and didn't draw real well perhaps because of rainy weather that day, the players had to cough up, in this case, $33 apiece, to pay the difference of the $1,000-3,000 guaranteed fee. That price varied, as was the case against Hammond, which cost each man $11 bucks — big dough back in 1925.

Bills began to pile up, leaving the group of cash-strapped player/owners no alternative but to take drastic measures to save their team. That's when the group offered to sell the franchise to Ole Haugsrud, who had been serving as the club's volunteer secretary-treasurer, for the sum of $1, in exchange for his commitment to assume the team's growing debt. Haugsrud agreed, and even structured an agreement right then on the spot with them for that next season which would pay each player $75 for a win, $60 for a tie and $50 for a loss. He then made the transaction legal by handing the gentlemen a crisp one dollar bill — which they in turn immediately cashed in to buy 20 nickel beers at a local pub to celebrate. It would be a drunken hangover they would all one day regret!

Ole was a young, ambitious 23-year-old Swedish entrepreneur who had inherited some money, owned some real-estate, and had some big ideas. While he was just happy to be a part of the team as a volunteer, he jumped at the chance to become the team's owner. He knew, however, that in order to become a successful franchise, he would need to make some drastic moves.

You see, at the time, the NFL had two serious flaws. First, was the fact that there was no draft, which allowed teams like Green Bay, Chicago and Philadelphia (which were known back then as the Big-Three), to corral all of the best talent by paying them a lot of money. Secondly, the league didn't mandate which teams should play one-another. That was left up to the individual franchises, who, in turn, were required only to make sure that they had at least seven games scheduled against anyone that they pleased. As a result, owners tried to play the best teams, with the marquis college players, thus ensuring them of a big draw, and an even bigger pay-day.

In 1925 Chicago Bears Owner, George Halas pulled off one of football's greatest coups by signing the great All-American Running Back from Illinois, Red Grange. This was a significant move, because at the time, pro football was considered to be quite inferior to the beloved college game. But the addition of the "Galloping Ghost" gave the league a ton of new credibility, as well as the fans a reason to come out and watch pro football. Grange, the greatest name in football, was everyone's hero, with only Babe Ruth ranking higher as a sports celebrity. After that, nearly every team in professional football was willing to pay big bucks to have the Bears come to their city and do battle. "Papa Bear" Halas obliged, and showcased Grange on a very profitable 20-city cross-country tour that year.

Shortly following Halas' tour, Grange's agent, C.C. Pyle (the C.C. apparently stood for "Cash and Carry"), a flamboyant New York business manager, started to renegotiate a new deal for his client's services. Knowing that he had structured an "out" clause in Grange's contract, he high-balled Halas for an unheard of five-figure contract, plus he wanted one-third ownership of the Bears for himself. Halas laughed, and Pyle said "Say good bye to Red Grange!"

With that, Pyle went to the NFL and requested a new expansion franchise in New York for Grange and himself. In fact, he had already taken out a five-year lease on Yankee Stadium. With the country's premier venue and the biggest star in pro football, Pyle reasoned that every franchise would profit greatly from the new addition. But Tim Mara, the owner of the New York Giants, which had just begun play the year before, didn't see it that way. His Giants were just across the Harlem River at the Polo Grounds, and he didn't want to be the No.2 show in town. So, the league denied Pyle his NFL franchise, which then inspired him to start his own rival league, which he called the American Football League, or "Grange League" as it was even referred to.

Pyle's competing eight-team AFL opened up shop that next season with all of the fan-fare of a presidential inauguration. Pyle, who would operate one of the franchises, the New York Yankees, gave Grange a fat new contract and made him the league's headliner. Red Grange, who was the star and savior of the NFL in 1925, had now become the NFL's biggest competitor only a few months later.

In addition to the Yankees, the other AFL teams of that 1926 season were the Philadelphia Quakers, Cleveland Panthers, Los Angeles Wildcats, Chicago Bulls, Boston Bulldogs, Rock Island Independents, Newark Bears and the Brooklyn Horsemen — who had Notre Dame's legendary Four Horsemen.

The NFL was now in serious trouble. Not only was there a serious rival threat to now contend with, but also the fact that Pyle was raiding the league's top box-office attractions off of the other NFL teams as well. Pyle then completely shocked the establishment by announcing that he had also signed All-American Stanford Fullback Ernie Nevers, the only other player on the planet who could possibly draw as well, if not better, than the mighty Grange.

Now, Haugsrud also had an ace of his own up his sleeve. It would be a wild-card so powerful that it would actually single-handedly rescue the struggling NFL from going extinct. Ole grew up in Duluth's twin-port sister city of Superior, Wis., and one of his best friends from high school was that very Ernie Nevers, who at the time, had graduated and was playing professional baseball as a pitcher with the St. Louis Browns. Ole went to Ernie and asked him if he was interested in giving up baseball and coming back to the gridiron. Nevers was skeptical, but listened. He trusted Ole, and saw that with Grange now playing, maybe pro football was a respectable way to make a living. Pyle had indeed offered Nevers a fat contract to come play in his new rival league, but he hadn't accepted the offer. He then told his old pal Ole that if he matched Pyle's offer, that he would come play for him in Duluth instead. With that they shook hands and made it official. Not only was Nevers going to receive the ridiculous sum of $15,000 per year (an amount almost unheard of in those days), but he would also get 10% of the team's gate receipts. It was big dough for a big star.

With that, the two got together and hammered out the particulars of a deal that would bring Nevers up to Duluth, where he would get his own team...literally. You see, Ole then renamed the Kelly's as the "Ernie Nevers' Duluth Eskimos." He figured that Ernie's name should be right out there on the logo for all to see.

Ole then went off to the league's meetings that August and confided in his friend and mentor, Giants Owner Tim Mara, to tell him the good news about signing Nevers. Mara then encouraged Ole to hold off before telling the entire group of owners, to see how the scheduling would evolve. He waited until league President Joe Carr was well into the scheduling process, and then sprung the announcement. "Gentlemen! I've got a surprise for you," exclaimed Carr, who had his arm around Ole. "This young man has just saved the National Football League!" With that, a celebration broke out, and

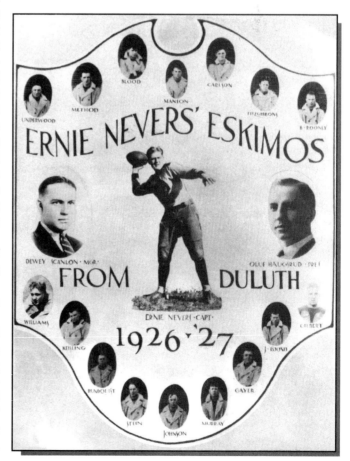

all of the shocked and elated owners demanded to throw out the first scheduling blueprint and start over.

The owners then clamored to schedule Haugsrud's new franchise onto their schedules as quickly as possible. But there was one stipulation. You see, because icy Duluth was not exactly on the beaten path, not to mention their less than desirable home stadium, the league designated the newly named Eskimos as a "road-team." The league figured that with Nevers on board, people would line up to buy tickets in cities big and small from coast to coast. And they were right. By the time Ole left the meeting he had lined up an amazing 19 league games with an additional 10 exhibition games — all the way from Chicago to Hartford and back to California. So eager were the owners that none of them batted an eye at Ole's guaranteed fee of $4,000 per game, plus a cut of the gate receipts.

The next step was to get back and quickly get the franchise organized. Dewey Scanlon remained with Haugsrud for every step of the way, and Ole rewarded him by keeping him on as the manager. Ole then decided to do something revolutionary. He announced to his players that, after considering Moose Lake and Solon Springs, the team's training camp was going to be held up in the Lake Superior port city of Two Harbors, about 25 miles northeast of Duluth along the scenic North Shore. (Although we take this for granted today, the fact that teams hold their camps in foreign locales, but back then, the Eskimos were the first professional team ever to do so.) They also became the first team to feature a distinctive emblem, a large white igloo, rather than just a numbered jersey. Ole then had a local clothing manufacturer, F.A. Patrick, custom tailor big white mackinaw trench coats for each player, emblazoned with the igloo logo on the back with the lettering "Ernie Nevers' Eskimos" underneath. Haugsrud even had big custom-imprinted trunks made, figuring that as long as they were going to be spending most of their time on the road, they might as well look good.

With that, the team met at the Spalding Hotel in Duluth to take a bus up the Lake Superior International Highway to Two Harbors. There, the group of some 30 players stayed at the Hotel Agate and practiced at the Horace Johnson Athletic Field twice daily for up three hours at a time. The training day started with a three-mile run, followed by a morning workout. Then, after lunch, the team practiced again, followed by dinner and class-room time diagramming plays on the blackboard. Camp was a raucous, yet physically demanding time. One player, a giant lineman named Oke Carlson, even got ready for the tough practices by consuming a breakfast of two dozen eggs, which was then topped off with a huge steak. (I'm sure Oke's roommate just loved the aroma at night!)

Nevers, who was given free reigns by Haugsrud to do whatever he felt necessary to make the team a winner, used the practice time to teach his new mates the offensive formation fittingly named the "Stanford Double Wing," which he learned under legendary Coach, Glen "Pop" Warner during his playing days at Stanford University. The offense was designed around the fullback (Nevers' position), who took the snap from center and dictated the plays. Predicated on deception and athleticism, Nevers thrived in this system. He could take the snap and choose whether to run it, hand the ball off for a reverse, or slip it to the quarterback for a pass. Nevers also assumed the coaching duties and redid the entire playbook. One of the first moves he made was to introduce the huddle, something totally foreign to the players at that time.

After two weeks of practices, the team boarded a bus and headed to Superior for its first exhibition game against the Bessemer-Ironwood Gogebic Panthers, a semi-pro Iron Range team from Michigan's Upper Peninsula. They checked into the West Duluth YMCA... but not for long.

"I got a call that night," Haugsrud would later recall, "inviting me to move my players out of there. It was an innocent mistake. The boys had somehow got the impression that there was a fire, and they went out and got the fire hose and sprayed the halls and stairs. I had to move them all to the Superior YMCA."

The inaugural game at Superior's Hislop Park was a homecoming of sorts for Nevers, who was a prep football, baseball and basketball star at Superior Central High School, which also used the same field for its home games. More than 3,000 fans showed up on that September 13th to see their local hero, with a couple thousand more catching a glimpse from behind the fences and also from on top of the railroad boxcars that were lined up along the tracks on both sides of the field.

The Panthers weren't a push-over team by any means. The Northland was a football hotbed at that time, and there was a lot of talent playing semi-pro ball around the area. The teams had played to four scoreless ties over the past couple of years, until Duluth finally beat them in 1925, by the score of 9-0. But with Ernie in the backfield that day, it was going to be a different story altogether. Wingback Doc Kelly scored the game's first touchdown early in the first quarter, only to see Ernie take over and wow the home-town crowd. Nevers came out and scored a pair of touchdowns in the second half, as he passed, ran and punted his Eskimos to a 25-0 blow-out. He did it all, averaging 50-yards on six punts, and even intercepting a key pass in the third quarter to end a Panther scoring drive.

By now the team had made all of its final cuts, whittling down the roster to just 15 men. Besides Nevers, the opening game roster included Wally Gilbert, Johnny "Blood" McNally, Doc Williams, Russ Method, brothers Cobb and Joe Rooney, Bill Stein, Bunk Harris, Jimmy Manion, Oke Carlson, Walt Kiesling, Jack Underwood, Charles "Doc" Kelly, Paul Fitzgibbons and Porky

WALLY GILBERT

Wally Gilbert is arguably one of Minnesota's greatest ever all-around athletes. A graduate of Duluth Denfeld High School, Gilbert went on to Valparaiso University in Indiana, where he served as captain of the football, basketball and baseball teams there. In football, he earned All-American honors starring as a halfback, punter and drop-kicker extraordinaire.

In the late 1920s and early 1930s he played third base for the Brooklyn Dodgers and Cincinnati Reds. When those same Dodgers moved to Los Angeles in 1957, the Sporting News named him as the starting third baseman on the all-time Dodger team. In addition to playing on several pro touring basketball teams, including with Two Harbors, the Duluth Tank Corps, the Denver Tigers and the Buffalo All-Americans, he was also a champion curler, back at the old Duluth Curling Club. But perhaps his most memorable role in professional Minnesota sports came on the gridiron, where he starred alongside future Hall of Famer's Ernie Nevers and Johnny Blood, as a halfback and kicker with the NFL's Duluth Eskimos in the late 1920s. Wally's deadly drop-kicks beat several teams, including the likes of the Green Bay Packers, and Chicago Cardinals. He once booted a record 61-yarder!

Late in the 1930s, Wally married his long-time sweetheart, Mary McKay, and settled down. But he didn't slow down! He continued to play and manage in the Northern League with both Wausau and Winnipeg, and when World War II broke out, he and some buddies organized a semipro baseball team out of Duluth.

Gilbert worked and lived in Duluth for the remainder of his life, until he passed in 1958. The obituary, in the Duluth News Tribune on Sept. 7th of that year, led with a fitting headline: "Duluth's greatest all-around athlete is dead." Wally was a true Northland legend.

JOHNNY "BLOOD" MCNALLY

Born on November 27, 1903, in New Richmond, Wis., Johnny "Blood" McNally was one of football's all-time greatest players. He was also one of the game's most colorful characters, playing the game on his own terms and having fun every step of the way.

At six feet tall and 185 pounds, McNally was a lightning quick running back, with hands that made him one of the finest receivers in the National Football League. He could throw, catch, run and punt with the best in the business. And, on the other side of the line, he was a ball hawking mad-man and a deadly tackler. He played pro football for a total of 22 years, but is most remembered in Minnesota football history for his exploits both as a student at St. John's University and also with the Duluth Eskimos in the late 1920s.

McNally grew up in New Richmond, Wis., the son of a wealthy family of newspaper publishers and paper mill owners. Incredibly, he never played any organized sports throughout high school, primarily because he was too small. He graduated at just the age of 14, and after a year of local prep school, was shipped off to St. John's University for some good Catholic disciplinary teachings. His father had also attended the school in the late 1800s, but ironically, was expelled for a harmless tobacco spitting incident which inadvertently found the back-side of an unsuspecting professor.

Johnny sprouted at St. John's and quickly got involved in sports, where, after three years, he earned letters in football baseball, track and basketball. But then he decided he needed a change of pace, so he up and transferred to Notre Dame.

In the spring of 1924 he received a 60-day suspension from Notre Dame for disciplinary problems, so he decided to make it permanent. From there he headed back to Minneapolis, where he and one of his football buddies from St. John's, Ralph Hanson, got jobs at a local newspaper. But it didn't pay much, and they wanted to get back out on the gridiron. So they decided to pick up some extra money by playing in a semipro city league in the Minneapolis area, by playing for a team called East 26th Street Liberties. But he didn't want to lose his remaining year of college eligibility by playing pro ball, so he decided to assume an alias.

"I used to get around town on my own motorcycle then, and so we both hopped on it and headed out to where this team practiced, some playground in back of a factory," he said. "On the way there, we passed a movie theater on Hennepin Avenue and up on the marquee I saw the name of the movie that was playing, 'Blood and Sand with Rudolph Valentino.' Ralph was behind me on the motorcycle and I turned my head and shouted, "That's it. I'll be Blood and you be Sand!" And so we went to the practice, tried out, and made the team, as Johnny Blood and Ralph Sand. And, of course, I kept it as a football name from that time on."

After helping the Liberties win the city championship, Blood ventured up to Michigan's Upper Peninsula to play a year of pro ball with the Ironwood Panthers, and from there he signed with his first NFL team, the Milwaukee Badgers, in 1925. Blood continued to bounce around after that, with his next stop being in Duluth, where he and Nevers forged one of the most dynamic backfield duos in history.

"Signing with the Duluth Eskimos is one of my great memories," said Blood, "because it was there that I got to play with Ernie Nevers, who was the star. No, he was the team! Ernie was a fine man, I admired and respected him. He was a fiery kind of guy, a different specimen really, and we had a pretty good football team up there, considering it was Duluth and not Chicago or New York."

He remained with the Eskimos for two seasons, and then signed on with the Pottsville Maroons. After a year there he joined the team that he would become most synonymous with, the Green Bay Packers, where he was a fixture on several NFL championship teams for some nine seasons.

In negotiating his first contract with Packer's owner Curly Lambeau, Blood asked for $100 a game. Lambeau countered with an even better offer of $110 a game, provided he agreed to a clause in his contract that forbade him from drinking after the Tuesday of each week there was a game scheduled. Blood had a compromise of his own. He would accept $100 if he could booze it up through Wednesday. Lambeau agreed.

Blood tore up the league, and even scored 13 touchdowns in 1931, a single-season record at the time. Before Don Hutson joined the Packer roster, Blood owned nearly all the major NFL pass-receiving records. It was also in Green Bay where Blood became famous for his soldier of fortune antics as well. It was said that he broke as many training rules as he did tackles, and ignored team curfews just as he did Prohibition.

"I was reckless, they said, on the football field," confessed Blood. "Reckless in a lot of things, I guess. I liked to have a good time back then: women, travel, a little drinking, loved to spend money. I had a lot of experiences. I was very uninhibited, that way all my life, even as a little kid. My mother would teach me Shakespeare and my father taught me sports. So I was a semi-split personality."

Once during a game, Blood checked into the huddle with a pass play directly from Lambeau. He then turned to Quarterback Arnie Herber and said: "Arnie, throw it in the direction of Mother Pierre's whorehouse." Herber, like Blood, was no stranger to the Green Bay nightlife, and knew he was going to be headed for the goal post at the northeast end of the stadium. The pass was there, and so was Blood for the touchdown.

Missed curfews and broken rules were just part of his daily routine. One time, when the Packers were leaving for a pivotal game in Chicago against the Bears, Lambeau realized that Blood had missed the train. Then, shortly after pulling out of Green Bay, the train came to a sudden halt. The players then opened their windows and saw Blood, who had parked his car smack in the middle of the railroad tracks to stop the steaming locomotive. With that, he moved his car, and jumped on board as if nothing had happened.

In 1937, Blood, after one too many run-in's with old Curly, moved on, this time to Pittsburgh. There, he became the player/coach for the Pirates (they would later be known as the Steelers). His debut was something the steel city fans will never forget, as he took the opening kickoff 92 yards for a touchdown against their cross-state rivals, the Philadelphia Eagles.

After a couple of years in Pittsburgh, Blood drifted to Kenosha and played there in 1941. From there he found himself in the Air Force, which took him to the China-India-Burma theater of operations as a sergeant and cryptographer. He returned to Green Bay in 1945, and at the age of 42, played what would be his final season of pro football.

Blood was a newspaper man's dream come true. Whether he was hopping freight trains for kicks, or gallivanting to all hours of the night, he was a character. From all of his travels and exploits he was eventually dubbed as the "Vagabond Halfback," a nickname that appropriately stuck for a man who had wandered all over the world. Whether in China, or in a Havana jail (for only one night), he was a legend.

When it was all said and done, he had managed to cram in 22 years of professional football, where the four-time All-NFL halfback tallied 59 touchdowns both rushing, receiving and passing and nearly 400 points in 15 seasons with five NFL teams. With that, he decided to go back to school. That's right, 26 years later he returned to St. John's to finish his degree and begin his new career as a teacher and coach. He was later replaced by another legendary football coach, John Gagliardi, who came in 1953 and has been there ever since.

A fabulous athlete and notorious free spirit, Blood was later enshrined as a charter member of the Pro Football Hall of Fame in 1963. Once referred to as a "Peter Pan who would never shed his eternal youth," Johnny Blood was a legendary figure in the early days of pro football. A proud playboy of the pro football world in the '20s and '30s, his slashing runs and amazing pass-catching abilities were simply ahead of his time. He died the day after his 82nd birthday on November 28, 1985, in Palm Springs, Calif.

Perhaps his wife, Marguerite, put it best when she said of her husband: "Even when Johnny does the expected, he does it in an unexpected way."

Rundquist.

After beating the Twin City All-Stars at St. Paul's Lexington Park, the Eskimos got ready to host the Kansas City Cowboys (Later the Dallas Cowboys) for their regular season opener up at Athletic Park in Duluth. The Zenith City fans were excited to finally see their boys in action, and came out in droves to root them on.

The Cowboys, who arrived into Minneapolis via train, stayed over their first night in Minneapolis and practiced on St. Thomas University's field. They came up the next night and trained at both Athletic Park, and also at Duluth Cathedral High School — where, in addition to instructing the Hilltoppers on technique and tactics, even used the prepsters as their scout-team to scrimmage against. The Eskimos, meanwhile, also trained at Athletic Park, but got in a few extra workouts at the Blaine School field across the pond in Superior.

Frank "Cub" LaJoy, the promoter and lease-holder of Athletic Park had but one thought of the big game that afternoon: "They nicked me for $500 in promoting this contest, but I'm hoping that the weatherman and the sports fans of the Twin Ports will pull me through on the sunny side."

On game day the Cowboys came riding into town... literally. You see, the Cowboys had a gimmick which had them traveling to every city dressed up in full cowboy regalia, complete with rented horses, and putting on a pre-game Saturday afternoon parade. In this case, the spectator-filled extravaganza, which included players from both teams, went along West Superior Street from downtown Duluth and up to the ballpark. (The Cowboys later rode horseback down Broadway Avenue in New York City to the tune of more than 50,000 fans.)

Both managers of the opposing clubs issued statements prior to the game: "This game means considerable to us and Ernie Nevers will put all his resources on the field in an attempt to win the game and by a comfortable score," said Eskimos Manager Dewey Scanlon. "With an array of powerful talent supporting him, Nevers is expected be at his best this afternoon, and I'm confident we will win."

The Cowboy's Manager was equally confident: "I've got a line that will rope and tie up Mr. Nevers every time he attempts to gallop through our front wall," he said. "Nevers will be never, never more when we get through with him."

More than 6,000 fans crowded into and around old Athletic Park to catch a glimpse of their Eskimos that afternoon. The stadium, which was actually a minor-league baseball park for the Duluth White Sox, was even retro-fitted with 800 additional box-seats to provide fans with more unobstructed views. Pretty amazing when you consider that this game would prove to be the team's only home game of the year.

The Eskimos, who averaged just over 200 pounds from wing to wing, huge for those days, then lined up to do battle. The only score of the game came in the second quarter when former St. Thomas star Walt Keisling stripped the ball away from Cowboy Quarterback Al Bloodgood as he was handing the ball off to Tex White. That's when Defensive End Jack Underwood picked up the loose ball and ran it into the end-zone for a touchdown. Ernie Nevers then kicked the extra point to make it 7-0. The game was an extremely rough and tumble affair, with a lot of skirmishes breaking out near the end. In fact, once, Nevers, who was retaliating for being choked, was even penalized 15 yards for unnecessary roughness, on a "slugging" call. The game came down to defense and field position, with Nevers, who boomed several 60-yard punts, proving to be the difference.

"The game was slowly played with numerous penalties and delays of various sorts dominating, to make the contest interesting and thrilling only in spots," wrote Cubby Campbell in the following day's edition of the Duluth News-Tribune. "The game as a whole lacked continuous excitement for the fans."

From there the Eskimos packed up to catch the train out of town — to the tune of 25 more games over the next four months, all on the road. But not all of the players from the old Kelly's team were able to pick up and do that. They had jobs and families, and wanted to play just for fun. So, Duluth fielded a team in a new semi-pro circuit called the Northwestern Professional Football League, which featured teams from Hibbing and Virginia, as well as several other teams from Wisconsin and Michigan. Fred Denfeld, who played with the Kelly's and was an All-American Guard at Navy, served as the team's head coach and manager. Among the former Kel's who stayed behind were Allan McDonald, Tommy Murphy, Ed Bratt, Roy Vexall and Michael Koziak. They were then joined by several other local stars including: Johnny Benda, the former Duluth Cathedral and future St. John's University Coach, as well as a trio of Denfeld High School prep stars in Tore Gernander, Bob Bratt and Swede Larson.

WALT KIESLING

Born in St. Paul in 1903, Walt Kiesling first starred on the gridiron as a guard at Cretin High School. He went on to play at St. Thomas College in the early 1920s, and from there jumped right into his long pro career with the Duluth Eskimos in 1926. "Big Kies" stayed in Duluth for two seasons before moving on to the Pottsville Maroons. Kiesling bounced around for several more years in the NFL after that, eventually playing with the Chicago Cardinals and Chicago Bears from 1929 to 1934, the Green Bay Packers from 1935 to 1936, and finally with the Pittsburgh Steelers from 1937-38. He was All-NFL in 1932 and was a member of the 1936 NFL Champion Packers.

"He was big like Babe Ruth, and a left-hander, too," said former teammate Johnny "Blood" McNally. "Like Ruth, he played his best when he had some belly on him." Despite his size, however, Kiesling bad remarkable speed, and was one of the first great pulling guards to play the game.

Kiesling later served as the Steelers head coach on four different occasions throughout the 1940s and 50s, and also worked as an assistant with the Green Bay Packers as well. He finally resigned his post with the Steelers in 1957 because of failing health. After 34 seasons of pro football, he died in 1962. Kiesling was later inducted into the Pro Football Hall of Fame in 1966.

Dick McCann, former director of the Hall of Fame, once said of Kiesling: "He didn't just watch pro football grow from the rocky sandlots. He shoved it along the way. He gave almost half a century to the game he loved."

The Ultimate Road Warriors

The team's first trip was to Green Bay, where they managed a 0-0 tie against the mighty Packers. From there they ventured over to Milwaukee, where they rallied to beat the Badgers, 7-6, on Nevers' record 62-yard touchdown pass to End Joe Rooney, followed by his game-winning extra point, with only seconds left in the game. What is so amazing about this is the fact that Nevers, despite his doctors orders, insisted on coming in to play during the second half despite having a ruptured appendix! "What else could I do?" Nevers recalled. "I had to put myself in."

From there the team spanked the Hammond, Ind., Pros, by the final of 26-0, thanks to a pair of scores each from Nevers and

Blood. Their next stop was in Racine, Wis., where the team met a tavern owner a couple days before the game who was extremely proud of his German Shepherd's sprinting ability. In fact, he was so confident that his hound was the fastest thing on four legs, that he was willing to place a wager to any member of the Eskimos team who thought he could beat the mongrel in a race. The players scraped together $75 and nominated their soldier of fortune Halfback, Johnny "Blood" McNally, who was just as celebrated for his off-the-field exploits as he was for his on-field heroics. With that, Blood took a few shots, calmly went out back, and proceeded to beat the hound at his own game. He then asked the owner if he was willing to go double-or-nothing on the team's game that Saturday against his Tornadoes. He agreed, and the Eskimos cashed in once again when Blood caught three touchdown passes from Nevers, as Duluth routed Racine, 21-0.

The traveling was chaotic, with the team seemingly always running to catch the next train. After the games, the players would often times take two showers — the first with their uniforms on, and the second with them off. "We'd beat them like rugs to get some of the water out, throw them into our bags, get dressed and catch a train," recalled Nevers of their dirty, smelly uniforms after the game. "Hell, most of the time we were only half-dressed when we boarded."

After suffering their first set-back, a 24-6 loss to the Chicago Bears, the Eskimos rebounded to beat Milwaukee, 7-6, on Nevers' early score. After the Chicago game, Bears' Owner George Halas called Eskimos Manager Dewey Scanlon and begged him to either trade or sell Fullback Paul Fitzgibbons (who's nickname was the "red-haired flash") to him. But Scanlon, who knew that Fitzgibbons was going to be the lead blocker for Nevers in the new offensive system, promptly sent a return telegram to Halas that read: "Nothing doing!"

From there the squad posted another 0-0 tie with the Detroit Panthers, followed by a hellacious week in mid-November that saw the team playing three games in just four nights on the Eastern seaboard. Now, with just 14 players in uniform, it was little wonder that the team went 0-3 during that stretch. After taking the ferry from Providence to New York, the team lost Game One of their East Coast swing to the Giants, 14-13, at the Polo Grounds. Nevers, who played hurt, scored both touchdowns in this one (the latter coming on nine straight rushes following his key interception), only to lose the game when he missed the extra point. After the game Giants Coach Steve Owen was in awe of Nevers. "I was wondering where Nevers was hurt," he said. "It could only have been his big toe..."

Said Haugsrud: "Mr. Mara looked at us and said, 'I don't know what you'd call this, a football team?' And Grantland Rice, the big sportswriter, said, 'Well, there's the Iron Men from the North.' And that's the way we were dubbed from there on."

From there Duluth traveled to Pennsylvania, where they lost a pair to both the Frankford Yellow Jackets, 10-0, and Pottsville Maroons, 13-0. In Pottsville, Blood, Kiesling and Rooney found the local tavern, where, for some reason, Blood and Rooney challenged each other to a friendly fist-fight. Kiesling, who served as the referee, then led them out to an alley, where Blood threw a big round-house right hook that landed squarely into the side of a brick wall — thereby breaking his hand. When they got back to the hotel and told Haugsrud, naturally, he was furious.

"I fired all three of them," he later said. "But that was in the morning. Well, I knew I needed them for the game, so I hired them back at noon-time. I'm probably the only manager who ever fired two Hall of Famers in one day!" (Kiesling and Blood would both later be enshrined in the Pro Football Hall of Fame.)

Later that day, when the team arrived at the stadium to play the Maroons, they saw that the fire department had been called out to soak the field. They did this very deliberately in an effort to slow down the lightning quick duo of Nevers and Blood. Once the game started, the Eskimos, upset with the wet field and tired of getting a bunch of bad calls from the local "homer" referees, decided to take matters into their own hands.

"Russ Method, a terrific blocker, threw a block at the referee that knocked him out," described Haugsrud. "Five of our linemen put five of their linemen out of action. Jimmy Manion had this trick of jumping into the air feet-first and kicking a guy in the teeth, and he did it to the umpire. Meanwhile, Johnny Blood just ran right over the field judge." When the smoke finally cleared, the one remaining official, who wasn't maimed, blew his whistle and called off the game. The Eskimos obliged and hit the road.

By now the team was so strapped for bodies that Haugsrud and Scanlon were even wearing uniforms and warming up with the team to make it look as if they had more players than they actually did. In an effort to fit in out on the field, Ole enjoyed going out before the game and kicking field goals with some of the other players — as a sort of pre-game exhibition. After a while he began to think he was pretty good. "Sometime we'll let you kick the extra point, Ole." said Nevers jokingly. Well, that next night, up 52-0 over the hapless St. Louis Gunners, Nevers, who had just scored a touchdown, threw Ole a headgear and called him in to kick the point-after. Ole, now really excited, ran in to line up. What he didn't realize was that the players had all gotten together and told the Gunners that this was their boss, and they were going to pull a prank on him. With that, the ball was hiked, Ole approached the ball to kick it, and POW! He was flattened and buried by the entire Gunner defensive line, who screamed in untouched through the open flood gates. While the players rolled around chuckling, it would be Ole, however, who would get the last laugh.

"Well, I was pretty mad," he said. "And when I went back to the hotel I got the biggest towel I could find and put my arm in it like a sling. And you know? I couldn't write a pay-check for a couple of weeks! The boys never put me in another ball game after that."

Next up was a trip back to Cleveland, where the team played a couple of exhibition games against Cleveland and Akron, as well as a

THE NORTHLAND CONNECTION:

(Maybe it's the water...)

Believe it or not, the NFL of the 1920s was littered with Duluthians! According to the publication "Pro Football: The Early Years," there were some 42 players who either played high school or sandlot football in or around Duluth. Maybe there's something funky in that Lake Superior water?)

Johnny Blood
Bob Bratt
Eddie Bratt
Walt Buland
Gene Carlson
Herb Clow
Fred Denfeld
Joe DuMoe
Billy DuMoe
Rod Dunn
George Engstrom
Paul Flinn
Wally Gilbert
Ken Harris
Art Johnson
Doc Kelly
Howard Kieley
Mike Koziak
Joe Kraker
Allen MacDonald
Mickey McDonnell
Bill McNellis
Russ Method
Tom Murphy
Ernie Nevers
Dick O'Donnell
Wally O'Neill
Bill O'Toole
Cobb Rooney
Joe Rooney
Bill Rooney
Porky Rundquist
Dewey Scanlon
Bill Stein
Leif Strand
Ray Suess
Red Sullivan
Tarzan Taylor
Jack Underwood
Roy Vexall
Dick Vick
Doc Williams

regular season contest versus the Canton Bulldogs. While there the team stayed at the Allerton Hotel in Cleveland.

"It was a kind of show business hotel," Haugsrud reminisced. "The Marx Brothers and 'Mack Sennett's Bathing Beauties' were there at the same time we were. The owner had a very strict rule to prevent hanky-panky: women only on even-numbered floors and men only on odd-numbered floors" This was just the kind of silly rule the mischievous Blood loved to break. "John just walked into the elevator," continued Haugsrud, "handed the elevator girl some change and asked her to buy him cigarettes. When she went to the cigar stand, he stole the elevator. Of course, he didn't stop it at a men's floor." He was finally caught, but not before raising enough hell to nearly get the entire team booted out of the joint!

Canton, who was led by a 38-year-old superstar, Jim Thorpe, played the Eskimos tough, but came up short, 10-2. Nevers, who, after dropping back to catch a punt, got tattoo'd by Thorpe, later said: "I felt as though I was being Pile-driven into the ground. I've never been hit so hard before or since."

After Canton, the team headed East, where they beat the Hartford Blues, 15-0, and tied the Providence Steam Rollers, 0-0. (Nevers scored all the points in the Hartford game, kicking five field goals of 42, 21, 28, 26, and 25 yards, an achievement that stood alone until 1951.)

Now, among Haugsrud's official duties as team owner, in addition to arranging transportation, carrying the water bucket, and keeping track of the players, was to collect money from the home team that they were playing against. This in itself often times proved to be a very difficult task.

"You couldn't collect the money in advance, because the gate receipts weren't all in," Haugsrud recalled. "I tried to collect at half-time because then I could threaten to pull my team off the field if I didn't get it." In one of the game's, against the Gunners, the opposing team's owner came over and dropped off a check for $3,000. But Ole quickly noticed that he was about $70 short. "I hollered to him, but he knew what was going on and started running." he said. "I chased him right across the football field and up the steps of the grandstand and across an open cause-way. Then he ran into the ladies' room. There was a fellow standing outside the door, and he said to me 'You can't go in there!' I said 'I'm going in!' And I did. I cornered him in a toilet stall and he gave me the $70 bucks."

After that the team headed back west, with a stop in Kansas City, for a rematch against the Cowboys in the regular season finale. This time though, KC got revenge, beating the Eskimos, 12-7. From there the Eskimos, who finished out of the playoffs with a modest 6-5-3 regular season record, made a post-season exhibition swing through California, where Nevers was treated like a folk-hero.

In the end, the club netted a profit of $4,000. But there were times when they were in the hole by twice that amount. "See, when we got paid off for a game, I would send the check back to a Duluth bank, and as we traveled, I would write checks on our account," explained Haugsrud. "But in Providence early one morning. I got a telegram at the hotel from the banker in Duluth. It read: 'OLE, YOU BETTER GET THOSE ESKIMOS HOME WHILE YOU STILL GOT ENOUGH BLUBBER MEAT TO FEED THEM!' It turned out that our checking account was about dry. What happened was that we had been paid $4,000 in New Britain, Conn., but when the Duluth bank put the check through, it bounced. And we had gotten $3,000 in Hartford, but that check also got kicked in the tail. So I called all the boys together at breakfast and read them that telegram telling us to come home. I'll always remember that Cobb Rooney got up and said, 'Ole, tell that banker to stick that telegram up his you-know-where! You just pay us $15 bucks a week to eat on, and pay our room rent and our transportation.' All of the other boys said, 'Amen! You can pay us our salary when you catch up.' "

By now injuries and fatigue were setting in and they were struggling to field a team. But in Sacramento they lost their star quarterback, Cobb Rooney, for a different reason. After nearly losing his eye in a game against Sacramento, Rooney had to spend the night in an area hospital. Two days later he showed up at Ole's hotel room in San Francisco with his head all bandaged up and a nurse along his side. "I want to introduce you to my future wife," he said. And with that he was gone too.

The team's amazing 117-day, 29-game barn-storming tour finally came to an end in early February of 1927. After traveling nearly 20,000 miles, once playing five games in eight days, the team gladly returned home to Duluth with an overall record of 19-7-3. Through it all they played hurt and played as a team. Broken fingers, sprained ankles and torn up knees were just ailments the men had to live with. Some players went above and beyond, such as Wingback Russ Method, who had his nose broken on numerous occasions throughout the season. (Method actually busted his snout 14 times over his career — a record believed to still be in tact even to this day!)

Nevers, the team's meal-ticket, was the hub of the Eskimos offensive attack. He set five league marks for rushing, passing, kicking and scoring, and was just a horse, playing nearly every minute of every game, calling the plays and handling the ball on almost every offensive play. Just how exhausted was he? When the season started he weighed 210 and at the finish he weighed 185.

He had single-handedly saved the league that year. His presence raised the league's attendance immeasurably, and as a result, the AFL's eight franchises went broke and folded after the season. All except for C. C. Pyle's New York Yankees that is, who, as a concession, were given membership into the NFL — giving old C.C. what he really wanted all along.

(Incidentally, that would be the first of three rival AFL's that would challenge the NFL over the next 50 years. The next AFL threat came in 1936, with franchises in Boston, Cleveland, New York, Pittsburgh, Brooklyn and Syracuse, and then again in 1960, when the Vikings joined, only to jump out at the last minute to play in the NFL instead.)

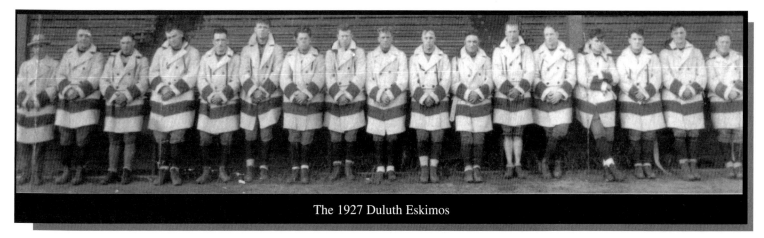

The 1927 Duluth Eskimos

The Beginning of the End

While the NFL survived the attack of the AFL in 1926, many of the weaker clubs soon found out that they couldn't afford to pay for the marquis teams like the Eskimos when they to came to town that next year. Consequently, 11 of the NFL's 22 franchises were forced to close up shop, which then left the remaining franchises to bulk up with out-of-work talent. Ironically, the Eskimos had priced themselves out of the market, and with just 11 teams to now play, Haugsrud could schedule only nine games. In the end he too, lost money.

Nevers earned All-Pro status for the second time in as many years in 1927, but his supporting cast just was unable to provide any consistency, and the team plummeted to a paltry 1-8 record. After losing to Green Bay, 20-0, in their opener, the Eskimos rebounded behind Nevers' 17-straight pass completions for a trio of touchdowns and pair of field goals to beat the Pottsville Maroons, 27-0. But from there, it got ugly as the team lost to Cleveland, New York, Providence, Pottsville, Frankford, Cleveland and Chicago.

In 1928, Haugsrud, unable to field a team, suspended the team's operations. While the league allowed him to let the franchise sit idle that year, essentially drawing a bye, they pressured him into selling his team. The NFL wanted to have their clubs located in the densely populated coastal cities, where there were more fans and less travel for the players.

After hearing the news, Nevers, who tallied an amazing 102 points in his two short years in Duluth, said good bye to his old friend, and headed back to Stanford. But, after spending a year working with Pop Warner's coaching staff, he returned to the NFL to join the Chicago Cardinals, where, in 1929, he set an NFL record by scoring all of his team's points in a 40-6 win over the cross-town rival Bears.

That next season Haugsrud reluctantly decided to sell his pride and joy to a group from Orange, New Jersey, where the Eskimos were renamed as the Tornadoes.

"But I didn't do so bad by selling," Haugsrud later explained. "You see, we negotiated the deal at a league meeting in Cleveland, and the fellows from the other clubs were anxious to see the deal settled. They wanted to get out of there because they didn't have enough money to stay three or four days in a high-priced hotel. I wanted $3,000 but the fellow from Orange wanted to give me $2,000. The others said to me 'Come on Swede. We've got to get going home!' So I said 'All right, but with one stipulation. The next time a franchise is granted in the state of Minnesota, I will have the first opportunity to bid for it.' In order to get out of there, they gave me a letter to that effect and over the years I kept letting the National Football League know about it. In 1961, when the Minnesota Vikings were created, I got 10% of the stock. The franchise cost $600,000, and for my share I paid $60,000."

Yup, Ole had gotten the last laugh once again. At his death in March of 1976, his shares were worth nearly $2 million. His original investment of a measly buck back in 1925 had become the deal of a lifetime.

JOE GUYON

Halfback Joe Guyon was one of the first Native Americans to star in the NFL. Guyon, who was born in Mahnomen, on the White Earth Reservation, later attended the Carlisle Indian School. where he played with the great Jim Thorpe. After leading Georgia Tech to a national collegiate championship, he played professionally for more than a decade with the Canton Bulldogs, Cleveland Indians, Oorang Indians, Rock Island Independents, Kansas City Cowboys, and New York Giants. He was inducted into the Pro Football Hall of Fame in 1966.

Meanwhile, the Tornadoes played just one season in Orange and then moved to Newark in 1930, where they finished dead last. In 1931 the league took the franchise back and put it on moth balls. But, that next year a group of New England businessmen, headed by George Preston Marshall, purchased the defunct team and moved it to Boston, where they were renamed as the Braves and played in Fenway Park. Two years later Mr. Marshall then moved his club to Washington D.C., where the Braves were renamed as the Redskins, and have remained ever since as one of pro football's most successful franchises. Incredibly, in 1998, the team, and its new stadium was sold to local businessman Daniel Snyder, for the unconscionable sum of $800 million — aproximitely $800 million times what old Ole paid for them, give or take a buck or two!

Years later Ole reminisced as to just how good his Eskimos really were. "When they selected the charter membership for the Pro Football Hall of Fame in Canton, Ohio, three of the first 17 men enshrined were on that team: Nevers, Blood and Kiesling," he said. "That should give you some idea of the talent we had."

In their own way, Ole and Ernie's Eskimos played a big part in making the NFL what it is today. Before Nevers came along, pro football was like the plague. College football was big-time, and wanted nothing to do with them. In fact, they even had an unwritten rule that if you played professionally, you could never get a college coaching job. Some coaches, such as legendary Chicago University skipper, Amos Alonzo Stagg, even took it a step further by declaring that if any of his boys went on to play pro ball after graduation, he would recall their varsity letter. As a result, the pro teams could get very little publicity for their games. The media at that time didn't want to make waves, so they stuck to covering the college gridiron. But Nevers changed all of that, bringing a new level of respectability and credibility to the game. It wasn't long before radio stations started to broadcast the games, and newspapers were running front-page stories about their local pro teams. Yup, the tiny Eskimos from Duluth, Minnesota, with their zany cast of characters, truly changed the face of professional football as we know it today.

The Minnesota Vikings have become an integral part of the fabric of Minnesota life for the past 40 years, bringing us all both joy and pain. For those of us who truly bleed purple, Sunday afternoons in Autumn are a religion all of their own. Named in honor of our Scandinavian heritage, the Vikings, were barbaric and ruthless marauders. It would be safe to say that many of those same qualities became prevalent during the genesis of creating this franchise some four decades ago.

While the concept of bringing a professional football team to Minnesota was a radical one back in 1960, it wasn't the first time our state had been a part of the NFL fraternity. In fact, the Duluth Kelly's, who later became the Eskimos, as well as the Minneapolis Marines, who later became the Red Jackets, were a part of pro football's beginnings back in the 1920s. Over the next several decades a smattering of teams also came here for exhibition games and to hold preseason camps, including the Chicago Cardinals, who held camp in Duluth back in the early 1940s. In addition, the New York Giants held their pre-season camp in St. Peter, at the campus of Gustavus Adolphus in the early 1950s, and the Dallas Cowboys did the same down in Northfield, on the campus of St. Olaf in 1960.

But this was a strange time in the world of Minnesota sports, and the thought of bringing a new franchise into a market that was booming, was going to be a difficult one. The state-of-the-state of Minnesota sports in 1960 was unlike any time in modern history. The new Minnesota Twins were just about to set up shop at the Met; the Gopher football team was coming off of its first national championship in nearly two decades; the Gopher baseball team had just won its second national championship in only four years; John Kundla's Gopher basketball team was playing decent, better than .500 ball over at the Barn; the Gopher hockey team was also doing well that year under John Mariucci, as several of the teams' stars, including John Mayasich and Jack McCartan, had just led Team USA to its first-ever gold medal in the Winter Olympics at Squaw Valley; the Minneapolis Millers and St. Paul Saints (winners of the league's Turner Cup championship that year) were leading the way for professional hockey in the state as members of the International Hockey League; and the six-time NBA world champion Minneapolis Lakers had just been uprooted to the city of Los Angeles in a very controversial move. Now to top all that off, the upstart Minnesota Vikings were attempting to build a brand new fan-base in a market that was, well, pretty much overloaded as far as sports options went.

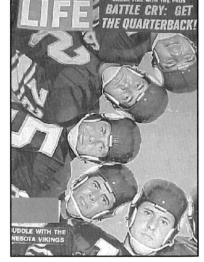

To make matters worse, at that time there were two rival leagues, the dominant NFL, and the upstart AFL, both competing for the rights to expand and counter-expand against one another in an attempt to gain as much market-share as possible. Minnesota's would-be franchise was caught right smack in the middle of this civil war, and in order for this group of NFL wannabe's to pull it off, they would need to build an alliance between a pair of bickering sisters — Minneapolis and St. Paul, who simply couldn't agree on a thing. That is where our story of the one of the NFL's most storied and successful franchises, the Minnesota Vikings, humbly begins.

The Makings of a Team

To fully understand the genesis of just how pro football came back to Minnesota in 1960, we must first go back to 1959, when a group of three local businessmen convinced the National Football League to allow the Chicago Cardinals to play two of their regular season games, against both the New York Giants and Philadelphia Eagles, in the newly constructed Metropolitan Stadium.

(Metropolitan Stadium, or the Met, as it was affectionately known, was built in 1956 on 164-acre farmland site in Bloomington, by the Baseball Committee of the Minneapolis Chamber of Commerce, with its first tenants being the Minneapolis Millers minor-league baseball team. [Bloomington was chosen as a Switzerland-like demilitarized zone which satisfied both of the rival sisters in knowing that neither one would rightfully be able to call the stadium their own.] The committee's intent though was to lure the New York [baseball] Giants, the Millers' major league affiliate, to move there. But, when the Giants decided to move to San Francisco instead, the group then convinced Calvin Griffith to move his Washington Senators here for the 1961 season. While the stadium was built for baseball, it could also house a football team, something that caught the attention of several very wealthy football boosters.)

Metropolitan Stadium

Enter the Minneapolis trio of H.P. Skoglund, a Swedish insurance tycoon, E.W. Boyer, a silver-haired northerner with a southern accent who ran local Ford dealership, and Max Winter, a hustler from North Minneapolis who, in addition to being a part-owner of the Minneapolis Lakers, was involved in a bunch of stuff including, restaurants, vending machines, real estate, boxing promotions, theater and even auto shows. This alliance of sorts put up nearly a quarter-million dollars for those two Cardinals games to show the league that this was indeed a good football town, and would therefore be a great market for one of their coveted expansion franchises. Now, in an effort to make sure that the Met was full of football fans for those two games, the group did everything from give tickets away to people on the streets to blitzing the airwaves with all the hype of a presidential election. While some of their strong-arming tactics were questionable, they needed to make sure that the league was thoroughly satisfied and confident that the area could support a team. (The funny part about having a bunch of non-football fans in the crowd was that whenever the team's did something dramatic out on the field, the seat-fillers just sat there lethargically, not knowing when or why to cheer — leaving the league officials who were in attendance to wonder if Minnesotans really knew anything about the game of football!)

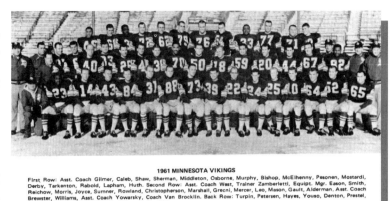

1961 MINNESOTA VIKINGS

First Row: Asst. Coach Gilmer, Caleb, Shaw, Sherman, Middleton, Osborne, Murphy, Bishop, McElhenny, Pesonen, Mostardi, Derby, Tarkenton, Rabold, Lapham, Huth. Second Row: Asst. Coach West, Trainer Zamberletti, Equipt. Mgr. Eason, Smith, Reichow, Morris, Joyce, Sumner, Rowland, Christopherson, Marshall, Grecni, Mercer, Leo, Mason, Gault, Alderman, Asst. Coach Brewster, Williams, Asst. Coach Yowarsky, Coach Van Brocklin. Back Row: Turpin, Petersen, Hayes, Youso, Denton, Prestel, Dickson, Rubke, Triplett, Shields, Culpepper, Hawkins.

Now here is where it gets a little bit confusing, so hang on. At the same time the group was trying to woo the NFL into coming to Minnesota, a newly formed rival circuit, the American Football League entered the fray. (The AFL began, in part because of Dallas oil millionaire Lamar Hunt's unsuccessful attempted to purchase the Chicago Cardinals just the year before, prompting his efforts to start a rival league. The Minnesota group then tried a different tact, and tried to convince Cardinals' owner Walter Wolfner to relocate his franchise to Minnesota, but he instead got gun-shy and moved the team to his hometown of St. Louis for the 1960 season.)

The AFL, considered by many to be a renegade league, even went as far as to set up shop at the Nicollet Hotel in downtown Minneapolis on the very day of the Cardinals vs. Giants game to conduct their organizational meetings regarding expansion. They wanted the lucrative Minnesota market and made no bones about it. The league featured a cast of eccentric characters and millionaires including, Houston's Bud Adams, Dallas' Lamar Hunt, New York sportscaster Harry Wismer, former Notre Dame Coach Frank Leahy (who represented Barron Hilton of the hotel dynasty), and a handful of celebrity jocks. The league, which was moving full-speed-ahead in expansion mode, had recruited the Minnesota threesome hard and was ready to offer them what would turn out to be their eighth new franchise right there on the spot.

Incredibly, that same afternoon, the head of the NFL's Expansion Committee, Bears Owner and Coach George Halas, sent a telegram to then sports editor of the Minneapolis newspaper, Charles Johnson, announcing the league's intentions to offer a franchise to the Minnesota group at its upcoming Winter Meeting in Miami. With both offers now in hand, the group had a decision to make. Knowing that the rival leagues were competing against one-another, and that this was just all part of their ongoing strategies, the group opted to accept the AFL's "bird-in-hand" offer to become new charter members, rather than take their chances on something getting fouled up a few months later in Miami. The group also felt the heat from the stadium group, who, along with their private bondholders who had invested millions, were anxious to rent out their new facility to another "major league" tenant. (Incidentally, Halas' decision to let the Minnesota group into the NFL fraternity was probably in his own best interests — and he knew it. Back then most of the team's were on the east and west coasts, leaving Chicago and Green Bay to own the Midwest. Halas knew that if the rival AFL landed a team just a few hundred miles away, the financial welfare of his Bears might suffer. His fan base would drop and future television revenues would be lost. So by letting Minnesota into his territory, the "Papa Bear" also made sure that the AFL stayed out.)

So, after paying their $25,000 deposit, the new Minneapolis—St. Paul AFL affiliate took part in the upcoming draft, which, coincidentally, was also held in Minneapolis. There, the group selected Wisconsin Quarterback Dale Hackbart with their first-round pick. But, when Hackbart found out that the group wanted no part of giving him a signing bonus, he said no thanks and headed north of the border, to the Canadian Football League's Winnipeg Blue-Bombers. (Ironically, five years later, Hackbart would sign with the Vikings as a defensive back.) Down, but certainly not out, the new ownership went to Miami, where the NFL was finally holding its Winter Meetings. There, after voting to make Pete Rozelle as its new commissioner, the NFL's Board of Owners voted for both Minnesota and Dallas to receive new expansion franchises. (Dallas would begin in 1960 and Minnesota in 1961, pursuant upon the team enlarging Metropolitan Stadium to 40,000 seats, and declaring that there would have to be 25,000 season ticket sales by the opening game.) Feeling confident, the trio then went back to the AFL, and much like Hackbart had done, said no thanks — even though it meant waiting an additional year to get a team with the NFL. League President Lamar Hunt reluctantly accepted the group's defection, and so was born the beginning of the Minnesota Vikings. (Incidentally, that eighth AFL franchise was given to a syndicate in Oakland led by Al Davis, whose Raiders would come back to haunt the Vikings in Super Bowl XI.)

Knowing that they were going to need additional financing to pay the $1 million franchise fee ($600,000 to join and $400,000 later), the group went out and added a couple of key investors. They knew that the team wasn't going to succeed without the active partnership of St. Paul, so they ventured across the Mississippi River and joined forces with Bernie Ridder, of the famed Knight-Ridder newspaper syndicate, who served as the publisher of both the Pioneer Press and Dispatch. The other partner was former Duluth Eskimos owner, Ole Haugsrud. Now Ole was the wildcard in the whole thing because, unlike the wealthy and powerful Ridder, he was simply "required" to be there. You see, when Ole sold his Eskimos back in 1930 to a group in New Jersey (the team would later become the present-day Washington Redskins), he made the NFL promise him that if the league ever expanded back to Minnesota, he would have the right of first refusal to be a part of the ownership group. Amazingly, 30 years later, the Duluth businessman was given his opportunity to purchase a 10% ownership stake in the new franchise. (Ole originally bought the franchise, then known as the Duluth Kelly's, back in 1924 for the whopping sum of $1!) With Ole's 10% and Ridder taking another 30%, the remaining 60% of the team's stock was divided equally among Skoglund, Winter and Boyer. They then voted to make Ridder as Chairman of the Board, Winter as President, Boyer as Vice President, Haugsrud as Secretary and Skoglund as Treasurer.

With that the team got organized. After learning that they would be playing in the Western Conference, along with the Baltimore Colts, Chicago Bears, Detroit Lions, Green Bay Packers, L.A. Rams and San Francisco 49ers, the team hired former Rams P.R. Director Bert Rose to be their General Manager. His main task was to figure out just how they were going to tap the local boosters in order to sell 25,000 season tickets in an already oversaturated sports market. (One of the major contributors in the start-up effort were the Minneapolis Minutemen, who helped to round-up a boat-load of season tick-

Norm "Dutch" Van Brocklin

Paul Flatley

et-holders required for admittance.) But first they needed a name. After much deliberation, they decided to go with "Vikings." Because of the predominantly Scandinavian make-up of the region, which is where the Vikings originally hailed from during the late 700s to about 1100, along with the area's frigid weather, it just seemed to fit. There was even a Norse term which, when translated, read "to go a-Viking," meant to fight fiercely as a pirate or warrior and conquer — that was something they could all relate to at that time. (Haugsrud then reportedly insisted that the team adopt the colors purple and white, which were, ironically, the same colors of his native Superior Central High School team.)

Their next step was to hire a coach, and start preparing for the team's first draft later that fall. Several quality candidates were considered, among there were: Northwestern University Coach Ara Parseghian, former Cleveland Browns Quarterback Otto Graham, San Diego Chargers Coach Sid Gillman (a minneapolis native), Winnipeg Blue-Bombers Coach Bud Grant, Philadelphia Eagles Assistant Coach Nick Skorich, and recently retired Eagles Quarterback Norm Van Brocklin. After careful deliberation and consultation with Pete Rozelle, the group decided on Van Brocklin, who, because he was a 12-year veteran and had just led his Eagles to the NFL championship, they felt would give the team instant credibility. "Dutch" as he was known, was very intelligent, very combative and very demanding. All were qualities that the group felt would be important in trying to mold a new group of untested rookies and washed up has-been's — which was precisely what they were going to get dealt in that opening draft.

Joe Thomas, formerly with the Rams' organization, was then brought in as the teams' chief scout to prepare for the upcoming chaos. There wasn't a bumper crop ripe for the picking that year, rather, a smattering of old and new. Held on December 27, 1960, the college draft yielded several key players who would go on to wear the purple proudly. With the first overall choice in that year's draft, the Vikings selected Tulane Running Back Tommy Mason. They next took North Carolina Linebacker Rip Hawkins, and at No.3 the team took a Quarterback out of the University of Georgia by the name of Francis Tarkenton. With their fourth and fifth picks, the team took a pair of defensive backs in Wyoming's Chuck Lamson and Pittsburgh's Ed Sharockman.

Following the college draft, an expansion draft was held, whereby the Vikings were allowed to select three players from the rosters of each NFL team. The teams, who were allowed to protect 30 of their 38 players, used the opportunity to cast-off may of their old duds and rejects. The Dutchman, Rose and Thomas all jumped in though, and by the time it was over, had came out with a few diamonds in the rough that had been foolishly discarded. Among them were 49ers star Running Back Hugh McElhenny and Detroit Tackle Grady Alderman. Additionally, the team made a couple of deals in exchange for their next years' first and second round draft picks with both the Cleveland Browns, for an undersized Defensive End by the name of Jim Marshall, and also with the New York Giants, for what they figured was going to be the quarterback of the future — George Shaw. All in all the Vikings wound up with 36 players, of whom the Dutchman, after seeing them up close, would refer to them fondly as "36 stiffs."

Off to Bemidji

With that the team headed north, 250 miles to Bemidji, where, on the third week of July, 1961, they officially opened their inaugural training camp. Many wondered just why the team had their camp so far away. That was simple, Dutch wanted obscurity and concealment, and in the midst of wild rice bogs, tamarack pine trees and Paul Bunyan's Big Blue Ox — Babe, that was exactly what he found.

Once there, Van Brocklin announced an open "cattle call" for any unsigned free agents. While Dutch was pleased to see a handful of former pro re-treads make the trek up to the great northwoods, he was also astonished to see what else crawled out from under the carpet and onto his practice field. Among the more than 150 walk-on's in attendance that week were a gnarly bunch of motley mercenaries which included random bartenders, truck drivers, bouncers, construction workers, soldiers of fortune, criminals, and drifters — basically anybody with a heartbeat and a jock-strap. But, after a couple of Van Brocklin's exhausting two-a-day workouts in the humidity and heat, most of the blue-collared wannabe's limped home. (One guy in particular who kept very busy during those few days patching people back together, was team trainer Fred Zamberletti, a man who, incredibly, is still with the team 40 years later.) It was now up to Dutch to sort through this collection of misfits and outcasts and put together a ball club that was going to compete against the best players the world had to offer.

The team got its first test when it ventured south, to Sioux Falls, S.D., where, on August 5th, they played their first-ever preseason game, losing 38-13, to the Dallas Cowboys, in front of just 4,954 fans. There were some highlights, and a bunch of lowlights, but all in all the

Gary Cuozzo

Vikings made it through OK that first preseason. Sure, they lost all five of their exhibition games, but they did show some promise. Van Brocklin absolutely hated to lose and took each loss as a personal insult on his ability to coach. He would go back to the drawing board after every game, and, while chain-smoking his Camel's, would go over each and every play, cursing and wondering just what in the world he had gotten himself into.

Their final preseason game would prove to be their first-ever home game at the Met, whereupon the Vikes came up just short in a 21-17 loss to the Rams. (The 41,200-seat stadium was unique because it was the only venue in the league where both team benches were on the same side of the field — an nuance which would make for some interesting scurmishes as the years went on.) The better than average crowd was excited to see their new team, and knew that it was going to be a building process. After all, the mighty Chicago Bears, the dreaded "Monsters of the Midway," were coming to town in just one week, and no one in the world expected them to spare any mercy on these "stiffs."

A Miracle at the Met

On September 17, 1961, the upstart Vikings christened Metropolitan Stadium by playing their first-ever regular season game against the Chicago Bears. While the Bears were revered as the reigning titans of the NFL, the lowly Vikings were just hoping to not embarrass themselves in front of the 32,236 fans who had come out to see them. What transpired was historic.

While the veteran George Shaw started out the game at quarterback, the Dutchman decided to bench him midway through the first quarter in favor of his rookie, Fran Tarkenton, whom he affectionately called the "Georgia Peach." Kicker Mike Mercer made history by scoring the team's first points, a 12-yard field goal, followed by Tarkenton's ever first touchdown pass, a 14-yarder to Tight End Bob Schnelker. Incredibly, Fran added numbers two and three in the third quarter and number four in the fourth. All in all he threw four TDs that afternoon, on 17 of 23 passing for 250 yards, and even ran one in just before the final gun for a fifth.

"Everything the NFL had to offer in the way of experience and power was opposing me just a few feet away, and here I was, a kid of 21, fresh out of college, being required to lead an untried team into this battle where we'd have to out-think and out-fight the old masters," said Tark.

The rookie's unorthodox "scrambling" (a term almost literally coined by the youngsters athleticism and ability to not get sacked) behind the line of scrimmage electrified the crowd and dissected the Bears defense, leaving their linemen simply dazed and confused. When it was all said and done, Halas' proud Bears didn't know what hit them. The Vikings went on to win the game convincingly, by the improbable score of 37-13. It would be safe to assume that one didn't want to know what was said behind the closed doors of the visiting lockerroom after the game.

"Sure, I helped get Minnesota in the league, but I didn't want to be this cooperative," said Halas sarcastically after the game.

That next week the Dallas Cowboys came to town, and, despite Tarkenton's solid performance, lost 21-7. They rebounded in a big way in Week Three, however, as the team took its first road-trip, to Baltimore, to take on Quarterback Johnny

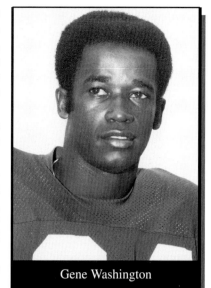

Gene Washington

Unitas and the mighty Colts. Van Brocklin decided to start Quarterback George Shaw in this one because he figured that since he used to play for the Colts, and was still fondly thought of by the local fans, would do better than the rookie Tarkenton. This one turned out to be a wild one with both teams scoring early and often. Behind Shaw's passing to Jerry Reichow, the running of rookie fullback Raymond Hayes, and the kicking of Mercer, who kicked a 20-yarder with 32 seconds left in the game to take the lead, the Vikes suddenly found themselves on the verge of upsetting the powerhouse Colts. That's when Unitas drove his club up to midfield by throwing quick out-patterns to his receivers along the sidelines. Then, with just one second remaining on the clock, Baltimore Kicker Steve Myhra calmly came out and booted the game-winning 52-yard field goal to give his squad a dramatic 34-33 victory. After the game Dutch was beside himself.

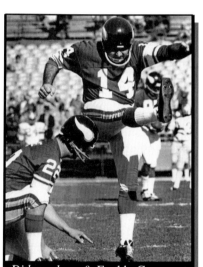

Did you know? Freddy Cox went on to invent the "Nerf Ball!"

"The coach was totally unpredictable," Tarkenton wrote of Van Brocklin in his book, "Don't Just Accept Defeat." "He could be the most charming guy in the world, and the next day he would be the most obnoxious. He could be sweet as a lamb or raise holy hell. You never knew which way he was coming from, so you were never in a stable situation."

Following that heart-breaking defeat the Purple then reverted to expansion-team form, losing five straight games to Dallas, San Francisco, Green Bay (twice) and Los Angeles, before finally getting a chance to even the score with the Colts. When Unitas and his all-star cast, which included the likes of Raymond Berry, Art Donovan, Jim Parker, "Big Daddy" Lipscomb and Gino Marchetti came to town this time, the Vikes were ready for them. A few days prior to the game, Dutch decided to cut his men some slack and announced that there would be no curfew for the weekend. Well rested and definitely recharged, the Vikes, with Tark, Mason and McElhenny tearing up the backfield, this time pulled off the upset, winning, 28-20, in front of 38,020 screaming Met Stadium fans.

After dropping a pair to Detroit and San Francisco over the next two weeks, the Vikings came back to beat a solid L.A. Rams club, 42-21. The team did lose its last two contests at Detroit and Chicago, but finished with a somewhat respectable rookie record of 3-11. The team's season finale at Chicago's Wrigley Field proved to be a barn-burner. McElhenny, who was honored at midfield by his former team prior to kick-off with a plaque that read: "Wouldn't football be a beautiful game if everyone played it the way Hugh McElhenny does?", responded diligently just a few minutes later by running back a punt 80 yards for a touchdown. He led the Vikes to a quick 21-0 lead, only to see the Bears rally back for a commanding 52-35 victory.

While the team really stepped it up a notch against the league's better teams, it still had a long way to go. Tarkenton passed for 1,997 yards and 19 touchdowns that season, while Jerry Reichow caught 50 balls for 859 yards and 11 touchdowns, and Hugh McElhenny, who finished with 570 yards rushing, was voted as the team's MVP. (The team also established its practice site at St. Paul's Midway Stadium, now home to the St. Paul Saints Baseball team.)

The Long Road to Respectability

Despite the acquisition of several key players in 1962 including, future All-Pro Center Mick Tingelhoff, Running Back Bill "Boom Boom" Brown, Tight End Steve Stonebreaker and Safety Bill Butler, as well as drafting Guard Larry Bowie and Linebacker Roy Winston, things somehow got worse for the squad. Although they started out 0-5, the team did manage to go on its first winning streak though, beating both Los Angeles, 38-14, and Philadelphia 31-21, in Weeks Six and Seven, but finished with just a 2-11-1 record. The porous defense allowed 410 points in just 14 games, but Tarkenton made it interesting as he fired another 22 touchdown passes that season, including a record 89-yarder to the hurdler, Charley Ferguson, against the Bears, a 74-yarder to Tommy Mason against the Eagles and a 60-yard bomb to Ferguson against the Steelers. Another pleasant surprise was the addition of Kicker Fred Cox, who beat out Mike Mercer after kicking a 43-yarder against Dallas. McElhenny and Reichow also became the

Bill "Boom Boom" Brown

Mick Tingelhoff

first Vikings ever to compete in the Pro Bowl that year, as the West defeated the East 31-30 at the L.A. Coliseum.

One of the bright spots on an otherwise dismal season was the inspired play of "Boom Boom" Brown, who, with his trademark military crew cut and deep guttural voice became one of the team's first fan-favorites. Brown, who ran like a Mack Truck without brakes, revolutionized the game perhaps without even trying. You see, back in the day, uprights were mounted right smack dab in the middle of the goal lines, to increase field goal accuracy for the kickers. As a result, players had to run around or in-between the two goal posts in order to get into the end-zone. Brown, on the other hand, had a habit of running into and even through them. His ensuing concussions, along with the fact that the goal posts were also hindering the league's prima-donna quarterbacks from throwing touchdown passes (which now affected TV ratings), was instrumental in the league's decision to move the goal posts back 10 yards to the end zone line.

Tarkenton, who was named as the team's MVP that season, was gaining quite a reputation around the league for his amazing ability to scramble behind enemy lines. His running around bought his receivers extra time to get open, and also set up other impromptu plays such as the lateral — which the team used quite a bit in pressure situations. When asked about it, the Georgia gun-slinger said he could-n't understand why so many pro quarterbacks just accepted sacks as part of the game when their pock-ets collapsed. Said Tark: "I'd sit there and I'd say, 'God, do something,' "

Now, Dutch, who was an old-school quarterback, accepted Tark's unorthodox style, but never real-ly got too comfortable with his improvisational antics. "Actually, Van Brocklin and I never had any real arguments about scrambling," Tarkenton said in Jim Klobuchar's 1995 book "Purple Hearts and Golden Memories." "Sometimes he'd chew on me in team meetings. But he didn't in public, except for that great line he used to have: 'I've told Tarkenton a hundred times, third and 18 is no time to be creative.' "I laughed every time I heard that. And, of course, he was exactly wrong. Third and 18 is the time to be creative. But he didn't really yell and scream when I tried to rescue a broken play. He made the obvious point that sometimes I caused it by leaving the pocket too early. How could I argue with that? What happened is that we had a young team. It was tough for the offensive linemen to hold out great pass rushers like Marchetti and Alex Karras and Roger Brown, Deacon Jones and people like that. The idea in football is to win. You'd like to do it with the artistic, order-ly plays drawn up in your playbook. But if it turns into a mess, it doesn't mean you have to throw up your hands and die. Quarterbacks of today, with the rare exceptions of the Steve Young's, won't do it the way I did. They're getting so much money the owners and coaches just won't let them risk their bodies by running with the ball or by doing all those crazy loops behind the line looking for a receiver. What was money in those days? I started at $12,000 a year. All I was doing by scrambling was trying to figure out a way to win on that play, buying some time or trying to save my skin. It wasn't planned. I didn't daydream ways to beat the rush while I was driving to work. I did it more than most quarterbacks of the time because we weren't competitive with a lot of the teams, and I had better reactions and quicker feet than most of the quarterbacks."

The Vikings started to show that they indeed had a pulse in 1963, as a new cast of characters came in and led the team to a much improved 5-8-1 record. Leading the charge was Northwestern Wide Receiver Paul Flatley, whose 51 catches for 867 yards were good enough to earn the NFL's rookie-of-the-year award. And while Hugh "The King" McElhenny decided to hang em' up, Halfback Tommy Mason, who finished fifth in the league with 763 yards rushing and seven touchdowns, filled his shoes admirably — even becoming the first Viking in team history to be named All-Pro. Also added to the roster were Defensive Backs Karl Kassulke and Terry Dillon, Quarterback Ron VanderKelen, and Running Back Phil King, who was acquired from the Giants. The team did lose their first and second round draft picks, however, Tackles Bobby Bell (a former Gopher All-American) and Jim Dunaway, to the rival American Football League.

The Purple began showing signs of respectability by taking four of five pre-season games and then going to win five more during the regular season. Tarkenton's offense generated 22 points per game, thanks in large part to his offensive line which was anchored by Tingelhoff, Alderman and Larry Bowie. The defense was also coming along, as players like Defensive End Jim Marshall and Cornerback Ed Sharockman, who had a dozen pick-offs over the past two seasons, were emerging as up-and-coming stars.

One of the team's biggest accomplishments that year was their late-season 17-17 tie with the would-be NFL Champion Chicago Bears, who needed a fourth quarter fumble recovery and a late touchdown to escape with the stale-mate. Minnesota made a nice run at the end of the season, finishing 2-1-1 in the final four games, which included wins over Detroit, 34-31, and Philadelphia, 34-13, to end the year with a respectable 5-8-1 record — by far their best to date.

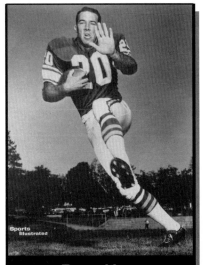
Tommy Mason

Beating the Pack and the now-infamous "Wrong Way Play"

The 1964 season got underway with the franchise making a major front-office maneuver, replacing General Manager Bert Rose with Jim Finks, a former NFL quarterback turned GM with the CFL's Calgary Stampede. Finks, who was well respected for recognizing and developing talent, would make a big impact on the team over the next several years. For starters though, the team made a huge addi-tion by drafting Gopher All-American Carl Eller, who, along with Jim Marshall, now made up half of the yet-to-be infamous "Purple People Eaters" defensive line. Behind Eller's defensive punch and the Pro Bowl backfield of Tarkenton, Mason and Brown, Minnesota went 8-5-1, including a 3-0-1 stretch over the last four games, to post their first winning season and get their fans excited about the team's future.

Minnesota got off to a roaring start that year. After an undefeated 5-0 preseason, they went on to beat the Colts, 34-24, in their opener. Then, after dropping the next two to Detroit and L.A., the team notched arguably its biggest win to date, beating the hated rivals from Green Bay for their first time ever. Coach Vince Lombardi, the meticulous planner and authoritarian, found no game plan to counter the Viking's black and blue smash-mouth style of football. After a back and forth game, the Purple were down by two points and found themselves with a fourth-and-22 desperation situation on their own 36-

yard line. The Pack knew Tark would scramble, so spread out their defense all over the field. The quarterback figured just that and, after simply telling everyone to "go deep," he bought enough time to heave a prayer that somehow found Tight End Gordie Smith at the 22-yard line. Then, with time ticking off the clock, Freddie "the foot" Cox came in and kicked the game-winning field goal to give his squad a 24-23 ball-game.

The team went on to finish second in the Western Conference that year, behind Baltimore, thanks to an offensive explosion in their final three games which produced 34, 30 and 41 points to beat the Rams, Giants and Bears, respectively, with the last two coming on the road. Tarkenton, who led an offense that, for the first time finally outscored its opposition, 355-296, passed for 22 touchdowns that season and was named as the MVP of the Pro Bowl. Meanwhile, Bill Brown rushed for 866 yards and seven TDs and also caught another 48 passes for nine TDs.

One of the most memorable plays in team history, which involved Jim Marshall, also happened that year. On October 25th, at Kezar Stadium in San Francisco, in a game against the 49ers, the now infamous "Wrong Way Play" took place, forever linking Marshall with a play he'd just as soon forget. It all started with a lob pass from San Francisco QB George Mira to Billy Kilmer (then a halfback) out of the Niner backfield. Marshall, who was charging in on a blitz, suddenly saw the ball fly out of Kilmer's hands. Immediately, he scooped up the loose ball and sprinted 60 yards to pay-dirt. Despite the frantic waving of his teammates along the sidelines, he was going to get six. He instead got two... for the Niners. When he got there he was quickly greeted by San Francisco Lineman, Bruce Bosley, who was the first to break the news by putting his arm around and say, "Thanks buddy, You ran into your own end zone!"

John Gilliam

It was at that moment that Marshall realized he had somehow lost his sense of direction and simply ran into the wrong end-zone, thus giving the Niners a two-point safety. "I had to jump over one of the 49ers' linemen to get to the ball, and after that, I didn't remember anything until I got to the end zone," said Marshall. The Vikings did win the game however, 27-22. Tommy Mason scored on a seven yarder in the second, Cox kicked a pair of field goals in the first and third, and Tark ran in an eight yarder in the fourth. The winning play of the game came late in the fourth though, thanks to, you guessed it, Jim Marshall. The Captain redeemed himself big-time by causing a key fumble that was picked up by Carl Eller, who then took it 45-yards into the end-zone to seal the victory for Minnesota.

Dave Osborn

(While the "Wrong Way Play" has lived on in infamy, even being voted as the hands-down No. 1 pick of NFL Films' list of "100 Greatest Follies," Marshall later capitalized on his sudden infamy by being booked on countless speaking engagements, made television appearances, and got advertising deals. Ironically, in 1963, Marshall returned a 49ers' fumble the "right way" for a touchdown!)

In 1965 the Met's capacity was expanded from 41,200 to 47,200 when a new grandstand was constructed on the stadium's east side, just in time for Baseball's All-Star game, and subsequent World Series appearance by the Twins against the L.A. Dodgers.

After going 5-0 in the preseason, the team's high expectations were cut short when the squad opened the regular season with a pair of losses to Baltimore and Detroit, ultimately settling for a somewhat disappointing 7-7 overall record. One of the bright spots that year was the addition of Cando, N.D., native Dave Osborn, who, as a 13th round draft pick, turned into one of the Purple's all-time great running backs. Minnesota also drafted Notre Dame Wide Receiver Jack Snow with their No.1 pick, but he refused to sign and was shipped to the Rams. Their No.2 pick, Wide Receiver Lance Rentzel, didn't produce the way that management would hope, although he did show signs of greatness by taking a kickoff 101 yards for a touchdown against the Colts.

They did come back to beat the Rams on Fred Cox's last-minute field goal, followed by a 40-14 victory over the Giants. From there they lost to the Bears, 45-37, no thanks to Chicago's All Pro Running Back Gale Sayers' four touchdowns. Then, against San Francisco, Paul Flatley played out of his head, making impossible catches all day to rack up eight passes for more than 200 yards and two touchdowns in a 42-41 victory. (Flatley, who wasn't afraid to take a mean hit, figured out that to make catches he simply had to let Tark see him when he was back scrambling around behind the line of scrimmage. It worked, and the duo became quite a force that year, hooking up 50 times for 896 yards.)

Perhaps the lowlight of the year came following a 41-21 loss to the Colts. After Johnny Unitas' back-up, Gary Cuozzo, torched the Vikes for five touchdown passes, Van Brocklin, in a rage, tendered his resignation. While many of the players cheered, the owners felt differently, and as a result, he un-resigned just one day later. Dutch returned just in time to lead his team to three straight losses, only to throw a tirade and watch his boys regroup to beat both Detroit and Chicago on the road, to finish the season at .500.

In 1966 Minnesota, Chicago, Green Bay and Detroit were all realigned to make up the newly formed Central Division (or Black and Blue Division) of the Western Conference. After a 1-3-1 pre-season, the Vikes came out looking flat. While Bill Brown played well, Tommy Mason, who came back following surgery in 1965, had clearly lost a step, and the offense sputtered. They didn't win a game until Week Five, a 31-7 win over L.A., and lost four of their final five games going out. The defense, led by the front four of Carl Eller, Gary Larsen, Jim Marshall and Paul Dickson, willed the team past the Green Bay Packers, 20-17, to provide one of the season's only rays of light. But, despite Van Brocklin's return that season, things just weren't the same between the coach and his players. Many felt that he had abandoned them when they were down that last season, and as a result the team played less than inspired football that year — limping to a paltry 4-9-1 record.

The end for Brocklin came after the last game of the season, a 41-28 loss to the Bears, in which Dutch and Tarkenton finally had it out with each other. Having long not seen eye-to-eye on how to run

Karl Kassulke

FRAN TARKENTON

Francis Asbury Tarkenton was born the son of a Georgia preacher on February 3, 1940, in Richmond, Va. Fran attended high school in Athens, Ga., where he excelled in both football and basketball. He went on to star as both an All-American and Academic All-American quarterback at the University of Georgia, where he graduated with a degree in Business in 1961.

Tarkenton was then selected in the third round of the NFL draft by the expansion Vikings in 1961. He made quite a statement in his first game, torching the mighty Chicago Bears for four touchdowns and running in another en route to leading Minnesota to a dramatic 37-13 win — one of the biggest upsets in NFL history. Fran would play five solid seasons in Minnesota, even having the phrase "scramble" coined after his unorthodox ways of running around to evade would-be sackers. He called his own plays and added a new dimension to the quarterback position by refusing to give up.

"Perhaps the best way I can sum up my scrambling activity, and also press home my deepest philosophies about fighting to win, is this way: I was talking to a writer one time, and he wondered why I scrambled. He said, 'I guess there's no sense standing back there and getting clobbered.' You know, I had never thought about that aspect of it, and I quickly corrected him by saying that there was only one reason to scramble - to win a ball game. The only thing I think about on a football field is winning."

But then, in 1966, after five stormy seasons with Dutch Van Brocklin's conservative and temperamental coaching style, Francis was traded to the New York Giants. The final straw came near the end of the 1966 season when Van Brocklin benched Tarkenton before the Atlanta game, apparently out of spite — knowing that his friends and family would be watching back home. Fran demanded to be traded and Vikings general manager Jim Finks pulled the trigger on a deal that sent him to the New York Giants for two first-round picks. The Giants desperately needed a marquis player much like their cross-town rival Jets had in Joe Namath.

Five years later, in 1972, Bud Grant engineered a deal that brought Fran back to Minnesota. By then he was a full-fledged celebrity. And his interests weren't confined to the playing field. Fran was a smart guy, and had already started to prepare for his life after football, where he was quite confident that he would become an even bigger star. He owned real estate, had countless major commercial endorsement deals, and he read the Wall Street Journal as avidly as he read his own team's play book. He was handsome, rich and articulate. The Republicans even begged him to run for public office. Yes, Fran had a plan, and football was just part of it.

He was also pretty damn tough. Despite being just six-feet tall and weighing in at a measly buck-eighty, he could take a hit. Once, in a game against the Lions, Detroit Defensive Tackle Dave Pureifory came plowing over the line unscathed and tattooed Tark square in the melon with his helmet. Fran crumbled. Then, after realizing that three of his front teeth had popped out, he jumped up, put his arm on giant tackle's shoulder and sarcastically whispered: "No hard feelings, Dave. I'm okay already..." And, just to spite him, he even came back in the second half to lead the Vikes to a 47-7 blow-out. After the game, Tark received nearly 60 stitches and endured several days with both the plastic surgeon and the dentist.

From 1973-1978, he led the team to an amazing 62-22-2 record, and guided them to three Super Bowls. In 1978, after 18 incredible seasons in the NFL, 13 of which were with Minnesota, Tark retired. At the time of his retirement, he owned nearly every one of the NFL's major passing records: most passing attempts (6,467), most completions (3,686), most passing yards (47,003), most games played (246), and most touchdown passes (342). He also rushed for 3,674 yards en route to scoring 32 touchdowns, a stat that made him the ultimate double-threat. (Eighteen years later, most have since been broken by Miami Dolphin's Quarterback Dan Marino.) And, for 15 consecutive seasons, he threw for more than 2,000 yards. He was a four-time All-NFL selection, played in nine Pro-Bowls, and was named as the league's MVP in 1975. In 1986 he was proudly inducted into the Pro Football Hall of Fame.

Fran was an A-typical quarterback who's dogged determination to keep trying in the face of failure, made him a fan-favorite. Back in the 1970s, the Vikings "golden era," he was every Minnesota kids' hero. Because he tried as hard as he did, sacrificed as much as he did, and, at times, carried the team on his back. He should be regarded as the best ever to wear the purple.

Today Fran and his wife Linda reside in the Atlanta area. They have four children and three grandchildren. After hosting TV's "That's Incredible," Fran became an incredibly successful businessman. In the past 20 years, he started and built 12 businesses. A highly sought after motivational speaker, Fran is also a board member of several major companies and has countless personal business interests throughout the world. "I'm a capitalist without apology," said Fran. If you want to see Tark today, just flip on the tube anytime after midnight, you'll probably find him hawking something!

Here is What a Few of His Teammates Had to Say About Him

"Fran was the greatest quarterback who ever played the game," said Bud Grant. "There's no question about that. Just look at his statistics. In addition to that, he could run with the ball!"

"He was our quarterback — the guy that made the offense go," said Chuck Foreman. "He was very bright and he understood the game forwards and backwards. Many times during the game he would create new plays in the huddle. In my opinion, he was one of the best quarterbacks to ever play the game."

"I personally liked Fran," said Carl Eller. "He was labeled as being selfish, but that was one of the qualities that I admired and respected most about him. I think that Fran knew most of all what he needed and wanted. Not only do I respect him, but I have a great admiration for him for that. In that same sense, what was good for Fran was also good for the Vikings, and that's where I differ from a lot of people. I think that Fran was good for the team, and I think that he cared about his teams. He was just a great Viking player. In some respects, Fran was bigger than the Vikings, but we eventually caught up to him."

"Fran knew how to use all of his people," said Jim Marshall. "He could drop the ball off to his backs when the receivers were covered, and he knew how to use his tight ends. He knew how to manipulate all of his people to accomplish the goal of winning. I think of him as a highly skilled, mechanical, technician. He was a great quarterback."

"Fran was a good quarterback," said Alan Page. "To be honest, my recollection of Fran was probably greater playing against him, than as a teammate. It was always a great challenge to get to him, and he made you work for everything you got against him."

"He was a really smart quarterback," said Ahmad Rashad. "With Fran and I, it was like we both had ESP. I could make up routes on the fly, and it was like the ball would be right there. Fran Tarkenton was simply the best there was."

the offense, as well as other philosophical differences, their tension's had reached a boiling point and both wanted an immediate change. As a result Dutch retired and Tark demanded to be traded. Van Brocklin would later resurface as Atlanta's head coach, while Tark got his wish and was sent packing to the Big Apple, to play for the Giants, who where desperate to find someone to come in and neutralize the popularity and glitz of their cross-town rivals' quarterback — Joe Namath, of the Jets. They paid a hefty price though, in exchange for a bunch of high draft picks. Among them was the foundation of a dynasty, including future All Pro Tackle Ron Yary, Michigan State's Running Back Clint Jones and Wide Receiver Gene Washington, as well as Wide Receiver Bob Grim, Corner Back Bobby Bryant and Guard Ed White.

Mel Triplett

"Maybe I'm just a pioneer-type coach, good with a new team," Dutch said. "I don't think it's going to work anymore. I think I'd better get out."

The final straw for Tark came on the last game of the season, when, in a televised game against his hometown Atlanta Falcons, in front of his friends and family, Dutch benched him in favor of young Bob Berry. Berry was picked off five times as the Falcons, in their first season, went on to beat Minnesota, 20-13.

The Dutchman, who finished his five-year tenure in Minnesota with a 29-51-4 record, produced solid football teams which played with a tough, competitive and creative style that was always entertaining. It was just time for him to go. He was a team player, and couldn't tolerate individualism and show-boating. He was also an old-school coach and didn't want to deal with people who challenged his bigotry's and tirades. With that, Max Winter ended the melodrama by calling his old friend and former point-guard, on his Minneapolis Lakers team, up in Winnipeg, who had turned down his offer to be the Vikings' first head coach. This time, Bud Grant said yes.

Enter Bud Grant

Bud felt comfortable with the management. He knew Max Winter, and he also knew Ole Haugsrud, who was a buddy of Bud's dad, Harry Grant Sr. So, after leading his Winnipeg Blue-Bombers to four Canadian Football League Grey Cup championships in just 10 years, the former Gopher legend came home to take the helm of the Minnesota Vikings. He would start out slow, but rebound in a huge way — ultimately taking his new team to four Super Bowls in less than a decade.

Bud was a hard-nosed kind of a guy who demanded excellence from his players. Bud set an early tone at training camp that year (camp had now moved from Bemidji to Mankato), and let his players know that things were going to be different under his watch. Right out of the gates, in an effort to get their undivided attention, he put them at attention, literally, before each game during the National Anthem. The shock value alone was enough for many of the players to know that this guy meant business. Grant's stoic expressions through the good times and the bad left the players to wonder just what in the hell was going on in the man's head. He didn't encourage coffee drinking or smoking, and even went as far as making sure that his players didn't get too dressed up out in the frigid below-zero temperatures at the old Met. He wanted them to concentrate on the game going on in front of them, not worrying about how cold they were. That attitude would give his teams a world class reputation for cold-weather invincibility like non other. Teams feared coming to Minnesota for the playoffs in December, and that was just what Bud wanted. Known for his discipline and precision, he was also considered to be a fair coach by his players. He gave every man a good shot and unlike Dutch, he never abused a man on the field or humiliated him in front of his peers — things that made him a "player's coach," and ultimately made him the only coach in league history to win more than 150 games in less than 20 seasons.

Bud had a solid nucleus of players to work from when he got to Minnesota, including the kind of men he loved: blue-collar tough guys who could hit and could play through pain in an effort to get their team a win. Guys like Jim Marshall, Mick Tingelhoff, Carl Eller, Bill Brown and Dave Osborn to name a few. Then, in addition to all of the high draft picks that Finks negotiated from the Tarkenton deal, he had also dealt 1st round draft choice Jack Snow to Los Angeles in exchange for Gary Larsen, the ex-Marine who learned to play ball at Concordia in Moorhead. Tommy Mason, and the temperamental receiver, Hal Bedsole were also traded in exchange for a pick that would translate into future Hall of Fame Defensive Tackle Alan Page. The "Purple People Eaters," which officially included Jim Marshall, Carl Eller, Alan Page and Gary Larsen, would now be in place to make the team's defense its trademark. "Offense sells tickets, but the defense wins the games," as Grant would say.

Despite all of these new players, there was one key component still missing — a quarterback. For that Finks and Grant went back to their Canadian roots and got a guy that they thought would fit in perfectly with this bunch. His name was Joe Kapp, who was then playing with Vancouver of the CFL. The son of a Mexican-American mother and German-American father, Kapp was tough as nails. His desire to win, coupled with his care-free attitude and fun-loving personality made him an instant fan-favorite in Minnesota. He was a warrior though, both on and off the field, as evidenced by the huge scar on his jaw from where he stopped a beer bottle one time. Though he lacked the flare that Tarkenton had out on the field, and despite the fact that his passes seldom took the form of a spiral when thrown, he had a lot of self-confidence. Kapp's physical shortcomings were far outweighed by his huge heart

Bud Grant

"I figure I can't scramble like Tarkenton, but I got to move around now and then," Kapp said, in response to comparisons. "I may not run with much speed, but I make up for it with a lot of desperation." With lines like that, it was no wonder that he fit right in with the fans as well as his new teammates.

Although Grant's NFL debut was a rocky one, as his Vikings lost their first four games in 1967, he did rebound to beat the defending and eventual repeating Super Bowl champion Packers, 10-7, for his first win. Kapp, and Running Back Dave Osborn, who rushed for 972 yards, emerged as the team's offensive leaders. The squad, which focused on improving their horrible turnover ratio and stupid mistakes from the year before, went just 3-8-3 that year, also beating the Giants and Steelers, while tying powerful Baltimore, Detroit and Chicago. But, four of the Vikings' eight losses were by five points or less, as Grant was on the verge of something special, and people could sense it. With his draft choices

Bobby Bryant

about to pan off big-time, he was planting the seeds that would help build the Vikings into a perennial Central Division champion.

With a year of Grant's conservative play-calling under their belts, and a new bunch of pieces in place, including the addition of new Offensive Coordinator Jerry Burns, the Vikings came out and posted a much improved 8-6 record in 1968, giving them their first divisional title. Ron Yary, the highly touted Offensive Tackle out of USC, would join the team that year as part of the Tarkenton deal, as would Safety Charlie West, Fullback Oscar Reed and Quarterback Bob Lee. Defensive Back Paul Krause also came over in a trade with the Redskins, while Wide Receiver John Henderson and Linebacker Wally Hilgenberg were claimed on waivers. Krause and West would join an already solid defensive secondary which was led by Defensive Backs Ed Sharockman, Earsell Mackbee, Dale Hackbart and Karl Kassulke.

After a 3-1 start, Minnesota lost three straight, won its next three, dropped two more, and then needed to win its final two games to have a shot at making it into the playoffs. After beating San Francisco, 30-20, the title hung in the balance as the Vikings went off to Philadelphia to meet Grant's former team, the Eagles.

"We had to win our last game against the Eagles to clinch it, and I remember it was snowing and icy," recalled Grant. "We ended up scoring a couple big play touchdowns on a bad field. Usually teams play conservatively on bad conditions, but I had played enough games on bad fields to know that you can make big plays on bad fields easier than on good fields. So we got a couple big plays and won the game. Then we sat in the locker room and listened to the outcome of the Packers vs. Bears game. The Pack won, 28-17, and we had our first divisional title. (Reporter) Sid Hartman was relaying the information over the phone to us. It was a great feeling."

The Vikes finished the season with a modest record of 8-6, then headed east, to face the mighty Baltimore Colts in the Western Conference Playoff Game. Led by Coach Don Shula, the Colts went on to defeat Minnesota in a rainy and muddy Memorial Stadium by the final of 24-14. Earl Morrall, who had taken over for Johnny Unitas, was the top ranked quarterback in the league that year, and made his presence felt. He threw a pair of TD passes on the day, while six-foot-seven, 300-pound Defensive End Bubba Smith tattooed Kapp to force a fumble which was then returned 60 yards for another score by Mike Curtis, to get the Colts up 21-0 in the third quarter. Kapp rallied the troops late in the game though, completing a record 26 of 44 passes for 287 yards, and throwing for a pair of touchdown passes to Tight End Billy Martin and "Boom Boom" Brown.

"It was a rough game," said Kapp, who took a bloody beating but played like a hero. "The Colts blitzed us with everything they had, sometimes with as many as a nine men at once, and it caused problems for us."

After the loss, the Vikings went on to play the loser of the Miami vs. Dallas game where they lost to the Cowboys, 17-13, in the NFL's "Runner-up Bowl." In that game, rookie Corner Bobby Bryant returned a punt 81 yards for a touchdown, and Fred Cox kicked two field goals to help Minnesota build a 13-0 lead. But Cowboy quarterbacks Don Meredith and Craig Morton each tossed touchdown passes to rally Dallas to victory.

The Vikings were a team on the rise and one of their emotional leaders, Jim Marshall, played an important role in taking them to the promised land the very next season. "Winning the divisional title in 1968 was very special." he said. "We worked very hard to get there, and we knew that we had a great core of guys that could go even further."

"40 for 60"

Minnesota finally turned the corner as one of the league's premier teams in 1969, going 12-2 and earning a trip to their first ever Super Bowl. Being seen on Sunday afternoons at the stadium was the "in" thing to do by this time, as tail-gating outside of the old Met took on a life of its own. The fans were crazy for the purple by now and they were front-page news on a daily basis. Led by their emotional leader, Joe Kapp, the Vikings embraced a new campaign slogan for the season called "40 for 60," which meant that 40 men playing together for 60 minutes, couldn't lose.

The season started out on a downer, however, as the Vikes lost their opener, 24-23, to Tarkenton and the New York Giants in Yankee Stadium. The Giants won off of a bunch of Minnesota miscue's, combined with some good old fashioned luck by Tark. Fran later described the desperate fourth quarter situation he was in as he tried to mount a comeback in Jim Klobuchar's 1995 book "Purple Hearts & Golden Memories:"

Stu Voigt

"If I wanted to get a pass off, I'd tell Greg Larson at Center to double up with the guard on Page," he said. "I'd double on Marshall with the left tackle and fullback. Against Eller I told the tight end to stay in and block with the right tackle. That meant I was doubling on everybody on their defensive line except Gary Larsen, who almost always stayed back looking for draws. So I never sent more than three people out on pass plays, a back and the two wideouts. That's all we had downfield and the Vikings were sitting back there with four defensive backs, including guys like Krause and Kassulke and Bobby Bryant, and we assigned six people to block three of their defensive linemen. I never saw a more clear confession on a football field in my life. We were saying 'you got us surrounded. We need pure luck to beat you.'"

"While I was going through my cadence behind Larson, I glanced at Eller and I nearly fainted," he added. "He was pawing the ground and practically snorting. If he ever got through he was going to tear my head off. Good old Carl, my ex-teammate. Right there I thought, 'My daddy was right, I should have entered the seminary.' "

Minnesota rebounded to pound Baltimore, 52-14, thanks to Kapp's amazing seven-touchdown performance. He hit everybody with one that "spiritual" day including: Dave Osborn, Bobby Grim, Kent Kramer, John Beasley, Jim Lindsey, and a pair to Gene Washington.

"I remember I had hurt my knee just before that season," said Kapp, "and the doctors' remedy was

JOE KAPP

Joe Kapp grew up as a sports fanatic in southern California. He attended the University of California at Berkeley, where he quarterbacked a Rose Bowl team, and even played on a couple of championship basketball teams for the Golden Bears. He. After graduating, he decided to head north of the border to try his luck in the Canadian Football League. There he would ultimately play for eight years with Calgary and then British Columbia, where he won a Grey Cup with the Lions.

From there Kapp was lured to Minnesota in 1967 by an old CFL colleague, Bud Grant, who was now coaching the Vikes. Minnesota had just dealt Fran Tarkenton and needed a veteran signal-caller. Kapp obliged and became an instant fan-favorite in Minnesota. Kapp was a throwback to when football was really a game and played simply because he loved it. He had the mentality of a linebacker and actually loved to punish his would-be tacklers by putting his head down and letting them have it. He occasionally threw spirals, but seemed to be able to will his team to victory on pure emotion and heart alone. He even championed the slogan "40 for 60," which meant that all 40 men needed to work in harmony for 60 minutes to win. It typified just the kind of team player he really was.

In 1969 Kapp led the Vikings to the Super Bowl and even turned down the team's MVP award, citing the fact that there was no most valuable player on a team of 40 men working together. After three seasons in Minnesota Kapp got into an ugly contract squabble and wound up being shipped off to the Boston Patriots, where he would play one more year before hanging up the cleats for good.

Kapp led the Vikings in passing all three years he was with the team, with 4,807 yards on 351 of 699 attempts. He also tossed 37 touchdowns while surrendering 47 interceptions. He left the game, not on his terms, but will always be remembered as one of the guttiest quarterbacks in NFL history.

He later became head football coach at his alma-matter, Cal, where, five years later, he got the acting bug and did some commercials (including one for Wheaties), as well as performed in a number Hollywood motion pictures. Today Joe and his wife reside in Los Gatos, Calif., and have four children. Joe is involved with a family restaurant called "Kapp's," in Mountain View, and does motivational speaking work.

What did it mean for you to be a Viking?
"Minnesota has the most wonderful, beautiful people — even if they're all blonde! It was a great three years, and we continued to improve and build the team every year. We showed the fans some spirit, and we didn't play the game with clean pants. We got down and rolled up our sleeves, and we had fun doing it."

On Leaving the Vikings for the Patriots
"I didn't want to go to Boston. I was 32 years old and I figured I was in my prime. I believe we would have won a Super Bowl in Minnesota if I could have stayed there. It didn't work out. That's a memory that I want to put out of my mind."

On "40 for 60?"
"Forty for sixty was the recipe that meant that every person counts, and it was unacceptable for anybody not to participate. I recognized the value of every person on the team. I started my college career on the bench as a substitute defensive end, and I learned to appreciate the guys that didn't get to play. So, I've always felt that as a team you are only as strong as your weakest player, not as strong as your star. I learned from my basketball coach that there is a value in not being the guy starting on the court or field. That's where the forty for sixty came up. It's the unsung guys that make you good. Our whole team attitude of forty for sixty was for real and we were a family."

Here is What a Few of His Teammates Had to Say About Him
"Joe was a football player who probably did not have a sense of what was good for Joe Kapp as an individual," said Carl Eller. "In other words, what Joe was about was what was good for the team. It didn't really matter whether it was good for Joe or not, he was a true team player."

"Joe was kind of a rebel, but maybe he over-rebelized," said Bud Grant. "I watched him as a player in Canada, and I knew he could play, so we got him down here to play for us in Minnesota. He was a tough guy for a quarterback. He really overstepped what you could do in that era. He played here for a couple years and then something else came up, and so he ended up in New England. It was too bad that Joe didn't just settle down and make the most of it where he was. You can't hold a team hostage all the time. He ended up playing with different teams and did well with all of them, but it was too bad he just didn't stay with one - the Vikings. He would've been better off. But he challenged the NFL contract system, so we let him go."

"Joe is a guy that you would want to be in an alley fight with," said Jim Marshall. "He would do anything that was necessary to get the ball down the field and to make something happen. He didn't throw the prettiest passes in the world, but, he threw winning passes. It didn't make any difference what his passes looked like, but they always got to his target. He made some great efforts in the short time he was with the Minnesota Vikings. He is one of my most dear friends, and I am so respectful of his ability and his qualifications. Most of all I'm respectful of the attitude and toughness that he brought to the team. No quarterback that I know of ever had that kind of toughness, period. I've seen him fight linebackers, and come out winning. I've seen him put guys like Jim Houston, one of the toughest all-pro defensive ends in the league, out of a game. He didn't care who you were, he was going to hit you as hard as you were going to hit him. As soon as that ball left his hand he was looking to deliver a blow to someone coming at him. You don't find that anymore. He was a genuine throwback to the earliest days of professional football."

"Joe Kapp was a great leader," said Alan Page. "He could make people do things in terms of their ability which they probably didn't think they were capable of. He brought out extraordinary qualities in people."

CARL ELLER

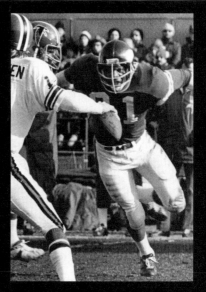

A native of Winston Salem, N.C., Carl Eller went on to star as two-time All-American Tackle for the Golden Gophers from 1961-63. The six-foot-six 260-pound terror was then selected by the Vikings with the sixth overall pick of the first round of the NFL draft. He went on to play 225 regular-season games over 15 years for the Vikings before spending one final season with the Seattle Seahawks in 1979. He was named All-Pro six times, was the NFL's Most Valuable Defensive Lineman twice, and played in six Pro Bowl games. Eller is the Vikings all-time sack leader, credited with 130 quarterback sacks, 44 from 1975-77 alone. He also recovered 23 fumbles, a number that still ranks fourth best in NFL history. His great speed, power and agility will one day find him a home in the Pro Football Hall of Fame.

Eller has very much become synonymous with football in Minnesota and will always be remembered not only for his big smile, but as a fierce competitor as well. In his first season at the U of M, he even played with a broken hand, tossing aside his cast that he wore in practices come game day. And football wasn't all Carl could do. He once played MacBeth at the Guthrie Theater and was even voted one of Esquire Magazine's "Best Dressed Jocks" in 1972. He also starred in a B-Movie about bikers called "The Black Six," with Mean Joe Greene and Mercury Morris. Eller has also been a huge inspiration and role-model to kids everywhere by speaking to them about the dangers of drugs. Today he works for the State of Minnesota and also operates a satellite communications company. He has three children and lives in the Minneapolis area.

What Did it Mean for You to Be a Gopher?
"Being a Golden Gopher was great," said Eller. "Going to the U was one of the better choices that I made in my life. Being on a metropolitan campus and being a part of the Saturday football scene at Memorial Stadium were wonderful experiences for me. Sure, it was a culture shock for me because I had come from a segregated town in North Carolina. Everything at the U was a new and incredible experience for me, and it was my first exposure to big-time football. Yes, it means a lot for me to be a Gopher."

What Did it Mean for You to Be a Viking?
"It still means a lot. But, truthfully, I felt I was totally misunderstood by the media. You see, when I played, I felt like I was an artist. I could have easily been the equivalent of a violinist, or a painter, or whatever. Football is a mental game, and I was a craftsman who had great skill and technique. The culmination of all those things made me a great player. Professional football was a real test of all my skills, and I looked at playing as a performance. In other words, when I would do things like putting on a pass rush, or stopping a double-team, or making a tackle behind the play, I had to push and test myself to the limit to do those kinds of things that were just barely humanly possible. I had to be quick off the ball, and I had to beat the opponent to the ball. Sometimes I had to beat two guys, and sometimes I would have to like hold one guy off with one arm and try to grab the quarterback with the other, all while trying to maintain my leverage, and all while watching out for the back who was coming to cut me at my knees. You had to do all that in a split second, and I took great pride in being able to do it well. I really felt like playing professional football was an art."

On the Purple People Eaters?
"The nickname was special because we were in it together. There was compassion among us, because we knew what each other guy was going through. If a guy was holding Jim or Alan or Lars or me, we knew what that meant, and we took care of each other. We all had to step up when the game was tight, and we stuck together. It was special."

Does Never Winning a Super Bowl Still Hurt?
"Well, we had four shots at winning the big one. People can look at it whatever way they want to, but the four losses never came off as a negative to me. I can say that we were champions of the National Football Conference three times and NFL once, we went to four Super Bowls, defeated some great teams, and lost to some of the best football teams ever in Miami, Oakland, Pittsburgh, and Kansas City. It wasn't like we took a dive in our Super Bowls, or anything like that. I have nothing to be ashamed of. I have nothing to regret. We lost four games fair and square. But we didn't lose because we didn't put our best effort out there. We didn't lose because we weren't the best team to make it there. Regardless of what anybody says, those were my greatest moments. Those games were great Vikings moments and a unforgettable part of the great Vikings' history. We never quit. It takes a lot of strength and character to come back time and time again. I think that says a lot more about the Vikings than some of the teams that actually won the Super Bowl."

Here is What a Few of His Teammates Had to Say About Him
"Carl was a very talented football player," said Alan Page. "He was strong, quick and agile, and he was a very intense football player."

"Moose was a great talent," said Bud Grant. "He got a lot of sacks and knocked down a lot of balls back then, he was just a dominant player. He played his best against the best players, and would dominate each team's top players that they put up against him."

"He was one of the biggest, strongest, toughest guys to come down the pike," said Jim Marshall. "When he wanted to destroy an opponent, I don't think there was anyone who could stop him. He was a great, great football player and I have so much respect for him. We played throughout our entire careers together. He was my roommate and one of my closest friends."

"He was the enforcer," said Chuck Foreman. "Carl wasn't just a great football player, he was a great athlete. He was also a very bright guy. He was probably the greatest defensive end that ever played the game."

"As great a player as Carl was, I always admired the confidence that he added to our team each time we went onto the football field," said Joe Kapp. "He was like a chieftain out there. He was as big, as fast and as tough as anybody in the league, and yet he had such a will and spirit to win. Confidence is what separates losing teams from winning teams and Carl passed that quality onto our team."

"He was an all-around athlete," said Bobby Bell. "I got recruited with Carl from Winston Salem. He was so tough and strong, that's why we named him the 'Moose'. He was a happy-go-lucky fun guy, and he was a guy you could coach. I remember playing that great Michigan State team where they had the No.1 offense in the country and we had the No.1 defense in the country. I think they were averaging something like 550 yards of offense per game, and at half-time they had like 26 yards — we shut them down, and Carl was just unstoppable. We unbalanced the line that game so he could come down to my side and double-down. Carl would drive their guy into the ground every play and our offense took over. He was the greatest."

to put it in a cast. Well, I did that for about 10 days, and finally I couldn't handle it anymore, so I went down to a tire store and cut the cast off to get ready to play football again. By the time I got ready to play, Gary Cuozzo had started the first game of the season. I thought Gary played well, but Bud (Grant) didn't. For the second game, we were matched against the Colts, and I got the chance to get the starting job back. We beat them, 52-14, and I threw seven touchdown passes. I had showed them what I could do and what we could do as a team. I was in my third season, and I had prepared myself — I studied the films from the Colts game the year before. That was a memorable game for me, and it was just the start of that season."

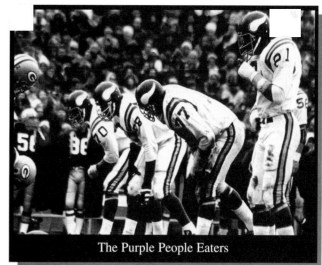
The Purple People Eaters

That next week, on October 5, 1969, against Green Bay, the Vikings made history by playing at the University of Minnesota's Memorial Stadium, because the Twins were playing the Baltimore Orioles in the American League playoffs that day at the Met. No problem though, as the Vikes went on to beat the Pack, 19-7.

From there Minnesota didn't look back, as the team's unstoppable defense led them to a record 12 consecutive victories. In Week 3, the "Purple People Eaters" sacked Bart Starr eight times, only to sandwich Chicago's Bobby Douglass nine times just four weeks later. In Week Eight the Vikings scored on their first nine possessions en route to a 51-3 win. In Week 10 Safety Paul Krause picked-off Pittsburgh Quarterback Dick Shiner and took off 77 yards for a touchdown. The score put the Vikes into the lead, and they went on to crush the Steelers, 52-14. In Week 12 they met the Rams out in L.A., who were riding an 11 game winning streak of their own. The Vikes took control early though and went on to beat the Rams 20-13. After beating the 49ers the next week, Minnesota found themselves with a 12-game winning streak —the NFL's longest in 35 years. Only a 10-3 loss in a torrential rainfall down in Atlanta, against Van Brocklin's Falcons nonetheless, in the season finale (with Grant resting many of his starters for the playoffs), prevented the team from winning 13 in a row.

The "Super Ball?"

Did you know that the history of the Super Bowl stems from the word "Super Ball?" That's right. Kansas City Chiefs owner and American Football League founder Lamar Hunt, a Texas oil millionaire, decided that the "AFL-NFL World Championship Game" was simply too dull a term to use on such a festive event. As the story goes, Hunt, who was playing with his daughter and her new bouncy "Super Ball," had an epiphany of sorts and decided to call the title game the "Super Bowl." Go figure!

The Vikings were by far the NFL's best team that year, scoring the most points in all of pro football and yielding the least by an unthinkable 379-133 margin (that average of 9.5 points a game allowed was the lowest since World War II). With their Western Conference championship in hand, they then prepared to battle the Rams in the playoffs.

On Dec. 27, in front of some 48,000 frozen fans at the Met, the Vikes played the Rams in a game that ranks as one of the most exciting ever in team history. The Rams, guided by their fiery Coach, George Allen, were led by defensive giants Merlin Olsen and Deacon Jones, as well as Quarterback, and NFL MVP, Roman Gabriel. L.A. went up early in this one, scoring early off the recovery of Bill Brown's fumble. Minnesota then came back behind a thunderous crowd that the players had never seen the likes of before. With the fans stomping and absolutely going nuts, the Vikes drove 75 yards to tie the score on Dave Osborn's tough one-yard dive up the middle. The Rams answered though, only to take a 17-7 lead on a field goal, followed by a two-yard touchdown pass from Roman Gabriel to Tight End Billy Truax just before half-time. The Vikings roared back in the third behind a 41-yard pass from Kapp to Gene Washington which set up another Osborn one-yarder to make it 17-14. Kapp took over late in the fourth quarter, capping a 65-yard drive by plunging into the end-zone for a two-yard touchdown. Then, with just a few moments left in the game, Carl Eller crashed into the end-zone to sack Gabriel for a safety to secure the dramatic 23-20 victory.

"That roar and togetherness was so great," recalled Grant "the unity of the fans with the team, that it just lifted you off the ground. Almost literally. I've never ever experienced a moment like that in all my years in athletics."

From there Minnesota went on to beat the Cleveland Browns, 27-7, in the NFL Championship Game, to become the first modern expansion franchise to advance to the Super Bowl. The stage was set. The field was slick, the sidelines out at the Met were stacked with snow, and the frigid eight degree temperature made the illusion of Minnesota's cold weather invincibility even more intimidating. Joe Kapp started it off by hitting Gene Washington for a 33-yard pick-up when he beat Cornerback Walt Sumner, who had slipped on the icy field. From there Kapp ran over a couple of Brown defenders to score on a seven-yarder, followed shortly thereafter by another Kapp to Washington bomb, this one covering 75 yards to give the Purple a 14-0 first quarter lead. After Fred Cox nailed a 30-yard field goal, Dave Osborn then chewed off 20 of his game-high 108 yards rushing by finding the back of the end-zone late in the second quarter. Cox then added another 32-yarder late to seal the team's first-ever NFL Championship victory.

After the game the team, bloodied, cold and battered, cried and celebrated with a champagne party in the lockerroom. For that moment, it was all about a bunch of kids, Black, White and Latino, who had come a long, long way. They would now go on to face the AFL champion Kansas City Chiefs in Super Bowl IV at New Orleans.

Super Bowl IV

More than 80,000 fans crowded into Louisiana's Tulane Stadium on January 11, 1970, to watch the Vikings do battle with the Chiefs in what would prove to be the AFL's last-ever game. That's because the 10-year-old AFL would merge that following season with the NFL, despite the notion by most gridiron fans that the AFL was inferior to the NFL with regards to quality of play. And, because the Jets dispelled that very notion just the year before by shocking the mighty Colts in Super Bowl III, many were expecting Minnesota to restore the balance of power back to the established NFL. The oddsmakers also agreed with that sentiment, declaring the Chiefs, who lost to Baltimore in Super Bowl I, as two-touchdown underdogs.

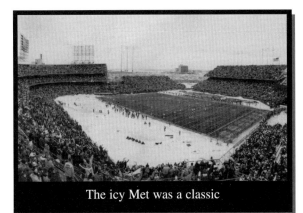
The icy Met was a classic

The pre-game controversy surrounding the game involved Chiefs Quarterback Len Dawson, who subsequently was called to testify in a federal sports gambling investigation. A cloud of suspicion surrounded many players and coaches who were angered by the timing of it all. Although Dawson was later cleared of any wrongdoing, he was reportedly devastated by the accusations. Many thought the distraction had killed any chances the Chiefs had to upset the Vikings. They were wrong.

The Vikings weren't without controversy as well that week. Kapp, bothered at suggestions made by the media that he lacked a classic throwing style, was quoted as saying: "Classics are for Greeks. Who is a classic quarterback? I think I can play some ball."

Before the game, a hot-air balloon with the Vikings logo on it crashed into the stands, nearly decapitating a group of nearby Sugar Bowl Princesses — perhaps a dreadful omen of things to come. The Chiefs, led by Dawson's short, precision passing picked apart the now world-famous "Purple People Eater" defense. On the other side of the ball, the Chiefs huge defensive linemen simply outmuscled the smaller Vikings on the line of scrimmage, stuffing Minnesota's highly touted running game. In addition, the Chiefs used an elaborate trapping scheme to neutralize the Vikings great pass rushers Alan Page and Carl Eller who were blitzing from the ends. To make matters worse, leading the way for the Chiefs defensively were a bunch of ex-Gophers: Bobby Bell, Aaron Brown and Bob Stein. Very methodically, and without flash, Kansas City dominated the game — capitalizing on five very costly Minnesota turn-overs.

Perhaps the opening kickoff as an indication of things to come for Minnesota, as Charlie West bobbled and lost the wind-blown offering, giving the Chiefs the ball deep in Viking territory. Jan Stenerud then kicked the first of his three field goals on the first half, ultimately giving the Chiefs a 9-0 lead midway through the second. Minnesota's Charlie West then fumbled the ball on the kickoff following Stenerud's third field goal at the Vikings' 19-yard line. A few plays later Kansas City's Running Back Mike Garrett scored on a five-yarder, as the Chiefs went into the locker room at half-time up 16-0.

The Vikings came out primed in the second half and appeared to be mounting a rally when they forced the Chiefs to punt, and then capped off a 69-yard, 10 play drive with a Dave Osborn four-yard touchdown run. Kapp drove the team down, hitting John Henderson, who finished with seven catches for 111 yards on the day, for a key first down to keep the drive alive. (Incredibly, Minnesota didn't even get a first down until the second half!) The Chiefs didn't flinch though, as Dawson drove down after the ensuing kick-off and tossed a short five-yard pass to Wide Receiver Otis Taylor at the 41, who then ran right through Vikings' defenders Earsell Mackbee and Karl Kassulke 40 yards and into the end-zone. It would prove to be the final nail in the coffin.

Minnesota had three possessions in the fourth quarter but couldn't capitalize, as each drive ended in an interception. The final blow to the Purple came midway through the fourth, when Kapp, battered and injured, had to be helped off the Tulane Stadium field after badly injuring his shoulder while being sacked, dramatizing the Viking's futility. Back-up Gary Cuozzo then came in and completed two passes: one to the Vikings and one to the Chiefs. Adding insult to injury was the Chiefs' bombastic coach, Hank Stram, who, while wired with a microphone during the game for NFL Films, said of the Vikings: "They can't figure us out. They don't know what they're doing. It's like a Chinese fire drill out there!"

Although the 23-7 loss to the Chiefs stunned the Minnesota faithful and most of the NFL, it did not diminish the accomplishments of a brilliant season.

"Unfortunately, in our first Super Bowl, we were in a cloud," said Jim Marshall. "I think we felt that there was no way we could lose. We were very confident that we could go out, perform, give our best, and win it all. I was deeply saddened at the loss to Kansas City, but it was a wonderful experience just getting there. It was different from the 1968 season when we were sitting on a bus and waiting to see if we had made the playoffs. We needed help from other teams to get into the playoffs and to win the conference title. But, in 1969, we made our own destiny, and we went all the way on our own.

Gary Larsen

Throughout the entire Super Bowl game, I felt that we were going to do something to pull it out, but it just didn't happen."

"In probing the films of three games, we couldn't find a weakness in their defense," said Grant in a post-game interview with Sid Hartman. "They have big, strong linemen, outstanding linebackers and a great secondary. "Most of the time you can find a defense where you can take advantage of some weaknesses. We didn't find any in Kansas City's. But don't take anything away from the Chiefs. They are one great football team."

"Kansas City had some really great players," said Kapp. "They definitely outweighed us, and they probably had more speed. They beat us on that day, but I'm not sure that they were a better team. We lost, but not convincingly. We did some things in that game that we hadn't done all season. For example, there had been a lot of shifting and using odd-man lines in the AFL. It was unusual to us, and we didn't really adjust well to their strategy. Also, we said 'ho-hum' to the whole Dawson gambling story that was going on, but I think they got some emotion out of that. The weather told our story that day. It was a cold, dreary day. Our only fire seemed to come at the end of the first half when we were down and then marched 70-some yards for a touchdown. We were starting to come back. Then they connected on a hitch pass and were able to score an easy one on a long run. We started to have to play catch-up, and we weren't that kind of team. We were a team that needed to get out and play our game from the opening bell. In the Super Bowl, we didn't do that. We missed our opportunity to be champions of the world, or at least I did. The rest of those guys got to go three more times! Still, that sea-

Ron Yary

son has its own special place for me."

After the season, Joe Kapp forever immortalized himself with a speech at an awards banquet. There, upon being presented the team's MVP award, Kapp, shocked the crowd by walking up to the podium and respectfully declining to accept it. Now, Joe so much epitomized "team player" that he even signed autographs with the phrase "Best wishes from ALL of the Vikings," followed by his name underneath. Knowing that, it was no wonder that he felt that no one single player could possibly be the most valuable of 40 men working together as a team. It was "40 for 60," and no one played harder in those 60 minutes than did Joe Kapp.

"I didn't plan it or anything, it was just down deep in me," said Kapp of his decision to turn down the award. "I just couldn't accept it. Hell, I was sitting at the same table as Jim Marshall. Tell me I was more valuable than Jim Marshall! Or Mick Tinglehoff. Tinglehoff was the most determined player I ever played with, and I thought so after seeing Dick Butkus finish the game with bite marks all over his body. Billy Brown? I mean is anybody tougher? I don't know, maybe Dave Osborn? What about Alan Page or Carl Eller or Gary Larsen? I turned down the MVP trophy with a very real belief that there wasn't any Vikings most valuable player."

(Ironically, following the season, Kapp became mired in a contract dispute and was consequently shipped off to the Patriots, where he played one more year before finally hanging em' up for good. The compensation for Kapp, by the way, was a first-round draft pick that was cashed in for future All-Pro Linebacker Jeff Siemon — a guy who would quickly turn out to be a leader of a team that was on the verge of going to three more Super Bowls.)

Jeff Siemon

Minnesota, now playing with Gary Cuozzo at the helm, opened the 1970 season by extracting a little revenge against the Chiefs, 27-10, in what was referred to as the Revenge Bowl. From there the Purple won nine of their first 10 games en route to a third straight Central Division crown on the strength of a stingy defense which allowed just 143 points. Among that season's many highlights was a demoralizing 54-13 win over the eventual Super Bowl champion Cowboys, thanks to Fred Cox's four field goals, and Ed Sharockman's 23-yard blocked punt return and 34-yard interception for a pair of touchdowns.

Against the Rams the Purple Gang allowed just five first downs in a 13-3 victory, while Clint Jones scored three touchdowns in a 24-20 victory over Detroit. They even beat up on their old pals, Joe Kapp and the Boston Patriots, 34-14, in Week 13, and Dutch Van Brocklin and the Atlanta Falcons, 37-7 in the season finale to finish the season with a 12-2 record, identical to 1969. Having outscored their opponents by a 334-143 margin, the Vikings, led by a defense that allowed just 14 touchdowns all season long, won 10 of their last 11 games.

With that, the highly favored Vikings hosted the San Francisco 49ers at the Met for what many figured to be just a warm-up to the Super Bowl. Boy were they wrong. There, just two days after Christmas, in just single-digit frigid temperatures, the Vikes got upset in one of the team's most crushing defeats of all-time.

The young 49ers, complete with sideline heaters, showed up dressed to the nines in face masks, snowmobile boots, and parkas. The Vikes, meanwhile, who by now found the tundra-like temperatures of Minnesota to be a real advantage, figured that this one was going to be like shooting fish in a barrel. Minnesota took an early lead when San Francisco fullback Ken Willard fumbled, and Paul Krause grabbed the ball out of midair and sprinted 22 yards for a touchdown. But Niners QB John Brodie mounted a rally. After a 30-yard punt return by Bruce Taylor, which led to a Brodie touchdown pass to Dick Witcher, Bruce Gossett added a 40-yard field goal, courtesy of a Dave Osborn fumble, to put the Niners ahead 10-3 at half-time. Then, midway through the fourth quarter, Steve Spurrier punted the Vikings back to their own one yard line. Pinned behind enemy lines, the Vikings were forced to give the ball back to the 49ers, who, this time, would make them pay. That's when Taylor returned the ensuing punt 23 yards to the Vikings 14-yard line. Now, with 1:20 remaining in the game, Brodie, on third-and-goal, scored the game-wining touchdown up the gut on a quarterback-sneak. Minnesota tried in vain to mount a come-back as Cuozzo hit Gene Washington on a 24-yard desperation scoring strike with just a second left on the clock. San Francisco, who capitalized on four crucial Minnesota turn-overs, had sleighed the dragon, 17-14. The nearly 45,000 freezing Met Stadium fans stood in utter disbelief.

The Unbelievable Alan Page

That next year the Vikings reloaded with some new talent. Among the new faces in camp were Defensive Tackle Doug Sutherland, Defensive End Bob Lurtsema, Guard Ed White, Tight End Stu Voigt, Defensive Backs Nate Wright and Jeff Wright, and Quarterback Norm Snead. Snead would prove not to be the solution the team was so desperately looking for that year at quarterback though. He was brought in to compete with Gary Cuozzo and Bob Lee for the starting job, and thanks to Grant's decision to play musical chairs, they all got to see some action that year.

In the first game of the season Gary Cuozzo got the nod, and responded by sparking the Vikings to a 16-13 victory over the Lions. Then, after a 20-17 rare home loss to the Bears, Norm Snead came off the bench to take over. While Snead led the Vikings to back-to-back shutouts over Buffalo and Philadelphia, Grant decided to shuffle the deck once more, this time putting Cuozzo back in for the next five games. Bobby Lee's number got called for four of the final five games of the season, assuring Grant of one thing — he needed a new quarterback.

Over that stretch Minnesota went on to win 11 out of 14, even going nine consecutive quarters at one point without surrendering a point. In addition, their defense, which was led by Tackle Alan Page, forced 33 fumbles and 27 interceptions, including seven by Charlie West and six each by Paul Krause and Ed Sharockman, en route to giving up just 139 points — an average of nine points a game. That awesome defense also tallied 49 quarterback sacks for 360 lost yards!

While the team did win their fourth straight NFC Central Division title, the quarterback problem was making more headlines than the team's unbelievable defense, just fueling the debate as to who was going to score the most points each game — the offense or the defense. Clint Jones did rush for 675 yards and Receiver Bob Grim was able to catch 45 passes for a modest 691 yards, but the offense was flat. It was the team's Achilles heel, and was about to become exposed and exploited.

The purple entered the playoffs that year with high hopes of returning to the Super Bowl. It was

In 1973 the Vikings drafted future baseball hall of famer Dave Winfield, as a tight end, based on pure talent alone.

ALAN PAGE

After starring on the 1966 Notre Dame national championship team, All-American Defensive Tackle Page was selected by the Vikings as the No.2 overall pick of the 1967 draft. The first rookie ever to start for Bud Grant, he would go on to become one of the greatest players the NFL would ever know. Page was selected as a unanimous All-Pro on six different occasions while receiving nine Pro Bowl invitations. From 1967-78 the anchor of the "Purple People Eaters" defense posted 108 career sacks, however, unofficial records show that he recorded 173 sacks. (Sacks weren't counted back then like they are today.) In addition, he also recovered 23 opponents' fumbles and blocked 28 kicks. Page was even the inspiration for the now-common pass-rushing statistic known as the "hurry," which was issued when he forced the quarterback throw the ball before he wanted to.

In 1971 he made history by becoming the first defensive player in NFL history of to win the league MVP. That season Page posted 10 sacks, 109 tackles, 35 assists, 42 hurries and three safeties. It might possibly have been the single-greatest season ever recorded by a defensive lineman.

Page was a nonconformist, often bucking heads with Coach Grant. Later in his career he began to attend Law School at the U of M, and even began running marathons. As a result, Page thinned down to about 230 pounds, which was very small for an NFL defensive tackle. When he went against the wishes of the coaching staff to keep his weight up, he was released on waivers for $100. Page then went on to play another three seasons with the Bears before retiring in 1981. When it was all said and done, the numbers were staggering. He had played in 236 straight games, was a four-time Defensive Player of the Year, All-NFL nine times, played in nine Pro-Bowls, recovered 23 fumbles, blocked 28 kicks and punts and recorded an amazing 173 sacks.

"There really isn't much to think about on a football field." said Page of his retirement. "Playing the game requires physical ability and a tremendous emotional commitment. Intellectually, it doesn't require much. There are a finite number of things that can take place on a football field. After 10 years, you probably have done most of them. Football to me became repetitious and boring."

When Page's career was over he had a homecoming of sorts. You see, he grew up in Canton, Ohio, now home to the Pro Football Hall of Fame, and actually worked on the construction crew that built the museum during one summer during the late 1960s. In 1988 he was inducted into that very Hall of Fame. However, he did it in typical Alan Page style, declining the opportunity to swap gridiron gossip, as most of the football brethren do at their induction's, and instead shocking the pro football establishment by choosing Willarene Beasley as his presenter, principal at Minneapolis North High School. Never in the Hall of Fame's history had a person not in the football fraternity made an induction speech. Page selected her because of the fact that she was an educator and, as a black woman, represented minorities. Alan's speech was about the values of education, not football; about learning to tackle issues, not quarterbacks; and about ABCs, not Xs and Os. "I wanted to take advantage of that recognition and use the day as a mechanism for something meaningful," Page said. Following her introduction, Alan launched the Page Education Foundation from the steps of the Hall of Fame.

On why Page decided to use that forum to speak of education rather than football, Page recalled a pre-season afternoon practice some years ago, when, during a defensive meeting, one of the coaches asked some of the players to read aloud from the playbook. It was at that moment that Page realized a couple of his teammates couldn't read, while several others were struggling to get by. "In that moment, listening to my teammates unable to read a simple playbook, everything crystallized for me," Page said. "I don't know why it took me so long to realize, but at that moment it became clear that this wasn't a dumb-jock problem, or an athletic problem. These men were supposed to learn to read in first, second, or third grade, long before they were football players. You think about something, and you think about it again, but you can't point your finger at it. Well, that day, I realized the problem I wanted to try to address was education. Pure and simple."

Today Page sits on the Minnesota Supreme Court. He had always battled adversity, and his journey to the bench would be no exception. By 1979, Page had earned his law degree and moved from the gridiron to private practice. Soon he was working in the attorney general's office. After spending several years there, he decided to seek an even higher office. Typically, new judges are appointed temporarily and then elected without competition. But, when his opportunity to run kept being denied, he sued then Governor Arne Carlson. A substitute Supreme Court then ruled in Page's favor, allowing him to run successfully, with opposition, in 1992. As a result, he became the first African-American to sit on the state's highest court — or on any Minnesota state appellate court, for that matter. Today, with his spectacles and trademark bow-tie, Associate Justice Page is a member of the Minnesota Supreme Court. He and his wife Diane live in the Twin Cities and have four children. He still logs about 60-miles a week in the sneakers and remains active in his Page Education Foundation, which to date has helped more than 1,100 minority students attend colleges in Minnesota.

What did it mean for you to be a Viking?
"To be honest with you, I never really thought about it in that context," said Page. "What I enjoyed and what I thought about, were the people that I worked with, being a part of a team, having great friends, and working with a lot of good people. That's really what was important to me. I suppose that I was fortunate to work with a number of talented people. Not only people like Jim Marshall, Carl Eller, Ahmad Rashad, and Chuck Foreman, but also Bobby Bryant, Charlie West, Clinton Jones, Gene Washington, and a whole host of others who were good friends, good people, and talented football players. I was very fortunate to be a part of all that."

On the Viking's Super Bowl Futility
"To be quite honest with you, I don't look back. My perspective is to look into the future. The fact that we didn't win four particular football games is not terribly significant in the grand scheme of things."

Here is What a Few of His Teammates Had to Say About Him
"As a football player, I feel very proud to have played with Alan Page," said Jim Marshall. "I think he was one of the guys that truly changed the game. They stopped calling holding (penalties) because Alan was so quick and elusive, and he was so disruptive to the other teams. They intentionally allowed holding on him, because that was the only way anybody could block him. They gave more freedom to offensive lineman in the way they used their hands, and a lot of that was because of his elusive play. Never in the history of the game, and I have looked at films since the beginning of organized football, has there been any rule changes like they made in the 10 years that Alan was out there. Everything changed with the advent of television, and people wanted to see a more potent offensive representation on the field. That handcuffed the defensive teams. Today football is more of a form of entertainment, rather than the sport that it was back in those days. I think a lot of that had to do with the play of Alan."

"Alan had a vision about his own personal life," said Carl Eller. "To a great extent, within his greatness, he saw his own limitations. He felt that he really had to do something significant outside of football. I think that Alan felt consumed by his own greatness on the field, and it was probably too much for him. He was a torch-bearer right from the very beginning."

Christmas day at the Met, and nearly 50,000 Minnesotans were on hand to watch the Vikes do battle with the hated Cowboys. Dallas had other ideas though, and jumped out to an early lead in this one, going up 6-3 after an early fumble recovery and an interception, which led to two Mike Clark field goals. After Freddy Cox answered on a 27-yarder, Dallas exploded in the third quarter for a pair of touchdowns. The first of the two scores came on Cliff Harris' interception which was returned 30 yards to the Minnesota 13. Then, on the next play, Running Back Duane Thomas took a hand-off up the middle for a 13-yard touchdown. The Vikes offense sputtered and was forced to punt again, which led to a Roger Staubach nine-yard touchdown pass to Bob Hayes. Minnesota rallied in the fourth behind an Alan Page safety followed by a six-yard touchdown pass from Cuozzo to Stu Voigt, but it was too little too late. Dallas hung on to beat the Vikes, 20-12. Once again, it was the team's inability to hold onto the ball that did them in. Five turnovers, including a pair interceptions each from Bob Lee, and Gary Quozzo, negated the fact that the Purple actually out-gained the Cowboys in total yardage 311-183.

Matt Blair

The undisputed bright spot of the season though was the inhuman play of Alan Page, who simply took his game to another level. In the Detroit game, Page, the first rookie ever to start for Grant, had a coming out party of sorts. You see, Alan Page was lightening quick, almost to the point that he made everyone else look like they are in slow motion. It would just so happen that in this particular game, the referees weren't that familiar with his ability to get across the line of scrimmage and wreak havoc on the opposing teams' offense. As a result, Page was called on two consecutive encroachment, or off-sides penalties, for what they perceived as him jumping over the line before the ball was snapped. Page went nuts, threw his arms in the air and demanded justice. He would get none, so he took out his rage on the defenseless Lions, who simply had no way of stopping him. Page released an onslaught of blitzes and bull-rushes that completely destroyed Detroit's game plan. His cat-like quickness proved to be no match for double and even triple teams that were thrown at him. His passion for the game was unparalleled and he hated to lose. That day he blew threw the line time after time and smothered the Lion's quarterback and halfbacks from sideline to sideline. He caused a couple of fumbles, had a few sacks and simply took all of the rhythm out of their passing attack. They were all so afraid of him that seemingly everyone on the line had one eye on him, which of course let Eller and Marshall have a feast of their own. When the Lions punted the ball away on that day, it wasn't for strategy, it was to get Page off the field and provide a little mercy for the team's offense. Coaches who later saw the game on film said Page's superhuman performance was a never-before seen case of one lineman somehow being able to dictate the flow of the game all by himself. Said one Lion after the game: "They could call this guy murder. We couldn't block him. He played like we weren't even there. He was unreal."

For his efforts, Page made history by becoming the first defensive player in NFL history of to win the league's MVP, something he later downplayed. "The MVP award was by somebody else's measure," he said. "Certainly 1971 was a good year for me, but there were other good ones in there too. For me, it was trying to be the best that I could be. That was something that was constant for me, and it wasn't something that took place one year and not in others. When I look back, I look on a whole career, not any one particular season. I had a lot of success in a lot of successful seasons."

Re-Enter Sir Francis

After the loss to Dallas, it became readily apparent that the team desperately needed a quarterback who could lead this team back to the Super Bowl. That's when Jim Finks picked up the phone and called New York Giants Owner Wellington Mara and asked him if his quarterback was in need of a new time zone. It just so happened that he did. The Giants were 4-10 that year, and Sir Francis made no bones about it, he wanted to escape from New York. When he found out that Minnesota wanted him, he jumped at the opportunity. When Finks called him and asked how he felt about it, Tark asked for the number of the first flight to the Minneapolis airport. So badly did Fran want to come back and play for a winner, with a big offensive line mind you, that he even agreed to take a pay-cut. The 30-year-old's salary would be just shy of $125,000. And with that, five years after he was cast off to the Big Apple, the Scrambler came home. To get him the Vikes gave up Quarterback Norm Snead, Flanker Bob Grim, Halfback Vince Clements and a pair of first and second draft choices. It was a steal. Francis had learned a lot about the art of quarterbacking in New York, and had grown up along the way. He was no longer the reckless scrambler that he used to be, and was desperate to lead a winning team to the promised land.

While he wasn't universally loved, and was criticized for often times looking too much after his own off-the-field personal interests, he said all the right things that made him a hero to so many. "There isn't any question in my mind that the Vikings are the best team in football," said Fran. "I just hope I can make a contribution to bring them to the Super Bowl."

Despite the celebrity of Tarkenton back at the helm, the Vikings didn't live up to their lofty expectations that year, limping their way to a very mediocre 7-7 record. Not only did Minnesota lose the divisional title to (Duluth native) Dan Devine's Green Bay Packers, they also lost their final two games to finish out of the playoffs for the first time in five years. The club did make a couple of upgrades along the way, dealing Gary Cuozzo to the Cardinals for Wide Receiver John Gilliam, and drafting a pair of promising rookies in Running Back Ed Marinaro and Linebacker Jeff Siemon.

The defense was slowed greatly that year due to the untimely injuries suffered by both Alan Page, who had a deep thigh bruise, and Carl Eller, who banged up his knee during the heartbreaking 16-14 loss to Miami in Week Three, and leading rusher Clint Jones, who broke a bone in his right elbow against Chicago early on. In addition, the usually reliable Freddy Cox also blew one victory by missing a 26-yarder, and cost the team three possible ties as well. Although the injuries messed up the defense that year, the team also had to play the toughest schedule in the league that year, facing six divisional champions along the way.

A classic example of just how the season went was against Washington, in their opener when the Vikings roughed up the Redskins in every statistical category, but lost the game on two mistakes

Sammy White

Ed Marinaro later went on to Hollywood, where he starred in "Hill Street Blues" among other series'.

which were both turned into touchdowns. They beat them in first downs, 26-11, total yards, 382-203, and total number of plays from scrimmage, 79-48. Tarkenton outplayed Redskins' QB Billy Kilmer every step of the way, but it was all in vain as Washington won 24-21.

From there the Vikes beat Detroit, 34-10, thanks to Dave Osborn's three touchdowns and Tarkenton's 40-yard TD toss to Gilliam. After losing to Miami and St. Louis, the Vikes rebounded to beat Denver, 23-20, on Tarkenton's 31-yard game-winning touchdown to Gene Washington with just 17 seconds remaining in the game. After losing to Chicago, 13-10, in Week Six, Minnesota rolled off four straight wins over Green Bay, 27-13, New Orleans, 37-6, Detroit, 16-14 and L.A., 45-41. Tark threw a pair of TDs against the Saints, Bobby Bryant blocked the game-winning field goal attempt in Detroit to save the day, and against the Rams, Fran threw for 319 yards and three long second-half touchdowns to: Bill Brown, for 76 yards, John Henderson, for 70 yards, and Gilliam, for 66 yards.

They lost three of their final four though, to Pittsburgh, Green Bay and San Francisco, beating just Chicago in Week 12, to finish at 7-7, good enough for just a third place finish in the NFC Central. Tark threw for 261 yards and a touchdown against the Bears, but it wasn't enough to salvage the season. Steeler Rookie of the Year Franco Harris was the difference against Pittsburgh, and against the Pack, the Vikes, whose only score came on a rare reverse to Tight End Stu Voigt, lost a crucial one, 23-7, in 18-degree below zero weather out at the Met that surely cost them a wild-card spot. Then, against the Niners, in the finale, the Vikings led, 17-6, going into the fourth thanks to Tarkenton's 18-yard TD pass to Ed Marinaro, his 31 yarder to Gilliam and a 43-yard field goal by Cox. But 49ers Quarterback John Brodie came in and threw a pair of touchdown passes to both Gene Washington and Dick Wichter in the final moments to ice it, 20-17.

It was a sad ending to a .500 season filled with bad luck and bad chemistry. Sure there were some key injuries and missed kicks along the way, but it was not Bud Grant football, and he would make darn sure his boys were ready to play that next season. Tark, who threw for 2,600 yards that year, had the receiver he needed in Gilliam, who posted over 1,000 receiving yards, but lacked the running threat to get his offense into high gear. Dave Osborn just wasn't going to cut it for the Vikes, who that following spring went out and drafted Running Back Chuck Foreman out of the University of Miami.

Super Bowl VII and Forty-Foreman

Minnesota recorded one of the greatest turn-arounds in pro football history in 1973, by posting a 12-2 record and advancing to their second Super Bowl in four years. Leading the way was the all-purpose wonder Chuck Foreman, who was named as the NFL's Rookie of the Year for his 1,163 yards both rushing and receiving. The offense was clicking because the ground game was forcing the defenses to respect them. Tarkenton, who was now thoroughly familiar with Grant's system, took advantage of the situation by throwing for nearly 3,000 yards and hooking up with John Gilliam 42 times for eight touchdowns.

As the 1973 season opened, the Vikings roster looked like this: Tarkenton at QB, John Gilliam as the go-to receiver, Foreman, Brown, Osborn and McClanahan in the backfield, Yary, Tingelhoff, Alderman, White and Sunde on the O-line, Page, Eller, Marshall and Gary Larsen on the D-Line, Siemon, Winston and Hilgenberg at linebackers, Krause, Bryant, Nate Wright and Jeff Wright in the defensive backfield and Freddy the foot doing his kicking thing. There was one guy who wasn't there though, Cornerback Karl Kassulke, who was involved in a motorcycle accident the day before practice started that summer and was tragically paralyzed for life. Karl, long known for his wild ways, turned his life around after that though, found religion and even fell in love with, and later married, the nurse who cared for him.

The Purple jumped out of the gates poised to do some damage in 1973, winning all five of their exhibition games. From there the squad ran off nine straight wins in the regular season before finally losing at Atlanta in Week 10. They rounded out the season by tattooing Chicago that next week, 31-13, getting shut-out badly at Cincinnati, 27-0, and rebounding to beat both Green Bay and the Giants both by the identical scores of 31-7, to finish out the regular season at 12-2. The defense was healthy and it showed. They were ready to make yet another run in the post-season.

On December 22, 1973, the Redskins came to town to face the Vikes in the first round of the playoffs. It would be a game remembered for two reasons. First, because of the team's great second half comeback, and secondly, because of Carl Eller's half-time motivational speaking seminar that ultimately caused the Vikings to have the aforementioned great second half comeback.

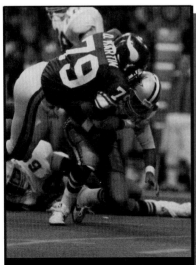

Doug Martin

Washington got on the board first in this one on a three-yard touchdown run by Larry Brown after Bob Brunet recovered Bobby Bryant's fumbled punt at the Minnesota 21-yard line. Cox added a field goal in the second, but the lethargic Vikes blew a chance to take a lead at the end of the half when Tarkenton threw an interception. At half-time, Eller, who played like a man possessed, went ballistic. He screamed, shouted, pounded his fist on metal doors, smashed a chalk board against the wall and challenged every man in that room to give it his all. He was tired of losing big games, and wanted more guts from everyone — right then and right there. The rest of the team sat in shock, staring silently, knowing that they had better step it up big-time, or they were going to have to deal with Carl after the game. And that's just what they did. Minnesota came out and took the lead in the second-half, thanks to Bill Brown's two-yard TD plunge which came on the heels of Oscar Reed's 46-yard scamper into the red-zone. Following a pair of Redskin field goals, Tarkenton capped a 71-yard drive with a 28-yard touchdown pass to Gilliam. Nate Wright then intercepted Billy Kilmer on the team's next offensive play, which led to Tarkenton again hitting Gilliam on an eight-yard touchdown pass. Freddy the foot came in to nail a 30-yarder late in the fourth to ice it for the Vikes as they hung on to win, 27-20.

That next week the Vikes headed to Irving, Texas, where they faced the Cowboys in the NFC Championship game. Minnesota came out and jumped all of the 'Boys in this one, thanks to an early Fred Cox field goal, followed by Chuck Foreman's five-yard TD run which capped a long, demoralizing 86-yard drive, mostly through the middle of the field. With two of their stars, Running Back Calvin

Hill and Defensive Tackle Bob Lilly, out of the game with injuries, Dallas just couldn't get going on either side of the ball.

Golden Richards finally put Dallas on the board early in the third quarter though when he returned a punt 63 yards for a touchdown, but Minnesota answered when Tark found John Gilliam open behind Cornerback Mel Renfro for a 54-yard touchdown pass. Dallas added a field goal to make it 17-10, but Quarterback Roger Staubach threw two of his four interceptions in the fourth quarter — one of them right into the awaiting arms of Bobby Bryant, who promptly took it 63 yards for a touchdown. Another interception set up a 34-yard field goal by Fred Cox. Walt Garrison terminated a forgettable day for Dallas when he fumbled the ball away at the Minnesota two-yard line late in the fourth to end it at 27-10 in favor of the Vikes.

With that, the Vikings found themselves in their second Super Bowl, this time at Houston's Rice Stadium, where, on January 13, 1974, they took on the Miami Dolphins. Yeah, the same Dolphins that had won 17 in a row just the year before to win Super Bowl VII. Their roster was a venerable who's-who of pro football: Bob Griese, Larry Csonka, Nick Buoniconti, Mercury Morris, Paul Warfield, Larry Little, Jim Langer (a native of Little Falls, Minn.), Garo Yepremian and, their fiery Coach, Don Shula.

"Benchwarmer Bob" Lurtsema

Much of the pre-game excitement and controversy the week before the big game centered around the Viking's miserable practice facilities at Delmar Field in Houston. Sparrows had moved in and built nests in the shower room, where most of the nozzles didn't work, nor did they spit out any hot water. The locker room didn't even have any lockers, just a bunch of rusty nails on the wall.

"This is shabby treatment. This is the Super Bowl, not some pickup game," Grant told reporters at a press conference. "The NFL sets up the practice facilities, and they had a year to do it right. Go look for yourselves, we don't have any lockers. Our seven coaches have to share one table for spreading out our clothes. These facilities definitely give the Dolphins the advantage." Meanwhile, the prima-donna Dolphins, on the other hand, were working out at the Houston Oilers' plush practice facilities. This was just what Grant wanted. He needed a juicy subplot to distract all of the hounding journalists and their endless questions about nothing, so he figured that this headline would be better than that involving of any of his players. Plus, it got his players fired up. They were already underdogs coming in, but now they were plenty pissed off about being treated like second-hand citizens to the glamour boys from Miami.

The reporters still hounded the players though, including Viking's Tackle Gary Larsen, who found the whole Super Bowl hyperbole to be a bit much. "I hope you don't think I'm a wise guy when I add that we've sweated a long time for this opportunity, and a whole bunch of people will be watching on TV," he quipped. "But there are 800 million Chinamen who don't give a damn about what happens in Houston this Sunday afternoon!"

Maybe Gary was on to something, but all those Americans who did care about the game saw nothing more than a good old fashioned butt-kicking, as the Dolphins thrashed the Vikes, and became the second team in NFL history to win back-to-back Super Bowls. On paper, the game seemed to be a mismatch from the opening kick-off. You had the 23rd ranked Vikings run defense up against a relentless Miami ground attack, and Miami wasted little time in exploiting Minnesota's weaknesses. Before the Vikings could manage a first down, the Fish were up by the score of 14-0.

Following two time-consuming 62 and 56 yard drives, Miami Fullback Larry Csonka plowed in first on a five-yard run, followed by a Jim Kiick one-yarder. Garo Yepremian then added a 28-yard field goal to make it 17-0 at the half. The Vikings' only chance to get back in the game came late in the first half when they drove down to the Miami five-yard line, only to see Dolphins' Middle Linebacker Nick Buoniconti crunch Oscar Reed on the next play, forcing a costly turnover.

Stu Voigt then got called for a clipping penalty during the kickoff to start the second half, negating John Gilliam's brilliant 65-yard return which would've given Minnesota the ball on the Miami 34-yard line. As a result, they were held on downs, and Csonka scored on a two-yard plunge on the next series to make it 24-0. Sir Francis, who set a Super Bowl record by completing 18 passes, then tried to mount a late comeback by capping a 40-yard drive on a four-yard TD run. He put together another drive with seconds to go, but it was foiled by Curtis Johnson's interception at the Miami goal line to end the game at 24-7. "Let's get one thing straight," said Grant. "When you get beat, you get beat. We were beaten just about every way by Miami, a great team."

Just how bad was it? Dolphins' Quarterback Bob Griese had to throw only seven passes that entire afternoon, completing six. The 71,882 fans in attendance that day watched Csonka, named as the game's MVP, set a Super Bowl record by rushing for 145 yards and two touchdowns on 33 carries to double the rushing yardage of the entire Minnesota backfield. "I've never tried to tackle anybody stronger," said Vikings' linebacker Jeff Siemon after the game. "Once he got going, he just carried you on his back. He has to be the strongest running back I've ever faced."

"I don't have many good memories of that Super Bowl game against Miami," recalled Foreman. "There's not much to say except that they beat us on both ends of the ball. Of all the Super Bowls I've played in, that was the only one that I could justify losing in my mind. The Miami Dolphins had more talent and a better unit than we had. Personally, it was an incredibly exciting time for me being Rookie of the Year and playing in my first Super Bowl and all. Miami was the only team that I have ever played against that I could honestly say that they were better than us. It was just a tough loss after coming off the great season that we had."

Trying for Redemption at Super Bowl IX

The Vikes came right back in 1974, and with the additions of Linebackers Fred McNeill and Matt Blair, finished with a solid 10-4 record. One guy who wasn't there at the opener, however, was General Manager Jim Finks. Finks, who, on the heals of being named as the NFL's Executive of the Year in 1973, wanted some ownership of team stock as part of his new contract. Board President Max Winter felt differently though, and with that, Finks resigned. It was a shocking announcement for a man who had done so much in not only building the team, but also with regards to player relations, trades, P.R., contract

Dave Huffman

CHUCK FOREMAN

Chuck Foreman was raised in Frederick, MD, just outside Washington D.C. He grew up playing football, basketball, and baseball , but loved the gridiron the most. Originally recruited as a defensive tackle, he made the switch to running back at the University of Miami, where he quickly broke all of the Hurricanes' freshman rushing records

In 1973 he was drafted by the Vikings as the 12th overall pick of the first round. The transition to the pros was a smooth one for the powerful running back, who, after rushing for 801 yards, catching 37 passes, and scoring four touchdowns, was named as the NFL's Rookie of the Year. Not only was he a bruising runner, but he had amazing hands — which made him one of the game's greatest all-time offensive weapons. When he had the ball in the open field it was all over. His now infamous 360-degree spins became his trademark, as he often-times left his would-be tacklers dazed and confused in his vapor trail.

"I am sometimes surprised when I look at film of myself," said Foreman of his unorthodox running style in Jim Klobuchar's book entitled "The First Fifteen Years." "I just do what's natural out there and live by instinct. It's like when you're riding your bicycle and all of a sudden, a mad dog starts chasing you. There's a little bit of fear in your heart, and you've got to get away. I look at running as an art."

In 1975, en route to leading the Vikings in rushing, receiving, and scoring, No. 44 also won the NFC scoring and receptions titles by hauling in 73 catches — the most ever by a running back. He followed that up the next year by rushing for 1,155 yards, including a 200-yard game against the Eagles, to be named as the NFC Player-of the-Year. Then, in 1978, Foreman, the hub of the Vikings offense for five seasons, suffered a knee injury which would ultimately lead to the premature end of an incredible career. He gained a career-low 749 yards that year, ultimately leading to him becoming a backup to Ted Brown in 1979. Chuck was then traded to New England in 1980, where he played one more season before finishing his career.

Without a doubt, Chuck "Forty-Fourman" was the greatest running back in Vikings history. There hasn't been a dominant, explosive or more versatile back since him to wear the purple. Chuck led the Vikings in rushing for six consecutive seasons, set team records for yards rushing, with 5,879, and combined yards rushing and receiving, with 8,936. All in all, he scored 53 rushing touchdowns, along with hauling in 350 catches for 3,156 receiving yards and 23 receiving touchdowns. There will be good ones that come and go, but no one will run the ball with the passion and desire like Chuck Foreman did. Period.

Today Chuck lives in the Twin Cities area and continues to work in the world of sports and business. He is also following his son Jay, a former star linebacker at the University of Nebraska, who is trying to follow his old man's footsteps in the world of pro football.

What did it mean for you to be a Viking?
"I was always a big fan of the 'Purple People Eaters.' I had to pinch myself when I was drafted by Minnesota. But before I came up here to join the Vikings, I actually did a lot of research on the NFL team and on the players. I wanted to know who played here and where they were from. I consider it to be a privilege to have been able to perform here."

On Super Bowl Futility?
"The games themselves were incredible to play in, but they weren't like they are today. Now they're like the greatest event in the history of the world. When you're standing out on that field at a Super Bowl game, you really realize just what you've accomplished. I was fortunate enough to be in three of those games. It was a great experience in my life, but certainly there was disappointment too, because, of course, we didn't win any of them."

On the Fans in Minnesota?
"When I played, the fans were really a part of the success of the team, simply because we were accessible. You know, we went out there in that cold weather, and they would stay out there with us for hours. That was a big reason why our teams were so close to each other back then. There are a lot of great people here in Minnesota, and of all the places I've been, Minnesota is second to none."

On Leaving Minnesota to Join the Patriots?
"It's just like what they do with thoroughbreds when they can't run anymore — they put them out to pasture. I really think I could have played a couple more years. But, that's just the nature of the game, and you know that at some point in time it's going to happen to everybody. Depression kind of set in because you realize it's coming to the end. We all know it's coming, but I think I could've played a couple more years."

Here is What a Few of His Teammates Had to Say About Him:
"I think that Chuck was one of the finest running backs in the history of the NFL," said Jim Marshall. "At the peak of his career, he was one of the most highly skilled running backs that ever played the game of football. He was a great player."

"His talent is still unrecognized," said Carl Eller. "He was one the best running backs ever. Chuck was so good the Vikings didn't realize how good he was. He was a great player, but as great as he was, I don't think the Vikings ever used his greatness to its fullest extent."

"It was too bad Chuck didn't play the game a little longer," said Bud Grant. "He was the best back in the league for five years. Running backs take a lot of wear and tear, and it was unfortunate that he got hurt."

"Chuck was the best all-around running back that I ever played with," said Ahmad Rashad. "He was an amazing athlete. He could block, tackle, run, catch, and score. Chuck Foreman could do everything."

"Chuck was just a great running back," said Alan Page. "He had the speed, talent, the moves, and he always came to play."

negotiations and community service. His replacement would be a Memphis millionaire by the name of Mike Lynn. Lynn, who made his fortune in the discount store business, was an extroverted pitchman who tried unsuccessfully to lure an NFL franchise to Tennessee. The Vikings' board thought that he would be a good fit, and, in the long, it was. Within a couple of years he knew of every nuance the game had to offer. He understood negotiating contracts, procedures and how to work the loopholes in order to land free agents that other teams couldn't touch.

Minnesota started strong that year, winning their first five games against Green Bay, Detroit, Chicago, Dallas and Houston before losing a pair to both Detroit and New England. (Against Dallas, Fred Cox made history — sort of. You see, he kicked a game-winning field goal that afternoon that soared high above the uprights. The Cowboys though differently, however, and made such a stink about it, claiming that it was went wide, that the league decided to extend the uprights to their current height.) They rebounded to beat Chicago and St. Louis, followed by another two-game losing streak to Green Bay and Los Angeles. From there they man-handled New Orleans, Atlanta and K.C. to finish the season at 10-4 and play host to the Cardinals for the first round of the playoffs.

Greg Coleman

It was a pretty good year for the Purple. Tarkenton, despite playing most of the season with a sore arm, which severely limited his passing options, still managed to toss 17 touchdown passes on 2,500 yards. Fran's playing style made it easy for him to move the ball around, with Foreman, Marinaro and Dave Osborn in the backfield. (Foreman stymied the sophomore jinx by rushing for 777 yards, catching 53 passes and leading the NFL with 15 touchdowns.) He had John Gilliam and Jimmy Lash as his deep threats, and when got desperate, he would just dump it off to his security blanket, "Chainsaw" Stu Voigt over the middle.

Primed and ready to make yet another run at the Super Bowl, the Vikes hosted St. Louis in what would prove to be a blow-out. After a scoreless first quarter, the Cards, who had been dominating the game, got on the board first when Jim Hart hit Jim Thomas on a 13-yard touchdown pass. Minnesota, answered back though, with Tarkenton hitting Gilliam on a 16-yarder to make it 7-7 at the half. Jeff Wright then intercepted a pass on the opening drive of the second half, which led to a Fred Cox field goal just five plays later. Two plays after that, Cards Running Back Terry Metcalf fumbled, only to see Nate Wright pick up the ball and run 20 yards for a touchdown to give the Vikings a 17-7 lead. After Minnesota held St. Louis on the next series, Tarkenton hit Gilliam for his second TD of the day, this one being of the 38-yard variety. Shortly thereafter, Foreman, who ran for 114 yards on the day, capped off a long Minnesota drive by taking in a four-yarder to finish off the Cardinals, 30-14.

Next up were the Los Angeles Rams, who were trying to prevent Minnesota from going to its third Super Bowl in just six years. After a scoreless first quarter, the Vikings got on the board first when Tarkenton hit Jim Lash on a 29-yard touchdown pass to go up 7-0. The Rams then answered with a 27-yard David Ray field goal to make it 7-3. After a scoreless third, Minnesota's defense turned the game around on a single play. Here's what went down. After Vikings Punter Mike Eischeid pinned the Rams down to their own one-yard line on a superb punt, the Rams began a long drive which was highlighted by Quarterback James Harris hitting Harold Jackson on a 73-yard pass play that ended with Safety Jeff Wright knocking him out of bounds at the Vikings' two-yard line. From there, Harris, on a key third down play, threw a pass intended for Tight End Pat Curran, but Linebacker Wally Hilgenberg stepped up and picked it off in the end-zone to save the day. Dave Osborn then capped a brilliant 15-play, 80-yard drive by leaping in from the four-yard line on what would prove to be the game-winning touchdown. The Rams came back midway through the fourth with a 44-yard TD pass from Harris to Jackson, but the Vikings maintained the ball and ran out the clock to preserve the 14-10 victory. One of the unsung heroes of the game was Tackle Ron Yary, who neutralized L.A.'s Pro Bowl Defensive End Jack Youngblood, in one of the most physical and barbaric confrontations perhaps in playoff history.

With that, the Vikes had earned themselves a trip to New Orleans' Tulane Stadium, and a date with the Pittsburgh Steelers in Super Bowl IX. The veteran Vikes were favored going in — after all this was their third trip in just six seasons, while the Steelers were rookies to the big dance.

The first half was dominated by both defenses: Minnesota's "Purple People Eaters" and Pittsburgh's "Steel Curtain," which was led by Defensive Tackle "Mean" Joe Greene. After a scoreless first quarter, the Steelers' Defensive End Dwight White pounced on a Dave Osborn fumbled hand-off in the end-zone for a safety to make it 2-0 at the half. The Vikings could've taken the lead before the half-time show, had it not been for an untimely Tarkenton interception that came on a pass he tried to thread to Gilliam near the goal line. The ball popped loose and into the hands of Pittsburgh's Mel Blount, leaving the 80,000-plus fans only to wonder what could've been.

By mid-game, a cold rain started to come down making the ground really slick. But Pittsburgh's equipment manager came prepared and saved the day for his squad by switching his players' artificial turf shoes to cleats over half-time. It was a subtle change, but a significant one nonetheless in the game's final outcome.

Then, to open the third quarter, Bill Brown fumbled the opening kick-off deep in Minnesota territory. The Steelers would make them pay, as Running Back Franco Harris ran it in just four plays later to make it 9-0. Then, midway through the fourth, Matt Blair blocked Bobby Walden's punt, and Safety Terry Brown recovered it in the end-zone to get Minnesota on the board at 9-6 (Cox shanked the extra-point). But, thanks to the running of Harris, who, upon running for a record 34 carries for 158 yards on the day, would be named as the game's MVP, and Rocky Bleier, who added 65 yards on 17 carries, the Steelers were able to charge right back. Starting on their own 34-yard line, Quarterback Terry Bradshaw capped a long drive deep into Minnesota real-estate that ended when he hit Receiver Larry Brown on a four-yard touchdown to put the game on ice. Harris appeared to have fumbled on the drive, but the referees controversially ruled that he was down before the ball popped out. (A television replay would say otherwise!) Pittsburgh's Mike Wagner even intercepted a last-minute Tarkenton pass in the game's final moments to prevent Minnesota from mounting a rally. After the game Grant summed it up as eloquently as he could: "All three sides had a bad day — the Vikings, Steelers and the officials..."

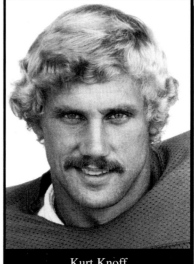

Kurt Knoff

The Viking's offense was stymied throughout the whole game, managing just nine first downs and only 17 yards rushing — both Super Bowl lows, not to mention their five horrific turnovers that were clearly the difference in the game. It wasn't much better through the air either, as Tarkenton, under constant pressure from Linemen Joe Greene, Ernie Holmes, Dwight White, and L.C. Greenwood, as well as Linebackers Jack Ham, Jack Lambert and Andy Russell, completed only 11 of 26 attempts for 102 yards, had six passes knocked down, and heaved three interceptions.

Perhaps the only good thing that came out of that week in the French Quarter happened before the big game even took place at the team's hotel. That's where legendary sportscaster Howard Cosell came to do an interview with Tarkenton. Cosell, who showed up dressed to the nines in his network logo'd blazer, began to do the interview. Before long, Wally Hilgenberg, Bob Lurtsema and Alan Page all spotted the goings on from a balcony just above the camera crew. Deciding to lighten the moment, the three each filled up their room's wastebaskets full of water and, on the count of three, proceeded to dump them on the head of the unsuspecting Cosell below. When Howie realized that his hairpiece looked like a wet kitty, he was none to pleased — shouting profanities that would have made a construction worker proud. Score one for the Purple!

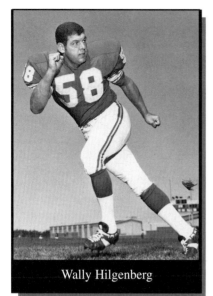
Wally Hilgenberg

Pearson Pushed-Off!

The Vikings team of 1975 was arguably the best ever. The team came out of the gates just smoking, winning its first 10 games. It wasn't until Week 11, when they got upset, 31-30, at Washington, did they even come back down to earth. They then beat Green Bay the following week, lost at Detroit in Week 13, 17-10, and rebounded to finish the regular season with a 35-13 waxing of Buffalo.

The Buffalo finale was an interesting one to say the least, particularly for Running Back Chuck Foreman, who, because of a snowball, lost the NFC's triple crown title (given to the league's rushing, receiving & scoring leader) to O.J. Simpson. Foreman came into the game with the opportunity to become the only player in NFL history to lead his conference in rushing and receptions, and also share the league record for touchdowns in a season. The conditions were horrible out at Rich Stadium. The snow was coming down like crazy, it was freezing out, and to top it off there were a ton of drunk fans who were heaving snowballs at the Vikings throughout the game. Despite all of this, Foreman was having a great game. By the third quarter he had already racked up 85 yards rushing, 10 receptions and four touchdowns. Tarkenton had even joked with the players in the huddle that if anyone got close to scoring, they should go out of bounds at the one-yard line so Chuck could get the TD. He needed just one more touchdown and a few more yards to beat Simpson, when POW!, he took a rock-filled snowball right in the face. The fans, who were already pissed about being clobbered, 28-6, certainly didn't want to see an opposing player beat their hometown hero's record in their own backyard. Foreman, who went down hard, returned to the game with blurred vision, and even caught another touchdown pass to tie Gale Sayers' and Simpson's touchdown records, but was forced to spend the fourth quarter on the bench unable to see out of his eye. Less than a minute later, Simpson scored on a 54-yard reception to win the touchdown record, and to make matters worse, the next day, St. Louis' Jim Otis, gained 69 yards to edge Foreman by six measly yards to earn conference rushing crown. Foreman did manage to hang on the league's reception title, however, with 73 catches, but he should've had the trifecta.

In addition to Foreman's brilliant season, Tarkenton had a career year as well, passing for 25 touchdowns and earning the league's coveted MVP award. Things were looking great for a repeat trip to the big dance. The offense was playing huge. They had outscored their opponents, 377-180, won nine games by 10 or more points, and were hitting on all cylinders. They were primed to finally win it all that year, that was, until the Dallas Cowboys came up with one of the most famous plays in the history of the NFL.

On December 28, 1975, the Vikes played host the hated Cowboys for the NFC Divisional Playoff game. Minnesota, a veteran laden team which had battle scars from three Super Bowls, was expected to finally win the Super Bowl this year, while the 10-4 Cowboys on the other hand, were a young wild-card team, with a cast of more than a dozen rookies. Sure they had lost Bob Lilly and Walt Garrison to retirement that year, but they did have an outstanding hard-hitting "Doomsday Defense," which was led by Ed "Too-Tall" Jones, Harvey Martin, Lee Roy Jordan and Safety Cliff Harris. It would go down as one of the greatest upsets in the history of sports, and without question the Vikings' undisputed worst game of all-time.

After a scoreless first quarter, something pivotal happened in the second quarter that would play an important role in the outcome of the game. Dallas felt that they were jobbed by the refs when Cowboy safety Cliff Harris, who was waiting to receive a Neil Clabo punt on his own four-yard-line, opted to let the ball sail into the end-zone for a touchback. However, the ball took a crazy bounce and Vikings linebacker, Fred McNeil jumped on it. Harris didn't know what was going on, but the officials claimed it touched his leg on the bounce, meaning that it was a live ball for anyone to claim. Dallas argued to no avail, and Chuck Foreman leaped over the goal line for a touchdown one minute later, making it 7-0.

After a missed 45-yard field goal attempt by Fred Cox, Dallas came back to tie it up on a Doug Dennison seven-yard TD run, and then took the lead on Toni Fritsch's 24-yard field goal to make it 10-7. But with five minutes to go in the game, Minnesota regained the lead when Brent McClanahan capped an 11 play, 70-yard touchdown drive by taking it in from the one-yard line.

Dallas' offense sputtered on the next series and was forced to punt. But they held the Vikings in check, thanks to Dallas Safety Charlie Waters, who blitzed and sacked Tarkenton for a three-yard loss on a key third down to force the Vikings to punt. The Cowboys then got the ball back on its own 15-yard line with just 1:51 remaining. Quarterback Roger Staubach started out his drive by hitting Drew Pearson for seven yards. Then, on fourth-and-16 from his own 25, he found Pearson again at mid-field for another first down. The play, which had Staubach faking a post pattern and instead hitting Pearson angling for the sideline, was aided by Cornerback Nate Wright. While the momentum of the pass probably would have carried Pearson out of bounds for an incompletion, the official ruled otherwise, declaring that Wright had forced him out. The Vikings, now frantically pointing their fingers and criss-cross-

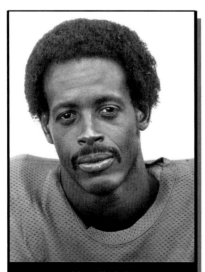
Nate Wright

PAUL KRAUSE

A native of Flint, Mich., Paul Krause went on to star as a defensive back and wide receiver at the University of Iowa. There, in addition to starring as an All-American center fielder on the baseball team, Krause received All-Conference football honors while playing for future Vikings Coach Jerry Burns, and alongside future Viking teammate Wally Hilgenberg. (He would've made it as a pro baseball player had he not torn up his shoulder in a football game against Michigan his senior year.)

In 1964 Krause was selected as a second-round draft choice of the Washington Redskins. The speedy rookie wasted little time making a name for himself in D.C., intercepting two passes in his very first game and going to lead the NFL with 12 interceptions. He soon became known as one of the league's best up-and-coming defenders. Four years and 28 interceptions later, the free safety was traded to the Vikings in exchange for Linebacker Marlin McKeever (McKeever came to the Vikes as part of the Tommy Mason deal with the Rams), and a seventh-round draft pick.

"To play for a winning football team is one of the greatest things that a player can experience," said Krause. "When I got to Minnesota, I was quite fortunate to play a part in a truly great defense. I was never really that great of a defender against the run, but with the pressure that our front four put on offenses, my objective in playing the run was to just stop the runner before he reached the goal line.

With the Vikings, Krause became a fixture back in the defensive secondary. He even intercepted passes in six consecutive games in his first season in Minnesota. His ball-hawking skills were legendary, making him the Deion Sanders of his day. He even came out as the holder for field goals and conversions, adding another element of danger to opposing teams who now had to watch for fake kicks. Among the many highlights that dotted the canvas of his brilliant career, came on Sept. 30, 1979, when he picked off a pass thrown by Detroit's Jeff Komlo to tie Emlen Tunnell's all-time interception's record. He then became the all-time leader with a pair of interceptions off of both Vince Ferragamo and Bob Lee against the Rams, at the L.A. Coliseum, on Dec. 2, 1979, nabbing No.'s 80 & 81, respectively. It was a huge relief, seeing as he had gone that entire 78' season without intercepting a pass — an event that happened just once in his career. Content, he retired from the game just a few weeks later.

He studied his opponents and became a student of the game. Prior to each game he and the other members of the secondary would end with the words "Ban the bomb!" a saying they would live by. He was the leader of a three-deep zone coverage defense that had the linebackers in the short territory while freeing up the defensive backs to contain deep receivers. The center fielder's natural instincts and reactions really flourished out in this system, allowing the crafty veteran to sit back and watch the quarterback's eyes, knowing just when to make his move.

"I would have to say that Paul Krause had the game down to a science," said Bud Grant. "His intuition and instinct for playing the receiver and the football was terrific. His ability to make a big play was almost constant ... he could turn a game around for us."

Krause's total of 81 career interceptions over his illustrious 16-year pro career (53 of which came while wearing the purple), is an all-time NFL record that will probably never be broken. He also ranks third all-time in interception return yardage, with 1,185, and scored three touchdowns as well. In addition, he was named to eight Pro Bowls, was voted All-NFL four times, and started at Safety in four Super Bowls. For his amazing efforts and contributions to the game, he was finally inducted into Pro Football Hall of Fame in the Summer of 1998. His presenter: his old Hawkeye coach, "Burnsie." It was a huge relief for Krause who had been denied a spot in the Hall several times prior because of a bias against the Vikings 0-4 Super Bowl record.

"You have to think interceptions," he said. "I analyzed quarterbacks. I knew some of the things they tried to do in certain situations. That wasn't gambling. It was being in the right place at the right time."

Today, Paul and his wife Pam, the parents of three children, reside in Lakeville, where he has many business interests including owning a golf course, land development, construction and real estate.

ing their arms, claimed it would have been impossible for Pearson to have landed in-bounds. But the referee stood firm, and the drive continued.

With that, Dallas now had a first down at the 50-yard line with 37 seconds left. After throwing a pair of incompletions to Receivers Golden Richards and Preston Pearson, Staubach then mishandled John Fitzgerald's poor snap and was dumped for a six-yard loss. Metropolitan Stadium was rocking. He got up though, and huddled his men at midfield. His bruised ribs from the week before were bothering him and Drew Pearson was exhausted. Pearson thought he could beat Wright, so Staubach told him to do just that. With that, he said a prayer and lined up against the "Purple People Eaters," who wanted to pulverize him.

There, with 24 seconds left on the clock, and after a bobbled snap, Staubach dropped back, pump-faked to keep Safety Paul Krause from coming over to offer double-coverage, and let go a desperation heave into the semi-darkness of the late afternoon Minnesota haze. The wobbly pass hung up there and was slightly under-thrown of the sprinting receiver. But Pearson, who was shoulder to shoulder with Cornerback Wright in a foot-race down the sidelines, somehow came back, adjusted to ball and miraculously caught the 50-yard prayer at the five-yard line and simply fell into the end-zone as time ran off the clock. With the ball pinned awkwardly in between his elbow and hip, the surprised receiver cautiously looked at the official for a penalty flag. But the offensive pass interference call never came. Pearson, who clearly pushed off of Wright, even knocking him down to gain better position on the play, had gotten away with murder. He then turned around, took a running start and fired the ball up at the Marlboro Man (cowboy advertisement) up on the scoreboard, as a sort of salute to all of Texas.

More than 47,000 fans in the old Met sat in silence, shock, and disbelief. Everyone thought that there would be a penalty called, and there was, only on Minnesota's Wright. The Vikings players went berserk. The fans started booing and screaming: "Pearson pushed off!" Then, in what some zealots later called "justifiable homicide" some drunk lunatic heaved a half-full "Corby's" Whiskey bottle from the 21st row of

JIM MARSHALL

Jim Marshall was born in 1937, in Danville, Ky., and attended East High School, in Columbus, Ohio. He went on to become an All-American Defensive End at Ohio State, and was one of the stars of the 1959 Rose Bowl title team that beat Oregon, 10-7. After playing in the CFL and then with the Cleveland Browns for one season, in 1960, he was acquired by the Vikings, where he anchored one side of the infamous "Purple People Eater" defensive line from 1961 - 1979. The two-time Pro-Bowler also served as the team's captain, an honor extremely fitting of the type of amazing player that he was.

When it as all said and done the numbers were astounding. From 1961 to 1979, over 19 seasons, he played in an NFL record 270 consecutive games, and 302 consecutive regular season and post season games. Like dog-years, in football-years, that's got to be close to a millennium. And one of the reasons he was able to survive that long down in the trenches was because of Bud Grant's willingness and understanding of what made each guy tick. He knew that Marshall hated to practice and would do anything he could go get out of it. So, every now and then, Bud would accommodate his "mystery" illnesses that would pop up in mid-week to let him take a sauna and get ready for Sunday.

Marshall's legend and lore includes several incredible stories that exemplify the many obstacles he hurdled over the course of his career. For example, a few months before joining the Browns, while stationed at an army training camp, Marshall was stricken with encephalitis. Although he lost over 40 pounds, he still reported to camp and insisted on playing. Jim was a warrior in the best sense of the word. He loved adventure and on more than one occasion it nearly killed him, literally. In 1964, while cleaning his gun, Marshall accidentally shot himself in the side. Once during training camp, he was hospitalized when a grape became lodged in his windpipe. Another time, while visiting the troops during the Vietnam War, he underwent a tonsillectomy that resulted in severe hemorrhaging.

In 1971, Marshall almost died in a snowmobile accident on a trip throughout the Grand Teton Mountains in Wyoming. After his snowmobile went over a cliff and nearly crushed him in the midst of a blizzard, his group was forced to burn $20 bills to keep warm on their three-day ordeal. Marshall later said, "It was the toughest thing I've ever encountered in my life, I thought we were all going to die." As a matter of fact, one member of his 16 person group did. Then, in 1980, Jim survived a near-fatal motorized hang-glider accident. He was an enigma, and that's why everybody loved him so much. It was if they wanted to live vicariously through him. It was if he was Superman.

How he played through all of those injuries that would keep 90% of today's players out of the lineup is unconscionable. He played for the love of the game and lived for Sundays. Perhaps former teammate Ahmad Rashad summed it up best when he described Marshall as "A Viking among men, and a giant among Vikings."

One of the initiation rituals for many Vikings rookies was to make the road-trip to training camp in Mankato, with Marshall behind the wheel. For most humans that trip took two hours, but Jim usually made it in about 45 minutes, with the rookies screaming the entire way down. He loved adventure, wherever it presented itself.

But there is also another side of Marshall — the one who studied Oriental philosophy, wrote poetry and even modeled men's clothes. He once took a brokerage test and was given a genius rating. He described life as "wonderful, with so many things to be enjoyed," he said. "I think too many times we restrict ourselves to a small box with a limited wish list on each wall. I like to raise my head above the walls and look out into the horizon and think about all the possibilities that are out there to better enjoy my life. That outlook makes life interesting. It gives you the opportunity to grow as a person. I want to enjoy everything as much as I can while I still occupy this physical body. Because, one day, when I no longer have this earthly vehicle, I want to feel as though I truly had an opportunity to enjoy everything that was available to me."

Today Jim is divorced and works in the inner city with at-risk youth. He formed a social service agency along with Oscar Reed, a Viking teammate, called Professional Sports Linkage. Jim described it as, "a service that has programs to help everyone from young people, to senior citizens, to new immigrants, to adjudicated youth - while they are incarcerated, all to create positive, tax-paying, productive members of our society."

Jim Marshall, the Captain, will always be remembered as a Vikings legend. Fittingly, on Nov. 28, 1999, in a game against the San Diego Chargers, the Vikings celebrated "Jim Marshall Day," officially retiring his No. 70 jersey in front of a thrilled and appreciative sell-out Metrodome crowd.

On his unbelievable durability and ability to play through pain, Marshall modestly replied, "I played because I loved the game."

"I would like to be thought of as a guy who gave everything he had to give on the football field and did whatever was necessary for his team to help win the game," he added. "I had fun doing it, and I tried to give the best that I could give to win."

Here is What a Few of His Teammates Had to Say About Him

"Jim Marshall was one of the finest athletes I have ever coached," said Bud Grant. "He had durability, and that was the greatest ability you could have. He was one of the finest competitors the Vikings have ever had. Period."

"He was the best," said Carl Eller. "He epitomized the term 'Viking.' I am still very good friends with Jim, and I cherish our friendship very dearly. Together we went through a lot out there and he was just a fabulous football player. He was so quick off the ball and was just fearless. I have a lot of respect for him as a player and as a person."

"Jim was a phenomenal football player and a really good friend," said Alan Page. "He is somebody who was dedicated and committed to the game of football and to his franchise. I guess the best way to describe him would be when you look up the definition of professional football in the dictionary, you should find Jim Marshall's name."

"Jim Marshall was our leader," said Chuck Foreman. "A guy that anybody would follow. He is a unique man in that he had the greatest mind control of anybody I've ever seen. He was the heart and soul of the Minnesota Vikings."

"Captain Marshall! Man, he was fearless," said Ahmad Rashad. "He was the epitome of a football captain. He should definitely be in the Pro Football Hall of Fame. No, they should have a separate wing in the Hall of Fame just for him."

"To me, aside from being a magnificent player, Jim was the spirit of the Vikings," said Joe Kapp. "He represented the essence of spirit and leadership. There would be no player who would stand up more for basic, fundamental, consistent values in team sport than Jim Marshall. He was always there for his teammates on and off the field, and he is a wonderful person."

the Met's right field bleachers and decked the Official, Armen Terzian, square in the noggin. Foreman ran to the aid of the bleeding ref and pleaded with the fans to remain calm. The game ended a few seconds later, but for Tarkenton, things got much, much worse. Shortly thereafter, he learned that his father, a Pentecostal Minister whose name was, ironically, Dallas, had died of a heart attack while watching the game on television.

(After the game the whiskey bottle was seized as evidence, and a search for the psychotic fan began. A $5,000 reward was offered, the Bloomington Police Department released a sketch of the perpetrator, game tapes were scrutinized and more than a dozen suspects were interrogated. Six months later, a 21-year-old kid from Golden Valley was picked out of a line-up by a couple of witnesses and charged with simple-assault and disorderly conduct. He pleaded guilty and was fined a whopping $100 bucks.)

"It was just a 'Hail Mary' pass," said Staubach very impromptu-like after the game, "a very, very lucky play." "I just threw it and prayed. I'll admit that we were very lucky on that play. But on the other hand, that touchdown we gave the Vikings in the second quarter had to be some kind of a fluke. If you take away that touchdown by the Vikings and our so-called lucky catch, we still would have won by a field goal and I think we deserved to."

"The touchdown pass was a prayer that was answered," said Bud Grant "From our side of the field, there is no question that Pearson shoved Nate Wright. It was as clear as day and night. He (Pearson) had nothing to lose. If they called a penalty on him, what had he lost? They would just line up and try another long pass. It was one chance in a hundred that he would get away with it, but it was the only chance he had."

"I had a clear view," said Tarkenton. "The man pushed his arm down and pushed Nate down. It definitely should have been offensive pass interference."

"It was very obvious," said Ron Yary, "that the officials were going to do all they could to make sure we didn't win this game."

"We all just stood on the sideline and watched Drew Pearson push Nate down," recalled Foreman. "That was probably the greatest football team that I ever played on. We were the best team in the NFL that year bar none. It was the toughest loss I ever experienced, and it happened on a blown call."

"I knew our only chance was to throw one long and hope for a miracle," said Cowboy's Coach Tom Landry.

"It was a lucky catch, but it was the most important catch of my career," said Pearson, who went on to start a Dallas-based marketing company (producing licensed hats) which, ironically, had a branch in Hopkins. "I never did push. There was contact on the play — two players running downfield, jostling for position, but there was no deliberate push."

In the era of modern football there are several historic and celebrated plays that will forever link certain teams with an era: Green Bay's "Ice Bowl," Pittsburgh's "Immaculate Reception" by Franco Harris, "The Catch" by Dwight Clark from Joe Montana, the Raiders' "Holy Roller" play, and even the Tennessee Titans' "Music City Miracle" to beat the Bills in 1999. But none was as big, or has become so much a part of the NFL's vocabulary than has the infamous "Hail Mary."

Joey Browner

Back to the Promised Land for One Last Time

The Vikings had every reason to come out feeling sorry for themselves in 1976. But with the memories of the "Hail Mary" still fresh in their minds, Minnesota instead came out and showed their true colors, posting a tremendous 11-2-1 regular season record, and yet another trip to the post-season. The defense, which allowed only three teams to score more than 13 points that season, led the team to its eighth division title in nine years on November 21, with a 17-10 win against the Packers. One of the bright spots for the defense that year was the addition of Cornerback Nate Allen, who loved to tear it up and make big hits. He even posted three of the team's 15 blocked kicks or punts that year. He also fit in well back there with Paul Krause, who was closing in on the all-time career interception record held by Emlen Tunnell.

Foreman, who had his best rushing year with 1,155 yards, and Tarkenton, who, with 2,961 passing yards, surpassed Johnny Unitas as the all-time leader in virtually every major passing category, were again the heroes on the offensive side of the ball. But they were joined that season by a couple of receivers who would make for a wonderful a one-two punch. Sammy White, who would earn Rookie of the Year honors, and veteran Ahmad Rashad, who, after a couple of stints with St. Louis, Buffalo, and Seattle, finally found a home in Minnesota. The team's core group of stars were aging however, and played with a sense of urgency that year. Key players such as Tarkenton, Marshall, Eller, Tingelhoff, Hilgenberg and Krause, all knew that this might be their last chance to make a run at the Super Bowl.

The season had its share of highlights, including Foreman's amazing 200-yard game against Philadelphia, as well as the nail-biter in Detroit, where the Vikes hung on to beat the Lions, 10-9, on a blown second half conversion. (The Vikings almost didn't make it to that game at all, after the team bus got hung up in traffic and showed up late to the game!) And then there was the 17-6 win at Pittsburgh, where the Vikings' defense played like they were possessed. They owned the Steelers that day, as Page blocked a field goal and a conversion, Eller blocked a field goal, and Nate Allen picked off a pair of Terry Bradshaw passes — one of which came on the heels of a Page's forced fumble which later led to Foreman's game-winning touchdown.

Foreman had emerged as one of the team's leaders that year, and even showed his stuff at a late-season lockerroom pow-wow that later became known simply as "The Talk." No. 44 was tired of losing in the post-season, and wanted his teammates to take a different tact. Tired of Grant's calm, disciplined, mythical style of play, he wanted his mates to "go crazy!" He knew they were getting old, and figured that by trying something different, like showing some real emotion and having fun out on the field, might be the difference in the team getting over the hump. His impassioned speech did get them to Pasadena. Unfortunately, they came home with the same results as in the three previous tries.

First up for the Purple were the Washington Redskins, who they faced in the first round of the playoffs out at the Met. This one proved to be a wild one right out of the gates as Brent McClanahan

Anthony "A.C." Carter

rumbled 41 yards on the first play from scrimmage. Just three plays later, Tarkenton found Stu Voigt, who plowed his way over two Redskins defenders en route to an 18-yard touchdown. After a Washington field goal by Mark Mosely, Tark hit Sammy White on a key third-and-9 play for a 27-yard touchdown to make it 14-3. From there Chuck Foreman capped a pair of 66 and 51-yard drives by scoring a pair of two and 30-yard touchdown runs. White added another TD of his own in the third, this one being a nine yarder following a 76-yard drive. Washington Quarterback Billy Kilmer rallied his squad back late but came up on the short end of a 35-20 ball game. With the win, the Vikes had earned themselves another title bout with the Rams for the NFC championship.

The Rams flew in to Minneapolis on Christmas Eve for the NFC title tilt with a business-like attitude. L.A. Defensive End Jack Youngblood vowed that this time his team was not going to be psyched-out by the frigid weather. Just how much did they want to make a statement to the Vikings on that 12-degree below zero wind-chilled day? They came out for their pre-game warm-ups in T-shirts, impressing the grounds-crew workers who were out trying to soften up the frozen turf with flame throwers. It didn't do much for the Viking's players though, who just thought that they were nuts.

The Rams came out swinging early in this one, driving the length of the field on the open-ing series behind the running of Lawrence McCutcheon. Then, after the Vikes held the Rams out of the end-zone on several key defensive stops, the Rams' Tom Dempsey came in and attempted a simple 26-yard field goal. That's when Nate Allen flew over the pile and blocked the kick, leav-ing Bobby Bryant to scoop up the bouncing ball and race 90 yards in the other direction for a touchdown.

From there Vikings Linebacker Matt Blair took over. First he recovered a John Cappelletti fumble to kill a Ram's drive at the Minnesota 21-yard line, and then proceeded to block a Rusty Jackson punt midway through the second. Freddy Cox gave Minnesota a 10-0 lead at the half thanks to a 25-yard boot, which was then followed by Chuck Foreman's third quarter 62-yard scamper off the right tackle to get down to the Ram's two-yard line. From there he simply ran it in to make it 17-0. The Rams didn't lie down though, as Cornerback Monte Jackson intercepted a Tarkenton offering and got his squad back in the game. They rallied behind McCutcheon's 10-yard score, followed by Quarterback Pat Haden's five-yard TD pass to Harold Jackson to make it 17-13. (A monster rush by the Viking's D-line forced Dempsey to rush his extra-point and it flut-tered off to the left.)

The Rams kept coming and reached the Vikings' 33 and 39-yard lines on their next two possessions. Wally Hilgenberg blitzed and sacked Haden to end the first threat, and with 2:31 to go, Bobby Bryant killed the Ram's final drive by nabbing his second interception of the day deep in Minnesota territory. A few minutes later, after Tarkenton found Foreman on a critical third down play, reserve Running Back Sammy Johnson ran it in to ice the 24-13 victory for Minnesota.

(At home, the Vikings just owned the Lambs. In the 13 games the two teams had played at Metropolitan Stadium since the Vikings came into the NFL, Minnesota had won 11 and tied two. And, for the third time since 1969, the Rams and Vikings had played the NFL or the NFC Championship Game at the Met, with L.A. going home losers each time. Rams Coach Chuck Knox swore that there was a Metropolitan Stadium jinx on him.)

With that, and to the dismay of millions of football fans across America (much like Buffalo of the '90s), the Vikings were going back for a fourth shot at the Lombardi Trophy against the perennial AFC playoff bridesmaids, the Oakland Raiders, in Super Bowl XI. The pregame hype was intense, but Grant, who said that he felt his team was as prepared for that game as they could have been for any game he had coached, knew that it was getting to be the end of the line. "There's an obsession with this team to win this game," added Tarkenton.

The Vikings, attempted to seek redemption from the Super Bowl gods under the scrutiny of an estimated 81 million television viewers along with the 103,438 fans at the Rose Bowl in Pasadena. Minnesota got the first break, when Fred McNeill blocked a Ray Guy punt, and the Vikings recovered at the Raider three-yard line. But the momentum shifted quickly when Oakland linebacker Phil Villapiano ducked under Minnesota's offensive line and stuck his helmet on the ball Fullback Brent McClanahan was car-rying, popping it out his arms and into the awaiting hands of his teammate Willie Hall just two plays later. (Incidentally, the player who made the defensive call which helped cause the McClanahan fum-ble was Oakland linebacker and Bloomington native, Monte Johnson, who grew up worshiping the Vikes and even sold programs at the Met as a kid.) The Raiders, long known for their physical, hard-hitting and even dirty cheap-shot style of play, took it to the Vikes early and often — giving them the confidence they would need to psyche-out Minnesota.

Led by Quarterback Ken Stabler, who completed 12 of 19 passes for 180 yards, and running back Clarence Davis, who gained 137 yards rushing, the Raiders quickly drove the length of the field to set up an Errol Mann 24-yard field goal. Before half-time they added a one-yard touchdown pass from Stabler to Dave Casper as well as a one-yard Pete Banaszak touchdown run. They were dominating the Vikings, holding them to a mere 86 total yards of offense in the first half, compared to 288 of their own.

In the second half, after another Mann field goal, Sir Francis finally put Minnesota on the board, capping a 68-yard drive by connecting with Sammy White on an eight-yard touchdown pass. However, two Raider interceptions led to another 13 points for the silver and black — one set up a two-yard

Fred McNeil

Banaszak touchdown run, and the other was a record 75-yard Willie Brown pick-off return to pay-dirt. Minnesota rallied to get to within 18 points when back-up quarterback Bobby Lee hit Stu Voigt on a 13-yarder. But it was way too little way too late, as the Raiders went on to crush the Vikes, 32-14. Thanks to the blocking up front by future Hall of Famers Art Shell and Gene Upshaw, Oakland amassed a Super Bowl-record 429 yards, while Fred Biletnikoff, who caught four passes for 79 yards, earned MVP honors.

Nine years after getting spanked by the Packers in Super Bowl II, 33-14, the Raiders had won football's biggest prize. But their victory would be obscured by the shadow of Minnesota's Super Bowl futility — a record four losses in eight years. It would mark the last time that the Vikings would get back to the big dance.

To add insult to injury, Raider Coach John Madden (a native of Austin Minn.) said that his team had played tougher games in the conference playoffs. Afterward, Tarkenton quipped: "What we're trying to do is run through all the American Football League clubs to see if there's one we can beat."

"The attitude of the press is ridiculous," quipped Page after the game. "What we've done all year to get here doesn't mean one thing. Now that we lost this game, we're a bunch of losers, a bunch of dogs. We're four-time losers so that means we're a lousy football team?"

"I still don't have good feelings about it," said Rashad. "It was one of those things where I thought that we changed everything that we did well during the season to try to do something different for one game, and when it didn't work it was just too late. In retrospect, I guess when you lose a game you don't have many good memories about it. For me, I figured that I had joined a team that had gone to four Super Bowls, so I thought that we'd be back three or four more times. The next thing you know, your career is over. There's something to be said about losing. It teaches you things, and everybody's got to lose at some point. It keeps you going."

Tommy Kramer

Enter Rookie Quarterback Tommy Kramer

At the end of the 1976 season, it was painfully obvious to most fans that the glory years of the Minnesota Vikings were a thing of the past. While there was an apparent changing of the guard on the horizon, the team did reload at the linebacker position when it got a late-round steal in drafting Scott Studwell with their ninth pick. The "Stud" would go on to be the leading tackler in team history.

But, just when everybody wrote this bunch of old-timers off as dog food, the Vikes pulled a rabbit out of their hats in 1977 and almost made it back to the big dance yet again. While a 9-5 record would be outstanding in many NFL camps, based on Minnesota standards, it was an off year. They posted just a 1-4 record against playoff-bound teams that season, but finished strong in winning three of their final four games. It was, however, just good enough to win another Central Division title on a tie-breaker over the Bears, and even get them back into the play-offs, where this crafty bunch of veterans could do some damage.

The season started out on a downer as the team lost its opener at Dallas, 16-10, to the Cowboys. From there the club won it next four before losing to L.A. Week Six. After beating Atlanta, 14-7, and losing to St. Louis 27-7, the unthinkable happened that next week in a 42-10 drubbing at the hands of Cincinnati, at the Met. That's when a 270-pound Defensive Tackle named Gary Burley busted through the Vikings' line and sacked Tarkenton so hard that he busted the scrambler's leg. As Tark was being carried off the field for the first time in 17 seasons, most thought that the Vikings run was officially over.

Back-up QB Bobby Lee was inserted into the starting lineup that next week, as the Vikes lost to Walter Payton and the Chicago Bears, 10-7. Payton, who got the team's only touchdown despite battling a bad case of the flu, was inhuman that day, gaining 275 yards on 40 carries, and breaking O.J. Simpson's single-game rushing record by two yards in the process.

After rebounding to beat Green Bay that next Sunday, on a harsh December afternoon at the Met, rookie first-round draft pick Tommy Kramer, a tobacco-chewing Texan, had his coming out party against the Niners. With Lee struggling and Minnesota trailing, 24-7, early in the fourth quarter, Grant finally gave in to the screaming fans' pleas of "We want Tommy!" — "We want Tommy!" to give the kid a shot. Just how would the 22-year-old Rice University honor student do under the pressure? Kramer calmly came in, completed nine of 13 passes for 188 yards, and tossed three touchdowns to Bob Tucker, Ahmad Rashad and Sammy White to spark the Vikings to a dramatic come-from-behind 28-27 victory. The Vikings had their quarterback of the future.

"I've been in pro football for 10 years," said All-Pro Tackle Ron Yary after the game, "but Tommy Kramer has unbelievable poise, a lot more than I do. He is going to be a great quarterback, one with great leadership qualifications and the ability to get the job done under the toughest situations."

With that, the Vikings, for the first time in a long time, had to hit the road for the playoffs. After dominating the Rams in the post-season at home over the past three years, it was now time to pay the piper in L.A. And, after a 35-3 pounding by those very Rams during the regular season, the Vikings came into this one as the rare underdogs.

By the time the game got going out in LA-LA land, the skies had opened up and a driving rainstorm turned the field into a sloppy, muddy mess. From that moment on, the game has lived in infamy as the "Mud Bowl." Chuck Foreman ran wild, and the Purple People Eaters came up big in this one, which turned out to be a classic. Grant opted to go back to the veteran Lee at quarterback, and he responded by leading the Purple to a thrilling 14-7 victory.

Foreman, who would run for 101 yards on the day, got the Vikes on the board first when he capped a 70-yard drive on a five-yard touchdown run up the middle. The Rams drove right back, but Quarterback Pat Haden was intercepted in the end zone, and Rafael Septien later missed a short field goal to keep them scoreless through three quarters. Then, early in the fourth, Manfred Moore's 21-yard punt return set up a one-yard touchdown plunge by Sammy Johnson to give the Vikings a 14-0 lead. L.A. rallied on Harold Jackson's one-yard touchdown catch from Haden, and even had a chance to tie it when Jim Jodat recovered an on-side kick with just 53 seconds left on the clock. But Haden again was

Teddy Brown

intercepted to seal it for the Purple.

Next up for the Vikes were the Cowboys, on a rainy New Year's Day at Texas Stadium, as Bud Grant and Tom Landry again squared off for the right to get to the promised land. This was their fourth NFC Championship meeting in just six seasons, and their stoic post-season chess matches had become legendary. One writer even described their coaching battles as a "collision of icebergs that usually created a loud thud, but nothing ever melted."

Dallas jumped out to an early lead in this one, when, on just the third play of the game, Vikings Running Back Robert Miller fumbled the ball and Defensive End Harvey Martin recovered at the Minnesota 39-yard line. Two plays later, Roger Staubach hit Golden Richards on a 32-yard touchdown pass. The margin increased to 13 points when Quarterback Danny White ran for a key first down in the punt formation, which later led to Robert Newhouse's five-yard touchdown run. (The extra-point was blocked.) Fred Cox then kicked a pair of second quarter field goals, which would later prove to be Minnesota's only points of the day.

The Cowboys put it away in the fourth when Martin recovered a Manfred Moore fumbled punt, which led to Tony Dorsett's 11-yard touchdown scamper. Defensive ends Harvey Martin and Ed (Too Tall) Jones held Minnesota's ground game to a paltry 66 yards, including 22 in the second half, as the Cowboys went on to crush the Vikings, 23-6, thus earning their fourth Super Bowl appearance.

Steve Jordan

The Rams Finally End the Jinx

While the drubbing by Dallas did mark the last time in what would be a decade that Minnesota would play in an NFC championship game, the 1978 Vikings did manage to again win the Central Division title, thanks to a tie-breaker with Green Bay. Tarkenton, now 38, returned for one final season, and, despite winning just one of their five last games, they got a ticket to the post-season to once again meet up with the Los Angeles Rams. There were a couple of key defections that year, including Kicker Fred Cox's retirement and Guard Ed White's decision to move on to San Diego.

But the biggest loss was that of future Hall of Famer Alan Page, who, despite slimming down to less than 220 pounds, was released and signed on with the rival Bears. It was an ugly end to a brilliant career. Page, who was now pursuing his law degree at the University of Minnesota, was also running marathons. His weight had dropped drastically, and so did his performance on the field. Grant, seemingly at an impasse, put the Pro Bowl Tackle on waivers, where he was quickly gobbled up by the Bears for the paltry sum of $100.

Despite finishing with a modest 8-7-1 record, the team did produce a couple of highlights that season, including beating both of the 1978 Super Bowl teams: Denver, 12-9, in overtime, and Dallas, 21-10. But there was also a lowlight of the year, which unfortunately came on a Monday night game between the Vikings and Bears in Chicago. Despite Minnesota's 24-20 victory, the team suffered a huge loss when Chuck Foreman, the nucleus of the team's offense for five years, suffered a severe season-ending knee injury which would ultimately lead to the premature ending of an otherwise spectacular career.

The veteran-laden squad then met the Rams in a first-round playoff game in Los Angels. With no mud or freezing Met Stadium jinxes, the Rams were finally poised to exact a little revenge on the Vikings, who had handed them four consecutive playoff losses. The Vikings got on the scoreboard in the first when Kicker Rick Danmeier nailed a 42-yarder early in the first. From there the Rams scored twice, first on Willie Miller's nine-yard pass from Pat Haden, followed by a Corral field goal. The Vikes later tied it up following Bobby Bryant's interception, which led to Ahmad Rashad's one-yard touchdown pass from Tarkenton with six seconds left in the second quarter. From there it was all Rams, as they simply overpowered Minnesota in the second half. A 21-yard punt return by Jackie Wallace set up Cullen Bryant's three-yard, go-ahead touchdown, which was proceeded by Haden's 27-yard touchdown pass to Ron Jessie, who danced through the Vikings' secondary for the last 20 yards. Jodat added a late touchdown run, but by then it was over. The Rams had finally exorcised the demons, 34-10.

The Changing of the Guard

When the 1979 Vikings hit the turf, they were without their long-time star quarterback. After 18 seasons, Fran Tarkenton finally decided to hang em' up — but not before rewriting the record books along the way. Among his many career NFL records he finished with included: most passing yards (47,003), most touchdown passes (343), most passing attempts (6,647) and most completions (3,686).

Rickey Young

The dismantling of the team really kicked into high gear this year. With Tarkenton, Tingelhoff and Cox gone to retirement, and Page off to the Bears, the Vikings also lost perennial Pro Bowler Carl Eller, who signed on with Seattle during the off-season. Additionally, Chuck Foreman, who was banged up in '78, would be relegated to backup duty behind No. 1 draft pick Teddy Brown. All in all, there were 10 key players from the team's glory years that would be gone by the end of the season.

Over the next two seasons the team would add some solid replacements though, including offensive linemen: David Huffman, Wes Hamilton, Jim Hough and Dennis Swilley, as well as Tight End Joe Senser. Doug Martin, Duck White, Mark Mullaney and Randy Holloway were brought in to anchor the defensive line, while John Turner, Keith Nord, Willie Teal and Tommy Hannon were added to bolster the defensive backfield. In addition, Halfback Rickey Young was added to the lineup, as were Quarterback Steve Dils, Kicker Rick Danmeier and Punter/Actor Greg Coleman.

Minnesota found themselves with a 4-4 record at the halfway point, but then lost three straight games to fall out of contention for the post-season. They would finish with a mediocre 7-9 ledger that year, clearly a sign that the times were definitely changing in the Twin Cities. The team did post some solid wins against some of the league's better teams though, including a 23-22 victory over the conference champion Bucs, who were torched by "Two-Minute Tommy's" three TD passes. That following Sunday, in a 27-21 overtime loss to the Rams, Kramer passed for 297 yards and three more touchdowns. Then, in the season finale, Kramer passed for 308 yards on an unconscionable 61 attempts, in a 27-23 loss to a very good New England team. The once-invincible Minnesota defense allowed 21 or more

AHMAD RASHAD

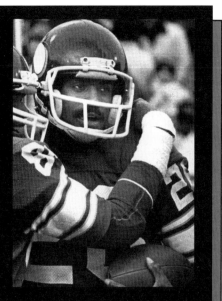

Formerly known as Bobby Moore, Viking's All-Pro Wide Receiver Ahmad Rashad grew up in Tacoma, Wash., and attended the University of Oregon on a basketball and football scholarship. After being drafted No.1 by the St. Louis Cardinals in 1972, Rashad was traded to the Bills two years later. After missing his second season in Buffalo due to an injury, he was acquired by Minnesota in a 1976 trade for, among others, "Bench-Warmer Bob" Lurtsema.

In Minnesota Rashad gelled immediately with Fran Tarkenton, and became a superstar. Today he ranks sixth on the Vikings all-time receiving list with 400 career receptions and 5,489 yards receiving. He had 13 100-yard receiving games from 1976-1982, won the NFC receptions title in 1977 and 1979, and from 1978-1981 was named to the Pro-Bowl. Perhaps his best season with the Vikings was in 1979, when he caught 80 balls for nine touchdowns and had 1,156 yards receiving. He still holds the NFL record for the longest non-scoring pass reception, when he hooked up with Cardinal Quarterback Jim Hart on a 98-yarder in 1972.

Today Rashad is one of America's most respected sports journalists. A star in the world of television, Rashad hosts several shows including the NBA's "Inside Stuff" and "Real TV". In addition he does NFL, NBA and Olympic broadcasting for several networks. And, if that weren't enough, he is married to Felicia Rashad, formerly "Claire Huxtable" of the Cosby show. When he has a spare moment, that is when he's not hanging out with guys like Michael Jordan, he even finds time to come back to Minnesota, where he still has a summer home in Lakeville. Once here, he often goes out with his best friend Bill Murray, either golfing or to watch the St. Paul Saints, of which Murray is a part-owner. Ahmad, Felisha, and their children currently reside in New York City and Connecticut.

What Did it Mean for You to Be a Viking?
"Minnesota will always be my home because that's where I had the chance to blossom as a player. I had the perfect coach in Bud Grant, the perfect quarterback in Fran Tarkenton, and it was just an ideal situation for me. It was the first time that I had gotten someplace where I felt like I had a kinship with the players and was a part of the team. Anytime you play a sport, you want people to respect your performance. I feel like my years in Minnesota were great, and I was on a real run there. I can't remember ever having too many bad games. I played some pretty good Sundays in Minnesota."

Do You Still Consider Yourself as a Minnesotan?
"I am a Minnesota Viking. When I look back on my career, I remember only playing for the Vikings. I know I played for St. Louis and Buffalo, but they don't count. The love affair went both ways I felt. I really enjoyed playing there, and I enjoyed the people. It really felt good to actually feel that love from the people because very few athletes get a chance to do that in their careers. I love it there and we will always have a home in Minnesota."

On His Last Game
"When I quit football after my last game, I never even went and cleared out my locker. When I drove away from the facility that day, it was like 'Hey man that's it, I'm gone...' I had prepared for my exit out of football, and I left the game on my terms. I said 'I'm going to quit,' and that means a lot, paying dividends the rest of my life. Plus, I felt like when I left, I left the fans wanting more rather than less. I had been All-Pro the year before, and it wasn't like my game was down at that point where people thought it was time for me to hang it up. It's sad because you see so many guys today that had unfulfilled athletic careers and just won't let go. I had a life outside of football and was eager to begin the next phase of my life. Football wasn't everything to me. During the season, I used to come home after games and play tennis. Years later, Bud put all my pads and everything in a box and sent it to me. I have no idea where all that stuff is today."

Here is What a Few of His Teammates Had to Say About Him
"He was the Baryshnikov of wide receivers," said Chuck Foreman. "I remember watching him run patterns, and he was just like a gazelle — smooth and fast. He was a great addition to the Vikings and played a very important role on our last Super Bowl team. He is somebody that I admire and respect. He is a great player and a great person."

"He found a home in Minnesota," said Bud Grant. "He was one of the finest receivers I ever coached. He and Sammy White were a great pair together."

"Ahmad was a great receiver and made a lot of amazing plays for us," said Jim Marshall. "He could catch anything thrown to him. He was unbelievable."

"Ahmad was a strong personality," said Carl Eller. "I think Ahmad, like both Alan Page and Fran Tarkenton, had a sense of what was best for him and what he needed to do outside and beyond football. Those are great qualities, and I think are part of a sense of survival. Some players have it and some don't. It's a unique characteristic and a very good quality. He was a great talent."

"Ahmad had great hands, great speed, and a great ability to get open," said Alan Page. "He was a great wide receiver."

"He sent me a couple nice telegrams when I broke his records with the Vikings, and that was definitely very nice," said Cris Carter. "He is very likable, receptive, and helpful. He is a person that I look up to on and off the field, not only as a great player, but also as a great broadcaster. I have always wanted to follow him not only in the Vikings record book, but also what he has done nationally, as far as being successful in the broadcast arena."

points in 10 of their 16 games — as many points as they had allowed in the 84 games from 1969 to 1974.

After the season, the exodus continued as Captain Jim Marshall, after 19 seasons and 270 consecutive games, decided to retire. His teammate, Paul Krause with his all-time interceptions record, also called it quits, as did Wally Hilgenberg. Chuck Foreman, the greatest runner in Vikings history, was also traded to New England.

Perhaps the biggest news of all that year came from off the field. That's where, after an eight-year campaign by team officials, the State Legislature passed a bill which would allow for a hotel and liquor tax to fund a new domed stadium in downtown Minneapolis. They also created the Metropolitan Sports Facilities Commission, a body which would oversee most of the process. Much of the decision came on the heels of the threat of the team relocating to Memphis or even New York, where the possibility of moving into Yankee Stadium was once discussed. The stadium, which had a small seating capacity, also lacked the necessary number of luxury boxes — a necessity which would produce much needed additional revenues. The ground-breaking ceremony came in early December as the team's wonderfully chilly home-field advantage out in the elements at the Met was about to become a thing of the past.

Ahmad's Miracle in Cleveland

After finishing out of the playoffs in 1979, the 1980 Vikings rebounded to win their 11th division championship — largely in part because of the amazing last-second catch of one Ahmad Rashad. The season started out slow for the Purple, winning just three of their first five, but finishing 6-2 in the second half. (One of the reasons the team did better in the latter part of the season was due to the team's posh new Eden Prairie practice facility, named Winter Park, in honor of team owner Max Winter, which was completed that fall.) The team went on a mid-season three-game winning streak in which they outscored the Redskins, Lions and Bucs, 111-44, and then, following a loss to the Pack, tallied wins against the Saints and Bucs to set the stage for one of the greatest plays in team history.

With their record sitting on the bubble at 8-6, the Vikes let it all hang out at the Met on December 14th in their second-to-last game of the season against Cleveland. If they won, they would clinch a divisional title and earn a trip to the post-season. If they lost, they would play a meaningless game against the Oilers in Week 16 and the season would be over. It was that simple.

The Browns, who, at 10-4 were a Super Bowl favorite, took a commanding 13-0 first-half lead on Brian Sipe's 18-yard touchdown pass to Calvin Hill, followed by a two-yard quarterback keeper midway through the second quarter. Tommy Kramer took over in the second half though, throwing for an amazing 456 yards and four TDs on 48 attempts. Senser notched the first one, a 31-yarder over the middle, only to see Cleveland raise their lead to 16-6 on a Cockroft 32-yard field goal. Rick Danmeier answered with a 24-yarder of his own, but Sipe found Miller in the end-zone midway through the fourth quarter to make it 23-9 in favor of the Browns.

Now, with less than two minutes to go in the ball game, and Kramer had thrown another touchdown pass, Minnesota got the ball back with about 90 seconds left when Bobby Bryant came up with a huge interception. Kramer then came in and capped a 47-yard drive by throwing his third touchdown of the afternoon, this one to Rashad, narrowing the score to 23-22. Cleveland then recovered Danmeier's attempted on-side kick, but the Vikings held and forced them to punt. The punt then sailed into the end-zone and Minnesota got the ball back at their own 20-yard line. With 23 seconds on the clock and no time outs, Touchdown Tommy Kramer came out to work his magic. His first play was a pass to Senser, who then lateraled to the awaiting Teddy Brown on the old hook-and-ladder. Brown promptly scampered 34-yards and out of bounds to kill the clock with just five seconds to go in the game.

With the crowd on their feet for the final play of the game, the Vikings called a "Squadron Right" play, which called for everyone to line up on the right side of the field and go deep. With that, Receivers Ahmad Rashad, Sammy White and Terry LeCount all lined up on the 46-yard line and, when the ball was snapped, took off towards the end-zone. Cleveland, who had most of their team down there waiting for them, knew what was coming. Kramer took the snap, dropped back (ironically, from almost the same spot on the same field where Staubach launched his "Hail Mary" only five years earlier), and let it go with everything he had. The ball came down into a heap of players, where it was tipped by Defensive Backs Thom Darden and Ron Bolton into the air and right into the awaiting left hand of Ahmad Rashad. With the clock at zero, Rashad, who was positioned at about the three-yard line, simply grabbed the ball and backpedaled around the swarm of colliding bodies and into the end-zone for the thrilling game-winner. The Met exploded in celebration.

With the division title in hand, the team went out and lost to Earl Campbell and the Houston Oilers, 20-16, in a meaningless game. The real prize came a few weeks later, when they would face the upstart Philadelphia Eagles in the first round of the playoffs. And it looked like it was going to be a blowout early in Philly, when, on the first drive of the game, Kramer threw a 30-yard touchdown pass to Sammy White. Then, in the second quarter, Minnesota went up 14-0 on Ted Brown's one-yard touchdown plunge. That's when Eagle's Quarterback Ron Jaworski took over, capping an 85-yard touchdown drive to the six-foot-eight Receiver Harold Carmichael, followed by a Wilber Montgomery eight-yard

The Hubert H. Humphrey Metrodome

touchdown run. The Vikings regained the lead on a safety, when Matt Blair and Doug Martin nailed Jaworski in his own end-zone, but let the floodgates open after that. A pair of fumbles and an untimely interception let Coach Dick Vermeil's Eagles come back to score 17 unanswered points, and win it going away, 31-16.

Farewell to the Old Met

Despite the team's early exit from the playoffs in 1980, the 1981 Vikings came in to the season with some high expectations. It was the final season for Metropolitan Stadium and the players wanted to send her off in style. But, when the team finished with a disappointing five-game losing streak to end with a 7-9 record, they found themselves out of the post-season. The last game came in a boring 10-6 loss to Kansas City, as the fans said good-by by ravaging the Met — taking with them whatever wasn't nailed down. (Actually, a lot of people even brought in tools with them, so they could take the nailed down stuff as well!) Kicker Rick Danmeier's two field goals would serve as the last points ever to be recorded on the big scoreboard in right field. (The old gal would be torn down and replaced with the nation's largest shopping center, the Mall of America.)

The season wasn't a total wash, however, as Kramer did engineer a couple of terrific back-to-back wins over the Chargers and Eagles in Weeks Six and Seven. At one point the team enjoyed a 7-4 record, but a blown 21-7 lead against the Falcons on a Monday nighter proved to be the beginning of the end. Teddy Brown couldn't find his groove and Kramer, who, despite finishing the year with 26 touchdown passes and 3,912 yards (second only to Chargers All Pro Dan Fouts), also tossed an NFC-high 24 interceptions. In addition, the defense was inconsistent throughout the season, even getting burned for 45 points in a 45-7 loss to the Lions at the Silverdome on December 12th.

With that, the Met was officially left for dead in favor of the new $68 million Hubert H. Humphrey Metrodome in downtown Minneapolis. (A facility with all of the character of a major home appliance.) The move was made by not only the Vikings, but also the Twins and Gophers, who all need-ed to compete with the revenues being generated by many of their competitors. Sure it was old, and dilapidated, but the Met had heart. In leaving her, they gave up so much. Gone was the infamous tail-gating. Gone were the snowmobile suits and ski-masks. Gone were flasks full of schnapps to keep warm. And gone was the best home-field advantage and most feared destination by opposing players in all of professional football during the months of November, December and January. With the old Brickyard being abandoned at the U of M campus, outdoor football in Minnesota was officially dead. Now the biggest thrill fans could get was watching someone lose their hair-piece as they tried to exit out of the Dome's tornado-like revolving doors!

Wade Wilson

STRIKE!

Despite their new 70-degree windless home deflating on them not once, but twice, the Vikings did pretty good in 1982. They finished with a 5-4 record, and even made the playoffs, despite the fact that the league went on strike that year. A dispute between the players and owners over issues such as free agency, pension and salary arbitration, resulted in an organized a labor strike against the NFL's owners. For nearly two months this nonsense went on, until the two parties finally got together and made some compromises. When the strike was finally settled, the league scrambled to salvage the season by creating a one-time, 16-team playoff tournament that would allow every team with a winning record into the post-season.

The Vikings christened the Metrodome by beating the Tampa Bay Bucs, 17-10, and went on to play some respectable football in the strike-shortened season. Then, in Week Nine, Minnesota found themselves playing the Cowboys, at the Dome, with the winners advancing on to the playoffs. The Vikings would go on to win the game by the final of 31-27, but not before Cowboys Running Back Tony Dorsett made history midway through the first half. That's when the speedy running back busted loose from his own one-yard line on a record 99-yard touch-down run. It was an ugly play for the Vikings secondary, who didn't even lay a finger on him. The 60,000 fans in attendance stood in shock, but Tommy Kramer saved the day by coming back in to throw for 242 yards and a pair of touchdowns to preserve the win.

From there the team hosted Atlanta in the first round of the playoffs, where they beat the Falcons, 30-24. Atlanta jumped up 7-0 in this one thanks to a blocked punt that Doug Rogers recovered for a touchdown in the Minnesota end zone. Minnesota came back to take the lead on a Sammy White 36-yard touchdown pass from Kramer, followed by a Danmeier 33-yard field goal. After that the Falcons roared back on a pair of scores starting with Kicker Mick Luckhurst, taking a lateral on a fake field goal and scrambling 17 yards for a TD in the third, followed by Bob Glazebrook's 35-yard interception for the other. The Vikes rallied though, first behind Danmeier's 39-yarder, proceeded by Receiver Sam McCullum's 11-yard touchdown pass from Kramer. Atlanta added a field goal late, but Teddy Brown's eight-yard TD scamper in the game's final moments iced it for the Vikes.

Next up were the Washington Redskins, in D.C., for a chance to get back to the Super Bowl. The Skins got on the board early in this one and jumped out to a quick 14-0 lead thanks to Joe Theismann's three-yard touchdown pass to Don Warren on the game's opening drive. From there the Skins drove 71 yards with Theismann hitting Alvin Garrett on a 46-yard pass to set up John Riggins, who tallied two of his game-high 185 rushing yards for a touchdown. Teddy Brown got the Purple back into the ball game late in the second quarter when he scored on an 18-yard run, but Theismann iced it just moments later when he found Garrett again for an 18-yarder of his own. The Skins, who would go on to win the Super Bowl, shut-out the Vikes in the second half and simply hung on for the 21-7 victory.

Bud Bids Adieu: Part I

In 1983 the Vikings made some "smart" additions to their roster by drafting Stanford Running Back Darrin Nelson at No.1 and Ivy League Tight End Steve Jordan at No. 7. In addition, future lawyer and Pro Bowler-to-be Offensive Tackle Tim Irwin was also added. But Kramer went out early in the season with a knee injury that year, and the team's performance suffered. With Rashad retiring, and Sammy White and Sam McCullum also suffering injuries, things did not bode well for this club. Kramer's back-up, Steve Dils, was serviceable, but couldn't hold a candle to Tommy. Nelson paid big dividends though, leading the team in both rushing and receiving. The Vikings had started at 6-2 only to lose six of the next seven games — adding up to a mediocre 8-8 record, good enough to place fourth in the NFC Central.

Shortly after the season, Bud Grant, possibly the greatest athlete ever to play and coach in the history of Minnesota sports, announced his resignation as the team's head coach. Not only was the entire state of Minnesota shocked by his announcement, but so too was the entire world of football.

After years of producing elite, well disciplined teams through the early 1970s, Grant's Vikings had gone just 44-42-1 over the previous six seasons and he was simply tired of all the mediocrity — not

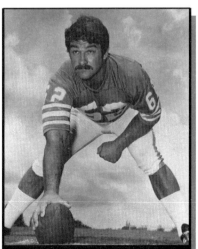

Little Falls native Jim Langer played for the Purple in 1981 before being inducted into the Hall of Fame.

Joe Senser

to mention all of the new politics surrounding the team's management structure. The gray-haired, crew-cutted warrior's exit from the game signified an end of one of the greatest era's of all time. Bud simply decided it was time to get out. He wanted to spend more time with his family and enjoy more of the outdoors in the summer and fall, hunting and fishing.

"In my mind, timing is the most important thing," he said. "I decided this was the time to quit. There wasn't any pressure on me. There are a lot of things I want to do while I still have my health."

The early 1980s were a tumultuous time for the Vikings. Much of the teams' infrastructure, personnel and personality was about to change. The Purple People Eaters were all gone, and in 1982, the Vikings lost much of their mystique when they moved indoors to the Metrodome, something Bud simply hated. The cold weather had always given Minnesota a psychological advantage, and now he was reduced to just standing on the sidelines of a big cozy greenhouse.

"The things that bothered me about going into the Dome is that it took some of the coaching out of it," said Grant. "Outside I could use the elements to my advantage. Things like the wind, sun, rain, snow or a even a frozen field."

"We knew we could play with numb fingers and frozen feet, which gave us an edge," added Ahmad Rashad. "A lot of times I caught passes without ever feeling the ball, just this heavy thump against my frozen hands."

Bud never allowed his players to use heaters on the sidelines or even wear gloves or turtlenecks under their jerseys. He wanted them to stay focused and theorized that if his players were thinking about getting warm then they weren't thinking about football.

"The Vikings always ran out for the warm-ups with this big facade, like we weren't cold," said Rashad in his book of the same name. "Of course, we were freezing. But the other teams didn't know that, not for sure. They would be looking at us out of the corners of their eyes, thinking 'How come these guys look so warm?' They must be some bad dudes!"

All in all, Grant was happy to be getting out on his terms, and he could now enjoy life from the stands, rather than the sidelines. They threw him a party on the Metrodome floor and showered him with enough gifts to fill a Cabella's catalog.

Kirk Lowdermilk

Bud Bids Adieu: Part II

When Bud left, he had asked that his longtime friend colleague, Jerry Burns, who had been his offensive coordinator for a number of years, be given the head coaching position. But the management group, who thought that the team needed some shaping up, figured differently, and hired the team's Receivers Coach, Les Steckel, a former Marine who clearly had a drill sergeant's mentality.

Steckel's preseason training camp was more like boot camp. He was intense, and wanted to win in his first coaching stint. While he did cut several key veterans from the roster, including Randy Holloway, Duck White and John Turner, he did bring in some promising young players as well. Among them were a couple of future Pro Bowl Defensive Backs in Joey Browner and Carl Lee. In addition to adding a pair of solid running backs from Baylor, Alfred Anderson and Allen Rice, former Saints Quarterback Archie Manning was also brought into camp to serve as Kramer's backup.

Steckel drove his players mercilessly, and the result was a pathetic 3-13 record — the worst in Viking's history. Things were bad from the get-go, as the team lost its final three pre-season games by a combined score of 91-17. From there it got worse as the team lost its first two games to the Chargers and Eagles. They did rebound to win their next two over Atlanta, 27-20, and Detroit, 29-28, only to see the bottom drop out for good. Minnesota lost five straight, and following a come-from-behind, 27-24, win over the lowly Bucs, lost their last five games by the brutal margins of: 45-17, 42-21, 34-3, 31-17, 51-7, and 38-14. In the 34-3 loss to Chicago, Manning was sacked 11 times. He was finally benched as an act of mercy.

The season was a joke and the players were lost. They used to joke that Sundays were days off, compared to the horrors they had to endure out on the practice field with Steckel. Mondays were the worst. That's when Steckel would set up his military obstacle course, complete with stations. The players had to advance through each station by completing an excruciating physical activity such as performing hundreds of sit-ups and pushups, or climbing ropes, or running sprints. One day Darrin Nelson simply had too much and passed out. The players started to become resentful and rebellious at that point, as they remembered fondly the relaxed practices that Grant put them through.

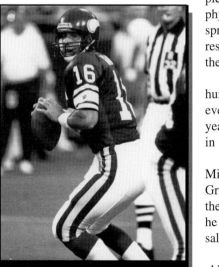

Rich Gannon

After being outscored 484 to 276, and not wanting to subject the loyal Vikings fans to any more humiliation and suffering, Steckel was canned. A public plea was issued for Grant's return, and to everyone's surprise, he came back. After sitting by and watching the team he had built for so many years crumble before his very eyes, Grant could take no more. He became moved by the sudden decline in the Vikings' public image during the down season and wanted to vindicate his team.

So, on December 18, 1984, 327 days after calling it quits, and after owner Max Winter and G.M. Mike Lynn begged him to resuscitate some life back into their franchise after its' disastrous season, Grant unretired. With Lou Holtz packing the Dome for Gopher games, Lynn needed a sure thing to keep the Purple faithful... faithful. They had made him an offer he simply couldn't refuse. Not only would he have the option to end the contract after just one season, it also guaranteed him a handsome deferred salary which would pay him, regardless of how long he stayed, for more than a decade.

"It's unusual, but we're in an unusual business and you have to have the opportunity to be unusual," said Bud. "I think I'm old enough now to claim a little senility."

With that it was Bud to the rescue. Not only did his return from the duck blinds and deer stands of Northern Minnesota prevent a mutiny by season ticket holders, it also enticed a bunch of free-agents from the now defunct United States Football League, or USFL (a rival pro league that operated for one season in 1985 before finally folding), to come to Minnesota. Among the additions to Bud's squad that year included a bunch of future Pro Bowlers in Wide Receiver Anthony Carter, Guard Gary Zimmerman and future sack-leader Keith Millard. They also drafted Cornerback Issiac Holt, Receiver Hassan Jones, Linebacker Jesse Solomon, Center Kirk Lowdermilk, Linebacker Dave Howard, and a kid who would turn into one of the top sackers in league history, Defensive End Chris Doleman. (Ironically, their first pick that year, Defensive End Gerald Robinson from Auburn, turned out to be a bust.) They even added future Hall of Famer Jan Stenerud to do the kicking. The rebuilding process was looking good and Grant liked what he saw.

He got his squad off to a 3-1 start that year and seemed headed for a complete turnaround. That's when they lost a pair to the Rams and Pack, beat the Chargers, but lost four of their next five to the Bears, Packers, Lions and Saints. Sitting at 5-7, the team then went on a two-game winning streak to get back to .500.

The first big win came over Philadelphia. Third-string Quarterback Wade Wilson, another young Texas gun-slinger, was in for rookie backup QB Steve Bono, who was in for Kramer — who was hurt. The game was ugly early, with the Vikings down 23-0 in the fourth quarter with just over eight minutes to play. Wilson came in and kicked off an amazing rally though, starting with a seven-yard touchdown pass to Allen Rice. The Purple then made it 23-14 just two minutes later when Willie Teal picked up a fumble and raced 65 yards into the end zone. Now pumped up, the Vikings defense held the Eagles, and forced them to punt. That's when Wilson capped a long scoring drive by hitting Anthony Carter on a 36-yard touchdown strike to get to within two points. After the defense held yet again, Minnesota got the ball back with just a few seconds to go. Wilson, calmly stepped up, and found Carter, or A.C. as he was affectionately known, on a dramatic 42-yard out pattern to pay-dirt. The Vikes had done the impossible, and eked out a thrilling 28-23 victory.

Minnesota then beat the Bucs 26-7 in Week 14, only to end their season with back-to-back losses to the Falcons and then to Philly, in the rematch at the Dome, to finish out of the playoffs at 7-9 — good for just third in the Central Division. For Grant it was a tough way to end the season. He didn't have a bunch of old veterans on his team like in years past, and he saw how the lure of money was changing the game. He found that the players were much more interested in their own highlights than were those of the team's. Drugs, greedy agents demanding playing-time for their clients, and off-the-field problems all contributed to his decision to not return to the bench in 1986.

Grant wanted to come back, rehabilitate his team and get it back on track. He had succeeded. With that, on January 6, 1986, only 384 days after his return, Bud, then the sixth winningest coach in NFL history, shocked the world one more time by announcing his re-retirement for the second time in as many years.

"I've been in professional sports for 36 years," said the 58-year-old Grant. "I think I'd like to enjoy the fruits of those endeavors."

His replacement this time was his old friend, Jerry Burns. Determined to hang em' up for good, he turned down other offers to coach in the NFL and started to plan his next hunting trip. His final stats were legendary. They included a regular season record of 158-96-5 in 18 seasons, 10 post-season victories, 12 playoff appearances, 11 divisional titles, one NFL Championship, three NFC Championships and four Super Bowl appearances. He would, of course, go on to become enshrined into the Pro Football Hall of Fame on July 31, 1994, where his long-time friend, Sid Hartman, served as his presenter.

VIKINGS' ALL-TIME FIRST-ROUND DRAFT PICKS

1961 Tommy Mason, RB, Tulane (No. 1 overall pick)
1962 No Choice — Traded to the Giants for QB George Shaw
1963 Jim Dunaway, DT, Mississippi State
1964 Carl Eller, DE, Minnesota
1965 Jack Snow, WR, Notre Dame
1966 Jerry Shay, DT, Purdue
1967 Clinton Jones, RB, Michigan State (choice from NY Giants for Tarkenton)
Gene Washington, WR, Michigan State
Alan Page, DT, Notre Dame (choice from Rams for Hal Bedsole & Tommy Mason)
1968 Ron Yary, T, USC (choice from NY Giants) (No. 1 overall pick)
No Choice — Traded to the New Orleans Saints for Gary Cuozzo
1969 No Choice — Traded to the New Orleans Saints for Gary Cuozzo
1970 John Ward, T, Oklahoma State
1971 Leo Hayden, RB, Ohio State
1972 Jeff Siemon, LB, Stanford (choice from New England)
No Choice — Traded to the Giants for Tarkenton
1973 Chuck Foreman, RB, Miami
1974 Fred McNeill, LB, UCLA (choice from Atlanta along with Bob Berry for Bob Lee and Lonnie Warwick)
Steve Riley, T, USC
1975 Mark Mullaney, DE, Colorado State
1976 James White, DT, Oklahoma State
1977 Tommy Kramer, QB, Rice
1978 Randy Holloway, DE, Pittsburgh
1979 Ted Brown, RB, North Carolina State
1980 Doug Martin, DT, Washington
1981 No Choice — Traded to the Baltimore Colts (for two 2nds and a 5th)
1982 Darrin Nelson, RB, Stanford
1983 Joey Browner, DB, USC
1984 Keith Millard, DE, Washington
1985 Chris Doleman, LB, Pittsburgh
1986 Gerald Robinson, DE, Auburn
1987 D.J. Dozier, RB, Penn State
1988 Randall McDaniel, G, Arizona State
1989 No Choice — Traded to the Steelers for LB Mike Merriweather
1990 No Choice — Traded to the Dallas Cowboys as part of the Herschel Walker trade
1991 No Choice — Traded to the Dallas Cowboys as part of the Herschel Walker trade
1992 No Choice — Traded to the Dallas Cowboys as part of the Herschel Walker trade
1993 Robert Smith, RB, Ohio State
1994 Dewayne Washington, CB, North Carolina State (choice from Denver in Gary Zimmerman trade)
Todd Steussie, T, California
1995 Derrick Alexander, DE, Florida State (choice from Denver through Atlanta in Chris Doleman trade)
Korey Stringer, T, Ohio State
1996 Duane Clemons, LB, California
1997 Dwayne Rudd, LB, Alabama
1998 Randy Moss, WR, Marshall
1999 Daunte Culpepper, QB, Central Florida (choice from Redskins in QB Brad Johnson trade)
Dimitrius Underwood, DE, Michigan State
2000 Chris Hovan, DT, Boston College

The Jerry Burns Era Begins

Jerry Burns, who had been the team's offensive coordinator since 1968, took over in 1986 with a crop of new talent ready to blossom. He was a player's coach, and unlike Grant, was buddies with many of his players. He would go to bat for them, no matter what, and that gave him a lot of credibility with them. Long known for his now infamous foul-mouthed language, "Burnsie," as he was affectionately known, wasn't afraid to get out there and mix it up either. He also assembled a tremendous coaching staff which included newcomers Pete Carroll, Marc Trestman and Tom Batta, as well veterans Bob Schnelker, who served as the offensive coordinator, and Floyd Peters, who ran the defense. Peters, a bald-headed warrior, was extremely popular with his men — particularly with guys like Browner, Millard, Doleman and Studwell, who all had a mean-streak in them.

Led by Tommy Kramer, the Vikes started to turn the corner that season, winning three of their first four, and three of their final four, to finish at 9-7. At times Kramer showed signs of brilliance, including throwing for nearly 500 yards in a 44-38 overtime shoot-out loss to the Redskins — making him the first quarterback in NFL history to pass for more than 450 yards twice in a career. He and Wade Wilson tossed 31 touchdown passes that year (24 by Kramer and seven by Wilson), as the team's high-octane offense, led by A.C., Steve Jordan, Darrin Nelson, Leo Lewis, and Hassan Jones, outscored its opponents by a team record margin of 398-273.

Despite their 9-7 finish, their best in six years, the team still had a ways to go. That's because the mighty Bears, led by Walter Payton, Jim McMahon, Richard Dent and Mike Ditka were still dominating the NFC Central, and doing that hideous "Super Bowl Shuffle."

EEK! Scabs!

In 1987 the players walked-out and declared a strike against the owners. This time, unlike the 1982 work stoppage, when the season was just delayed, the league called their bluff of solidarity by allowing former players, has-been's, wannabe's and rejects to come out to training camp. These replacement players, or "scabs" as they were referred to, got to not only try out with the big-leaguer's, they actually got to play in games that really counted. To make matters worse, Mike Lynn, who figured this was all going to just blow over, didn't go out and recruit any quality players with the vigor of other GM's from around the league. The decision would be costly. Lynn's late cattle-call for try-outs, which he held in Memphis, resulted in the Vikings fielding the worst group of slugs in the entire league.

The Vikings hit the field that year, scabs, slugs and all, to play some superficial football. The games were a joke, but had to be played regardless of what the fans thought. The owners weren't going to cave in and wanted to show the players that they were expendable, and that they weren't bigger than the game itself. With that, the Vikings surprised everyone by beating the Lions and Rams in their first two games. But then the bottom fell out as the team got outscored, 70-33, and lost three straight to the Pack, Bears and Bucs. Lynn started to panic. Luckily though, by then the league had come to its senses and resolved the little spat with its players. The public black eye it took was growing every day and they needed to get the real product back on the field. So, the training camps opened back up for the "real" players and the season resumed. The wins and losses counted though, as the Vikes prepared to salvage a season that started out like a bad science fiction movie.

A couple of newcomers hit camp that year that would prove to be pretty good. Among them were LSU Defensive Tackle Henry Thomas, Defensive Back Reggie Rutland of Georgia Tech and Washington Fullback Rick Fenney. Adding them to a team which would send Carter, Jordan, Doleman, Browner, Studwell and Zimmerman to the Pro Bowl, they looked pretty darn good on paper. They came out and won five of six, but then lost three out of four late in the season. Those losses, coupled with the three that the scabs had left for them, resulted in a mediocre 8-7 record. But, in a year that didn't make sense anyway, they somehow backed into the playoffs as a road wild-card team.

Their opponents for the post-season would be the New Orleans Saints, who were making their first-ever playoff appearance. It showed, as the Vikes came out showed no mercy on the league's top-ranked defense. The Saints actually got on the board first in this one, with QB Bobby Hebert firing a 10-yard touchdown pass to Eric Martin to make it 7-0. But from there it was all Minnesota, who by this time had Quarterback Wade Wilson playing for an injured Tommy Kramer. Led by the defense's four four interceptions, two fumble recoveries and relentless pressure on Hebert, the Vikes exploded for 44 points. They ran everything but the kitchen sink at the hapless Saints, and incredibly, most of it worked.

Anthony Carter started the onslaught when he returned a punt 84 yards for a touchdown, then the longest return in post-season history. After Steve Jordan's five-yard touchdown pass from Wade Wilson in the second, Carter got on the board for the second time when he hauled in a 10-yard halfback pass for a touchdown from Allen Rice. By half-time it was already 31-10, thanks to Wilson's 44-yard prayer which was answered by Hassan Jones on the second quarter's final play. By the fourth, another young quarterback by the name of Rich Gannon even got in the game. Kicker Chuck Nelson then hit his third field goal of the day, followed by Running Back D.J. Dozier's 18-yard scoring scamper late in the game, to give the Vikes a demoralizing 44-10 victory.

Next stop for the Purple was San Francisco's Candlestick Park, where the Vikes would face the Super Bowl veteran Joe Montana and the 49ers in round two. After exchanging field goals in the first,

Jim McMahon

CRIS CARTER

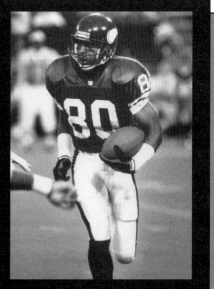

Cris Carter was born in Troy, Ohio, on November 25, 1965. He graduated from Middletown High School in 1983, where he caught 80 passes for over 2,000 yards, and earned Parade All-American honors as a senior. He also excelled as an all-state basketball player, scoring over 1,600 points during his prep career. (His older brother Butch went on to play for seven years in the NBA and later went on to become the head coach of the Toronto Raptors.)

Heavily recruited out of high school, Cris chose to go to Ohio State, where he earned first-team All-American honors in 1986. When it was all said and done, Carter would finish as the Buckeyes' all-time leader in receptions, with 168, and touchdown catches, with 27. while ranking No. 2 in receiving yards, with 2,725.

Cris went on to be selected in the fourth round of the 1987 supplemental draft by the Philadelphia Eagles. After three productive years in Philly, then-Head Coach Buddy Ryan, for some insane reason, released Carter, citing irreconcilable differences. C.C. was then immediately claimed off the waiver wire by the Vikings. Philadelphia's blunder was Minnesota's gain. Now the Purple had two Carters, Cris and long-time Viking great, Anthony, to form one of the most lethal receiving tandems in the league. Cris got some sweet revenge against his old mates on November 15th that year when he nabbed six receptions for 151 yards, including a 78-yarder for a TD.

"I was really excited about the possibility of playing in Minnesota because I knew about the tremendous tradition that the Vikings had built over the years," said Carter. "But I was most excited about the opportunity to play with Anthony Carter."

In 1991, Cris led the Vikings in receptions with 72 and added 962 receiving yards with five touchdowns. That next year, after leading the club in receptions, receiving yards and TD's, he knew he had made it to the big time when he was selected as a member of John Madden's notorious "All-Madden" team. In 1993 he played in his first Pro Bowl, and in 1994 he set the NFL's all-time receptions record, with 122. Showing that 1994 wasn't a fluke, CC went on to catch another incredible 122 balls for the second consecutive year in 95', giving him the most catches ever in the NFL over a two-year span.

"I think that season I accomplished even more than in 1994 by catching 122 again, as well as catching 17 touchdowns," said Carter. "That might be the best year that I have ever had as a pro."

In 1996, Carter made his fourth Pro Bowl team in his eighth season with the Vikes. Perhaps his biggest accomplishment that season came during the off-season, when he was ordained as a minister. Since then he has simply dominated the world of professional football. Week in and week out he continues to amaze fans everywhere by making spectacular one-handed finger-tip catches. He has a sixth sense as to where the sideline is, and always seems to somehow drag both feet to make sure he is in bounds.

Today Cris owns virtually all the Vikings receiving records and is still going strong. He also took on the role of tutoring then rookie Randy Moss, in 1998, showing the ropes along the way. Today the duo is the most feared in the NFL. Among Carter's club records after his first 198 games through the 1999 season, he ranks first in receptions with 926, first in touchdown catches with 114, and first in receiving yards with 11,714. (In addition, thanks to his nine receptions for a career-high 168 yards in the Vikings' 13-7 victory over the Miami Dolphins in Week Two of the 2000 season, Carter broke Darrin Nelson's long-standing team record of 10,365 combined yards. Then, in Week Three, against the Patriots, he caught his 942nd career reception, pulling him past Art Monk to get to No.2 all-time behind just Jerry Rice.)

In 1999 Carter was honored by being named as the NFL's Man of the Year, by receiving the Walter Payton Award. He was recognized for his efforts in the community with his Cris Carter's CAUSE (Christian Athletes for Spiritual Empowerment), as well as for his tireless work with inner-city schools, the Special Olympics, the Boy Scouts and the Make-A-Wish Foundation.

"It really means a lot to me," said Carter of the award. "The fact that it brings a lot of attention to so many of the children's charitable programs that I am associated with is very gratifying."

As for now, Cris is currently the star receiver on the 2000 Vikings. He lives in Boca Raton, Fla., during the off-season with his wife Melanie, and their two children, but has big plans for life-after-football, including pursuing a career in broadcasting.

On Owning all of the Vikings Receiving Records
"It's really nice because those records are pretty substantial, and the players who played before me were phenomenal. That gives the records a lot of credence and value in my mind. It's always nice to be compared to great people of the past and also with people who are still playing in the league. Growing up and watching Ahmad (Rashad) and Sammy (White) catch passes in those blustery days at old Metropolitan Stadium, to me is unbelievable. It's nice to have been able to have seen some of their incredible careers, along with guys like Anthony Carter, and know that I was be able to pass them up. This means a lot to me."

Which catch do you remember the most?
"Against Atlanta in 1991. I was running a corner flag pattern, and the defender had the better position on the ball. Wade Wilson threw it, and I was on the other side of the defender, but I somehow able to put one hand on his back, keep my balance, dive over the other side of him, and catch it with my right hand. I landed on the five-yard-line and rolled into the end zone for a touchdown. That by far was my best catch ever. Besides the ability to compete in the man-on-man battles, I would like also to be remembered for some of the more remarkable catches that I have made as a Viking."

On Minnesota's Fans?
"I really enjoy the fans in Minnesota. They're great, and I love playing before them. It seems that they have warmed up to me as my performances have gotten better. I feel that they have shown their appreciation toward me and have always been very respectful of me. It has always given me a sense of confidence in my ability, knowing that, during tough situations, the fans are behind me. Because a lot of times in certain situations, they know that I'm going to get the ball, and it's nice knowing they are behind me. In Minnesota, the fans really know their sports, are very knowledgeable, and they know the history of their sports heroes. There is just a great football tradition here — which makes rivalries like against the Packers even better."

On the Dome?
"I like the temperature and the consistency with regards to the wind. I've gotten used to the dead spots in the ceiling and on the turf and being able to see the ball out of the lights. I like how the fans are so close in the end zones, so I really like playing in the Metrodome. I'm not so sure that I would be so fond of playing outside in Minneapolis in December."

On Minnesota?
"I'm not a big fan of the Minnesota weather, and I only live here during the season, but I can definitely see the appealing aspects of guys wanting to live here as far as the quality of life goes. When my family and I are here, we definitely love it, and we have become very comfortable in our second home. I really wouldn't want to play anywhere else besides Minnesota. The people are very cordial, and it's a pleasure for my family and I to be Minnesotans."

Jack Del Rio

the Vikings broke the game wide-open in the second, going on a 17-0 run. Leading the charge was Wade Wilson, who found Tight End Carl Hilton on a seven-yard touchdown pass, followed by rookie Cornerback Reggie Rutland's 45-yard interception return for a touchdown. Rutland, along with fellow DB's Joey Browner, Carl Lee and John Harris, did a wonderful job of stopping All-Pro Receiver Jerry Rice, who finished with just three catches for 27 yards on the day.

The Niners didn't lie down though, as Safety Jeff Fuller answered by returning a 48-yard touchdown interception of his own midway through the third. But Wilson responded, this time with a five-yard touchdown pass to Hassan Jones, capping a long Minnesota drive. From there the Vikings defense, which was led by Millard, Martin and Doleman, took over, even knocking Montana out of the game. And, although his understudy, Steve Young, did come in to throw a late touchdown pass, the rally was snubbed by Kicker Chuck Nelson, who nailed his fifth field-goal of the afternoon to ice the 36-24 upset victory. While Wilson finished the day with nearly 300 yards passing and a pair of touchdowns, the real hero was A.C. Carter, who broke an NFL playoff record by grabbing 10 passes, many of them nearly inhuman, for 227 yards.

And just like that, the Vikings, pre-season 75-to-1 longshots to make it to the Super Bowl, found themselves back in the NFC Championship game facing the Redskins and their world-famous "Hawgs" defense, at Washington's RFK Stadium. With the fans still intoxicated over the Twins winning the World Series earlier that Fall, and the Vikes just one game away from the Super Bowl, Minnesota sports fans were riding high.

The Redskins drew first blood early in the opening frame by driving 98 yards in eight plays and scoring on Quarterback Doug Williams' 42-yard pass out of the backfield to Running Back Kelvin Bryant. Minnesota then answered just before half-time to tie it when Wilson hit Leo Lewis with a 23-yard touchdown strike. Washington rallied back to take the lead early in the third though, thanks to an Ali Haji-Sheikh field goal which was set up by Linebacker Mel Kaufman's interception deep in Minnesota territory. But Anthony Carter's 26-yard punt return to midfield set up Chuck Nelson's tying field goal early in the fourth. The Skins were getting great field position all day, thanks in large part to the fact that Punter Greg Coleman was injured and his backup, Bucky Scribner, just didn't have the same kind of power that Coleman did.

Sean Salisbury

From there Washington assembled an impressive 70-yard, 18-play drive that culminated with a seven-yard touchdown pass from Williams to Receiver Gary Clark with 5:06 showing on the clock. Minnesota had one last shot, and began its long drive to get back the equalizer. The Skins, who held Minnesota to just 76 yards rushing en route to registering eight sacks on the day, were relentless in their pursuit of Wilson. The Vikes drove all the way down to the Redskin six-yard line, but, on fourth-down, with just seconds remaining in the game, Wade Wilson's game-tying pass to Darrin Nelson came up short. Nelson, who was racing toward the left corner of the end-zone on an out pattern, reached, but couldn't hang on to the low, but catchable pass, which bounced harmlessly off his hands and onto the turf to end the game, 17-10. Nelson, who was fighting the flu, later admitted that he should've had it.

The Curse of the Niners

The Vikings were back in the saddle as one of the teams to beat in 1988. In addition to looking good on the field, they had also gone through a face-lift in the front-office. Four newcomers were added to the Board of Directors that year. Joining Max Winter, John Skoglund, Jack Steele and Sheldon Kaplan were Irwin Jacobs, Twins Owner Carl Pohlad, Wheelock Whitney and Jaye Dyer.

The team's core group of talented youngsters had stepped up that year and were ready to lead the team back to the post-season. And that's just what they did, winning 11 games to finish runner-up, for the third time in as many years, to the Bears in the NFC Central. The team's defense was a force to be reckoned with, while the defense, which outscored Dallas, Indy, Detroit and New Orleans, by a 123-9 margin during a late-season stretch, was hitting on all cylinders. With the post-season hanging in the balance on the season's last game, the Purple came out and beat Chicago for the second time of the year on Walker Lee Ashley's 84-yard interception return to give the club a thrilling 28-27 win.

Keith Millard

First up for Minnesota was Los Angeles, a team that had given the club some troubles in recent years, in a wild-card game. Thanks to Joey Browner's pair of first-quarter interceptions off Rams Quarterback Jim Everett, which set up back-to-back touchdowns less than 30 seconds apart, the Vikings took the lead in this one and never looked back. The first pick led to a 73-yard drive which was capped by Alfred Anderson's seven-yard touchdown run, followed immediately by Allen Rice's one-yard touchdown plunge. Everett rallied back to cut the margin in half at the intermission when he found Tight End Damone Johnson in the end-zone, but Minnesota hung tough. Anderson scored his second of the afternoon early in the third on another one-yarder, followed by Wade Wilson's five-yard scoring strike to Tight End Carl Hilton to ice it late in the fourth. Everett tried to mount a late rally when he threw his second TD of the day late in the game, but it wasn't enough as the Vikings went on to take the game, 28-17.

That next week the Purple ventured west to Candlestick Park, where the powerful 49ers eagerly awaited to avenge their early exit upset dealt to them by these very Vikings the year before. This one got ugly early as San Francisco got off to a quick 21-3 lead by half-time, thanks to Jerry Rice's three touchdown catches from Joe Montana. The Niners were dominant. Not only was their offense almost unstoppable, their defense had already registered five sacks in the first half alone. Minnesota answered late in the third on Hassan Jones' eight-yard touchdown pass from Wilson, but the Niners were just too much in this one. They unleashed their ground game in the second half as Roger Craig scored a pair of fourth quarter scores on runs of both four and 80 yards to seal the Vikings fate, 34-9.

The Herschel Walker Fiasco

In 1989, following a mediocre 2-2 start, GM Mike Lynn had a light bulb go off above his head. His team, complete with nine Pro Bowlers, was, on paper, rock solid. The defense, bolstered by free-agent Linebacker Mike Merriweather, was one of the league's best. The team's three outstanding quarterbacks: Kramer, Wilson and Gannon, had a bunch of weapons at their disposal in A.C., Jones and Jordan, and a seasoned offensive line the just got better with the addition of Guard Randall McDaniel. What he didn't have though, was a dominant running back. Someone who could get downfield in a hurry and be able to spread the defense for those potent wide receivers. Darrin Nelson was good, but Lynn thought that the missing piece to the puzzle was still out there. He knew that to get past the elite teams like the Niners, he would need a star unlike Minnesotans had ever seen before. He reasoned that first-round draft picks were expensive, took time to develop, and often-times didn't pan out, while free-agency was an all-together different headache. He knew that if he wanted to get over the hump, he was going to have to do something way outside the box. With that, on October 12, 1989, Lynn went out and made the biggest trade in league history.

Brad Johnson

The winners in this Texas-sized bounty of players and draft picks were none other than the hated Dallas Cowboys, who made the deal of a lifetime by shipping Herschel Walker up the river. In exchange the Cowboys got five players: Darrin Nelson, Jesse Solomon, Issiac Holt, David Howard and Max Stewart, as well as eight draft choices, including three first-rounders, three seconds, a third and a sixth. (Nelson ultimately refused to report to Dallas, and instead successfully lobbied to be traded to the Chargers.) In addition to Walker, the Vikings also got some draft picks in return including, Mike Jones, a third-rounder, Reggie Thornton, a fifth, Pat Newman, a 10th, and a third-rounder in 1991 who turned out to be Wide Receiver Jake Reed.

Jake Reed

(This deal might have been the biggest rip-off since a bunch of conniving settlers conned the island of Manhattan out from underneath some unsuspecting Native Americans for a string of beads a couple hundred years ago. But hey, at least the beads improved their image, right? If only the same were true in this case!)

At first Minnesotans were giddy. Sure, there were skeptics who thought we way overpaid, but most thought that this blockbuster gamble was going to pay off with a long awaited Super Bowl ring. "Judge this deal," said the smiling Lynn to the media on the day of the trade, "on whether we get to the Super Bowl with Herschel Walker on the roster. If we do, the deal was a success. If we don't, it wasn't."

Now, in defense of Herschel Walker, at the time he was a marquis running back in the National Football League. He was a two-time 1,000-yard rusher in Tom Landry's offense, and had all the star-power to boot. He had been an enigma from the time he earned the Heisman Trophy back at the University of Georgia until he shocked the NFL by signing with the New Jersey Generals of the upstart United States Football League. Here was a guy who did 1,000 push-ups and sit-ups every morning. He was a running back with the speed of a sprinter and the chiseled body of a linebacker. He was handsome, rich and had a southern drawl that made women swoon. But Jimmy Johnson was the new man behind the bench in Big-D that year, and he knew that he had to start his rebuilding process. And by unloading Herschel, and his multi-million dollar salary, his last-place Cowboys were able to complete one of the fastest turn-arounds in sports history — winning three Super Bowls just a few years later.

Just how would this man perform under all of this scrutiny? I mean the GM himself said that if the team didn't win it was on Herschel's shoulders. Well, the Herschel Walker story got off to an incredible start. Chapter one was Pulitzer material — but from there the story gets real ugly, real quick.

Amidst the fan-fare of a rock-star, Walker joined the team just in time for their Week Six matchup against rival Green Bay, at the Dome. He was given just a few plays to learn for his debut, perhaps enough to give the locals a sneak preview taste of what was to come. They wasted little time in bringing him into the game though, giving him his first carry on a second down play midway through the first. With the 62,000-plus fans waiting anxiously, Walker took the hand-off, busted through the line and took off towards the Packer secondary. He dodged a couple of would-be tacklers, even lost a shoe, and sprinted 47-yards until finally being brought down deep in Green Bay territory. The crowd went nuts. This is what they had paid to see. It even got better. Herschel even returned a kick-off for a touchdown, but had it called back on a penalty, only to return it deep again on the next play. All in all he ran wild for 148 yards that day, making Mike Lynn look, briefly, like a genius. Walker, ever the smoothie, knew just what to say afterwards. "It was the Viking offensive line," he said modestly.

But how would Walker fit into this cast of super-egos? The Vikes were a team filled with superstars, who had a lot of off-the-field baggage. Kramer and Millard found their way onto the front page more than once for events non-football related, while guys like Anthony Carter found themselves out of the limelight, and Wilson wanted to be the starter — creating a quarterback controversy.

The team did get through it though. After beating Cincinnati, 29-21, on Christmas Day at the Dome, Minnesota finished with a respectable 10-6 record — good enough for the team's 12th Central Division title and a return trip to San Francisco, where they would one again face the mighty Niners. They would be ready this year. Their defense, which racked up the second-most sacks in league history, with 71, would be waiting for Montana and Rice.

But, after Minnesota jumped ahead on Rich Karlis' 38-yard first quarter field goal, Montana and Rice took over. Joe and Jerry scoffed at the Viking's defense, hooking up for a pair of 72 and 13-yard touch-down passes in the first half alone. And, unfortunately, Montana was just getting started, as

Chris Doleman

VIKINGS' ALL-TIME PRO BOWLERS

1961   Hugh McElhenny (HB), Jerry Reichow (E)
1962   Tommy Mason (HB)
1963   Tommy Mason (HB), Grady Alderman (T), Rip Hawkins
1964   Tommy Mason (HB, Grady Alderman (T), Mick Tinglehoff (C),
       Fran Tarkenton (QB), Bill Brown (RB)
1965   Grady Alderman (T), Mick Tinglehoff (C), Fran Tarkenton (QB),
       Bill Brown (RB)
1966   Paul Flatley (E), Mick Tinglehoff (C), Grady Alderman (T),
       Milt Sunde (G)
1967   Mick Tinglehoff (C), Grady Alderman (T), Bill Brown (RB)
1968   Mick Tinglehoff (C), Bill Brown (RB), Carl Eller (DE), Jim
       Marshall (DE), Alan Page (DT)
1969   Mick Tinglehoff (C), Carl Eller (DE), Jim Marshall (DE), Alan
       Page (DT), Gene Washington (WR), Joe Kapp (QB), Paul
       Krause (S), Gary Larsen (DT)
1970   Fred Cox (K), Carl Eller (DE), Carl Kassulke (S), Gary Larsen
       (DT), Dave Osborn (HB), Alan Page (DT), Gene
       Washington, (WR)
1971   Carl Eller (DE), Alan Page (DT), Paul Krause (S), Ron Yary (T),
       Bob Grim (WR)
1972   John Gilliam (WR), Alan Page (DT), Paul Krause (S), Ron Yary (T)
1973   Chuck Foreman (RB), John Gilliam (WR), Paul Krause (S), Alan
       Page (DT), Jeff Siemon (LB), Ron Yary (T), Carl Eller (DE)
1974   Carl Eller (DE), Chuck Foreman (RB), John Gilliam (WR), Paul
       Krause (S), Alan Page (DT), Fran Tarkenton (QB), Ron Yary (T)
1975   Bobby Bryant (DB), Chuck Foreman (RB), John Gilliam (WR),
       Paul Krause (S), Alan Page (DT), Fran Tarkenton (QB), Jeff
       Siemon (LB), Ron Yary (T), Ed White (G)
1976   Jeff Siemon (LB), Ron Yary (T), Ed White (G), Chuck Foreman
       (RB), Sammy White (WR), Alan Page (DT), Fran Tarkenton (QB)
1977   Jeff Siemon (LB), Chuck Foreman (RB), Matt Blair (LB), Sammy
       White (WR), Ed White (G), Ron Yary (T)
1978   Matt Blair (LB), Ahmad Rashad (WR)
1979   Matt Blair (LB), Ahmad Rashad (WR)
1980   Matt Blair (LB), Ahmad Rashad (WR)
1981   Matt Blair (LB), Ahmad Rashad (WR)
1982   Matt Blair (LB)
1984   Jan Stenerud (K)
1985   Joey Browner (S)
1986   Tommy Kramer (QB), Joey Browner (S), Steve Jordan (TE)
1987   Joey Browner (S), Chris Doleman (DE), Scott Studwell (LB),
       Anthony Carter (WR), Steve Jordan (TE), Gary Zimmerman (T)
1988   Joey Browner (S), Chris Doleman (DE), Carl Lee (DB), Anthony
       Carter (WR), Keith Millard (DT), Scott Studwell (LB), Wade
       Wilson (QB), Steve Jordan (TE)
1989   Joey Browner (S), Chris Doleman (DE), Carl Lee (DB), Keith
       Millard (DT), Steve Jordan (TE), Randall McDaniel (G), Gary
       Zimmerman (T)
1990   Joey Browner (S), Chris Doleman (DE), Carl Lee (DB), Steve
       Jordan (TE), Randall McDaniel (G)
1991   Steve Jordan (TE), Randall McDaniel (G), Henry Thomas (DT)
1992   Chris Doleman (DE), Randall McDaniel (G), Audray McMillian
       (CB), Todd Scott (DB), Henry Thomas (DT), Gary Zimmerman (T)
1993   Chris Doleman (DE), Randall McDaniel (G), Cris Carter (WR),
       John Randle (DT)
1994   Cris Carter (WR), Randall McDaniel (G), John Randle (DT), Jack
       Del Rio (LB) Fuad Reviez (K), Warren Moon (QB)
1995   Cris Carter (WR), Randall McDaniel (G), John Randle (DT),
       Warren Moon (QB)
1996   Cris Carter (WR), Randall McDaniel (G), John Randle (DT)
1997   Cris Carter (WR), Randall McDaniel (G), John Randle (DT),
       Todd Steussie (T)
1998   Cris Carter (WR), Gary Anderson (K), Jeff Christy (C), Randall
       Cunningham (QB), Ed McDaniel (LB), Robert Smith (RB),
       Todd Steussie (T), Randall McDaniel (G), Randy Moss (WR)
1999   Cris Carter (WR), Randy Moss (WR), Randall McDaniel (G),
       Jeff Christy (C), Mitch Berger (P)

he then found Brent Jones and John Taylor for two more to make it 27-3 by half-time. Karlis added another 44-yarder in the third, but San Fran answered right back, first with Ronnie Lott's 58-yard interception return for a touchdown, followed by Running Back Roger Craig's four-yard TD plunge late in the fourth. Rick Fenney found his way into the end-zone during the game's final moments, but this one was a blow-out as the Super Bowl champion to-be 49ers won it going away, 41-13.

Herschel's Wild Ride

The Vikings' off-the-field problems escalated in 1990. In addition to several key players keeping the team's public relation's department up all night on more than one occasion, the players weren't gelling together as a group. The result was a lousy 6-10 record, good for last place in the Central. Despite a five-game winning streak throughout November, the team had a pair of five and four-game losing streaks to ensure their position in the conference cellar.

One bright spot that year though, came courtesy of Philadelphia Eagles' Coach Buddy Ryan, who decided that Wide Receiver Cris Carter, and his 11 touchdown catches that season, was just not cut out to be an NFL football player. Ryan then foolishly dumped Carter on the waiver wire, where, back in Minneapolis, the Vikings player-personnel triumvant of Frank Gilliam, Jerry Reichow and Jeff Diamond, quickly snatched him up for a whopping $100.

Going into the 1991 season, the Vikings had plenty of incentive to get to the big dance. That's because, for the first time ever, the Super Bowl was held in their own backyard at the Metrodome. Apparently that wasn't incentive enough though, as the team started out at 2-4, and finished with a .500 record of 8-8. With all that complacent talent, and Herschel's fat contract, it wasn't long before heads started to roll. (Incidentally, the Redskins beat the Bills by the final score of 37-24, to win Super Bowl XXVI at the Dome.)

A new ownership group came in near the end of the season and made their intentions clear that they were going to be making some changes. Pohlad and Jacobs were bought out by a new group which was led by Roger Headrick, a former corporate executive with Exxon and Pillsbury, who was named as the President and CEO of the team, replacing Mike Lynn as the man in charge of day-to-day operations. (Lynn would receive a handsome buy-out and try his hand in starting a developmental football league in Europe. And why not, he had already successfully experimented with the idea by having his Vikings play a couple of exhibition games in both Sweden and London a few years earlier.)

Next to go was Burnsie, who, after finding himself stuck between a rock and a hard place, decided to do the honorable thing and retire. Despite his six-year campaign which produced a solid 52-43 record, along with three post-season appearances, he realized that this team was in disarray. Another guy who hit the road was Herschel, who had been making headlines not for scoring touchdowns, but for trying out the Olympic Bobsledding team.

Lynn's experiment had officially gone awry. And while Herschel did post some decent numbers for the Purple, leading the team in rushing with 669, 770, and 825 yards respectively over his three seasons in Minnesota, he was often criticized for his running style. The experts said he was a "north-south" runner, and not an "east-west" kind of a guy, meaning that he was a square peg trying to be shoved head-first into a round hole. His toughness was questioned too, as he often-times went into the line turning his back before he had to. By then he was detested by many fans who simply blamed him for the team's demise. His first-person answers of "Herschel thinks Herschel had a good game..." drove people nuts, ultimately leaving management no other choice but to wash their hands of a terrible deal gone sour. (Walker was released and signed by the Philadelphia Eagles, where he played for a few years before, ironically, returning to the Dallas Cowboys, who, thanks in large part to the players and draft picks that they had suckered away from Minnesota, had built a dynasty — complete with a trio of Super Bowl titles in 1993, 1994 and 1996.)

Randall McDaniel

There's a New Sheriff in Town

The new management needed to reload quickly, and they needed a new coach to make it all happen. By passing popular assistant Pete Carroll, the group went back to San Francisco, where they hired away then Stanford University Head Coach and former 49er Assistant, Dennis Green, to be the team's fifth-ever coach. Denny's first order of business was to turn around a franchise in turmoil, and believe it or not, that's just what he did.

While Burnsie found success by befriending many of his players, the first words out of Green's mouth when he came to Minnesota were: "There's a new sheriff in town." He knew that the team was lacking a strong leader, and that was what he aimed to be. He commanded respect, and he got it. That next season things were noticeably different in Viking country, and the team responded by doing a 180-degree about-face. He came in and cleaned house big-time, even getting rid of veterans Wade Wilson, Keith Millard and Joey Browner, in an effort to show the younger players that he meant business. By the start of the season there were 17 new faces on the squad.

Among the additions were high-stepping 49er Running Back Roger Craig, and a kid Green once recruited for Stanford, Darrin Nelson, who returned after his stint in San Diego. They also went out and scoured the Plan B free-agency pool, which yielded Linebacker Jack Del Rio, and Corners Vencie Glenn and Anthony Parker.

Tony Dungy

There was also a core group of players ready to step up. Among them were the Carters (Anthony and Cris), Tight End Steve Jordan, Halfback Terry Allen (who would rush for 1,200 yards on a pair of bad knees), Linebackers Mike Merriweather and Carlos Jenkins, Wide Receiver Jake Reed, Cornerbacks Todd Scott, Audray McMillian and Carl Lee, and Defensive Tackles Henry Thomas, Al Noga and a kid from Texas with the energy of a Tasmanian Devil by the name of John Randle.

Green felt good about his prospects, and decided to initiate the very mobile Rich Gannon as his starting quarterback with the former CFL star Sean Salisbury as his backup. On the other side of the ball, Defensive Coordinator Tony Dungy, a former Gopher Quarterback, created a ball-hawking, sack-machine that produced no less than eight defensive touchdowns.

The result? The 1992 Vikings jumped out of the gates by winning all four of their exhibition games by a combined score of 140-6, and went on to win five of their first six regular season games. From there they won seven of their eight conference games, losing only to the Lions, 31-17, in Pontiac. Then, on December 20, 1992 the Vikings beat the Pittsburgh Steelers, 6-3, at Three Rivers Stadium, to cap an 11-5 record, thus earning the franchise's 13th divisional crown.

One of the highlights of the season included a memorable comeback victory in the Metrodome against Mike Ditka and the Chicago Bears. Down 20-0 in the second, Todd Scott kicked off a comeback like none seen before in the teflon tent, when he picked off a Jim Harbaugh offering and returned it 80 yards for a touchdown. The score would start a rally that led Minnesota back to an amazing 21-20 victory, nearly giving Ditka a heart-attack on the sidelines.

With that the team found themselves playing host to the defending Super Bowl champion Washington Redskins in the first round of the playoffs, at the Metrodome. Terry Allen got the Vikes on the board first when he capped a long, 79-yard drive by plowing in from the one-yard line to make it 7-0. But the Skins defense took over after that, allowing Minnesota to generate just 69 total yards for the rest of the game. After former Gopher Chip Lohmiller's 44-yard field goal, Ernest Byner scored on a three-yard run to make it 10-7. Reserve Running Back Brian Mitchell, who would tally more than 200 all-purpose yards on the day, then broke the game wide-open late in the second quarter when he took a fake punt on fourth down and raced 36 yards — setting up an eight-yard jaunt just a few plays later. From there Quarterback Mark Rypien capped a long drive when he found Receiver Gary Clark on a 24-yard scoring strike to ice it, 24-7. It was the second home loss to the Redskins that season.

Green's Regime

Despite the team's solid season and conference crown, Green wanted to continue to make changes within his team's infrastructure. His first move was to remove Jack Burns as his offensive coordinator and replaced him with Brian Billick. With free agency, escalating salaries and a salary cap to contend with, more and more blue-chip players were trading places. Among the players to defect in 1993 were Offensive Linemen Gary Zimmerman (who was dealt to Denver for three high draft picks), Kirk Lowdermilk and Brian Habib, D-Tackle Al Noga, QB Rich Gannon, Running Back Darrin Nelson, Receiver Hassan Jones and Linebacker Mike Merriweather. But the team did add a couple of great players in first-rounder Robert Smith, a sprinter-turned running back out of Ohio State, and second-rounder Qadry Ismail, a Wide Receiver out of Syracuse. In addition, they rescued an out-of-work fullback by the name of Scottie Graham, who was working in an Ohio pharmacy. But perhaps the biggest pickup of all was former Chicago Bear cast-off Jim McMahon, who was brought in to compete with Gannon

Denny Green

JOHN RANDLE

Born on December 12, 1967, John Randle grew up in the small town of Mumford, located in south central Texas. John and his two brothers grew up pretty fast. They were raised in a small wooden home by a single mother who worked as a maid. "It'd get so windy," he said, "and in the winter the wind would blow through the cracks in the house and under the house, and we'd put eight or nine blankets around us and still be cold." He went on to explain how he and his brothers would hang a bucket of water from a rusty nail on the back wall, from which they would take sponge baths.

John grew up loving sports, but amazingly, he didn't even touch a football until he was a freshman in high school. "Because we lived so far out in the country, and didn't have a car, it was always a big hassle to get a ride into town," he said. "Then, every night after practice I would have to try to get a ride back home — usually around midnight. Dealing with that was really tough." He persevered though, and went on to earn all-district and all-state offensive and defensive lineman honors at Hearne High School, where he also participated in track.

Out of high school, John enrolled at Trinity Valley Community College in Athens, Tex. After two years, the sociology major moved on to play at Texas A&I, a Division II school, where in 1990 he earned all-conference as well as Little All-America honors as a senior. After proving he could play big-time football, John wanted to follow his big brother Ervin's footsteps into the promised land of the NFL. (Ervin played linebacker for eight seasons with the Tampa Bay Buc's and Kansas City Chiefs) But, after waiting and watching 331 players get drafted ahead of him, he was devastated.

The 6'1", 270-pound pesky inside pass rusher seemed to be a square peg trying to fit in a round hole. They thought he was too small to be a defensive tackle and wasn't the prototypical defensive end like a Lawrence Taylor or a Bruce Smith. This just made him want to work even harder. After a couple of NFL tryouts, John was invited to the Vikings training camp. He felt that this would be a good match, because Minnesota featured small, quick defensive linemen. He fought and fought, until he had made the team as a free agent.

In 1991 he started eight games — recording nine sacks. He had arrived. But he wasn't just happy to be there. In 1992, John and his bookend tackle counterpart, Henry Thomas, started to redefine the rules of the game. Teams had always built their defensive ideologies upon the premise that the fastest route to the passer was by speed-rushing giant defensive ends from the outside. Minnesota's two partners in crime were much smaller, quicker, and had better technique. They figured that the shortest route to point-A was by bull-rushing, and by blowing gaps through guards and centers on the line.

"John is the toughest player I play," said Packers quarterback Brett Favre. "On artificial turf he's unblockable." He even started to wear face paint, which soon became the sack-artist's calling card.

"The 'war-paint' is about having fun, getting ready, and getting excited about playing the game of football in a military style," said Randle. "I smear the paint and rub it into different spots and I think it reflects my emotions. It's a combination of "Braveheart," different military movies where guys get ready for combat with the war paint, and also from watching Jesse "The Body" Ventura in the movie "Predator." All of those get me fired up to go into battle!" (In 1999, the NFL, or *"No Fun League,"* banned Randle from wearing the paint, citing it wasn't sportsmanlike to wear.)

When you are double and even triple-teamed the way Randle is, you have to go above and beyond the call of duty. That's why he is a student of the game who works hard and studies his opponents in detail. Why you might ask? Because John is what you might call on the football field, somewhat of a "talker." He feels that by talking to his opponent lined up across from him, he gains a psychological advantage. "I am one intense guy," he said. "When I'm playing out on the field, I'm giving it my all. I think the best way to describe myself is that I'm like Dr. Jekyll and Mr. Hyde on and off the field. On the playing field I'm going to do whatever I can to help my team win. But, when I come off the field I'm just another quiet, shy guy who tries to stay low-key and out of the spotlight. Out there on the battlefield I need every edge I can get, and if that means getting under my opponents skin, then so be it. I do whatever it takes to out-psyche the guy across from me. I love to talk it up out there! If guys are thinking about me, then they're not thinking about the game that's going on, and that's good for the Vikings!"

One of the preeminent pass rushers in the history of the game, No.93 is as humble as he is tenacious, and he hasn't forgotten where he came from. Even with his newly found fortune, his modest upbringing hasn't changed him. "I've chopped cotton, picked watermelons, built fences, worked on an assembly line, worked in an oil field, built scaffolding," he said. "You know what? Those jobs are harder than football. So I'll never take it easy in football. I remember how I grew up." Aside from his new truck, he has a very modest $200,000 home in Texas with a swimming pool and a weight room. "I don't need anything more," said John. "I've got a 24-hour grocery store nearby. I've got a Wal-Mart. I've got a Target. I've got a Whataburger. This is all I need."

"To me being a Viking is like being a part of a great legacy," he said, "It's an honor to be a part of what Alan Page, Jim Marshall, Carl Eller, and all of the Purple People Eaters started back in the 1970's. Those guys were great defensive linemen and pass rushers, and it's a privilege to be able to take the reins from those guys who started such a great tradition. With free agency today, there aren't too many guys who are able to stay with one team throughout their entire careers. So, I'm lucky and I feel very honored."

Currently this Tasmanian Devil anchors the Viking's Defensive line. He was recently engaged and has a home both here and in Texas. His numbers continue to boggle the mind. In the decade of the '90s, he has recorded 107 sacks, 462 tackles, 23 forced fumbles, five fumble recoveries and 30 stuffs behind enemy lines. Certain athletes in Minnesota "Get it" while others simply don't. Certainly Kirby Puckett, Kevin Garnett and Neal Broten got it, and John Randle gets it too. The fans have embraced him and rewarded him by making him one of their all-time favorites. He appreciates where he came from and knows that if it wasn't for some hard work and determination back in training camp in 1990, he wouldn't even be here today.

"I am glad that I can give back to the fans in some way, and for me, playing hard on every play is how I can give back," said Randle. "By encouraging my teammates to do the same so that we can win is my ultimate goal every time I step onto the field. For me it's all about respect, and I want to give the fans as much respect as possible - they deserve it. Because of that, I take every game very personal and that is why I hate to lose — I don't want to let anybody down. At first I wanted to win for me, but now I really want to win the them."

"My whole career has truly been a dream for me," he added. "My personal life, my athletic career, everything — it's been unreal. I never could have imagined so many wonderful things would happen to me and I am very thankful for that. I honestly feel welcome here, and the way I have been treated here has been just amazing."

and Salisbury for the starting quarterback job.

McMahon played quite a bit that year. And, though he wasn't the spark-plug of years before — slower, more injury prone — he did manage to toss nine touchdowns and lead the squad to wins in eight of the 11 games he started. The Vikings were a solid 6-2 against NFC Central foes, but weak against everyone else, losing five of eight outside of the division to finish at 9-7.

There were some highlights that season, including the team's thrilling come-from-behind victory to beat the hated Pack early in the season at the Dome. Down 13-12 late in the fourth quarter, McMahon rallied the Purple back by heaving a deep pass downfield. There, a kid by the name of Eric Guliford came down with his first NFL catch. With time running out Kicker Fuad Reveiz ran out and nailed a 22-yarder to give Minnesota a thrilling 15-13 win.

All in all the team finished the season strong by winning four of its last five games, including a 13-0 shut-out over Detroit, beating Green Bay in Milwaukee, 21-17, knocking off the Chiefs, 30-10, and narrowly beating the Redskins, 14-9, at RFK on New Year's Eve to back into the post-season for the second time in as many years.

Their playoff wild-card opponents this year would be a very good New York Giants ball club, on the road at the New Jersey Meadowlands. And, had it not been for the artificial turf, this one might have been Mud Bowl II. That's because the game was held during a torrential downpour, complete with hurricane-like winds in near-freezing temperatures. But hey, that was Viking football right? Wrong.

Darrin Nelson

Nearly 78,000 psychotic Giants fans braved the elements to watch their Giants do battle with the Vikes that day, as it became a matter of wind. You see, all of the points that were scored that afternoon, came when the team had the wind at their backs. The Giants led 3-0 after Jeff Treadwell's 26-yard field goal in the first, but Minnesota came back to take a 10-7 lead in the second, when Jim McMahon found Cris Carter on a 40-yard touchdown pass, followed by Fuad Reveiz's 52-yard wind-aided field goal.

But the Giants rallied behind their defense, which knocked McMahon out of the game twice with concussions. Jimmy-Mac kept getting up though, and came back in to replace Salisbury on both occasions. It would be to no avail though, as New York, led by their bruising Running Back Rodney Hampton's two touchdown runs, dominated the third quarter to take a 17-10 lead. His first, a 52-yarder, came on their opening possession of the quarter, and his second, a two-yard plunge, came after a short 21-yard punt gave the Giants the ball at the Minnesota 26-yard line.

Robert Griffith

The Vikings, perhaps rattled by the elements, had a couple of key off-sides penalties called on them to keep the Giants drives alive. Minnesota had a chance to tie it up, but when Cris Carter fumbled his long pass reception trying to get into the end-zone, it was over. New York hung on to win, 17-10, handing Denny Green his second consecutive first-round playoff loss in as many years.

Out with Jimmy-Mac and in With the Moon

Green, frustrated with the erratic play of his three-headed quarterback monster of Rich Gannon, Wade Wilson, and Jim McMahon, set out to find a dependable No.1 go-to guy. After unsuccessfully wooing Miami QB Scott Mitchell (who, luckily for us, opted to go to Detroit, where, after receiving a boat-load of money, never lived up to his high expectations), Green went out and acquired Houston Oilers signal-caller, Warren Moon. Moon, the master of the high scoring run-and-shoot offense, was getting up in years, but still had a lot of life left in his arm. This made Carter, Reed, Ismail and Terry Allen very excited to say the least. He then installed a young Brad Johnson as his back-up. With that, the new-look team set out to do some damage.

Moon would receive some good protection that year as well, from first-rounder Todd Steussie, a Tackle out of Cal, who fit in right away on the offensive line along with Randall McDaniel, Jeff Christy, Todd Kalis, John Gerak, and Chris Hinton, who replaced long-time tackle-turned lawyer, Tim Irwin. The team also drafted Cornerback DeWayne Washington, in the first round and Tight End Andrew Jordan in the sixth, as compensation for the Gary Zimmerman trade a few years prior.

Despite Moon's two interceptions which ultimately led to Green Bay being able rally back and beat the Vikes, 16-10, in Game One, Minnesota went on to win seven of its first nine games. Then, in mid-November, they fell flat on their faces by losing three straight to New England, New York and Tampa, with the latter two coming at home. They rebounded to win three of their last four against Chicago, Detroit, Buffalo and San Francisco, however, to clinch Green's second Central Division crown.

Moon wasted little time in torching the competition in 1994, shattering nearly every one of the team's major single-season passing records in the process. His league-leading 4,264 yards and 371 completions were huge. The recipients of all that good will were Cris Carter, who shattered Packers' Receiver Sterling Sharpe's NFL single-season record of 112 catches by hauling in 122 balls, and Jake Reed, who added 85 of his own. The tandem set an NFL record for receptions that year with 207, breaking the previous record held by Houston's Haywood Jeffries and Drew Hill with 190 receptions in 1991. (Both duos had the luxury of Quarterback Warren Moon throwing them the ball.) Carter also set a team record for receiving yards in a season with 1,256, breaking former teammate Anthony Carter's record of 1,225 yards in 1988. He averaged 10.3 yards per catch while finding the end-zone seven times.

Carter emerged as a superstar that season, at times carrying the team on his back. On September 9, C.C. caught three touchdown passes in the first half against the Dolphins. Later that season, on October 2, he single-handedly took care of the Phoenix Cardinals when he caught a team record 14 passes for 167 yards. Then against the Bears, Carter had two touchdown catches, including the overtime game-winner on a 65-yard bomb from Moon, thus earning NFC offensive Player of the Week hon-

Brian Billick with Brad Johnson
& Warren Moon

Randall Cunningham

ors. He scored the first ever two-point conversion in team history on September 18 against the Bears, and he also led the team in 100-yard receiving games that year with five. Carter became the first Vikings player in history to have three seasons with 70-or-more receptions, and at season's end, had caught at least one pass in 54 consecutive games, including the playoffs. For his efforts, No. 80 was selected to the Pro Bowl for the second straight season, his first as a starter, as well as earning All-Pro and All-NFC recognition.

"It was nice to break the NFL record, but, for me, I wasn't all that wrapped up in it," said Carter. "It was a great year for us as a team, and winning the NFC Central was a great accomplishment for everyone. It was especially great to have Warren Moon with us as well. It was Warren's first year and we were experimenting and getting used to one another on the field. Our timing and cohesiveness was just great. Warren was just a phenomenal quarterback."

Just how tough was the Central that year? With Minnesota being joined by Chicago, Detroit and Green Bay in the playoffs, it marked the first time in league history that a division had placed four teams in the post-season. And, it would be those same gritty Bears that the Vikes would host in their first-round wild-card playoff game at the Dome. This would be a cake-walk right? I mean they had beaten Chicago six straight times. Think again.

Despite their fourth-place conference finish, Chicago was not to be taken lightly. They were led by former Cretin High School star Quarterback Steve Walsh, who would play huge in front of his home-town fans, completing 15 of 23 passes for 221 yards and two touchdowns. Minnesota jumped out to a quick 3-0 lead in the first on "Fuad-o-matic's" 29-yarder. But the Bears, who had turnovers on their first two possessions, came back with a pair of second quarter scores from both Lewis Tillman, who capped a long drive with a one-yard dive, and by Walsh, who hit Tight End Keith Jennings on a nine-yarder in the end-zone. The Vikings then cut Chicago's margin to 14-9 just 19 seconds before the half on Moon's four-yard touchdown pass to Cris Carter, but the Bears roared back in the third on Raymont Harris's 29-yard touchdown run. After another Reviez field-goal, Walsh made it 28-12 late in that same quarter when he found Jeff Graham with a 21-yard touchdown pass.

Vikings' third-down specialist Amp Lee came in and tried to mount a late rally when he caught an acrobatic 11-yard TD pass from Moon midway through the fourth, but when Bears DB Kevin Minniefield scooped up a fumble and raced 48 yards for a touchdown, the 35-18 upset was complete. The Vikes had really stunk up the joint. Their defense, which logged seven touchdowns and had held its opponents to only 68 rushing yards per game up to that point — the fourth lowest in NFL history — simply couldn't shut down Walsh. Even John Randle, who registered 13.5 sacks that year was neutralized. They just couldn't capitalize — as evidenced by their two turnovers which produced just three points in the ball game. Conversely, the Bears shut down Minnesota's running game, and forced Moon, who was playing injured, to go to the air far too frequently — 52 times to be exact.

With three straight playoff defeats, including a pair in the Dome, pigskin prognosticators from International Falls to Winona began to wonder if Green had what it took to get this team back to the big dance.

Trying to Get Over the Hump

The 1995 Vikings finished with just a .500 record at 8-8. They shocked the locals that year though, by announcing that Robert Smith would become the team's No.1 running back. In so doing, they hastily released Terry Allen, afraid that the 1,000-yard rusher's two surgically-repaired knees simply wouldn't hold up on the Metrodome's tough turf. (Boy were they wrong! Allen went on to become a Pro Bowler with the Skins.)

After losing Game One to the Bears, Minnesota rebounded to win three of their next four over Detroit, Pittsburgh and Houston. But they lost three straight after that to Tampa Bay, Green Bay and Chicago — all conference foes. They went on to win six of their next seven, however, giving themselves a shot at earning a wild-card spot at season's end. After dropping a heart-breaker to the Niners, 37-30, at San Francisco in Week 15, the Vikes went into their season finale needing a win over the lowly Bengals, along with a little help from some other teams, to get into the post-season.

With that the team then ventured to Cincinnati, where, upon leading, 24-3, at half-time, learned that Atlanta had won earlier that day, thereby eliminating Minnesota's playoff hopes. The players, dejected, fell apart and gave up 24 unanswered second half points to suffer one of the team's ugliest losses in franchise history.

Things got better in 1996, despite the loss of Defensive Coordinator Tony Dungy, who was hired to serve as Tampa Bay's new head coach. It was a tough battle to get back to the post-season though. Green Bay was emerging as a real power behind Quarterback Brett Favre, and every week the competition seemed to get harder. To make matters worse, Warren Moon went down with a high ankle sprain in the season opener against Detroit. The team won the game though, 17-13, thanks to the efforts of backup Brad Johnson, who finally got his big break after getting some seasoning that off-season across the pond in the World League.

Korey Stringer

Johnson led the Vikes to an early 4-0 record with big wins against Atlanta, Chicago and Green Bay. Moon returned midway through the season but was clearly hampered by injuries. After the team went through a horrible 2-6 stretch in midseason, Johnson was once again given the reins. The youngster made the most of his opportunity by leading the team to three straight wins over Arizona, Detroit and Tampa, suffering only a loss in the season finale at Green Bay. With their 8-8 record, the team had earned another trip to the post-season, this time as a wild-card draw against the hated Cowboys, in Dallas.

On December 28, 1996, the Vikes suited up to take on the Cowboys. And, in hindsight, maybe that wasn't such a good idea. The 'Boys pounded the Vikes that day, showing no mercy whatsoever. They came out and scored 37 points before Minnesota could even get on the board in the third quarter. Perhaps an indicator of just how the day was going to go happened in the first quarter, when Amp Lee caught a short pass over the middle and appeared to be well on his way to a 43-yard touchdown. But, from out of nowhere came Safety George Teague, who caught him from behind at the goal-line and stripped the ball out of his hands which went through the back of the end-zone for a touchback. Later, Running Back Emmitt Smith ran 37 yards for a touchdown, and just a few moments later, Teague intercepted a Johnson pass and returned it 29 yards for a touchdown to put Dallas up 24-0. Minnesota did get a couple of insignificant TDs late however, as Johnson ran for one and hit Carter for another.

All in all the Dallas defense forced five Viking turnovers, and on offense, Quarterback Troy Aikman ran for one touchdown, passed for another, and threw for 178 yards. Receiver Michael Irvin caught eight balls for 103 yards and Emmitt Smith scored a pair of touchdowns en route to rushing for 116 yards on 17 carries. And, not to be left out, Dallas Kicker Chris Boniol added four field goals to rub a little salt in Minnesota's wounds. When the blitzing was over, the scoreboard read Dallas 40, Minnesota 15.

Robert Smith

No Room for Crybabies

After the playoff loss to Dallas, rumblings of Green being on the hot-seat began to race through the media. Tired of the frivolous criticism which had persecuted him unjustly for the better part of five years, Green fired back by writing a controversial tell-all biography entitled "No Room for Crybabies." The book, which not only lashed out at the team's ownership group, but also at the media — who he claimed was conspiring to get him fired, even had a detailed plan on how he might go about suing the team for a piece of ownership. While it shocked the sports world, it also united Green with his players.

Johnson became the team's full-time quarterback in 1997 when Moon, after being crucified in the media for an alleged domestic abuse incident with his wife, opted to get out of Dodge by signing a free agent deal with Seattle. Johnson's back-up was none other than former Philadelphia Eagles great, Randall Cunningham, who came out of retirement from running his granite-laying business to join the team.

Minnesota came out swinging that year, winning their first two at Buffalo and Chicago. Then, after dropping a pair to Tampa Bay and Green Bay, they rebounded to string together a six-game winning streak. At 8-2 the team was poised to do some damage as one of the league's elite teams. But, like so may times in years past, the team's bubble burst as they went on a five-game losing streak. While the streak did include a two-point loss to the Jets, a six-pointer to the Pack and just a one-pointer in the final minute against the Lions, they did manage to beat the Colts, 39-28, in the season finale to finish with an 8-7 record and earn a post-season trip. Late in the season Johnson went down with an injury and Cunningham's number was called. He looked great, having emerged from his days as a "scrambler," to looking very comfortable as a pocket-passer.

Gary Anderson

From there Cunningham led Minnesota to a thrilling come-from-behind, wild-card victory over the NFC East champion New York Giants, at the Meadowlands. There, in one of the all-time classics, the Vikes found themselves on the wrong-side of a 19-3 deficit by half-time. The Giants jumped out all over the Purple by capitalizing on three Cunningham turnovers which led to three Brad Daluiso field goals, and a Danny Kanell touchdown pass to Tight End Aaron Pierce. The Vikings came back though, starting with LeRoy Hoard's four-yard touchdown run in the third quarter. After exchanging field goals in the final quarter, the Giants still had a nine-point lead with a minute-and-a-half to go in the game. That's when Cunningham hooked up with Jake Reed on a 30-yard touchdown pass to get to within two points. In desperation, Green called out for Vikings Kicker Eddie Murray to try an on-side kick. Murray lined up everyone to his left and kicked it into the Meadowlands turf. Then, incredibly, after a goofy bounce off of Giants Receiver Chris Calloway, Vikings special-team God Chris Walsh somehow came up with the ball from underneath a scrum at midfield. Elated, the Vikings offense ran onto the field, drove down into Giants territory and promptly called Eddie Murray back onto the field, where he kicked the 24-yard game-winning field goal to ice the 23-22 miracle for the Vikes.

Green, now with his first playoff win in five tries under his belt, felt good about his chances that next week against his old mates in San Francisco. That's right, Minnesota was headed back out to the "Stick" to face the dreaded 49ers. Except this time the Niners were without their two of their biggest weapons, Wide Receiver Jerry Rice and Running Back Garrison Hearst, who were both nursing injuries.

It didn't matter though, because backups J.J. Stokes, Terrell Owens and Terry Kirby filled in brilliantly, as the Niners jumped out to a quick 7-0 lead on Fullback William Floyd's one-yard touchdown run early in the first. Minnesota answered right back when Cunningham threw a spectacular 66-yard touchdown pass to Cris Carter to make it 7-7. From there San Fran scored 17 straight points on Terry Kirby's short TD run, a Gary Anderson field goal and a perfectly timed Ken Norton, Jr., interception return for a 23-yard touchdown off of Cunningham.

Cunningham rallied back in the second half, however, as he hit Carter on an eight-yarder for his second touchdown of the day to make it 31-14. But Minnesota's running game couldn't get jump-started as Robert Smith and Co. managed just 57 yards on the afternoon. San Francisco Quarterback Steve Young then took over, first hitting Terrell Owens on a 15-yard hitch pass that found the back of the end-zone, followed by a leading a well-orchestrated time-consuming drive which resulted in Terry Kirby's second short touchdown run of the day. Young, who rushed for 37-yards and passed for another 224 on the day was, at times, unstoppable. Cunningham found rookie Matthew Hatchette on a 13-yard scoring strike late in the fourth, but by then it was over. Cunningham, who threw for 331 yards and three touchdowns, had to watch his season end in disgust as the Niners hung on to take it, 38-22.

Red's Dream Season

That off-season was one of the wildest and most bizarre on record up in Minnie. An ownership strug-

Eddie McDaniel

Chris Walsh

gle emerged that was comparable only to a really bad soap-opera. First, you had Vikings President Roger Headrick leading a mystery group of investors to buy the team. Then best-selling spy novelist Tom Clancy came to town with all the hoopla of a presidential inauguration.

"Why buy the Vikings?" said Clancy. "Why not? It's a good team, a lovely area. Minneapolis is one of the nicest cities in the country. And... they were available."

He was the white knight. He was famous, smart and had the big bucks to get this team some big talent. Or did he. It turned out that Clancy was a bit cash-poor, so after all of the hub-bub, a Texas billionaire by the name of Red McCombs calmly stepped in. Now, Timberwolves owner Glen Taylor entered the fray as well, making the Vikings board entertain three offers from each competing suitor. But, in the end, they chose McCombs, who, in addition to previously owning the Denver Nuggets and San Antonio Spurs, made his fortune selling cars. The reported asking price was in the $250 million range, a bargain compared to the fact that Houston's expansion franchise was sold for a record $700 million just the following year.

Promising to restore "Purple Pride" to Minnesota, the first thing old Red did was to give Denny Green a new fat contract extension. And the first thing Denny Green did was to give the 34-year-old Randall Cunningham a fat contract extension. All in all Red ponied up about $80 million to ensure that in addition to Cunningham, Robert Smith, Cris Carter, John Randle and Todd Steussie were all also taken care of. With everyone fat and happy, the Vikings set out to play some football.

The 1998 season would prove to be a very profitable one for Minnesota's tenacious Defensive Tackle John Randle. The five-time pro bowler signed a five-year, $32.5 million deal which included a $10 million signing bonus. His $6.5 million average salary made him the third-highest paid player in the NFL (Behind only quarterbacks Steve Young and Brett Favre), and the highest-paid defensive player in league history. It was money well spent for a guy who had 71 tackles and 15.5 sacks in 1998 — en route to earning his first NFL sack title. Since 1991, his career sack total of 85.5 was tops in the NFL, surpassing the likes of league superstars such as Reggie White, Leslie O'Neal, and Neil Smith during that same time span.

Signing Randle wasn't an easy thing for the Vikings to do. A small-market team doesn't always have the resources available to sign the most highly coveted free agents, particularly players of his caliber. A bidding war started to break out with teams such as the Dolphins, Broncos, and Eagles leading the charge. But with the enormous TV contract that the NFL just signed — which raised the salary cap, the purple knew what they had to do with their designated 'transition player.' "If there's a player that's worthy of this kind of contract, it's John," said Vikings V.P. Jeff Diamond. "He's the heart and soul of our defense. You start from that premise and you say 'We've got to do whatever it takes to sign this guy.' "

The Vikings also made a very bold statement in the draft that year by selecting Marshall University Wide Receiver Randy Moss with their first-round pick. Moss, a sure-fire lottery pick who saw his stock plummet in the draft because of some off-the-field problems he encountered as a high schooler that scared off a lot of teams, was an absolute steal with the 20th pick in the draft. The six-foot-five former sprinter would make an instant statement in Minnesota, earning Rookie of the Year honors, rewriting the record books along the way. Denny liked his team's chances at the on-set.

"We feel like this is going to be our year," said Coach Green. "We've got a clear-cut goal for ourselves and that's to become the Super bowl champions. We feel it's realistic. We feel it's attainable."

Tom Clancy's Epic Tale

Perhaps it was divine intervention that Tom Clancy's bid to buy the Vikes fell through. I mean could this guy really be trusted, or was he just looking for some more material? Did you know that in his 1991 techno-thriller "The Sum of All Fears," Clancy conjured up a sinister scene at a fictional Super Bowl in Denver, where, during the game, terrorists detonated a 120-kiloton bomb, thereby leveling the city and killing countless thousands? Oh, and by the way, in case you were wondering, the team that was winning the big game before getting hideously blown to smithereens... Our Minnesota Vikings!

Moss wasted little time in letting everyone from Minnesota know that he had officially arrived. He caught his first NFL regular season pass on the third play of the game, an 11 yard bullet from Brad Johnson. His next catch, two drives later in the first quarter, went for a 48-yard touchdown. It was what would become vintage Moss. Johnson under-threw a long pass in which most viewers thought would surely be intercepted by the opposing cornerback. But Randy somehow turned in mid-air, came back for the ball, and with his long arms bumped the ball up like a volleyball over the outstretched defender and back into his own hands as he landed in the end-zone for six points.

Mitch Berger

Throughout the game the Buccaneer defensive backs were visibly intimidated by Randy's size and speed. While most rookies get hit, or "jacked up" off the line of scrimmage, in order to slow them down before they can get open running their routes, Randy was getting a 10-yard cushion. They were giving the rookie speedster the kind of respect usually reserved for All-Pro's.

The Vikings continued to roll against the Bucs, as Moss and Johnson hooked up again midway through the second quarter on a 31-yard touchdown, giving him his second score of the day. All in all Randy finished with four receptions for 95 yards and a pair of TDs, while Cris Carter added two more as the Vikes went on the crush the Bucs by the final score of 31-7.

From there the Vikes just dominated their opposition. In Game Two Randall Cunningham came in for Brad Johnson, who injured his leg, and hit Carter for a 19-yard game-winning TD to secure a 38-31 victory. Cunningham and Moss connected immediately, hooking up for a pair of touchdowns in wins over both Detroit and Chicago. Against the Lions Randy caught five balls for 37 yards, including a 5-yard touchdown pass in between double-coverage in the back of the end-zone, as the stingy Minnesota defense held Lions All Pro running back Barry Sanders to just 69 yards and guided the team to a 29-6 victory. Then, against Chicago, Moss somehow leaped and hovered above a trio of Bears defenders only to come down with a miraculous 44-yard come-from-behind game-winning touchdown strike from Cunningham.

Week Five saw Minnie traveling to rival Green Bay, where Moss put on a show that left the cheeseheads utterly speechless. Moss used the nationally televised Monday Night Football game as his coming out party, en route to torching the defending NFC champions for 190 receiving yards and a pair of touchdowns. (It would've been three had it not been for a 75-yard TD negated by a holding penalty.) Green Bay's sold-out Lambeau Field was as quiet as a Sunday mass after Cunningham threw for record 442 yards, including a couple of 52 and 44-yard bombs to Moss, as the Vikes rolled to a 37-24 win.

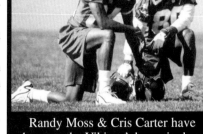

Randy Moss & Cris Carter have become the Vikings' dynamic duo.

"He's a big guy and has great leaping ability," said Packers safety Darren Sharper, who Moss burned throughout game. "He doesn't play like a rookie, I'll tell you that."

After pummeling the Skins, 41-7, behind Smith and Hoard's three scores in Game Six, the Vikings traveled to Detroit for a rematch against the Lions. Minnesota got ahead early and was able to use its running game to tire the Lions defense. Robert Smith rushed for 134 yards in this 34-13 blow-out, Cornerback Jimmy Hitchcock returned a 79-yard interception for a touchdown, and both Carter and Reed each tallied as well.

The undefeated Vikings then hit a bump in the road in Week Eight, as their conference rivals from Tampa Bay pulled off a major upset. The Bucs, outstanding running back duo of Mike Alstott and Warrick Dunn rushed for 243 yards collectively in this one, while Cunningham threw for 291 yards and a pair of TDs to Jake Reed. But the Bucs defense held off a last-minute Vikings surge to preserve a nail-biting 27-24 victory.

After rebounding to win their next two games over both New Orleans and Cincinnati by the scores of 31-24, and 24-3 respectively, Minnesota was off to their best start since 1975 and looking good. Their offensive line was solid. Their defense, led by Randle up front and Eddie McDaniel and Dwayne Rudd at Linebackers, was among the best in the league. Running back Robert Smith was having a career year. The defense was looking good, having allowed the second fewest points in the NFC (170), and Cunningham, who was named as the NFC's Player of the Month for October, had emerged as the catalyst for this high-octane offense. No one knew how to handle this potent air attack which was scoring at a record pace, not even Brett Favre and the Green Bay Packers, who got lit up by the Vikings yet again in Week 11 by the final of 28-14. As if to prove that his two touchdowns weren't a fluke back in Week Five, Moss wowed the Metrodome crowd with eight catches for 153 yards, including a 49-yard touchdown with 3:17 left on the clock to seal the deal.

Then, on Thanksgiving weekend, Moss gave Minnesotans a whole bunch to be thankful for — a nationally televised 46-36 drubbing of the hated Dallas Cowboys, in Texas. While Randy had performed like a champ before in the limelight, this game will stand out forever as his "break-out" game of all-time. In an offensive explosion, Moss tortured the Cowboys for three 50-plus yard touchdown strikes, not to mention drawing a 50-yard interference penalty that set up another score. While Dallas, who did get three TD runs from Emmitt Smith, cried that the loss was simply because their Pro Bowl cornerback Deion Sanders was out with a sore foot, fans from around the country knew better.

Back in Minnesota, they were rejoicing about their new go-to-guy, Randy Moss, who had simply gobbled up the Thanksgiving day competition. Fans everywhere had just witnessed one of the single-greatest offensive performances in pro football history — three catches for 163 yards and three touchdowns, giving Moss a record 11 TDs on the year while pushing him over 1,000 yards receiving. After the game Moss, who received NFC Offensive Player of the Week and Month honors, tried to keep it all in perspective.

"Luckily Deion was hurt, but injuries happen," said Moss. "A lot of people wanted to see our match-up but I had to make it happen anyway. It was a great game and I'm just glad that we came out on top."

With the win, Moss and his Vikes had all but locked up their first Central Division crown in five years. Emotions were running high after the big game, as football fans everywhere could sense that something special was happening in Minnesota. Suddenly, everyone was picking the Vikings to win the Super Bowl.

With the division crown in hand, and the home-dome field playoff advantage secure, the Vikes went out and tried to have fun in their remaining few games. With the pressure off, Minnesota blew up Chicago 48-22, with the help of Rudd's 94-yard fumble return for a touchdown. Moss was again huge as he scored three touchdowns on eight catches for 106 yards — proving he could carry the load as both Carter and Reed had to sit this one out with injuries.

Now on auto-pilot, the Vikes cruised to several easy victories over Baltimore, 38-28, Jacksonville, 50-10, and Tennessee, 26-26, to finish out the franchise's best-ever regular season record at 15-1. In those final three games, Moss tallied a total of 14 catches for 193 yards and three touchdowns. For the season, Minnesota's offense had now set a new NFL single-season record for total points, with 556, a statistic that scared the daylights out of any team that would have to face this offensive juggernaut in the playoffs.

After a well deserved playoff bye-week of rest, the Vikes hosted the upstart Arizona Cardinals in the NFC divisional semifinals at the Dome. For Minnesota, the expectations were at an all-time high. Seemingly anything short of the Super Bowl would now be considered as a failure. And while they were no stranger to the post-season, as Coach Green had led them to the playoffs in six of the last seven seasons, incredibly they had just one win to show for it.

Feeling the pressure, the Vikes came out and dominated the young Cards. While Quarterback Jake Plummer played heroically for Arizona, his two first-half interceptions, which both led to Vikings scores, rattled his confidence. Minnesota came out and built a 24-7 half-time lead and never looked back. Cunningham threw for 236 yards and tossed three touchdown passes on the day — one to Tight End Andrew Glover, another to LeRoy Hoard and a third to Moss. Robert Smith added 124 yards on the ground, and Kicker Gary Anderson continued his perfect season with a pair field goals and five extra points. Running Back Mario Bates tallied three touchdowns for the Cardinals, but it wasn't nearly enough as the Vikes cruised to a 41-21 blowout victory. With the win Minnesota had earned themselves a ticket to the final-four of pro football, the NFC Championship Game.

Next up for the Purple were the high flying Atlanta Falcons, who, like Minnesota, were used to playing on artificial turf in a deafening domed stadium. The game got underway in Minneapolis with Minnesota looking like it was going to blow it wide open. After Atlanta's Pro Bowl Running Back Jamal Anderson scored on a five-yard pass from Chris Chandler to give his club a 7-0 lead, the Vikes rallied. Cunningham was on fire, hitting Moss, Carter and Reed all over the field. Robert Smith and LeRoy Hoard were carrying the load up the middle, and the defense was holding its own. Minnesota made it

Todd Steussie

Randy Moss going up and beating Charles Woodson

20-7 thanks to Cunningham's one-yard TD run, a pair of Anderson field goals, and Moss' 31-yard touchdown strike. But Atlanta battled back behind Wide Receiver Terrence Mathis' 14-yard touchdown pass from Chandler to make it 20-14 at half-time.

After a Morten Andersen 27-yard field goal made it 20-17 in the third, things heated up in the fourth. Cunningham then found Matthew Hatchette on a five-yard slant to give them some breathing room. After another Morten Andersen field goal, the game then came to a climax late in the fourth quarter when the Vikings had a chance to ice the Falcons once and for all. All they had to do was kick a 30-yard field goal and put the game out of reach. The good news was that Minnesota kicker Gary Anderson had set an amazing NFL record that year by not missing a single field goal during the entire season. The bad news was that his luck unfortunately ran out right then and right there in the biggest game of his life. He missed the kick, and Atlanta, behind Chandler's amazing drive downfield in the game's final minutes, rallied back. He then tossed his second touchdown pass of the day to Terrence Mathis with just 49 seconds left in the game to tie it up at 27-27.

Then Minnesota did something that no one could figure out. Knowing that they had lost a couple of key players to injury, Green, despite having a time-out left, opted to play it safe by instructing Cunningham to simply take a knee on both third and fourth downs, instead of going for a long bomb to win the game. The crowd boo'd to no avail and the grudge-match went into overtime. There, after both teams failed to score in their opening drives, Atlanta, behind Chandler's leg injury that had him limping badly, drove deep into Minnesota territory on a quick, tactical drive. As the clock ran down to just a few seconds, they called time-out, brought in Morten Andersen and said a prayer. Anderson, the old veteran war-horse, calmly came in and kicked the 38-yard game-winner with ease. As the ball sailed through the uprights, the Falcons stormed the field. With that, Atlanta had upset the mighty Vikes, 30-27, thus earning themselves a trip to Super Bowl XXXIII in Miami.

The 64,060 Metrodome fans stood in complete disbelief, shock and horror. With the exception of the "Hail Mary" back in 1975, it was probably the worst loss in the history of the franchise. It was a sad ending to an otherwise brilliant season. Cunningham stepped it up huge that year, passing for 3,704 yards and 34 touchdowns. So did Carter and Reed. But Moss was the big story. No. 84, who finished with 69 receptions for 1,313 yards and a league leading 17 touchdowns (10 of which came on plays over 40 yards), was named as the Rookie of the Year. In addition to also making a serious case for being named as the league's MVP, he also became the only rookie to be named as a starter, alongside teammate Cris Carter, for the NFC in the Pro Bowl in Hawaii.

Vikings' All-Time Coaches		
1961-66	Norm Van Brocklin	29-51-3
1967-83	Bud Grant	151-87-5
1984	Les Steckel	3-13-0
1985	Bud Grant	7-9-0
1986-91	Jerry Burns	52-43-0
1992-Present	Dennis Green	81-47-1

Coming Up Short

The 1999 Vikes traveled to Atlanta for their much-anticipated rematch against the same Falcons who had so mercilessly upset them that last January. With the hype running high, Minnesota hung its pride on the line and rallied to beat the "dirty birds" by the final of 17-14. It wasn't pretty, but it was a "W," as the Falcons were done in, ironically, by the man who drove the dagger through the hearts of Vikings fans everywhere, Kicker Morten Andersen, who missed two field goals in the game. Minnesota's only touchdowns on the day, a two-yard TD catch by Carter, and a one-yard TD run by Hoard, came on the heels of a pair of "Moss-induced" pass interference calls which amounted to 76 yards of real-estate for the Purple.

While Game Two may have officially been billed as Minnesota vs. Oakland, the media had hyped it up as the Randy Moss vs. Charles Woodson show. (Moss and Woodson were both Heisman Trophy candidates, with Woodson ultimately bringing home the hardware.) The meeting between the two second-year phenoms didn't produce an afternoon of fireworks — rather, just one amazing play. It happened midway through the second quarter when Cunningham dropped back from the Raiders' 34-yard-line and lofted a hanging spiral to Moss on the right sideline. Moss, who was running back towards to ball, leaped over Woodson and somehow made a miraculous one-handed 29-yard grab to give the Vikings a first down at the five yard line. The Vikes fell apart after that big play however, as the Raiders scored on four consecutive drives to turn a 10-3 deficit into a 22-17 victory.

Dimitrius... had some issues

The Purple traveled to Green Bay that following week to face the Pack, who incidentally, in an effort to give themselves a fighting chance against Moss that season, selected three tall cornerbacks with their first three picks of the 98' draft. Moss, who capped an 80-yard drive by catching what appeared to be the game-winning touchdown with just under two minutes on the clock, was out-done by Green Bay QB Brett Favre, who threw up a miraculous 23-yard game-winning touchdown on fourth-and-1 with 12 seconds remaining in the game to give his club a dramatic 23-10 victory.

With a 1-2 record, and Tampa Bay in town for Week Four, Moss caught a pair of 61 and 27-yard touchdown passes on the Vikings' first two drives of the game, as Minnesota went on to beat the Bucs 21-14. The Vikings went into a slump after that though, losing their next two by just two points each to conference rivals Chicago and Detroit. In the Detroit game, Cunningham just wasn't getting it done. So Denny decided to put in the newly acquired Jeff George at Quarterback. It would be the smartest move he ever made.

That next week George came in and torched the once mighty San Francisco 49ers by the score of 40-16. In Week Eight the Vikes headed west to Denver, to face the two-time defending Super Bowl champion Broncos. This one was a wild one, with the game coming down to a defining moment on a pivotal third-and-10 play late in the game. That's when Moss somehow caught a loose ball that had just been deflected off of both Cris Carter and Denver Cornerback Ray Crockett. The incredible play saved the drive and led to an emotional 23-20 Minnesota victory.

Next up for the Purple was a hyped-up Monday Night Football matchup against the Dallas

Cowboys, and the best coverage cornerback in the game, Deion Sanders, who, this time, was healthy. Dallas jumped out to a quick 17-0 first-half lead, but when All Pro running back Emmitt Smith was forced to leave the game with an injury, the Vikes mounted a comeback. Moss, whose second TD of the day, a spectacular 47-yard bomb from George with 5:10 remaining in the game, helped to rally the team back to an amazing 27-17 victory. But the real excitement came on Cris Carter's game-winning TD grab amidst the back-drop of some premature pyrotechnics. That's right, the dude who shoots the cannon after touchdowns got excited and blew it off as the ball was in mid-air. But it was no problem for C.C., who hauled it in like it was nothing.

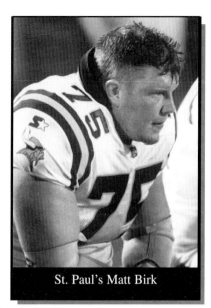
St. Paul's Matt Birk

With the momentum on their side the Vikes went on a roll, winning their next two over both Chicago and San Diego. Against the Bears Moss was absolutely phenomenal, posting a career-high 12 catches for 204 yards, while teammate Cris Carter added nine catches for 141 yards and three touchdowns, as the Vikings hung on to beat the Bears in a wild one, 27-24.

After getting a much needed rest over their bye week, the Vikes' high-powered offense revved up and produced a season-high 485 yards in a 35-27 victory over the Chargers. While the offense of old had seemed to be back on track for the Purple, it was the team's shaky defense that was causing the fans to get nervous. The Vikings then hit a couple of road blocks in both Tampa Bay and Kansas City. Down, but not out, Minnesota came back in Week 15 to beat the Packers at the Metrodome, 24-20, thanks to a pair of Moss TDs, including a dramatic 57-yard bomb from George late in the second quarter.

With their playoff lives in jeopardy, the Vikings next traveled to the Big Apple, where they took on the New York Giants. The highlight of the game came late in the third quarter on a razzle-dazzle play called "Z-pass-right." George handed the ball off to Moss on a reverse. Moss faked the run and instead pulled up and threw a perfect strike to a streaking Cris Carter for a 27-yard touchdown. The Purple held on for a 34-17 win, thus guaranteeing them a shot in the post-season.

Jimmy Kleinsasser

In the final regular season game of the year, the Vikes went on to beat a very good Detroit team by the final score of 24-17. The game was important for Minnesota, who, with the win, was awarded a home-field first-round playoff game. The Vikings would now host the Cowboys in the first-round of the playoffs. The Cowboys, of whom the Vikings had seemingly owned over the past two seasons, would be out for revenge.

The game was back and forth, but behind Robert Smith's team playoff-record 140 yards rushing, and Randy Moss' 127 yards receiving, the Vikings dug out of an early 10-3 hole, scored the game's final 24 points, and advanced to the NFC's final four for the third straight season. With the victory, the Vikings would now face the upstart St. Louis Rams in the second round. It would be a tough battle playing in St. Louis' noisy domed stadium, but the Purple embraced the challenge.

The Rams, much like the Vikings, were an explosive team with an explosive offense. All predictions were that it was going to be a shoot-out, and that, was a huge understatement! When the smoke had cleared after this one was over, the Rams were declared the victors by the final score of 49-37. The Vikes, despite going into the lockerroom at half-time up 17-14, were completely thrashed in the second half. St. Louis came right out of the gates inflicting a 35-0 second-half run that started with Tony Horne's 95-yard momentum-swinging kickoff return for a TD to open the half.

Just how frustrated was Moss, who caught nine passes for 188 yards and scored a pair of touchdowns? Late in the fourth quarter, Moss, after lobbying to the official about what he felt was a blatantly blown pass-interference call on him just the play before, went over to the sidelines, grabbed a water bottle, and proceeded to soak the official. Although it was harmless, the commissioner's office responded sternly by fining him a whopping $40,000. (Moss cleared his head that off-season by going to Hawaii, where he earned MVP honors at the 50th annual Pro Bowl by setting two single game records with nine receptions for 212 yards, while also adding a 25-yard touchdown catch from Carolina's Steve Beuerlein.)

It was yet another ugly ending, heart-breaking loss, as the Vikings found themselves with an early post-season exit for the second frustrating year in a row. Something drastic needed to be done that next year. It was the beginning of the new millennium, and several of the team's veterans were on their last legs. Just how would Denny respond? After unsuccessfully signing Jeff George, who hit the road for Washington, and not being able to woo Dan Marino out of retirement, Denny declared that his prized pupil, rookie QB Daunte Culpepper, was going to be his starter for the home opener against the Bears.

Daunte's Inferno

The media went nuts that off-season. Talk-radio was filled with nothing but Purple chat. Green, who had selected Culpepper with the 11th overall pick of the 1999 draft, was in the hot-seat. You see, he had received that pick when he traded Brad Johnson to the Redskins, and opted to select the young quarterback out of Central Florida University, over Defense End and future Tennessee Titan Rookie of the Year, Jevon Kearse. In addition, Green's other first-round pick was squandered when the team selected Michigan State's Dimitrius Underwood, who lasted all of one day at training camp before going AWOL. But Green stuck to his guns, and assured the fans that Daunte was going to be something special. So, after Culpepper waited in the wings in 1999, he came out and started for the Purple in 2000. How did he do? Daunte was, in a word, spectacular. The six-foot-four, 265-pound hulk ran for nearly 100 yards en route to running for a record three touchdowns, in leading the Vikings to a thrilling 30-27 victory over Chicago. Green's quarterback of the future had arrived.

Daunte Culpepper

2000 and Beyond

Perhaps it was famous writer and fellow Minnesotan F. Scott Fitzgerald who said it best when he said, "Show me a hero and I'll write you a tragedy." While the Vikings are certainly not a tragedy, having won 15 divisional titles and made 22 playoff appearances in their 40-year existence, they have suffered through four tragic Super Bowl defeats. But surrounding that entire story, have been countless heroes. Men who have battled bravely and worn the purple proudly. What started as a colorful expansion team, has blossomed into one of professional sports' most successful and well-respected franchises. Sure, their identity has evolved from the glory days of the feared Purple People Eaters and their snowy exploits out at the old Met doing battle in the Black and Blue Division, to a home-dome field advantage of a different kind. It might be sterile and ugly, but it is deafeningly loud, and in its own way, has a bizarre sort of charm and beauty.

As we enter the new millennium, it is an exciting and yet pivotal time in the franchise's storied history. The team, under its new owner, wants a new stadium. Vailed threats of relocation run amok, and as fans, we are left to wonder. While many are adamant against their tax dollars being spent towards aiding millionaires and billionairs, others see the Vikings as a valuable resource that should be saved at all costs. The team needs more luxury suites, more seating, more signage, more concessions, more parking, more of everything. But the citizens of Minnesota have said no. Where does that leave our beloved Purple? There have been many new stadiums financed primarily with tax dollars and public contributions over the past decade, as well as several privately built ones. Miami, Washington, Charlotte and soon to be New England, have all found a way to get it done, and that's just in football. In baseball, hockey and basketball, countless other cities have found a way to keep up with the Joneses. Let's just hope that cooler heads prevail in the upcoming years, so that we can keep this wonderful organization right where it belongs — as a vital part of our identity right here in Minnesota.

Denny Green was signed to a multi-year contract extension in the Fall of 2000, securing him through 2004. With Denny steering the ship, these Vikings will continue to be a force in the NFL for years to come. SKOL!

CHARLES SCHULZ

"Good Grief!" World famous cartoonist Charles Schulz was born in Minneapolis on November 26, 1922, and grew up in St. Paul as a big Gopher Football fan. After graduating from St. Paul Central High, Schulz went on to art school in Minneapolis. There, he created a comic strip about the adventures of a group of preschoolers (including a kid named Charlie Brown) called "Li'l Folks," which appeared in the St. Paul Pioneer Press in 1947.

United Features Syndicate bought the strip in 1950 and renamed it "Peanuts" because 'Li'l Folks' sounded too much like another cartoon, "Li'l Abner." Seven newspapers carried the original "Peanuts" cartoon strip on October 2, 1950, and the numbers have grown ever since.

He later moved on to California, where he became one of the world's most famous cartoonists. The multiple Emmy winner's cartoons are now read by several hundred million people in 68 countries, who speak 26 different languages. (Charlie Brown is Carolius Niger and Snoopy is Snupius in the Latin version.) He was one of the top 10 highest-paid entertainers in the U.S., and has built an empire surrounding that lovable pooch, Snoopy.

Today, the Minnesota Cartoonists League meets at O'Gara's piano bar in St. Paul under an original portrait of Snoopy drawn and signed by Charles himself. The reason they meet there is because that building was, from 1942 to 1952, Charles Schulz's father's barbershop. Schulz tragically died early in the year 2000, but his memories live on forever.

"A League of Their Own"

It is by all means a very compelling story. Countless women from across the country, leaving everything behind all for the opportunity to play a game that has otherwise been off-limits to them. I am talking, of course, about women's football, and the amazing phenomenon happening right here, in Minnesota, in the year 2000.

That's right, the Women's Professional Football League, or WPFL, is headquartered out of the Twin Cities, and is finally giving women a chance to lace em' up and crack some skulls. Fad? Think not. Women from as far away as California and Florida have picked up, left their families, quit their jobs and moved to sunny Minnesota — all for the chance to be pioneers of a sport that will offer them no health insurance in case of an injury, force them to suffer through occasional practices in the dark, encourage them to recruit their own fans to attend their games, and pay them next to nothing. Welcome to the world of women's pro football, a sport that actually has roots that go back much, much further than you might think.

Believe it or not, organized women's football has been around for more than a century in the Land of 10,000 Lakes. In as far back as 1898 a group of women on the campus of St. Cloud State (then St. Cloud Teachers College) fielded a football team, and in 1923 a group of women on the campus of Gustavus Adolphus made history.

That's right, on Friday, November 1, 1923, an event that was billed as the "First Women's Football Classic," was conceived by a group of fraternity boys. The young men, who had convinced a group of campus co-ed's to play a harmless game, were astonished to see that their little ploy would receive so much nation-wide publicity.

Gustavus women who played in the 1920s

The ladies, who borrowed uniforms from the men's team, divided into two teams: the "Heavies" and the "Leans," and began two weeks of rigorous practicing. The game,

which proved to be the first ever recorded contest between a group of exclusively women, was played in front of several hundred onlookers in some bitterly cold St. Peter weather. While the two teams battled to a 6-6 tie, that next week Gustavus was, according to the school paper, "spread-eagled over every sports page in the country from the Atlantic to the Pacific."

Incredibly, national newspapers from around the world, including the Boston Herald, New York Times, LA Times and London Times, all covered the event with feature stories. With so much publicity, talk of a rematch soon emerged — but was shot-down when a smallpox epidemic broke out on campus.

Other women's teams soon popped up around the world of football, mostly as a publicity stunts though. Such was the case with the NFL's Frankford Yellow Jackets, who, in 1926, featured women's teams as their half-time entertainment.

Following the Great Depression and then W.W.II, women's pro football was restricted to sandlot status. Then, in 1965, a Ohio talent agent by the name of Sid Friedman started a women's semi-pro tackle football league, which he called the Women's Professional Football League. What started as two teams, one in Cleveland and another in Akron, who barnstormed around the area as a sort of gimmick, later evolved into an eight-team circuit which included clubs from as far away as New York and Pennsylvania.

In 1974 a woman named Patricia Barzi Palinkas made history by becoming the first woman ever to play on a professional men's football team, when she suited up for the semi-pro Orlando Panthers.

During that same era of the early 1970s, another pro circuit started up called the National Women's Football League. The NWFL's inaugural lineup featured several clubs from across the country, including: the Los Angeles Dandelions, California Mustangs, Detroit Demons, Columbus Pacesetters, Toledo Troopers, Dallas Bluebonnets and Fort Worth Shamrocks.

So successful was the start-up league that Toledo Troopers' star Halfback Linda Jefferson was named as Women's Sports magazine's 1975 Athlete of the Year. The five-time 1,000-yard rusher, who led the Troopers to an amazing 39-1-1 record over that same time span, even competed on ABC's then-popular "Women's Superstars" television show.

By 1976 the NWFL had blossomed into three divisions and featured teams from as far away as San Diego, Houston, Philadelphia, Oklahoma City and San Antonio. From there, a couple of rival spin-off leagues popped up, includ-

Gustavus women's football in the 1920s: the "Heavy's" vs. the "Lean's"

Minnesota golfing legend Patty Berg also played quarterback for her neighborhood team, the "50th St. Tigers."

ing the Western States Women's Professional Football League, which featured such clever team names as the Tucson Wild Kittens, Phoenix Cowgirls and Long Beach Queens. Both leagues ultimately went through some financial hardships though, and were toast by the early 1980s.

The game soon emerged overseas, however, with the American Football Association of Germany being formed in the late 1980s, and growing into a 10-team league, even culminating with the winners playing in the "Ladies Bowl." Go figure. There was also a Japanese circuit, and even the West Australian Football League, which was formed in 1987 and boasted of seven teams as well.

By the 1990s, despite the fact that women's rugby and flag football had grown quite popular both intramurally, on college campuses, as well as in city leagues throughout the country, no serious attempt at organizing a pro women's league in the US had proven effective.

But, after seeing the success of other women's teams in the sports of hockey, soccer, fast-pitch softball and basketball (which spawned the extremely popular WNBA), it was only a matter of time before someone tried to get female football back into the spotlight. That someone was former Minnesota Vikings Cornerback, John "J.T." Turner, who, along with business partner Terry Sullivan, launched the Women's Professional Football League (WPFL) in the Fall of 1999, out of their Edina-based World-Wide Sports offices.

The group, which also runs the (men's) semipro Mid-America Football League and promotes small-college all-star games, started the league with just two charter franchises — the Minnesota Vixens and the Lake Michigan Minx. After try-outs at Augsburg College, the squad of 45 women then started practices at Park Center High School. Some 2,000 fans showed up to see them play at Midway Stadium, and then again at the Dome, where the Vixens lost to the Minx, 23-20, on a last-second field goal. These ladies were for real!

From there, the League then initiated an inaugural "No Limits Barnstorming Tour," which featured games in St. Paul, Minneapolis, Chicago, Green Bay, New York, and Miami, concluding with an exhibition game at the "NFL Experience" during Super Bowl XXXIV in Atlanta.

Tentatively, there are several cities who have paid the reported $50,000 franchise fee and have committed to join the league for the 2000 season, including: the Colorado Valkyries, Chicago Blaze, Milwaukee Minx, Atlanta Amazons, Austin Rose, Dallas Wildcatz, Daytona Beach Barracudas, Houston Energy, Miami Fury, Nashville Dream, New England Storm, New York Sharks, Rochester Galaxy and Tampa Tempest.

The Vixens vs. Minx

The Vixens, who will play their future games in both the Metrodome and also at Midway Stadium in St. Paul, will sport uniforms featuring a red fox, with their team colors being "Arctic" white and "Fox-foot" black. In addition, they will play a 10-game schedule as members of the Central Division of the WPFL's American Football Conference, along with Colorado, Chicago and Milwaukee.

Seeing the popularity of other physical women's sports, the athletes seemed ready for the emergence of full-contact football. Not only are these courageous women mothers, wives and daughters, they are also doctors, lawyers, teachers, police officers, firefighters, students and secretary's. And, if things go right, they can also add to their resumes the impressive titles of defensive tackle, quarterback and nose guard — all for the hope of being a part of the next big thing in the world of sports entertainment. Are you ready for some football? Stay tuned!

THE MINNESOTA STATE "SCREAMING EAGLES"

Craig T. Nelson, A.K.A. "Hayden Fox," was the fictitious head coach of the late 1980s and early 1990s ABC show "Coach," which chronicled the life and times of a bumbling coach, his bone-head assistants, "Luther" and "Dauber," and their mythical college football team — the "Minnesota State Screaming Eagles."

The show used to use old Gopher football video footage from the Metrodome that was even color enhanced to make the maroon jerseys appear as purple.

I don't think that Minnesota State, Mankato's decision to change their name from Mankato State University had anything to do with the television show being cancelled. Or maybe it did! Who Knows?

Indoor football, with all of its razzle-dazzle and high-scoring shoot-outs, is a relatively new phenomenon to the world of sports. It was conceived back in 1985, when Jim Foster, a pro football marketing guru, had a vision while watching an indoor soccer game. Knowing that he wouldn't stand a chance at competing head-to-head with the NFL, he decided, instead, to create an indoor football hybrid that would take place during the summertime.

In so doing, he decided to apply the best of traditional American football, with a couple of new twists. Among the things differentiating itself from the classic gridiron game would be: playing in a 50-yard indoor field (inside hockey and basketball arenas); using eight (instead of 12) two-way iron-man players; allowing two-point drop kicks (goal posts are nine-feet wide — half of the width of the NFL's); not allowing any punting; featuring foam rubber padded side-boards (there is no out of bounds) and also installing rebound nets where players can catch the ball off of the net and play it live. Additionally, of the eight players per side, three could be wide receivers, and all could be in motion before the snap — even running towards the line of scrimmage. With rules like that, it was no wonder that the fans loved the often 100-point shoot-outs!

Foster then organized a new four-team league which hit the astro-turf in 1987. The teams, which included: the Chicago Bruisers, Denver Dynamite, Pittsburgh Gladiators and Washington D.C. Commandos, played a 13-game regular season schedule, culminating with an "ArenaBowl" Championship game.

The league fared well, as more and more teams came and went, into and out of the league, over the next decade. Then, in 1996, the AFL moved into Minneapolis, where the Minnesota Fighting Pike were born. The Pikes, who made the Target Center their home, went out and signed former Gopher Quarterback Rickey Foggie, who had been playing in the Canadian Football League for the past eight years, to lead them in their inaugural campaign.

Quarterback Rickey Foggie

The Pikes came right out of the gates swinging, as they won their first-ever game against the Texas Terror, on the road, 36-24. Former Gopher Wide Receiver Tony Levine caught the team's first touchdown pass, a 17-yarder from Foggie early in the first half. Levine, like the other players, had to get used to playing both ways.

"It's an adventure, put it that way," said Levine of his (two-way) receiver/linebacker duties. "Defense is really not my thing. I stand back there and try to fake it the best I can and hope the ball carrier doesn't come around my area."

The team signed several kids with Minnesota roots, all part of the organization's effort to attract more fans to an already crowded sports-entertainment market.

"I think it's great to have local players on our team," said Pike Coach Ray Jauch. "Nowadays fans can't identify with a team because they don't know the players. We want to make this a team for the fans and having players from Minnesota helps us do that. It helps give us stability."

In Game Two, against the Iowa Barnstormers, 15,000 fans showed up at Target Center to root on the state's newest team. And, despite losing the game, 43-59, the Pikes put on an unbelievable show. One of the early stars of the season was Kicker Mike Vanderjagt, who went on to star for the NFL's Indianapolis Colts.

The Pikes in action

The Iowa loss would, unfortunately, be the first of eight straight defeats for the Pikes, who finally got back on track with a 44-40 thriller against Connecticut in Week 10. They then lost a pair to both Orlando and Texas, 15-56 and 51-54, respectively, but finished out the season strong with wins over both San Jose, 40-31, and Memphis, 50-25.

When it was all said and done the team had put up a modest 4-10 record, while posting no home victories. Regrettably, it would prove to be the team's first and only season in Minnesota. That's right, the team, citing financial difficulties, folded after that season.

They played well though. They were entertaining and they put up a lot of numbers. Rickey Foggie was the team's leading passer, going 224-443 for 2,668 yards and tossing 40 touchdowns, while also adding four rushing touchdowns as well. (To put it into perspective as to just how much the team passed instead of rushed the ball, Harry Jackson ended the season as the team's leading rusher with a whopping 26 yards!) Foggie's favorite targets that season were Wide Receivers Reggie Brown, who caught 79 passes for 964 yards and 17 touchdowns, and Alvin Ashley, who

The Minnesota Fighting Pike's One and Only 1996 Schedule

at Texas	36-24	W
Iowa Barnstormers	43-59	L
St. Louis Stamped	22-59	L
at Albany	30-85	L
Tampa Bay	16-21	L
Anaheim	23-49	L
Arizona	27-59	L
at Florida	28-63	L
Milwaukee	49-61	L
at Connecticut	44-40	W
at Orlando	15-56	L
Texas	51-54	L
at San Jose	40-31	W
at Memphis	50-25	W

nabbed 69 balls for 971 yards and 19 touchdowns.

"I felt like I had a good reception from the fans, and it was great to be able to come back to the Twin Cities," said Foggie, who later went on to star for the New Jersey Red Dogs, where, against the Albany Firebirds in the playoffs that next season, he threw for 446 yards and a record nine touchdowns. "We had a lot of fun that year, but it was unfortunate that we didn't get to win any games at home. I was disappointed that my Pike experience wasn't a successful situation, but I was glad to get back into the atmosphere of having the Twin Cities fans come out and watch me perform again."

That wasn't the end of indoor arena football in Minnesota, however, with several other teams coming and going throughout the '90s as well. Among them were the Professional Indoor Football League's (PIFL) Minnesota Monsters, and the Indoor Football League's (IFL) Mankato Purple Rage and Duluth-Superior Lumberjacks.

The PIFL, which, in addition to the Monsters, featured the Green Bay Bombers, Honolulu Hurricanes, Louisiana Bayou Beast, Madison Mad Dogs, Texas Bullets and Utah Catzz. The league spent two seasons here during the late-1990s, and when they folded, about half of the team's players headed north to play for the upstart IFL Lumberjacks.

The IFL, which competes with the Arena football league but has gone to smaller markets to find its own niche, was actually started by Kelly Ecklund, a Neenah, Wis. trucking company executive. Ecklund originally tried to buy the Fighting Pike and move them to Green Bay, but when that fell through, he decided to purchase two franchises, in Green Bay and Madison, to play in the Atlanta-based Indoor Professional Football League (IPFL). But, when he found himself having to pay for rival clubs to travel to Wisconsin to play his teams because they had no money, he decided to simply start his own league, the IFL. (Today the IFL is a rival league to the AFL's "AF2," a secondary small-market league.)

Minnesota Stallions

Eventually, the AFL sued the smaller league, alleging that they had infringed on their patented and proprietary ideas. The IFL eventually settled though, and agreed not to use the AFLs giant goal-line rebound nets, in which players can catch attempted kicks to run back on the fly.

Duluth's franchise began play in the spacious Duluth Entertainment and Convention Center (DECC), and has been very well received in the port city. More than 5,000 fans showed up for the team's 1999 inaugural home-opener, which they won, 47-40, over the Steel Valley Smash of Wheeling, W.V. The Jacks went 2-10 in their initial IFL campaign though, and as a result, decided to clean house. They brought in a new owner, John Torzewski, a new coach, Ed Holden, and an overhauled roster that included only one significant name from the inaugural season, Quarterback Bob DeMeyer, a 30-year-old school teacher from Superior, who played briefly for Las Vegas in the AFL back in 1995.

By and large, indoor football is a great alternative to the NFL. It just might be the perfect amalgam of monster trucks, hockey, all-star wrestling, and football — all under an air-conditioned roof. Before the games there are clinics for the kids; during the games the music blares to a deafening tone; and afterwards, the players stay for autographs while the fans come onto the field to hang out. It might be a lot to ask of a guy who might make a couple hundred bucks per game, but the players — like the fans, just love still being a part of the game.

The Mid-America Football League

Semi-pro football has roots that extend all they way back to the turn of the century in Minnesota. From the old St. Paul Ideals and Berman's, to the Minneapolis Staley's and Marines, the Land of 10,000 Lakes has seen it all. And now, as we head into the new millennium, there has been a new crop of semi-pro league's that have sprung up — offering local kids an opportunity to hook up with a number of very talented, hard-hitting regional clubs.

One is the the upstart Great Plains Football League (GPFL), a minor league/semi-pro circuit that plays clubs from around the upper midwest, including: the Alexandria Mustangs, Woodbury Warriors, Anoka County K-9's, Rochester Dragons, Minnesota Stallions (Windom), St. Cloud Thunderbirds and Minneapolis Wolfpack.

Another, and perhaps the most successful to date in Minnesota, has been the Mid-America Football League (MFL), a six-team circuit which has included several Minnesota entries over the greater part of the 1990s, including: the St. Paul Wranglers, St. Paul Pigs, St. Paul Sting, Minneapolis Lumberjacks, Minnesota Maulers and Twin Cities Talons. (Some of the GPFL teams play in the MFL as well.)

Today the "Maffle" is affiliated with numerous other nationwide semi-professional teams, including nearly 40 in the Midwest alone. While the players receive little in the way of compensation, rather, it is an opportunity for them to stay sharp and hone their skills. The teams aren't extravagant either, as they play and practice at local high school football fields, and live within a modest fixed budget. While all of the players have day jobs, they also all have dreams.

The league is a tremendous stepping-stone for those individuals with the ability to play at the next level, but just need some more exposure. A lot of the league's players are former semi-pro, and Division II & III alumni, who, because of injuries or bad luck, are now transition players. While many of the players have gone on to play in the "show," including 1998 MFL Player of the Year Keith Williams, a speedy cornerback who went on to sign a contract with the Green Bay Packers, others just see the league as an outlet to continue playing the sport they love.

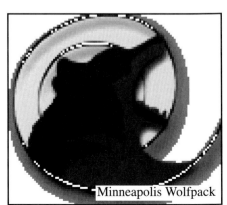

Minneapolis Wolfpack

LEROY NEIMAN

Minnesota's very own LeRoy Neiman is one of America's premier artists. He is without question the most famous sports artist of the 21st century, and has painted nearly every famous American athlete over his career. Neiman was born on June 8, 1921, in St. Paul, and grew up playing hockey and sandlot football at the Uniondale Playgrounds in the Frog Town neighborhood of the city.

He loved sports and painting as a kid, and used to love going to see the Gophers play at old Memorial Stadium by either hitchhiking or hopping street-cars.

"Bernie Bierman was such a great coach, and Bronko Nagurski was my all-time favorite," said Neiman in a recent phone interview. "They were so good in those days during the Depression, and we used to love to watch them whenever he could get the chance."

Neiman attended Washington High School in the late 1930s, until going into the Army. After his discharge from the Service, in 1946, Neiman enrolled in courses in basic drawing techniques at the St. Paul Gallery and School of Art. There, he learned the principles of composition espoused by the French Impressionist Paul Cezanne, one of his early influences. Neiman later moved to Chicago and entered the School of the Art Institute of Chicago, where he would go on to become a teacher as well.

It was also in the Windy City where Nieman caught his first big break. You see, while he was an art student, he used to love going to watch the Bears games out at Wrigley Field, where he could watch his boyhood idol, Bronko Nagurski.

Once, at a game, he decided to jump over the railing to get down to the field, where he could take out his sketchbook and draw Nagurski from the sidelines. Suddenly, a cop came up to him and tried to kick him out. But just then, legendary Bears Owner, George Halas, came over and saw what he was painting, and told the cop to back off and let him stay. Halas loved his artwork and from that point on, he made sure to let him down onto the sidelines to sketch his Bears. That, ironically, was the start of his amazing sports art career.

After gaining recognition early in his career as a contributing artist for Playboy, in the 1950s, Neiman went on to become one of the world's most recognized figures. He is especially well known for his renditions of sports scenes that feature his trademark brushing techniques with vivid color explosions that burst off the canvas. He was the official artist at five Olympiads, and has become good friends with everyone from Mohammed Ali to Wayne Gretzky. It has been estimated that the more than 150,000 Neiman prints that have been purchased to date around the world have an estimated market value exceeding $400 million.

Fran Tarkenton

Today Neiman lives in New York City, and continues to do what he loves most, paint, and watch sporting events. He has written nearly a dozen books, given millions to charity and to museums, and shows no signs of slowing down. In 1995 he gave the School of the Arts at Columbia University a gift of $6 million to create the LeRoy Neiman Center for Print Studies. After speaking with him this past summer, he told me that he had just finished painting such legends as Shaquille O'Neal, Mike Piazza, Mark McGwire, Sammy Sosa and Joe DiMaggio.

Plans are currently in the works for creating a museum in his honor that would showcase his paintings in downtown St. Paul — a gesture fit for one of our country's greatest ever artists, and a true American hero.

Gophers vs. Hawkeyes

JERRY SEEMAN: NFL DIRECTOR OF OFFICIATING

Fridley resident Jerry Seeman, the NFL's long-time Senior Director of Officiating, retire after the 2000 season as the league's highest ranking official.

After 12 years as a college official, Seeman joined the NFL in 1975 and spent 16 years as a line judge, head linesman and referee. He worked two Super Bowls, including Super Bowl XXV, which was his last game. As the Director, he oversaw the return of instant replay, which came back in 1999, modernized the training and grading system of officials and increased communication between his office and NFL teams.

"I had a vision and a dream when I took this position and am leaving it knowing that I made a real difference," said Seeman. "While I am excited about coming home to retire in (Fridley) Minnesota with my wife Marilyn, our three sons and five grandchildren, finally choosing to hang em' up after all these years was one of the most difficult emotional, gut-wrenching decisions I have ever made."

With roots which can be traced back for nearly 125 years, the University of Minnesota Golden Gopher football program has a long and epic history dotted with peaks and valleys. While the Gophers of today are an up and coming force to be reckoned with in the Big Ten, many don't realize what a powerhouse program this used to be. Did you know that in the first half of the century alone, the Gophers won five national championships, 16 conference titles and posted 11 undefeated seasons?

In those days the Gophers were referred to by the rest of the football world as the "Giants of the North." There wasn't a young boy in the state who didn't dream about one day playing football at Memorial Stadium. For the lucky few who could actually get down to University Avenue to see them, they were truly the "Legends of the Fall." For everyone else, which included a loyal following of fans throughout the Midwest, sitting around and listening to the action on the radio was pure heaven. Back in the day, the Tribune Newspaper had a section called the "Peach," which was delivered all the way to the Dakotas and even into Montana, where Gopher fans anxiously awaited to read all about their beloved team. The Gopher football program wreaks of a tradition that has become woven into the very fabric of our state's rich history. So let's go back, way back to the beginning, and see how far these Golden Gophers have come — and just how far Coach Mason has his eyes set on taking them into this new 21st century.

The Early Years

The University of Minnesota was founded along the banks of the Mississippi River in Minneapolis back in 1851, fully seven years before the "Minnesota Territory" had even achieved statehood. By the latter part of the 1870s, the new sport of football had migrated west and popped up on campus at the intramural level. The student newspaper, the Ariel, first made mention of this new college fad in October of 1878, referring to it as an "all-absorbing amusement." The article went on to describe the new rugby-like sport as a "barbaric charade which featured 15 men on a side engaged in a jaw-to-jaw, man-to-man style of combat on the line of scrimmage, while a ball carrier tried to run around or go over the battle area." Back then, when the ball carrier started to run, the linemen squared off in man-to-man brawls. When the runner attempted to cross the line of scrimmage, he could be picked up and carried back toward his own goal until his teammates halted the effort by whichever means possible. Defenders could simply hold on to the ball carriers legs and pull, while the offense pushed, sometimes getting leverage while grasping arms, or even hair. "We are anxiously waiting for some one to get his head knocked off," the Ariel stated. (I wonder if they had any accidental dismemberment insurance back in the day?) It even went on to describe an "inter-class" freshman vs. sophomore scrimmage having to be canceled due to the "non-arrival of the ball," which was apparently a hard item to come by back then.

With the increasing popularity and interest in sports during that time, the University formed an Athletic Association, for the purpose of fostering all athletic endeavors, but especially football. It didn't catch on right away though. Just a year later, an editorial in the Ariel reported that while football had reached a high standing among eastern universities, "our University seems perfectly dead in this respect."

History was finally made on September 29th, 1882 when the U of M, Carleton and Hamline were to take part in a "Field Day," which included a number of track events, that been scheduled at the Colonel King State Fairgrounds (near Riverside and Franklin in South Minneapolis). While the Gophers were supposed to play Carleton in a friendly game, they wound up playing against Hamline instead, due to the fact that Carleton insisted upon playing by the rules of rugby. With Carleton respectfully declining, Hamline thus agreed to play in what would become the first intercollegiate football game in Minnesota history. That historic first game saw the Gophers win 4-0 in "55 minutes of hard play," thanks to the efforts of team captain A.J. Baldwin, who scored all four Gopher points. Spectators came out to watch the game, with "many ladies from both institutions so thoughtful as to bring elegant floral offerings to the victors." Hamline then issued a challenge for a rematch, later getting revenge when they beat the Gophers 2-0 just a few weeks later on a controversial last-minute score.

In the fall of 1883 Professor Thomas Peebles, an Irish immigrant who played football at Princeton, came to the U of M to teach philosophy. Knowing that he was well versed in the school of American football, which was first originally played at Princeton back in 1869, the Gopher players asked him to be their coach for an upcoming game against Carleton. The boys then hopped the train for Northfield, and once there, realized that Carleton, in addition to allowing their faculty to play, once again insisted upon using a big old fashioned round, inflated, rugby ball — instead of an oval football. Despite the U's protest, the game was played with Carleton winning by the final score of 4-2. They later went on to beat Hamline again that season, 5-0, only to lose to a group of ex-collegians by the final of 4-2. Peebles got the team organized, and even got them practicing on their own practice field — a sandy burr which is the ground now occupied by Folwell Hall, in the heart of campus.

In addition to Hamline, Carleton and Shattuck Military Academy, the Gophers also began to play against some of the other local teams, including Macalaster, the Minneapolis Football Club, the Eastern College Alumni Team (former stars from Yale, Harvard, Dartmouth and Princeton — all native sons of the state of Minnesota), Minneapolis High School, St. Paul Central High School, and the Northfield-Carleton Farmers Alliance Football Association.

In the fall of 1885, Frederick Jones, a former star football player at Yale, arrived on campus via a

Alf Pillsbury

brief teaching and coaching stint at Shattuck Military Academy. Jones, who would later earn the nick-name as the "Father of Minnesota Football," was asked to help coach the Gopher's squad. Jones, who would go on to serve as the Dean of the University's Law School, was schooled in the rugby style of football played at Yale, while Peebles was a student of the soccer-style system, which created somewhat of a battle of wills. This rivalry, however, was quickly ended when Alf Pillsbury, or "Pilly" as he was known (son of John Pillsbury, the former governor of the state, and heir to the famous flour company bearing his name), arrived on campus with his brand new shiny rugby ball. Because balls were in such short supply in those days, it was just understood that they would pursue the rugby style of play to make things a whole lot easier. Pilly became the team's first star, an honor he would hold for an amazing eight years (due to attending law school after his undergraduate studies). One might say that there were advantages to having your own ball back in the day!

Pudge Heffelfinger

Because Jones was at Shattuck prior to coming to the U of M, it was only natural that a rival-ry be kindled with the prepsters from Faribault. One day, as the team was about to board the train to Faribault to play the Shads, Pilly, who was counting his players before departing, observed that his squad was one man short. As he looked up into the crowd of anxious on-lookers and fans who had come to see the team off at the train depot, he noticed a big, six-foot-three, 200-pound kid standing in the dis-tance. Pilly had a light bulb go off above his head, and went over to talk to him. The kid's name was Walter (Pudge) Heffelfinger, a Minneapolis Central High School student who had come down to root on the Gophers for their trip. Pilly asked him if he wanted to suit up and join them on their trip, and the rest they say, is history. (Back then there were no eligibility rules about things like this.) Heffelfinger, who ran and got a change of clothes, was enlisted for the game and pressed into action. He even wound up playing his entire senior year of high school with the Gophers. (After Pudge played for Minnesota for one year, he then went out east to Yale, where he became a three-time All-American guard and regarded by most as the nation's best college football player. He would later become America's first-ever professional football player, when he was paid to play for an Eastern team, and is today enshrined in the Pro Football Hall of Fame.)

The first known action photo of a Gopher game took place around the turn of the century.

In 1888, the Gophers hosted a return visit by the Shads in one of their biggest games of the year, beating them 14-0. That next day the Ariel stated: "Everybody turned out, and faculty, students, and small boys united to encourage the home team with mighty yelling. The unusual noise, together with the surprisingly mountainous contour of the campus, disconcerted the visitors, and gave the victory to the home team." The game was followed by a bus ride around the city, as the University and Shattuck Yells ("yells" were the predecessor to modern-day cheerleaders) combined to make the day "hideous till supper time."

The Gophers' were heralded as "champions of the Northwest" in 1890 when they commenced their first out-of-state competition. After first beating Iowa's Grinnell College, 18-13, Minnesota then went on to beat the University of Wisconsin, 63-0, starting a tradition that has become the longest running rivalry in major college foot-ball history. The game was not without its share of controversy though, as Pillsbury, who was not only the quarterback but also the team's best runner, devised a play where he handed the ball off to a running back and then got it right back on a lateral. This razzle-dazzle play was extremely controversial at the time, and led to the changing of many of the rules which involved carrying the ball — which had now started to replace the exclusively kicking game. (Back then there was no forward or lateral passing, only backwards passes, and always through the hands of the quarterback to a halfback, for a running play, or to the fullback, for a punt or a drop kick.)

Minnesota's program got serious in the early 1890s, as the team's management began a fund-raising drive to improve itself. Among the items on its agenda were building a new ball-field (which would eventually become Northrop Field), employ a trainer, and start a daily train-ing table — which was established at Johnson's Restaurant. There, the men ate together and were quizzed on strategy and signal drills. The team also got new uniforms, those being of the wool turtleneck sweater variety. In addition, the basement of the campus YMCA served as the team's new locker room, where one bathtub was shared for the entire team. The new tactics and amenities paid instant dividends though, as the team's first undefeated, untied record came in 1892, when they beat Michigan, 14-6, Northwestern, 16-12, and Iowa, 42-4. For their efforts, the team was officially named as the winners of their first-ever conference title, the newly-formed Intercollegiate Athletic Association of the Northwest.

The Gophers went undefeated again that next year, but received no accolades because the Athletic Association was disbanded due to financial problems, as well as pressures from the public regarding the increasing level of violence in the game. Seeing that something needed to be done about the game's lack of control, Purdue University President James H. Smart, along with the presidents of six other universities (Minnesota, University of Chicago, Illinois, Michigan, Northwestern, and Wisconsin), met on January 11, 1895, to create the new Western Conference. (Minnesota was considered a Far West team by the East back in the day, since anything west of the Hudson River was still considered wild frontier land.) The Western Conference then became the Big Seven Conference, and later the Big Eight, Nine, Ten & Eleven. Indiana and Iowa joined the conference in 1899, followed by Ohio State in 1912.)

In 1895 Pudge Heffelfinger returned from an illustrious career at Yale University to take a one-year coaching stint at Minnesota. After posting a modest 7-3 record, which included losses to Michigan, Purdue and Grinnell, he decided to turn pro full time.

From then until the turn of the century, the Gophers went through a dismal stretch. One of the more memorable games during this era though, was an 11-10 loss

Minnesota's first game against Wisconsin

Dr. Henry Williams

to Illinois on Thanksgiving Day, 1898, which was played in 12 below zero conditions at Northrop Field. Despite a blizzard dumping several feet of deep snow on the field, then student manager, John Pillsbury, hired a crew that worked through the night to clear it with horse-drawn plows. The game was even delayed several times while the officials searched inside the snow-banks for the often-buried football. The star of this era was John Harrison, a left end from Minneapolis Central who became the first Gopher to earn All-Western Conference honors.

Enter the Good Doctor

Something, or rather someone, big happened to Minnesota in 1900. That was the year that University officials, after a string of one-year coaching stints from a variety of former players, hired Dr. Henry L. Williams on a part-time basis as its football and track coach. Williams, a former star player and teammate of Heffelfinger at Yale University, who then attended medical school at the University of Pennsylvania, accepted a three-year, $2,500 contract, with the understanding that he also be able to carry on his medical practice. Williams, whose three-year commitment ultimately turned into the University's first full-time coaching job, which would last for more than 22 years, marked the beginning of a new football era in Minnesota during which the Gophers would win or share eight conference titles over the next 16-seasons. Additionally, Williams was the innovator of several football innovations that would place him among the immortals of the game. Among his contributions to the sport included: the advent of the Forward Pass (which became legal in 1905); Criss-Cross Plays, which halfbacks and ends passed the ball back and forth to each other while going in opposite directions; Revolving Wedges; Tackle-Back formations, On-Side Quarterback Kicks; and perhaps most importantly was the now infamous "Minnesota Shift," which was the forerunner of all quick shifts since implemented in the game, and long considered as the most devastating offensive weapon introduced into modern football.

Under Williams' tutelage, Minnesota, who was led by Quarterback Gilmore Dobie, won the newly formed Big Nine Conference title in 1900, finishing with an undefeated 10-0-2 record. After beating the likes of Illinois, Northwestern, Wisconsin, Nebraska, North Dakota University, Grinnell, Carleton, Ames College and St. Paul Central, they tied Chicago and Minneapolis Central High School. Minneapolis Central, who held the Gophers to a 0-0 stalemate, featured a couple of future Gopher stars in-waiting: Sig Harris and Bobby Marshall.

The good doctor had turned around the slumping program, and brought to it a new sense of style. He even held the team's pre-season camp at Lake Minnetonka, just to give the kids a fresh outlook each season. With each of the starters towering at least six-feet tall, this team was dubbed as the "Giants of the North." With the forward pass not yet legal, Williams' early teams featured a ground attack similar to that of a battering-ram. In this system, the runner had to just get behind his offensive linemen, who would simply lock arms and mow down any defender who got in their way.

Football was a barbaric game in those days and as a result, was really coming under fire. Due to the pressure that coaches were putting on their teams to "win at any price," gridiron injuries and even deaths were on the rise. The public was calling for the abolition of the sport, which soon caught the attention of then-President Theodore Roosevelt. Teddy called upon radical change for the game, and the coaches listened. New rule changes set by faculty representatives included: shortening the halves from 40 minutes to 30, required at least six players on the line of scrimmage, legalizing the forward pass, establishing a neutral zone, and forbidding certain types of hurdling and violent tackling.

The 1902 Gophers, after outscoring their opponents 299-23, generated a lot of enthusiasm on campus. Against Grinnell that year, Robert Liggett scored seven touchdowns! The only points they gave up that season were to Michigan, in a game that they lost 23-6. (Michigan would go on to slaughter Stanford, 49-0, in the first-ever Rose Bowl that year.) School spirit skyrocketed in 1903, when the U of M plowed over everybody, and even got to exact a little revenge on the national champion Michigan Wolverines, whom they battled to a historic 6-6 tie. That game, more so perhaps than any other at that time, would put Minnesota on the football map. It would also be the start of an amazing rivalry that would forever linked together by a small, brown piece of crockery — the Little Brown Jug, which has become one of college football's most enduring trophies.

Cheerleading was Born in Minnesota

In the fall of 1898, then student Johnny Campbell offered to lead organized cheers at football games. This offer came after three straight losses, and a subsequent editorial in the school paper that said, "Any plan that would stir up enthusiasm for athletics would be helpful." Campbell had a plan, and he began to lead organized cheers at the home game against Northwestern. Minnesota won 17-6, and much of the credit went to Campbell and his "yell leaders." At that late-season game, the tradition of cheerleading was born.

Johnny Campbell

Rah-Rah-Rah for Ski-U-Mah!

The Legend of the Little Brown Jug

On October 31, Halloween day, 1903, the undefeated Gophers hosted the undefeated Michigan Wolverines at Northrop Field. The game had all the hype of a modern day Super Bowl going in, and left the fans begging for more when the final whistle was blown. A huge bonfire was lit for thousands of fans the night before this classic showdown of titans, which featured a couple of would-be coaching legends: Fielding H. (Hurry Up) Yost and Dr. Henry L. Williams. Yost's "Point-a-Minute" Michigan juggernaut came in with a three year, 29-game unbeaten and untied winning streak. (The team literally averaged about 60 points per 60-minute game while yielding just a couple of touchdowns during the entire streak!) Williams' squad was no slouch either, having won 10 straight coming in, including a 75-0 rout of Iowa, an 85-0 pasting of Hamline and a 112-0 shellacking of Macalester.

The pre-game build-up was tremendous, and the fans got there early. Northrop's 20,000 wooden seats were filled beyond her capacity, while thousands of other die-hard fans scrambled onto neighboring roof-tops in hopes of catching a glimpse. One newspaper account read: "By nine in the morning the trees and telegraph poles overlooking Northrop Field began to fill and by ten not a point of vantage from which the field could be seen was left unoccupied."

The game got underway that Saturday afternoon with the Gophers outplaying the Wolverines in a scoreless first half — piling up 17 first downs to the Wolverines' three. A disallowed safety and a missed place-kick were all that Michigan could muster as Minnesota's defense played big. Willie Heston, Michigan's All-American Running Back was held in check during the first half by a venerable United Nations-like defense that included the likes of a 140-pound Jewish Quarterback/Cornerback named Sig Harris, a pair of Chippewa Native American and African American Defensive Ends in Ed Rogers and Bobby Marshall, respectively, along with an assortment of Germans, Italians and Swedes. (Incidentally, Marshall became just the first African American to play in the conference.)

The second half was another story though, as Heston, who finished his collegiate career with 93 TDs, finally capped off a solid Michigan drive on a one yard touchdown plunge to make it 5-0. (Touchdowns were worth five points back then.) The extra point was good and the lead now stood at 6-0. The Gophers mounted a comeback, but by then nearly all of their starting running backs — Earl Current, James Irsfield and Otto Davies, had each gone out with injuries. Even Harris' 43-yard kick-off return in the third quarter couldn't get the Maroon and Gold on the board. Since no one had been able to score a touchdown against Michigan up to that point in the season, things started to look bleak.

The Little Brown Jug

On defense, Harris was a one-man wrecking crew, making game-saving tackles all day on Heston. On one play, an end-around, he hit Heston so hard that both of them were knocked unconscious. They were both revived however, and both continued to play. Coach Williams, ever the innovator, had shut down Heston by devising a seven-man defensive line (teams of this era had consisted of nine-man lines), with the other four players dispersed behind — like modern-day defensive backs. Even if Heston broke through the line, he would have four others there to deal with. It is something we take for granted today, but back in the day it was revolutionary.

After another series, Minnesota's Freddie Burgan returned a short punt to the Michigan 38-yard line. (Punting was the one area of Michigan's game that was rusty, after all, up until this game they had not punted all season long — they never needed to!) With the good field position, things started to look up. Fred "Germany" Schacht, a huge 210-pound lineman and All-American from Fergus Falls, who was now

playing running back, along with Winona's James Kremer, alternated on carrying the ball deep into Wolverine territory. Then, on third and "last down," from the Michigan three, Egil Boeckmann, on a cross-buck, dove straight through the hole offensive Tackle Dan Smith had opened for him into an area of the end zone nicknamed "coffin corner." (Back in the day team's had three downs to go five yards for a first down on the 110-yard field.) With the score 6-5, the drama began to unfold with regards to the matter of the extra point.

In those days, an extra point had to be attempted from behind the spot where the touchdown was scored, unless a team made successful "punt-out," in which case the extra point could then be attempted from a better angle. The Gophers did just that, thanks to the leg of Kremer, who punted it straight up in the air from his 15-yard line and straight down to the awaiting Burgan, who came down with the "jump-ball" in the end zone. Burgan then held on for dear life as he squeezed the cradled ball like a baby, despite the viscous beating he immediately took by the awaiting Michigan players in an attempt to make him drop it. Having now earned the right to try the extra point from a much better angle, team captain Ed Rogers, with Harris holding, calmly came out and kicked it through the uprights for the tie.

It was at that point, despite the fact that there were still a couple of minutes remaining on the clock, that the crowd went nuts and stormed the field. In the pandemonium both coaches conceded the tie, as the festivities, which finally culminated in a downtown Minneapolis parade well into the night, officially began. Streetcars lined up to take the mob of fans downtown to celebrate, as they yelled "Ski-U-Mah!" all the way there. Minnesota was now being heralded as the new "Champions of the West." After the smoke had cleared that next day, the clean-up began. That's when Oscar Munson, a Norwegian immigrant who served as the team's equipment manager, made a discovery of sorts. It had appeared that in the mayhem, the Wolverines had left behind their big water jug. Munson took the jug and, in his thick Scandinavian accent whereupon "j's" were sometimes pronounced as "y's," presented it to Louis Cooke (as in Cooke Hall), then the head of the athletic department, proclaiming: "Jost left his Yug..." (Michigan, fearing some sort of diabolical contamination from the rival Minnesotans, actually brought its own drinking water in a barrel from Ann Arbor. Then, on the morning of the

BOBBY MARSHALL

Bobby Marshall was the first great African American sports legend of Minnesota. The Minneapolis Central High School star went on to become the first man of color to play in the Big Nine (later the Big Ten) as an End for the Gophers. From 1904-06 he led the team to an amazing record of 27-2, while outscoring their opponent 1,238-63. In 1906 he even kicked a game-winning 60-yard field goal in the rain and mud to beat the University of Chicago, 4-2 (field goals counted 4 points back then). He received All-Western honors for all three of his years in Minnesota.

In addition to football, he earned all-conference honors as a first baseman on the baseball team and lettered in track as a sprinter. As a professional, he was a star in football, baseball, boxing and even hockey, where, in 1908, he became the first African American to play professionally, when he suited up for the semi-pro Minneapolis Wanderers, and later with the Hillsdale Hockey Club in Pennsylvania. In baseball he played for the Colored Gophers and the Chicago Leland Giants professional Negro-League teams, and on the gridiron he played professionally with the Minneapolis Deans, Minneapolis Marines, Duluth Eskimos and Rock Island Independents.

He was such an incredible athlete, that after retiring from playing pro football at the age of 44, he even made a comeback at that age of 50 to play in an exhibition game at Nicollet Park. Marshall was such a durable athlete that he never sustained a major injury in nearly 30 years of football. He later became a grain inspector for the state of Minnesota and died on Aug. 27, 1968, at the age of 88. In 1971 he was inducted into the College Football Hall of Fame, and several years later was also named to the National Football Foundation's Hall of Fame. He will undoubtedly be remembered as one of Minnesota's greatest ever all-around athletes.

John McGovern

game, Wolverine team manager Tommy Roberts went out to the Busy Bee Variety Store, on Hennepin Avenue, where he purchased the five gallon water jug for the sum of 30¢.)

Cooke then sent word to Yost back in Ann Arbor, telling him that he had left his water jug behind. "If you want your Jug, you'll have win it back," he said sarcastically. Yost accepted the challenge and thus the Little Brown Jug tradition was born. (Yost would have to wait six years, however, to reclaim the Jug. Due to scheduling problems, the Wolverines and Gophers did not play each other again until 1909. In 1910, Michigan, who had won the Jug back the year before, left the conference in protest against the abolishing of the training table, among other things, and Minnesota didn't have a chance to win it back until 1919. That year the Gophers, lead by their star Arnie Oss, stormed into Ann Arbor and spanked the Wolverines, 34-7, on their own Ferry Field. When Minnesota asked for the symbolic trophy at the end of the game, Michigan mysteriously couldn't find it. But the Gopher players persisted, until Wolverine equipment manager Henry Hatch came up with it after a short time, saying that he found it "overgrown behind a clump of shrubbery near the gym." (In reality it was found padlocked inside a trophy case inside the gymnasium!)

Cooke, who kept the jug on his desk for those first six years, even went ahead and painted the score of the game on it with a big "6" for Minnesota, dwarfing a little "6" for Michigan. Under that he painted the caption: "Michigan Jug — Captured by Oscar on October 31, 1903." (Scores of each game have since been added to the vessel, which was later repainted brown with both a maroon and blue "M" on each side, representing the colors of the two Universities.) Cooke once mused of the strange power within the stoneware crock, "I sometimes think that the jug has been filled with spirits, not alcoholic, but the disembodied spirits of the countless players who have fought for it on the gridiron..." It is without question the most famous of all college rivalry trophies, and no other inanimate object can come close to the aura of tradition like that of the Little Brown Jug.

Simply Dominant

After outscoring their opponents 618-12 in 1903, the Gophers once again went undefeated in 1904, even bettering their scoring margin of the year before to an amazing 725-12. (Those 725 points remain second all-time to only Harvard's record of 765 back in 1886.) One of the highlights of the season came against Grinnell, whom the Gophers thrashed, 146-0. At the time it broke what was referred to as the "World's Scoring Record," with the previous honor being held by Michigan, who had previously beaten West Virginia, 130-0. Against Wisconsin that year Minnesota racked up an amazing 1,183 yards of offense! The Gophers were led that season by All-American Center Moses Strathern, from Hastings.

In 1905 the forward pass was finally legalized, making the game much more exciting and much more tactical. The Gophers suffered their first loss in two years when they were beaten in by Wisconsin, 16-12. The heartbreaking contest featured by long runs by Wisconsin's All-American Running Back Ralph Vanderboom, and Minnesota's star Halfback Joe Cutting. They did manage to go 10-1 that year, even outscoring their opponents 542-22. As far as Doc Williams' first five-year report card, a not too shabby 52-3-3 overall record.

From there the team went on to win Big Eight crowns in 1906, 1909, 1910, 1911 and 1915, while only once losing more than two of their seven games. (Under President Theodore Roosevelt's sports initiative recommendation, teams now only played seven-game schedules.) The U of M won the conference title in 1906, on Bobby Marshall's 60-yard kick at the buzzer to defeat Amos Alonzo Stagg's University of Chicago Maroons, 4-2. (A field goal counted four points at the time.) Their only loss that year, 17-0, came against Pop Warner's famous Carlisle Indians, who were led by future NFL Hall of Famer, Jim Thorpe. The Gophers came back to beat the Indians that next year though, behind the legendary running of Minnesota's Left End, Ed Chestnut, who recovered an Indian fumble on the Gopher goal line and raced 100 yards for the game-winning touchdown.

Five-foot-five Gopher Quarterback Johnny McGovern, a native of Arlington, Minn., was the first to finally get a hang of this new forward passing thing, and for his efforts was named as the team's first consensus Walter Camp All-American in 1909. McGovern was also a terror on defense, a great passer and receiver, a talented punter and drop-kicker, and an overall excellent field general. McGovern, despite having a broken collarbone, played heroically against Michigan that year, only to come up short as the team was beaten, 15-6, for its only loss. In 1910 the game was divided into four equal quarters, instead of two halves. Leading the charge that year was Tackle James Walker, a Minneapolis native who became Minnesota's second consensus Walter Camp All-American.

In 1913 Clark Shaughnessy earned All-American honors as a fullback and tackle. (Shaughnessy would later become known for his coaching exploits, as he coached Tulane, Loyola, Chicago, Stanford, Maryland, Pittsburgh and finally the Los Angeles Rams. A student of the game, he studied military tactics for strategy and is also credited with inventing the "Man in Motion T—Formation.") Another interesting thing happened in 1914. That was the first year that the University featured a homecoming game, complete with a campus bon fire to evoke a plethora of school spirit.

The 1903 Gophers outscored their opponents by an unbelievable 618 to 12 margin

The Gophers of 1915 featured perhaps one of the toughest offense backfields in college football prior to World War I: the trio of two-time All-American End Bert Baston of St. Louis Park, Half Back Arnold 'Pudge' Wyman and ace Running Back and team captain, Bernie Bierman. (Incidentally, Bierman took over the captain's position from All-American End Lorin Solon, who was ruled ineligible when it was found out that he played pro baseball under an assumed name. Solon scored four touchdowns in the Gopher's win over Iowa State just prior to the Illinois game.) Next up were the Illini, and due in large part to Bierman's untimely sprained ankle, the Illini managed to eke out a 6-6 tie with the Gophers. Minnesota drew first blood in the opening quarter of the game when Joe Sprafka scored on a 29-yard run around the left end. Kicker Al Quist then failed to convert what could have been the winning point, as Illinois answered by scoring in the second quarter on a fourth down pass from Bart Macomber to Potsy Clark. When Macomber's extra point kick went wide, the score remained tied. The Gophers outplayed the Illini down in the sweltering heat of Champagne for the rest of the game, but just couldn't get into the end-zone.

Bierman's ankle would recover though, and thanks to his two touchdowns and four pass interceptions, Minnesota went on to defeat Wisconsin, 20-3, to finish the season unbeaten and tied for a share of the Big Nine crown. Wyman to Baston was the ultimate dynamic duo that year, as Baston, a tireless work-horse with tremendous leaping ability, had established himself as one of the game's premier receivers.

All-American Quarterback Clare (Shorty) Long, led the 1916 Gophers to what Walter Camp, the era's preeminent football expert, had called the "most perfect team of history." After blowing out nearly everyone that season, including a 67-0 thrashing of Iowa, and an 81-0 spanking of South Dakota, Coach Bob Zuppke's Fighting Illini, led by the Papa Bear himself, George Halas, came to town. Despite being considered as three-touchdown underdogs, Illinois would catch the Gophers off guard. The Illini came out and did something unheard of — they passed on first down. In addition, Zuppke had scouted and capitalized on a bizarre Gopher superstition whereby he learned that they opened each game by giving the pigskin to Sprafka, Wyman and Long, always in succession and always in the same order. Zuppke then had his defense key in on those three in succession, with each being stopped cold. On fourth down Minnesota was forced to punt, and so began what was considered at the time by many to be the greatest upset in college football history. The strategy was brilliant, and the Illini pulled off the upset of the century right in front of such legendary prognosticators as Walter Camp, E. C. Patterson of Colliers Magazine and Grantland Rice, who each made the trek to Minneapolis to see the squad first hand.

Bert Baston

Down 7-0 early in the first, Wyman threw an interception into the hands of Illinois' Kraft, who ran 55 yards for a TD. Minnesota got on the board in the second half on a key fourth down play when Sprafka shot into the end-zone from the five. Wyman booted the extra point and the Gophers added a safety late, but came up short, 14-9. With the loss, the embarrassed and dejected Gophers, who were 35-1 odds-on favorites going in, finished in a tie for second in the conference and out of the national championship running. It was even rumored that before the ugly upset that Camp was going to name as many as seven Gophers to his prestigious All-American team. The next day the Chicago Tribune's big front page headline read: "HOLD ON TIGHT WHEN YOU READ THIS!"

The Gophers rebounded that next week, crushing the University of Wisconsin, 54-0, followed by the University of Chicago, 49-0, thus giving legendary coach Amos Alonzo Stagg the worst defeat of his career. After the game a Chicago sports writer commented on the visiting Gophers: "It is impossible to single out one individual star, for every player on the team was a star."

In 1917 the Gophers went 5-1, losing just once to Wisconsin. Leading the way that year was All-American George Hauser, who allowed just one first down all season at the defensive tackle position. World War I soon came on though and Williams lost most of his good prospects to military service. In 1918, despite the fact that several games were played under quarantine — because of an influenza epidemic, Minnesota had a good year, even beating up on Carleton so badly that they were forced to punt 50 times during the game! Another outstanding year was 1919, when the speedy Half Back Arnie Oss suited up for the Gophers. Oss single-handedly beat Indiana, and then had the game of his life against Michigan, scoring on an amazing 67-yard zig-zag run en route to crushing the Wolverines by the final of 34-7. For the first time since 1903, the Little Brown Jug would come home.

Harold Hanson

After Williams posted just average teams in both 1920 and 1921, the University Athletic Board, which had a lot of power in those days, fired him as the team's head coach. One of the final straws came in 1921 when Williams finally gave in to demands that he put numbers on his players' uniforms. Instead of using the one and two digit variety, however, he instead put four digits on each player so that the fans were just as confused as the team's opposition. It was a bitter ending for one of Minnesota's greatest coaches. Many didn't realize it, but Williams never had more than one assistant through all his years behind the bench, and through it all continued to practice medicine full-time. Sadly, he died only 10 years later, in 1931.

There was a great deal of speculation with regards to the good doctor's successor as football coach at Minnesota. Rumors ran rampant with the front-runner appearing to be former quarterback and then current St. Thomas College head coach, Johnny McGovern. But, in a shocker, the University regents decided to go with William H. Spaulding, then coach of Kalamazoo Normal School in Michigan. Spaulding, who played his football at Wabash College, was an unknown, causing a lot of dissension amongst the Maroon and Gold faithful.

Spaulding got off to a respectable start. One of the more emotional games of his tenure however, came on November 17, 1923, when the Gophers played their last game ever at Northrop Field, defeating a much heavier Iowa squad, 20-7. Earl Martineau scored two of the three Gopher touchdowns, while passing to Ray Eklund for the other.

Perhaps the highlight of Spaulding's three-year tenure came in 1924, when the Gophers, led by All-Americans Ray Eklund, an end from Minneapolis East, and the "Flying Frenchman," Running Back Earl Martineau of Minneapolis West, upset of a formidable Illinois team, 20-7, which featured three-time All-American Halfback Red Grange in its backfield. That game would forever go down in history, not only because of the victory, but because it marked the dedication of Minnesota's newly constructed 55,000-seat Memorial Stadium, or "Brick House" as it would become affectionately known — which paid tribute to the men and women who served in W.W.I. Grange, otherwise known as the "Galloping Ghost," had ironically just christened Illinois' new

Back in the day, fans even climbed the telegraph poles to catch a glimpse

ED WIDSETH

Ed Widseth grew up on a dairy farm in the sleepy northwestern Minnesota town of Crookston. Despite having very little prep football experience, he came to the University of Minnesota and quickly emerged as a star tackle. He became the anchor of an amazing defensive line that led the Gophers to three national championships from 1934 through 1936, of which he was twice named as an All-American.

After playing in the College All-Star game of 1937, the fearsome tackler went on to play five seasons with the NFL's New York Giants, winning all-pro honors three of those years. In 1953 he was inducted into the College Football Hall of Fame, and he was the only Minnesota player named to the National Football Foundation's 11-man All-America squad for the 25 seasons from 1924 through 1948.

After his gridiron career ended in 1941, Widseth spent some time as a recreational specialist in the military. Upon returning home, he became head football coach at St. Thomas, where he coached the Tommies for two years, before entering the food business. For nearly 50 years he owned and operated Hart's Fairway Foods on Central Av. NE in Minneapolis. He died in 1998 at the age of 86.

"If it wasn't for playing football at the ag school in Crookston, I would have spent my life on the farm, milking cows," Widseth later said. "I sure would have never seen New York and a lot of other places."

Memorial Stadium in Champaign just a few weeks earlier by scoring six touchdowns against a fearsome Michigan squad.

Grange opened the scoring in the game when he took the pigskin into the end-zone from around the right end for a touchdown. He then kicked the extra point to make it 7-0 for Illinois. Minnesota would get 20 unanswered points that day though, thanks in large part to the efforts of Running Back Clarence Schutte. After Malcolm Graham's 27-yard double pass reception, Schutte plunged over for a one-yard touchdown to tie it up. Shutte then scored again on a 31-yarder near the end of the first half, followed by yet another five-yard touchdown late in the third after a 34-yard scamper deep into enemy territory. Schutte showed up the great Grange on this day as he finished the afternoon with 282 yards on 32 carries for three TDs. While Minnesota, incredibly, had played the game with just 12 men, Illinois responded by not scheduling the Gophers on their docket for the next 17 years.

Minnesota's hopes for a conference title were dashed on the final Saturday of that season when Michigan, despite being held to just 66 yards rushing, beat the Gophers, 10-0, in Ann Arbor. After three years though, and a modest 11-7-4 record, it had appeared that the nay-sayer's would get their wish. Spaulding was fired at the close of the 1924 season, only to be rehired that next season as UCLA's new head coach. Taking his place was Dr. Clarence W. Spears, a former All-American guard at Dartmouth who had coached at the University of Virginia. Spears had a reputation for being a tough, stern disciplinarian, who played to win. With just a handful of holdovers, Spears dove in with a bunch of youngsters and started the rebuilding process. The early star of the Gophers during this era was a kid by the name of Herb Joesting, a sophomore fullback who would become known simply as the "Owatonna Thunderbolt."

The 1925 Gophers rolled over North Dakota University, Grinnell College and Wabash College, before getting beat by the defending national

Bronko Nagurski

champs from Notre Dame, 19-7. Knute Rockne's Irish, even without the recently graduated legendary "Four Horsemen," waged a terrific battle against the Gophers, who, despite Herb Joesting's brilliant running and Harold Almquist's early touchdown, came up short before the capacity crowd at Memorial Stadium. Even in defeat, Minnesota's fans were pleased at the solid performance. That quickly changed the next week though, when Spears, despite being up 12-0 in the fourth quarter against Wisconsin, sent in an entire team of substitutes who let the cheese-heads back in the game to tie it at 12-12. (The rules at that time dictated that players leaving the game in any quarter could not return to the line-up during the same quarter, so Spears was unable to get his regulars back into the game.) The Gophers came back to beat Butler College, 33-7, and Iowa, 33-0, before being blanked by Michigan, 35-0. (Incidentally, in 1926 the Gophers played Michigan twice, becoming just the first team to ever play a double-header against a conference foe. The Wolverines unfortunately won both games. So big was that Michigan away game, that back home in Minneapolis, reports of the game were telegraphed back and the scrubs

Herb Joesting

who didn't travel, reenacted the plays, live, to the home fans who had gathered to root them on.)

The 1927 season was a special one in Minnesota history, as it marked the entry of International Falls' Fullback/Tackle, Bronko Nagurski into varsity competition. The "Bronk" would go on to become arguably the greatest all-around football player ever to play the game, at any level, eventually landing in the Pro Football Hall of Fame. Led by Nagurski, Quarterback Fred Hovde, All-America Guard Harold Hanson, and a trio of running backs in Herb Joesting, Mally Nydahl and Shorty Almquist, the 1927 Gophers had their most successful season under Dr. Spears. In their first undefeated campaign since 1915, Minnesota, despite a pair of ties with Notre Dame, 7-7, (on Nagurski's forced fumble which set up Herb Joesting's fourth-quarter, fourth-down pass to Len Walsh), and Indiana,14-14, went on to earn a share of the conference crown with Illinois by defeating Michigan, 13-7 (as Joesting and All-American End Kenneth Haycraft tallied for the Gophers in this one, as more than 10,000 fans made the trip to Ann Arbor to watch the Gophers reclaim the Jug), Iowa, 38-0, Wisconsin, 13-7, North Dakota University, 57-10, Oklahoma Aggies, 40-0, and Drake University, 27-6. The Bronk made his presence felt on the field that year by literally knocking out several blockers and passers by running them over.

In 1928 Bronko single-handedly beat the top-ranked Wisconsin Badgers, terrorizing them up an down the field with ferocious hits and bone crunching running. He forced and recovered the fumble that set up his 6-0 game-winning touchdown, then saved the day by running down from behind Wisconsin's speedy Bo Cusinier, who was bound for the end-zone late in the game. Then, with time running out, Nagurski intercepted a Wisconsin pass to ice it for the Goph's. Oh, and did I mention that Nagurski played the entire game with his back in a metal brace to protect his broken ribs he was playing with?

Despite the brilliant efforts of All-Americans Bronko Nagurski, End Ken Haycraft and Guard George Gibson, a pair of third place conference finishes in both 1928 and 1929 were not enough to satisfy the Maroon and Gold faithful. (The Gophers lost only four games in those two seasons by a total of just five points.) As a result, the colorful Dr. Spears, after five respectable seasons in Minnesota, resigned to become the head coach at the University of Oregon. University President Lotus Coffman then shocked everyone by announcing that Herbert Orrin (Fritz) Crisler, an assistant to Amos Alonzo Stagg at the University of Chicago, would become the Gopher's new coach and athletic director. The selection was once again a controversial one, as the football faithful in Minnesota were unsure of a man who had no head coaching experience.

Crisler scored big points with the alumni, however, in naming his assistant coaches: Bert Baston, Sig Harris and Frank McCormick. His first season was a trying one though, as he remained under the intense media pressure that went along with having the top sports coaching position in the Midwest. The players were having a hard time adjusting from Spears' military-like practices, to Crisler's quiet and subtle style, which included no profanity.

In 1930 Fritz had some promising rookies in Fullback Jack Manders and Tackle Marshall Wells, as well as some solid holdovers from the Spears era, including: All-American Guard Clarence (Biggie) Munn, Elmer (Bull) Apmann, Pete Somers, Allen (Tuck) Teeter, Lloyd (Snapper) Stein and Clint Riebeth. The team wasted little time in making a name for itself by spank-

BERNIE BIERMAN

Born in 1894 to German parents on a farm near Springfield, Minn., Bernie Bierman's boyhood home was in Litchfield. As a youngster, Bernie had to overcome a bone infection in his leg that kept him bed-ridden and on crutches. But, after going through several operations to correct the problem, he quickly emerged as a prep star in football, baseball, basketball and track at Litchfield High School. (His family later moved to Detroit Lakes, and as evidence of his stature as a local legend, all three communities claimed him as their own home-town hero!) From there he decided to follow in his big brother Alfred's footsteps and play ball at the University of Minnesota. There, as an All-Conference halfback, Bernie captained the undefeated 1915 Big Ten title team.

Bierman was a three-sport letterman at the U of M, also starring on the basketball team and running track as well. After graduating, he went on to become a successful high school coach in Bill___ Montana before going off to fight in World War I., as a Captain in the Marines. "The Marine Corps taught me discipline, organization and to love life," Bierman would later say.

Returning from the service in 1919, he took over as the head coach at Montana University, where he remained until 1922. Bierman left coaching after that season to work for a Minneapolis bond house, but came back that next year to become an assistant under former Gopher teammate, Clark Shaughnessy, at Tulane University. After a couple of seasons in New Orleans, he headed west, to take over as the head coach at Mississippi A&M. Two years later, he returned to serve as the head coach of Tulane. He guided the Green Wave from 1927 to 1932, posting a 39-10-1 record and even leading the squad to a 1931 Rose Bowl appearance.

In 1932 Bierman came home to be named as the head coach the University of Minnesota, where he became a living legend. Known as the "Gray Eagle," for his prematurely gray hair, Bernie could flat-out coach. He could also recruit, which he did like no other in the program's history. His rosters were loaded with big Minnesota farm kids and leather-tough kids from the neighborhoods of Minneapolis and St. Paul. He trained them mercilessly, sometimes six days a week for as long as he felt necessary.

During his first ten years as head coach (1932-41), better known as the "Golden Era," the Gophers not only won seven Big Ten titles, they went undefeated for five of those seasons winning as many national championships. During that amazing span, the Maroon and Gold went three straight seasons and half way through a fourth without a defeat, losing just eight conference games during that unbelievable stretch.

"Bernie was a task master and you had to survive to play for him," said former player Bud Grant. "You were tested all the time and the people who survived, played. It was like the Marines. A lot of people went by the wayside. If you could survive the practices and scrimmages and not get hurt, then you could play. Bernie was from a different era of football back then."

His players were schooled in practice and on timing to such a degree that Bierman would inspect their footsteps in the grass to see if they went where they were supposed to go as blockers, tacklers, or runners. They also got a good dose of Bierman's philosophy, whether they wanted it or not: "There's only one thing worse than going into a game convinced you can't win," said Bierman. "That's going into a game convinced you can't lose."

In 1942, Bierman rejoined the military for a three-year stint to serve in W.W.II. He then returned to the University of Minnesota for six more seasons before finally retiring from coaching in 1950. With a 93-35-6 coaching record, Bernie was without question the greatest college football coach in Gopher history. A recipient of numerous Coach of the Year awards, he was later inducted into the College Football Hall of Fame.

Asked about the secret to his success, the Gray Eagle said this: "There's nothing secret about blocking, tackling and hard charging. That's fundamental. Given a reasonable share of material that has speed, brains, some brawn and a burning desire to give — and school it as thoroughly as possible in these fundamentals — then, with a few good breaks, you're bound to win once in a while."

Upon his retirement, he spent some time as a color commentator on Gopher radio broadcasts. He later moved to California, where, in 1977 he died at the age of 82.

Dick Smith

ing South Dakota State, 48-0, in its season opener. But, after a 33-7 loss to a very mediocre Vanderbilt squad, Fritz found himself in the hot-seat. To make matters worse, Pop Warner's top-ranked Stanford Indians were coming to town that next Saturday to battle his Gophers. Crisler remained calm though, and thanks to the efforts of All-American triple-threat Guard Biggie Munn, who punted, ran, and passed, Minnesota held the Indians to a scoreless tie in what was considered as one of the biggest upsets of the day.

The Gophers squeezed out a 6-0 victory over Indiana that next week, but then lost, 27-6, to a great Northwestern team which had tied Michigan for the Conference title. The highlight of the Northwestern game was Kenny MacDougall's 51-yard touchdown run through the entire Wildcat defense. After smashing South Dakota, 59-0, the Gophers lost a heartbreaker to Michigan 7-6, only to drop a 14-0 decision to Wisconsin in the final game of the season.

Minnesota closed out the 1931 season with a fifth place, 3-2 conference finish. Perhaps their biggest game of the year came against Ohio State, in what was considered to be the first ever post-season charity game. More than 40,000 fans showed up to watch Jack Manders score a pair of TDs as the Gophers beat the Buckeyes, 19-7, at the Brickyard. Proceeds raised from the game then went to the families of thousands of needy unemployed men and women during the Depression.

With the mediocre season, Crisler, after just two years at the helm, was replaced by one of Minnesota's most famous of prodigal sons, Litchfield's Bernie Bierman. (Crisler would later coach at Princeton and then at Michigan, where he became one of the conference's most successful all-time coaches.) Bierman, who had been the captain of the 1915 Gopher squad, later coached at the University of Montana, Mississippi A&M and Tulane. In fact, he had just led Tulane to a 21-12 loss to USC in the Rose Bowl only the year before. Bert Baston, the two-time All-America End, stayed on as an assistant with Bierman, as did former teammate George Hauser.

Enter the "Gray Eagle"

By 1932 the country was mired in the Great Depression, and unemployment was running wild. It was during this troubled time, however, that the Gophers would emerge as "America's Team." Perhaps it was because people found a new sense of pride in following the Gophers as a form of cheap entertainment, but for whatever the reason, they were definitely the team of the decade.

A brilliant football tactician, Bierman was a strict disciplinarian and a perfectionist at his trade — so much so even, that his hair turned prematurely gray, thus earning him the nickname of the "Gray Eagle." Bernie demanded a lot out his troops that first season, immediately putting them on a conditioning program like they had never seen before. Bierman refused to allow his players to make stupid mental mistakes and ran them through months of grueling practice sessions to make sure that they got it right.

At the beginning of training camp, Tailback Myron Ubl suffered an injury. His replacement would be a small, speedy kid from Rice Lake, Wis., who, after four years in Dinkytown, would go down as one of the all-time greats — Francis "Pug" Lund. The Pug would play a big role in the team's success that season, as the Gophers opened the Bierman era with a 12-0 win over South Dakota. Minnesota then dropped a 7-0 decision to Purdue, only to rebound for a 7-6 victory over Nebraska on a touchdown by Jack

Memorial Stadium

Manders. Manders, who would go on to become one of the Chicago Bears' greatest all-time place kickers, also added the extra point.

Lund and Manders tore it up that season. In a 21-6 win over Iowa, Lund hit Brad Robinson on a pair of touchdowns, and in a 7-0 victory over Northwestern Lund connected with Bob Tenner for the game-winner. Then, along with Pug's 233 yards rushing, Manders scored three touchdowns in a 26-0 victory over Mississippi. After losing to Wisconsin, 20-13, on a last-second play, followed by a 3-0 loss to Michigan, in a game played in below-zero temperatures, the Gophers finished their season with a respectable 5-3 record. That loss was significant for one reason and one reason only. It would be the last Gopher loss over the better part of the next four years.

Bierman came back with a renewed vigor in 1933. His practices became more intense, he became more demanding, and he simply

Ken Haycraft

wouldn't tolerate ineptitude. If a player screwed up, the "Prussian General," as he became known, would simply say, "Take a lap around the field and make up your mind if you're going to do it right!" He even ended each practice by lining up the offense on the 20-yard line and have them run 15 perfect plays right down the field. If someone goofed during the drill on play No. 14, the whole team would start all over again from the 20. In addition, the last formality of the day meant having the entire team run laps around the field. As players passed Bierman, he would call out their names in the order with which they could hit the showers. If you practiced hard that day, your name got called early. If you messed up... you ran! It was an exhausting ritual that forced the players to try harder than ever to get it right.

The 1933 season was a pivotal one for the Gophers, as they definitely turned the corner into becoming one of football's greatest dynasties. One of the first things that Bernie did that year as to change the color of the squad's uniforms to gold. That year the "Golden Gophers," as they were tabbed by local sports radio legend Halsey Hall, hit the gridiron with a new sense of purpose. (Incidentally, not only did Bierman change the uniforms to give the team a new sense of pride and identity, but also, for a bit of camouflage! "It was hard for teams to pick up the ball with our players wearing those mustard-colored uniforms," Bierman later quipped.)

The junior class of Lund, Milt Bruhn, Butch Larson and Phil Bengston was joined by a supporting cast of sophomores led by Fullback Sheldon Beise, Quarterback Glenn Seidel, Babe LeVoir, and Dick

Smith. In addition, George Svendsen and Bill Bevan returned home from Oregon, where they had gone to play for Doc Spears. Bierman also devised a new, revolutionary blocking strategy for his Gophers which entailed "hole" blocking. Rather than assigning his blockers to specific linemen, he assigned them to block in specific areas, or holes, where the play was going to be run, regardless of which defensemen were in their way.

Led by Lund, who gained more yards than did all of his opposing teams' backfields that season, the team responded by putting together their first undefeated season since 1927. While the squad won four games, including a 7-3 win over eastern power Pittsburgh, thanks to a pair of Babe LeVoir interceptions and Bob Tenner's late TD, they also tied four games. One of them was to the likes of an undefeated Michigan squad, 0-0, whereupon a Bill Bevan game-winning field goal attempt fell short in the game's final moments. The final game of the season was a wild one as the Gophers, on Pug Lund's one yard TD plunge late, beat Wisconsin, 6-3, in a freezing, windy blizzard at Memorial Stadium. The 4-0-4 Gophers finished in second place that year, with the cream of their young crop of talent ready to rise up and take over.

"You men have it in you to be champions," said Bierman before the start of the 1934 season. So dedicated were the players, that Pug Lund, after badly breaking his often-dislocated finger (from a prep pole-vaulting accident) in training camp, even opted to have it amputated so that it wouldn't slow him down and hurt the team. A couple of new additions were thrown into the mix that year as well.

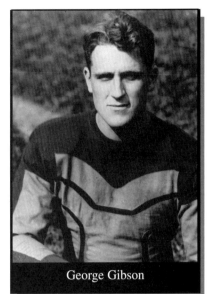

George Gibson

One was a bone-crushing fullback by the name of Stan Kostka, a large Pole from South St. Paul, who joined the Gophers after spending a year in Oregon, who played behind Beise. (Like a runaway tank, Kostka quickly became known as the "Hammer of the North.") The other was a big kid by the name of Ed Widseth, who had grown up in the tiny potato farming town of Gonvick, in Northwestern Minnesota. Widseth, whose family immigrated from Norway, was too busy helping out on the family potato farm to attend high school, so never got around to enrolling until he was 19. He finally graduated from Crookston High School, and made his way south, to Minneapolis, where the future three-time All-American would go down as one of the greatest tackles in the history of college football. With team captain and Center Roy Oen as the only 1933 regular lost to graduation, the '34 Gophers, two-deep at literally every position, knew that they were on the verge of something special.

North Dakota State was the team's first casualty, losing by the score of 56-12. Kostka was the story in this game, as he came in to spell Beise, and finished with four touchdowns. George Roscoe, backup to Pug Lund, also scored a pair of touchdowns, including a 76-yard punt return. Kosta didn't stop there though, scoring another pair that next week in a 20-0 romp over Nebraska. All-American Guard, Bill Bevan, also intercepted a pass and took it 28 yards for a touchdown in this one as well. (Just how tough was Bevan? He was the last known player in the Big Ten to play without a helmet!) After that, Minnesota boarded the train out east to Pittsburgh, where their upcoming clash with the Panthers was billed as the undisputed "game of the year," with national championship implications riding on its outcome.

Butch Larson

Ever the psychologist, Bierman's true colors came out for all to see in this epic game. Knowing that Pittsburgh was unofficially considered as a "semi-pro" program back in those days, due to the speculation that its kids received some form of "compensation" for playing, Bierman figured that many of them weren't as dedicated to the game as his tired, hungry and broke Gophers were. With that, he devised a game plan wherein he would simply punish the Panthers by giving them the ball over and over again, until they cracked under his team's enormous defensive pressure. By the start of the third quarter Pittsburgh was up 7-0 on Mike Nicksick's 64-yard touchdown run, while the Gophers hadn't even made a first down. In fact, they were punting the ball on third and even second downs just to tire out their offense. Never fretting though, Bierman knew his gamble would pay off. By now, when his Gophers laid their blocks, they could hear their opponents across the line groan in pain.

Late in the third, Pug Lund, who was somehow playing with a severely injured thigh, punted his 13th ball of the game deep into Panther territory and into the arms of an awaiting receiver. It just so happened that at that exact moment Ed Widseth showed up to say hello, as he delivered one of the hardest hits in Gopher history on the poor, unsuspecting sap. The ball flew out and into the arms of another All-American End, Butch Larson. This time the Gophers, with great field position, marched into the end-zone behind a trick play from Lund, who faked an end-around, and instead pitched the ball to End Julie Alphonse on a naked reverse that turned into a 22-yard touchdown. (Bill Bevan converted to knot the score at seven points apiece.) After more punishment by the Gophers' defense, which had knocked just about all of the steam out of the Panthers offense, the Gophers got the ball back and headed downfield. Then, on fourth down, from the Pitt 17-yard line, Kostka took the snap and faked a run, only instead he handed off to Quarterback

PUG LUND

Born and raised in Rice Lake, Wis., Francis "Pug" Lund was a four-sport prep star at Rice Lake High School. In 1931 he headed West, to the University of Minnesota, where before he played football and ran track. The All-American running back would go on to become one of college football's biggest stars. Perhaps his biggest game came in 1934 against the University of Pittsburgh, where he took a lateral and then threw the game-winning touchdown pass to Robert Tenner late in the fourth quarter to give the Gophers their first undefeated national championship. He rejected the many offers to play pro football, and instead began a career in both the automotive and insurance industry.

BUD WILKINSON

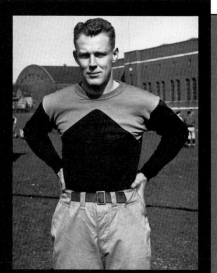

Born in 1916, in Minneapolis, Bud Wilkinson attended the Shattuck School in Faribault. There, he quickly emerged as a brilliant student-athlete both on the gridiron, as a quarterback & guard, and on the ice, as a hockey goaltender. So good was Wilkinson as a goalie, that in 1932, he led Shattuck to an undefeated record and in the process, he went unscored upon over the entire season. He graduated in 1933 as Cum Laude with the rank of First Lieutenant, and headed north, to the University of Minnesota, where he would emerge once again as one of the school's all-time greats.

Bud distinguished himself in football and hockey in Gold Country, even finding time to also letter in golf. As a guard on the 1934 and '35 undefeated national championship teams, he was termed by the famous writer Grantland Rice as "The best offensive guard in college football." Due to injuries, Bernie Bierman asked Wilkinson if he would switch from guard to quarterback that next year. He did, and in 1936, Bud directed Minnesota to their third straight undefeated national championship.

When it was all said and done, Wilkinson had done it all. Not only was he an All-American goalie on the Gopher Hockey team, but he had also garnered back-to-back All-American honors on the gridiron. In addition, he also won the school's highest honor for scholastics and sports — the Big Ten Medal of Honor.

Following graduation, he played in the college All-Star game, quarterbacking the collegiates to a 7-0 victory over the Green Bay Packers, the first time in history the All-Stars had beaten the pros. He also played on the Galloping Gophers, an all-star basketball team that traveled around the Midwest playing independent teams, including the Harlem Globetrotters, whom they defeated.

From there Wilkinson went on to Syracuse University, where, in addition to serving as an assistant football coach under Ossie Solem, he earned his Masters Degree in English. He returned to Minnesota briefly as an assistant to Bernie Bierman before being commissioned in the US Navy.

After the war, he was considered for the Gopher coaching job, but he turned it down instead going to the University of Oklahoma, where he would become the team's head coach in 1947. At OU Wilkinson would forever change the game, and in the process become one of college football's greatest ever coaches.

After tying for the 1947 championship, the Sooners won 12 straight conference championships. Additionally, in between 1953 and 1957, his teams won 47 consecutive games over five straight undefeated seasons — an all-time national record. His teams also appeared in eight Sugar & Orange Bowl games, and he was named as the Coach of the Year on numerous occasions as well. His record at OU was an astounding 145-29-4, with three national titles to boot. At the time of his retirement, in 1963, Bud had become the 'Winningest' coach in college football.

He was also an innovator. He is credited for creating the "Swinging Gate" formation and a 1950s version of the "no-huddle" offense which he called the "Go-Go offense" He also didn't believe in red-shirting, and he graduated an incredible 90% of his student-athletes.

His coaching accolades are too many to mention. Among the major ones include being inducted into the College Football and National Football Coaches Hall of Fames, being elected president of the American Football Coaches Association and receiving the Sports Illustrated Silver Anniversary All-American Award in 1962. (In 1983, his No. 22 was also the first Shattuck football jersey ever to be retired.)

After retiring, he even ran for senate in 1964, where despite winning the Republican primary, lost the general election. Then, after a career in TV broadcasting, among other business interests, Wilkinson later coached in the NFL for the St. Louis Cardinals in 1978 and 1979. He hung em' up after just two sub-par seasons behind the bench though, and returned to the TV booth, where he was an analyst for both ESPN and ABC.

In addition to later becoming OU's Athletic Director, Wilkinson led quite a celebrated life after football. He was a consultant to President Nixon and a member of the White House Staff from 1969-1971. He was a special consultant to President Kennedy on physical fitness from 1961-1964, and he served as the Republican National Committeeman for Oklahoma during the late 1960s.

Then, in 1994, after battling heart problems, Wilkinson died at the of 77 in St. Louis. He will always be regarded as one of Minnesota's greatest all-time athletes, coaches and humanitarians.

Glenn Seidel, who then pitched it to Lund around the right end. Pug then pulled up short and fired a bullet to Bob Tenner, who trotted into the end-zone from the 10. This classic variation of the famous "buck lateral" series made it 13-7 in favor of the Gophers. Pittsburgh rallied late, but after being stopped four straight times by Bevin up the middle, this one was over.

After rolling Iowa, 48-12, in a game which saw Kostka score three touchdowns and Julius Alfonse rush for two more, the Gophers then pounded Michigan, 34-0, thanks to touchdowns from five different players. Michigan, who was led by future U.S. President, Center Gerald Ford, was a team that required yet another tactical adjustment by Bierman, as his club went into half-time tied at 0-0. That's when the Gray Eagle went to the blackboard, as he did so often, and diagrammed out each adjustment that needed to made to counter the Wolverine defense. With that, the superbly conditioned Gophers, who held the Wolverines to just 56 total yards of offense, cruised to the shut-out victory.

After blanking Indiana, 30-0 (The Hoosiers got a whopping zero yards of total offense on the day!), and rolling Chicago, 35-7, the Gophers wrapped up their undefeated season by white-washing a Wisconsin team coached by Dr. Clarence Spears, 34-0. Lund, the featured attraction in Bierman's single-wing attack, had now earned the label "Ironman of the Big Ten." He proudly ended his collegiate career in style by scoring a pair of touchdowns on the cheese-heads, including a 59-yarder up the gut. Dick Smith also scored on 25-yard tackle-eligible pass from George Roscoe, while Babe LeVoir and Whitman Rork each tallied against the Badgers as well.

(In making his annual All-American announcement, Grantland Rice wrote of Lund: "As a ball carrier, passer, kicker, blocker and tackler, he has carried out a heavy assignment. He has been battered and broken up — teeth knocked out, finger amputated, thumb broken — but through all this blasting barrage, Lund has carried on." Later, in 1959, Sports Illustrated named Lund as a Silver Anniversary All-American.)

With that, for the first time in school history, Minnesota was declared as national champions. They also captured their first conference title since 1915, as Lund, Larson and Bevan were all named as All-Americans. So awesome were the 1934 Gophers that they needed to pass just 36 times throughout the entire season, completing 15. Conversely, their defense allowed only 28 pass completions over the season, en route to intercepting 21. Oh yeah, the offense, which outscored its opponents that year 270-38, and averaged better than five touchdowns per game, also pounded out 300 yards of rushing each Saturday as well. Bierman knew how to recruit in his own backyard, and Minnesota was producing serious talent back in the day. So deep were the Gophers at every position that no longer did they have to platoon each player to play both offense and defense for all 60 minutes — giving them a much needed rest to recharge their batteries between plays. (This revolutionary system of two offensive and defensive units, didn't catch on with the rest of the football world until the mid 1940s.) So good was the second team, that, in an attempt to get bumped up to the first team, they used to have bloody scrimmages after practice which often led to fist-fights.

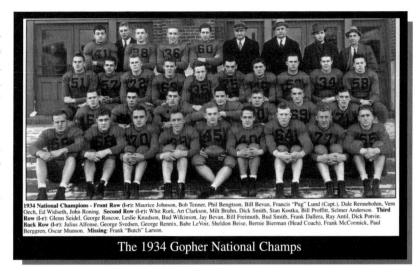

1934 National Champions - Front Row (l-r): Maurice Johnson, Bob Tenner, Phil Bengtson, Bill Bevan, Francis "Pug" Lund (Capt.), Dale Rennebohm, Vern Oech, Ed Widseth, John Roning. Second Row (l-r): Whit Rork, Art Clarkson, Milt Bruhn, Dick Smith, Stan Kostka, Bill Proffitt, Selmer Anderson. Third Row (l-r): Glenn Seidel, George Roscoe, Leslie Knudson, Bud Wilkinson, Jay Bevan, Bill Freimuth, Bud Smith, Frank Dallera, Ray Antil, Dick Potvin. Back Row (l-r): Julius Alfonse, George Svedsen, George Rennix, Babe LeVoir, Sheldon Beise, Bernie Bierman (Head Coach), Frank McCormick, Paul Berggren, Oscar Munson. Missing: Frank "Butch" Larson.

The 1934 Gopher National Champs

"My job could be much simpler in selecting the 1934 Collier's All-America team," said Grantland Rice, "by naming the entire University of Minnesota eleven, one of the greatest, if not the greatest, football teams I ever saw." The team, which Rice dubbed the "Destroyers," had officially ushered in the most amazing period in Minnesota's gridiron history — the "Golden Era," which, over the next decade would bring the Gophers a total of five national championships and six Big Ten Conference titles.

Back to Back

Bill Bevan

The prospects for the 1935 season were rough, as the team found itself behind the eight-ball even before the team played its first down. Fully 11 lettermen were not to be seen when Fall practice got under way. While seven players had completed their three years of eligibility (Pug Lund, Butch Larson and Bill Bevan, along with Bob Tenner, Phil Bengston, John Ronning and Maurice Johnson), three more lost their eligibility due to a Big Ten transfer rule. The players, George Svendsen, Stan Kostka, and Art Carleson, were all ruled ineligible that season by the conference eligibility board for playing a year of freshman football at Oregon, be-fore transferring to Minnesota. The 11th player was Halfback Julie Alphonse, who failed to make the team due to scholastic difficulties.

The revamped line, which featured Ray King and Dwight Reed at Ends, Dick Smith and Ed Widseth at Tackles, Vern Oech and Shattuck's Bud Wilkinson at Guards and Dale Rennebohm at Center, never missed a beat though, as the Gophers ventured out to repeat as Big Ten and national champions.

After beating North Dakota State, 26-6, with Halfback George Roscoe tossing a pair of TDs to both Ray King and Dwight Reed, the Gophers headed to Lincoln to do battle with the Cornhuskers. There, in the sizzling heat, the Gophers played in what would become one of the classics. George Roscoe quieted the capacity crowd of 37,000 screaming Husker fans by taking the opening kickoff 74-yards deep into Nebraska territory. Sheldon Beise and Roscoe then pounded it down to the three-yard line, only to see the Nebraska line thwart off three touchdown plunges. Then, on fourth down, Seidel lateralled to Beise, who, in turn, faked a dive into the line and instead lateralled it back to Seidel, who then pitched it over to Roscoe, who ran it in around the right end to score. Bud Wilkinson failed to convert, but the Goph's were up 6-0.

Nebraska's defense hung tough in this one, preventing Minnesota on several occasions deep in their own real-estate. The Huskers took the lead on a second quarter 33-yard Jerry LaNoue touchdown run, only to see the Gophers rally behind Roscoe's punt that pinned Nebraska inside their own five-yard line. Then, after holding their offense in check, the Gophers forced a poor punt and got the ball back on the 15-yard line. From there LeVoir and Roscoe drove it down to the five, as Roscoe, who ran for 128 yards that day, took it in for his second score of the afternoon to give Minnesota what would turn out to be the game winner. Wilkinson again failed to convert, but this Gopher defense hung on, despite a desperate rally in the fourth quarter which included a fumbled punt recovery on the Gopher one-yard line. That's when future All-American End Ray King zoned in like a missile and blitzed Husker Halfback Lloyd Cardwell for a loss, even knocking him out cold. Finally, on the fourth down, Husker QB Bauer had Gus Scherer open for a sure touchdown, only to see Dale Rennebohm bat the ball away to ice the game.

The victory over Nebraska was short-lived though, as the Gophers received another jolt just that next week when Quarterback Glenn Seidel suffered a season-ending broken collarbone on a late, touchdown saving tackle, in a 20-0 win over Tulane. Tuffy Thompson and Sheldon Beise each tallied in the game, while Bud Wilkinson gave Minnesota its other touchdown by blocking a punt and then scooping it up and trotting 35 yards into the endzone. Bierman revamped his backfield for the upcoming game against Northwestern by moving Babe LeVoir to Quarterback, George Roscoe to Left Half from Right Half, while George Rennix was put in at Right Halfback. Roscoe, like his predecessor, Pug

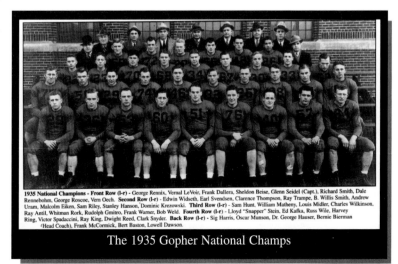

1935 National Champions - Front Row (l-r) - George Rennix, Vernal LeVoir, Frank Dallera, Sheldon Beise, Glenn Seidel (Capt.), Richard Smith, Dale Rennebohm, George Roscoe, Vern Oech. Second Row (l-r) - Edwin Widseth, Earl Svendsen, Clarence Thompson, Ray Trampe, B. Willis Smith, Andrew Uram, Malcolm Eiken, Sam Riley, Stanley Hanson, Dominic Krezowski. Third Row (l-r) - Sam Hunt, William Matheny, Louis Midler, Charles Wilkinson, Ray Antil, Whitman Rork, Rudolph Gmitro, Frank Warner, Bob Weld. Fourth Row (l-r) - Lloyd "Snapper" Stein, Ed Kafka, Russ Wile, Harvey Ring, Victor Spadaccini, Ray King, Dwight Reed, Clark Snyder. Back Row (l-r) - Sig Harris, Oscar Munson, Dr. George Hauser, Bernie Bierman (Head Coach), Frank McCormick, Bert Baston, Lowell Dawson.

The 1935 Gopher National Champs

Lund, was playing a mean Left Half — the key position in Bierman's single-wing attack.

Minnesota then went on to defeat Northwestern, 21-13, behind Thompson's two touchdowns, and Purdue, 29-7, thanks to touchdowns from Thompson, King and Roscoe. Minnesota, now feeling the week-in and week-out pressure of having every team bring their A-Games in an attempt to knock-off the defending national champs, now ventured south to Iowa City, where they took on a very talented Hawkeye squad. Now, Iowa's fans were still upset about their loss from the year before, when they felt that Sheldon Beise deliberately knocked their star Halfback, Ozzie Simmons, out of the game with a cheap-shot. This, of course, was false, as many speculated that the Oz was just acting, but it led to some good drama. Amidst the hostility, Iowa's Governor Clyde Herring added fuel to the fire when he made a statement to the Associated Press that went out to newspapers throughout the country the day before the game. His quote said in effect, that if any Gophers tried to injure Simmons, or any other Hawkeye player this year, that Iowa's spectators at the game would act accordingly.

This statement shocked Coach Bierman, as well as the hoards of Minnesotans who made the trek to Iowa to watch the game. Fearing a mob would break out, Minnesota's Governor, Floyd Olson, stepped in. While many were demanding that he rush National Guardsmen to Iowa City to protect our boys, cooler heads prevailed. In a diplomatic attempt to ease the pre-game tension that had turned into a border war, Governor Olson sent Governor Herring a telegram that read: "I will bet you a Minnesota prize hog against an Iowa prize hog that Minnesota wins." Herring enthusiastically accepted, and thus was born the "Floyd of Rosedale" traveling trophy. The Gophers, who went on to beat the Hawkeyes on a pair of Beise and Thompson touchdowns, then became the proud owners of an award-winning prized porker which was donated by the owner of Rosedale Farms, near Fort Dodge, Iowa. (The hog, who was actually the brother of the celebrity swine from the Will Rogers movie "State Fair," was then named after our beloved Governor, Floyd!) Some years later, after Floyd (the pig) passed on to hog-heaven, a St. Paul artist named Charles Brioschi was commissioned to create a bronze statue of the porker. Today, the last Saturday of every college football season means that the winning team will be able to bring Floyd home with them for one year of bragging rights.

Minnesota then handed Michigan the most lop-sided spanking in team history, crushing the Wolverines, 40-0, in Ann Arbor. Andy Uram and little Rudy Gmitro ran wild in this one, tallying three touchdowns on an amazing total of 460 yards from scrimmage, while Biese and Thompson, who returned a kick-off for an 85-yard TD, also tallied in this blowout as well. The Goph's then finished the season undefeated and ran their string of victories to 17 straight by defeating Wisconsin, 33-7, before a capacity crowd at the Brick Yard. While Biese and Uram each scored, it was once again the 150-pound halfback, Rudy Gmitro, who was the hero, as he electrified the crowd by returning a kick-off 80 yards to pay-dirt. (Incidentally, in the win over Wisconsin, Minnesota scored what might have been the ultimate football play. The next morning's paper showed a photo of Beise's touchdown run, in which all 11 Badgers were on the ground at the same time after being pancaked by their Gopher blockers.) With the win, Minnesota won its second consecutive Big Ten title and was again named as national champions. Dick Smith, Bud Wilkinson and Ed Widseth all earned unanimous All-American honors, while Sheldon Beise and Ray King were named to several mythical squads.

Governor's Floyd Olson & Clyde Herring with Floyd of Rosedale

Floyd of Rosedale... A.D.

Three in a Row

With Washington and Texas being added to the Gophers' schedule, Minnesota had a serious task ahead of them in 1936. With Roscoe, Beise and LeVoir gone to graduation, Bierman once again rebuilt his backfield with a little creativity. This time, he took All-American Guard Bud Wilkinson, and moved him to Quarterback, where he could guide Julie Alphonse (who had now regained his scholastic eligibility), Uram, Vic Spadacinni and Gmitro in his backfield. The backfield was also bolstered by a couple of impact sophomores in Larry Buhler and Wilbur Moore.

The season started off on a wild and crazy adventure that almost never got off the ground. On their way to the University of Washington for their season opener, the Gophers, who were spending the night in Missoula, Montana, woke up to find that their hotel was burning to the ground. While the Gophers luckily escaped without incident, the team was forced to return to their train where they spent the remainder of the evening. Perhaps inspired by their near-death experiences, Minnesota rallied in the fourth to beat the Huskies, 14-7, thanks to a pair of touchdown passes from both Alfonse to Wilkinson and the other from Uram to Ray King. Alfonse also intercepted three passes in the victory.

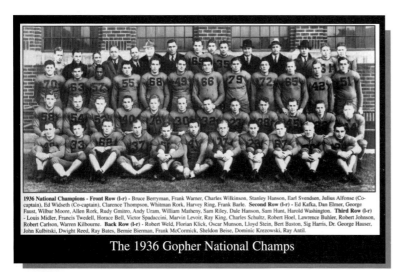

1936 National Champions - Front Row (l-r) - Bruce Berryman, Frank Warner, Charles Wilkinson, Stanley Hanson, Earl Svendsen, Julius Alfonse (Co-captain), Ed Widseth (Co-captain), Clarence Thompson, Whitman Rork, Harvey Ring, Frank Barle. Second Row (l-r) - Ed Kafka, Dan Elmer, George Faust, Wilbur Moore, Allen Rork, Rudy Gmitro, Andy Uram, William Matheny, Sam Riley, Dale Hanson, Sam Hunt, Harold Washington. Third Row (l-r) - Louis Midler, Francis Twedell, Horace Bell, Victor Spadaccini, Marvin Levoir, Ray King, Charles Schultz, Robert Hoel, Lawrence Buhler, Robert Johnson, Robert Carlson, Warren Kilbourne. Back Row (l-r) - Robert Weld, Florian Klick, Oscar Munson, Lloyd Stein, Bert Baston, Sig Harris, Dr. George Hauser, John Kulbitski, Dwight Reed, Ray Bates, Bernie Bierman, Frank McCormick, Sheldon Beise, Dominic Krezowski, Ray Antil.

The 1936 Gopher National Champs

The Gophers then narrowly beat a veteran Nebraska team, 7-0, when Wilkinson caught a short Husker punt and then pitched it to Andy Uram, who bolted down the sideline for a dramatic 78-yard game-winning touchdown with less than a minute to go. After that, Minnesota rolled over Michigan, 26-0, and blanked Purdue, 33-0, as the team ran its unbeaten streak to 28 games and counting. Next up was Northwestern, in Evanston, Illinois, where the Gophers rolled up 243 yards to the Wildcats' 120, but still wound up on the losing end of a 6-0 wet and windy grudge-match. The Cats, who won the game on a late fourth quarter touchdown plunge from Running Back Steve Toth, wound up on the receiving end of a very controversial 15-yard roughing penalty by Ed Widseth, that put the ball on the one-yard line. Northwestern then held off three frantic Minnesota drives that all ended inside their 20-yard line, to preserve what was considered to be one of the biggest upsets in college football history. After the game Widseth insisted that he had not deserved the penalty, and Coach Bierman, after studying the game films, agreed. To put the game into perspective, the A.P. stated that the biggest shock in the world of sports that year was Max Schmeling's knock-out of Joe Louis. No. 2 was Northwestern's upset of the Gophers.

Determined to come back, the Gophers rallied that next week to squash Iowa, 52-0, before closing out the season with wins over Texas, 47-19, and Wisconsin, 24-0. Now, with the Gophers' strong finish, coupled with Northwestern's 26-0 drubbing by Notre Dame, the Associated Press voted that the Gophers were indeed once again the best in the land. So, despite their controversial loss to the Big Ten champion Wildcats, the Gophers, who were rewarded for playing a tough non-conference schedule, had made the improbable national championship three-peat a reality. Leading the post-season award barrage that year was Ed Widseth, who for the third time in his collegiate career, was named as a unanimous All-American. Joining him on other All-American squads were Bud Wilkinson, Andy Uram, Ray King and Julius Alfonse. Notably absent from the list was George Roscoe, who was one of the best natural athletes Minnesota ever produced. (Even today, no team has won three consecutive national titles since the Gophers from 1934-36!)

Minnesota finished undefeated in the Big Ten in 1937, but losing non-conference games to Nebraska and Notre Dame eliminated them from making it four national championships in a row. Led by a couple of sophomore running backs, in Marty Christiansen and Harold Van Every, the Gophers came out with a season opening 69-7 mauling of North Dakota State. Van Every led the team with 147 yards, including a dramatic 76-yard touchdown run.

Andy Uram

Minnesota then only got nine points against Nebraska, those coming on a touchdown pass from Uram to Spadacinni, and a field goal by Horace Bell, as the Cornhuskers scored a pair of touchdowns on key fumble recoveries and came from behind to win, 14-9. The Gophers then beat Indiana, 6-0, on Wilbur Moore's TD, and then creamed Michigan, 39-6, for Bierman's fourth straight Little Brown Jug. In that game Gmitro scored twice and Van Every hit Spadacinni for the clincher. The downside to that game was that Andy Uram broke his arm and was done for the season. To add insult to injury, the team then lost a 7-6 heart-breaker to Notre Dame, as they came back for a second quarter TD on a buck lateral pass that went from Christiansen to Gmitro to Van Every, who then hit All-American Ray King, only to see kicker George Faust's try for the tying point get blocked.

Biggie Munn

After rolling over Iowa, 35-10, Minnesota eked out a bitterly contested match against Northwestern, 7-0, on a touchdown pass from Van Every to King. Wisconsin was then beaten, 13-6, on touchdowns from Bill Matheny and Marty Christiansen to end the season as Big Ten champs.

With Van Every, Christiansen and Moore returning on offense, combined with a solid defense built around Captain Francis Twedell, at Guard, and All-American Butch Nash at End, the Gophers looked to repeat as Big Ten champs in 1938. After beating Washington and Nebraska in their first two games, Minnesota opened their conference schedule by beating Purdue, 7-0, thanks to a Marty Christiansen and Wilbur Moore's 80-yard touchdown march. The Gophers then eked out a 7-6 victory over Michigan, who's new coach was none other than former Gopher skipper Fritz Crisler. The defense was the key in this one, as Eveleth's John Mariucci (the future Godfather of Minnesota hockey) blocked the extra point of Michigan's early touchdown. Wayzata's Harold Van Every, playing with a ruptured kidney, then led the come-from-behind victory by first forcing and recovering a fumble, which led to him throwing a nine-yard tying touchdown pass to Wilbur Moore. George Faust then kicked the game-winning extra point for the rights to the coveted Jug.

The Gophers then met up with their old nemesis from Evanston, the Northwestern Wildcats, who once again had Minnesota's number — this time winning, 6-3. Minnesota then beat Iowa for the eighth consecutive time, 28-0, on a pair of Sonny Franck and Bob Paffrath touchdowns, before falling once again to Notre Dame. In a game that clearly defined what is meant by the "luck of the Irish," Notre Dame posted more touchdowns (three) than it did first downs (two). The Gophers played solid football, but lost, 19-0, on three well executed touchdown plays. (The jinx ended when the schedule makers finally took the Irish off of Minnesota's schedule — it would be 40 years until the two teams met again!)

Bierman punished his players mercilessly that week, getting them so pissed-off at him that they wanted to deck him. The team then took out their frustrations on Wisconsin, with Larry Buhler leading the charge on a 27-yard TD run up the middle to guide the Gophers to a 21-0 victory, and their fourth Big Ten title in five years. Bierman's mind tricks worked every time.

Down in the Dumps

Despite the return of Van Every, Bob Paffrath and Sonny Franck, along with the arrival of a sophomore Running Back named Bruce Smith, 1939 would have to be considered a disaster. After all, it was the beginning of W.W.II. and people's minds were on other, more important issues. While football took a back-seat during the late 1930s and early 1940s, the game, as they say, must still go on. With that, the season opened with the Maroon and Gold annihilating Arizona, 62-0, as Bruce Smith and Franck each got a pair of touchdowns in the win.

The Gophers then dropped a 6-0 decision to Nebraska that next week, followed by a 13-13 tie with Purdue. Shortly thereafter, Minnesota lost to Ohio State, 23-20, as Joe Mernik's tying field goal attempt in the final minutes hit the crossbar. The wheels had come off this well-oiled machine, and before they knew it, they had lost to both Northwestern, 14-7, and Iowa, 13-9. In the Iowa game, Van Every intercepted a pass late in the fourth which had apparently clinched the victory for Minnesota, but a controversial interference penalty was called from 50 yards away from the play and the Hawkeye's

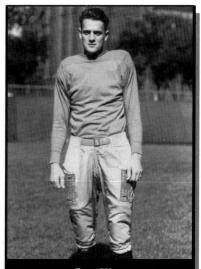

Ray King

BRUCE SMITH

Perhaps famed Minnesota author F. Scott Fitzgerald was thinking of Bruce Smith when once wrote the famous line: "Show me a hero and I will show you a tragedy."

Bruce Smith grew up in Faribault and like his father, Lucius, went on to stardom as a half-back at the University of Minnesota. The blonde haired, blue-eyed Adonis was the prototypical boy-hood idol. He was lightning quick and could run through defenders like a tank. He was a clutch player, who often played hurt and sacrificed his body for the good of the team.

Three times in 1940 alone he scored game-winning touchdowns when his team was behind, including his now infamous 80-yard weak-side reverse through the mud and rain to beat Michigan, 7-6, which made him a virtual house-hold name. Against Iowa in 1941, an injured Smith, after begging to come in late in the game, incredibly, passed or ran for every Minnesota touchdown in a 34-13 win.

The marquis triple-threat tailback of his era, Smith epitomized the single-wing offense and could seemingly do it all. In 1941 the team captain led the Gophers to their second consecutive unde-feated, national championship. For his efforts, Smith, on the day after the Japanese had attacked Pearl Harbor, became Minnesota's first, and only, Heisman Trophy winner, beating out Notre Dame Running Back, Angelo Bertelli.

After graduating, the All-American halfback went on to garner MVP honors in the College All-Star game against the Chicago Bears that summer. That next year, before going off to fight in W.W.II, Smith first went to Hollywood, where he starred in the movie "Smith of Minnesota," about a small-town family whose son becomes an All-American halfback. (A book on his life was also written, appropriately entitled "The Game Breaker.")

Smith went on to become a Navy fighter pilot, where he also played service football for the Great Lakes Navy team. He returned home in 1945, and signed on with the Green Bay Packers and later with the Los Angeles Rams. He played for four years in the NFL, mostly on defense, but injuries prevented him from performing up to his unbelievable collegiate standards.

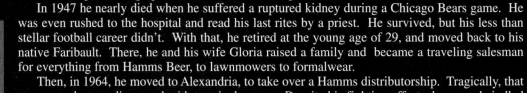

In 1947 he nearly died when he suffered a ruptured kidney during a Chicago Bears game. He was even rushed to the hospital and read his last rites by a priest. He survived, but his less than stellar football career didn't. With that, he retired at the young age of 29, and moved back to his native Faribault. There, he and his wife Gloria raised a family and became a traveling salesman for everything from Hamms Beer, to lawnmowers to formalwear.

Then, in 1964, he moved to Alexandria, to take over a Hamms distributorship. Tragically, that same year he was diagnosed with terminal cancer. Despite his fighting efforts, he soon dwindled from 200 to 90 pounds. On August 26, 1967, at the tender age of 47, Smith finally succumbed to his disease. It was a true tragedy for a real American hero.

He was inducted into the College Football Hall of Fame in 1972, and in 1977, Smith's No.54 became the first Minnesota number to be officially removed from the roster.

"I only have to tell you that when I played against Bruce Smith at Minnesota, he was a pow-erful, hard running back of 205 pounds, and a magnificent specimen of a man," said Michigan All-American Running Back Tommy Harmon. "In fact, I don't know of a man who would better fit the description of an All-American than Bruce Smith. Not only was he a great talent as a football player, but he was a clean living, religious, fine guy off the field as well. He was a champion in the true sense of the word."

scored on the next drive to win it. They did manage to shut down Michigan's star Running Back Tommy Harmon, as Van Every, Franck and Smith each found the end-zone to secure a 20-7 victory over the Wolverines. A 23-7 comeback win over Wisconsin in the final game was inspired by touchdowns from Marty Christiansen, Bruce Smith and Bob Sweiger, as well as a blocked punt for a safety by Bob Fitch. Despite the strong finish, the Gophers finished with a 3-4-1 record and an ugly 7th place conference standing. (Van Every, who earned all-conference honors, would later be named a Silver Anniversary All-America by Sports Illustrated.)

Back to the Promised Land

The 1940 season was a big turn-around in Gopherville, as Minnesota rebounded to finish with an undefeated 8-0 record, another Big Ten title, and yes, their fourth national championship. It would be a story-book season for the Gophers, as they would once again return Bernie Bierman to the promised land. The Gopher line was solid this year with Bill Johnson and Bob Fitch at Ends, Dick Wildung and Urban Odson at Tackles, Bill Kuusisto and Helge Pukema at Guards and Bob Bjorkland at Center. In the backfield were Bruce Smith and George Franck, followed by Bob Paffrath at Quarterback and Bob Sweiger in the Fullback slot.

The season opened with Washington coming to town, as Sonny Franck's second touchdown of the afternoon, a 98-yard kickoff return, iced a 19-14 victory for the men of gold. Nebraska then came to the Brick House and shut-down Franck and Smith, only to see William Daley and William Johnson, who caught a 42-yard TD from Smith, gain nearly 300 yards on the ground in leading the Gophers

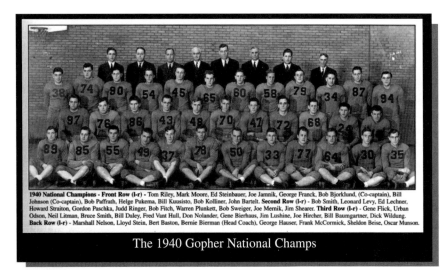

1940 National Champions - Front Row (l-r) - Tom Riley, Mark Moore, Ed Steinbauer, Joe Jamnik, George Franck, Bob Bjorklund, (Co-captain), Bill Johnson (Co-captain), Bob Paffrath, Helge Pukema, Bill Kuusisto, Bob Kolliner, John Bartelt. **Second Row (l-r) -** Bob Smith, Leonard Levy, Ed Lechner, Howard Straiton, Gordon Paschka, Judd Ringer, Bob Fitch, Warren Plunkett, Bob Sweiger, Joe Mernik, Jim Shearer. **Third Row (l-r) -** Gene Flick, Urban Odson, Neil Litman, Bruce Smith, Bill Daley, Fred Vant Hull, Don Nolander, Gene Bierhaus, Jim Lushine, Joe Hircher, Bill Baumgartner, Dick Wildung. **Back Row (l-r) -** Marshall Nelson, Lloyd Stein, Bert Baston, Bernie Bierman (Head Coach), George Hauser, Frank McCormick, Sheldon Beise, Oscar Munson.

The 1940 Gopher National Champs

to a 13-7 victory. Then, at Ohio State, Smith took over, scoring both of Minnesota's touchdowns en route to racking up 134 yards rushing. Franck might have been the hero though, as he made a game-saving play by tackling Buckeye Quarterback Don Scott out of bounds on the Gopher one-yard line as the clock struck zero.

Franck then showed why he was a unanimous All-American selection that year by scoring four touchdowns, two of them on passes from Bruce Smith, in a 34-6 scorching of the Hawkeyes. The celebration would not be long-lived, however; as pesky Northwestern was on deck — a team that had owned the Gophers over the past few seasons. In another barn-burner, the Gophers finally got the monkey off their back by rallying to beat the Cats, 13-12, thanks to a pair of Bob Sweiger touchdown runs combined with a Joe Mernik place-kick. Amazingly, it was Minnesota's first victory at Dyche Stadium in 11 years.

Next up were the undefeated Michigan Wolverines. Led by Bruce Smith's 205 total yards and game-winning 80-yard weak-side reverse touchdown (followed by what would prove to be the game-winning extra-point by Mernik), Minnesota held off the Wolverines by the final score of 7-6 in front of nearly 60,000 Brick House fans. This one came down to a missed Wolverine point-after attempt by Harmon, as the Gopher defense, which fought off four drives that began on a first down inside their own five-yard line, hung on to preserve the victory amidst the memorable Armistice Day blizzard. While Michigan's Heisman Trophy winning running back, Tommy Harmon, did manage to throw a TD pass to Quarterback Forest Evashevski (later to become Iowa's greatest coach) to give Michigan the lead at 6-0, he was once again shut-out, incredibly having never scored against the Gophers in his three varsity seasons as a Wolverine. He did have one last shot at ending the Minnesota jinx, when Michigan End Ed Frutig blocked a Franck punt to give his team the ball on the Gopher three-yard line. But, after three Harmon plunges up the middle, the score remained 7-6, with Minnesota once again keeping the Little Brown Jug.

Dick Wildung

George Franck

(Now, the wonderful part about this particular game was that it finally vindicated Bruce Smith's father's 1910 vow of revenge. You see, the "Myth of Smith" was a legend that began 30 years prior when Smith's dad, Lucius, played End for the Gophers. That year, because of Lucius' missed block while playing Tackle, a position he was thrown into that afternoon due to an injury, Michigan scored the only touchdown of the day and beat Minnesota, 6-0. Lucius took the big game so hard that he vowed to have a son who would one day avenge the tragic loss. His promise came true in 1940 on his son's 80-yard game-winning touchdown. In fact, it was such a compelling story that a Hollywood screenwriter decided to make a movie about it a few years later, entitled: "The Smiths of Minnesota.")

The Golden Gophers then went on to beat Purdue, 33-6, as Franck exploded for an 85-yard opening kick-off runback for a touchdown to send an early message. Then, in the final game of the season, Minnesota defeated Wisconsin, 22-13, as Bill Daley and Bruce Smith each scored on touchdown runs, while George Franck added another on a 20-yard interception return. With the win Minnesota had earned their fourth national championship in seven years. Sonny Franck and Tackle Urban Odson were also both named as All-Americans. (Just how much did this 1940 title team rely on its running game vs. the passing attack? Well, consider this, in the three-game stretch that featured Nebraska, Ohio State and Iowa, Minnesota threw a grand total of three passes... for a grand total of three touchdowns. How's that for pass proficiency?)

The "Talking Play"

With Franck gone to the New York Giants, of the NFL, the 1941 team was all Bruce Smith's. The Captain would lead the defending national champs back to the promised land once again that year, accomplishing something that had never been done before. He became the first and only Gopher ever to win the Heisman Trophy, emblematic of the nation's best collegiate player.

Smith kicked off the season by scoring both of Minnesota's touchdowns in the team's 14-6 victory, and fourth straight over Washington. The Gophers then pummeled Pittsburgh, 34-6, with Smith's understudy, Bud Higgins, scoring three touchdowns. From there the team rolled over the Illini in the Big Ten opener, as Fullback Bill Daley's 72-yard opening-drive touchdown run was just the beginning of a 39-0 pasting.

Then, as was the case the year before, Michigan and Northwestern proved to be the team's biggest foes. The Wolverines were on deck first, and thanks to Bruce Smith's 43-yard pass to sophomore Herman Frickey, which set up Frickey's ensuing game-winning touchdown, Minnesota hung on to win by that same score. Half Back Bill Daley also intercepted a pair of key passes down the stretch to ice it for the Gophers. The Michigan victory proved costly though, as Smith's right knee would be injured just a few plays later. He did manage to play briefly in the first quarter of the Northwestern game, but with Frickey also sidelined, Bierman was forced to concoct a makeshift backfield which featured a pair of Fullbacks in Bill Daley and Bob Sweiger, along with a pair of Quarterbacks in Bill Garnaas and Warren Plunkett.

The Gophers got on the board first in this wild one, thanks to a safety on a poor snap from center. Northwestern took the lead late in the first though, when future NFL great Otto Graham hit Bud Hasse on a touchdown pass to take a 7-2 lead. The game roared back and forth, until Bierman, who needed to do something desperate to get his team back in it, instructed his quarterback to run the "talking play." The now-infamous "talking play" was a

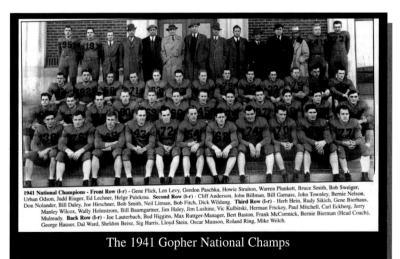

1941 National Champions - Front Row (l-r) - Gene Flick, Len Levy, Gordon Paschka, Howie Straiton, Warren Plunkett, Bruce Smith, Bob Sweiger, Urban Odson, Judd Ringer, Ed Lechner, Helge Pulekma. Second Row (l-r) - Cliff Anderson, John Billman, Bill Garnaas, John Townley, Bernie Nelson, Don Nolander, Bill Daley, Joe Hirschner, Bob Smith, Neil Litman, Bob Fitch, Dick Wildung. Third Row (l-r) - Herb Hein, Rudy Sikich, Gene Bierhaus, Manley Wilcox, Wally Holmstrom, Bill Baumgartner, Jim Haley, Jim Lushine, Vic Kulbitski, Herman Frickey, Paul Mitchell, Carl Eckberg, Jerry Mulready. Back Row (l-r) - Joe Lauterbach, Bud Higgins, Max Ruttger-Manager, Bert Baston, Frank McCormick, Bernie Bierman (Head Coach), George Hauser, Dal Ward, Sheldon Beise, Sig Harris, Lloyd Stein, Oscar Munson, Roland Ring, Mike Welch.

The 1941 Gopher National Champs

Urban Odson

gadget play intended for use only in a desperate scoring emergency. Such was the case at that very moment late in the third quarter after Ed Lechner had blocked a Bill DeCorrevont punt on the Wildcat's 41-yard line. The play started inconspicuously enough when, as planned, the Gophers' first play in the series was just "teaser" run with Bob Sweiger running for no gain over to the left sidelines. What this did was necessitate bringing the ball in 1 -yards to the center hash mark to start the next play. At this point the Northwestern defensive players, like the countless other times after a play during the game, were loose and even engaged in conversation while they waited for the Gophers to simply set up at the line of scrimmage.

To assist in Northwestern's relaxed mood, the Gophers stood around "talking" and distracting the officials. Then, without warning, Minnesota quickly lined up with everyone standing totally still on the line to the right of Center Gene Flick, who stood nonchalantly facing his own end-zone. Suddenly, Flick grabbed the ball and pitched a shovel-pass to Bud Higgins (a scat back from Minneapolis Washburn who weighed not too much more than the football), who then raced clear across the length of the field before he got an opening to make the 90-degree turn toward the Wildcat end-zone. Once he got open, he flew by the stunned and flatfooted Wildcat defense and into open field. Tackle Urban Odson made a couple of key blocks along the way on the final two defenders, as Higgens went on to score what would become one of the most controversial touchdowns in college football history. Northwestern, now furious, complained in vain to the officials, who had been pre-warned in advance by the Gopher coaches that they may run the play that afternoon. The extra point was missed, but the Gophers hung on to win by a narrow 8-7 margin.

After the big win, Minnesota made sure not to let their guard down against Nebraska. Bob Sweiger's first half touchdown run followed by Bill Garnaas' fourth-quarter field-goal would be all the offense the Gophers would need as they rolled to a 9-0 victory. Bruce Smith returned with a vengeance that next week against Iowa, where he ran or passed for all the Gopher scores, including a couple of TDs to Bill Daley, in the 34-13 win. Incredibly, Smith, who was still injured, begged Bierman to put him in the game after the Gophers hadn't produced a single yard on the ground.

Minnesota then pounded the hapless Badgers, 41-6, winning not only the undisputed Big Ten title, but also their fifth national championship. With the win, Bernie Bierman also became the winningest coach in school history. Bruce Smith, the great triple-threat star, was selected as a unanimous All-American and later was awarded the Heisman. In addition, Tackle Dick Wildung and Quarterback Bill Garnaas were also selected to various All-America squads.

From the Great Depression to the second world war, this was truly the "Golden Era" for Minnesota football. In the 10-year span from 1932-1941, Bierman's Gophers won six Big Ten championships, five national championships and had five undefeated seasons en route to posting an amazing 63-12-5 record.

The Turbulent War Years

World War II would deny Minnesota their sixth national championship in nine years due to the fact that most of the players were forced to enlist in the service. Even Bierman himself, who was a Captain in W.W.I, joined the Marine Corps, where he coached a training camp team called the Iowa Seahawks. Assistant Coach George Hauser handled the coaching duties in his absence, trying to salvage something out of a season which saw some 350 college and universities around the country suspend their athletic programs altogether during the war. Incredibly, the Gophers, who, after beating Pittsburgh 50-7, thanks to Bill Daley's four touchdowns, in their 1942 season opener, had their string of 18 straight victories over the past four seasons broken by none other than their own coach, Bernie Bierman. That's right, Bierman's service team, the Seahawks, who won the game 7-6, were even led by a bunch of former Gophers including George Svendsen, Gene Flick, Judd Ringer and Charlie Schultz, as well as a number of professionals.

Bud Grant

Bill Daley

(During the war period many collegiate players transferred to schools that had Naval programs, which permitted them to finish their careers before going into service. As a result, a lot of the countries' premier players found themselves playing on rival teams. Among them was Fullback Bill Daley, who was transferred to a military base in Ann Arbor in 1942 and later earned All-American honors at Michigan. In addition, End Herb Hein, who, after playing the 1942 season with the Gophers, became an All-American at Northwestern in 1943.)

From there the Gophers lost to Illinois 20-13, beat Nebraska 15-2, and then beat Michigan for the ninth straight time on place-kicker Bill Garnaas' impromptu drop-kick. They would beat Iowa but lose to both Wisconsin and Indiana to finish the season with a very modest 5-4 record, good for just fourth in the Big Ten. Tackle Dick Wildung was honored as an All-American that year, as the country really had more important things to worry about other than football. The 1943 season should also be remembered as the year Minnesota's line was anchored by a young kid named Vern Gagne, who would go on to put the sport of wrestling on the map, both collegiately, where he won two national championships as a heavyweight for the Gophers, but also professionally, where he helped to pioneer a form of entertainment that today generates billions of dollars of revenue.

The Gophers were anything but a football power through the mid-1940s, averaging just five wins per year through 1947. There were highlights along the way though, like in 1943, when Wayne "Red" Williams led the nation in total-yards, with 1,467, while averaging 167-yards per game. In one of those games, against Iowa, he tallied four touchdowns. In 1944 Minnesota eked out some fourth-quarter heroics over Indiana and Wisconsin. The Hoosiers were beaten, 19-14, with Merlin Kispert scoring the winning touchdown, while the Badgers were edged, 28-26, in a wild one that ended in the final moments with Bob Kasper finding Bill Marcotte in the end-zone.

In 1945 Bernie Bierman returned home from the Marine Corps to find that college football had changed. Freshmen were now rubbing elbows with 25-year-old servicemen who had been toughened by both combat and the rigors of Army football. This new, older athlete, was also much less receptive to stern discipline — long the hallmark of Bierman's coaching philosophy. As a result, Bierman was less connected with his new Gopher squad, and the record book reflected that. Struggling with the transition to the new T-formation from the old single-wing was one of the major reasons that the team posted just a 4-5 record that year. After beating Missouri, Nebraska, Fort Warren and Northwestern, the bottom fell out as the Gophers lost the rest of their games to Ohio State, 20-7, Michigan, 26-0, Indiana, 49-0, Wisconsin, 26-12, and Iowa, 20-19.

The "49ers" Hit Campus

In 1946 a new batch of freshmen hit the campus who would later become known as the "49ers," for the year in which they were to graduate. They were mixed in with an unusual crop of talent to say the least, with many of them playing on the varsity as freshman under a World War II ruling making first year men eligible for Big Ten competition. (Prior to the war freshmen weren't allowed to play.)

Players like Bud Grant and Billy Bye, who hadn't played collegiately but did play for the Great Lakes Naval Station, were joined with pre-war college guys such as Chuck Avery, Herman Frickey, Herb Hein, Bill Baumgartner and Judd Ringer. Veterans Bill Carroll, Warren Beson, Dean Widseth and Bill Elliott were also joined by newcomers such as Gordy Soltau, Ken Beiersdorf, Bill Thiele, Buster Mealey, Gene Fritz and Jim Malosky. Then, there were high schoolers, like Clayton Tonnemaker, and a kid named Leo Nomellini, who hadn't even played high school football, but was encouraged to walk-on by a former player that he served with in the Air Force. The enormously big and tough Nomellini signed up and, amazingly, when the starting tackle had to leave the opening game of the season with an injured leg, "Leo the Lion" found himself playing for the Minnesota Gophers in what would prove to be the first football game of his life!

Bierman started out using the veteran players but with freshmen still eligible under the war-time rules, he began to play the youngsters. They would prove to be instrumental in three upset wins on the team's final three Saturdays over Purdue, Iowa and Wisconsin — where Billy Bye scored the game's only touchdown to give the Maroon and Gold a 6-0 win. They opened that season with a big win over Nebraska, 38-6, then split the remaining games for a 5-4 record.

In 1947 Minnesota opened the season with wins over Washington, Nebraska and Northwestern. In the Washington game, End Bud Grant provided the heroics when he took a Husky fumble into the end-zone for what would prove to be the game-winner. From there the Rose Bowl champions from Illinois whipped the boys in gold by the final score of 40-13. Michigan, despite Ev Faunce's big day on the ground, which included Minnesota's only touchdown, narrowly escaped with the Little Brown Jug by winning, 13-6, while victories over Pittsburgh, 29-0, Purdue, 26-21, and Wisconsin, 21-0, plus a 13-7 loss to Iowa, left Minnesota with a 6-3 season. Against Purdue it was all Billy Bye and Bud Hausken, who each scored a pair of TDs, while Hausken and Bill Thiele each returned interceptions for touchdowns against the Badgers that next week.

JOHN MARIUCCI

In 1936, John Mariucci left Eveleth and the Iron Range and headed south to the University of Minnesota, where he starred as an offensive and defensive end under Bernie Bierman. Despite playing in between a pair of bookend National titles in 1936 and 1940, he did lead the squad to a Big Ten title on the gridiron in 1938.

"I believe I have the only lineman in America who can extract people's teeth with his fists on the line of scrimmage," joked Bierman of the hulking brute.

Maroosh also starred as an All-American defenseman on the Gopher hockey team, where, in 1940 he captained the AAU National Championship team. Mariucci would then go on to star as the caption of the Chicago Blackhawks. There, as one of just a handful of Americans playing in the NHL, he quickly earned the reputation as one of the league's all-time toughest brawlers. Maroosh came home in 1952, and wound up coaching the Gopher Hockey team for 14 years. The hockey half of Williams Arena was later named in his honor as Mariucci Arena. After his death in 1988, he was forever known as the "Godfather of Minnesota Hockey."

Running Back Ev Faunce kicked off the 1948 season with a 67-yard TD run to lead the Gophers past Washington, 20-0. They then went on to beat Nebraska in the home-opener, 39-13, followed by a 19-16 loss to Northwestern despite a couple of scores from Dale Warner and Ken Beiersdorf. After beating Illinois, 6-0, on a fourth quarter 53-yard pass from Bemidji's Dick Lawrence to Vern Gagne, the Gophers lost to the defending national champs from Michigan, 27-14, despite being held to just 22 yards rushing by Nomellini and Tonnemaker. Minnesota then rallied from behind in a pair of wins over both Indiana and Purdue, 30-7, and, 34-6, respectively, and went on to beat Iowa, 28-21, thanks to Billy Bye's three touchdowns and Ev Faunce's game-winner. In the finale, the Gophers blanked Wisconsin, 16-0, in the rain and sleet, behind Ken Beiersdorf's two touchdowns and Gordy Soltau's field goal, to finish with a 7-2 record. Tackle Leo Nomellini was named to the All-American team that year as the Gophers knew that they were on the verge of turning the corner.

The Bacon Slab

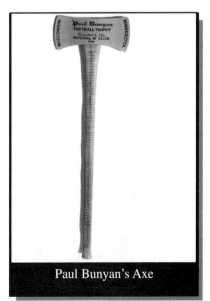

Paul Bunyan's Axe

LEO NOMELLINI

Born in Lucca, Italy, Leo Nomellini grew up in a tough neighborhood outside of Chicago, where, incredibly, he never played high school football. He was convinced to try out for the Gophers, however, and blossomed very quickly into one of the school's all-time greats. In 1949, the bruising defensive tackle led the Gophers to a short-lived No.1 ranking, even anchoring a defense that allowed just 80 points all season. Nicknamed "The Lion," Nomellini would go on to earn All-American honors that same year. Described as "One of the most magnificent specimens ever to play the game" by Bernie Bierman, Leo was truly a man among boys out on the gridiron.

So good of an athlete was Nomellini, that for the heck of it, his teammate Vern Gagne, himself a national heavyweight champion, convinced him to get into wrestling. He did, and believe it or not, in just one year wound up finishing second overall in the Big Ten, losing to Ohio State's Bill Miller, whom he had pinned earlier in the season.

Nomellini graduated in 1950 and was the first pick of the San Francisco 49ers. There, he would go on to star for 14 seasons in the NFL, never missing a game along the way. At 6-3 and 265 pounds, he was the third fastest player on the team, making him the true prototypical lineman of his era.

Later in his career, he hooked up with his old buddy Verne Gagne, and the two of them then teamed up to become tag-team partners in the ring. He even won the world championship in 1956, a title he held for seven months.

In addition, the 10-time Pro Bowler became one of the few players ever to be named All-Pro both on offense and defense, winning offensive honors in 1951 and 1952, and defensive laurels in 1953, 1954, 1957, and 1959. In 1969 Nomellini was inducted into the Pro Football Hall of Fame, and later was named to College Football Hall of Fame as well. One of the best pass rushers the game has ever seen,

Incidentally, after beating the cheese-heads, a new tradition was started for one of college football's greatest rivalries — "Paul Bunyan's Ax," honoring the Midwest's greatest lumberjack. While the teams, which first played one another back in 1890, had been vying for a "Bacon Slab" since 1930, the schools decided to create a new traveling trophy in 1948 that was symbolic of their competitive traditions. Today the six-foot long handle proudly displays the scores of all 110 games, the longest rivalry in the history of Division 1-A football. (The "Slab of Bacon," which originated back in 1930, was a block of black walnut wood that had a big football carved on one end, and an "M" or "W," depending on which way it was held, carved into the other. The concept was that the annual winners would "bring home the bacon." The two schools were set to have a symbolic presentation of the trophy after their big game in 1930, but, a post-game melee spilled onto the field following the Gophers' victory, and in the mess, the trophy was lost forever. Or so we thought! You see, that supposedly lost "Slab of Bacon" made the headlines in 1994, when it was "mysteriously" found in an old storage room deep inside Camp Randall Stadium at the University of Wisconsin. Somehow, incredibly, even though the slab has been "lost" since 1946, the scores of every Gopher-Badger game from 1930 to 1970 were printed on the back of it! Hey Cheese-heads, are there ghosts in your stadium or just what's the deal with that?)

By 1949 those 49er kids were finally all grown up and ready to take on the world. And while the expectations were running high for this talented bunch of over-achievers, in the end, they would turn out to be the right men in the wrong place at the worst possible time. Although this was primarily a senior-laden team, some pretty good sophomores had moved up in the depth chart throughout the year, including Dick Gregory, Wayne Robinson, Dick Mundinger, George Hudak, Bob Thompson and Art Edling.

The group, which had come so far, frustrated and even angered Bierman, who, due to philosophical differences, felt that they never reached their full potential. Times were different after the war, and kids of this era simply did not consider football to be the most important thing in lives, considering what they had lived through and seen overseas. Bierman's authoritative approach to the game also didn't hold much water with this group, who, unlike the kids from years past, never had to rely on the University for a good campus job to live on. In the post-war economic boom, jobs were plentiful, and, along with the G.I. Bill, student-athletes were enjoying a new sense of independence rarely seen before.

With that, Minnesota opened the season with a 48-20 spanking of Washington. The Huskies, who were led by future NFL Hall of Fame Running Back Hugh McElhenny, who ran back the opening kickoff 98 yards for a touchdown, were simply no match for Gophers Billy Bye and Ralph McAllister, however, as each scored a pair touchdowns on the afternoon. Minnesota then rolled over Nebraska, 28-6, thanks to junior Fullback Dave Skrien's two touchdowns, Northwestern, 21-7, and Ohio State, 27-0, as Billy Bye, Dick Gregory, Jim Malosky and Ken Beiersdorf all scored to give the Gophers a No. 3 national ranking.

Billy Bye

Michigan upset the Gophers that next week, 14-7, but still left them hope for the Rose Bowl since every Big Ten team had lost at least one game up to that point. Bierman, upset with their attitudes, worked his players mercilessly in practice that next week. But instead of inspiring them, like in years past, it backfired, and it showed on the field.

"I've never gone through such a tough week of practice in my life," Tonnemaker would later say. "He absolutely killed us in practice that week."

The 26-point underdogs from West Lafayette then came to Memorial Stadium and pulled off one of their program's biggest upsets of all-time that day, piling up 354 yards of offense en route to a 13-7 victory. Lawrence was able to tally a touchdown late, but it wasn't enough as the Gopher's suddenly saw their Rose Bowl dreams all but evaporate. Embarrassed and upset, the Prussian General tried a different tact that next week. "We will have fun the rest of the way," said Bierman, whose Gophers responded by crushing Iowa 55-7 that following Saturday. They didn't stop there though, as they went on next beat Pittsburgh, 24-7, and then closed out their season with a 14-6 victory over Wisconsin.

The sad footnote to an underachieved 7-2 season came on Jan. 1, 1950, when Ohio State, whose only loss that year, a 27-0 butt-kicking, came from the Golden Gophers, beat the University of California, 17-14, to win the Rose Bowl. Tonnemaker joined Nomellini that year as unanimous choices for every All-American team, as both would go on to brilliant pro careers with Green Bay and San Francisco, respectively. Gordy Soltau also ended up in San Francisco as a kicker, and Bud Grant, in

VERNE GAGNE

Verne Gagne was born in Corcoran, Minnesota, and grew up in Hamel during the Depression, attending a one-room school house. A tremendous athlete, he grew up loving sports. "At the age of 10 I knew that I wanted to be a football player and a wrestler," said Gagne. Later he transferred to Wayzata High School for one year, ultimately graduating from Robbinsdale High School in 1943. There he earned all-state honors in football, and, even though he weighed only 185 pounds, he also won the state heavyweight wrestling championship.

During the early 1940s, because of World War II taking so many young men, the University needed football players. So, Gagne was recruited by Bernie Bierman to play for the Gophers. But his main sport quickly became wrestling. After winning the Big Ten heavyweight wrestling title in 1944 as a freshman, he went into the Marine Corps. There, Gagne also played football for the El Toro Marine team in 1944 and 1945. He returned to the U of M to continue playing football, where, in 1949, the star End was selected to play in the College All-Star Game. As a wrestler, Verne became arguably the greatest grappler to ever come out of Minnesota. He won the Big Ten heavyweight championship four times and won two NCAA national championships as both a heavyweight and as a 191-pounder. The two-time All-American also wrestled on the 1948 Olympic team.

After college he was drafted as a defensive end by the Chicago Bears. But, because Halas wanted him to give up a year of eligibility and sign a contract as a junior, Gagne passed and that next season signed with Curly Lambeau's Green Bay Packers. Verne played for the Pack throughout the 1949 pre-season, but just before the first regular season game, Lambeau informed him that because the Bears still owned his rights and wouldn't release him, he was ineligible to play. Gagne then said "to heck with football" and went into the sport that would make him one of the most celebrated and recognizable athletes of his day, professional wrestling.

Verne spent a life-time participating and promoting the sport that he loved, a sport that was born in Minneapolis, "All Star Wrestling." Verne was a local celebrity and became a local hero to a lot of people around the country. He was a daily feature in all the old newspapers and became synonymous with the sport.

"In pro wrestling back then, there were a lot of great wrestlers like myself, who came out of major universities and wanted to continue in the sport," said Gagne. "Sure there were famous guys we wrestled, like Gorgeous George back in the late 40's and early 50's, but back then it was more like collegiate wrestling. Today there are no 'wrestlers' in wrestling."

"We did a TV show called "All Star Wrestling" that we broadcasted from the old Calhoun Beach Hotel, starting in 1950 and going all the way until 1992, never missing a week. The program was syndicated all over the United States, in the far east and all over the world. During the 60's, 70's and 80's it was the highest rated television show in Twin Cities, period. With a 26-share rating, we beat every sit-com, the Vikings, the Twins, everybody. We had no idea that it would grow as big as it did. We even drew the biggest crowd ever at Madison Square Garden. I was traveling the country and making more money than Joe DiMaggio and Mickey Mantle."

The grand grappler retired in 1981 but had more than a few come-backs with his son, and tag-team partner, Greg Gagne. Verne was an entertainer and one of the most successful ones at that. Verne was always one of the "good guys," making him one of the sport's all-time favorites.

"Gopher Football was pretty exciting back in those days," said Gagne. "When we were growing up as kids and listening to the Gopher Football team winning the national championships in the 30's and 40's, every kid wanted to play football for the Gophers. I never dreamt that I would have a chance to go to college. I was very fortunate."

addition to playing pro basketball with the Minneapolis Lakers, went on to play with the Philadelphia Eagles, where he became a star receiver. (Bud earned nine letters during his tenure at the U of M, starring on the basketball and baseball teams as well.) Wayne Robinson, Vern Gagne, Dave Skrien, Larry Olsonoski and Floyd Jaszewski all later played pro ball as well, while Quarterback Jim Malosky went on to become one of the country's winningest all-time coaches at the University of Minnesota-Duluth.

Bernie's Swan Song

A combination of graduation and the return of the freshman ineligibility rule (because of the Korean War), the Gophers were looking pretty thin in 1950. You knew it was going to be bad when Washington, who had always been a doormat to the Gophers, finally ended the hex after losing seven straight, and won 28-13. They did manage to beat Purdue, 27-13, and tie the Rose Bowl bound Michigan Wolverines, 7-7, but lost seven games that year to finish with a dismal 1-7-1 record. With the future looking bleak and the press hounding him, Bierman, who was also upset about being passed over by Ike Armstrong as the new Athletic Director, finally came to the realization that he was simply out of touch with a new generation of kids that wanted no part of his old-school regime. With that, Bernie, who had posted a modest 30-23-1 postwar record, reluctantly decided to step down as the Gopher's head coach. He would be remembered as the greatest ever to coach at Minnesota.

One of the few things Bierman was negligent of, was recruiting mostly just kids from his own backyard. Back in the day he could get away with that. There was a lot of talent in the Midwest, and kids didn't want to venture too far away from home. But in the new era of competitive college athletics, universities were now scouring the countrysides armed with big scholarships in search of the best talent they could find. Minnesota finally got wise to this, and, in an effort to get the local kids to

Gopher National Championships

1934	8-0 overall	5-0 Big Ten
1935	8-0 overall	5-0 Big Ten
1936	7-1 overall	4-1 Big Ten
1940	8-0 overall	6-0 Big Ten
1941	8-0 overall	5-0 Big Ten
1960	8-2 overall	6-1 Big Ten

Paul Giel

Dick McNamara

stay put, started its own scholarship program called the Williams Fund.

Enter the Winona Phantom

In 1951 the Gophers hired former Ohio State head coach Wes Fesler, a three-time All-American End for the Buckeyes, to take over the reigns and right the ship. It would be a formidable task, but he did have one thing going for him — the Winona Phantom. One of those freshman who was ineligible in 1950 was a kid from Winona who would go on to become one of Minnesota's greatest ever athletes, rewriting the record books along the way. His name was Paul Giel, one of the first benefactors of that new scholarship fund.

The 1951 squad struggled to say the least. After starting out the season with losses to Washington and California, Coach Fesler moved Giel from Quarterback to Left Half, where the speedster's running and passing potential could be better utilized under the team's new single-wing offense. That next week, against Nebraska, Giel scored on a short run in the first, lateralled to Fullback Ron Wallin for a second, completed a 53-yard pass to End Bill Foss for a third, and then busted around the end late in the game on a seven-yarder to score his second TD of the day, en route to leading the Gophers to an impressive 26-7 victory.

Giel added two more against Iowa in a 20-20 tie, and then led the Gophers to a 16-14 win over Indiana. He electrified the crowd with a 64-yard touchdown run in a 19-13 loss to Purdue, and got enough yardage in the 32-6 loss to Wisconsin to bring his total yardage for the season to over 1,000 yards, ultimately setting a new Conference record. Percy Zachary, George Hudak, Kermit Klefsaas, Don Swanson, Jerry Helgeson, John Baumgartner, Jimmy Soltau, Chuck Swanum, Gino Cappelletti and Gordy Holz all contributed that year, as the team finished with a dismal 2-6-1 record.

By 1952 Giel was having ball... literally. He passed the ball, caught the ball, ran the ball, kicked the ball, and even held the ball for PATs. In addition, he called the plays and emerged as the leader both on and off the field. That season the Gophers improved to finish with a 4-3-2 record, highlighted by a couple of big upset wins and last-minute thrillers. After losing a couple of non-conference games to Washington and Cal, the Gophers rebounded to beat Northwestern, as Giel hit Don Swanson for the tying touchdown in the last 17 seconds of the game. Kicker Gino Cappelletti added the winning point for the victory. Minnesota then upset the nationally ranked defending champs from Illinois, 13-7, as Giel hit Bob McNamara for one touchdown and Mel Holme ran for another.

After losing to Michigan, 21-0, Minnesota upset Iowa 17-7 at Memorial Stadium. Down 7-0 in the fourth, Giel caught a leaping one-handed catch from Don Swanson and sprinted 38 yards for the tying touchdown. After recovering a pair of Iowa fumbles that resulted in both a field goal and a touchdown pass by Swanson, the Gopher defense simply hung on for the win. That next Saturday the Gophers had to settle for a 14-14 tie against a tough Purdue team, which could've been beaten had Cappelletti's field goal attempt late in the fourth not missed by a foot. Giel then led his squad past Nebraska, 13-7, by throwing for one and running in another.

Gordy Soltau

Then, in the season finale against Wisconsin, Giel, handled the ball 54 times and either passed or ran for all of Minnesota's touchdowns in a thrilling 21-21 tie. In a game filled with fumbles and interceptions, the ball, incredibly, switched hands five times in the last two minutes of the game. For Giel, who was selected as the conference MVP and received All-American honors, the loss was bitter knowing that if his squad had won they would've taken the Big Ten title. (Incidentally, at the end of the season, the football gods decided to legislate against platoon football, something which had been allowed in the post-war years.)

Optimism was running high in the Land of 10,000 Lakes in 1954, as the Gophers looked poised to finally make a run for the roses. Minnesota got off to a very slow start that year, and was just 1-3 (They lost to USC, 17-7, Michigan State, 21-0, and Illinois, 27-7, and beat Northwestern, 30-13.) heading into the big Michigan game. The game was significant because it was the Silver Anniversary of the Little Brown Jug, and many of the stars from 1903, including Sig Harris and Ed Rogers, were on hand for the festivities. Fesler knew it was a big game, and came down hard on his players that week. He knew that if they were to win though, it would come down to the play of one man — Paul Giel.

Bob McNamara

Giel, who had the power to call his own plays and audible at the line whenever he felt necessary, was ready to make history, and turn the season's misfortunes around that Saturday. In what many have called the greatest-ever single performance in Gopher history, Giel single-handedly crushed the Wolverines. The game opened with Minnesota kicking off and got exciting early when Gordy Holz recovered a Michigan fumble on their own 29-yard line. Just four plays later Giel called his own number, and after deking out several Wolverines, found himself standing in the end-zone with his squad up 7-0. He would repeat that feat yet again in the first quarter, leading a 62-yard drive which was capped by another run around the end to make it 14-0.

Giel provided more heroics in the third when he returned a punt 41 yards down to the Michigan 34-yard line. From there, after nice runs by McNamara and Holme, Giel hit Bob Rutford in the end-zone to make it 20-0, as the Gophers added a late safety to make the final score 22-0, and regain the precious Jug that had eluded them for a decade. Giel set a Big Ten record that day by handling the ball on 53 of 63 offensive plays, of which he ran for 112 yards. He also completed 13 of 18 passes for another 169 yards, returned one kickoff for 24-yards and four punts for 59-yards. Oh yeah, on defense he also intercepted a pair of Michigan passes to end a couple of key drives.

It was an unbelievable performance from an unbelievable player. "They had kicked us around pretty good in those previous years and I really wanted to beat them badly," Giel later said. "From a personal standpoint, I would have to say that it was my best all-around game ever."

The Gophers went on to beat Pittsburgh, 35-14, behind Giel's three touchdowns, and Indiana, 28-20, before getting shut out by Iowa, 21-0. They ended the season by once again tying Wisconsin, 21-21, this time fumbling on the Badger two-yard line with just a minute to go, to finish with a 4-4-1 record — far short of pre-season expectations.

Giel averaged more than 100 yards per game that year, and for his efforts was again named as a unanimous All-American. In addition to being awarded the prestigious Big Ten Medal of Honor, he was given the Walter Camp Award for "Back of the Year," and was chosen UPI's "Player of the Year." He also finished as the runner-up to Notre Dame's Johnny Lattner for the coveted Heisman Trophy, an award many felt he would've won had he been on a better team. In his three seasons at Minnesota, he scored 22 touchdowns, threw 13 touchdown passes, and racked up 5,094 all-purpose yards. What's even more amazing was that Giel was also named as an All-American Pitcher on the Gopher baseball team. In fact, after his senior year, he even decided to forego a certain star-studded career in the NFL to instead play major league baseball, with the New York Giants, Pittsburgh Pirates and later with his hometown Minnesota Twins. (Giel would later take over as the University's Athletic Director in 1972.)

At the end of the season, Coach Fesler resigned his post to accept an executive position with a Minneapolis radio station. And with that, for the second time in three years, Minnesota found itself looking for a new head football coach.

CLAYTON TONNEMAKER

Clayton Tonnemaker, like the great Pudge Heffelfinger before him back in the late 1800s, unofficially played for the Gophers even as a high school student. The recruiters had spotted him absolutely dominating his Minneapolis Edison High School team's opponents, and wanted to get him up to play with the big boys as soon as possible. With that, the young Center took the street car down to campus to get a taste of spring football. Being that it was not legal to allow a high schooler to train with a college team, the Gophers did not mention or acknowledge him being there. Once, in a Saturday scrimmage, Tonnemaker intercepted a pass and run it back for a touchdown. Excited, he ran out that night to pick up a copy of an early edition of the Sunday newspaper to read about his accomplishments. When he opened it up though, all he read about was how another "different" center on the team made a spectacular interception return for a touchdown!

The Ogilvie, Minn., native then joined up that Fall and went on to become an All-American center and linebacker at the U of M from 1946 to 1949. That next summer, after captaining a college all-star team that upset the NFL Champion Philadelphia Eagles, he went on to play professionally in the NFL with the Green Bay Packers for several seasons in the early 1950s. He was later inducted into the College Football Hall of Fame.

Enter the "Autumn Warrior"

With the resignation of Fesler as Minnesota's football coach, rumors ran wild about reports that former Gopher star Bud Wilkinson, who was coaching at Oklahoma at the time, was going to be named as the team's new skipper. It never happened, however, and in late January of 1954, Gopher athletic director Ike Armstrong announced that Mississippi State Head Coach Murray Warmath had been selected to fill the vacant the post. The choice of Warmath, a virtual unknown, was unacceptable to many Gopher fans, who, in addition to being upset about hiring a coach who was not a member of the Big Ten family, were reeling about the University's inability to lure their native son, Wilkinson, back to campus.

Warmath, who had played at Tennessee under General Bob Neyland, later coached at Army and Mississippi State. He brought four "Dixie" assistants with him, but opted to keep Butch Nash on staff, a popular move on his part. A student of the split "T" offense, complete with a plethora of flankers spread out behind the line, Warmath did pretty darn good in his first year, even quieting a few of his critics. Warmath showed his military roots by announcing that the team would have practice every morning at 6:30 a.m., something that went over about as good as a warm beer on a hot day with the players.

In addition to Bob McNamara, there were several other standouts from the Fesler era on the squad including Gino Cappelletti, John Baumgartner, Don Swanson and Jimmy Soltau. There were also a couple of promising young sophomores in Dick "Pinky" McNamara — Bob's younger brother, Center Dean Maas and future All-American Tackle Bob Hobert. The team rallied behind their new coach and finished with a very surprising 7-2 record that year, with wins over Nebraska, Pittsburgh, Northwestern, Illinois, Michigan State, Oregon State and Iowa, and just a pair of losses to both Michigan and Wisconsin. Chants of "Mac and Cappy" (McNamara and Cappelletti) were abound at Memorial Stadium that year, as the Gopher faithful liked what they saw.

Leading the way for the Gophers in 1954 was team captain and Running Back Bob McNamara, who had fully recovered from knee surgery just the year before to receive All-American honors. Big Mac's tough running accounted for at least three Gopher victories that year. He ran for one score in the opening 19-7 win over Nebraska, returned a punt 65 yards for a TD to turn a close game with Pitt into a 46-7 rout, scored twice in the 26-7 win over Northwestern, added another in the 19-6 victory over the Illini, put in two more in the 19-13 win over Michigan State, and tallied a pair in the 44-6 crushing of Oregon State.

Then, against Iowa, McNamara gained 209 first half yards alone, and scored the first two Gopher touchdowns — a 36-yard run around the left end, followed by an 89-yard kickoff return which Warmath later called the "greatest exhibition of one man against eleven he had ever witnessed." The game, which was deadlocked for the third time at 20-20 late, got crazy when an 85-yard Iowa touchdown run was nullified for a clipping penalty. Then, an Iowa fumble in their own end-zone gave the Gophers a safety, which, with the two points, was enough to give them a well-deserved 22-20 victory.

Bob Hobert

Warmath was pleased with his first season in Minnie, but knew that he would have a lot of work to do. His next few years at the Gopher helm would be a saga like non other. He made no bones about the unpopular fact that Minnesota's home-grown talent was simply not going to cut it an longer in the Big Ten. With that, he literally became a pioneer- of sorts, by going way outside the box and recruiting young African American men from out East and down South to come to Minnesota. While it proved to be an unpopular move at first, most became pretty accepting of it when, in 1960, he brought Minnesota it's first national championship in nearly 20 years.

Warmath's second year, 1955, was a rebuilding one, as his Gophers posted just three wins and twice as many losses, en route to registering a dismal 2-5 Big Ten record. Washington squashed Minnesota, 30-0, in the opener, while an errant fumble cost them a tie in the 7-6 loss against Purdue. Missed conversions were big factors in the 21-13 and 14-13 losses to both Illinois and Michigan respectively. On the bright side, Fullback Dick Borstad tallied in the 18-7 win over Northwestern, while Halfback Bob Schultz scored a pair of touchdowns in the 21-6 upset victory of Wisconsin. Perhaps the highlight of the season came against mighty USC, when the Gophers upset the Trojans, 25-19, in a classic snow-fest at old Memorial. Richard Borstad scored twice and Quarterback Don Swanson added another on a 65-yard keeper to "ice" it for Minnesota.

The 1956 Gophers had to face a quarterback controversy at the start of the season when incumbent QB Dick Larson was joined in the backfield by Bobby Cox, a transfer from the University of Washington. After smoking Washington 34-14, and rallying to beat Purdue, 21-14,

BOBBY BELL

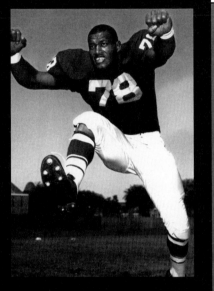

Growing up in Shelby, N.C., Bobby Bell was a star on his high school football, baseball and basketball teams. It was out on the gridiron though where the powerful quarterback made his mark. When he was recruited to Minnesota, he had every intention of being the Golden Gophers' signal caller. But, when he got there, Coach Warmath told him that he was going to convert him to be a tackle, because Sandy Stephens was the quarterback. Bell was stunned. At first, he didn't even know how to get into a lineman's stance, but he went into it with an open mind. How opened minded you might ask? By the time he graduated, the two-time All American had become the best tackle in all of college football.

His transition from QB to tackle was hailed by sportswriters of the day as one of the modern wonders of college football. He led the Gophers to a 22-6-1 record during his tenure in Minnesota, which included a national championship and Rose Bowl victory. The two-time All American was also awarded the prestigious Outland Trophy his senior year, recognizing him as the nation's top interior lineman. In addition, he won the conference MVP and finished third in the Heisman voting.

Bobby Bell was a physical specimen. He was six-feet-four, weighed 225 pounds, ran a 4.4, and sported a 28-inch waist. The amazing athlete was even recruited by several other U of M teams including the gymnastics, baseball and basketball teams. He chose the hard-court, where he even became the first African-American to play a varsity game for the Gopher basketball team. One time, Gopher Hockey Coach John Mariucci even tried to talk him into playing goalie for him.

"He told me that I had the quickest reflexes that he'd ever seen and that I was going to be the first black hockey player in the country," said Bell. "Now, coming from North Carolina I had never even seen hockey before. So, when we got out on the ice and someone nearly took my head off with a puck, I told him that the only way I'd get out there is if he turned the net around in the other direction!"

After graduating, Bell was drafted in the second round by the Minnesota Vikings. But, he decided to play instead for the Kansas City Chiefs of the rival AFL, where, in 1970, he led his squad past his old linemate and friend Carl Eller, who was starring for those very Vikings in the Super Bowl.

As a pro in the NFL, Bell made another transition, this time to linebacker There he played for 13 seasons, earning All-Pro honors for eight consecutive years, and becoming the Chiefs' first inductee into the Pro Football Hall of Fame in 1983. He was later elected to the College Football Hall of Fame and was also named to the AFL's all-time team in 1969. Bobby Bell was undoubtedly the greatest lineman and probably the greatest athlete ever to wear the maroon and gold.

"I thought I had died and gone to heaven when I arrived at the University of Minnesota," said Bell of his alma mater. "Coming from North Carolina, I remember the first time I ever saw snow, it was so exciting. Being on campus as a Gopher was one of the most exciting things in my life. Playing in those Saturday football games was just so great. The fans and everybody were just really involved in the game. The night before the football game, we would stay at a hotel in St. Paul. Then, on Saturday, we would drive down University Avenue with a police escort, and it was just wall-to-wall people everywhere yelling and screaming for us. My heart started to pound like crazy. I was so excited, and my stomach was churning. I couldn't wait to get my uniform on. Getting off that bus and seeing all the people hanging out of the frat house windows was incredible. Seeing all that excitement in one place was fantastic. Everybody was so into it! Tickets to our games were no where to be found. I had so much fun there, and to this day I have a real love for the University of Minnesota."

Bobby is currently retired and lives in Lee's Summit, Mo., where he travels all over the world as a motivational speaker.

Here is What a Few of Bobby's Teammates Had to Say About Him:
"Bobby was probably the most versatile player that I ever had the pleasure of playing with," said Sandy Stephens. "I don't know of anyone else who could have gone from quarterback to tackle. When he came in, the only place we had open was at left tackle, and coach Warmath realized that since he was such a good athlete, he had to play him somewhere. Bobby said that he just came here to play and didn't care where it was that he played. He was one of the only guys that could throw the ball five yards further than me, and I could throw 80 yards."

"He was one of the most naturally-talented athletes that I ever saw," said Carl Eller. "He was a person who really worked hard, but he had a lot of stuff to start with. He had speed and stamina, and he was a person that really enjoyed the game. Bobby made it look like fun, because he was so talented. He probably had talents that were maybe never really totally challenged, and that was the kind of guy that he was — just a tremendous player."

on Ken Bombardier's fourth-quarter TD, Minnesota managed just a 0-0 tie with Northwestern. From there the Maroon and Gold went on a three-game winning streak which began with a 16-13 win over Illinois, thanks to Cox's long punt return which led to Dick Borstad's game-winning field goal. Cox again played the hero that next Saturday when he led the Gophers to a 20-7 victory thanks to his two fourth-quarter touchdowns.

While Borstad's late field goal was enough to get past Pittsburgh, 9-6, in Week Six, the unbeaten Gophers were upset by the Hawkeyes the following weekend. Fumbles and penalties plagued the Gophers all day, as Iowa hung on for a 7-0 victory at Memorial Stadium. Minnesota rebounded to edge Michigan State, 14-13, on Blakley's fourth-quarter touchdown run, but managed just a 13-13 tie with Wisconsin in the season finale. With that, the 6-1-2 Gophers painfully watched Iowa pound Oregon State in the Rose Bowl, as their successful season somehow ended as a disappointment.

With Tackle Bob Hobert (who anchored a defense that gave up just 87 points in 1956), Center Dean Maas and Half Back Pinky McNamara being the only regulars lost to graduation, the 1957 Gophers, which featured Cox, Larson, Blakley, Borstad and Jon Jelacic, were feeling good about their prospects that year.

Murray Warmath

But, despite the high expectations of the '57 Gophers, in the end it was a season that just wasn't meant to be. Their potent offense, which put 201 points on the board, had to contend with a porous defense that surrendered 188 points as well. When it was all said and done, Minnesota had finished the season with a 4-5 record. It would be the start of a miserable pair of seasons in Gopherland, in terms of won-lost records, which would then be followed by one of the most amazing turn-around's in college football history. Through this journey, one man, Murray Warmath, would have to endure a lot.

The Good, the Bad and the Ugly

With victories over Washington and Northwestern along with a 21-17 win over Purdue, the Gophers started out their season at 3-0. But then the team traveled to Champaign, where they soon got a big taste of reality. Going into the game against the Illini the Gophers were feeling confident. They had been tabbed as 13-point favorites and even had their star Quarterback, Bobby Cox, featured on the cover of Sports Illustrated. When it was over though, the Gophers had been embarrassed, losing 34-13, and scoring only on a couple of mop-up touchdowns against the Illini's scrubs late in the fourth. To compound matters, Cox's ankles were hurt and slowed him down, while Larson was also banged up at Safety to make an already thin secondary even more suspect. After losing to Michigan that next week, the team managed to beat lowly Indiana, 34-0, at old Memorial, before dropping the rest of their games against Iowa, Michigan State and Wisconsin.

The next year, 1958, the bottom fell out for the Gophers, who posted the worst season in modern history with just one win, against Michigan State, and eight losses. With their disappointing record, Warmath's critics had resurfaced big-time. So much was the pressure from the masses that Warmath even considered taking the head coaching position at Arkansas. Unfortunately, it didn't get any better in 1959 either, when the team went just 2-7, beating only lowly Indiana and Vanderbilt. By now there were loud cries from throughout the local sports world calling for Warmath's head. Even his own boosters, the "M" Club, felt that it would be best for both sides to part ways. If that weren't enough, a couple of local businessmen made an effort to buy off the remainder of his contract. It got so bad that Warmath's home even became a target for vandals.

Things were ugly in Gold Country all right, but somehow Warmath, ever the tactician, knew what he was doing. He knew that he needed to not only recruit outside of Minnesota, but also recruit a new kind of player. Through that bad stretch he had gone out and landed some of the most promising young African American men from around the country that college football would ever know. Among them were a crop of Pennsylvanians which included Quarterback Sandy Stephens, and a pair of Halfbacks — Judge Dickson and Bill Munsey. He also recruited a couple of future NFL Pro Bowl Defensive Ends out of North Carolina in Bobby Bell and Carl Eller.

"It became obvious," said Warmath in the 1972 book "Gold Glory," "that we couldn't win with just Minnesota boys, because of the small population of the state and the short season."

Joining that star-studded recruiting class for the 1960 campaign were a couple of other out-staters who would make an impact that year: Ends Bob Deegan and Tom Hall, Guard John Mulvena, Linebacker Julian Hook and Quarterback "Smoky" Joe Salem. They, along with home-grown holdovers Guard Tom Brown, Fullback Roger Hagberg, Tackle Frank Brixius and Center Greg Larson, would join together to become a team of destiny. On the horizon was a turn-around which would become the most dramatic in Gopher history

The Coming Out Party

After starting out the 1960 season with an embarrassing 19-7 pre-season loss to the alumni squad, Minnesota got its house in order by whipping the Nebraska Cornhuskers, 26-14, in Lincoln. Stephens led the charge in this one, running three yards for one touchdown while passing to Dave Mulholland for another. Jim Rogers also scored on a short

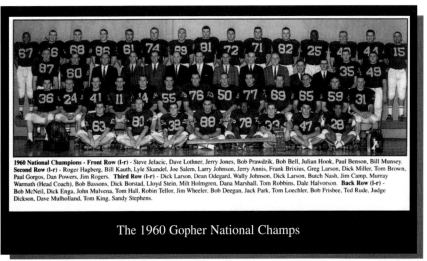

1960 National Champions - Front Row (l-r) - Steve Jelacic, Dave Lothner, Jerry Jones, Bob Prawdzik, Bob Bell, Julian Hook, Paul Benson, Bill Munsey. **Second Row (l-r)** - Roger Hagberg, Bill Kauth, Lyle Skandel, Joe Salem, Larry Johnson, Jerry Annis, Frank Brixius, Greg Larson, Dick Miller, Tom Brown. **Third Row (l-r)** - Dick Larson, Dean Odegard, Wally Johnson, Dick Larson, Butch Nash, Jim Camp, Murray Warmath (Head Coach), Bob Bassons, Dick Borstad, Lloyd Stein, Milt Holmgren, Dana Marshall, Tom Robbins, Dale Halvorson. **Back Row (l-r)** - Bob McNeil, Dick Enga, John Mulvena, Tom Hall, Robin Tellor, Jim Wheeler, Bob Deegan, Jack Park, Tom Loechler, Bob Frisbee, Ted Rude, Judge Dickson, Dave Mulholland, Tom King, Sandy Stephens.

The 1960 Gopher National Champs

TD run following a fumble recovery, and the speedy defensive back, Bill Munsey, added a 42-yard interception return for the final score of the game. That following week Minnesota spanked Indiana, 42-0, thanks to touchdowns from Roger Hagberg, on a short run around end, Bob Deegan, who caught a 46-yard TD from Stephens, Linebacker Jerry Annis who returned an interception, Stephens, on a short dive over the middle, and Dave Lothner, on a pass from Salem.

The Gophers won their third straight over Northwestern that next Saturday, 7-0. Tom Brown led the defensive surge to shut-out the Wildcats, while Sandy Stephens' lone four-yard touchdown run was enough to give Minnesota the victory. The winning drive began with Salem, who, after three successive hand-offs at midfield to Munsey, faked a draw and instead pulled up to hit Deegan on a 40-yard pass. Then, on third down, Stephens came back in and rushed it into the end-zone. Next up were the Illini, a team Minnesota would hang on to beat, 21-10, on a fourth quarter rally. Quarterback Larry Johnson led the late charge for the men of gold, as Stephens came in to cap a 66-yard game-winning scoring drive with nine-yard touchdown — his third on the day.

At 4-0, Minnesota was starting to gain some respect in gridiron circles. They would make some more believers that next week, when they blanked a very good Michigan team, 10-0, at Ann Arbor. Defense was the key to the team's big win that day, as they forced five fumbles and held the Wolverines to just 76 yards rushing and 68 yards passing. Jim Rogers finished a 44-yard scoring drive when he ran in what would prove to be the game-winner from the two yard line.

Kansas State then fell to the Gophers, 48-7, setting up an epic showdown between the suddenly No.2 ranked Gophers and the No.1 ranked Iowa Hawkeyes. Forest Evashevski's Hawk's had owned the Gophers over the last five years, surrendering just 21 points over that time period. More than 65,000 Gopher fans somehow jammed into 53,000-seat Memorial Stadium on that November 5th to see history. Iowa took the opening kickoff to mid-field, only to see Tom Brown so dominate the Hawkeye Center, that when it came time for him to long-snap the ball back to his punter, he nervously floated it straight over his head. Minnesota then promptly recovered the ball at the 14-yard line and let Stephens later pitch it to Munsey, who scored from seven yards out to make it 7-0. Iowa came back on a field goal, and later, in the second half, went 55 yards for a touchdown to take a 10-7 lead. Joe Salem then came off the bench and hit Hagberg on a couple of key passes, which set up yet another Stephens touchdown run from inside the 10. Then, in the fourth, Tackle Jim Wheeler forced and recovered his own fumble, which then setup a Hagberg 42-yard touchdown run on the very next play. Bobby Bell later recovered a Hawkeye fumble deep in Iowa territory which set up a Salem touchdown run to make the final score 27-10 for Minnesota.

Against Iowa Tom Brown was an animal. "Brownie" had been stuffing the Hawkeye linemen all day and was just dominating both sides of the line. On one particular third-down play, with the ball on the Gopher five-yard line, Brown fired through the line just as the ball was snapped and knocked the center into the quarterback, who then flew back into the fullback — pancaking all three of them on their butts on one play for a five-yard loss. After that game Brown proudly hoisted Floyd of Rosedale over his head for all to see.

With the big win, Minnesota found itself as the number one team in the land. That's when last-place Purdue came to town and wrecked everything. Purdue Quarterback, and future Minnesota Twin, Bernie Allen led the Boilermakers on a pair of first half 80 and 25-yard touchdown drives to give his squad a 14-0 lead. Johnson then led the Gophers back in the third on a 40-yard pass to Deegan, followed up by a 27-yard touchdown run by Munsey. Stephens then hit Munsey on a two-point conversion to make it 14-8. But after a Johnson interception, Purdue was able to drive and kick a 35-yard field goal. Minnesota rallied in the fourth behind a 27-yard, Stephens to Hall pass which set up a Hagberg touchdown. But when the Gophers fumbled in their own end-zone late in the game, Purdue was able to secure the 28-14 upset.

Down, but not out, the Gophers traveled to Wisconsin for the final game of the regular season with a Big Ten title and possible Rose Bowl berth laying in the balance. Minnesota "rose" to occasion that afternoon, scoring a pair early and a pair late, as their top-rated defense shut down the Badgers to secure a 26-7 victory.

Judge Dickson

With that, the Gophers found themselves at the top of both the AP and UPI final polls, declaring them as consensus national champions for the first time in two decades. And, although they had a better record, the Gophers did have to share the Big Ten title with Iowa. This was due to the fact that their early rout of Indiana, who was on probation for recruiting violations, did not count in the final standings. (The irony there was that the Hoosiers' coach was a man named Phil Dickens, Warmath's roommate at Tennessee.) Fittingly, for his perseverance and courage, Warmath received full vindication by being named as Coach of the Year. Bud Wilkinson would later comment on Warmath's achievement: "What he did under that pressure was one of the greatest things to happen to college coaching in a long, long time."

With their Big Ten title, their first since the invasion of Pearl Harbor, the Gophers would now have to sit back and wait to find out if, and where, they would be spending New Year's Day. You see, at the time, the Big Ten — Pacific Coast Rose Bowl pact was not in effect, which therefore allowed the PAC-10 champion, Washington, to choose its opponent. Luckily, they chose Minnesota, and the Gophers were off to Pasadena to face the Huskies in their first-ever Rose Bowl.

Once there, the Gophers were showered by well-wishers who simply couldn't get enough of this Cinderella story. When the game got going though, it became a different tale. Washington, unlike the star-struck Gophers, had been there before, crushing Wisconsin just the year before by the final of 44-8.

Nearly 100,000 fans were on hand to watch what would later be considered to be a tale of two

TOM BROWN

Tom Brown grew up loving sports and went on to star in football, track, and swimming a Minneapolis Central High School. After winning the state championship in the shot-put and discuss, the heavily recruited prep football and track star decided to attend the University of Minnesota, where he not only ran track, but also played offensive and defensive tackle on the Gopher football team.

In 1960, Tom's senior year, the Gophers tied for the Big Ten title, were voted national champions and went to the Rose Bowl — where they ultimately lost to Washington. The defensive unit allowed only 88 points that entire season. One of the stars of that team was the "Rock of Gibraltar," Tom Brown. His Herculean strength was legendary, and his ability to blast holes in opposing defensive lines made him an easy pick for the Outland Trophy, recognizing him as the best lineman in the country. He was also named as the Big Ten MVP, a first team All-American, and runner-up in the Heisman Trophy voting.

After his collegiate career, Tom was drafted by the Baltimore Colts in the NFL as well as the British Columbia Lions in the Canadian Football League. "I didn't want to move to Baltimore," said Brown. "I thought that the Great Northwest would fit my outdoor lifestyle much better." So he headed north of the border, where, in 1964, he led the Lions to the Grey Cup championship and was named as the team's MVP. He would win one more Grey Cup during his tenure in B.C. before having to retire prematurely due to a neck injury in 1967.

"Being a Gopher was a very prominent part of my life," said Brown. "Growing up there, I used to follow everything at the University even though there wasn't a lot of TV at the time. When I saw all of the other kids not only from Minnesota, but from other states trying to get into the University to play sports, it made me want to go there even more. I wouldn't trade my experiences there for anything."

Today Tom and his wife live in Bellingham, Washington, in a cabin overlooking the Pacific Ocean. Years ago he ran a river rafting company, but now he works in Vancouver and runs the sales and marketing for a plastics fabrication company. "I love the outdoors, the ocean, the Orcas, the mountains, river rafting — it's so beautiful up here."

Here's What a Few of Tom's Teammates Had to Say About Him:
"He was one of the strongest, most agile players that I ever witnessed playing on the football field," said Sandy Stephens. "I remember the game against Iowa when he knocked down the All-American center, the quarterback, and the fullback — all on the same play. I'll never forget that play as long as I live!"

"He was a great athlete and a great lineman," said Carl Eller. "He was a great lineman in the sense that he was built like a lineman. He was so strong and had big upper-body and trunk strength, with so much quickness. He was the picture offensive and defensive lineman. He was so quick and tough, he would just come at you with a great charge. He was a really great player."

"Tom was originally recruited as a running back," said Bobby Bell. "Coach Warmath decided to take this strong, quick guy with good speed and move him into the line. He was a quick, very quiet, content, strong, solid football player. If you wanted somebody on your football team, that was the guy you wanted. He didn't say too much, but he got the job done."

"Tom Brown scared more people on a football field than any player in Minnesota history," said former Coach Murray Warmath. "He was a one-man interior line."

halves. The game got underway with the Huskies scoring early on a 34-yard field goal by George Fleming. From there they went on to score a pair of touchdowns in the second quarter, thanks in large part to the efforts of Quarterback Bob Schloredt, who threw for one and ran in the other from 31-yards out to give his squad a 17-0 half-time lead.

The Gophers, meanwhile, could muster just two first downs the entire half, while Stephens' interception didn't help much either. It was a different story in the second though, as the Gophers came out and rallied behind a Bob Deegan fumble recovery which set up an 18-yard touchdown pitch from Stephens to Munsey. Minnesota threatened to get back in the game by driving to the Washington six-yard line midway through the fourth, but were held when Stephens was blitzed for a 13-yard loss. The Gophers then tried a little razzle-dazzle by going for a fake field-goal on fourth-down, but came up short when Stephens, the holder, pulled up and threw an interception on a pass intended for Tom Hall at the Husky one yard line. The Gophers got the ball back late, but were unable to get past the 35-yard line. Washington added a field goal to ice it, but the Gophers, who ended the game with 60 more total yards than the Huskies, came up on the short side of a 17-7 loss.

"We didn't play as well as we could, and on that day we played one of the best football teams I've seen in 18 years at Minnesota," Warmath would later say. "But as the game wore on, we started coming on fast and they were fading. Another 15 minutes and we maybe would have won."

"We made some stupid mistakes in that Rose Bowl game, but we knew we had a good team," said Stephens. "After the game, I recall that I had never felt so bad after losing. However, it was a fantastic experience for me. The Rose Bowl was everything I thought it would be and more. The whole first half we were sort of awe struck, but the second half we were ready to play. I think they only got one first down in the entire second half, and that was off a long quarterback sneak. We just couldn't get any offensive momentum going at that point, and we couldn't overcome Washington. I don't want to take anything away from the Huskies, they were a fine team. But they were just a better football team on that day. We lost the game, but were still national champions, and they can't take that away from us."

"The year before we finished near the bottom of the Big Ten, but we were actually very close to winning a lot of close games that we lost," said Tom Brown. "So, Murray Warmath got us all together and told us that we needed that extra little effort to cross that thin line between winning and losing. Beating the No.2 ranked Nebraska Cornhuskers in a pre-season game really built our confidence, and from then on we felt like we could do some real good things that season. The Big Ten at that time was very dominant on the national football scene."

Despite losing the Rose Bowl, the Gophers still remained as National Champs, due to the fact that the voting was done prior to the post-season. That wasn't the only award the team would win either as Bobby Bell and Tom Brown each earned All-American honors. Brown, who also received the Outland Trophy, as the best interior lineman in the nation, went on to be named as the Big Ten MVP, and even finished as the runner-up in the Heisman Trophy voting — a first for a lineman.

Another Run for the Roses
The defending national champs from Minnesota weren't going to sneak up on anyone in 1961 like they had done the year before. The Gophers, who lost a few key players to graduation, including Tom Brown and Joe Salem, still had a nucleus of stars in Bobby Bell, Sandy Stephens, Bill Munsey, Judge Dickson, and a new sophomore Tackle by the name of Carl Eller, who stood six-foot-

SANDY STEPHENS

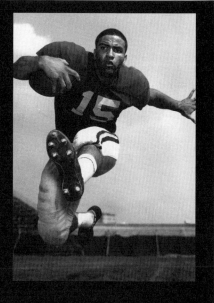

Sandy Stephens grew up in Uniontown, Pa., where upon graduating from high school, had more than 50 football scholarships from colleges and universities (eight from the Big Ten alone), around the country. Sandy felt pretty strong about his football roots: "We always felt that those of us who lived in Western Pennsylvania had the best high school football in the country, bar none — including Ohio and Texas too!"

Stephens was a tremendously gifted all-around prep athlete, earning nine letters in football, basketball, and track. He garnered high school All-American honors in football, was an All-State basketball player, and, although he never played high school baseball, was a good enough pitcher and centerfielder to be romanced by several major league baseball teams, including his home state Philadelphia Phillies, who drafted him regardless.

With assurances that he would be given a shot at quarterback, as well as the opportunity to play baseball, Stephens enrolled at University of Minnesota in the fall of 1958. With that, he packed up and made the trek to Minnesota, alongside his friend Judge Dickson, a fullback from nearby Clairton, Pa. (Sandy's boyhood pal, halfback Bill Munsey, arrived a year later.)

"We felt the University of Minnesota was interested in us as men and not just as football players," said Sandy. "I wanted to measure how good I could be playing in the best college conference in the nation. Also, being black, I knew there were many other top colleges that would allow me to play quarterback. (Warmath) guaranteed me a chance."

He hit campus in a big way and became an instant celebrity, later serving as the catalyst in leading the team to the 1960 National Championship, and narrowly missing it once again by just two points in '61. He would also be named as the MVP of the 1961 Rose Bowl, he led the Gophers past UCLA, 21-3.

Still considered by many to be one of the greatest players ever to wear the maroon and gold, Sandy will always be a football legend in Gold Country. From 1959-1961 the first real option quarterback in big-time college football threw for nearly 1,500 yards and rushed for an amazing 20 touchdowns. He led the Gophers in total offense and scoring all three years he played, and in an era of platoon football, Stephens also played safety, punted and returned kicks.

In 1961 he was named as the Big Ten's MVP, and also became just the first African American to earn All-American honors as a quarterback. In addition, he finished fourth in the balloting for the Heisman Trophy.

"I was proud to be the first black All-American quarterback," said Sandy. "Doug Williams was the second, and he played 17 years after me."

After college, Sandy was drafted in the first round by the New York Titans of the American Football League. "At the time the Titans didn't want a black man playing quarterback," said Stephens. "Cleveland had my NFL rights, but the NFL still wasn't ready for a black quarterback. So, I was forced to play in Canada." With the promise that he would be given a chance to be the signal caller, Sandy went north of the border and signed on with the Montreal Alouettes.

After three successful years in Canada, Sandy's life was abruptly changed when he was involved in a nearly fatal car accident. The doctors said that he wasn't supposed to ever walk again, but Sandy was determined to come back. He fought hard to rehabilitate himself and in 1964, Sandy's old teammate, Bobby Bell, asked his Chiefs coach, Hank Stram, to give his old friend a shot at a comeback. He did, and Sandy overcame the unbelievable odds against him by playing with Kansas City for two seasons, both as a defensive back as well as a quarterback, before retiring from the game in 1970.

In 1997, Sandy was inducted into the Rose Bowl Hall of Fame. "Getting this honor now, after all these years, is thrilling and definitely a high point in my life," said Stephens.

Sandy was the greatest quarterback to ever wear the maroon and gold. He blessed the University of Minnesota football program with his talents and leadership like no other, before or since. Tragically, Sandy died of an apparent heart attack in June of 2000. He was 59 years old.

"I loved everything about being a member of the University of Minnesota football team," recalled Stephens. "In fact, the only negative thing that I remembered about coming to Minnesota, was the fact that a gopher was their mascot. I almost didn't come to Minnesota because of that nickname. In Pennsylvania, being a gopher didn't mean anything good. It meant you'd 'go-fer' anything!"

"I hope that they'll remember the championship teams that we had," he added. "That's my biggest thing. I have always been a team player. The only reason that you achieve accolades is because of the teammates that you have, and I had great teammates all the way through. We were all champions."

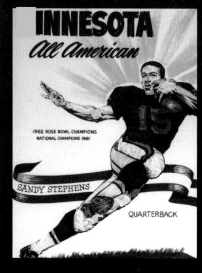

Here is What a Few of Sandy's Teammates Had to Say About Him:
"Sandy was a great quarterback," said Bobby Bell. "If they would've given Sandy the opportunity to have played in the NFL, he would have been the first black quarterback in league — that's how good he was. He was a player that just wanted to win. He had the quickness, the speed, the arm, and the agility. Defenses couldn't pin him down and contain him because he was so fast and so smart. He could beat you in a lot of ways, but especially one-on-one. He was so versatile; he would punt, pass, run, and do just about anything for the team. He hated to lose. I don't care if you were playing ping-pong, he wanted to beat you. He drove us to win and to be national champions. He was an all-around fun guy to play with and a tremendous competitor."

"He was a great leader and commanded a lot of respect from everybody," said Tom Brown. "His teammates really liked him and always played hard for him."

"He was the field general, in the truest sense of the word," said Carl Eller. "He was in command out on the field, and there was no question about it. We had total confidence in him and we knew that he could get it done. He would tell us in the huddle that we were going to either run over my side or over Bobby Bell's side, and we would do it. He was just a fabulous football player."

five and weighed in at 240 pounds. Eller and Bell, a pair of outstanding tandem bookend Tackles from North Carolina, would anchor the Gopher defense and eventually lead the squad back to Pasadena.

"Goldie" Gopher Returns To ASADENA!

The team's season opener against Missouri attracted a lot of national interest because the Tigers were the team that Minnesota had climbed over to earn the number one ranking in the polls after the last week of the 1960 season. The playing conditions that day were less than desirable, to say the least. "It was the worst game in terms of weather conditions that I ever played in," said Stephens. "It was just awful, and it was so cold that I couldn't feel the ball when it was centered." Amidst constant rain and wind, the Tigers hung tough and upset the Gophers by the score of 6-0.

Minnesota won six in a row after the sorry Missouri opener, starting with Oregon, who they rallied to beat, 14-7. Stephens scored both Minnesota touchdowns in this one, with the speedster from Fairmont, Jimmy Cairns, adding a two-pointer for good measure. Then, against Northwestern, Stephens tallied on a one-yarder, while Judge Dickson added a 31-yard field goal of his own to give the Gophers a 10-3 victory. In Champaign, Stephens beat the Fighting Illini all by himself, passing for four touchdowns and scoring a fifth on a short run.

In the 23-20 win over Michigan, Stephens, who was married just two days prior, played one of his best games ever, racking up over 300 all-purpose yards in another come-from-behind victory. The game started out horribly though, as Stephens coughed up two balls that led to Michigan touchdowns early on. Trailing 13-0, Stephens rolled out on his own 37-yard line, and behind the brilliant blocking of Cairns, sped 63 yards into the end-zone. He then hit End John Campbell with a two-point conversion pass. After a third quarter Wolverine touchdown to make it 20-8, Stephens struck again, hitting Jack Campbell on a 46-yard TD pass. Minnesota then had a touchdown called back on a penalty, only to have Judge Dickson recover a Benny McRae fumble and then go in on a one-yarder to score the winning touchdown just a few plays later on a key fourth down. With under a minute to go, Stephen's then hit Tom Hall for the two-pointer to ice it, and even saved the day in the final seconds of the game when he deflected a sure touchdown pass on defense.

Then there was the 13-0 shutout over the then top-ranked Michigan State Spartans at Memorial Stadium, where Munsey, who had recovered from an injury that sidelined him from the Wolverine game the week before, scored both touchdowns for the Gophers.

Next up was Iowa. After giving up an early safety, Tom Loechler's field goal early in the second gave Minnesota a 3-2 lead. Then, in the third, Stephens tallied on a 39-yarder, followed by a touchdown on a blocked punt by Dick Enga, which was recovered in the end zone by John Campbell to give the Gophers a 16-9 victory.

Purdue was next, as an all-time record crowd of 67,081 crammed into Memorial Stadium to watch the Gophers beat the Boilers, 10-7. Minnesota went ahead 10-0 on Tom Loechler's 25-yard field goal, followed by Stephens four-yard score. The Boilermakers rallied back to score, but the Gopher defense, which yielded just 27 yards of rushing on the day, stood firm in preserving the win in one of the most bruising battles in Gopher history.

Now only the Wisconsin Badgers stood in the way of the Gophers' first perfect Big Ten record since 1941. But Wisconsin coach Milt Bruhn, an ex-Gopher, had a different idea, as his Quarterback, Ron Miller, connected with Pat Richter for two touchdowns in leading his Badgers past Minnesota, 28-21. In the loss, Sandy Stephens and End Tom Hall combined for an 80-yard touchdown bomb, followed by Jerry Jones' 22-yard score. Stephens then connected with Al Fischer with just under two minutes to go, but it was too little too late.

Normally a 6-1 Big Ten record would make a solid case for winning the title, but, in 1961, the undefeated Ohio State Buckeyes would receive that honor. Then, in a bizarre twist of fate, Woody Hayes' Ohio State Buckeyes, who were invited to play the UCLA Bruins in the Rose Bowl, declined the invitation. If an official Big Ten-West Coast agreement been in effect at that time, Minnesota would have been ineligible to play in the big game two years in a row — but there was no such contract that year. As a result, the Rose Bowl committee selected the Gophers, and for the second time in as many years, they were off to Pasadena for a run at the roses.

"This time," Warmath would later say in an interview, "we stayed at a monastery where we were isolated and could get a lot of rest. We were better prepared mentally because it was a team of veterans. We had a more professional attitude, and we wanted to redeem ourselves for what happened the year before. UCLA was not as good a team as Washington the year before, but we played an excellent game."

Incidentally, the pressure was on to perform well for the camera during this game. That's because it was the first college football game to be televised nationally in color.

Reminiscent of the '61 Rose Bowl, when Washington scored a field goal on the opening drive, UCLA would also strike first in 1962. After being held deep in Gopher territory, the Bruins settled for a 28-yard field goal by Bob Smith just seven minutes into the game. The 98,214 fans that had poured into Pasadena's Rose Bowl to see the game could sense early on that Minnesota wasn't just happy to be there. That would be all the scoring the Bruins would do that day against the stingy Minnesota defense. The Gophers, haunted by the previous year's finale, rallied back late in the first on a one-yard touchdown plunge by Stephens, which was made possible by Dickson's fumble recovery a few plays prior. Coach Warmath had decided early that he wasn't going to play as conservatively on this go-round, and his Gophers went for it on several pivotal fourth down plays, picking up a first down on one, and scoring on another. Just before the half, Stephens marched the Gophers 75 yards for a second touchdown, with Munsey scoring on a reverse.

Dominating the game with their amazing defense, the Gophers looked poised in the second half. Stephens led the Gophers on an incredible 84-yard scoring drive late in the final period, scoring his second touchdown of the game from two yards out. The 19-play drive ate up 11 minutes off the clock, leaving little time for UCLA to do anything but wonder what could have been. The Gophers controlled every aspect of the game, compiling 21 first downs while holding UCLA to eight. Led by the outstanding defensive play of Bell and Eller, Minnesota held the Bruins to a paltry

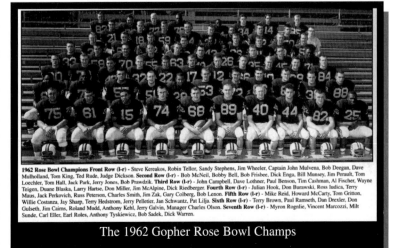

1962 Rose Bowl Champions Front Row (l-r) - Steve Kereakos, Robin Tellor, Sandy Stephens, Jim Wheeler, Captain John Mulvena, Bob Deegan, Dave Mulholland, Tom King, Ted Rude, Judge Dickson. Second Row (l-r) - Bob McNeil, Bobby Bell, Bob Frisbee, Dick Enga, Bill Munsey, Jim Perault, Tom Loechler, Tom Hall, Jack Park, Jerry Jones, Bob Prawdzik. Third Row (l-r) - John Campbell, Dave Lothner, Paul Benson, Tim Cashman, Al Fischer, Wayne Teigen, Duane Blaska, Larry Hartse, Don Miller, Jim McAlpine, Dick Riedberger. Fourth Row (l-r) - Julian Hook, Don Burawski, Ross Iudica, Terry Maus, Jack Perkovich, Russ Peterson, Charles Smith, Jim Zak, Gary Colberg, Bob Lenon. Fifth Row (l-r) - Mike Reid, Howard McCarty, Tom Gritton, Willie Costanza, Jay Sharp, Terry Hedstrom, Jerry Pelletier, Jan Schwantz, Pat Lilja. Sixth Row (l-r) - Terry Brown, Paul Ramseth, Dan Drexler, Don Gulseth, Jim Cairns, Roland Mudd, Anthony Kehl, Jerry Galvin, Manager Charles Olson. Seventh Row (l-r) - Myron Rognlie, Vincent Marcozzi, Milt Sunde, Carl Eller, Earl Roles, Anthony Tyskiewicz, Bob Sadek, Dick Warren.

The 1962 Gopher Rose Bowl Champs

Carl Eller

107 yards of total offense and a mere field goal. Minnesota would not be denied in their second run for the roses, winning the game, 21-3, for the team's first and only Rose Bowl victory. As coach Warmath was carried off the field, it was said that his smile could be seen all the way back in Minnesota.

"We went out the year before and lost to Washington, so this year we were going to win the Rose Bowl, no matter what," said Bobby Bell. "We beat UCLA pretty bad, and I have to say it was amazing. It was one of the greatest things that ever happened to me in college. I was playing with cracked ribs during the game, but at the time I didn't care because I wanted to win so badly. I can remember our defensive coach was saying to us, 'hey, if you let these guys run three or four yards up the middle, then we are not players at all, we might as well pack up, put our dresses back on, and go home.' Their running back, All-American, Charlie Smith, was a great player, but every time he got close to that line, we were all over him. We shut him down completely. It was great, and when it was over, we were sitting on top of the world."

"It wouldn't have mattered who we would have played this go around," added Big Ten MVP, Sandy Stephens. "I would have died before I lost that game, even if I had to win it all by myself. We just completely dominated UCLA from the point after they made that opening field goal. The game started out similar to the Rose Bowl of the year before, and that shocked us and woke us up pretty quick. That was the first and last time UCLA would score on us that day."

"I don't know if this is something that is very well known," said Carl Eller, "but I think that a lot of the senior players weren't sure if they even wanted to go back to the Rose Bowl in 1961. We actually had a team meeting on whether or not we should even go. Many of the players didn't want to go if Coach Warmath, who was a task-master, was going to lock them up in a retreat again when they were right down the street from Hollywood. Now, I was only a sophomore at the time, so I didn't have a voice on the team like the juniors and seniors did, but I felt like there was a mutiny going on. So, I stepped up and said, 'Hey guys, I don't want you to rob me of my chance to go to the Rose Bowl.' I didn't care what hotel we stayed at, I just wanted to go to the Rose Bowl! I think in retrospect, he (Warmath) probably did relax a little bit on us out there, and we had a great time that year. We had a very strong team in 1962, and we just overpowered UCLA, physically dominating them. It was a tremendous experience."

After the season several Gophers were honored, including Bell, who was once again named as a unanimous All-American, and was also awarded the prestigious Outland Trophy, recognizing him as the nation's top interior lineman. Sandy Stephens also became the first African American ever to be named as an All-American Quarterback.

Insanity at Camp Randall

With Stephens gone, Duane Blaska took over the quarterbacking duties in 1962. He was joined by a solid backfield that year as well, with Bill Munsey, Jerry Jones, Jim Cairns, Bill McMillan, Bill Crockett and Jerry Pelletier. It would be the defense, however, that would be the trademark of this team, which posted an amazing five shut-outs that season. Anchored by future Minnesota Viking's All-Pro Carl Eller, the Gophers' defense allowed just 58 yards of rushing per game against Big Ten opposition, while surrendering a mere 61 points in nine games. More than half of those points even came in one game, a 34-22 upset by Northwestern.

After opening the season with a tough 0-0 standoff with Missouri, Minnesota went on to blank Navy, 21-0 (Navy had negative 31 yards rushing!), before being upset by a pesky Northwestern team. They rebounded to post a pair of 17-0 shut-outs over Illinois and Michigan (Michigan was held to negative 46 yards rushing as well!), followed by wins over Michigan State, 28-7, Iowa, 10-0, and Purdue, 7-6. With a 5-1 Big Ten record, the Gophers needed a win at Wisconsin to secure the conference title and a repeat trip to Pasadena. The Badgers, also at 5-1, were ready and waiting when the Gophers came to mix it up at Camp Randall Stadium in Madison.

Unfortunately, what followed could be considered to be one of the most bizarre and disturbing games ever played in college football history. When the dust finally settled, it became clear that the officials, not the players, played a pivotal role in a game that will long be remembered for all of the wrong reasons in Gold Country.

The Gophers opened the scoring in the second quarter, with Duane Blaska connecting with Jimmy Cairns on a 15 yard scoring strike.

Defensive End Aaron Brown went on to be drafted in the first round by the KC Chiefs, where he played professionally for nine seasons.

The extra point was no good, as Quarterback Ron VanderKelen then rallied his Badgers back with a 65-yard scoring drive to take at 7-6 lead.

In the second half, the game started to turn into a penalty-filled freak-show, capped by the Gophers being penalized 15 yards for illegally aiding the advance of a runner, Bill Munsey. Minnesota settled for a Collin Versich 32-yard field goal, and the scoreboard read: Minnesota 9, Wisconsin 7.

The Gophers later punted, and the coverage team, seeing the ball hit a Badger player, jumped on the loose ball rolling in the end zone, and claimed a touchdown. The officials didn't see it that way, however, and returned the ball to Wisconsin out on the 20-yard line. The Gophers, dejected, assumed that the refs probably just didn't see it, and figured they would get it right the next time. Wrong! Then it happened — an event that will live in infamy! On the Gopher 43 yard-line, VanderKelen dropped back to pass and was sacked hard by Bell. The ball then flew into the awaiting arms of Gopher John Perkovich, only to have the referee, Robert Jones, nullify the interception. Incredibly, he even called Bell for roughing the passer. At this point, Coach Warmath could no longer contain himself. The 15-yard roughing call suddenly turned into 30 when the ref slapped the Gopher bench with an additional unsportsmanlike conduct penalty. So, instead of Minnesota having the ball at mid-field, the Badgers now had a first down on the Minnesota 13-yard line with less than two minutes to go. Three plays later Wisconsin scored to make it 14-9.

Then, amazingly, the officials, who were feeling the heat, decided to even things up and let the Gophers back into the contest by first calling the Badgers for a personal foul penalty on the ensuing kickoff, followed shortly thereafter by a pair of pass interference calls. Suddenly, with a minute to go in the game, the Gophers found themselves with a first down on the Wisconsin 14. Now it gets weird.

Mysteriously, all communications from the press box to the Gopher bench disappeared, and the assistant coaches who had the bird's eye views were silenced with jammed head-sets. So, on first down, Blaska, not knowing otherwise, went for it all. But, his floater was picked-off in the end zone to kill the rally. Wisconsin had won the Big Ten championship. The irate Gopher fans had just witnessed their third straight Rose Bowl appearance vanish before their very eyes.

"I was called for roughing the Badger quarterback," said Bell, who would go on to receive All-American honors for the second straight year, "but you could see on the film that he still had the ball in his hands, so it couldn't have been roughing. It was a blown call. It was a mess, and they ended up getting about 45 yards out of the whole thing, which ultimately led to them winning the game. It was the craziest game I ever played in. I bet that I've received hundreds of letters and newspaper clippings from around the country about that one play, and people still want to talk to me about it. The referee's name was Robert Jones. I will never forget that guy."

The run was over. For three glorious seasons in the early 1960s, Minnesota had produced a very respectable 22-6-1 record, entitling them to a National Championship, a Big Ten title, and a Rose Bowl victory. The next few years would take a toll on Warmath. The team lost a lot of key seniors from the 1962 team, and 1963 was viewed as a rebuilding year. They did have Carl "Moose" Eller, then a senior, Captain Milt Sunde, as well as a sophomore Defensive End named Aaron Brown, who would go on to become one of the great ones. One highlight did come against the team's first-ever meeting with Army, as the Gophers spanked the Cadets, 24-8, thanks to the passing of Quarterback Bob Sadek and

Bob Stein

the running of Fullback Mike Reid. After finishing up the season with a promising 14-0 blanking of Wisconsin, the Gophers packed it in with a humbling 3-6 record, good for ninth in the Big Ten. "Moose" Eller went on to receive All-American honors that year, and would go on to become the backbone of the Vikings' legendary "Purple People Eaters" defense.

That next year the team was led by a young quarterback named John Hankinson, who had a plethora of targets to throw to that year including, Kenny Last, Kent Kramer, Ray Whitlow, Billy Crockett and even Aaron Brown, who, platooning at tight end, caught a school record

Karl Mecklenberg

27 balls that year. Minnesota put together a couple of winning seasons in 1964 and 1965, going 5-4 and 5-4-1 respectively. Aaron Brown, who, despite suffering a broken jaw on the opening play of the game against Washington State in 1965 but insisted on playing — coming out only to spit blood when he had to, was named as an All-American. Brown was so tough that he even finished the season with his mouth wired shut! That 1965 team, which beat Indiana, 42-18, Iowa, 14-3, Michigan, 14-13, Northwestern, 27-22, and Wisconsin, 42-7, came on strong to finish tied for third place in the Big Ten. By the time team captain John Hankinson graduated that season, he had broken nearly every Minnesota passing record, including setting a single-season total offense plateau of 1,583 yards. ("Hank" would go on to play in the NFL with the Vikings, later producing three amazing kids who would all go on to play professional hockey in the NHL.)

Warmath was forced to rebuild yet again in 1966, this time with Curt Wilson as his Quarterback. Wilson, a good running QB, was helped out that year by Warmath's decision to change to the "I" formation. The more high powered offensive attack began to take shape late in the season, as Minnesota, who tallied wins against Stanford, Iowa, Ohio State and Northwestern, finished their campaign with a 4-5-1 record, good for fifth in the Big Ten.

The nucleus of that team returned in 1967, and so was a renewed interest in Gopher football. The fans were again coming out to see this group who showed some real promise early on. Warmath had shifted Curtis Wilson, his starting Quarterback from 1966, to Halfback, and instead rotated Ray Stephens, Sandy's younger brother, Walter Bowser and Phil Hagen into the fold.

The Gophers kicked off the season with a very unimpressive 13-12 win over Utah, followed by an even more unimpressive 7-0 loss to Nebraska. They rebounded though, beating SMU, 23-3, and the Illini, 10-7. Next up were the defending Big Ten champs from Michigan State, who came to campus riding a 16-game unbeaten streak. Warmath shook it up in this one, switching Wilson back to quarterback, and letting the Spartan scouts know that they were going to be utilizing his running skills that Saturday. Luckily for Murray, they took the bait, as the decoy Wilson torched MSU by passing for 264 yards and three touchdowns, including a pair to Chip Litten and another to Hubie Bryant, en route to a huge 21-0 upset victory. George Kemp and Jim Carter did most of the damage on the ground, combining for more than 100 yards rushing, while the Minnesota defense, anchored by All-American End Bob Stein, McKinley Boston, Dick Enderle and Del Jessen, shut-down the Spartan's high-octane offense.

Minnesota kept it going that next week, coming from behind to take a 20-15 win over Michigan, followed by a 10-0 shut-out over Iowa. They then suffered a mental lapse against Purdue in Week Eight, getting crushed 41-12. With the Big Ten title hanging in the balance, the undefeated Indiana Hoosiers came to town to let it all hang out. Minnesota opened the scoring in this one, on Wilson's six-yard touchdown run in the second quarter. It would be just the first of four rushing touchdowns on the day for Wilson, who also passed for one as well to his favorite receiver, Charlie Sanders.

With the win, the Gophers found themselves in somewhat of a quagmire. You see, going into the last week of the season, the Gophers were in a position to win a share of the Big Ten title if they beat Wisconsin. Indiana, who was playing Purdue,

1967 Big Ten Champions- Front Row (l-r) - Del Jessen, Bob Stein, Maurice Forte, Bob Brothen, Randy Rajala, Bobby Lee, Dave Baldridge, Dick Peterson, Larry Carlson, John Bergstrom, Wayne King, Noel Jenke. Second Row (l-r) - Ezell Jones, Charles (Chip) Litten, Curtis Wilson, Hubie Bryant, McKinley Boston, Bob Bedney, Tom Sakal, John Williams, Ed Duren, Charley Sanders, Ron Klick, Gordon (Miko) Condo. Third Row (l-r) - Tom Fink, Dennis Hale, Tim McGovern, Asst. Coach, Bob Gongola, Asst. Coach, Mike McGee, Asst. Coach, Butch Nash, Asst. Coach, Don Grammer, Asst. Coach, Head Coach Murray Warmath, Denver Crawford, Asst. Coach, Jerry Annis, Asst. Coach, Mike Reid, Asst. Coach, Lloyd Stein, Trainer Andy Brown, Ray Stephens, Ron Kamzelski. Back Row (l-r) - Jon Hammer, John Wintermute, John Darkenwald, Steve Lundeen, Mike Curtis, Phil Hagen, Leon Trawick, Jim Carter, Anthony (Jim) Pahula, Dave Nixon, George Kemp, Bill Laakso, Dick Enderle.

The 1967 Co-Big Ten Champs

Gopher All-Americans

Year	Name	Position
1903	Fred Schact*	Tackle
1909	Johnny McGovern*	Quarterback
1910	James Walker*	Tackle
1915	Bert Baston	End
1916	Bert Baston*	End
	C.I. "Shorty" Long	Quarterback
1917	George Hauser*	Tackle
1923	Ray Ecklund*	End
	Earl Martineau	Halfback
1926	Herb Joesting*	Fullback
1927	Herb Joesting*	Fullback
	Harold Hanson	Guard
1928	George Gibson	Guard
	Kenneth Haycraft	End
1929	Bronko Nagurski**	Fullback & Tackle
1931	Clarence "Biggie" Munn*	Guard
1933	Frank "Butch" Larson	End
1934	Frank "Butch" Larson*	End
	Francis "Pug" Lund*	Halfback
	Bill Bevan*	Guard
1935	Charles "Bud" Wilkinson	Guard
	Ed Widseth*	Tackle
	Dick Smith	Tackle
1936	Ed Widseth**	Tackle
1937	Ray King	End
	Andy Uram	Fullback
1938	Francis Twedell	Guard
1940	Urban Odson*	Tackle
	George Franck*	Halfback
1941	Bruce Smith*	Halfback
	Dick Wildung*	Tackle
1942	Dick Wildung*	Tackle
1943	Bill Daley#	Fullback
	Herb Hein#	End
1948	Leo Nomellini*	Tackle
1949	Leo Nomellini*	Tackle
	Clayton Tonnemaker**	Center
1952	Paul Giel	Halfback
1953	Paul Giel**	Halfback
1954	Bob McNamara	Halfback
1956	Bob Hobert	Tackle
1960	Tom Brown**	Guard
1961	Sandy Stephens*	Quarterback
	Bobby Bell	Tackle
1962	Bobby Bell**	Tackle
1963	Carl Eller*	Tackle
1965	Aaron Brown*	End
1967	Bob Stein	End
1971	Doug Kingsriter	End
1997	Lemanzer Williams	Def. End
1999	Tyrone Carter	Safety
	Ben Hamilton	Center

*   *Consensus All-American*
** *Unanimous Consensus All-American*

was in the identical position. However, if Minnesota lost their game, and finished second in the conference, they would get to go to the Rose Bowl. Confusing? Here's how it went down. Because Purdue was ineligible to go to the Rose Bowl that year (due to the fact that there was a rule at that time which declared that a team couldn't go two years in a row), the second place team would get to go instead. Well, the Gophers wound up beating the Badgers, 21-14, but it also so happened that Indiana upset Purdue, 19-14. With both Minnesota and Indiana now tied for the Big Ten title, along with Purdue (who was ineligible to go the Rose Bowl), the committee selected the Hoosiers to go over the Gophers because "they had never been there before." It was a rip-off, and everyone in Minnesota knew it.

Minnesota bounced back for a 6-4 overall record in 1968, finishing at 5-2 in the conference standings — good enough for a third place tie. After dropping the first two to USC and Nebraska, the U of M rallied to beat Wake Forest, 24-19, Illinois, 17-10, and Michigan State, 14-13. They then got beat by both Michigan and Iowa, 33-20, and, 35-28, respectively, only to bounce back with wins over Purdue, 27-13 (Running Back Jim Carter led the charge in upsetting the No.1 ranked Boilermakers), Indiana, 20-6, and Wisconsin, 23-15.

Leading the way for the Gophers that year was St. Louis Park's Bob Stein, who, for the second year in a row, received both All-American and Academic All-American honors. (Stein, who went on to play Defensive End for the Kansas City Chiefs and Minnesota Vikings, would later become the President of the NBA's Minnesota Timberwolves.)

The next three years would also be the last three for Coach Murray Warmath. That regime included three losing seasons starting in 1969, when Minnesota finished at 4-5-1, good for fourth in the Big Ten. In 1970 they wound up with a 3-6-1 record, while in 1971, they could muster just a 4-7 mark. One game of note in 1970, against Michigan State, saw Gopher Corner Walter Bowser run back 140 yards worth of interceptions, while D-Back Jeff Wright picked off three of his own in the 23-13 victory. Fittingly, on the last drive of the last game of the 1971 season against Wisconsin, the boys of gold gave their coach a proper send-off by presenting him with a last-minute game-winning touchdown, courtesy of Craig Curry's pass to Mel Anderson, to eke out a 23-21 victory over the Cheese-Heads.

One bright spot over those otherwise dismal last two seasons, was the outstanding play of Quarterback Craig Curry, who led the Big Ten in total offense over both of those years, including throwing a record nine touchdown passes in 1971. Another emerging star was junior Doug Kingsriter, an All-American Tight End from Richfield who made the one-handed grab his trademark on the gridiron.

Other great players from that era included: Walt Bowser, Jim Carter, Ernie Cook, Mo Forte, Phil Hagen, Kevin Hamm, Noel Jenke, Del Jessen, George Kemp, Wayne King, Bill Light, Chip Litten, Barry Mayer, Ray Parson, Doug Roalstad, Ray Stephens, John Wintermute and Jeff Wright, just to name a few.

Times were tough in Gold Country, and Warmath knew it. The numbers were down in the stands, and it didn't take a rocket scientist to figure out that there was a direct correlation between the dwindling fan base at old Memorial and a very good "other" football team which was now tearing up the National Football League down in Bloomington's Metropolitan Stadium. With that, Warmath, after 18 seasons in Gold Country, resigned. A man of dignity, toughness and pride, the Autumn Warrior took a program in shambles and built it into a national champion, and for that he should be remembered as one of the great ones.

Re-Enter Paul Giel and a Man Named Cal

Times, they were a changin' in Minnesota during the tumultuous early 1970s. The war in Vietnam was raging and college kids had more important things to be worrying about than playing football. Gopher football was hurting, and needed a shot in the arm. Pressure was on from all sides to win. Bill

Doug Kingsriter

Musselman, the Gophers new young basketball coach, came along in 1971 and led a rag-tag bunch all the way to the school's first Big Ten championship since the 1930's. The football program now needed a new coach of their own to come in and turn it around 180 degrees, like Musselman had done at Williams Arena.

The answer came in the form of former Gopher All-American Paul Giel, who, after several years of pitching in the big-leagues, and a stint at WCCO Radio, came in to serve as the University's new Athletic Director. Giel came in and rounded up a lot of corporate support from local businesses, like Midwest Federal and Twin City Federal, to get the program off to a clean start. They were instrumental in helping the program to upgrade its facilities, which would include the future construction of the Bierman Building — complete with a training field, locker rooms and weight rooms. In addition, Giel decided to retrofit his new team with some classic golden colored uniforms, reminiscent of those dominant Gopher squads of the 1930s.

The next thing he did was to hire a new coach, and he did just that in landing former Gopher Defensive End, Cal Stoll, who had just led Wake Forest to back-to-back conference championships down in North Carolina. Stoll, who first learned the game playing six-man football up in tiny Tower City, North Dakota, was elated to come home to his alma mater. To his new post Stoll brought more than 20 years of coaching experience, and from the looks of his squad, he was going to need every bit of it. He had the support of the fans though. After all, he was the first "M" man since Bernie Bierman to come back as the school's head coach.

Stoll's Gophers got off to a rocky start in 1972, losing their first five games to Indiana, Colorado, Nebraska, Kansas and Purdue. They finally got in to the win column on November 21st, piling up more than 400 total yards of offense to beat Iowa, 43-14. After a 42-0 shut-out at the hands of Michigan, and a 27-19 loss to Ohio State, the Gophers rebounded to finish the season with three straight wins over Northwestern, 35-29 (a game which the team racked up nearly 500 yards of total offense), Michigan State, 14-10, and Wisconsin, 14-6. Fullback John King led the charge for the Gophers that season, as he pounded the opposition and set several rushing records along the way. With a modest 4-7 record under their belts, the Gophers were poised to do even better that next year.

TONY DUNGY

As a quarterback from 1973-76, Tony Dungy finished his career near the top of almost every Gopher passing category. In addition to his incredible on-field performance, he was also a two-time Academic All-Big Ten selection. From there Dungy went on to sign with the Pittsburgh Steelers, where he played safety for two seasons. His best season was in 1978, when he posted six interceptions (second in the AFC) and helped top lead his Steelers over the Dallas Cowboys in Super Bowl XIII.

In 1980 he returned home to Minnesota, where he took over as the team's defensive backs coach. Soon after that he returned to Pittsburgh, where after a stint as an assistant, he became the league's youngest defensive coordinator at the age of 28. He would stay with the Steelers under Coach Chuck Noll for eight seasons before finally moving on as an assistant with the Kansas City Chiefs. After three years in KC, he came back to Minnesota, this time as a the Vikings' defensive coordinator. From 1992-95 Dungy worked his magic, ultimately turning the Vikings' defense into one of the league's best. His trademark for forcing turnovers became legendary and, as a result, it wasn't long before he got a call from the struggling Tampa Bay Buccaneers asking him to serve as their head coach. Tony immediately turned the program around, and in 1999, after leading his team to a pair of playoff appearances, guided his Buc's to the NFC Championship game. Today the Buccaneer's have the best defense in the NFL and are considered as one of the league's elite teams. Dungy, who is as modest as ever, has quietly emerged as the league's brightest young head coach.

"The University of Minnesota is really where I got my start," said Dungy of his alma mater. "I owe a lot to Head Coach Cal Stoll. He helped shape some of my values and some of the things I wanted to do in my life. The 'U' is where I developed a lot of the values that I carry with me today"

One of the stories of the 1973 season was the improbable saga of freshman Running Back Larry Powell, who tore it up that year, only to nearly lose his life the next. Powell, the crown jewel of Stoll's recruiting class, came out of Michigan that year and made his presence felt with his blinding speed. However, Powell contracted French Polio during that off-season, dropping down to a mere 115 pounds, and nearly died. He did recover, but sadly, he never played football again.

"I think if Larry Powell had stayed healthy, he would have won the Heisman Trophy," Stoll later said. "I know that sounds far-fetched, but that's how good he was. He was the best running back I ever recruited. Many scouts liked him better than Tony Dorsett, who was a contemporary. We might have gotten over the hump if Larry hadn't had such rotten luck. I'm serious. He was that good."

The Gophers, behind Powell's running, did manage to improve their record to an impressive 7-4 that season, even finishing third in the Big Ten. Among their victims were Indiana, 24-3, Iowa, 31-23, Northwestern, 52-43, Purdue, 34-7, Illinois, 19-16, and Wisconsin, 19-17. The school's two conference losses came at the hands of Michigan, who won 34-7, and Ohio State, 56-7. During the 1970s, those two schools would absolutely dominate the world of college football. While John King was the work-horse, carrying the ball on the ground, and Receiver Mike Jones dominated through the air, the leader of the team was a kid by the name of Tony Dungy. Dungy, a speedy and very crafty quarterback, would lead the Gophers for the next three years. (Today, after spending time as the Minnesota Vikings Defensive Coordinator, he is the head coach of the NFL's Tampa Bay Buccaneers.)

In 1974 Rick Upchurch hit the gridiron. He would go on to become one of the greats at Minnesota, setting several rushing records along the way. The Gophers slipped to 2-6 in the Big Ten that year, beating only Iowa and Purdue, ultimately finishing in just 7th place. One highlight though came on the last game of the season, when Upchurch returned a kick-off a record 100 yards against Wisconsin.

The 1975 season was more of the same for the Gophers, who managed just a 3-5 record that year. Dungy did throw 15 touchdowns though, en route to leading his team to wins over Iowa, 31-7,

Rick Upchurch

Marion Barber

Northwestern, 33-9, and Wisconsin, 24-3. Minnesota then rebounded in 1976, behind the running of Jim Perkins and the passing of Dungy, who capped his illustrious career with two single-season and six career Gopher records for passing and total offense, to finish with a much improved 4-4 record in the Big Ten. Among the team's wins that year were against Indiana, 21-13, Illinois, 29-14, Michigan State, 14-10, and Northwestern, 38-10.

Bowl-Bound at Last

Cal Stoll's most exciting season was without question the year of 1977. That was the year Minnesota finally turned the corner, and gave the football faithful on campus a reason to once again get excited. After beating lowly Western Michigan, 10-7, in the season opener, the Gophers got waxed by Ohio State, 38-7, in Columbus, with their only touchdown coming on an amazing Bobby Weber 100-yard kick-off return for a touchdown.

They mounted a nice pair of victories over their next two games at Memorial Stadium against UCLA and Washington though, beating them 27-13, and 19-17, respectively. Those two Western power-houses would later battle for the Pac-8 Rose Bowl berth, with the Huskies eventually getting the nod to go to Pasadena and beating the eventual Big Ten champs from Michigan. After suffering an 18-6 setback against Iowa, the Gophers rallied back to beat a respectable Northwestern team by the final score of 13-7.

What followed that next Saturday, October 22nd, at old Memorial, was one of the most special moments in Gopher history. The No. 1-ranked Michigan Wolverines had come to town, with an offense that sizzled and a defense that had not been shut out in 113 games. Both of those things would change on that day though. The Gopher faithful hadn't forgotten about the thrashing they had received just a year earlier, when Michigan buried the Gophers, 45-0, in Ann Arbor, and they also remembered the last time they had won the Little Brown Jug, way back in 1967. All of these factors went into the making of one of the program's biggest upsets of all-time, which would ultimately foil Michigan's national championship hopes.

Thanks to sophomore Quarterback Mark Carlson and a pair of Michiganders, Paul Rogind, who tallied three field goals, and Marion Barber, who scored the game's only touchdown, a four-yard run up the middle, the Gophers blanked the era's most dominant team by the final score of 16-0. The Minnesota defense was huge in this game, all but shutting down Michigan Quarterback Rick Leach, a player that Coach Bo Schembechler would, at the time, call his "best ever." Led by Linebacker Michael Hunt, who would be named as the National Defensive Player of the Week, and Defensive End Mark Merrill, who forced an early fumble which led to a Gopher score, Minnesota never let Michigan into the game. They held the Wolverines to 80 net yards rushing, and just 122 yards passing — most of which came late in the game against the Gophers' "prevent-zone" pass defense.

"Unless you've been there, you can't know the feeling," Stoll said following the big win. "There is nothing like it."

The emotional win would get the best of them, however, as the Hoosiers ambushed the Gophers that very next week, 34-22, in Bloomington, followed by a disappointing 29-10 loss at home against Michigan State. They would rebound though against a very good Illinois team in Week 10, thanks in large part to the running of Rochester's Kent Kitzmann, who carried the ball a record 57 times for 266 yards in the Gophers' 21-0 triumph over the Illini in Champaign.

On one second half drive, Kitzmann carried the ball 13 consecutive times, never once losing yardage. "The line was great," said Kitzmann. "My job was probably easier than theirs, considering the way they knocked people off the line of scrimmage."

Kitzmann took "only" 40 hand-off's against Wisconsin the following week, rushing this time for 154 yards in a 13-7 win. Freshman Running Back Marion Barber's 33-yard game-winning touchdown run was the big play though, as the Gophers, with the win, clinched an invitation to play in the inaugural Hall of Fame Bowl.

The 7-4 Gophers then headed south, to Birmingham, Alabama, where they would face the University of Maryland in the teams' first bowl appearance since the 1962 Rose Bowl win in Pasadena. With thousands of Gopher faithful on hand amidst the 47,000 fans at Legion Field, Minnesota took its opening drive 66 yards in 11 plays to take a 7-0 lead. Scoring for the Gophers was Tailback Marion Barber, on a one-yard plunge, followed by Paul Rogind's extra point.

The Terrapins later connected on a 32-yard field goal, followed by a 69-yard touchdown drive midway through the second which was finished by Running Back George Scott's two-yard plunge over the middle. The Maroon & Gold, now down by three, let the wheels come off just two plays later by fumbling the ball on their own 14-yard line. Scott again made them pay, this time scoring his second touchdown of the day on a one-yard TD to make it 17-7 at the intermission. From there the Terrapin defense simply shut down the Gophers' offensive attack. Despite Kitzman's 76-yards rushing, Jeff Anhorn's 49-yards receiving, and Quarterback Wendell Avery's 130 yards through the air, Minnesota was held to just 268 total yards of offense for the game. Following a scoreless second half, which featured several valiant Gopher rallies that just came up short, the game ended as a 17-7 loss.

Mike Shanahan was the Gopher's Offensive Coordinator in 1979.

Minnesota finished the 1977 season with a modest record of 7-5, and a fifth place Big Ten finish. They would go 5-6 in 1978, finishing fifth in the conference yet again that year. Quarterback Mark Carlson proved to be a solid performer in the pocket, while Receiver Elmer Bailey hauled in 27 balls for a modest 464 yards. In addition, Marion Barber lit it up on the ground, rushing for a school record 1,237 yards and eight touchdowns. Highlighting the year were wins over Toledo, 38-12, Iowa, 22-20, Northwestern, 38-14, Indiana, 32-31, and Illinois, 24-6. The low-point of the year came on the season finale, when the lowly Badgers upset the Gophers, 48-10, at Wisconsin to conclude the 1978 season.

Jim Fahnhorst

Keith Fahnhorst

Coming on the heels of Cal Stoll's best year, the crushing defeat left Minnesota no other choice but to start searching for a new coach.

In his seven seasons on campus Cal Stoll's teams won 39 games and lost 39 games. His .500% record had its share of ups and downs, but was not impressive enough to earn him an eighth campaign behind the Gopher bench. Making matters even more difficult for Stoll was what was later referred to as the "Big Two" and the "Little Eight." The "Big Two" were Ohio State and Michigan, who won every football title in that 70s decade, while the "Little Eight" was simply everyone else — including Minnesota. With Woody Hayes at Ohio State and Bo Schembechler at Michigan, it gave teams little hope of ever getting over the hump. Incredibly, during the Stoll years, only Minnesota, Purdue and Michigan State managed to win even one game from the "Big Two." To his credit though, Stoll outlasted all the other "Little Eight" coaches from the time he came into the conference back in 1972. Minnesota was 27-29 against Big Ten teams from 1972-78. However, if you were to exclude the Ohio State and Michigan games, they were a respectable 26-16. That translates to paltry 1-13 against the "Big Two," with the Michigan upset in 1977 being the only exception.

"Catching them was almost impossible," Stoll would later say of the "Big Two." "It's like running the mile, only they have a half-mile head start. And they aren't going to slow down."

Welcome Back Smoky Joe

Stoll's replacement in Gold Country would be none other than former Gopher Rose Bowl Quarterback, Joe Salem. "Smoky Joe," who had been an assistant with the Gophers in the mid-1960s, had moved on to coach at both South Dakota and Northern Arizona.

Anxious to return to his alma mater, Salem opened his 1979 campaign with a 24-10 win over Ohio University, only to drop the next two to Ohio State and USC. They rebounded though, beating both Northwestern, 38-8, and Purdue, 31-14, before losing a tough one to Michigan, 31-21. They rallied to beat Iowa, 24-7, and then tied Illinois at 17-apiece. From there the Gophers lost their final three games to

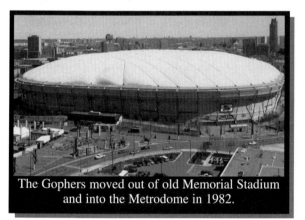

The Gophers moved out of old Memorial Stadium and into the Metrodome in 1982.

Indiana, Michigan State and Wisconsin, to finish with a 4-6-1 record — good for just sixth in the Big Ten. Mark Carlson threw for 2,188 yards that year, while Running Back Garry White tallied 1,021 all-purpose yards.

The 1980 season would be another average year in Minneapolis, with the Gophers finishing with a marginal 5-6 record, and a fifth place finish in the Big Ten. Garry White and Marion Barber combined to form one of the conference's most respected backfields, while Tim Salem (Joe's son) passed for nearly 900 yards on the year. The team did manage wins over Ohio, 38-14, Northwestern, 49-21, Iowa, 24-6, Illinois, 21-18, and Indiana, 31-7. Three-time All-Big Ten Running Back Marion Barber, who ran for a school record 3,087 yards, went on to a successful career with the NFL's New York Jets.

Salem's 1981 Gopher squad got off to its best start in years by winning their first three games over Ohio, 19-17, Purdue, 16-13, and Oregon State, 42-12, a game which saw Quarterback Mike Hohensee pass for five touchdowns. From there the Gophers suffered a pair of losses to both Illinois and Indiana, sandwiched by a win over Northwestern in the middle. It was a tough final stretch for the Gophers, who, despite upsetting Ohio State, behind Hohensee's 444 yards of passing and five touchdown tosses, and Chester Cooper's 182 yards of receiving, lost the remainder of their games to Michigan, Michigan State and Wisconsin.

The 26-21 loss to Wisconsin, which took place on November 21, 1981, would prove to be one the saddest games in the history of Gopher football. That's because it proved to be the last game ever at Memorial Stadium.

The last points ever scored by the Gophers in the old Brick House came when Hohensee hooked up with Chester Cooper on a four-yard touchdown pass in the fourth quarter to give Minnesota a 21-20 lead. Unfortunately though, the Cheese-Heads rallied behind reserve Quarterback Randy Wright, who connected with Michael Jones on a seven-yard touchdown pass with just under a minute to go in the game to give the Badgers the victory.

Hohensee, who passed for 2,412 yards, also set a single-season record for touchdown passes that year, with 20. In addition, Running Back Frank Jacobs ran for 636 yards, while Wide Receiver Chester Cooper hauled in over 1,000 receiving yards and six TDs that year, en route to leading the team to a respectable 6-5 record, good for sixth place in the very tough Big Ten.

Enter "Sweet Lou"

The 1982 Gophers took a big leap of faith by abandoning the Brick House and moving off-campus to the newly constructed Metrodome in downtown Minneapolis. How would the Gophers respond to playing in this new, sterile, 70-degree artificial environment? Well, it started out like it was going to be the

Lou Holtz

RICKEY FOGGIE

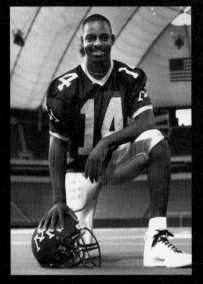

Rickey Foggie was born and raised in Waterloo, S.C., where he grew up as one of nine siblings in a family that loved sports. At Laurens High School he was an all-stater in both football and basketball, and, in his senior year, he led his high school football team to the state championship.

After being heavily recruited in both sports, Foggie came on board at Minnesota in 1983, following the disastrous 1-10 Gopher season under Joe Salem. As a freshman, he led the team in both rushing and passing and showed great promise by redefining the conventional rules of the quarterback position. For his career he remains the university's all-time leader in total offense, with 7,312 yards. He is still No. 8 all-time in rushing with 2,150 yards, and ranks third all-time in career yards passing, with 5,162 yards. From 1984-1987 he scored 160 points, putting him ninth all-time in that category. He also ranks No. 2 for most touchdown passes, with 34, and is third in rushing touchdowns, with 25. Throughout his career he completed 311 passes, good enough for fifth all-time, while amassing an amazing 16.8 yard average gain per completion, tops in school history. Playing the option, Foggie became only the third quarterback in college history to run over 2,000 yards and pass for over 4,000 yards. By the time he left Gold Country, the Gophers had not only gone to two bowl games, but he had returned the program to its old glory.

When Rickey finished his tenure at Minnesota, he headed north of the border to play in the Canadian Football League, first with the British Columbia Lions, then the Toronto Argonauts, where he won a Grey Cup, and lastly the Edmonton Eskimos. From there he headed to Memphis, when the CFL expanded to the United States. Then Rickey had a homecoming of sorts when he came back to Minnesota to play with the new Fighting Pike of the Arena Football League. In 1996, after only one season in the Target Center, the Pike folded. Foggie headed east and began his 10th year of professional football with the New Jersey Red Dogs of the same arena league.

"Once I learned the great tradition of the school and its winning success, it all kind of sunk in," said Foggie of his alma mater. "Coach Holtz brought back a lot of the tradition. To be able to play in front of sellout crowds for our first two years was great. I felt that we brought a college football atmosphere back to the U of M. The fans were great, and it always meant a lot to me that they supported me the way that they did. Maroon and gold is something that I will never be able to get out of my system, and I am always proud to say that I am a Gopher."

best thing since sliced bread. The men of gold opened with three straight victories over Ohio, Purdue and Washington State, even outscoring the schools by the insane margin of 134-24. This Astroturf thing was going to be way better than that old dump of a stadium back on University Avenue, right? Wrong! Minnesota took a nose-dive after that, losing the remainder of their final eight games and finished dead last in the Big Ten.

It didn't get any better that next year either. In fact it got worse, as the team finished with a miserable 1-10 record and yet another spot in the Big Ten cellar. Minnesota was so bad that year that they allowed 4,951 yards in total offense while fumbling 30 times and throwing 25 interceptions, en route to being outscored by their opponents 518-181. (One of the stars of this era, however, was New Brighton Guard Randy Rasmussen, who went on to star in the NFL with both the Steelers and Vikes.)

With that, Salem was canned. While he would return to his native South Dakota, to become the president of a liquor company, the Gophers needed to hire a new head coach, and quickly, before the recruiting season was awash. Giel knew he had to right this ship, or his job would be on the line too. But he needed some heavy artillery to get it done this time. The big gun he was able to woo into the northwoods that year, would be none other than Arkansas Head Coach, Lou Holtz. Holtz, who had just taken the Razorbacks to six consecutive bowl games, was considered by many to be one of college football's premier coaches.

"Sweet Lou," who came in amidst the hype and fan-fair of a rock star, took the campus by storm. Holtz fever was everywhere and with it came a renewed sense of pride the Gopher football program hadn't seen in decades. Holtz could recruit, coach and preach to the masses better than anyone. He could sell ice in the North Pole and sand in the desert, and before it was all said and done, thousands upon thousands of fans would follow him like the Pied Piper into that big teflon tent otherwise known as the Metrodome to watch their Gophers make an about face.

In 1984, his first year at the helm, Holtz began one of the greatest turn-arounds the program would ever see. The last-place Gophers hit the field against Rice in their opener, and behind the amazing play of freshman Quarterback Rickey Foggie, who would go on to rush for 647 yards, pass for 1,036 and toss 10 touchdown passes that season, Minnesota ended their eight-game losing streak by beating the Owls, 31-24. The team hit a few bumps in the road from there, losing three straight to Nebraska, Purdue and Ohio State, before rebounding to beat Indiana and Wisconsin, 33-24 and 17-14, respectively. Then, after losing their next four to Northwestern, Michigan State, Illinois and Michigan, the team rallied to beat rival Iowa by the final score of 23-17. With the team excitedly hoisting Floyd of Rosedale above their heads down on the Metrodome floor, people just knew that this was going to be the beginning of something special.

The "Fog" Rolls in to Shreveport

In 1985 the upstart Gophers greatly improved to finish with a 7-5 record, which included the program's first post-season bowl appearance in nearly a decade. Leading the charge once again was Rickey Foggie, who tore up the Big Ten that year. There have been quite a few memorable T-formation quarterbacks at the University of Minnesota, but none of them was as versatile a performer as was Rickey Foggie. Foggie could run, pass, scramble, and wreak havoc on opposing defenses — making up the rules as he went along.

Led by Foggie, who scored three touchdowns on 140 yards rushing while throwing for another 157, the Maroon and Gold kicked off the season with a 28-14 win over Wichita State. From there, the Gophers crushed Montana, 62-17, as Foggie again played masterfully. The Gophers piled up over 500 yards of offense as Valdez Baylor rushed for 89 yards and two touchdowns and Ricky Foggie scored three TDs and passed for another to Mel Anderson.

Minnesota, despite Foggie's TD pass to Kevin Starks late in the game, then lost a heartbreaker to the top-ranked Oklahoma Sooners, 13-7, in Week Three. The team rebounded though by pouncing all over Purdue, 45-15, as Foggie threw for 212 yards and a TD, while rushing for 47 yards and another touchdown. The Goph's went on to beat Northwestern in Week Five, 21-10, behind nearly 300 yards of total offense from Foggie, in addition to 102 yards receiving and a TD from Tight End Kevin Starks. In Week Seven they beat Indiana, 22-7, in a game that featured Valdez Baylor rushing for a career high 141 yards and a TD, along with three Chip Lohmiller field goals.

Minnesota then lost a pair of nail-biters, one to Ohio State at Homecoming, 23-19, and the other to Michigan State, 31-26. Foggie scored the only two touchdowns in the Buckeye game, and then sat out the Spartan game with a pulled groin, as backup QB Alan Holt came up just short in leading the team back from a huge deficit. In Week Nine, the Gophers beat Wisconsin, 27-18, in a game that was highlighted by an 89-yard record-setting TD bomb from Foggie to Mel Anderson. The Gophers finished out the season on a huge downer though, getting pummeled by both Michigan, 48-7, who was led by Quarterback Jim Harbaugh, and Big Ten champion Iowa, 31-9. Despite finishing only fifth in the Big Ten with a 4-4 record, the Gophers got invited to once again go "bowling," something that hadn't occurred on campus since 1977.

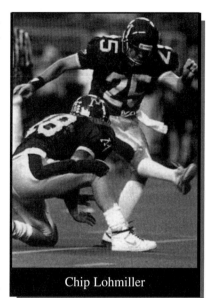

Chip Lohmiller

With that, Minnesota was off to Shreveport, La., to meet the Clemson Tigers in the 10th annual Independence Bowl. Nearly 43,000 fans, many of whom made the trip from the Gopher State, crowded into Independence Stadium to watch the big game. Now, in a bit of off-the-field drama, Coach Holtz controversially opted to exercise a little-known secret clause (which would later become known affectionately as the "Notre Dame Clause") in his contract which entitled him to step down to take the head coaching position at Notre Dame, should it become available. It did, and he went, leaving his Defensive Coordinator, John Gutekunst, to take over as head coach of the team. "Gutie," who had served as an assistant at both Duke and Virginia Tech before joining Holtz at Arkansas and then Minnesota, was eager and excited to make the most of his "golden" opportunity.

"Lou's got to be one of the top five greatest college coaches of all time, without question," said Foggie regarding the coach's decision to leave. "Everywhere Holtz has been, he's won. He turned our "U" football program around and got people in the stands. He was able to recruit good athletes to come in and make us competitive again. His greatest asset was to be able to recruit and to motivate his players to go out and win at all costs. I just wish he would've stayed at Minnesota longer, because there's no telling where the program would be today if he had."

"This was a big change for us, but, because Gutie was already on the staff, we were familiar with him, and we kind of knew what to expect," Foggie added. "But, going from Lou Holtz, who was a fiery, up-tempo guy, to Gutie, who was a more laid-back kind of coach, was a big change. Gutie wasn't the motivator that Coach Holtz was, but he knew the X's and O's of the game, and he was a good guy."

With "Gutie" at the helm, the Gophers took to the field and made a statement on the game's first play from scrimmage. That's when Clemson QB Rodney Williams hit wide Receiver Ray Williams on a screen pass. Williams, upon being tattooed by Gopher defender Doug Mueller, then proceeded to cough up the ball at the Tiger 39-yard line. Minnesota took over and began to drive downfield behind Ed Penn's

25-yard run, which got the Gophers down to the Clemson five-yard line. But after a holding penalty, they could only muster a field goal attempt. Kicker Chip Lohmiller came in, but was wide-right on a 22-yarder, keeping the score at double-bagels. But two plays later, Clemson again fumbled on their own 26-yard-line. After a failed attempt to get the ball into the end-zone, Lohmiller came in and this time drilled a 22-yarder through the uprights to put the Gophers up 3-0.

In the second quarter, after forcing the Tigers to punt, the Gophers put together an impressive drive that started with two David Puk nine-yard scampers up the middle. Foggie then hit Tight End Craig Otto on another nine-yarder to get to their own 43, followed by 15 and 20-yard runs by Baylor. Finally, on third-and-four, at the Tiger nine, Foggie hit Anderson on a nine-yard scoring strike, and the Gophers went up 10-0. Clemson rallied back in the third though, thanks to a pair of Jeff Treadwell field goals to make it 10-6. Then, behind the running of Clemson tailback Kenny Flowers, the Tigers drove and scored on a Jennings touchdown catch to take a three-point lead, 13-10.

The valiant Gophers came back in the fourth though, behind their leader, Foggie, whose running and passing sparked an 85-yard drive that was capped by another Lohmiller "Chip-shot" to tie the game at 13 apiece. After the Gopher defense forced the Tigers to punt, Foggie came out and lined up in the shotgun formation. He started out the drive on a 10-yard pass to Anderson, followed by a 16-yard Baylor run to the Clemson 36. Foggie then hit flanker Gary Couch on a 14-yarder, quickly followed by a Baylor run that gave him 12 more of his team-high 98 yards. Now, with the Gophers at the seven-yard line,
Fullback David Puk rumbled down to the one. That was all Baylor needed to launch himself into the end-zone as the Gophers took a seven-point lead.

But the Gophers weren't out of the hot water yet. Faced with a fourth-and-six at their own 39, Clemson pulled off a fake punt to stay alive. Then on fourth and 12, Williams completed a 21-yarder to Jennings to reach the Gopher 31-yard line. So, with 90 seconds left in the game, the Tigers tried a trick play. Williams tossed a long, backward pass to wide Receiver Ray Williams, who then turned around and lofted a pass of his own to Tight End Jim Riggs near the goal line. That's when Cornerback Donovan Small dove, and just barely got his finger on the ball enough to deflect it out of bounds and preserve the Gopher victory.

"When they first threw that ball out wide," said Small, who was named the Defensive Player of the Game, "I was going to come up to try to tackle the guy. I thought it was a screen pass. But just out of the corner of my eye I saw this Clemson guy running really hard downfield. I wondered why that guy was running so hard, so I decided I'd better try to catch up to him."

"I have fond memories of that game because I always wanted to attend Clemson," added Foggie, who threw for 123 yards and a touchdown in the game. "But the Clemson coach told my high school coach that I was too slow to run their offense. So there was a definite revenge factor there for me personally. I knew a lot of the guys that played for Clemson, and to go out and play well and to beat those guys was just really satisfying for me. Minnesota hadn't been to a bowl game for a while, so to win it was a really special experience for everyone."

Peter Najarian

For the season Foggie accounted for 1,821 yards in total offense and was named to the All-Big Ten team. Baylor led the team in rushing with 680 yards, while

Brian Williams

Lohmiller led the team in scoring with 75 points. In addition, Linebacker Peter Najarian, who described the win as the "greatest feeling I've ever had," was the Golden Gophers' top tackler (for the third straight season) with 133 total hits.

"Give Me Liberty..."

The beginning of the 1986 season brought more hype and hoopla to campus than perhaps every before. That season a kid from Rochester hit campus by the name of Darrell Thompson, and by the time he was done four years later, he would own most every rushing record in the books. "Darrell and Rickey" became quite the dynamic duo that year, as the upstart Gophers earned their second straight post-season trip to a bowl game.

It was John Gutekunst's first full season as head coach at the U of M, and the Gophers were anxious to show the football world that their Independence Bowl victory over Clemson the year before was no fluke.

The season got underway against Bowling Green, as Thompson made an immediate impact by rushing for 205 yards and scoring four touchdowns en route to a 31-7 victory. Thompson was for real. But, from there the season hit a few bumps in the road, including a giant pothole in the shape of the University of Oklahoma, who crushed the Goph's by the ugly score of 63-0. The men of gold followed that up with a 24-20 loss to tiny Pacific University, despite two more touchdowns by Thompson. From there the Gophers went on a roll, beating Purdue, 36-9 (as Rickey Foggie scored three rushing touchdowns and passed to Mel Anderson for another), Northwestern, 44-23 (led by Thompson's 176 yards rushing and two touchdowns, as well as Mel Anderson's 90-yard kickoff return for another), and Indiana in a squeaker, 19-17 (where Thompson ran wild for another 191 yards to set up Chip Lohmiller's 21-yard game-wining field goal with two seconds to go in the game).

Minnesota ran into some more trouble in Week Seven, when they got shutout by Ohio State, 33-0, thanks to the Buckeyes defense, which was led by future NFL star, Chris Spielman. The squad then lost to Michigan State that next Saturday by the final of 52-23, in a real wild one. But the Gophers rebounded as they had done all season long in Week Nine, this time defeating the Wisconsin Badgers, 27-20, to retain Paul Bunyan's Axe. In that game, Foggie threw a 27-yard strike to Dennis Carter for the go-ahead touchdown, while Thompson rushed for 117 yards to become the first Gopher frosh to run for 1,000 yards.

Next up, No. 2 ranked Michigan, who had beaten Minnesota the past eight seasons. The Michigan game, in all of its pomp and circumstance, would prove to be one of the greatest ever for the University of Minnesota. After back and forth scoring the entire game, it all came down to the wire in this one. Down 17-16 with just over two minutes to go in the game, Michigan Coach Bo Schembechler opted to go for the tie instead of a two-pointer to win. He succeeded, and with the game now all tied-up, Minnesota drove the ball downfield. Then with 47 seconds left, Foggie took off from the Michigan 48 and ran for 31 yards to the Michigan 17. The stage was now set for Woodbury Kicker Chip Lohmiller, and the "Chipper" came through in a big way, nailing a 30-yarder as time ran out to give the Gophers a dramatic 20-17 victory, as well as the coveted Little Brown Jug. "I knew once we got it inside the 40, Chip could put It through," said Foggie. "He's got a great leg." In addition, Linebacker Larry Joyner, who sparked the defense with 11 tackles and forced two fumbles, was named as the Defensive Player of the Week.

Despite Chip Lohmiller's record 62-yard field goal, the Gophers finished out their season by losing to Iowa, 30-27. It didn't matter though, as the Gophers still earned a berth in the Liberty Bowl, where they would face the University of Tennessee, right in the Vol's own backyard of Memphis.

The game got underway with the Volunteers jumping ahead 14-0 on two Jeff Francis touchdown passes. The first came to Joey Clinkscales in the left flat as he beat both Cornerback Matt Martinez and Safety Steve Franklin to scoot into the end zone for an 18-yard touchdown. After a second quarter Foggie fumble at midfield, Francis dumped a screen pass to Fullback William Howard who promptly took it to the house to make it 14-0. The Gophers came close twice in the half — once to the Vols' six-yard line, where Foggie came up short on a sneak, and then again when Thompson fumbled on the Vols' 33-yard line. Minnesota's only points came on a Lohmiller 27-yard field goal that ended a 70-yard drive at the end of the half.

When the third quarter opened, Foggie appeared to be a man on a mission. The junior quarterback led Minnesota on a 10-play, 88-yard drive that was capped by an 11-yard quarterback-keeper for a touchdown. Then, Thompson added a two-point conversion to make the score 14-11. Still in the third, behind 38 of Thompson's game-high 136 yards, the Gophers started a long march down to the Tennessee 14. But,

Two Harbors native Lloyd "Snapper" Stein starred as a Center for the Gophers from 1928-30, and then went on to serve as the team's head trainer for more than 40 years.

a holding call nullified their touchdown hopes, and Minnesota had to settle for another field goal by Lohmiller.

Tied at 14-apiece in the fourth, the Vol's cruised upfield on a 67-yard drive that was capped by Clinkscales' second TD catch of the game less than two minutes later. With Tennessee up, 21-14, the Gophers tried to rally. Their next drive got stalled on their own 49-yard line, but after an exchange of punts Minnesota got the ball back at midfield largely because of two great plays by freshman linebacker Jon Leverenz — who forced a two-yard loss on a first-down play, and then broke up a key third-down pass. So, with Foggie and Thompson poised for the upset, they tried one last drive to win it all. The final rally, a seven-play drive, started out well, but unfortunately ended near midfield when Foggie's fourth-down pass to Waconia's Ron Goetz fell incomplete. Tennessee took over with 16 seconds left and simply ran out the clock to win it. Minnesota out-gained Tennessee in the game 374-324, but, in the end, the final score

The Bierman Football Complex

read 21-14 in favor of the Vols.

The Gophers played well, despite having to do battle deep inside enemy turf. For the season, they finished at 6-6 and tied for third in the Big Ten with a 5-3 record. Thompson, who led the conference in rushing that year, also set a new Gopher single-season rushing mark with 1,240 yards.

"It was a big deal because you grow up watching the bowl games on TV, and when you finally get to play in one, it is a very special event," said Thompson, who was named to the All-Big Ten team. "I mean, only the year before I was playing for Rochester John Marshall High School, and now here I was starting at running back in the Liberty Bowl, it was an exciting time."

Foggie set a new University of Minnesota career total yardage record by reaching the 5,118 mark. Lohmiller, who set a new team record by nailing a 62-yard field goal against Iowa, was named to the All-Big Ten team. Bruce Holmes, a senior linebacker, who led the team with 118 tackles also made the All-Big Ten team. In addition, there were a lot of players on that team who deserve credit for the team's outstanding season, including Ray Hitchcock, Jim Hobbins and Norries Wilson who anchored a veteran offensive line, as well as defenders Donovan Small, Anthony Burke, Larry Joyner, Don Pollard, Matt Martinez, Steve Thompson, and Duane Dutrieuille.

The Slide to Mediocrity

The Gophers were feeling pretty good about their prospects in 1987. The team had felt that despite losing their bowl bid, they were solid behind Coach Gutie. The team picked up where they left off in 86', winning their first three games against three mediocre schools: Northern Iowa, Cal and Central Michigan. But when they beat Purdue, 21-19, in Week Four to go 4-0, people started to sense that this group might be once again flirting with the post-season. That's where the good news stops and the bad news starts. The Gophers would win just two more games during that entire season, against both Northwestern, 45-33, and Wisconsin, 22-19. One loss in particular, a 27-17 come-from-behind thriller in Week Eight, was orchestrated by a young Illini Quarterback by the name of Jeff George, who came in and rallied the team back from three scores down in the fourth to beat the Gophers.

Minnesota did finish the season with a 6-5 record, but due to their cream puff schedule, were not in consideration for any bowl games. One highlight of mention from that year came against Michigan, in Week Nine, when Darrell Thompson set a Big Ten record with a 98-yard touchdown run. His 200 yards that day were the most ever surrendered by a Wolverine team. For the season Darrell ran for 1,229 yards and tallied 13 touchdowns, while his tag-team partner, Rickey Foggie, threw for 1,232 yards and eight TDs, even running in six more touchdowns on the ground.

In 1988 the bottom fell out, as the Gophers finished ninth in the Big Ten with an awful 0-6-2 record. With Foggie gone to the pro ranks, Thompson was left to fend for himself. Behind the blocking of future NFL star Center Brian Williams, he did manage to rush for 910 yards and post nine touchdowns that year, while his new Quarterback, Scott Schaffner, threw for 1,234 yards and seven TDs. You knew it was going to be bad when the

DARRELL THOMPSON

Minnesota has always been known to represent the "three yards and a cloud of dust" mentality of Big Ten football, which was anchored by a sound running game. There have been so many great running backs through the years in Gold Country but none of them could run like Darrell Thompson, who rewrote the record books during his tenure at the U of M. With his 6'1", 220-pound, frame combined with his 4.4 speed and acceleration, Thompson was an elusive yet punishing running back.

Born and raised in Rochester, Thompson went on to become a three-sport star at John Marshall High School. A star forward on the basketball team, Darrell also earned all-state honors in track, where he ran the 100, 200, and 400 meters, and even anchored the 1985 state championship mile relay team. But his main sport was football. His senior year he rushed for over 1,000 yards, scored 102 points and averaged an amazing 9.7 yards per carry. Not only was he all-state in football, he was also an All-American as well. In fact, Darrell was the state's most highly recruited football player ever, and was wooed by nearly every major college in the country.

He wasted little time in making a name for himself in Gold Country, becoming the only running back in Big Ten history to go over 1,000-yards as a freshman and a sophomore. In 1987, after scoring a 98-yard touchdown run (the longest run from scrimmage in Big Ten history), he became the first player ever to gain more than 200 yards in a game against the Michigan Wolverines.

"Daarreelll...Daarreelll...Daarreelll" were familiar chants at the Dome from 1986-89, as the powerful halfback soon emerged as one of the team's all-time fan-favorites. When it was all said and done, Darrell had rushed for 4,654 yards on 936 attempts, and scored 40 touchdowns, making him the school's all-time leader in all three categories. He also scored 262 total points, placing second on the all-time scoring list behind only Kicker Chip Lohmiller.

After a phenomenal senior campaign, Darrell was drafted in the first round by the Green Bay Packers. He went on to play for five seasons with the Pack, rushing for 1,641 yards and eight touchdowns before finally hanging up the spikes in 1995. Because he was hampered by injuries throughout much of his pro career and was often forced to play out of his natural position, at fullback, he was never able to truly showcase his talents in the NFL. Today he and his family reside in the Twin Cities, and in addition to doing color commentary for Gopher telecasts, he manages several youth programs and charitable foundations.

"I took a lot of pride in being a Gopher," said Thompson. "It was really an amazing experience for me to play at the University and to be so well regarded by the fans. It was truly an honor to play for them, and it is something I will never forget. In fact, I'd like to see more kids from Minnesota experiencing the same pleasure that I had there. Athletes can carve out a real nice niche in the community if they do."

team started off the season with a pair of ugly losses to Washington State, 41-9, and Miami of Ohio, 35-3. They did rebound to beat Northern Illinois in non-conference action, but lost to everyone else except Northwestern and Illinois, who they managed to tie at 28-28 and 27-27 respectively.

The 1989 and 1990 Gopher teams made a solid recovery to get back to respectability. Both clubs finished with identical 6-5 overall records, good for fifth and sixth in the conference, respectively. Thompson rounded out his glorious career in Gold Country at the end of the 1989 campaign, literally rewriting the record book on the way out. Darrell now owned nearly every rushing record on campus, including Total Rushing Yards (4,654), Rushing Touchdowns (40), All Purpose Yards (5,109) while ranking second in Career Points Scored (262). The 1989 team did manage to beat Purdue, 35-15, Northwestern, 20-18, Wisconsin, 24-20, and Iowa, 43-7.

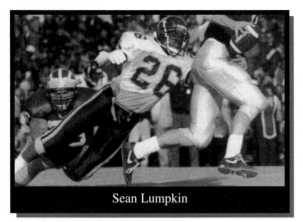
Sean Lumpkin

Meanwhile, the 1990 club was able to upend Purdue, 19-7, Northwestern, 35-25, Indiana, 12-0, Wisconsin, 21-3, and Iowa, 31-24. Beating the Rose Bowl bound Hawkeyes, and keeping Floyd around the Bierman Complex for the second year in a row would have to rate as one of the highlights of the Gutekunst era.

In 1991 the Gophers sunk to last place in the Big Ten, with a paltry 2-9 overall record. Their only Big Ten win came against Purdue, a team they were able to edge out by the whopping final of 6-3, thanks to a nine-yard touchdown run by Quarterback Marquel Fleetwood. The extra point, however, was another story. Highlights from this year included a 58-0 beating on national television by Quarterback Kordell Stewart and the defending national champs from Colorado, and a 52-6 drubbing by Quarterback Elvis Grbac and the Michigan Wolverines at the Dome. Let's not forget about the 34-8 loss to Indiana, or the 35-6 pasting by Ohio State either. All in all it was not a good year to be a Gopher Football fan, but there were some great performances from Quarterback Marquel Fleetwood, who passed for 1,642 yards and six TDs, and Running Backs Chuck Rios and Antonio Carter, who combined for more than 1,000 yards on the ground. In addition, Sean Lumpkin was a star in the defensive backfield that year, eventually going on to play with the NFL's New Orleans Saints.

After the 1991 season, Gutie was let go and Texas Christian University Head Coach Jim Wacker was brought in to clean up the mess. A winner of two national Coach of the year wards, Wacker was known for his ability to rebuild and run clean programs. Coming in like a Texas twister, full of energy and a sharp wit to boot, Wacker was an instant fan-favorite. In his first year on campus he succeeded in unseating two of Minnesota's biggest rivals, the Iowa Hawkeyes, 28-13, in the 91' season finale, and then the Rose Bowl bound Wisconsin Badgers in both 1993 and 1994.

Wacker's team's struggled though, finishing 10th in 1992, eighth in 1993, 11th in 1994, 10th in 1995 and ninth in 1996. His best year was 1993, when his team went on a three game Big Ten winning streak, beating Purdue, 59-56, Northwestern, 28-26, and Wisconsin, 17-14. In the end, Wacker's team's ultimately just didn't get the job done. After five seasons behind the Gopher bench, his record stood at a paltry 16-39.

There were some great football players to pass through during that era though, including Running Back Chris Darkins, who, in addition to running for 294 yards against Purdue in 1995, ran for 3,235 career yards from 1992-95, good for second all-time. Others would include Quarterbacks Cory Sauter and Tim Schade. Sauter holds the record for all-time career passing yards with 6,834, and career touchdowns with 40, while Schade ranks fifth in that category with 22 TDs. Receivers Tutu Atwell and Ryan Thelwell rank No.1 and No.2 respectively for career receptions with 171 and 136, while Chuck Rios, Omar Douglas and Aaron Osterman rank No.'s 3, 4 and 5 as well in that same category. In addition, all but Rios, who is a running back, also rank in the top-five all-time for career receiving yards, with Atwell leading the list at 2,640 yards. There was also All-American Lemanzer Williams, who, from 1994-97 became the team's career leader in sacks, with 132. In addition, Linebacker Craig Sauer went on to play with the Atlanta Falcons, in Super Bowl XXXII, while Tackle Mike Giovinette went on to play with the Tampa Bay Bucs as well.

Wacker, however, would be remembered for other positive things, like running a tight ship, and demanding excellence on both the field and in the classroom, where his teams finished at the top of the Academic All-Big Ten selections for three straight years. In 1996 Wacker was let go, later becoming the Athletic Director at Southwest Texas State University.

In 1997 Glen Mason took over the reigns as the University's newest Head Coach. Mason, who spent nine seasons turning around the fortunes of the University of Kansas' football program, led the Jayhawks to a top-ten national ranking in 1995. A former linebacker on Ohio State's 1970 Big Ten championship team, Mason knew what it would take to turn the program around, and that is exactly what he has done.

Mason's immediate impact was felt during his inaugural campaign in gold country, when the Gophers finished fifth in total defense in the Big Ten, the program's best effort in more than a dozen years. Minnesota broke or tied a total of 28 school records during that season, which, at 3-9, was slowly showing signs of life. Led by Quarterback Corey Sauter and Running Back Thomas Hamner, the Gophers kicked off the season with a 17-3 loss at Hawaii, followed by Mason's first win as a Gopher, a 53-29 shellacking of Iowa State. They followed that up with a 20-17 win over Memphis, and then lost a heart-breaker to Houston that next Saturday by the final of 45-43, as Sauter threw for 368 yards and three touchdowns in the defeat.

The Gophers struggled from there on in, losing to Michigan State, 31-10, Purdue, 59-43, Penn State, 16-15, Wisconsin, 22-21, Michigan, 24-3, and Ohio State, 31-3. Many of those game were closer than they looked on paper, particularly the Penn State game, which would've been one of the biggest upsets of the year. They rebounded that next week against Indiana, beating the Hoosiers, 24-12, only to get shut-out by Iowa in the season finale, 31-0.

In 1998 the Gophers began to turn the corner, finishing with an improved 5-6 record, good for seventh in the Big Ten. Quarterback Billy Cockerham, Receiver Tutu Atwell and Running Back Thomas Hamner provided one of the most solid 1-2-3 punches in the conference that season, and all would eventually go on to play in the NFL. The team won its first three games that year against Arkansas State, 17-14, Houston, 14-7, and Memphis, 41-14. Against Arkansas State, Safety Tyrone Carter returned the opening kick-off 86-yards for a touchdown. Then, after a Thomas Hamner score late in the second, Gopher Kicker Adam Bailey came in to boot the game-winner with no time left on the clock. Billy Cockerham's two touchdown passes to Luke Leverson and Ron Johnson were enough to seal the deal against Houston, while Hamner, Cockerham and Byron Evans each ran for touchdowns to lead the Gophers past Memphis.

After suffering set-backs to Purdue, 56-21, Penn State, 37-27, and Ohio State, 45-15, Minnesota came back to beat Michigan State, 19-18. Luke Leverson caught a pair of TDs each against Purdue, Penn State and Michigan State, while Andy Persby found Antoine Henderson in the end-zone for the lone highlight against OSU. Minnesota then lost a couple of very close games starting with Michigan, who won 15-10, Wisconsin, 26-7, and Indiana, 20-19. The Gophers, who got an early fumble recovery for a touchdown from Trevis Graham, hung tough with Michigan, finally getting beat on a late safety and field goal in the fourth quarter. Leverson's 53-yard TD was the only offense Minnesota could

Lemanzer Williams

muster with Wisconsin, and against Indiana, Hamner scored once and Ron Johnson tallied twice in the narrow defeat. The team did finish on a high note, however, beating Iowa on the last game of the season, 49-7, at the Dome. Cockerham and Leverson each scored a pair of touchdowns in this one, while Hamner added 148 yards and an early touchdown on the ground.

Nearly securing the school's first bowl game appearance since 1986, the Gophers finished the 1998 season ranked 43rd in the final Sagarin national computer rankings, the program's best since 1985 (31st). While Mason-coached teams have had an impressive track record for moving the ball and scoring points, they are also known for their tenacious defense. Mason's Gophers ranked fourth in the Big Ten and 13th in the nation in rushing defense in 1998 by allowing just 104 yards per game. Not bad compared to 1996, the year before his arrival, when that squad gave up a porous 247 yards rushing per outing. Then, on offense, the Maroon and Gold ranked seventh in the Big Ten in rushing, with an average of 141 yards per game, compared to the 1996 team which finished at the bottom of the barrel with just 104 yards per game on the ground.

Thomas Hamner

The transformation of the program under Coach Mason has been evident in the team's steady improvement in most every key statistical category on both sides of the football. The change is particularly noticeable down in the trenches, where he has made a commitment from the get-go to play a more physical style of smash-mouth football. He is also doing well recruiting, and even getting a lot of the home-grown talent to stay put, something previous coaches struggled with.

The 1999 Gophers surpassed everyone's expectations, finishing the season with a greatly improved 8-4 record. In addition, the Gophers made their first post-season appearance since 1986, by being selected to play in the Sun Bowl. The band-wagon jumpers were out in force in 1999, as the once empty Metrodome suddenly got a lot noisier. The team was led by a cast of future pros including: Running Back Thomas Hamner, Quarterback Billy Cockerham, Safety Tyrone Carter, Receiver Luke Leverson, Linebacker Parc Williams, Center Ben Hamilton and Defensive End Karon Riley.

The Gophers, thanks to Cockerham's two rushing touchdowns and 89-yard TD pass to Antoine Henderson, pummeled Ohio University, 33-7, in their opening non-conference game. From there the team beat Louisiana-Monroe, 35-0, thanks in large part to Hamner's three touchdown runs along with Willie Middlebrooks' 26-yard TD interception return. The Gophers were gaining confidence, and it showed big-time in their 55-7 pounding of Illinois State. Cockerham again led the charge with a pair of rushing touchdowns along with two more through the air to both Ron Johnson and Henderson.

The Gophers continued their roll by man-handling Northwestern, 33-14, at Evanston. Cockerham, continuing his amazing offensive output, ran in a two-yarder, and also hit Hamner on a 64-yard touchdown pass. Hamner and Leverson each added scores on the ground as well as the Gophers cruised to victory.

Against Wisconsin the Gophers got a dose of reality, losing a heart-breaker, 20-17, at the Dome. Arland Bruce opened the scoring in the first on a nice 24-yard TD pass from Cockerham, only to see Heisman winner Ron Dayne get the equalizer midway through the second on a three-yard plunge. Hamner then put Minnesota back on top when he caught a sweet 49-yard touchdown pass from Cockerham. After Wisconsin scored again late in the third on an 81-yard bomb from Brooks Bollinger to Nick Davis, followed by Dan Nystrom's field goal, the Gophers were up by six. But, after a pair of Vital Pisetsky field goals in the fourth, the final one coming as time ran off the clock, Wisconsin found themselves hanging on for a thrilling three point victory.

The Gophers rebounded that next Saturday against Illinois though, beating the Illini in Champaign, 37-7. Leverson's 74-yard punt return for a touchdown late in the first got things going. Cockerham then hit Jermaine Mays on a six-yard TD strike, followed by Nystrom's first of three field goals on the day to put Minnesota up 17-0. Hamner and Evans each then scored in the second half as the Gophers cruised to the easy win.

Minnesota then suffered another gut-wrenching loss at the Dome, this time to Ohio State, 17-20. Down 7-0 in the first, Cockerham scored on a nine-yard run around the end to even it up. After a Nystrom field goal to go ahead, OSU answered on Michael Wiley's second touchdown run of the day midway through the third. Hamner answered with a seven-yarder of his own, only to see Buckeye Kicker Dan Stultz nail a pair of field goals late in the fourth to ice it for Ohio State.

Mason's squad again rallied back, this time to beat Purdue, 33-28, giving the Gopher fans an extra bonus for their Homecoming dollar. This one, like Wisconsin and OSU, would also come down to the wire. Down 14-0 in the first, Hamner scored on a nine-yard run up the middle late in the second. The Boilers then went up 24-7 in the third, only to see Minnesota start their improbable fourth quarter comeback. Cockerham started it by capping a long Gopher drive early in the period on a one-yard dive, only to see Purdue's Montrell Lowe answer with a one-yarder of his own just three minutes later. Thomas Hamner then got busy, scoring on a brilliant 60-yard run through a maze of Boiler defenders. Purdue Quarterback Drew Brees then hit Randall Lane for a touchdown with just five minutes to go to take a 28-26 lead. The Gophers, down but not out, drove 80 yards on 12 plays and got what would prove to be the game-winner at 2:39 of the fourth when Cockerham found Johnson on a 12-yard game-winning touchdown pass.

Chris Darkins

With the win, the Gophers were primed and ready to take on No.2 ranked Penn State, in what would prove to be one of the greatest games in the history of Gopher football. The Penn State crowd was ecstatic. Not only were they were just three wins away from a trip to the national championship game in the Sugar Bowl, but their legendary coach, Joe Paterno, was coaching in his 400th game in Happy Valley. It was also homecoming, which meant that the partying had started early on that morning and the fans would be juiced.

The Nittany Lions got on the board first, when Mike Cerimele busted through the Minnesota line on a five-yard plunge early in the opening quarter. Nystrom answered for the Gophers at 4:59 of the first with a 27-yard field goal. They then took the lead early in the second when Ron Johnson caught a 25-yard touchdown pass from Cockerham to go up 10-7. Penn State answered though, as QB Kevin Thompson found Bryant Johnson in the back of the end-zone with a 17-yard TD pass, followed by a

Glen Mason

Travis Forney 44-yard field goal to take the lead early in the fourth. Hamner then put the Gophers back on top when he capped off a seven-play, 71-yard drive by hauling in a beautiful 49-yard touchdown pass from Cockerham.

The Lions roared back though, and despite being held out of the end-zone, did manage to take the lead back with a 44-yard field goal midway through the final quarter. Then, after both teams exchanged punts, Minnesota got the ball with just under two minutes in the game. Cockerham drove the team down the field and had his prayer's answered with 1:22 on the clock. Faced with a fourth down and 16 yards to go for the first down from Penn State's 40-yard-line, Cockerham heaved a "Hail Mary," which somehow bounced off Ron Johnson's hands and right over to Arland Bruce, who grabbed the ball out of the air for a 27-yard gain, and a first down on Penn State's 13-yard line.

"When Ron tipped it, I just saw the ball hanging in the air saying, like 'Come get me, come get me!' " Bruce said after the game. "I just grabbed it. It just hung there, in slow motion, like it was meant to be."

After a few plays to run down the clock, the Gophers were ready to go for broke. That's when Freshman Kicker Dan Nystrom came out and made history, kicking a 32-yarder straight through the uprights as time expired to give Minnesota the unbelievable 24-23 victory. The shocked crowd stood in silence as the Gophers mobbed Nystrom at midfield. For the first time in Gopher history, the team would return home with the Liberty Bell traveling trophy.

"This program went from a losing program to a winning program today," said Thomas Hamner after the win. "We knocked off the No.2 team, a great Penn State team, at home. It doesn't get any better than that."

After doing the improbable, the Gophers came back that next week and crushed Indiana, 44-20, in Minneapolis. Cockerham scored a pair of short touchdowns while also throwing a 39-yarder to Ron Johnson, and Cornerback Jimmy Wyrick tallied on a 61-yard interception return to spark the Minnesota victory.

Next up were the Iowa Hawkeyes, at Iowa City, in a game which had post-season implications written all over it. But, thanks to some more fourth quarter heroics by Arland Bruce, who scored what proved to be the 73-yard game-winning touchdown run at the 9:15 mark of the fourth quarter, the Gophers rallied to beat the Hawks, 25-21. Nystrom kicked his third field goal of the day with just over three minutes to go to ice it for Minnesota. With the win, the Gophers found themselves ranked in the top-20 of every college poll in the nation.

Sun Burned

With the win, the Gophers were invited to play the Oregon Ducks in the Sun Bowl, on Dec. 31, 1999, in El Paso, Texas. It would be the team's first bowl appearance since 1986, when Darrell Thompson and Rickey Foggie came up short against Tennessee in the Liberty Bowl. Droves of Gopher fans made the trek south to see the game, giving the program a much needed boost.

The Gophers got on the board first in this one, when Cockerham, after hitting Leverson on a 36-yarder, capped a seven-play, 62-yard drive by finding Ron Johnson in the back of the end-zone for a one-yard touchdown. Oregon's Quarterback Joey Harrington answered by scoring on a five-yard keeper, only to see Cockerham strike again early in the third — this time to Arland Bruce with a 38-yard TD pass on the final play of an 80-yard drive (Nystrom's kick failed). Harrington then added his second score of the game just a few minutes later, on another one-yard keeper, followed by a Villegas field goal at the 3:11 mark of the third to go up 17-13. The drive was kept alive when the Gophers were stung with a key pass interference penalty on a fourth down. Then, after a 10-play, 72-yard drive, Cockerham, after hitting Leverson a key third down strike for 34-yards, threw his second touchdown of the afternoon to Johnson, this one measuring just seven yards to put the Gophers up 20-17. The Ducks rallied back though, behind both Running Backs Reuben Droughns and Herman Ho Ching, and Harrington, who led the team down-field 87-yards on 12 long and methodical plays.

Then, with just over three minutes to go in the game, the Gophers were poised to win it. All they had to do was hold Oregon in a do-or-die fourth-down and 11 situation on the Gopher 44-yard line. Harrington came up huge though, connecting first with Tony Harltey on a 23-yard pass,

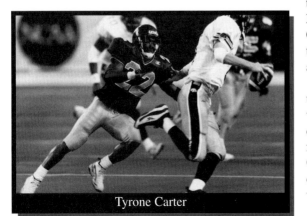
Tyrone Carter

Kicker Dan Nystrom's game winning field goal to beat Penn State

After 50 years, Ray Christenson will retire as a genuine broadcasting legend.

and then again three plays later to Receiver Keenan Howey, on a 10-yard touchdown strike with a minute and a half to go in the ball game, to give his squad a 24-17 lead. The Gophers, down but not out, would get the ball back twice after what would eventually prove to be the game-winner. The first of the two late drives ended when Cockerham fumbled after being sacked at the Oregon 45-yard line, while the second came with just 12 seconds to go with Minnesota trying to start a last-second rally from their own eight-yard line. The Ducks held though, and went on to win by the final score of 24-20.

Incredibly, after the game Billy Cockerham, Dyron Russ and Ryan Rindels were named as the game's Most Valuable Player, Most Valuable Lineman and Most Valuable Special Teams Player, respectively. Did anyone mention to the awards people that these guys were all members of the losing team? That's just how the game went that afternoon, it was a game that the Gophers should've won, and could've won, had they just caught a few breaks along the way.

"We won all three awards, but I'd trade all three of them in for the team trophy," said Coach Mason after the game.

It was a bitter loss, but a tremendous shot in the arm for a program that has completed a 180-degree turn in the right direction. Their 8-4 finish was the best in years, and the prospects for the program are brighter than ever. After the season both Tyrone Carter, who finished as the NCAA's all-time leading tackler (529) and was named as the country's top defensive back, and Billy Cockerham, were both drafted by the Vikings, while Thomas Hamner, who became the team's second all-time leading rusher, signed with the Philadelphia Eagles.

The Gophers of 2000 are poised to do better than ever. Behind Mason, and a young crop of talent, this team is officially a contender. Freshman Quarterback Asad Abdul-Khaliq will lead a very potent offense by taking his snaps from pre-season All-American Ben Hamilton. Abdul-Khaliq's favorite target out on the field will undoubtedly be six-foot-three Wide Receiver Ron Johnson, a returning two-year starter who has emerged as one of the top receivers in the nation. Johnson, who has great speed, size, hands and the strength to go up and take the ball away from his defenders, also led the team in receptions (43), receiving yards (574), and receiving touchdowns (7) in 1999. In the backfield will be the highly touted freshman Running Back from St. Paul, Thomas Tapeh, who will be ready to step it up in 2000 as well. On the other side of the ball the Gophers have eight starters returning, including pre-season All-American Defensive End Karon Riley, who led the Big Ten in sacks in 1999 (16), defensive backs Trevis Graham, Delvin Jones and Willie Middlebrooks, as well as four-year starting linebacker Sean Hoffman. In addition, Mason landed one of the biggest marqis blue-chip recruits in the nation in Dominique Sims, a Safety from De La Salle High School in Minneapolis, who is expected to do great things for the Maroon and Gold in the upcoming years.

The University of Minnesota's Golden Gopher football program is one of the most storied and successful in American history. What began in the 1870s, is now entering into its third century looking better than ever. From Nagurski to Giel, and from Bierman to Thompson, the tradition and ora only continues to grow and prosper. It will be a fun ride to see how far Mr. Mason can take this new crop of kids into the new millennium. Surely the ghosts of Gopher past are looking on proudly at the success and optimism of their fabled tradition.

Gophers in the Professional Ranks

1. George Abramson, T, Green Bay 1925
2. Julie Alfonse, QB, Cleveland 1937-38
3. Chet Anderson, TE, Pittsburgh 1967
4. Thtu Atwell, WR, Detroit 1998
5. Elmer Bailey, WR, Miami 1980-81, Baltimore 1982
6. Marion Barber, RB, NY Jets 1981-89
7. Bert Baston, E, Cleveland 1920-21
8. Bill Baumgartner, E, Baltimore 1947
9. Doug Beaudoin, S, NE1976-79, Miami 1980, SD'81
10. Bobby Bell, LB, Kansas City 1963-74
11. Warren Beson, C, Baltimore 1949
12. John Billman, G, Brooklyn 1946, Chicago 1947
13. Bert Bisbee, RB, Milwaukee 1922
14. Bob Bjorklund, C, Philadelphia 1941
15. Brian Bonner, LB, Washington 1988-89
16. McKinley Boston, LB, NY Giants 1968-69
17. Aaron Brown, DE, KC1966-72, GB 1973-74
18. Arland Bruce, WR, Kansas City 2000-
19. Bob Bruggers, LB, Miami 1967-68, SD1968-71
20. Hubie Bryant, WR, Pitt 1970, NE 1971-72
21. Bart Buetow, DT, NY Giants 1973, Minn 1976
22. Larry Buhler, FB, Green Bay 1939-41
23. John Campbell, LB, MN 1964, Pitt 1965-69
24. Geno Cappelletti, FL-K, Boston 1960-70
25. Ralph Capron, RB, Chicago 1920
26. Jay Carroll, TE, Tampa Bay 1984-85
27. Jim Carter, LB, Green Bay 1970-78
28. Tony Carter, RB, Chicago 1994-97, NE 1998 -
29. Tyrone Carter, DB, Minnesota 2000-
30. Marty Christiansen, FB, Chicago 1940
31. Billy Cockerham QB, Minnesota 2000-
32. Bill Daley, FB, Miami 1946, Brooklyn 1946, Chicago 1947, NYYankees 1948
33. Ken Dallafior, G, San Diego 1985, Detroit 1986-90
34. Chris Darkins, RB, Green Bay 1996-98
35. Jerome Davis, DE, Detroit 1997-99, Denver 1999-
36. Omar Douglas, WR, NY Giants 1994-97
37. Tony Dungy, QB-DB, Pittsburgh 1977-78, SF 1979
38. Mert Dunnigan, T, Minneapolis 1924, Mil. 1925-26
39. Walt Dunnigan, E, Green Bay 1922
40. Mark Dusbabek, LB, Hous. 1987-88, MN 1989-91
41. Ben Dvorak, RB, Minneapolis 1921-22
42. Gus Ekberg, E, Minneapolis 1921
43. Carl Eller, DE, Vikings 1964-78, Seattle 1979
44. Dick Enderle, G, Atlanta 1969-71, NY Giants 1972-75, San Francisco 1976, Green Bay 1976
45. Jim Fahnhorst, LB, San Francisco 1984-90
46. Keith Fahnhorst, T, San Francisco 1974-85
47. Mike Falls, G, Dallas 1960-61
48. George Faust, QB, Chicago 1939
49. Paul Faust, LB, Minnesota 1967
50. Paul Flynn, E, Minneapolis 1922-23
51. Fred Foggie, DB, Pitt. 1994-95, Carolina 1995-96
52. George Franck, FB, NY Giants 1941, 1945-47
53. Bill Garnans, RB, Pittsburgh 1946-48
54. Chet Gay, T, Buffalo 1925, Racine 1926, Mil. 1926
55. George Gibson, G, Minneapolis 1930
56. Gale Gillingham, OG, Green Bay 1966-76
57. Mike Giovinetti, OL, Tampa Bay 1996
58. Kerry Glenn, DB, Jets 1985-89, Miami 1991-92
59. Bud Grant, E, Philadelphia 1951-52
60. Gary Hadd, DT, Detroit, Phoenix 1989
61. Roger Hagberg, FB, Oakland 1965-69
62. Tom Hall, SE, Det. 1962-63, MN 1964-66, NO '67
63. Thomas Hamner, RB, Philadelphia, 2000-
64. Carl Hanke, E, Hammond 1921-23, Chi. 1922-24
65. Ron Hanson, C, Washington 1951
66. Hal Hanson, G, Frankford 1928-30, Minn. 1930
67. Alex Hass, TE, St. Louis, 2000
68. Rodney Heath, CB, Cincinnati 1999-
69. Craig Hendrickson, OT, Buffalo 1994
70. Matt Herkenhoff, T, Kansas City 1976-85
71. Ray Hitchcock, C, Washington 1987-89
72. Gordy Holz, T, Denver 1960-63, NY Jets 1964
73. Michael Hunt, LB, Green Bay 1978-80
74. Elner Irgens, E, Minneapolis 1921-24
75. Floyd Jaszewski, T, Detroit 1950-51
76. Jon Jelacic, DE, NY Giants 1958, Oak 1961-64
77. Noel Jenke, LB, MN 1971, Atlanta 1972, GB 1974
78. Herb Joesting, FB, Minneapolis 1929-30, Frankford 1930-31, Chicago 1931-32
79. Bill Johnson, E, Green Bay 1941
80. Dick Johnson, TE, Kansas City 1963
81. Ezell Jones, T, Boston 1969-70
82. Rube Juster, T, Boston 1946
83. Wayne Kakota, C, Minneapolis 1930
84. Wally Kersten, T, LA 1962, Tampa Bay 1965
85. Wally Kilbourne, T, Green Bay 1939
86. Doug Kingsriter, TE, Minnesota 1973-75
87. Stan Kostka, FB, Brooklyn 1935
88. Kent Kramer, TE, San Francisco 1966, New Orleans 1967, MN 1969-70, Philad4phia 1971-74
89. Bill Kuusisto, G, Green Bay 1941-46
90. Greg Larson, C, NY Giants 1961-73
91. Ed Lechner, G, NY Giants 1942
92. Jon Leverenz, LB, Washington 1990
93. Len Levy, G, Cleveland, 1945, LA1946,
94. Carl Lidberg, FB, Green Bay 1926-30
95. Chip Lohmiller, K, Washington 1988-94, New Orleans 1995, St. Louis 1996
96. Sean Lumpkin, DB, New Orleans 1992-97
97. Tom MacLeod, LB, GB1973, Baltimore 1974-78
98. Al Maeder, T, Minneapolis 1929
99. Frank Marchlewski, C, LA Rams 1965-69, Atlanta 1966-68, Buffalo 1970
100. Billy Martin, HB, Chicago 1962-64
101. Joe Mattern, HB, Cleveland 1920, Minn. 1922
102. Karl Mecklenburg, E, Denver 1983-94
103. Jon Michals, DE, New York 2000-
104. Bob McNamara, RB, Denver 1960-61
105. Jon Melander, OL, New England 1991, Cincinnati 1992, Denver 1993-94
106. Mark Merrill, LB, NY Jets 1978-79, Chicago 1979, Denver 1981-82, Buffalo 1983-84, LA 1984
107. Lou Midler, G, Pittsburgh 1939, Green Bay 1940
108. Eddie Miles, LB, Pittsburgh 1990
109. Paul Mitchell, T, LA Dons 1946-48
110. Wilbur Moore, RB, Washington 1939-46
111. Greg Murtha, T, Baltimore 1982
112. Bronko Nagurski, FB-T, Chicago 1930-37 & '43
113. Pete Najarian, LB, SF, MN TB 1987-89
114. Steve Neils, LB, St. Louis 1974-80
115. Don Nolander, C, LA Dons 1946
116. Leo Nomellini, T, San Francisco 1950-63
117. Olaf Noreene, RB, Evansville 1921
118. Mally Nydall, FB-QB, Minneapolis 1929-30
119. John O'Brien, RB, Minneapolis 1929
120. Dick O'Donnell, E, Duluth 1923, GB 1924-30
121. Urban Odson, T, Green Bay 1946-49
122. Vern Oech, T, Chicago 1936
123. Earl Ohigren, E, Green Bay 1942
124. Larry Olsonoski, G, GB 1948-49, NY 1949
125. Bob Paffrath, RB, Miami 1946, Brooklyn 1946
126. Ray Parsons, T, Detroit 1971
127. Gordon Paschka, FB-G, Pitt 1943, NY 1947
128. Roger Pattison, G, Kenosha 1924
129. Winfield Pederson, T, NY Giants 1941 & 1945
130. Art Pharmer, PB, Minn. 1930, Frankford 1930-31
131. Warren Plunkett, QB, Cleveland 1942
132. Darrell Rackley, TE, Atlanta 2000-
133. Randy Rasmussen, C, Pitt 1984-85, MN 1988-89
134. Josh Rawlings, T, Kansas City 2000 -
135. Matt Reem, OG, Washington 1996-97
136. Pete Regnier, HB, Mpls 1921-22, GB 1922
137. Steve Rhem, WR, NO 1994-96, Phil 1997-98
138. Wayne Robinson, LB, Philadelphia 1952-56
139. Jim Rush, HB, Minneapolis 1922
140. Arnie Sandberg, HB, LA Buccaneers 1926
141. Charlie Sanders, TE, Detroit 1968-77
142. Craig Sauer, LB, Atlanta 1996-99, MN 2000 -
143. Cory Sauter, QB, Arizona 1998, Detroit 1999 -
144. Bob Schmidt, T-C, NY Giants 1959-60, Houston 1961-63, Boston 1964-65, Buffalo 1966-67
145. Jeff Sehuh, LB, Cincinnati 1981-85
146. Charles Schultz, T, Green Bay 1939-41
147. Rudy Sikich, T, Cleveland 1945
148. Keith Simons, T, KC 1976-77, St. Louis 1978-79
149. Dave Simonson, T, Baltimore 1974, NY Giants 1975, Houston, Seattle 1976, Detroit 1977
150. Mark Slater, C, San Diego 1978, Phil 1979-83
151. Bruce Smith, HB, GB1945-48, LA Rams 1948
152. Gordy Soltan, K-E, San Francisco 1950-58
153. Bob Soltis, DB, Boston 1960-61
154. Vie Spadaccini, QB, Cleveland 1938-40
155. Randy Staten, DE, NY Giants 1967
156. Bob Stein, LB, Kansas City 1969-72, LA Rams 1973-74, San Diego 1974, Minnesota 1975
157. Mac Stephens, LB, NY Jets, 1990
158. Steve Stewart, LB, Atlanta 1978, Green Bay 1979
159. Milt Sunde, G, Minnesota 1964-74
160. Bud Svendsen, G, GB 1937-39, Brook. 1940-43
161. George Svendsen, C, Green Bay 1935-41
162. Bob Sweiger, HB, NY 1946-48, Chicago 1949
163. Stan Sytsma, LB, Atlanta 1980
164. Bob Tanner, E, Frankford 1930
165. Al Teeter, E, Staten Island 1932
166. Bob Tenner, E, Green Bay 1935
167. Chris Thome, OL, Cleveland 1991-92
168. Ryan Thelwell, WR, SF 1998, SD 1998-NO2000-
170. Darrell Thompson, RB, Green Bay 1990-95
171. Festus Tierney, G, Ham. 1922, MN 1923-24
172. Rex Tobin, E, Duluth 1925
173. Steve Tobin, C, NY Giants 1980
174. Clayton Tonnemaker, C, Green Bay 1950-54
175. George Thttle, E, Green Bay 1927
176. Fred Twedell, G, Green Bay 1939
177. Rick Upchurch, WR, Denver 1975-83
178. Andy Uram, HB, Green Bay 1938-43
179. Rube Ursella, QB, Rock Island 1920 & 1924-25, Minneapolis 1921, Akron 1926, Hammond 1926
180. Harold Van Every, HB, Green Bay 1940-41
181. Fred Van Hull, G, Green Bay 1942
182. Ellery White, HB, LA Buccaneers, 1926
183. Ed Widseth, T, NY Giants 1937-40
184. Dick Wildung, G, Green Bay 1946-53
185. Ben Williams, DE, Minnesota Vikings 1998-99
186. Brian Williams, C, New York Giants 1989-
187. John Williams, T, Balt. 1968-71, LA 1972-79
188. Lamanzer Williams, DE, Jax 1998-99, KC 2000 -
189. Vern Winfield, G, Philadelphia 1972-73
190. Troy Wolkow, OL, New England 1988
191. Jeff Wright, DB, Minnesota 1971-77
192. Arne Wyman, FB, Rock Island 1920
193. Jimmy Wyrick, CB, Detroit 2000-

BRONKO NAGURSKI

The legend of Bronko Nagurski began back in 1926, when then-Gopher Coach Clarence "Doc" Spears was on a recruiting trip up in northern Minnesota. One day, while driving through International Falls, he saw a hulk of a man plowing a field — without a horse. When the curious Spears stopped to ask for directions, instead of using his finger, the kid just lifted the enormous plow and pointed with it! That young man wasn't Paul Bunyan... it was Bronko Nagurski.

Bronislau Nagurski was born Nov. 3, 1908, on the Canadian side of Rainy Lake in Rainy River, Ontario. At the age of four, his family moved to International Falls, just a slap-shot away on the other side of the US border. His nickname supposedly came about when his first-grade teacher, after not being able to understand his mother's thick Ukrainian accent, called the youngster "Bronko," and the name stuck.

He grew up loving all sports, but, amazingly, in his two years of prep football at International Falls High School, his sophomore and junior years, he never played on a team that won a game. In fact, he even transferred to neighboring Bemidji High School for his senior year, because he was upset when his principal canceled the team's trip to a district tournament when a couple of other players required some disciplining. There, the transfer student was ruled ineligible to play football, but he did manage to play basketball and run track however. It was hardly the kind of a prep career that would have attracted college recruiters, even in those days.

Following high school, the "Bronk" headed south, to wear the Maroon and Gold at the University of Minnesota. (In reality, he met Doc Spears while he was up north fishing, and convinced him to come to the University.) Once there, Spears' greatest dilemma quickly became deciding where to play his new star. Then he finally figured it out — he would play him everywhere. And that's exactly what he did. Bronko would go on to play tackle, fullback, defensive end, offensive end, line-backer and even passed the ball as a quarterback.

He was a massive man for his time, measuring six-feet-two and weighing in at 235 pounds. He had giant hands, donned a size-19 neck and could even run a 10.3 100-yard dash. He literally became the fullback no one could tackle and the tackle no runner could escape. As a sophomore Bronko first got noticed by the national press when he forced and recovered a late-game fumble against a heavily favored Notre Dame team, which led to a game-tying Gopher touchdown. During his junior year, wearing a steel plate to protect a couple of broken vertebrae, he almost single-handedly defeated Wisconsin when, in addition to intercepting three passes and making numerous touchdown-saving tackles, he forced a fumble and ran it in for the game-winning score.

So talented was the powerful Nagurski that he would go on to earn All-America honors at three different positions. Sportswriters decided after his senior season in 1929 that he was the best Fullback and Tackle in the nation, making him the only player in college football history ever to be named a first-team consensus All-American at two different positions in the same season. Incredibly, he was even named as an End on a few other All-America teams! Over his illustrious three year career in Gold Country, the Gophers lost only a total of four games, and none of them by more than two points.

In the fall of 1930, Bronko graduated and became THE "Monster of the Midway," when he signed on with the NFL's Chicago Bears for the then-pricey, Depression-era sum of $5,000. The Bronk reached super-stardom status in the Windy City, where he would lead the team to three NFL championships during his eight-year tenure.

It was also in Chicago where the bruising fullback's exploits soon took on legendary proportions. Papa Bear Halas, the team's owner, recalled a game against Washington at Wrigley Field, where Nagurski barreled up the middle, sent two linebackers flying in different directions, trampled two defensive backs, ran through the end-zone and bounced off the goal-post, finally bulldozing into the brick wall that bordered the dugout used by the Chicago Cubs — even cracking it. "That last guy hit me awful hard..." the dazed Nagurski would say upon reaching the sidelines.

One tall tale had him falling out of bounds during a game one time, and toppling a policeman's horse standing along the sideline. Another had the Bronk missing a wild tackle and shearing the fender off a Model-T Ford that was parked near the sidelines.

As a runner, Nagurski didn't bother with dazzle and finesse, and as a lineman he never bothered to learn great technique. Instead, he simply used his brute strength and over-power his opponents. In other words, he was about as subtle as a Mack Truck. When he ran, he simply tucked the ball under his arm, lowered his giant shoulders, and charged full speed ahead — ramming through and over people.

"I was OK, I guess," Bronko would say years later. "I wasn't pretty, but I did all right. Our teams won most of the time, so that was good. I know I'd love to do it all over again. I never enjoyed anything as much as I did playing football. I felt like it was something I was born to do."

Bronko wasn't the only star running back on the team though, as future Hall of Famer Red Grange was also in the Bears' backfield. In fact, Bronko even took over in the backfield for another future Hall of Famer, the former Duluth Eskimo great, Ernie Nevers. "Halas stockpiled backs and he believed in spreading it around," Nagurski told Sports Illustrated in 1984. "Plus, he wanted to keep me fresh for defense, where I'd put in a full afternoon."

"I have said it a thousand times, Bronko Nagurski was the greatest player I ever saw, and I saw a lot of them in my lifetime," Grange would later say. "Running into him was like getting an electric shock. If you tried to tackle him anywhere above the ankles, you were liable to get killed."

Overall, he was a clutch player who did whatever it took to get his team a victory. He threw the winning touchdown pass in the 1932 playoff game against the Portsmouth Spartans, and that next season he led the Bears to another NFL championship when he tossed a pair of touchdown passes in Chicago's 23-21 victory over the New York Giants.

"Here's a check for $10,000, Nagurski" said G. A. Richards, owner of the Detroit Lions. "Not to play for the Lions, but just to quit and get the hell out of the league. You're ruining my team!"

In 1937, Nagurski, upset about his salary being decreased throughout the 1930s from the original $5,000 to $4,500 in 1931 and $3,700 by 1932, decided to retire, and pursue a career in pro wrestling. The Bronk had gotten into wrestling a few years earlier, but found it tough to juggle both careers. In one three-week stretch that year, he played in five Bears games and wrestled in eight cities: Portland. Vancouver, Seattle, Phoenix, L.A., Oakland, Salt Lake City and Philadelphia. Life in the ring was not as glamorous as he had hoped, but it was a living.

"I wrestled guys like Jim Londos, Strangler Lewis and others," said Bronko. "But they weren't in their prime then. I never liked wrestling. At that time, there wasn't a lot of money in it. And it was a sport where you worked every night and traveled a lot. I had a family at the time and didn't want to be away from home. But we were just getting out of the Depression in those days and we needed the money. The promoters told me I would make a million in no time. But it didn't happen."

Then, in 1943, because of player shortages caused by World War II, the Bears issued an S.O.S. to Nagurski to return for one final season. He agreed, and fittingly, at the age of 35, even scored the game-winning touchdown of the NFL title game against the Washington Redskins. He hung em' up for good after that season though, finishing his amazing NFL career with 242 points scored on 4,301 yards rushing. The six-time All-Pro even averaged nearly five yards per carry, a remarkable feat.

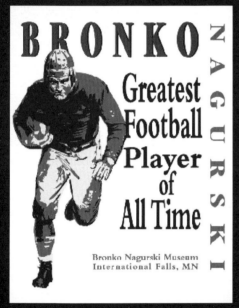

"My greatest thrill in football was the day Bronko announced his retirement," said Green Bay Hall of Fame Fullback Clarke Hinkle. "There's no question he was the most bruising fullback football has ever seen. I know, because I've still got the bruises!"

After wrestling professionally for more than a dozen years — a career he would later call "degrading," Nagurski returned to International Falls with his wife Eileen to raise their six children. (One of his boys, Bronko, Jr., played football at Notre Dame and later in the CFL.) There, quietly and unassumingly, he became the most famous gas station owner in town. He could now finally live in peace and privacy, and enjoy the fruits of his labor. He loved the outdoors, and was an avid hunter and fisherman. He even liked the cold weather. "We don't have summer," Bronko once explained of his beloved hometown, "just a season in the middle of the year when the sledding is poor."

He would later do some endorsements, including a couple of $50 deals for promoting Wheaties and Camel Cigarettes — which included a carton of smokes a week. "I bought Kools and gave the Camels away," he later said jokingly.

Tragically, on Jan. 7, 1990, Bronko died at the age of 81. His awards and honors include being named as a charter member of the Pro Football and College Football Halls of Fame, and being elected to the Football Writers Association of America's All-Time team. In 1995 that same group also voted to have his name attached to college football's Defensive Player of the Year award, called the "Nagurski Trophy."

In 1979 his No. 72 was retired by the U of M, and Sports Illustrated later named Bronko as Minnesota's Greatest Athlete of the Century. In addition, in 1992, International Falls honored is most famous son by opening the "Bronko Nagurski Museum," the only museum in America dedicated to a single player. That same year the Gophers' practice facility was renamed as the Gibson-Nagurski Football Complex, after Bronk and his teammate, 1928 All-American Guard George Gibson. Perhaps the biggest honor came years ago though, when his old high school renamed themselves as the International Falls "Broncos."

Legendary Notre Dame Coach Knute Rockne called him "the only football player I ever saw who could have played every position," and George Halas said he was "the greatest fullback who ever lived. He was absolutely unstoppable."

Bronko Nagurski was larger than life, and his size 22 Super Bowl ring, the biggest ever made, was proof! Perhaps no name has become more synonymous in the history of the sport than his. Nothing says leather helmets and high-top cleats louder than Bronko Nagurski. With his barrel chest and tree trunk legs, he became one of America's most colorful all-time characters and greatest sports heroes.

Perhaps Grantland Rice, once the most respected football authority in the nation, summed him up best when he was asked to select an all-time All-Star team. "That's easy. I'd pick 11 Bronko Nagurski's. I honestly don't think it would be a contest. The 11 Nagurski's would be a mop-up. It would be something close to murder and massacre. For the Bronk could star at any position on the field — with 228 pounds of authority to back him up."

He was truly a Bronko that could never broken.

THE MINNESOTA INTERCOLLEGIATE CONFERENCE

In the early 1900's the organization and control of football was for the most part student-centered. Issues such as eligibility restrictions, scheduling procedures, awarding championships, and the establishment of consistent rules and regulations were sporadic at best. As a result, conferences and associations began to appear in an attempt to formalize athletic competition.

One such organization was the Tri-State Conference, which was made up of colleges from both Minnesota and the Dakotas. In 1919, after a heated debate between the two state factions regarding rule changes and eligibility, the Minnesota contingent broke away and formed its own conference called the Minnesota Intercollegiate Athletic Conference. The MIAC's first charter members included: Carleton College, Gustavus Adolphus College, Hamline University, Macalester College, St. John's University, St. Olaf College and the University of St. Thomas. (Concordia College-Moorhead joined the conference in 1921, Augsburg College in 1924 and St. Mary's University in 1926. Bethel College later joined in 1977.) In addition, St. Mary's ended its MIAC football run in the 1960s, as did the UM-Duluth, which had originally joined the MIAC in 1950, but later made the jump to the Northern Sun Intercollegiate Conference in 1976.

Recognized as one of the toughest and most prestigious NCAA Division III intercollegiate athletic conferences in the country, today, the MIAC sponsors championships in 23 sports — 12 for men and 11 for women. And, because its members are all private undergraduate colleges, none of them can offer athletic scholarships to its student athletes. So it really is about the kids, and football.

All-Time MIAC Champions

Year	Champion	Year	Champion	Year	Champion
1920	Hamline	1946	Gustavus	1974	Concordia
1921	Hamline	1947	Macalester		St. John's
1922	St. Olaf		St. Thomas	1975	St. John's
	St. Thomas	1948	St. Thomas	1976	St. John's
1923	St. Olaf	1949	St. Thomas	1977	St. John's
1924	Carleton	1950	Gustavus	1978	Concordia
1925	Macalester	1951	Gustavus		St. Olaf
1926	Gustavus	1952	Concordia	1979	Concordia
1927	Gustavus		Gustavus		St. John's
1928	Augsburg	1953	Gustavus		St. Olaf
	St. Mary's		St. John's		St. Thomas
1929	St. Thomas	1954	Gustavus	1980	Concordia
1930	St. Olaf	1955	Gustavus	1981	Concordia
	St. Thomas	1956	St. Thomas	1982	St. John's
1931	Concordia	1957	Concordia	1983	St. Thomas
1932	St. John's	1958	Gustavus	1984	Hamline
1933	Gustavus	1959	Gustavus	1985	St. John's
1934	Concordia	1960	UM-Duluth	1986	Concordia
1935	Gustavus	1961	UM-Duluth	1987	Gustavus
	St. John's	1962	St. John's	1988	Concordia
	St. Olaf	1963	St. John's		Hamline
1936	Gustavus	1964	Concordia	1989	St. John's
	St. John's	1965	St. John's	1990	Concordia
1937	Gustavus	1966	Hamline		St. Thomas
1938	St. John's	1967	Gustavus	1991	St. John's
1939	St. Thomas	1968	Gustavus	1992	Carleton
1940	Gustavus	1969	Concordia	1993	St. John's
1941	St. Thomas	1970	Concordia	1994	St. John's
1942	Concordia	1971	Gustavus	1995	Concordia
	St. Thomas		St. John's		St. John's
1943	No Champion	1972	Gustavus	1996	St. John's
1944	No Champion	1973	UM-Duluth	1997	Augsburg
1945	Gustavus		St. Thomas	1998	St. John's
				1999	St. John's

M.I.A.C.
Minnesota Intercollegiate Athletic Conference

All-Time MIAC Titles
(Won or Shared)

School	No.	Last Title
St. John's	24	1999
Gustavus	22	1987
Concordia	17	1995
St. Thomas	14	1990
St. Olaf	6	1935
Hamline	5	1988
UM-Duluth	3	1973
Carleton	2	1992
Macalester	2	1947
Augsburg	2	1997
St. Mary's	1	1928
Bethel	0	x

NCAA Division III Football
All-Time Top 25 Winning Pct.

1)	Plymouth State	.702
3)	**St. John's**	**.681**
11)	**Concordia-M'head**	**.626**
17)	**St. Thomas**	**.608**
25)	**Gustavus**	**.605**

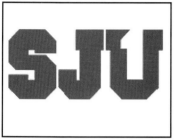

Founded in 1857, St. John's University has a long tradition of football success. The gridiron game first began at the school informally during the late 1890s. The first official game, however, was played on October 27, 1900, and ended in a 5-0 loss to St. Cloud High School on the gravel mall in front of the Abbey Church.

The team fared much better that next season though as they twice defeated St. Cloud High School, 11-6 and 11-0, St. Cloud Normal School, 17-6, and St. Thomas, 16-0. In 1905 Harry Comeau took over as head coach, and led the Johnnies to a pair of undefeated (1-0 & 2-0) seasons. In 1908 Bill Brennan assumed the role of head coach, and oversaw the drainage of the cranberry marsh, which was completed in preparation for the new football field, called the "Natural Bowl."

In 1910 football was abolished at SJU, with the reasons cited as "promoting unfriendliness towards other schools," and that football "didn't inspire school loyalty." The game returned to campus, however, in 1920, following W.W.I., with the new-look Johnnies joining the newly formed MIAC.

One of the early stars of this era was Johnny "Blood" McNally, who, after becoming became the Johnnies' first four sport letter-winner, went on to become one of the first superstars of the NFL. (After playing for the Duluth Eskimos, he later won several NFL titles with the Green Bay Packers. The 15-year NFL veteran was later enshrined as a charter member of the Pro Football Hall of Fame.)

St. John's 1901 squad

In 1925 Bill Houle was named as the team's new coach, and his star player was Guard George Durenburger, who went on to become the school's first all-conference player. Houle took the program to another level during his tenure in Collegeville, inspiring kids from across the state to try-out for his club.

In 1930 Duluth native Joe Benda took over behind the bench, and wasted little time in making his mark. The former Notre Dame player instilled a big chunk of the Fighting Irish's offense into the Johnnie playbook, a move that greatly improved the team's showing. By 1932 the team had achieved celebrity status on campus, as they outscored their opponents, 109-0, in seven games that year to win their first MIAC title. It would be the first of three for Benda, who added conference crowns in 1935 and 1936 as well.

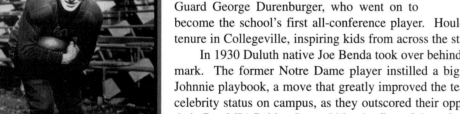

Johnny "Blood" McNally

George Durenburger replaced Benda in 1937 for what would prove to be a three-year stint behind the bench, and promptly led SJU to another MIAC crown in 1938. The star of that team was Halfback Edward Callanan, the Johnnies' first Little All-American. Benda returned in 1941 and led the Johnnies through the 1940s. His best years of the decade came in 1948 and '49, when he led the team to a pair of six-win seasons. Benda, after suffering from Hodgkins Disease, tragically died in 1950 at the age of just 45.

That same year Johnny "Blood" McNally came home at the age of 46 to finish his degree and also to assume the role of head coach at his alma mater. He would stay for three years in all, leading the team to a pair of four-win, and one five-win seasons, with the latter coming in 1952.

Then, in 1953 something happened in Collegeville that would forever change the school's identity forever — John Gagliardi was hired as the team's new coach. Incredibly, he has been there ever since! "Gags" got his first victory that year in a 22-6 win over St. Mary's. It would be the first of many, many more wins to come for the young coach.

Leading the way that year was the program's first great halfback, Jim Lehman (the father of Minnesota golfer Tom Lehman), who led the country in scoring and later went on to play with the Baltimore Colts. Lehman, behind the blocking of three-time all-conference Guard, Chuck Froehle, led the team to a 6-2 record that year — good for another MIAC championship.

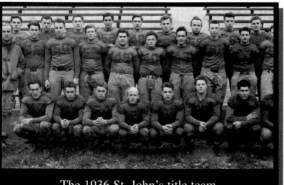

The 1936 St. John's title team

Despite a couple of six and seven win seasons in 1954 & 1955, the Johnnies were unable to bring home any conference crowns. One highlight of the '54 season came against Augustana, as Lehman, later named as the conference's MVP, scored a record five touchdowns. Gagliardi continued to lead to program into prominence, however, winning another MIAC title in 1962, when he led the team to its first undefeated 9-0 record.

The coach's pedigree was further heightened in 1963, when he led SJU to another undefeated 10-0 season, and an improbable

Halfback Jim Lehman... as in the father of golfing great, Tom

JOHN GAGLIARDI

John Gagliardi was born in 1927, the son of an Italian-born body shop owner in Trinidad, Colo. To fully understand this man's life-long calling of coaching, you have to go way back to Trinidad Catholic High School. Gagliardi's storied coaching career ironically began when his high school coach was drafted into World War II. Without a coach, the school was just going to drop the football program until "Gags" talked the administration into letting him do the coaching. Gagliardi, the teams' captain, took over the reins at the age of 16. Even at that young age people could see the man had a gift for teaching, working with young people, and instilling in them a winning attitude.

His teams would win several conference titles. Upon graduating, he put himself through school at Colorado College, where he coached the high school team for two more seasons and then took over as Colorado College's head coach for his junior and senior seasons.

After graduation from C.C. in 1949, the 22-year-old Gags accepted the college coaching position at Carroll College, a small Catholic liberal arts school in Helena, Mont. He coached not only the football program, but also the basketball and baseball programs as well. Inheriting a Carroll College athletic program in utter disarray, he turned things around in a hurry, leading the football and basketball teams to three straight championships.

His success drew the attention of another small Catholic college — St. John's University, where Gagliardi would go on to become a living legend. As we head into the new millennium, Gagliardi will begin his 52nd season as a collegiate head coach and 48th season in Collegeville. The winningest active coach in college football history, Gagliardi currently owns an amazing 364-107-11 career record. He is now just 44 wins away from the all-time collegiate win record of 408, set by former Grambling Head Coach Eddie Robinson. (He would've broken the record years ago, but the cold Minnesota weather prevented him from playing as many games as Robinson did down in the deep south.)

Nearly a half-century later, Gagliardi's teams still set the standard for MIAC competitors. He has coached three national championship teams (1963, 1965 and 1976), won 23 conference titles and has led his teams to 32 post-season appearances. In the past 38 years, SJU has been nationally ranked 36 times and it owns a 21-11 post-season record.

Gagliardi has built one of the nation's top NCAA Division III programs. The attitude and winning tradition he instills in his players is unprecedented. He has been the subject of books, countless national television, magazine and newspaper articles, and even appeared on the cover of Sports Illustrated's 1992 College Football Spectacular. In addition, he was ranked #19 on the Star Tribune's 100 Most Important Sports Figures of the Century List and #18 on Sports Illustrated's 50 Greatest Sports Figures from Minnesota.

Among his numerous awards and achievements, Gagliardi has been inducted into the Minnesota and Montana Halls of Fame and is featured in the College Football Hall of Fame. Perhaps his greatest honor came in 1993 though, when the NCAA honored the coach by naming the Division III equivalent of the Heisman Trophy after him. The "Gagliardi Trophy" is now given annually to the outstanding NCAA Division III football player.

Gagliardi's success is attributable to more than mere football strategy and tactics. He is an astute judge of talent. He creates an environment of fun and high expectations, and he concentrates on methods and practices that truly focus on winning football games. John Gagliardi has built a legacy that is unrivaled in college football, and what's frightening for all the other MIAC schools, is that he may just be getting his second wind.

"I dared to do a lot of things that no one else dared to do, like the way we practice," said Gags. "We've never gone 'full-go' in practice I am proud of the fact that I saved a lot of guys from permanent injuries because of that. I've been a lucky guy and I've always had great athletes to make me look good along the way."

John and his wife Peggy live in Collegeville and have four children: Johnny, Nancy, Gina and Jim —who is an assistant coach at SJU.

national title in a 33-27 win over Prairie View A&M (Texas) in the 1963 NAIA Championship game.

St. John's was led that year by Halfback Bob Spinner, who won his second straight MIAC scoring crown in the season finale against St. Thomas, who they trounced, 32-6. From there, it was off to the small-college playoffs, where St. John's met the College of Emporia (Kansas). It wasn't even close though, as the Johnnies dominated the game, 54-0, en route to waltzing through the playoffs and advancing to the title game. Held in Sacramento, Calif., the championship tilt was labeled as the "Camellia Bowl," where the Johnnies met Prairie View A&M.

Now, Prairie View A&M was the dominant Black college team in America at the time. They played a big-time schedule against teams like Grambling State and Florida A&M and fared well against them all. Prairie View had some great players on their team, including future NFL All-Pro Wide Receiver Otis Taylor and Quarterback Jim Kearney, who both went on to play for more than a decade with the Kansas City Chiefs.

Prairie View also had 40 "free-ride" football scholarships for their players, while the Johnnies, on the other hand, had none. The only thing the Johnnies did have in their favor, was the a-typical California weather on that day, which was a chilly 39 degrees — downright freezing to a Texan.

The Panthers scored first on a 29 yard rollout by Halfback Jimmy Hall. The underdog Johnnies answered though, on Bob Spinner's 41 yard punt return in the second, making it 7-6. But the Panthers came back on Jim Kearney's 61-yard pass to Otis Taylor, to make it 14-6.

St. John's defensive back John McCormick then returned an interception 44 yards, and Johnny Quarterback Craig Muyres hooked up with halfback Bernie Beckman to make it 14-13 at the half.

Then, in the third, the Johnnies took the lead for good on Muyres' 23-yard pass to Hardy Reyerson. Muyres then hit Ken Roering for the extra point and St. John's led 20-14. Late in the same period, Beckman, off a double reverse, connected with Roering on an 18-yard touchdown to give SJU some cushion.

The Panthers rallied back in the fourth though, as Kearney threw a 14 yard TD pass to Halfback Doug Broadus, cutting the margin to 26-21. But the Johnies answered, this time on a 19-yard Muyres to Reyerson aerial, followed by a Spinner extra point catch. Prairie View scored on an Ezell Seals one yard plunge, with only 2:15 to go in the game, but it was too little too late, as Roering recovered the Prairie View on-side kick to run out the clock. The Johnnies had done it, beating the Panthers 33-27, as the 12,220 fans, many of whom had make the trek from Minnesota, went wild.

Beckman, the smallest man on the field, ran for 52 yards, caught three passes for 43 yards, including a conversion and played brilliant defense, was named as the game's MVP.

"It was a tremendous win for us," said Gagliardi. "Prairie View is the best team we played all year. Believe me, we knew we weren't going to be playing St. Catherine's! I mean it, it was like

John Gagliardi & Eddie Robinson, are College football's No.1 & No.2 all-time winningest coaches.

coming back after two nine-count knock-downs. And the second knock-down really had us hanging on the ropes. I give credit to the team. They managed to come through with the big play when it was needed all season, especially Craig Muyres, who I believe is the best clutch quarterback in the United States."

After posting a modest 4-3 record in 1964, the Johnnies, who were led by MIAC MVP, Halfback Rich Froehle, roared back in 1965 to finish at 11-0. With their conference title in hand, they then went on to the post-season, where they first beat Fairmont State, 28-7, and then crushed Linfield College of Oregon, 35-0, to win their second NAIA Championship. Amazingly, the Johnnies allowed only 27 points to be scored against them that entire season!

The team went through a couple mediocre seasons in the late 1960s until finally going 8-1-1 in 1969, capping the season with a 21-0 win over Simpson College to win the inaugural "Mineral Bowl" game.

Gags had the troops back on track in 1971, as they went 8-1 and won yet another conference title. Their only loss that year came on a last-minute touchdown in a 22-21 loss to Duluth. (One of the stars of this era was Tight End Dave Arnold, who tallied a record 32 touchdowns from 1969-72.)

They then went on to win three consecutive MIAC titles from 1974-76. The '76 season was a special one, as the Johnnies capped a 20-game winning streak by winning their third national title, this one being the NCAA Division III championship. The team rolled through the playoffs, first pounding Augustana, 46-7, and then Buena Vista, 61-0, to earn a trip to the "Alonzo Stagg Bowl" in Phoenix City, Ala., to face Towson State. (Against Augustana, Quarterback Jeff Norman threw for five touchdowns, and Running Back Tim Schmitz ran wild for 530 yards on the ground.)

Then, in the "Stagg Bowl," behind Normans' two touchdown passes to Tim Schmitz and Jim Roeder, as well as a pair of rushing TDs from Schmitz, the Johnnies jumped out to a 28-0 lead by the end of the third quarter. Towsen State came back to tie it up though, on some fourth quarter dramatics. Norman led the rally back, however, as he hit Roeder on a long pass to get to the one-yard line. From there, Norman kicked the game-winning field goal with just three seconds remaining on the clock to give SJU the dramatic 31-28 national championship victory.

Following the game Gagliardi was named as the NCAA Division III Coach of the Year, Norman was designated the Offensive Player of the Year, and Schmitz, who tallied 17 touchdowns and more than 1,000 yards that season (nearly 4,000 over his career), was named as an All-American.

The team continued to dominate throughout the

Johnnie Pride

GAGLIARDI'S UNORTHODOX COACHING METHODS HAVE BEEN DISTILLED INTO A SERIES OF "WINNING WITH NO's"

The Overall Program
- No athletic scholarships.
- No big staff, just four assistant coaches.
- No coordinators.
- No freshmen or junior-varsity program.
- No discipline problems.
- No insisting on being called "Coach."
- No players cut.
- No pampering athletes.
- No one persuaded to come out or stay out.
- No hazing tolerated.

The Season
- No staff or player meetings.
- No film sessions after Monday
- No special diet.
- No training table — team eats with other students.
- No signs in dressing rooms.
- No slogans.
- No superstitions.
- No play-books.
- No statistics posted.
- No newspaper clippings posted.

The Practices
- No practice pants issued — shorts or sweats worn at all practices.
- No agility drills.
- No lengthy calisthenics (about three minutes.)
- No pre-practice drills — players do what they want or need to do.
- No practice apparatus or gadgets.
- No blocking sleds.
- No blocking or tackling dummies.
- No tackling.
- No laps or wind sprints.
- No special coaching clothes worn.
- No use of the words "hit," "kill," etc...
- No clip boards.
- No whistles.
- No practice on Mondays.
- No drills.
- No Spring practice.
- No practice in rain, extreme heat or cold.
- No long practices — varies from 30 to 90 minutes.
- No practice under the lights.
- No water or rest denied when players want it.
- No insisting underclassmen carry equipment other than their own.

The Games
- No big deal when we score — we expect to score.
- No Gatorade celebrations.
- No trash talking tolerated.
- No player NOT played in rout.
- No cheap-shots or foul play tolerated.
- No counting tackles.
- No precision pre-game drills.
- No special pre-game meals.
- No computer analysis.
- No cheerleaders.

The Off-Season
- No meetings
- No between season practices or conditioning.
- No weightlifting program

The Results
- No player has not graduated.
- No disciplinary problems.
- No player lost through ineligibility.
- No class has NOT had at least one prospective pro player.
- No small college has larger crowd support.
- No team has fewer injuries.
- No team has fewer penalties.
- No small college coach has won more games.

1970s and '80s, winning titles in 1977, 1979 and 1982. The '82 season saw the team go undefeated, losing only to Northwestern (Iowa), 33-28, in the first round of the D-III national playoffs.

They won additional crowns in 1985 and 1989, as the team advanced to the final four of the Division III playoffs that year as well. After beating Simpson, 42-35, and Central, 27-24, the Johnnies finally lost to Dayton, 28-0. (One of the stars of that team was legendary Wide Receiver Todd Fultz, whose 77 catches proved to be the difference on several clutch plays throughout that season.)

Then, in 1991, the Johnnies made it back to the Division III final four, this time defeating Coe College, 75-2, in the first round (setting a NCAA record for most points scored in a playoff game), followed by a second round win over UW-LaCrosse, 29-10, before once again bowing out to Dayton, 19-7, in the semifinals.

In 1993 Coach Gagliardi won his 300th game as a college coach, when his Johnnies pulverized Bethel, 77-12. After that historic event the eyes of the sports world were suddenly on Gagliardi.

"It was just a big relief and I was glad to get it over with," said Gagliardi. "We were in the middle of the season and there was so much build-up towards it. I never had so much attention in my life, it was hard to get anything done that week! I'm sure the big-time coaches were used to all the attention, but I didn't really like it. As far as being in the fraternity, those people are so great. Never in my wildest dreams did I ever think that I would be mentioned in the same sentence with them. But you have to remember, you couldn't win all those games without a lot of great players through the years."

That 1993 squad not only went undefeated, they also became the first college team since the 1904 Gophers to score more than 700 points in a season, averaging an unthinkable 61.5 points per game. For their efforts, they advanced to the Division III playoffs, where, after beating Wartburg, 32-26, and Albion, 47-16, they got smoked by Mount Union, 56-8, in the semis.

They made it back to the final four of the Division III playoffs in 1994, this time losing to Albion, 19-16, in Collegeville, after first beating Central Iowa, 51-21, and Wartburg, 42-14, in the quarterfinals. That next year, in the process of leading his team

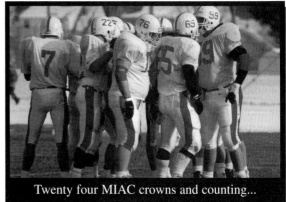
Twenty four MIAC crowns and counting...

St. John's Career Records

Category	Player	No.	Years
Rushing	Tim Schmitz	3,933	1974-77
Passing	Kurt Ramler	8,134	1993-96
Receiving	Chris Palmer	3,162	1992-95
Receptions	Adam Herbst	207	1995-98
TD Catches	Adam Herbst	41	1995-98
Points Scored	Jeff Norman	346	1974-77

to yet another MIAC title, Gagliardi won his 324th game, moving him into second place past Alabama's Bear Bryant on the all-time collegiate victory list.

In 1996 SJU went undefeated in the MIAC and again advanced into the NCAA national quarterfinals, where, after beating Simpson, 21-18, they lost to LaCrosse, 37-30. After going 6-4 in 1997, the Johnnies came back in 1998 by winning another conference crown, and again advancing into the postseason. This time, however, after beating Pacific Lutheran (Wash.), 33-20, they lost to Eau Claire, 10-7.

Incredibly, they did it again in 1999, bringing another MIAC title to the shores of Lake Sagatagan, and advancing yet again into the post-season, where, after beating UW-Steven's Point, 23-10, and Central Iowa, 10-9, they lost to Pacific Lutheran in the semifinals by the score of 19-9.

The Johnnies have posted a 96-16-2 overall record in the 1990s, one of the best records at any level of college football. In that time, SJU has won seven MIAC titles and has advanced to the national quarterfinals six times. In the 89-year history of the program, SJU has collected 24 MIAC crowns and registered a dominant 460-206-24 overall record for a .684 winning percentage. This program is, in a word, a dynasty. Period.

College Football's 300 Win Club

There have been more than 25,000 head coaches in the history of college football, of which just seven have won more than 300 games:

1. Eddie Robinson, Grambling: 408
2. **John Gagliardi, St. John's University: 364**
3. Paul "Bear" Bryant, Alabama: 323
4. Pop Warner, Temple: 319
4. Joe Paterno, Penn State: 319
6. Amos Alonzo Stagg, Pacific: 314
7. Bobby Bowden, Florida State: 304

The Johnnies' 1976 national championship

Augsburg Auggies

Founded in 1872, Augsburg College fielded its first football team back in 1926, thanks to an outpouring of support, both moral and financial, from alumni and businessmen in the Augsburg neighborhood near downtown Minneapolis. Augsburg's first team finished with a modest 1-3-1 record, garnering a 13-13 tie against St. John's and a 27-0 victory at Concordia-Moorhead in the final game of the season.

That next season, the Auggies finished with a 4-2 record, good for a second place tie in the MIAC with Macalester. By 1928, the Auggies, who finished with a 4-1-2 record under Coach Conrad Eklund, earned a share of the conference crown with St. Mary's.

The 1928 Auggie title team

"In reviewing Augsburg's football history, one notes with pleasure and satisfaction the very commendable record that the school's teams have established," noted the school paper, the Echo, in its Dec. 6, 1928 issue. "Augsburg, during its first year in the conference, was considered an easy mark by the other schools, but some of them were doomed to an unpleasant surprise. Augsburg soon set a precedent in making upsets that they still adhere to, and copped fourth place. Last year they earned second place in the final standings and this year capped the climax by tying for the championship. No wonder there is much cause for rejoicing about the campus. Coach Con Eklund and his assistants, Lyle Crose and Ray Eklund, are to be commended for their untiring efforts in the development of the team. They rightfully deserve praise, with the team, for giving the Auggies this their best year in state football."

In 1935, then-Athletic Director James Pederson made an announcement that would dramatically change college football history. Instead of fielding an intercollegiate varsity football team, he instead decided to field an intramural squad instead. "The purpose of the plan is to give playing experience to a greater number of students than was possible under the old system," the Echo would later report.

Sig Helmeland

"Coach Jim Pederson has decided to enter the ranks of the pioneers, whether he knows it or not," said the Echo a week later. "His athletic program, which places almost all the emphasis on intramural competition, is being tried for the first time in this part of the country. Other colleges are intensely interested in the results of this policy, and may adopt it if it proves successful at Augsburg."

Augsburg did manage to play one intercollegiate game in 1936, with the "Augsburg All-Stars," a collection of the best intramural players, ultimately losing to St. Thomas, 12-6.

In 1939, after pressure from both students and alumni for the school to return to intercollegiate competition, the sport was reinstated. Former Gopher star Dan Elmer took over the Auggie program in 1939, and despite a winless first season, there was still optimism for the future.

The war years of the 1940s took their toll on college athletics, and as a result, the football program was curtailed until 1946. That year former Auggie sports legend Edor Nelson, after spending six months in a German prison camp, returned to take over the football squad. He would coach the Auggie's for 23 seasons, compiling a 56-118-10 record before retiring in 1969.

In 1955, Nelson's Auggie football team accomplished a major goal, finishing 4-4 - the first .500 record for the school since football returned to the campus. The 1957 team also finished 4-4, highlighted by the school's first-ever victory over St. Thomas, the defending league champions, 7-6. The win broke a 12-game losing streak to the Tommies.

The early 1960s were perhaps Nelson's most successful, as his teams went 5-3 (1960), 4-4 (1961), 3-5 (1962) and 4-3-1 (1963). Then, in 1964, the Auggies went 6-3, earning a coveted runner-up spot in the MIAC standings.

Bill Caris took over the coaching duties in 1972, and over his four year tenure behind the Auggie bench, he produced a solid 19-19 mark. Caris came right out the blocks swinging during that first season, posting a pair of back-to-back shutouts at Wisconsin-River Falls and Wisconsin-Eau Claire, 27-0 and 20-0, respectively. The 1973 squad then put together a school-record five-game winning streak en route to finishing with a 7-2 mark.

The college received a huge boost in 1984, when the football, softball and soccer teams were given a new on-campus home with the opening of Anderson-Nelson Field. The structure, named for legendary Coaches Ernie Anderson and Edor Nelson, featured an artificial-turf surface (which came from the Metrodome) that gave home teams a unique advantage. Then, in the early 1990s, the facility was retro-fitted with a seasonal air-supported dome, giving them optimum weather conditions year-round.

Jack Osberg, who had earned Lutheran All-American honors as a two-way lineman from 1958-61, was named head coach at Augsburg in 1991. After graduating from Augsburg in 1962, the Minneapolis Washburn High School graduate began his coaching career at Minneapolis Roosevelt High School, serving seven years as an assistant coach (1962-70), before taking one year off (1968-69) to serve as a graduate assis-

Captain Arthur Hauser
All-State End

Edward Connoly
All-State Center

Augsburg's early stars

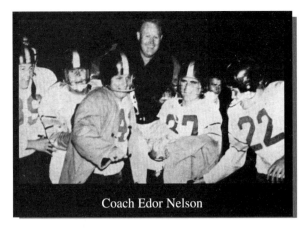

Coach Edor Nelson

tant on Bob Devaney's staff at Nebraska. (While at Roosevelt, he coached a student-athlete who would later earn fame on both a statewide and national level — James Janos, aka Minnesota Gov. Jesse "The Body" Ventura!) He later served as an assistant at Augsburg on two separate occasions.

Osberg's task was clear — he needed to lead a resurrection of the Auggie football program. The program was in dire straits; the Auggies had won just seven games in the seven seasons before Osberg took over, including two winless seasons — 0-9-1 in 1987 and 0-10 in 1990. The Auggies slowly moved out of the cellar that year, winning two games in 1991, three in 1992 and five games in both 1993 and 1994. The 1995 team finished 6-4, including a 28-7 win over St. Thomas — just the second Auggie win over the Tommies since 1970.

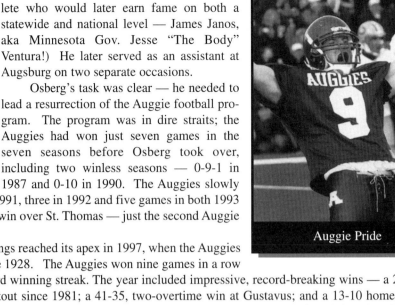

Auggie Pride

The decade-long move up the conference standings reached its apex in 1997, when the Auggies went 10-2 and won the MIAC title for the first time since 1928. The Auggies won nine games in a row after a league-opening loss at St. Thomas, a school record winning streak. The year included impressive, record-breaking wins — a 20-10 win over St. John's; a 42-0 shutout of St. Olaf, the first shutout since 1981; a 41-35, two-overtime win at Gustavus; and a 13-10 home win over Concordia to vault the Auggies into sole possession of first place. The title was clinched with a 56-22 thrashing of Bethel at the Metrodome. (The dramatic win over the Johnnies, under the lights at Anderson-Nelson Field, was Augsburg's first win over the northern power since 1980.)

With the conference championship, Augsburg reached the post-season for the first time in school history, qualifying for the NCAA Division III national playoffs. There, the Auggies reached the quarterfinal round of the playoffs, beating Concordia-Moorhead, 34-22, at the Fargodome, before ultimately falling to Simpson (Iowa), by the ugly score of 61-21.

During their run to the top of the MIAC standings, the Auggies became known throughout the ranks of Division III football as a great passing team. Quarterback Derrin Lamker, who took advantage of his quick artificial-turf home surface, earned the MIAC's Player of the Year honors in the team's championship season, completing a career in which he threw for 6,624 yards (1993-97), completing 550 of 1022 passes for 46 touchdowns. His favorite target all year long was junior Wide Receiver Scott Hvistendahl, who was just about unstoppable.

In 1998, Hvistendahl made college football history when he beat San Francisco 49ers legend Jerry Rice's the all-time NCAA record (all-divisions) for career receiving yards while he was at Mississippi Valley State from 1981-84. Hvistendahl, the most dominant receiver in MIAC history (holding all but one conference receiving record, 265 career receptions for 4,268 yards in MIAC play), entered the 1998 season with 2,836 career receiving yards, fully 1,857 yards short of Rice's 15-year old record of 4,693 yards.

Four times during that magical season, Hvistendahl eclipsed the 200-yard mark, including a school-record 271-yard, eight-catch, four-touchdown performance in the season-opener against Mayville State (N.D.). By the home finale against Bethel, Hvistendahl broke the old NCAA Division III record of 4,311 yards. He entered the season finale, Friday, Nov. 13, 1998 in the Metrodome against Concordia-Moorhead, 227 yards away from Rice's mark. Without the coaching staff purposely aiming plays at Hvistendahl until the final drive of his career, he somehow ended up beating Rice by just three yards, tallying 230 on the afternoon, to finish his illustrious career with a national-record 4,696 yards on 285 receptions, including 40 touchdowns.

Augsburg All-Americans

Tom Hofflander	1956	E
Bob Anderson	1995	DT
Scott Hvistendahl	1996-98	WR
Martin Hlinka	1998	K
Jake Kern	1997, 99	DB
Ted Schultz	1997	TE

Career Leaders

Rushing	Yards	Years	
Marty Alger	2,026	1991-9	

Passing	Yards	Years	
Derrin Lamker	6.624	1993-97	

Receiving	Yards	TDs	Years
Scott Hvistendahl	4,696	40	1994-98

"Years from now, my record will probably be broken four or five times, the way things are going," Hvistendahl said. "But it will still be neat to say to my grandkids that I was the first person to break Jerry Rice's record. He was one of the best players ever to play the game and his record stood for 14 years. That will be the special part. It was great to break the record in the last five minutes of my last game ever."

Hvistendahl became the first Auggie — and just the second MIAC player — to win the Gagliardi Trophy, given by the St. John's University J-Club and Jostens, Inc., to the national player of the year in Division III football. He was also a finalist for the other Division III national player of the year trophy, the Melberger Award. He was named to the first team of every Division III All-America team, and played as part of a Division III all-star team in the Aztec Bowl in Monterrey, Mexico. In addition, he twice earned GTE Academic All-America second-team honors. (Incidentally, the Cannon Falls, Minn. native went on to play professional football with the Arena League's Quad City Steamwheelers.)

Scott Hvistendahl set the NCAA's All-Time Receiving Yards record

Augsburg is a program on the way up. Other Auggies who have gone on through the years to play professionally include Don Nelson, Jim Pederson and David Warnke. Over the past decade, Augsburg has become a consistent threat to claim the MIAC championship, as Osberg, who has a 40-41 career record heading into the new millennium, has been able to build a consistent top-five team in conference play.

Bethel College, in Arden Hills, began its four-year Christian liberal arts instruction in 1947, but can trace its roots all the way back to Bethel Seminary, which was founded in 1871.

In the fall of 1947, Bethel Academy (which is now known as Bethel College and Seminary) made the decision to finally organize an intercollegiate football program. With the return of all of the GI's from World War II, there was plenty of talent to choose from. After conducting try-outs, the team played its first game on Sept. 19, 1947, losing to Rochester on Edwards Field. The team went 1-3 that year, but laying a solid gridiron foundation for years to come.

The Royals won their first Gopher Conference title in 1958 with a 5-3-0 record. Then, in 1975, they posted an outstanding 7-2 record to win the Tri-State Conference championship.

In 1977 Bethel College joined the MIAC, where they have competed ever since. The team has

Kim Walker

steadily improved through the years, and in the 1990s have taken off. The team had a pair of back-to-back third place finishes in 1990 & 1991, followed by another third place, 7-3 record in 1994. They bettered that in 1996, going 9-1, to finish in second place, and did it again in 1998, this time going 8-2.

Over the past 50 years, Bethel has had 14 head coaches. One of those coaches was former Vikings Defensive Back Karl Kassulke, who, after becoming paralyzed in a motorcycle accident, went on to serve as an assistant coach from his wheelchair along the sidelines.

They have also had eight game fields.

Bethel vs. Macalester

Among the venues the team played in prior to getting their recently built and dedicated Armstrong Stadium included: the Old Campus Mud Bowl, Highland Stadium, Hamline, Ramsey High School, Midway Stadium, Bremer Field and Roseville High School. The Royals (or "Indians" as they were previously known) have also held their practices at various locations, the State Fair grounds, Luther Seminary, and Fairview Community Center in Roseville for the 1996 season.

As we head into the new millennium, Head Coach Steve Johnson enters his 11th season at the controls of the Bethel football program. Under Coach Johnson's leadership, the Royals have had winning records in the MIAC in eight of the past nine years. Johnson has also twice been selected MIAC

Jeremy Belisle

Coach of the Year — after the 1989 and 1996 seasons. He was also selected as the West Region Coach of the Year after the 1996 season. The team is poised to do well into the next century as well. Free Safety Kirk Midthun is a two-time All-MIAC, and, in a game in early 2000, against Gustavus, Bethel Cornerback Ben Mathews set an all-division NCAA record by picking off five interceptions, en route to leading his team to a 14-13 come-from-behind victory.

Today, hundreds of Bethel players have had the opportunity to feel the impact of being a part of the Bethel Football Family, an intimate and caring group of young men.

Bethel College All-Americans

Name	Year	Position
Jim Nelson	1963	Running Back
Ray Sheperd	1963	Lineman
Kevin Hallstrom	1976	Defensive Back
Jack Negen	1990	Wide Receiver
Vincent Hooper	1993	Wide Receiver
Jeremy Tvedt	1996	Running Back

Bethel's Career Rushing Leaders

Name	Yds	Att	Avg	Years
Jeremy Tvedt	3,351	676	4.9	1993-96
Chris Wiens	2,969	572	5.2	1989-92

Bethel's Career Receiving Leaders

Name	Yds	Rec	Avg	Years
Jeremy Belisle	3,001	191	15.7	1996-00
Jack Negen	1,913	132	14.5	1989-91

Bethel's Career Passing Leaders

Name	Yds	Comp/Att	Years
Matt Lundeen	6,080	470/888	1994-97
Trent Anderson	5,436	434/817	1987-90

Kirk Midthun

Founded in 1866, Carleton College is one of Minnesota's finest higher institutes for learning. Although the program became a charter member of the MIAC in 1919, Carleton's gridiron history goes back much, much further. All the way back to 1881 to be exact. That was the year the Knights beat Seabury Seminary in their first-ever game. Then, in 1888, Carleton was beaten by Shattuck for the Northwest Championship, losing 48-16 to the Cadets. The team went on to win Minnesota Athletic Conference championships in 1897, 1899 and again in 1905.

The Knights continued to play well through the war era of the late 1910s, even playing tough against the University of Minnesota. Carleton's most famous football victory perhaps came against Amos Alonzo Stagg's mighty University of Chicago team, back in 1916. In 1918, at the height of W.W.I., Carleton and St. Olaf joined forces to form a unified football team. The combined team played just one game, a 59-0 thrashing at the hands of the mighty Gophers. They decided that was enough, and separated after that. In 1919 the rivalry was born, and Carleton beat St. Olaf 15-7 to capture the first-ever "Goat Trophy." After the war, Carleton, now solo, went on to win their first MIAC title in 1924, under Coach C.J. Hunt.

1—Hilton; 2—Burnquist; 3—Anderson; 4—Lundeen; 5—Harris; 6—Goldsbury; 7—Robertson; 8—Couper; 9—Wilcox; 10—Fath; 11—Harsh; 12—Brubaker; 13—McCarthy; 14—Strang; 15—McCulloch; 16—Rose; 17—Hayes.
CARLETON (MINN.) COLLEGE FOOT BALL TEAM.
Carleton's 1901 squad

In 1925 the team switched from the MIAC to the Midwest Conference. In 1932 the Knights headed east to play Army, at West Point, where the Cadets spanked them, 57-0. Then, in 1934 former University of Minnesota All-American Guard George Gibson took over as the team's new coach. He would stay for just five years, but did manage to lead them to an undefeated Co-championship of the Midwest Conference in 1936. That same year Carleton made a strong showing in losing to Division One power Iowa, 14-0.

Immediately prior to World War II, Knights stars Donald Senior and Richard Raiter were named as Little All-Americans. Carleton had no football teams in the mid-1940s, as Wally Hass and other coaches had left the campus for military service. Hass continued to coach through the late 1940s and into the mid-1950s though. In 1954 he produced an undefeated team that was one of the program's best ever.

Warren Beson took over in 1956 and relinquished the reigns to Mel Taube in 1959, who stayed in Northfield for a decade. Then, in 1973, Carleton beat St. Olaf, 16-14, to win the famed Goat Trophy, albeit the first time in 10 years.

Dale Quist was named as the new head coach in 1970, and remained until 1978. In 1976 Quarterback Bruce Johnston finished among the top 10 college players in the nation in both total offense and passing.

In the fall of 1977, Carleton hosted the first and only NCAA-sanctioned metric football game, which was appropriately called the "Metric Bowl." The game was the brainchild of chemistry professor Jerry Mohrig, who was teaching a course in the metric system and was intrigued by the idea of measuring a game like football, which is so conscious of distance, in meters. Cross-town rival St. Olaf College, at that time in a different athletic conference, agreed to participate in the non-conference game. The field, extended to measure 100 meters long by 53 meters wide, was marked off in 10-meter lines. All statistics were kept metrically, and the players' weight and height was listed in kilograms and centimeters in the game program. Even some female students took part as "cheerleaders," wearing T-shirts declaring "Drop back 10 meters and punt." Ten thousand fans (about 8,000 more than for a regular game) filled the stadium to see the Oles thrash the Knights, 42-0. The event even garnered national media attention from the likes of Sports Illustrated, NBC and the New York Times.

In 1979 Bob Sullivan, a St. John's grad, took over as head coach, and he has been there ever since. In 1983 he presided over Carleton's switch back from the Midwest Conference to the MIAC. One of the highlights of his tenure was Carleton's 1986 39-11 upset of St. Thomas, then-ranked No. 1 in Division III at the time. The team was led by Running Back Dan Nienhuis, who went on to be named as the MIAC's MVP.

"That game gave us an immediate credibility," said Sullivan, "it was

Ted Kluender holds the school career record with 50 TD passes.

Carleton Football Honor Roll

Dan Nienhuis	1986	Running Back	MIAC MVP
Tim Nielson	1988	Quarterback	MIAC MVP
Jim Bradford	1989-91	Wide Receiver	All-American
Scott Bunnell	1989	Tackle	All-American
Scott Hanks	1992	Tight End	All-American
Watie White	1992	Defensive End	All-American
Art Gilliland	1992	Free Safety	All-American
Geoff Morse	1992	Center	All-American

Career Leaders

Rushing	Yards	Years	
Adam Henry	3,482	1990-93	

Receiving	Yards	TDs	Years
Jim Bradford	3,719	32	1988-91

Passing	Yards	Years	
C.G. Shoap	5,429	1994-97	
Ted Kluender	5,058	1989-93	

Total Offense	Yards	Years	
Tim Nielson	5,606	1985-88	

Tackles	No.	Years	
Scott Klein	359	1993-96	

the game of our lives." The St. Paul Pioneer Press even dubbed the game as the "upset of the decade."

The next honor came in 1992, when Carleton went 9-2 and won just its second ever MIAC title. That season, which earned Sullivan MIAC Coach of the Year honors, was sealed by a heart-stopping 21-20 victory over Gustavus Adolphus College at the Metrodome. From there the team made its first-ever NCAA playoff bid, losing to Central Iowa, 20-8, in the first round.

"There's nothing like a title game, and it was especially nice that we earned an undisputed title," Sullivan said.

In 1993 the game of the year came against St. Olaf, in the 70th anniversary of the Goat Trophy. This one was a wild one, with more than 1,140 yards of total offense hurled on the field. The Knights, behind Quarterback Ryan Becker's 291 yards and five touchdowns, came from behind to win, 51-48, in the game's final moments.

The Knights continued to improve throughout the 1990s, frequently packing Laird Stadium, which, with 7,500 seats, ranks as the 11th largest stadium in NCAA D-III. Bob Sullivan, who recently won his 100th game, has emerged as Carleton's all-time winningest football coach.

The Goat Trophy
(St. Olaf vs. Carleton)

Adam Henry rushed for
a school record 3,482 yards.

Gustavus Adolphus College

Founded in St. Peter in 1862 by Swedish immigrants, Gustavus Adolphus College bears the name of the famous 15th century Swedish monarch, Gustav II Adolph, better known as the "Warrior King." Fittingly, today's Gusties boast one of the premier Division III football program's in the nation.

The first game in Gustavus history was in 1896 when the Gusties beat St. Peter High School, 8-0. The team repeated its success in its first official intercollegiate game held in 1902, with an 11-6 upset of Mankato Normal (now Minnesota State, Mankato).

The rapid development of Gustavus football came to a screeching halt in 1904, however. The college administration, concerned that athletics were taking precedence over academics, eliminated all sports as an official part of campus life. Although the total restriction was lifted in 1910, the ban on football remained in effect until 1917.

The end of football prohibition at Gustavus was followed by the establishment of the Minnesota Intercollegiate Athletic Conference in 1919. Gustavus was a charter member of the MIAC, and with the exception of a brief period during the 1940s, has been part of the conference ever since.

The 1920s was also an era of a couple of college football "firsts" for the program. On December 1, 1923, the tiny school made newspapers and newsreels across the country when they hosted the first women's football game in history. Two teams of Gustie women, the "Heavy's" and the "Lean's," who were chosen by a group of campus fraternity boys, battled to a 6-6 tie. The women, who dressed the part, and took the game quite seriously, practiced and trained diligently to prepare for the much ballyhooed event.

Gustavus' first ever team hit the field around 1900

Then, in September of 1929, Gustavus beat St. Paul Phalen Lutheran, 14-0, in what would prove to be the first game in state history under the lights, giving the local fans an evening of entertainment like they had never seen before.

The undefeated 7-0 1926 team, under the tutelage of new Coach George Myrum, won the school's first MIAC title, allowing only three points all season. It would be the first of many more to come. The 1920s and 30s were a period of dominance under Myrum, who led the team to six titles in all during this era (1926, 1927, 1933, 1935, 1936 and 1937).

Russell Buckley

One of the stars of the late 1930s was Wendell Butcher, the "Worthington Walloper." Butcher led the Gusties to three straight crowns and played every minute of every game in that same span. He was leading scorer in the conference his junior and senior years and was also leading rusher and leading passer. He was elected to three All State teams and was named Little All - American in 1937. He later went on to play professionally with the Brooklyn Dodgers of the old AFL for six years.

The War years were led by a pair of Gustie coaches in John Roning, who led the team to a 1940 conference crown, and Ted Lindenberg, who guided the squad to back-to-back undefeated championship seasons following W.W.II in 1945 and 1946.

In 1947 new Coach Lloyd Hollingsworth took over the reigns. He bought new plastic helmets, getting rid of the old leather ones and thought they should be dressed up a little bit. So he called then-Michigan AD Fritz Crisler and asked if they could use their winged logo that the Wolverines used. He agreed and the rest is history.

(One of the early stars of Hollingsworth's era was Running Back Harold "Swen" Swanson, who was selected as a member of a college all-star team and played in the Little Olympic Bowl in Gilmore Stadium, LA.)

Hollingsworth would take the Gusties on an incredible ride during the 1950s, leading them to an amazing eight conference championships throughout the decade.

One of the more storied squads was the 1950 group, which finished the regular season with a 9-0-0 record before losing NAIA Playoff games to UW-LaCrosse, 20-13, and Texas Abilene Christian, 13-7, in what was billed as the "Refrigerator Bowl," a promotion for the Evansville, Ind., appliance industry. The game was played in a muddy downpour, where the Gusties... got "iced." (Stars of that team included Quarterback Tom Zweiner, End Haldo Norma, Center Kenny Quist, Halfback Gene Payne and Little All-American Tackle Cal Roberts.)

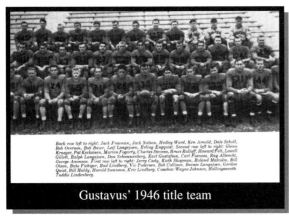

Gustavus' 1946 title team

Back row left to right: Jack Freeman, Jack Nelson, Hedley Ward, Ken Arnold, Dale Scholl, Bob Overson, Bob Baier, Leif Langsjoen, Erling Engquist. Second row left to right: Glenn Krueger, Pat Keckeisen, Marvin Fogarty, Charles Stevens, Bruce Rolloff, Howard Felt, Lowell Gillett, Ralph Langsjoen, Don Schwausberg, Earl Gustafson, Carl Fossess, Ray Albrecht, George Aronson. First row left to right: Jerry Cady, Kieth Skogman, Roland Malcolm, Bill Olson, Babe Fiebiger, Bud Lindberg, Vic Pedersen, Bob Collison, Ronnie Langsjoen, Gordon Quist, Bill Holdy, Harold Swanson, Eric Lindberg. Coaches: Wayne Johnson, Hollingsworth, Tuddie Lindenberg.

In 1953 the NFL's New York Giants held their preseason camp at the Gustavus campus, which was really quite a big deal at the time. Thousands of dignitaries from the world of Minnesota football came to watch the team, which was led by Tom Landry, Frank Gifford and Emlin Tunnell. They often times scrimmaged the Packers at Minneapolis' Parade Stadium and also played intersquad games in front of nearly 10,000 fans in both St. Peter, in what was called the "Green Giant Bowl," and also in Austin, to play the "Spam Bowl."

The Gusties dominated the 1950s, even making several post-season runs as well. One of the better ones came in 1958, when the 8-1-0 squad went on to lose to Arizona State, 41-12, in the NAIA Playoffs. (One of the stars of the late '50s was Little All-American Defensive Lineman Bill Beck, who went on to play briefly for both the New York Giants and the Dallas Texans of the fledgling AFL.)

In 1961 Don Roberts took over from Hollingsworth behind the bench. The 1952 all-conference lineman from Appleton did OK, posting a modest 18-26 record over what would prove to be a five-year stint. Roberts would make his mark in St. Peter another way, however, as a fixture behind the bench of the hockey team, where, 30 years later, he retired as the winningest hockey coach in NCAA Division III history.

Jack "Jocko" Nelson became the head football coach in 1966, leading the squad to a pair of conference titles in both 1967 and 1968. He remained for just five seasons, however, posting an

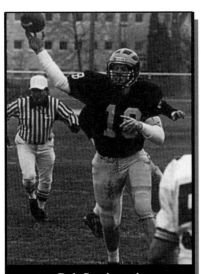

Bob Southworth

Gustavus Football Honor Roll

Career Leaders
Rushing Yards: 3,315, Tom Dahlberg, 1969-72
Touchdowns: 37, Jay Schoenebeck, 1976-79
Passing Yards: 7,085 Bob Southworth, 1995-98
Passing Touchdowns: 59, Bob Southworth, 1995-98
Receptions: 159, Chris Swansson, 1995-98
Receiving Yards: 1,996, Chris Swansson, 1995-98
Receiving Touchdowns: 25, Chris Swansson, 1995-98
Points: 222, Jay Schoenebeck, 1976-79

Gustavus All-Americans
1937 Wendell Butcher (back — AP & Collier's Eye)
1939 Russell Buckley (halfback — AP, 2nd team)
1946 Vic Pedersen (tackle — AP, 2nd team)
1947 Gerry Cady (tackle — AP, 2nd team)
1949 Red Malcolm (fullback — AP, 2nd team)
1950 Cal Roberts (tackle — AP, 1st team)
1951 Haldo Norman (offensive end—AP 1st team)
1952 Cal Roberts (defensive tackle — AP 2nd)
1953 Roger Carlson (fullback — AP 2nd team)
1954 Gene Neiguard — AP 1st team)
1954 Jack Henderson (center — NAIA)
1955 Jack Henderson (center —NAIA)
1958 Jack Westin (end — NAIA 1st team)
1958 Bob Swiggum (quarterback — NAIA, 3rd)
1958 Bill Rill (center — NAIA, 1st team)
1959 Bill Beck (tackle — NAIA, 1st team, AP 2nd)
1966 Rick Jaeger (center — NAIA, 1st team)
1967 Rick Jaeger (linebacker — AP 1st team,)
1969 Greg Johnson (linebacker — NAIA 2nd team)
1970 Greg Johnson (cornerback — NAIA 2nd team)
1972 Tom Dahlberg (back — NAIA 2nd team)
1979 Jay Schoenebeck (running back—NAIA 2nd)
1980 Dave Najarian (linebacker —NAIA 2nd team)
1983 Kurt Ploeger (defensive line —NAIA 1st team)
1984 Kurt Ploeger (def. line — Kodak 1st team)
1997 Ryan Boutwell (kicker — FB Gazette 1st)

The Gusties have won
22 MIAC championships

outstanding overall record of 32 wins, 11 losses and four ties.

Coach Dennis Raarup took over in 1971, and wasted little time in making a name for himself, leading the Gusties to undefeated conference titles in both 1971 and '72. The star of this era was Little All-American Fullback Tom Dahlberg, who carried the ball 35 times for 238 yards and two touchdowns as Gustavus beat Hamline 20-7 to clinch the '72 MIAC title. (Dahlberg's 238 yard effort was the school's single game rushing mark until 1979 when current Gustie football coach Jay Schoenebeck rushed for 339 yards against Macalester.) Another standout of that era was three-time all-conference Defensive End Jim Goodwin, who, in 1972, became the first Gustavus player to be named to the Parade Magazine Preseason All-America team.

The late 1970s and

JOCKO NELSON

Jack "Jocko" Nelson was a coaching legend. The head football coach at Gustavus from 1966-71, his 1967 and 1968 Gusty teams were MIAC Champions and his overall record was 32 wins, 11 losses and four ties.

Nelson was a prep star at Hibbing, where he played basketball, football, track and baseball. After a stint in the U.S. Navy, Nelson attended Gustavus in 1946, lettering in football, basketball, hockey, track and baseball, and also squeezed in a season of pro baseball with the Braves between his sophomore and junior years.

Following graduation he taught and coached football and basketball at Grand Marais and Mora High Schools for four years, was then an assistant coach at Utah State (1955-58), University of Colorado (1958-59), and Univ. of Michigan (1959-66) before returning to Gustavus. In 1971 Jocko headed north, to assume the position of linebacker and special teams coach for the Minnesota Vikings, under Head Coach Bud Grant. During that time he also owned and operated a family business, Jocko's Clearwater Lodge, on the Gunflint Trail. He remained with the Vikings until his untimely death on November 19, 1978.

Travis Prunty

1980s weren't as prolific as the 1950s and '60s, but some good teams came through nonetheless. The 1987 season was perhaps the most exciting of all those seasons. Picked in the preseason to finish no higher than the middle of the MIAC, the "Cardiac Kid" Gusties in Coach Denny Raarup's final year, fashioned a series of last-minute come-from-behind victories to finish the regular season with a 10-0 record and a MIAC championship. Their only loss came to Central Iowa, 17-3, in the first round the NCAA Playoffs.

Steve Byrne came in for the 1988 campaign and stayed through 1993, posting a solid 27-32 record. Then, in 1994, Jay Schoenebeck took over, and has remained on campus ever since. The Green Bay native recently completed his sixth season as the head coach of the Golden Gusties, compiling a mark of 29-31 overall and 26-28 in the MIAC. Schoenebeck's squads have been ranked in the Division III Top 25 in each of the last two seasons while registering a record of 15-5 overall and 13-5 in the MIAC.

Gustavus ranks second in the conference by either winning or sharing the football title 22 times, amassing an amazing record of 402-260-21 along the way. In addition, the team's winning percentage of .605 is the 19th highest percentage in all of Division III football.

The University of St. Thomas

Founded in 1885, in what was once a farmer's field, the University of St. Thomas originally began as St. Thomas Aquinas Seminary. From those original 62 students, the school has evolved into Minnesota's largest independent university with more than 11,000 students. With a rich football tradition that goes all the way back to the turn of the century, St. Thomas has been a small college football power in Minnesota for more than 100 years.

In 1893, St. Thomas started having intramural football teams on campus, with games played on the seminary grounds. That same year, a group of St. Thomas students got together with a group from Macalester College for a an informal game. Macalester won, 10-0, and beat the early Toms twice after that in both 1894 and 1895.

Due to the influence of students, who were clamoring for a varsity team up until the turn of the century, and with the backing of Father John Dunphy, the school's first athletic director, St. Thomas fielded its first official varsity football team in 1904. Coached by M.A. Healy, the team, named the "Saints," went 4-0, beating Macalester, Hamline, Shattuck and Carleton by a combined 63-6 score.

In 1905, led by star running back I.A. O'Shaughnessy and new coach Ed Rodgers, a Native American and former Gopher All-American End, the St. Thomas team went on its first out-of-state tour to play the University of North Dakota and North Dakota Agricultural College. The

Saints blanked the ag school but lost, 17-11, to UND.

At the time, St. Thomas was a military school much-like West Point, where the players were often called "Cadets" by their fans. Rodgers, who was also attending law school, coached through 1909, compiling a 13-9-1 record with a title in the old Minnesota State Conference in 1907.

Robert Saxton replaced Rodgers as coach in 1910, guiding St. Thomas to a 5-0 season. He was then replaced by John Ryan, who stepped in to post a pair of unbeaten championship teams in 1911-12. Stephen O'Rourke then took the helm in 1913 and helped build what probably was the greatest St. Thomas team in the school's early history. The team went 9-0, outscored its opposition 378-7 (a total point record that will never be touched) and handily won the state title. The highlight of the season was beating St. John's, 93-0, the worst beating St. Thomas has ever given to an opponent.

From 1915 until 1920, St. Thomas, along with many other colleges, lost players and coaches to the military during the first World War. St. Thomas played abbreviated schedules of only 4-6 games, had players of lesser quality, and played musical coaches, having a different mentor each season. From 1915 until 1919 the "Saints" were 14-10-3.

In 1920, St. Thomas joined the newly formed Minnesota Intercollegiate Conference. Under Robert (Brick) Hilger, a former St. Thomas player, the rebuilding Saints were only 1-3 in conference play, finishing fifth, and were 2-5-1 overall.

Two years later, the squad jelled for Joe Brandy, tying St. Olaf for the MIAC crown. Brandy managed to put together successful teams, but from 1923 until 1926 St. Thomas was ineligible to compete for the MIAC title because of failure to schedule enough games with other conference teams.

Frank Mach

One of the team's stars during this era was 250-pound Tackle Walt Kiesling, from Cretin High School, who would to go on to stardom in the pros, with the Duluth Eskimos, Chicago Bears and later as a coach of the Pittsburgh Steelers. The 12-year veteran would later be enshrined into the Pro Football Hall of Fame.

Following Brandy's resignation as coach in 1926, St. Thomas got a new athletic director — Father John P. Foley, who hired Robert Schmidt as the team's next head coach. After two losing seasons, the second seeing St. Thomas win only one game, Gillen replaced Schmidt with Ron Gibbs in 1928, then replaced Gibbs with Joe Boland for the 1929 season. Boland. a former Notre Dame star, introduced the "Notre Dame offense" — an offensive formation Knute Rockne had made famous at South Bend. Boland brought two other ex-Irish players, Frank Mayer and Ray Mock as assistants. Mayer had a one-year stint as a Green Bay Packer before coming to St. Thomas.

In Boland's first season, his brand of football brought the MIAC title back to St. Thomas with a 5-1 conference tally, and an 8-1 overall record. During the next four seasons, Boland's teams were MIAC runners-up, never losing more than three games each season. Key players of this era were quarterback Jimmy Gardner, known for his scrambling and quick, accurate passes; fullback Johnny Marturano, a fleet runner who once scored four TDs in a 1930 contest with Augsburg; and ambidextrous quarterback Pat Coyne.

St. Thomas Football All-Americans

Name	(Year)	Position	Honor
Jim Fitzharris	1941	End	Little All-American
Ted Moliter	1944	End	Little All-American
Jack Salscheider	1948	Back	Little All-American
Frank Mach	1953	End	Catholic Small College
DuWayne Deitz	1954	Tackle	Catholic Small College
Mark Dienhart	1973,74	Tackle	NAIA 1st Team
Ron Olsonoski	1975	Linebacker	NAIA 1st Team
Tom Kelly	1977	Guard	NAIA 2nd Team
Jim Gustafson	1982	Receiver	NAIA 1st Team
Mark McDonald	1983	End	NAIA 1st Team
Neal Guggemos	1984, 85	DB	Kodak All-American
Brian Biehn	1986	Receiver	Football News
Gary Trettel	1989,90	Halfback	Kodak All-American
Kevin DeVore	1990,91	Guard	Kodak All-American
Ryan Davis	1994,95	TE	1st Team D-III
Aaron Harper	1996	DE	2nd Team D-III
Ryan Collins	1996,97	TE	1st Team D-III
Steve Nolander	1998	Safety	3rd Team D-III

Wilbur Eaton and George Barsi followed Boland with one-season coaching stints which saw St. Thomas retain its hold on the MIAC No.2 spot. Jack Sterret coached the team, then known as the "Purple Tide," in 1935 and 1936. After a frustrating 1936 campaign, Sterret was replaced in 1937 by Nic Musty, a former Tommy and medical student. Musty was also named as the school's athletic director and head basketball coach. The Tommies prospered behind Musty, winning the MIAC title in 1939 and falling no lower than second in 1940. Musty recruited such fine players as Steve "Wiggly" Quiggley, a fullback who earned his nickname by running zig-zags to escape enemy tackles; "Joltin Joe" Wegner, a fullback who preferred to crash through opposing defensive lines; and halfback "Short Cut" Ignatius, a diminutive player with exceptional speed.

After the 1940 season, Musty gave up coaching to begin his career in medicine, leaving his coaching duties in the hands of another ex-Tommie, "Wee" Walsh, who had been assistant under Musty. Walsh coached the St. Thomas gridders for only three seasons under difficult circumstances, but was the most successful head coach at St. Thomas up to that time.

DuWayne Dietz

Walsh coached the Tide through the early 1940s, and despite of the shortages of able players because of the war, he produced three championship teams and compiled a tremendous 22-1 record. So good were Walsh's teams that they never gave up more than seven points per game. Some of the stars of this era included Tackles Joe Holzer and Frank Wambach, Lineman John Knox, All-MIAC Ends Dick Jewett and Jim Fitzharris, Center Gene O'Brien, and Fullbacks Gill Dapper and Bob Pates.

After Walsh left St. Thomas to join the service, former Gopher All-American Ed Widseth stepped in for the 1945 season, where he posted a modest 3-2 record. He was in turn replaced by Frank Deig that next year, who was also named as the school's athletic director. Deig would coach for 12 seasons at St. Thomas, winning 57 games and capturing four MIAC crowns.

In Deig's second season, the Toms tied Macalester for the MIAC crown, and that next season they won the title outright. That year, St. Thomas won the first ever game in the newly constructed O'Shaughnessy Stadium, a 33-0 white-washing of Augsburg on Saturday afternoon, Sept. 25, 1948. In fact, the Tommies won all four of their home games that year — three by shutout.

They were then invited to play in the 1949 New Year's Day Cigar Bowl in Tampa. The Tommies were stocked with several All-MIAC stars, including Quarterback Ed Krowka and All-American Fullback Jack Salscheider.

Vince Lombardi Jr.

The Tommies vs. the Johnnies is the MIAC's biggest rivalry

Played at Phillips Field in Tampa, the Tommies faced the 1948 Cigar Bowl champs from Missouri Valley University. The Vikings were a tough, physical team and opened the game by jumping out to a quick 13-0 half-time lead. The Tommies came back to tie it though, and even had a chance to win it on Krowka's 65-yard bomb which went through Salscheider's finger tips and into the end zone with less than a minute in the game. The game, which would prove to be the school's only bowl game, ever, ended in a 13-13 tie. (St. Thomas was the first four-year college ever to play in a post-season bowl game from Minnesota.)

Several of the stars of that team went on to get drafted in the NFL, including Salscheider, a Little All-American who later played for two seasons with the New York Giants. (He still holds the team record for kickoff returns, with a 100-yarder in the books.) Others included Don Simensen, who went on to play Tackle for the Rams and Vikings, under Coach Norm Van Brocklin; Jim "Popcorn" Brandt, a gifted Cornerback and punt returner who later played for seven years with the Pittsburgh Steelers; and Ed Krowka, a three-time All-MIAC quarterback who signed with the Detroit Lions, and was projected to be the backup to Hall of Famer Bobby Layne, but a heart murmer cut his career short.

Others from that team who didn't go on but could've included: Center Richard Pappenfus, Tackle Jim White, who turned down offers to play with the New York Giants to instead become a doctor, and Receiver Smitty Eggleston, who could've played pro ball as well.

The Tommies won a third consecutive MIAC crown that next year, with one of the highlights of the season coming in Collegeville, against the Johnnies in the season finale with a 19-game conference win streak and the MIAC championship on the line. The Johnnies rallied to take a six- point-lead in the final quarter, but St. Thomas drove down field and scored near the end to tie it. Don Simonsen, or "Big Si," as he was known, made what proved to be the winning PAT kick in a 25-24 Tommie win. Simonsen later said jokingly, "It was the biggest game between two Catholic schools, and a Lutheran made the winning kick."

Deig would claim one more title team seven years later, in 1956, when his squad, led by All-MIAC End Frank Mach, went undefeated.

Deig retired after the 1957 season as the winningest St. Thomas football coach, but died shortly thereafter at the age of 52. He was replaced by ex-Packer End Nate Harlan that next season, as the Tommies struggled to rebuild during this era.

Harlan's best teams were the 1961-62 squads which were both 5-2 in conference play and 6-3 overall. One of the stars of those teams was Fullback Vince Lombardi Jr., son of the late, great ex-Packer Coach Vince Lombardi Sr. Then, in 1969, in Harlan's last season, the Toms finished 1-9. DuWayne Deitz, a former Tommy star replaced Harlan.

Mark Dienhart

Deitz slowly guided the Tommies out of the conference cellar, and in 1973 led the Tom's to a 9-1 mark, good for a share of the MIAC title with Minnesota-Duluth. Fullback Dan Boisen rushed for 1,010 yards, second in the NAIA that year, and joined Tackles Mark Dienhart, Mike Julius and Ron Ormberg, Fullback John Goebel and Cornerback Jim Kempainen as All-MIAC selections. Dienhart and Julius were drafted by the Buffalo Bills and Chicago Bears, respectively, after the season.

The 1976 season saw the Toms, who were led by two-time 1,000-yard rusher Dave Gervais, tying for second in the conference with a 5-2 mark. Deitz then won his second MIAC title in 1979 when the Toms finished in a four-way tie for first. All in all Deitz coached 11 seasons in St. Paul, posting a modest 52-52-1 overall record. In addition, Linebacker Ron Olsonowski, Guard Tom Kelly and Tackle Doug Groebner each earned All-American honors under his tutelage.

Longtime assistant Mark Dienhart took over as St. Thomas' head coach in 1981 and promptly led the squad to a 7-2 record. Then, just two years later he led the squad to an undefeated conference championship, and a trip to the post-season, where the Tom's lost in the first round of the NAIA play-offs to Northwestern of Iowa.

Vic Wallace was hired in 1987 to replace Dienhart, who, in his six seasons, went 44-15-1 for an outstanding .742 winning percentage. In addition, four of his players garnered All-American honors, including Receiver Jim Gustafson, Defensive End Mark McDonald, Cornerback Neal Guggemos and Receiver Brian Biehn.

Running Back Gary Trettel is St. Thomas' all-time leading rusher with 3,724 yards

Neal Guggemos went on to play
for the Vikings

Wallace struggled initially, but finally got the program on track in 1990, when he led them to a MIAC title with an 8-3 overall record, which included a home win over rival St. John's. That squad also made the school's first ever NCAA playoff appearance, where it edged Wisconsin-Whitewater, 24-23, in the first round, only to lose a heart-breaker to Central (Iowa), 33-32, in the quarterfinals.

Wallace put together a solid 6-3 club in 1991, but went 3-7 in 1992. The highlight of that season came on O'Shaughnessy Field, where the Tommies played the Johnnies in a classic. While the Tommies had lost 37-7 to Augsburg that previous week, a team that had lost to the Johnnies 55-0 earlier in the season, the Tommies felt optimistic going into the game. A fumble returned for a touchdown made it 12-7 in favor of the Johnnies. St. Thomas opted against a field goal later in the second half and instead scored a touchdown and two-point conversion to take a 15-12 lead. The Johnnies fell short on a pair of second-half drives and the game came to a dramatic end when a Tommie defender deflected a pass in the end zone to preserve the three-point St. Thomas victory.

A couple of the stars of this era were Halfback Gary Trettel and Offensive Guard Kevin DeVore, who both earned All-American honors. He was replaced in 1993 by former Tommie Mal Scanlan, who came out smoking in his rookie campaign — leading the team to an 8-1, runner-up finish in the MIAC. The leader of this team was Quarterback Tom Stallings, who, before it was all said and done, would finish his illustrious career at St. Thomas with nearly 30 school, conference or NCAA records.

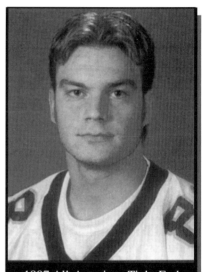

1997 All-American Tight End
Ryan Collins now plays for the
NFL's Cleveland Browns

St. Thomas had another strong season in 1994, but four losses by a combined 11 points led to a mediocre 4-6 ledger. The Toms were 6-4 in 1995, including a win over MIAC co-champ Concordia. A couple of stars during this era were All-American Ryan Davis, who set an NCAA record for single-season catches by a tight end, with 75, and three-time Academic All-American Cornerback Curt Behrns, who finished as UST's career tackles leader with 360.

The Tommies came out the gates at 7-0 in 1996, but lost two of their final three games to finish at 8-2 — good for just third-place in the MIAC. That year Quarterback Chris Esterley finished his illustrious career as the No.2 passer in MIAC history with 7,709 yards, 71 TDs and a gaudy 61% completion rate. UST had two All-Americans in '96-junior TE Ryan Collins, who in his first season as a starter had 55 catches for 820 yards and 10 TDs; and senior DE Aaron Harper, who had 14 sacks in nine games and won the Mike Stam Award as the MIAC's Most Valuable Lineman.

Jim Gustafson went on to play
with the Vikings

The 1997 Tommies again started well, going 5-0 before a 33-27 loss at Bethel denied them a chance to tie for the MIAC championship. They did end a four-year losing streak to St. John's, rallying to a 31-27 win in the season finale in the Metrodome. They drove 90 yards in the final three minutes to pull out the dramatic victory. (Collins repeated as All-American and even went on to play on the Minnesota Vikings' practice squad and later with the Cleveland Browns.)

Scanlan resigned prior to the 1998 season after compiling an impressive 34-16 record, and was replaced by long-time assistant and former player, Don Roney. Roney then led the Toms to a 7-3 record that year, closing out the season with six straight victories. A couple of the stars of that team were senior Halfback Ben Duffey, who closed out his career with 1,991 rushing yards, and junior Safety Steve Nolander, who picked off eight passes while returning two for touchdowns.

The 1999 Tommies finished with a very strong 7-2 record, tying for second place in the MIAC. The future looks bright for the 14-time MIAC champions from St. Thomas, who, in 2001, will play St. John's for the 100th time. There will surely be chants of "Go Back to the Woods," by fans wearing purple, and retorts of "Go Back to the City," by the fans in red. While the teams used to always play this classic on Thanksgiving Day, this one will surely rekindle the state's oldest and richest football rivalry — at any level.

St. Thomas' Career Leaders

Category	Name	No./Yards	Years
Rushing	Gary Trettel	3,724	1988-90
Passing	Chris Esterly	7,709	1989-93
Total Offense	Chris Esterly	7,549	1989-93
Receptions	Jim Gustafson	174	1979-82
Receiving	Ryan Davis	2,652	1993-95
Most Points	Gary Trettel	195	1988-90
Most Tackles	Curt Behrns	360	1992-95

Quarterback Tom Stallings was
named as the National Small
College Player of the Week
by Sports Illustrated after his
602-yard passing game
vs. Bethel in 1993

St. Olaf was founded in 1874 as a co-ed, residential, four-year private liberal arts college. The school began playing football on an informal basis as far back as 1900, and by 1917 the team was regularly playing local high school and college clubs.

Now, during this W.W.I era, many schools had a student-army training corps. To consolidate, and take advantage of the lack of man-power, the two military teams of St. Olaf and Carleton joined forces and played as a combined team.

The combined squad, in addition to playing many of the local prep and high schools, did play one official game together which turned out to be a 59-0 pounding by the Golden Gophers. Then a flu epidemic hit campus and the union was disbanded. St. Olaf still wanted to play though, and competed on an intramural basis that next year. Their school's first official team then hit the field that following year in 1919, right after the war.

By 1922 the undefeated Oles had won their first MIAC title, sharing the crown with St. Thomas. They then followed that up with a repeat performance in 1923. The star during this era was Ole Ade Christianson, who later took over the team's coaching duties in 1927. He would go on to become a St. Olaf legend.

During the mid-1920s the Oles were a gridiron force in Minnesota. They were led by a tremendous backfield that was among the school's best ever: Cully Swanson, Frank Cleve, Whitey Thevehold and Eng Lysne. So good was Swanson, the team's quarterback, that he set a record by passing for better than 200 yards in 10 straight games — a feat almost unheard of in that day and age. So astounding was his accomplishment that it even made it into "Ripley's Believe it or Not."

In 1930 Coach Christianson led the team to an undefeated 8-0 record, which was good for the program's third MIAC title. He added another one in 1935 as well, this time sharing the crown with Gustavus and St. John's.

"He was a tremendous builder of our football program and was the pioneer and mentor for all of us," said long-time Ole Coach Tom Porter." "If you were to mention one name with St. Olaf Football, it would have to be Ade Christianson. He was a real legend and a helluva ball player and coach."

In 1931 the now-infamous "Goat Trophy" traveling trophy with Carleton was originated. Since their break-up back in 1918, the teams had fostered an intense rivalry. (The story of the trophy goes back to a local clothing store, the "Toggery," who donated it to the club after they beat Carleton, 25-6, in that year's game.) One of the stars of the early 1930s was Halfback Syl Saumer, who signed to play with the Boston Braves in the United States Professional League, in 1934.

The 1904 St. Olaf squad

The school took time off during the early 1940s for W.W.II, and resumed competition in the late 1940s. One of the stars of that era was Tom Porter, a former Stillwater High School star, who went on to star for the Oles as an All-Conference Guard and Linebacker. After posting an outstanding club in 1946, which battled for the title, the club made a drastic change. That's when, in 1952, the school dropped out of the MIAC and joined the Midwest Conference.

As members of the Midwest Conference, the Oles fared very well. In 1953 the team went undefeated and was nationally ranked. They added another title in 1956, and in 1958 Porter came home to assume the team's coaching duties — a position he would hold for an amazing 33 years.

St. Olaf Career Leaders

Category	Name	No./Yards	Years
Rushing	Ole Gunderson	4,060	1969-71
Passing	Keith Karpinske	5,078	1990-93
Total Offense	Keith Karpinske	5,300	1990-93
Receptions	Tom Buslee	155	1990-93
Receiving	Tom Buslee	2,454	1990-93
Most Points	Ole Gunderson	362	1988-90
Interceptions	Steve Ashley	21	1968-70

Something unique then happened in 1960. That was the year that the Dallas Cowboys decided to hold their preseason training camp on the campus of St. Olaf. It was a star-studded affair with such legends as Don Meredith and Receiver Don Howten wowing the crowds. The liked the cool weather and had easy access to the other teams who also had training camps in the area. Perhaps one other reason for the team coming there was the fact that H. P. Skoglund, one of the Viking's original owners who was also on the St. Olaf Board of Regents, was buddies with Giants owner, Tim Mara.

As a result, several of the Oles got noticed by the Giant's scouts. One of those players was Fullback & Linebacker Bill Winter, who, in 1962, became the first Ole to play big-time pro football when he made the Giant's starting lineup as a rookie that year.

The team won back-to-back Midwest Conference crowns in 1960 and '61, and added another in 1966. By the late 1960s the team was set to break out, thanks to efforts of one man, Running Back Ole Gunderson, who rushed for over 4,000 yards and scored 362 points in just three seasons in Northfield — an amazing accomplishment when you also consider he played just eight games per season. From 1969-71 St. Olaf went 25-2-1, and won three straight conference crowns over that same span. (In one game against Monmouth, in 1969, Gunderson rushed for an incredible 356 yards! He went

Coach Tom Porter
is a St. Olaf legend

Ole Pride

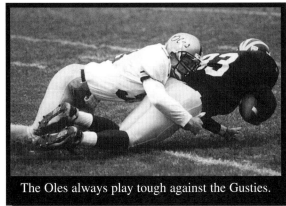

The Oles always play tough against the Gusties.

on to tally a record 132 points that season.) Another star of this era was Safety Steve Ashley, who picked off 21 balls from 1969-71 as well.

The Oles then decided to re-join the MIAC in the mid-1970s, and celebrated by playing in the first-ever "Metric Bowl," against Carleton. The event, which saw both squads play in the first and only all-metric game, even had the players listed in centimeters and kilograms instead of pounds and inches. And, while the Ole's crushed the Knights, 43-0, to win yet another Goat Trophy, the game reported nationally in such media outlets as Sports Illustrated, NBC and the New York Times.

In 1978 a pair of linemen led the charge for the Oles, Defensive Tackle Nate Bergeland and Offensive Tackle Steve Lidke, who both started every game for the team until graduating in 1981. The group led the team to a pair of co-MIAC crowns in both 1978 and '79, even guiding the club to a rare post-season appearance in 1978, where St. Olaf lost to UM-Morris, 23-10, in the quarterfinals of the D-III Playoffs

The team fared OK through the 1980s, and was led by several stars in the 1990s. Among them was Quarterback Keith Karpinske, who rewrote the record books during his tenure in Northfield from 1990-93. The gun-slinger threw for more than 5,000 yards over that time frame, many of them to Receiver Tom Buslee, who caught 155 balls for nearly 2,500 yards. In 1993 alone, Karpinske tossed 2,559 yards — with more than 1,300 of them finding their way into Buslee's sure hands. One of the classics that season came in the Goat game, against Carleton, where Karpinske tossed for 342 yards and four touchdowns, while adding another pair of his own on the ground in a heart-breaking 51-38 loss.

The Ole's avenged that loss in 1996 thanks to Ryan Hollom's 85-yard kick-off return for a touchdown, followed by Paul Minkler's 12-yarder late in the fourth, to give the team a dramatic 14-12 win.

That next year former Apple Valley High School Coach Paul Miller took over as the team's new skipper. And, with his motto for student-athletes and education, the team seems destined for success in the future: act with "class" on and off the field; be the best one can be as an athlete, student, and person; give great effort and never give up; be an unselfish player and individual; and graduate.

That's right coach,
the Oles are No. 1

Hamline University

Founded back in 1854, when Minnesota was still a territory, Hamline was the state's first university. Football was then started on an informal basis at the school back in the late 1870s, with the first game ever in taking place in 1887, a 21-0 loss to Macalester. The Pipers' first win came four years later against the Gophers, whom they beat 4-0 in 1891.

The team continued to play the game through W.W. I, and became an original member of the MIAC in 1920. The Pipers went on to win that inaugural title and then repeated again in 1921 to make it two in a row. The team wouldn't win another MIAC title, however, until 1966, when they posted a solid 6-1 record.

The star of that team was time All-MIAC linebacker and league MVP, Jerry Smith, who was later tragically killed in Vietnam. (Today the team honors him by presenting the Jerry Smith Award annually to the most courageous senior.)

Another star from that era was linebacker and Grand Meadow native Duane Benson, who, after being named as the MIAC's MVP in 1967, went on to play profes-

Hamline Career Leaders			
Category	Name	No./Yards	Years
Rushing	Monroe Walker	2,898	1977-80
Passing	Jay Schneider	5,465	1991-94
Total Offense	Jay Schneider	5,769	1991-94
Receptions	R.T. Taylor	175	1992-95
Receiving	Dave Abrahamson	2,697	1985-88
Touchdowns	Dave Hawkinson	24	1982-85
Most Tackles	Butch Lee	317	1981-85
Most Points	Gary Potter	195	1982-85

Duane Benson went on to
star in the NFL.

Hamline All-Americans

1955	Dick Donlin
1968	Larry Hegerle
1974	Steve Lindgren
1976	Bob Fletcher
1982	Bret Felknor
1984	Kevin Graslewicz
	Gary Potter
1985	Ed Hitchcock
1988	Jeremi Glynn
	Dave Abrahamson
1989	John Voss
	Lester Glenna
1990	Lester Glenna
	Robert Jacobson
1995	Rick Thurston

sionally with both the Oakland Raiders and Houston Oilers.

Another tragedy involving a Hamline star took place that next decade. That's when Steve Lindgren, a 1975 All-American in both football and track, was killed in an automobile accident while preparing to play with the NFL's St. Louis Cardinals. His No. 73 was later retired from the Piper roster and an award was also named after him which is given annually to the outstanding senior male athlete.

In 1978 Dick Tressel took over as the team's new head coach and incredibly, he has been there ever since. Hamline fared well during this era, with Running Back Monroe Walker leading the way with 2,898 yards rushing from 1977-80. By 1984 the Pipers had once again reached the pinnacle of success. They posted an undefeated 9-0-1 record that year en route to earning their fourth-ever MIAC crown. For his efforts, Tressel was named as National Coach of the Year. The leader of that team was Halfback Dave Hawkinson, who scored a record 24 touchdowns. They would add another crown in 1988, recording an equally impressive 8-1 mark that year as well.

Through the early 1990s the Pipers were led by Quarterback Jay Schneider, who from 1991-94, tossed a school record 5,465 yards. The benefactor of many of those yards was R.T. Taylor, who hauled in 175 catches during that same time.

Hamline Coach Dick Tressel

Hamline's Head Coach Dick Tressel was a product of some pretty good thorough-bred football lineage in his family. Dick, who played his college football for his late father, Lee Tressel, at Baldwin-Wallace College in Berea, Ohio, earned four letters both as a defensive back and as a baseball player. In 1978 Dick took over as Hamline's Head Coach, and was also named as the National Coach of the Year in 1984, matching his father, who earned the honor in 1978. In addition, Dick's younger brother Jim, who coaches at Youngstown State University, in Ohio, was also coach of the year in 1991 and 1994. The Tressel trio holds every college coaching record for father-son and sons that are kept, including each having more than 100 victories and being named National Coach of the Year.

"Growing up in a close family football atmosphere kind of made my decision to go into coaching an easy one," said Dick, who's son's Mike, Ben and Luke all played collegiately as well — Mike as a cornerback at Cornell, Ben as a quarterback at Hamline and Luke also as a cornerback at Hamline.

Brendan Swanson

Coach Tressel has established Hamline as a real contender in the MIAC. As of the year 2000, the coach, who also doubles as the school's Men's Athletic Director, holds a 120-86-2 career record at the school and shows no signs of slowing down.

Heading into the new millennium, Hamline's all-time record since their first-ever game against Macalester back in 1887 is a solid 376-360-29. That initial game also spawned one of college football's oldest traveling trophies: the "Old Paint Bucket," which, prior to W.W.II, was called the "Old Sprinkling Can." Commemorating one of college football's oldest rivalries, the Bucket was conceived as a good-will gesture in an attempt to halt the once popular custom of rebel students who mischievously painted profanity on one-another's campus. The Bucket, which features an "H" one side and an "M" on another, also has the annual scores painted on its sides. Since 1965 the Bucket has remained on Hamline's campus for all but three years, and the overall record has Hamline ahead 55-40, with four ties. In the year 2000 the 100th meeting between the two teams will take place, stay tuned!

Brian Swanson and John Cleveland

Concordia College, Moorhead

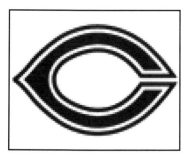

The University of Concordia was founded in 1891 in Moorhead as a mostly Norwegian Lutheran school. The Cobbers have featured one of the MIAC's strongest programs, consistently fielding tough, competitive teams. The school won its first MIAC title in 1931, and through the years won another 16, with the last one coming in 1995. (1934, 1942, 1952, 1957, 1964, 1969, 1970, 1974, 1978, 1979, 1980, 1981, 1986, 1988, and 1990)

One of the coaching legends at Concordia was Jake Christiansen, who from 1941 until his retirement in 1969, won 145 games and lost only 66. One of the highlights of his tenure came in 1964, when his squad won an NAIA national championship. After winning the conference crown that year, the Cobbers represented the MIAC in the ninth annual Small College Playoffs (NAIA) by defeating Linfield, OR, 28-6 in the semifinals and tying Sam Houston of Texas 7-7 in the NAIA title game to earn NAIA co-champion honors.

Cobber Pride

In all, with an 11-year stint at Valparaiso (Ind.) University before coaching at Concordia, Christiansen won 197 games. Concordia's football stadium was named in honor of the Northfield native, who was also a five-sport star at St. Olaf. He retired in 1969 and died in 1992.

He was replaced by former Cobber Captain and 1960 MIAC MVP Jim Christopherson, who has become a coaching legend in his own right, leading the Cobbers to 11 MIAC championships. (Christopherson went on to play professional football for the Vikings for two years, and even led them in scoring in 1962.)

The Cobbers earned national championship runner-up honors in 1969 when they beat Hilldale, Mich., 27-0, only to lose to Texas A & I, 32-7. They finally won it all in 1978, however, as they first rolled over Northwestern, IA, 49-0, followed by Linfield, Ore., 24-23, and then Findlay, Ohio, 7-0, to earn the coveted NAIA National Championship. (Among the stars of the 11-1 National Champion 1978 squad were all conference players: Al Holm, Bob Beliveau, Paul Weida, Kurt Christensen, Dave Klug and Mike Lee.)

Legendary Coach Jim Christopherson

The earned NAIA Co-champion honors in 1981, after beating Westminster, 23-17, and then tying Austin, 24-24. (Among the stars of the 11-0-2 National Co-Champion 1981 squad were All-Americans Jim Klug and Dave Rosengren, as well as all conference players Bob Vangerud, Dwight Hintermeister, Bruce Rimmereid and Dan Olson.)

In 1986 Concordia won the MIAC and went on to beat UW-Steven's Point, 24-15, in the first round of the NAIA playoffs, Central Iowa, 17-14, in the quarterfinals, and then lost to Augustana, 41-17, in the NCAA Division III semifinals. Then, in 1988 the Cobbers won another title, and again advanced to the post-season where they lost this time to Central College, 7-0, in the first round.

They made it back to the post-season yet again in 1995, and despite Chad Johnson's 63-yard interception return for a touchdown, the Cobbers got waxed by Wisconsin-LaCrosse, 45-7, up at the Fargodome. Most recently, Concordia advanced to the post-season in 1997, where they were beaten by Augsburg, 34-22.

Today the Cobbers continue to be led by long-time Coach Jim Christopherson, who has compiled a 214-95-7 record, placing him third in wins among active Division III coaches. He has been voted by conference coaches as MIAC Coach of the Year six times and in 1981 was named the NAIA National Coach of the Year. The Cobbers are one of the MIAC's strongest and most storied programs, and only continue to get better.

Macalester College

Founded in 1874, Macalester College has long been one of Minnesota's premier higher learning institutions. Macalester's football program started in 1887 and it's first win came that year over Hamline, 21-0. The teams now play for the "Old Paint Bucket," a traveling trophy which has roots tracing back for nearly a century.

The school posted some solid seasons through the early 1900s, and even played well against the Gophers on several occasions. They joined the MIAC in 1920, and quickly emerged as one of the state's premier teams. The Scots won their first MIAC crown in 1925, after posting a 5-2-1 record under Coach Frank Mayer. They would add another title in 1947 under Coach Dwight Steussy, this time registering a 5-0-1 mark, but that would unfortunately be the school's last.

Macalester has since seen its fair share of ups and downs in league play, but hasn't gotten back to the promised land in quite some time. Some of the low-points of the school's gridiron history came in the 1970s, when the team won just eight games, while losing 92. In fact, from 1975-79, the team went winless. Since 1989, the team has won just 12 games while losing 97, even going winless from 1992-94.

Today the club is led by third-year coach, Dennis Czech, a former running back for the Scot's in the early 80s, who is still ranked No.2 on the school's all-time career rushing list with 2,394 yards.

The Cretin High School grad has high hopes for his alma mater. "Macalester's football program can be successful again," said Czech. "I am familiar with the college and realize the value of a Macalester education. I believe I will be able to effectively communicate the unique aspects of a Macalester education to prospective recruits in a positive light. I also hope to generate essential alumni support for the program."

In addition, the Scots recently hired former NFL Pro Bowl Cornerback Irv Cross, to serve as the schools athletic director. Cross, who starred for the Eagles and Rams throughout the 1960s, also does color commentary for the Minnesota Vikings, and gives the school a ton of credibility in the world of student-athletes.

Macalester was a MIAC force back in the day

THE NORTHERN SUN INTERCOLLEGIATE CONFERENCE

In 1923 a junior college sports conference was organized in Minnesota, consisting of the teacher's colleges and the junior colleges (e.g., junior colleges at Duluth, Virginia, Hibbing, Itasca and Rochester and teachers colleges at Winona, Mankato, St. Cloud, Moorhead, Bemidji, and Duluth.) The purpose was to place the junior colleges and teacher's colleges on an equal basis regarding eligibility of athletes, scholastic requirements, length of participation of athletes, and regulation of transfer students.

The Northern Intercollegiate Conference (NIC) began in 1932 as the Northern Teacher's Athletic Conference. Charter members included Bemidji State University, Mankato State University, Moorhead State University, St. Cloud State University, and Winona State University. In 1942 the conference name was changed to the State Teacher's College Conference of Minnesota, and then switched again in 1962 to the Northern Sun Intercollegiate Conference.

The University of Minnesota-Morris joined the NSIC in 1966, followed by Southwest State in 1969 and UM-Duluth in 1975, while Crookston and Concordia-St. Paul were added in 1999. (Mankato and St. Cloud later withdrew to join the North Central Conference.) In addition, in the year 2000 the NSIC reached an agreement with The Quarterback Club of Excelsior Springs, Missouri to provide a team for its annual post-season NCAA Division II playoff football game, the "Mineral Water Bowl."

Conference Members

Team	Nickname	Location	Joined NSIC
Bemidji State	Beavers	Bemidji, Minn.	1932
Moorhead State	Dragons	Moorhead, Minn.	1932
Northern State	Wolves	Aberdeen, S.D.	1978
Southwest State	Mustangs	Marshall, Minn.	1969
Minn.-Duluth	Bulldogs	Duluth, Minn.	1932/1976
Minn.-Morris	Cougars	Morris, Minn.	1966
Winona State	Warriors	Winona, Minn.	1932
Wayne State	Wildcats	Wayne, Neb.	1998
Minn.-Crookston	Golden Eagles	Crookston, Minn.	1999
Concordia-St. Paul	Comets	St. Paul, Minn.	1999

All-Time NSIC Titles

	Titles	Last Title
Moorhead State	14	1995
St. Cloud State	14	1970
Mankato State	13	1968
UM-Duluth	12	1996
Winona State	12	1998
UM-Morris	8	1987
Michigan Tech	7	1974
Bemidji State	4	1959
Northern State	2	1992
Southwest State	1	1990

All-Time NSIC Champions

Year	Champion
1932	UM-Duluth, Moorhead State, Mankato State, St. Cloud State
1933	St. Cloud State
1934	UM-Duluth
1935	Moorhead State, Mankato State
1936	St. Cloud State
1937	UM-Duluth
1938	Mankato State, UM-Duluth
1939	Winona State
1940	St. Cloud State
1941	St. Cloud State
1942	Mankato State, St. Cloud State
1943	No Football
1944	No Football
1945	No Football
1946	Mankato State, UM-Duluth
1947	Winona State, Bemidji State
1948	Mankato State, UM-Duluth
1949	Mankato State
1950	Mankato State, Bemidji State
1951	St. Cloud State
1952	Moorhead State, Mankato State, St. Cloud State
1953	St. Cloud State
1954	St. Cloud State
1955	St. Cloud State
1956	Winona State
1957	Winona State, Bemidji State
1958	Mankato State
1959	Bemidji State, Mankato State, Michigan Tech
1960	Mankato State
1961	Mankato State
1962	Winona State
1963	Michigan Tech
1964	Winona State
1965	Michigan Tech
1966	Moorhead State
1967	St. Cloud State
1968	Mankato State, Winona State
1969	Michigan Tech
1970	Michigan Tech, UM-Morris, St. Cloud
1971	Moorhead State
1972	Michigan Tech
1973	Moorhead State
1974	Michigan Tech
1975	UM-Morris
1976	UM-Morris
1977	UM-Morris
1978	UM-Morris
1979	Moorhead State, UM-Duluth
1980	UM-Duluth
1981	Moorhead State
1982	Moorhead State
1983	Winona State
1984	Moorhead State, UM-Morris
1985	UM-Duluth
1986	UM-Morris
1987	UM-Morris
1988	Moorhead State
1989	Moorhead State
1990	Southwest State, UM-Duluth, Northern State
1991	Moorhead State
1992	Northern State
1993	Winona State
1994	Winona State
1995	Moorhead State, UM-Duluth
1996	UM-Duluth
1997	Winona State
1998	Winona State
1999	Northern State

The history of the University of Minnesota-Duluth dates back to 1895, when it was founded as the Duluth State Teachers College. The school's first football team was fielded in 1930 under the tutelage of Frank Kovach, an industrial arts specialist, who organized and coached the first squad that would later evolve into one of the most successful college programs in the land.

Kovach led his troops to a 0-3-2 record that inaugural campaign, which included a pair of ties against Itasca Junior College, 0-0, and a 6-6 deadlock with Duluth Junior College. Kovach left the Bulldogs that next year and handed the reigns to Lloyd Peterson, beginning an era that would continue through the 1957 season.

In 1932 Duluth found itself jammed in a four-way tie for first place in the Northern Intercollegiate Conference, their first taste of championship football, and in 1934 they captured their first outright title. The latter part of the 1930s was one of the

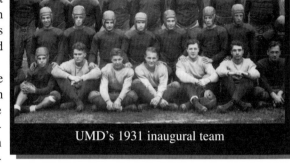

UMD's 1931 inaugural team

NFL Draft Picks from UM-Duluth

Player	Pos	Year	Round	Team
Brent Griffith	OT	1990	7th	Buffalo
Dave Viaene	DT	1988	8th	Houston
Ted McKnight	RB	1977	2nd	Oakland
Terry Egerdahl	RB	1976	6th	Minnesota
Dick Voltzke	FB	1969	14th	Green Bay
Vern Emerson	OT	1968	12th	St. Louis

Other Bulldogs in the NFL:

Lou Barle	FB	Detroit, Cleveland, 1938-39
Tom Adams	TE	Minnesota, 1962
Dick Pesonen	DB	Green Bay, Minnesota, New York Giants, 1960-64
Dan Devine	Coach	Green Bay, 1971-1974

most successful eras in Bulldog history as from 1934 through 1939, the Dogs amassed an impressive 31-7-2 record with another pair of titles coming again in 1937 and 1938.

The program then went through a rough stretch during the pre-World War II days. The 1941 campaign was the worst in the school's history to that point with a 1-6 record. When calm was restored, however, the Bulldogs made a quick comeback as they tied for the NIC crown in 1946 and again in 1948.

Duluth State Teachers College played an independent schedule in 1949 and then traded in their green and gold colors in 1950 to become the Maroon & Gold of the University of Minnesota-Duluth, where they then aligned themselves with the Minnesota Intercollegiate Athletic Conference (MIAC). The 1951 season came down to a showdown between UMD and Gustavus Adolphus, where, in the midst of below-freezing wintry weather, the Gusties stopped the Bulldogs' final

drive to bring home their first MIAC championship. The following season was a forgettable one in the Zenith City, as UMD suffered through a frustrating 0-7-1 season.

The mid-1950s proved to be a rebuilding period for the program. In 1957 Peterson stepped down after nearly a quarter-century of coaching the Bulldogs. His replacement was a Crosby-Ironton native who had worked wonders at Morris and Morningside High Schools, Jim Malosky, who would quickly restore respectability to the program. Malosky, a former Gopher star quarterback under legendary Coach Bernie Bierman, wasted little time in turning the ship around, and within three years, the Bulldogs had earned an MIAC championship. Malosky lost his first two games in 1958, both on the road, but his team won its home opener in a 22-6 decision over Hamline on Sept. 27, 1958. It would be the first of many for the coach.

UMD made it back-to-back titles in 1961 as

Mike Petrich

JIM MALOSKY

UM-Duluth Football and Jim Malosky are synonymous with one-another. In a word, Malosky, is a legend. The Crosby-Ironton native, who originally starred as a quarterback under Coach Bernie Bierman at the University of Minnesota during the late 1940s, started his illustrious coaching career both at Morris and Morningside High Schools. Then, in 1958, Malosky took over at UMD, where he would become a coaching icon. He coached the Bulldogs until 1997, when, after suffering a stroke and going through a knee replacement, he decided to retire.

When it was all said and done, he had very quietly won more games than any other NCAA Division II football coach in history, leaving behind an amazing 255-125-13 record. Over his 30-year tenure, Malosky's teams won three MIAC titles and six Northern Sun Conference championships. In addition, he ranks 11th on the all-time college coaches victory list — right up there with the likes of Pop Warner, Bear Bryant, Joe Paterno and Bobby Bowden.

well, but the program slumped again in the mid-1960s with three successive sub-.500 seasons. The Bulldogs were nosed out for the crown in 1967 with a 7-1-1 record, but again fell below the .500 mark in 1968 and 1969.

Then, after nearly a 30-year absence, UMD dropped out of the MIAC and rejoined the Northern (Sun) Intercollegiate Conference in 1976. Since that time, the Bulldogs have yet to suffer a losing season on the field of play against league opponents. During that span, UMD has also amassed a 152-69-5 overall record, including a perfect 10-0-0 mark in 1980, and have captured eight NSIC championships.

Heading into the 1999 season, UMD's all-time winning percentage (.614) ranked as the 11th best in all of NCAA football.

With 40-plus years of coaching experience under his belt, Malosky took a medical leave of absence in 1998 and officially retired one year later. In the summer of 1998, former Division III Coach of the Year from Wisconsin-Eau Claire, Bob Nielson, was named as the fourth full-time head coach in 67 years of Bulldog football. Nielson has already shown great strides in leading the program back to dominance.

DULUTH HALL OF FAME

1968: Ole Haugsrud
      Bronko Nagurski
1969: Ernie Nevers
      Wally Gilbert
1970: John Mariucci
1975: Bud Grant
1976: Dan Devine
1977: Mickey MacDonell
1979: Tuffy Leemans
      Gordy Soltau
1982: Frank (Butch) Larson
1983: Gino Cappelletti
      Norm Kragseth
      Mertz Mortorelli
1989: Doug Sutherland

DAN DEVINE

One of UMD's most prominent alumni would have to be 1942 Proctor High School grad, Dan Devine, who, after starring as a quarterback and guard on the Bulldogs football and basketball teams in the late 1940s, went on to coaching stardom. After a brief stint as an assistant coach at Michigan State, he later assumed the head coaching jobs with Arizona State (1955-1957) and Missouri (1958-1970). In 1971 he took over as the new skipper for the Green Bay Packers, where, after three years, he posted a very modest 25-28-4 record, and was voted as NFC coach-of the-year in 1972. From there the coach headed east, to South Bend, Ind., where he guided the Fighting Irish of Notre Dame from 1975-80. His career collegiate record was a very impressive 173-84-8, and was highlighted in 1977, when his Notre Dame squad won the national championship. All in all he guided teams to seven bowl game victories, which included two Cotton and two Gator Bowls plus the Orange, Sugar and Bluebonnet Bowls. Devine was elected to the National Football Foundation Hall of Fame in 1985.

Today, the Bulldogs, along with Northern Sun Intercollegiate Conference (NSIC) members: Bemidji State, Concordia College (St. Paul), Minnesota-Crookston, Minnesota-Morris, Moorhead State, Northern State (SD), Southwest State (MN), Wayne State College (NE) and Winona State make up one of the strongest programs in all of NCAA Division II football. All in all, UMD has harvested several outstanding football players throughout its rich 67-year history, which has included a formidable 346-219-24 overall record. The 2000 Bulldogs return 45 lettermen, including 17 starters, from the 1999 club, which posted a 3-8 overall record and a 3-5 NSIC mark. The program continues to get better and better and truly has a tremendous future out on Griggs Field under Coach Nielson.

DOUG SUTHERLAND

A name familiar to all Minnesota Vikings fans during the glory years of the 1970s, Former Defensive Tackle Doug Sutherland is now in his sixth year as an assistant with the UMD coaching staff. Born in Superior, WI, Sutherland was a four-year football letterman and a two-time All-Wisconsin State University Conference pick while attending Superior State University (now known as the University of Wisconsin-Superior).

From there Sutherland went on to star for more than a dozen years in the NFL, which included stints with the New Orleans Saints (1970), Minnesota Vikings (1971-80) and Seattle Seahawks (1981). Selected in the 14th round by the Saints in the 1970 NFL draft, Sutherland was used at offensive guard and linebacker in New Orleans but was switched to defensive tackle when he was traded to the Vikings in 1971. He landed a starting assignment in 1974 and maintained that role for the next seven seasons, until retiring from the NFL just prior to start of the 1982 season. Today, Sutherland, who is employed by a real estate firm in Superior, and his wife, Kriss, have three daughters.

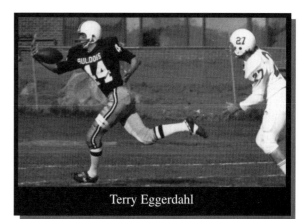

Terry Eggerdahl

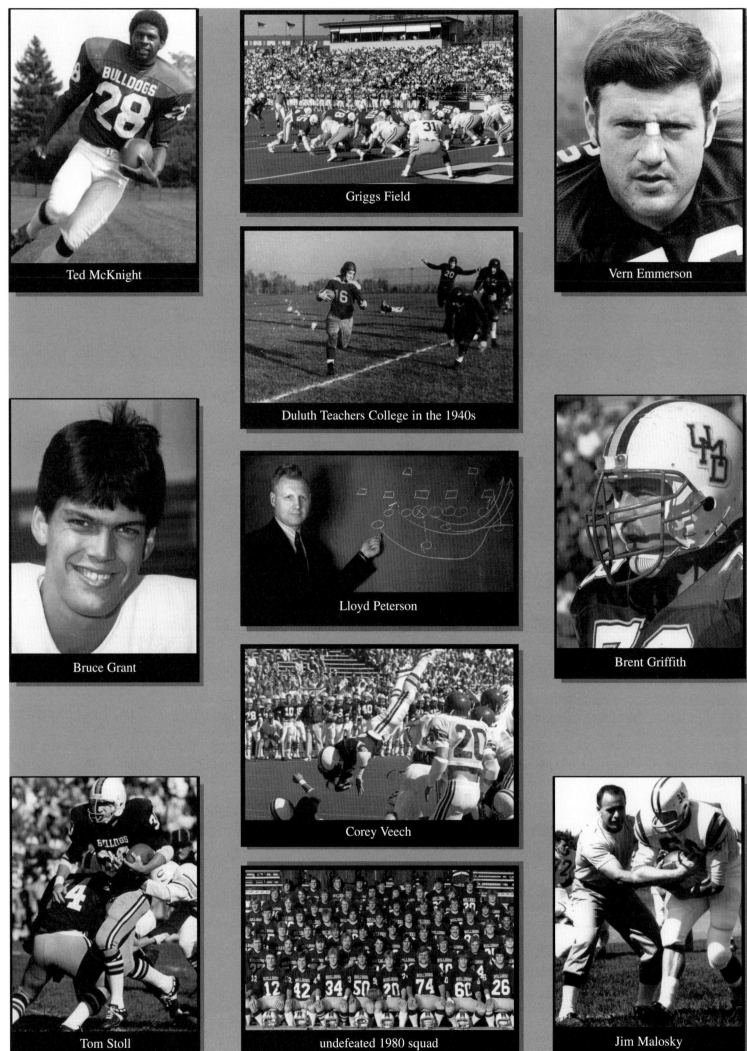

Ted McKnight

Griggs Field

Vern Emmerson

Duluth Teachers College in the 1940s

Bruce Grant

Lloyd Peterson

Brent Griffith

Tom Stoll

Corey Veech

undefeated 1980 squad

Jim Malosky

Bemidji State began as a state Normal School in 1919 and soon became one of the leading teachers' colleges in the region. By the 1930s and '40s the school was bustling with students from across Minnesota, the Dakota's and even Canada.

Bemidji's first football team was fielded in 1926 under the tutelage of Coach R.E. Mendenhall. The team's first ever game came that season against Cass Lake, who beat the Beavers 33-0. The team's first win came two games later against that same Cass Lake squad, 13-0, as the team finished its inaugural campaign with a 1-2-1 record.

The Beavers started out 3-0 that next season, beating the likes of Itasca J.C., Grand Rapids and St. Cloud Cathedral by the combined score of 64-0. They went on to beat Park Rapids and Crookston as well, to finish the year with a very respectable 5-3 record. The Beavers, now led by Coach Eldon Mason, followed that up with an undefeated 4-0-2 record in 1928, beating the likes of Cass Lake, St. Cloud Tech, Hibbing J. C., and Crookston A.C. Their two ties came against Hibbing J. C. and Virginia J.C. Incredibly, the team allowed just six points all year, which came in the opening game victory over Cass Lake, 32-6.

Mason handed the reigns to Jack Sterrett in 1931, who in turn passed them to R. B Frost in 1935. Frost stayed until 1938, when Jolly Erickson assumed the position. Erickson would stay in Bemidji through 1954, becoming almost as big as another local legend, Paul Bunyon, along the way. Jolly guided the 4-3 1947 squad to its first ever conference crown, and added another in 1950, when that team went 4-1-1 as well. When it was all said and done, Jolly, in 17 years, had racked up 53 wins, 53 losses and five ties, to become the school's all-time winningest coach.

BEMIDJI STATE ALL-AMERICANS

1990	Ray Betton, RB - NAIA*
	Larry Filippi, LB - NAIA*
1989	John Grooski, RB - NAIA*
	Dan Soltau, OL - NAIA*
1986	Al Wolden, RB - NAIA (2nd Team)
1985	Rich Schwartz, DB - NAIA (2nd Team)
1977	Dave Patten, DL - NAIA (2nd Team)
1976	Ed Acosta, RB - NAIA (1st Team)
1966	Ron Diagiacomo, RB - NAIA*
1965	David Odegaard, E - NAIA (2nd Team)
1964	Don Thompson, HB - All District
1959	Dennis Price, RB - NAIA (3rd Team)
1958	Guy Vena, FB - NAIA*
1956	Harold Dreseher, E - NAIA*

Honorable mention for All-American consideration

Coach Chet Anderson

Chet Erickson took over in 1955, and would stay for 10 years in all, posting a solid 43-34-5 record during his tenure. He led the Beavers to a pair of conference championships as well, in both 1957 and 1959.

The Beavers played some decent football throughout the 1960s, under both Anderson, and his predecessor, Don Palm. Palm would serve as head coach from 1966-68, before handing the job over to James Malmquist, who led the Beavers until 1973, when Larry Mortier took over. Don Turner assumed the role of head coach the following year, and produced several good squads, including the 1976 and '77 teams, which each went 6-4. Sparky Adams replaced Turner in 1978, and stayed until 1982, when John Peterson was named to the helm.

The 1982 squad posted just a 2-8 record, but did garner an exciting win on Oct. 9, against UM-Morris during the annual homecoming game. That's when the Beaver defense made a dramatic goal line stand in the contest's final minutes to preserve a 14-10 win.

Peterson turned the program around in the mid-1980s, going from the 0-10 disaster of 1981, to the 8-3 squad of 1984. In 1989 Kris Diaz took over as the team's new coach, leading the squad to a modest 4-5 record. One of the highlights that season came against Winona State, when BSU Halfback John Gronski scored a pair of fourth-quarter TDs to give the Beavers a come-from-behind 21-14 win.

In 1991 the Beavers managed to eke out another thriller over UM Morris, 28-25, thanks to Quarterback Marty Follis' 35-yard TD pass with 1:21 remaining in the game to David Schmidt, for what proved to be the game-winner. Follis added some more

THE BATTLE AXE

Awarded annually to the winner of the Bemidji State and Moorhead State Dragons game, the "Battle Axe" is one of Division II college football's oldest traveling trophies. The 1948 Bemidji Football Homecoming Committee thought that something symbolic was needed to add color to the festivities. They then decided that an axe would serve as a suitable trophy to mark the annual Beaver-Dragon grid clash which is always hotly contested. The axe, which originated at the native village of Mount Hagon, New Guinea, was obtained through a series of shrewd trades with the natives. It was hand made and polished under water by the maker.

In 1948 the teams fought to the bitter end for possession of the weapon, with Moorhead State winning 13-6. While Bemidji State's longest reign controlling the axe was from 1955 until 1962, the Dragons, however, lead the all-time series, 33-20. That tradition of hard work and determination continues annually when the Beavers and Dragons take the field to battle for the axe.

heroics that next season, this time diving into the end-zone with just 13 seconds remaining in the game to give his squad a thrilling 28-27 win over Moorhead State.

The 1993 season was another disaster, as the team got smoked in every game. While the 1994 team wasn't much better — it did manage to win once. The 1995 squad showed improvement, winning three games, including a dramatic 25-24 win over Northern State. BSU scored 18 points in the final 6:37 of regulation, capped by Cullen Garrity's 39-yard field goal with 3:33 remaining in the game to mark one of the biggest comeback wins the program had ever seen.

Ty Houglum and the "Catch"

Former North Dakota assistant Jeff Tesch was named as Bemidji State's 15th head football coach in May of 1996, replacing Diaz behind the bench. The program received another big boost that year as well, when Chet Anderson Stadium (capacity 4,000), was dedicated to the former Beaver football and wrestling coach. The eastern end zone sits on the shores of Lake Bemidji.

Beaver football fans will never forget "The Catch" made by Ty Houglum on Sept. 6, 1997. Trailing St. John's 21-19 with :15 seconds remaining in the game, Pat O'Connor connected with Houglum on a 47-yard touchdown pass as time expired, lifting the Beavers to a 25-21 victory before a home crowd of 3,278 fans at Chet Anderson Stadium. The scoring play capped a 13-point fourth quarter comeback by BSU, and gave Coach Jeff Tesch his first non-conference victory as the Beaver head coach.

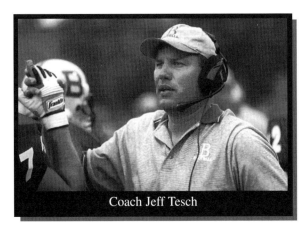

Coach Jeff Tesch

That next year the Beavers went 6-4 and posted their biggest win of the season against St. Thomas. BSU rallied from a 21-12 fourth-quarter deficit in this one thanks to a pair of fourth quarter touchdowns, including Chris Meyer's one-yard TD plunge which proved to be the game-winner with just minutes to go. BSU's stingy defense then sealed the win by holding the Tommies to a minus-six total yards in the final quarter.

Tesch's commitment to hard work and dedication have reaped the benefits of success on and off the field. A former free agent wide receiver with the Atlanta Falcons and a graduate of Moorhead State University, Tesch has the program on the right track. In his 19 years of coaching, he has produced 10 All-Americans, and five NFL draft selections, two of which are still active professional players.

Among them are former BSU rushing record holder Al Wolden (Gonvick, MN.), who played for the Chicago Bears during the 1987 strike season, and former Beaver standout quarterback, Ben Morie who signed a contract to play professional football with the Fargo Freeze of the Indoor Football League (IFL) in 2000. Morie, a two time all Northern Sun Intercollegiate Conference Second Team selection, led the Beavers to two winning seasons while with the team (6-4 in 1998 and 8-3 in 1999), and set several records at BSU including: career touchdown passes, 35, breaking the old mark of 29, set by Tom Peterson from 1984-85, and single season passing yards, with 2,322, breaking the old mark of 1,922 set by Scott Longenecker in 1977.

The Beavers continue to be one of the NSIC's up and coming programs that will only get better and better under the tutelage and leadership of Coach Tesch.

Bemidji's legendary "Paul Bunyan" and his trusty blue ox, "Babe."

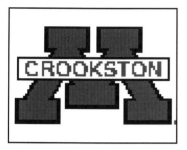

While Crookston was founded in 1966 as a two-year school, and later became a four-year institution in 1993, the school's roots go back to the 1920s, when it was known as the Northwest School of Agriculture. In 1929 a young running back from nearby Gonvick named Ed Widseth enrolled in the school. While he had never played the game before, he learned it at the school and soon emerged as a star. That next year he headed south, to the University of Minnesota, where he captained the 1936 National Championship Team. He went on to earn All-American honors and later played for five years with the New York Giants and was even named as the NFL's MVP in 1938.

Today the Golden Eagles, who are members of the NSIC and are NCAA D-II in status, give an annual Ed Widseth Scholarship award to a student athlete who epitomizes outstanding athletic leadership and academic achievements. In 1997 UM-Crookston and Crookston High School honored Widseth by dedicating the football field in his name.

Scott Oliver has been the head coach at Crookston for the past six seasons. Prior to becoming head coach, he served for eight seasons as the school's head hockey coach and football team's defensive coordinator. (His hockey teams posted a 204-49 record during his tenure, including two NJCAA national hockey championships.) Oliver is a former football captain at Moorhead State as a linebacker who later played with the Winnipeg Blue Bombers and Toronto Argonauts in the CFL

Ed Widseth

UM-Crookston's All-Americans

Name	Pos	Year	Hometown
Gary Wagner	RB	1972	Crookston, MN
Mark Linnel	C	1973	So. St. Paul, MN
Mike Spiva	WR	1976	Warren, OH
Dana Powers	DB	1976	Moorhead, MN
Al Standberg	DB	1978	Strathcona, MN
Jay Gustufson	DE	1982	Gary, MN
Rick Spaeth	OT	1985	Mahnomen, MN
Kirk Rongen	OT	1989	Crookston, MN
Craig Talberg	DB	1990	Princeton, MN
Kenny Bond	DT	1992	Winnipeg, Man.
Derrick Sanders	RB	1993	Milwaukee, WI
Mark Olsonawski	RB	1998	Hallock, MN
Jeremy Klien	DL	1998	Roseau, MN
Jason Lindquist	LB	1997	Dalton, MN
Cory Schreifels	NG	1997	Cold Spring, MN
Derrick Sanders	RB	1995	Milwaukee, WI

UM-Crookston's Career Records

Category	No.	Player	Years
Total Offense	3,067	Scott Strohmeier	1996-97
Rushing Yards	2,656	Mark Olsonawski	1995-98
Receptions	148	Mark Olsonawski	1995-98
Receiving Yds	1,629	Mark Olsonawski	1995-98
Touchdowns	15	Carl Aho	1995-98

Moorhead State University

The Moorhead State Dragons have a long gridiron history in Minnesota dating all the way back to the early 1900s. The team fared well through the first quarter of the century, and in 1928 the Dragons even pounded Park Region Junior College by the ugly score of 92-0! They went on to win their first Northern Sun Intercollegiate Conference championship in 1932, the conference's inaugural season, and won another 13 titles over the next 63 years — winning their most recent in 1995. (During, one stretch, from 1981-83, the team won three straight conference titles and rode a 12-game winning streak.)

One of the team's biggest rivals is Bemidji State, with whom they share one of the state's oldest traveling trophies, the "Battle Axe." Originating in 1948, the tradition is an annual rite of passage for the two teams, which usually play on homecoming. Moorhead State won the initial game, 13-6, and presently leads the all-time series: 32 to 15 with three ties.

Today the Dragons are led by Coach Ralph Michell, who, after 17 years of serving as a head coach (seven behind the Moorhead State bench), could be considered the dean of the Northern Sun Intercollegiate Conference.

Moorhead State Career Leaders

Category	Player	Years	No.
Rushing Yds	Grover Moore	1995-98	4,059
Total Yds	Mark Reed	1978-80	4,056
Receptions	Michael Howard	1980-82	123
Receiving TDs	Bob Jones	1989-91	34
Receiving Yds	Michael Howard	1980-82	2,132
Touchdowns:	Michael Howard	1980-82	23

Appointed coach at MSU April 5, 1993 as a replacement for the retiring Ross Fortier, Michell became the school's 14th skipper. The former Macalester star wasted little time in making a name for himself, becoming just the first coach in 71 years to debut with a winning season. He has since posted a 34-25-2 overall record, an NSIC championship and a post-season playoff appearance in 1995. He was also named as the NSIC Coach of the Year in 1994. In the school's history, their current record stands at 184-135-9 for an impressive .577 winning percentage.

Southwest State University

Southwest State University

Marshall's Southwest State University has been playing football in the NSIC since 1968 and has been one of the strongest programs in the conference's history.

The Mustangs, who play in the 5,000 seat Mattke Field, have won the Northern Sun Intercollegiate Conference Championship one time, in 1990. That year the team went on to play in the post-season, losing to Carson Newman University, 35-6, in Jefferson City, Tenn. The team also made it to the NAIA Quarterfinals in 1987 as well, that time losing at home to Mesa State, 49-7.

Several outstanding players have come through their program, however, including record-setting Quarterback Jeff Loots, who today stars for the Oklahoma City Wranglers of the Arena Football League. Another star was Wide Receiver Alvin Ashley, who set an all-time collegiate football record in 1993 by scoring six touchdowns in a 48-42 win over Michigan Tech at the Metrodome. Ashley finished his SSU career with school career records of 252 receptions for 4,335 yards, 59 receiving TDs (then a record), 392 points, 660 punt-return yards and 1,650 kick-return yards.

Today Coach Curt Strasheim, a former SSU quarterback back in the late 1970s, leads the Mustangs, as they continue to produce top players and winning teams.

James Ashley   Randy Haycraft   Greg Delaine

Wayne Hawkins   Jim Connor   Alvin Ashley

Southwest State's All-Americans

Southwest State All-Americans

1978	Paul Litwicki, LB
1980	Curt Strasheim, QB
	Joe Dittrich, WR
1981	Curt Strasheim, QB
	Paul Chondek, TE
1983	Randy Haycraft TE
1985	Juan Mitchell, TE
	Mike Roggenbuck, LB
1987	James Ashley WR
1988	Carl Douglas, DB
	Jim Connor, DL
1989	Jim Connor, DL
	Carl Douglas, DB
	John Lankas, OL
	Robert Lipsey, RB
	Walter Sutton, WR
	John Wallert, DL
1990	Greg Delaine, DL
	Wayne Hawkins, WR
	Jeff Loots, QB
	Dave Pederson, OL
	Darick Jordan, LB
1991	Wayne Hawkins, WR
	Jeff Loots, QB
	Greg Delaine, DL
	Alvin Ashley, WR
1992	Jeff Loots, QB
	Alvin Ashley WR
	Darick Jordan, DL
	Jason Hanson, DL
	Glenn Mogensen, LB
	Preston Cunningham, WR
	Martez Williams, WR
1998	Jason Jacobs, DL
1999	Jason Jacobs, DL
	Nate Rudolph, LB
	Russ Barclay, DB

THE UPPER MIDWEST ATHLETIC CONFERENCE

An affiliate of the National Association of Intercollegiate Athletics (NAIA), the Upper Midwest Athletic Conference (UMAC) is also affiliated with the National Christian College Athletic Association (NCCAA). Several of the schools located in Minnesota play various MIAC schools, and provide countless kids the opportunity to play ball at the next level.

School	Nickname	Location
Martin Luther	Knights	New Ulm
Crown	Crusaders	St. Bonifacius
Northwestern	Eagles	St. Paul
St. Scholastica	Saints	Duluth

NFL Draft Picks

1991 Walter Sutton, WR, 10th round, Atlanta

1992 Wayne Hawkins, WR 7th round, New England

Winona State University

Founded in 1858 Winona State University has had football on its campus on an informal basis for more than a century. The Warriors first joined the Northern Sun Intercollegiate Conference, however, in 1932, and have since won 12 conference titles, (1939, 1947, 1956, 1957, 1962, 1964, 1968, 1983, 1993, 1994, 1997, 1998), with the first coming in 1939 and the most recent being in 1998.

Today, under Head Coach Tom Sawyer, Winona State is one of the up-and-coming schools in the NSIC, consistently producing solid squads, and affording kids from across the midwest the opportunity to play big-time Division II college football.

The University of Minnesota-Morris

The University of Minnesota-Morris first joined the NSIC in 1966. All in all the Cougars have won eight conference titles, absolutely dominating the Northern Sun Intercollegiate Conference during a couple of stretches in the mid-1970s and mid-1980s. The school won its first NSIC crown in 1970, and then won four in a row from 1975-1978, followed by another three victories in 1984, '86 and '87.

The team made several playoff runs in that era as well. In 1977 Morris beat Albion in the quarter-finals, 13-10, and then lost to Wabash in the semifinals, 37-21. That next year they beat St. Olaf, 23-10, in the quarterfinals, but lost in the semis, 35-14, to Wittenberg. In 1979 Morris lost to Ithaca 27-25 in the quarterfinals, only to rebound that next season by beating Dubuque, 41-35, in the quarters but losing to Dayton, 28-0, in the semis. Then, in 1981, Morris lost to Lawrence, 21-14, in overtime in the quarterfinals to end their post-season run.

Today Ken Crandall, a former wide receiver at Fort Hays State University, is entering his second season as Head Football Coach with the Cougars. Said the 12th skipper in program history: "We are exited to continue the progress that we have made in the past two years. We have some great student-athletes that will not settle for anything but success." Hard work and commitment means....."Cougar Pride!"

Concordia University, St. Paul

Established in 1893 in St. Paul, Concordia University is a private, four-year liberal arts school of the Lutheran Church. True to its vision to be an exemplary Christian university in athletics as well as academics, in 1993, Concordia built Gangelhoff Center, a state-of-the-art athletic facility that quickly became the hub of its athletics program.

Football first began at Concordia back in 1969, when the Comets, as they were then known, went 4-4 in the Tri-Lakes Conference, with their first-ever coming against Golden Valley Lutheran. One of the highlights of that season came in a win against the Stillwater Prison team. (Perhaps that's where they got the inspiration for the movie "The Longest Yard!") The team fared well through the 1970s, and peaked in 1977, when the 9-1 Comets, led by All-American Halfback and career rushing leading leader LeRoy McBrayer, won the Conference title. In 1991 the team scored a big upset when they knocked off MIAC power Augsburg, a big boost for the program.

From 1976-91, the team, which continues to play at old Griffin Stadium, has won four Twin River Conference and six Upper Midwest Conference championships. In 1999, the team made the jump to join the Division II Northern Sun Conference. With the move, the team changed its name from the Comets to the Golden Bears. Since then, they have fared well in the new conference, even upsetting the likes of perennial powers UMD and Bemidji State. Presently the Bears are led by Coach Shannon Currier, a native of Cosmos, Minn., who played quarterback at Hamline in the early 1990s before heading off to take a couple of assistant coaching positions with Bemidji State, UM-Crookston and Southwest State.

"It's an honor and a challenge to take this job," Currier said. "I feel we're a program on the move with a lot of potential. As a team, we made great progress in our inaugural season, and I'm looking forward to more of the same in the next season."

THE NORTH CENTRAL CONFERENCE

Widely acclaimed as one of the top NCAA Division II athletic conferences, the North Central Conference has a rich and strong tradition which began in the Fall of 1921.

Member Schools

St. Cloud State	South Dakota State
MN State, Mankato	South Dakota
Augustana	Northern Colorado
Morningside	North Dakota State
Nebraska-Omaha	North Dakota

Founded in 1896, St. Cloud State University was once known primarily as a teacher's college. The school has been playing football, albeit on an informal basis, for more than a century now, having played its first recorded game back in 1890. That year St. Cloud played a group of the school's alumni in a game held at the Central Minnesota Fair.

By the turn of the century the team was playing several area schools including, Sauk Centre High School, the semi-pro Northern Pacific Apostles from St. Paul, the U of M Medical School, North Dakota State and Carleton College. In 1900 there were only 35 male students enrolled on campus, but the team still managed to field a winning team— beating Alexandria High School, 36-6, and Litchfield High School, 16-6.

In 1904 George "Red" Lynch was hired to serve as the team's new coach. In 1909 the Bear Cats (they weren't known as the Huskies until the 1930s) won their first "intercollegiate" title en route to beating St. John's, Mankato and Little Falls, as well as Alexandria and Mechanic Arts High Schools. Their only loss that year came against Fargo College, 28-0. World War I caused the sport to be stopped in the late 1910s, before it resumed with a one-game schedule in 1919.

Don Tolbert

By 1920 the Bear Cats were rolling, and even posted a 5-2 record that included a pair of victories over St. John's and a 13-7 season ending victory over Winona State.

In 1923 a joint teachers and junior college sports conference was organized called the Minnesota State College Conference. It consisted of the junior colleges at Duluth, Virginia, Hibbing, Itasca and Rochester, as well as the teachers colleges from Winona, Mankato, St. Cloud, Moorhead, Bemidji, and Duluth. The purpose was to place the junior colleges and teacher's colleges on an equal basis regarding eligibility of athletes, scholastic requirements, length of participation of athletes, and regulation of transfer students.

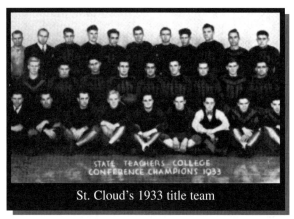

St. Cloud's 1933 title team

In 1925 the first annual homecoming game was held against the Winona State Bulldogs, and that next season St. Cloud won their first Minnesota State College Conference title thanks to a stellar 6-0-1 record. That championship season ended with a thrilling 7-6 win over arch-rival Mankato State as Felix Kamrowski came out to kick the game-winning extra point in the game's final moments. The squad posted another 6-0-1 record in 1927, thus earning a second conference title.

Coach Lynch stepped down in 1928, although remaining as an instructor with the University until his retirement in 1953. His replacement was John Weismann, who enjoyed immediate success by posting winning seasons in 1929, 1930 and 1932, before winning the school's first Northern Intercollegiate Conference crown in 1932, with a 4-3 record. (The Northern Teacher's Athletic Conference changed its name to the NIC that season.)

Then, in 1933, Lynch un-retired, and returned to the sidelines to once again work his magic. In 1933, Halfback Don Tolbert led SCSU to a perfect 7-0 record and its second consecutive NIC title. But, in 1935, Lynch stepped down for good and handed the reigns to Warren Kasch. Kasch wasted little time in making a name for himself on campus, by guiding the Huskies to a 6-0-1 record in 1936 and another NIC crown.

The 1937 season was a special one at SCSU as the Huskies saw completion of Selke Field, which was dedicated at the Homecoming Game on October 23, of that year. The distinctive 3500-foot granite wall, which still surrounds the field, was a product of local quarries.

In 1940, SCSU was blessed with the emergence of Lou Filippi. A speedy halfback, Filippi led the Huskies to NIC

Keith Nord went on to play with the Minnesota Vikings

LOU FILIPPI

Lou Filippi was the first St. Cloud State athlete to go on to earn national recognition. The early 1940s belonged to Filippi, who earned 14 athletic letters in football, basketball, baseball and track. The All-American halfback and two-time conference MVP handled the ball on nearly every play out of the single wing formation, leading his squad to 1940-41-42 conference championships. Only W.W.II kept him out of an NFL career. He is considered by many to be the school's greatest all-around athlete.

St. Cloud State Career Records

Category	Name	No.	Years
Yards Rushing	Harry Jackson	4,889	1986-89
Yards Passing	Tom Nelson	6,474	1980-83
TD Passes	Tom Nelson	43	1980-83
Receptions	Mike McKinney	202	1995-98
Receiving Yards	John Kimbrough	2,878	1973-75
TD Receptions	John Kimbrough	28	1973-76
	Mike McKinney	28	1995-98
Touchdowns	Harry Jackson	40	1986-89
Points Scored	Harry Jackson	240	1986-89
Interceptions	Dan Neubauer	19	1977-80
Tackles	Joe Robidou	361	1977-80

Lenny Johnson

crowns in 1940, 1941 (7-0) and 1942 (6-0). (At 7-0, SCSU, who was also led by Quarterback Fritz Bierhaus, was one of only seven undefeated teams in the nation during the 1941 season.) A four-sport athlete at SCSU, Filippi earned a total of 14 varsity letters before he graduated in 1943. One of the school's first football All-Americans, he later signed a professional football contract in 1942, but never got to play pro ball because of his participation in World War II. (Another star of this era was Fullback and co-captain Don Klein, who also earned All-Conference honors as well.)

In 1942 the Northern Intercollegiate Conference's name was changed to the State Teacher's College Conference of Minnesota. It would mark the post-war era on campus, which saw little with regards to football prosperity. The next great era came in the 1950s under the leadership of Coach Les Luymes. In his first season, Luymes directed the Huskies to a 5-2 record and yet another NIC title. He led SCSU to a string of NIC crowns in 1952, 1953, 1954 and 1955. Luymes would retire after the 1955 season with an overall record of 29-11.

Harry Jackson

Some of the stars of this era included: Bill Campbell and Mel Fisher, both two-time all conference halfbacks who were also named as the Conference MVP's; Hinckley's Stanley Petersen, another two-time All-Conference halfback who set season records for most touchdowns with 11 in 1952 and total points with 66 also in 1952; and St. Cloud Tech High School prep legend, Scott Harry Peterson, who won the conference scoring title in both 1955 and '56.

Jack Wink took over the coaching duties in 1956 and stayed with the program until Rod Anfenson was named head coach in 1965. (The conference also switched its name back to the Northern Intercollegiate Conference in 1962.) One of the highlights of this era came in '56, when Dick Lange scored on a record 96-yard touchdown run against Mankato. The Longest TD Reception in school history also came in 1966, when Mark Brenden hit Walt Rhodes on a 90 yarder against Morningside. Husky Halfback Gary Bahr, who, in addition to being named as the conference MVP, rushed for 1,093 yards in 1967, and propelled the team to an 8-1 record and an NIC title that year as well.

A couple of other stars of this era included Tony Jackson, who won the conference MVP in 1960, and Tackle Lenny Johnson, who earned Little All-American honors in 1968 — becoming SCSUs first nationally recognized All-American football player.

Mike Simpson replaced Anfenson as the Huskies' new coach in 1971, leading the club for what would prove to be 10 seasons, until 1982, racking up a very solid 59-54-1 career record along the way. Among the many standouts during this era included: John Kimbrough, who went on to play with the Buffalo Bills, Oakland Raiders and New England Patriots; and Cornerback Keith Nord, who went on to enjoy a successful pro football playing career with the Minnesota Vikings.

Another player of note was Quarterback Chuck Wilson, a graduate of Minneapolis North High School, who led the Huskies from 1971-74. The two-time conference MVP currently ranks fifth on SCSU's career all-purpose yardage chart with 5,042 yards and is fifth in all-time passing with 256 completions for 3,595 yards and 34 touchdowns. He ranked third in NCAA Division II in total offense in 1974, and in 1975, Chuck had a free agent tryout with the New York Jets.

In 1983, St. Cloud State turned the page on yet another chapter of its rich football history when it named Noel Martin as the team's new head coach. The program joined the North Central Conference that year, one of the nation's premier NCAA Division II circuits.

The Huskies wasted little time in tearing up the NCC, post-

Mark Schwegman

St. Cloud State All-Americans

1941	Lou Filippi (AP Little American)
1967	Lenny Johnson (NAIA)
1978	Carl Larson (NAIA)
1985	Mike Lambrecht (Kodak All-American)
	Dave Solon (Football News Second Team)
1987	Harry Jackson (Football News Second Team)
	Mark Schwegman (Football News Third Team)
1988	Harry Jackson (Football News Second Team)
	Clarence Williams, Jr. (Football Gazette H.M.)
	Rick Rodgers (Football Gazette H.M.)
1989	Harry Jackson (Football Gazette First Team)
1994	Dave Dahlstrom (Football Gazette H.M.)
	Troy Kluck (Football Gazette H.M.)
	Dave Dahlstrom (Football Gazette H.M.)
1995	Randy Martin (Football Gazette First Team)
1996	Randy Martin (Football Gazette First Team)
	Mike McKinney (Football Gazette First Team)
1997	John DesRoches (Associated Press)
1998	Mike McKinney (Football Gazette Second Team)

Todd Bouman is now the Vikings'
No. 3 quarterback

ing a 6-5 record in 1985, followed by a pair of outstanding 7-4 records in both 1987 and 1988. St. Cloud reached the pinnacle in 1989, registering an amazing 10-2 overall record and an 8-1 mark in the conference.

That fabled 1989 North Central Conference championship season was one that will never be forgotten in the Granite City. SCSU opened the season with a 28-0 win over Wayne State before suffering a 31-24 loss to Augustana. The loss inspired the Huskies though, as they reeled off eight straight wins over Mankato, 23-7 (to win the "Traveling Training Kit" trophy), Northern Colorado, 24-10, UN-Omaha, 24-15, SDSU, 13-10, NDSU, 20-13, North Dakota, 31-18, South Dakota, 28-25, and Morningside, 58-7. Harry Jackson set a school record by rushing for 1,777 yards that season, which was highlighted by a record 337-yard performance against USD! With their first-ever NCC title in hand, the team received its first-ever invitation to the NCAA Division II Football playoffs. With that, the team, led by All-American Halfback Harry Jackson, Cornerback Rick Rodgers and Defensive Tackle Clarence Williams, Jr., played host for its first-ever post-season game at historic Selke Field, where the Huskies exacted a little revenge over the Vikings, beating them, 27-20. Then, in the second round game, the Huskies were outmatched in a slug-fest, losing a tough one to eventual national champion Mississippi College, by the final score of 55-24.

Randy Martin

Over the past two decades, the Huskies have had several Conference MVP's including: Tackle Mike Lambrecht in 1985, Cornerback Tom Mazur in 1987, Halfback Harry Jackson and Guard Jon Tommervik in 1989, Cornerback Brad LaCombe in 1992, Receiver Mike McKinney in 1997 and Halfback Randy Martin in both 1995-96. Just how good was Martin? On Oct. 12, 1996, he single-handidly beat Mankato when he scored a record seven touchdowns for 42 points!

Strong defenses have also been an SCSU trademark throughout the 1980s and 1990s, due in large part to the performances of such defensive stalwarts as Rick Rodgers, Clarence Williams, Jr., Mike Lambrecht and Brad LaCombe. Over that same period the Huskies have produced 16 All-Americans, including two Harlon Hill trophy finalists (Randy Martin and Harry Jackson). Most recently, wide receiver Mike McKinney earned All-America honors in 1997 and 1998. In addition, Quarterback Todd Bouman is now the No.3 signal caller for the Minnesota Vikings!

The SCSU story added another chapter in 1999 as Randy Hedberg became the 11th coach in the history of the University's football program. A former offensive coordinator at the University of North Dakota, Hedberg a Parshall, N.D. native, was drafted by the NFL's Tampa Bay Buccaneers in 1977, where he played through 1978, before going on to play with the Oakland Raiders in 1979 and the Green Bay Packers in 1980.

For the past century St. Cloud State has continued to build on its rich tradition of gridiron success, and has its sites set on only getting better in the years to come.

THE TRAVELING TRAINING KIT

Inaugurated in 1978, the Traveling Training Kit signifies the rivalry between the two Minnesota members of the North Central Conference - Minnesota State University and State Cloud State University. The trophy features the MSU logo on a purple background on one side and the St. Cloud State logo on a red background on the other side. The winner of each year's game takes home the coveted kit. Minnesota State University and St. Cloud State University have been playing each other since the 1923 season. The 2000 meeting between the two clubs will mark the 64th time the Huskies and the Mavericks have squared off to do battle. St. Cloud State leads the series by a 31-29-4 margin, but "The Kit" remains in MSU's hands following a 28-20 win by the Mavericks in a game played in St. Cloud in 1999.

Minnesota State, Mankato

In 1868 Mankato Normal School first opened its doors in the picturesque river valley town of Mankato, with its primary role being to train teachers for work in rural schools throughout Southern Minnesota. In 1921 the school became Mankato State Teachers College and was authorized by the State to offer a four-year curriculum.

Unofficially, the school began playing football around the turn of the century against several local high school teams, as well as Gustavus, who they played as far back as 1902. The school's first official football team hit the field in 1922, under the tutelage of Coach Hugh Jameson, who led the team to an outstanding 4-0 inaugural record. After shutting out Rochester High School, the Indians, as they were then known, matched both Owatonna and Parker College to a pair of 0-0 ties. From there the team allowed just its first points of the season in a 21-6 drubbing over Blue Earth High School, followed by a pair of 27-0 and 20-6 victories over both Pillsbury Academy and Rochester Junior College.

C.P. Blakeslee took over behind the bench in 1924 and led the team until 1934. The team performed well throughout the 1920s and early 30's, with the highlight coming in both 1931 and 32. Mankato won back-to-back Little Ten Conference championships in those two seasons, posting 5-1-1 and 4-1-1 records, respectively.

Emmett Lowery was named as the team's third skipper in 1935, and despite staying for just one year, he led the club to a 5-2 record — good for their first (newly formed) Northern Conference title. Jim Carter then took over in 1936, leading the club for what would prove to be 11 seasons. His first conference title came in 1942, which was then followed by a an amazing stretch during the late 1940s that really put the program on the map. While football was suspended during the War years from 1943-45, Mankato came back in 1946 ready to play. Carter led the squad to another conference title in 1946, followed by a pair of crowns in both 1948 and '49.

In 1950 Earl Myers was named as Mankato's new coach, and he quickly picked up where Carter left off, winning NIC titles in 1950 and again in 1952. In 1953 Myers was replaced by Bob Otto, who would remain on campus until 1969.

Tight End Bob Bruer went on to play with the Vikes from 1980-84.

A couple of the stars of the 1950s were Bob Will, who led the team in total yards and touchdowns as a senior in 1955 (and later went on to play major league baseball with the Cubs); Al Blanshan, a lineman who was also a four-time wrestling All-American; and Receiver Lee Loewen, who went on to compete as an Olympic hurdler.

With enrollment at the school averaging some 700 students through the 1930s and 40's, a surge in the late 1950s strained the capacity of the tiny Valley Campus. So, a new campus on the hilltop overlooking the city began, and with it came a growing reputation for academic and athletic excellence.

With that, the program began to step up its recruiting effort and start to play bigger and better opponents. In 1957 Mankato State Teachers College became Mankato State College. The name change was celebrated by the football team bringing home four straight conference crowns from 1958-61, going 24-11 along the way. In 1962 the program got a huge boost when the newly constructed 7,200-seat Blakeslee Stadium, named for former football Coach, C.P. Blakeslee, was dedicated on campus.

One of the stars of the late 1960s was Bernie Maczuga, a stand-out running back and defensive back from 1966-69 who broke some 12 school records during his tenure at MSU including: career (3,129) and single-season rushing yards (1,490, 1969), most carries in a game (48 vs. Michigan Tech in '67), most rushing yards in a game (219 vs. UMD in '69), most points in a game (24 vs. MTU in '67) and single-season interceptions (7, 1967). In 1969 he was named as the conference's MVP.

BLAKESLEE STADIUM

Mankato State's spacious 7,000-seat Blakeslee Stadium, named for former coach, A.D. & professor C. P. Blakeslee, is a great place to play football — just ask the Minnesota Vikings, who have been coming there to stay in Gage Dormitory since 1965 for their preseason training camp. Only the Green Bay Packers, with 42 straight seasons at St. Norbert College in DePere, Wis., have a longer training camp tenure than the Vikings' 35 years on the campus of Minnesota State, Mankato.

Otto added another championship in 1968, before stepping down that next year to John Coatta. Coatta then guided the program through a decent stretch during the early 1970s, until 1976, when Al Sandona took over after an off-year in 1976. (One of the stars of that era was Tight End Bob Bruer, who, after catching 85 balls for 10 touchdowns and 1,271 receiving yards at MSU, went on to play professionally for five years with the Vikings.)

That same year the school went through some major changes. It went from College status to an official University, joined the Northern Intercollegiate Conference, replaced Coach Coatta with Al Sandona, and even decided to get politically correct and change their mascot from the "Indians" to the "Mavericks."

Sandona posted some decent numbers over what would prove to be a four year stint, before giving way to Dan Runkle in 1981. Runkle has since become a Maverick legend, now entering his 20th season at MSU as we embark on the 21st Century.

Runkle, who earned ten letters in football, basketball, and baseball at Illinois College, had previously coached at the University of Utah, the University of South Dakota, Northern Arizona University, and the University of Minnesota, under Head Coach Joe Salem, before taking over at MSU.

In his rookie campaign, Runkle promptly led the Mavericks to a 5-5-0 record. Following a four-year span in which the club went 15-29, the MSU program began to take off in 1986. The Mavericks won six out of their last seven games to give them their

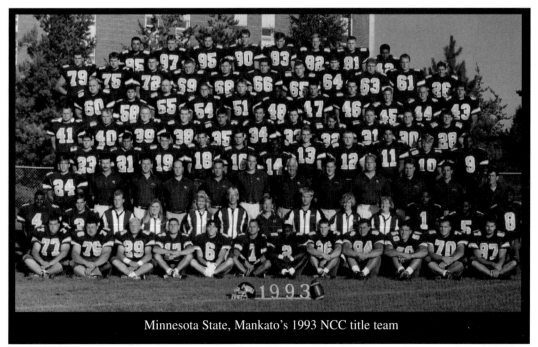

Minnesota State, Mankato's 1993 NCC title team

Tywan Mitchell went on to play with the NFL's Arizona Cardinals

first winning season in nearly a decade. The Mavericks, who finished 6-4-1 and earned their best-ever (at that point) finish in the North Central Conference with a 6-3 league record, only foreshadowed what was about to come the next year.

Minnesota State Career Records

Category	Name	Yards	Years
Passing Yds	John Hebgen	9,433	1993-96
Rushing Yds	Bernie Maczuga	3,129	1967-69
Receiving Yds	Josh Nelson	3,484	1991-94

The 1987 Mavericks went 9-3 and Runkle was tabbed NCC Coach of the Year for guiding his team to an 8-1 league mark and the school's first-ever NCC title. From there the Mavs got a taste of some post-season action, ultimately losing a heart-breaker to Portland State, 28-21, to end their season. But, in addition to setting school records for rushing offense, total offense, and wins in a season, Runkle was also named NCAA Division II North Central Region Coach of the year.

Mankato State produced several players that went on to play professionally during the 1980s, including: Offensive Tackle Phil Driscoll (1976-80) who played with the Dolphins, Offensive Guard Jeff Reinke, (1982-85), who played with the Raiders and Bengals, as well as Running Back Larry Brown (1981-85), Offensive Guard Mark Hanson (1983-86), and Defensive Tackle Ted Elliott (1884-86).

Runkle led his squad back into post-season action again in 1991, this time winning their first round match against Northern Colorado, 27-24, only to lose once again to Portland State in the quarterfinals, this time 37-27, to round out their year. Runkle was then named the NCAA Division II "Co-Coach of the Year" by the Football Gazette.

The 1993 team claimed the school's second NCC title, and, in addition to establishing 49 school records, also set four North Central Conference records, produced four All-Americans and advanced to the NCAA Division II quarterfinals. This time the team got out of the first round by crushing Missouri Southern, 34-13, only to get spanked by North Dakota in the quarterfinals, 54-21.

After getting off to a 2-4 start, his 1994 team proceeded to win the last five games for a 7-4 mark and earned a share for third place in the final league standings. In lead-

Head Coach Dan Runkle

ing a team that has become an annual contender for post-season play, Runkle's teams have built a 40-29-0 (.580) record in the past six seasons.

And never let it be said that Runkle, whose career record stands at 88-89-2 (.497) has earned him the distinction as the school's all-time winningest football coach, is not flexible. While his option-oriented rushing teams of the late 1980's established most of the school rushing and total offense records, his "high-tech" offensive teams of the 1990's have established school and conference marks for passing and total offense.

Under the Runkle regime, the MSU football program has grown in many areas in addition to success in the win column. Some 38 MSU players have been named All-NCC First Team and 24 players have received All-America honors. In addition, Jamie Pass, in 1993, and Wide Receiver Josh Nelsen, in 1994, were finalists for the Harlon Hill Award as the best player in NCAA Division II football. (Also, Quarterback John Hebgen was a regional finalist for the award in 1996, and Tywan Mitchell, a three-time All-American Wide Receiver, was a regional finalist for the award in 1998.)

But success during the "Runkle Era" has not been limited to the field of play. The entire MSU coaching staff stresses the "student-athlete" concept and with more than 30 players achieving GPA's of 3.00 of better during the 1996 season, one can see evidence of this philosophy.

Mankato State University is fortunate to have one of the most respected football coaches in all of NCAA Division II in Head Coach Dan Runkle. He has taken an independent, noncompetitive program and built it into one that contends year in and year out for a league championship in what quite possibly might be the toughest NCAA Division II conference in the country. In 1999 the coach got notched his 100th career victory, surely just the beginning of many, many more to come in the future.

Minnesota State All-Americans

Name	Pos.	Year
Cory Czepa %	DL	1998
Tywan Mitchell #&%^	WR	1998
Tywan Mitchell #%	WR	1997
Ed Machovec %	OL	1997
Tywan Mitchell #&%^	WR	1996
Greg Janacek &%	PK	1996
Andy Mazurek %	C	1996
John Hebgen %	QB	1996
Mark Erickson %	RB	1995
John Davis %	WR	1995
Josh Nelsen %^*	WR	1994
Stephen Henley *%	LB	1994
Jamie Pass %*^	QB	1993
Stephen Henley *&%^	LB	1993
Kenny Navitsky *	DB	1993
Josh Nelsen *&%^	WR	1993
Steve Connelly %	DL	1992
Dave Klawitter %	DB	1992
John Kelling &%#	DB	1991
Mike Ritacco %	LB	1991
J.R. Buckley &%	LB	1989
Chuck Gilbert %	DE	1989
George Brown %	DB	1989
Duane Goldammer &$	OL	1987
Scott Annexstad $	OL	1987
Darryl Wills %	DB	1987
Jeff Spann &	LB	1986
Mark Hanson %	OL	1986
Marty Kranz &	DB	1973
Jim Lietzke &	LB	1967

&-AP Little All-American
#-AFCA All-American
%-Football Gazette All-American
*C.M. Frank All-American
$-NFL Draft Board All-American
CoSIDA Division II All-American

Quarterback Jamie Pass broke or tied 19 MSU records and also established four North Central Conference marks.

High school football has a long and storied tradition in Minnesota dating way back to the Fall of 1877. That's when C.C. Camp, captain of the powerhouse Yale University football team, and cousin to the famous Walter Camp — Yale's legendary football coach, came to Faribault's prestigious Shattuck preparatory school to teach Greek. Football, which had been quite popular on the East Coast, was just in its infancy in Minnesota during this time. So Camp took it upon himself to give his new friends and colleagues in southern Minnesota a quick lesson in how the gridiron game was played. He marked off a field according to Rugby regulations, set up some crude goal posts and tossed out a rugby ball. The first players to try the new game were Shattuck cadets, teachers, and Seabury divinity students — who also lived on campus.

The team's first official game came against Carleton College on October 29, 1884, whom they went on to beat by the final score of 24-0. The rugby-like rules were slowly being adapted into what we know today as American football. But back then, the terms were a little bit different. Drop-kicks were all the rage, the center was called the "snapper-back" and all the other linemen were called "rushers." In addition, a touchdown counted for just four points, while a "goal after a touchdown" was worth two.

By the early 1890's Shattuck preparatory school was playing mostly college schools, with occasional contests against some of the local prep and high schools. They were even beating up on the University of Minnesota, as well as colleges such as Hamline, Macalester, St. Thomas, Carleton and St. Olaf. One of the reasons for their early success was due to the fact that they were permitted to allow their coach and other members of the faculty (many of whom played collegiately out East) to play with them.

Over the next few years football grew quickly both in southern Minnesota and also in the Twin Cities. The oldest recorded game between two high schools came in October of 1894, when Northfield pounded Faribault 104-0. Other high schools to field squads on the gridiron in the late 1890s were Owatonnna, Sleepy Eye, Sauk Centre, Redwood Falls, Mankato, Minneapolis East and West High Schools, St. Paul Central and St. Paul Mechanic Arts.

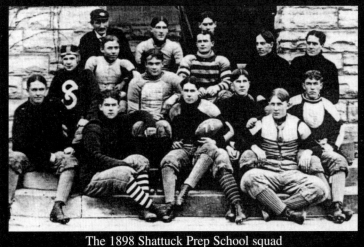

The 1898 Shattuck Prep School squad

The prep game grew and grew and by the turn of the 20th century it was found in nearly every small town in the Land of 10,000 Lakes. Some of the earlier schools to begin programs during the early 1900s were Cambridge, Fairmont, Mahnomen, Litchfield, Duluth, Hibbing, Stillwater, Montevideo, International Falls, White Bear Lake, Fergus Falls, Thief River Falls, Rochester, Aitkin, Austin, Tracy, Winona, Madelia, St. Cloud, LeCenter, Granite Falls, Little Falls and LeSueur. The Twin Cities had several schools playing in both Minneapolis and St. Paul, but Minneapolis Central High School was definitely in a league of their own by this time, even playing the Big Seven Conference champions from the University of Minnesota to a tough 0-0 tie.

In 1908 the Shattuck School again showed why they were the kings of gridiron when they won the Northwest Preparatory School Championship by defeating Pillsbury Academy (Owatonna), and then the Western Preparatory title by defeating the Middle State champs from Chicago's Lake Forest Academy.

The 1911 Litchfield High School, led by a young halfback named Bernie Bierman, was declared as the state's mythical champs when they beat a solid Hutchinson team. Later, in 1915, Anoka High School was declared as the state's gridiron champion.

Football, as well as many other prep sports got a boost that next year, in 1916, when the Minnesota State High School League was first organized as the State High School Athletic Association. Its primary purposes were to both promote amateur sports and to establish uniform eligibility rules for interscholastic contests. Football, with all of its' "house-rules" which were played and interpreted differently in nearly every small town throughout the state, was difficult to regulate into conformity. There were 152 schools participating in the sport that year, certainly a handful for an organization just in its infancy.

By the 1920s high school football was, in many cases, the biggest show in town for many small communities. While there were no "official" rankings or sanctioned playoff championships to speak of, there were local tournaments and locally proclaimed mythical titles. One such was the Northern Minnesota title, which was won regularly by Duluth Denfeld High School, who was led by their star halfback, Swede Larson.

Following W.W.I in the early 1920s, a number of outstanding teams emerged throughout the state, all of them claiming to be State Champions — Alexandria and Worthington to mention a few, as well as the 1922 Duluth Cathedral squad, which was led by future Notre Dame and St. John's star Joe Benda. Many of these teams were loaded with war veterans returning home to get their high school

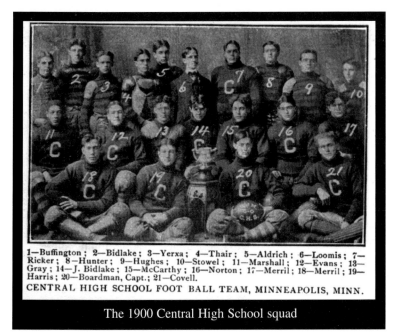

1—Buffington; 2—Bidlake; 3—Yerxa; 4—Thair; 5—Aldrich; 6—Loomis; 7—Ricker; 8—Hunter; 9—Hughes; 10—Stowel; 11—Marshall; 12—Evans; 13—Gray; 14—J. Bidlake; 15—McCarthy; 16—Norton; 17—Merril; 18—Merril; 19—Harris; 20—Boardman, Capt.; 21—Covell.
CENTRAL HIGH SCHOOL FOOT BALL TEAM, MINNEAPOLIS, MINN.

The 1900 Central High School squad

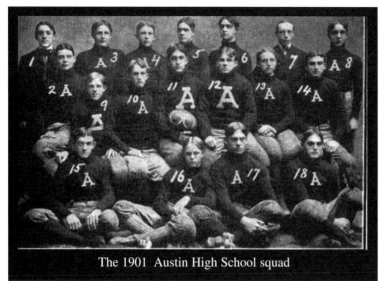

The 1901 Austin High School squad

diplomas. One of the favorite stunts for a young man who wanted to play another year of football in this era was to drop-out during his senior year after the football season, only to return the next Fall to graduate. This illegal "red shirting" loop-hole was very common back in the day, because the State High School League had not yet set up, or could police the necessary restrictions on games and eligibility.

Most games during this period were played on Saturday afternoons. That changed though with the rise of interest in Gopher Football during the Bernie Bierman era. With everyone wanting to stay home and listen to the Gopher games on the radio each Saturday afternoon, high school football attendance dropped drastically. So, games were eventually moved to Fridays. Soon, with the advent of night football under the lights, high school games on Friday nights became the family thing to do across the state. Some schools, who couldn't afford lights, even scheduled early Saturday morning games so that fans could get home to listen to the Gophers.

One of the powerhouses of this era was Montevideo High School. Having the good fortune of being located directly along the Milwaukee Railroad line, the team was able to schedule games with teams from all over the Midwest. (Since transportation was a big factor both logistically and financially in scheduling teams back then, games were often scheduled wherever one could find a suitable opponent. Sometimes, at the end of a season, an undefeated team would challenge another undefeated squad and claim it was for the Mythical State Championship.) Montevideo had built a tremendous football dynasty in those years, and in 1926 laid claim to the title after first beating the South Dakota champs from Aberdeen, and then the Twin City Champs from St. Paul Johnson. Each team came to town on trains jammed pack with fans and banners flying out the windows. People traveled there from all over the state just to see these games.

Due to the boom in popularity of college football in this era, coaching strategies were constantly changing and evolving to stay competitive. High school coaches often-times went to summer clinics during their off-season's to learn new formations and coaching techniques. There, they would copy one-another and then implement their new strategies for the upcoming seasons. There was the double-wing attack as perfected by George Myrum at Gustavus Adolphus, which featured among other things: using the quarterback and fullback handling the ball, full spins and half spins, a man-in-motion, balanced and unbalanced lines, positioning of backs as to depth and width, and even quick-kicks — with one man holding the ball and another man punting it. Then, with the coming of Bernie Bierman at the U of M, almost everyone swung over to single-wing, along with the box formation, which was used so successfully by Knute Rockne at Notre Dame. Variations came and went, such as the buck-lateral series with fullback spinners, which was used so effectively by Michigan's Fritz Crisler. (The T-formations, split and winged, didn't come until the 1940s, when the Chicago Bears, among other NFL teams perfected it.)

Into the 1930s six-man football began to become quite popular throughout the state. Much of the reason for this was because small towns often didn't have the man-power to field 11-man squads, but still wanted to play and compete. In six-man ball, all of the players were eligible to run, carry or pass the ball. Field goals were worth four points, and 15 yards were required for a first-down on the 80-yard fields.

In 1937 Minnesota had 237 high school programs playing 11-man football, with just five playing six-man ball: Ada, Bird Island, Buffalo Lake, Hector and Twin Valley. By 1941 there were more than 400

The 1942 State Mythical Champs from Coleraine High School

Bud Wilkinson starred for Shattuck in the early 1930s.

high school teams playing football in Minnesota, and 169 of them were playing six-man ball. After W.W.II, seven and eight man football teams began to pop up. By 1957 there were 321 11-man teams, 135 eight-man teams and 12 six-man teams. In 1959 just seven teams remained in six-man, and they all played in the "Longbow League." The league disbanded the next year with Longville winning the title with a 6-0 record, as the schools then evolved into eight-man football.

Into the late 1940s, local newspaper scribe Ted Peterson, who wrote for the Star and the Tribune for nearly half a century, became Minnesota's premier pigskin prognosticator. His weekly column entitled "No-Can-Pick-'Em" was the final word in prep football rankings. Starting in 1947, Peterson began rating local football teams, selected all-state squads and had the dubious honor of naming the state's annual "Mythical Champion." All undefeated teams were considered for each class, and then it would come down to his judgment based on toughness of schedule, margin of victory and number of all-star players. So if a team was ranked No. 1 back then, it was because Ted picked them to be there. There was not formal playoff system like we know of today to determine a state champion. Every Fall he would go non-stop throughout the four corners of the state, through the elements, traveling up to 5,000 miles in September and October alone, to witness countless teams in battle first-hand.

"Over the years I've covered football games in 80 degree temperatures, among hordes of mosquitoes, to others held in below zero temperatures in torrential rains, in hail, sleet and raging snow storms," said Peterson. "Never forgotten will be a game in Eveleth where mud was so deep we borrowed a pair of old football shoes. Before long the field itself was a sea of mud so deep the head of an Eveleth halfback actually disappeared on a tackle. There was an officials' time out while towels and water were needed to get the mud out of the eyes, mouth, nose and ears of the player."

He would also select the "Prep Games of the Week," an honor which later meant state-wide radio coverage and an instant spot on the football map for the two lucky squads. Peterson recalled that when a team was selected as the game of the week, it often-times meant that thousands of spectators would show up — regardless of their bleacher's seating capacity. One such "never-to-be-forgotten" prep game of the week was at Bemidji, where the underdog Lumberjacks took on an International Falls team led by a guy named Bronko Nagurski. Peterson, whose pre-game story mentioned the Broncos as the favorite, was walking by the Bemidji dressing room when he overheard legendary coach Ken (Red) Wilson giving a rousing pre-game speech which included the question: "And do you know why Ted Peterson drove those 230 miles all the way up here? It was just so he could see you kids get licked!" Determined to show Mr.

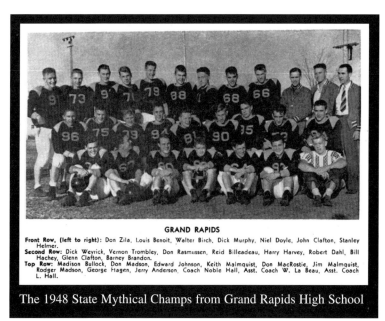

GRAND RAPIDS

Front Row, (left to right): Don Zila, Louis Benoit, Walter Birch, Dick Murphy, Niel Doyle, John Clafton, Stanley Helmer.
Second Row: Dick Weyrick, Vernon Trombley, Don Rasmussen, Reid Billeadeau, Harry Harvey, Robert Dahl, Bill Hachey, Glenn Clafton, Barney Brandon.
Top Row: Madison Bullock, Don Madson, Edward Johnson, Keith Malmquist, Don MacRostie, Jim Malmquist, Rodger Madson, George Hagen, Jerry Anderson, Coach Noble Hall, Asst. Coach W. La Beau, Asst. Coach L. Hall.

The 1948 State Mythical Champs from Grand Rapids High School

Peterson was dead wrong, the Jacks pounded I-Falls 35-6. During the fourth quarter, an International Falls running back attempted a sweep around his right end and a Bemidji defender actually permitted the ball carrier to run by until he was directly in front of Peterson, who was standing on the sidelines. Then, with a devastating tackle he dumped the ball carrier at his feet so hard that he had to jump out of the way. That little Bemidji player, his face dirty and smeared with blood, one knee on the chest of the International Falls player, looked up and said, "Huh, Mr. Peterson and you thought we were going to be licked!"

Being on the road so much also meant having to be able to write his stories and get them into the paper on deadline. This meant often-times just stopping at people's homes and asking to use the telephone just to call in and dictate his story to an editor back at the paper. On one occasion he was invited into a families' home to use a phone that was placed at the head of a huge kitchen table. The man of the house took a seat beside him, the mother took the other side, and a dozen kids of assorted sizes sat around in the other seats. Peterson recalled that they didn't make a sound as they listened to him dictate his lengthy story in detail over the phone. When he was finished the man of the house said calmly, "That was better than television..."

High school football back in the day was certainly no picnic. Coaches, who were also full-time teachers, were paid next to nothing and were usually overworked and underappreciated. In addition, schools had little or no budget for equipment, so kids had to fend for themselves as far as getting things like cleats and sometimes even helmets.

Front Row (left to right): Bob Hilgers, Jim Coult, Rog Thomas, Burnett Mens, Ron Olson, Allan Ledebur, Ron Jaqua, Ray Meyer, Edw. Ells, Richard Rose.
Second Row: Gene Myers, Glen Personius, Quinn Peterson, Tom Johnson, Byron Holcomb, Ron Craven, Jack Musser, Darrell Miedke, Ron Strom, Robert Bennett, Jim Duncan, Richard Weber, Rog Stevens.
Back Row: Rodney Stinc, Charles Keck, Allan Lidke, Bob Zemke, Vincent Style, David Johnson, Bill Cox, Doug Keasling.

The 1951 Fairmont High School squad

"Jerseys, usually of wool, were something to be patched again and again for a general rag-a-muffin appearance by the end of the season," recalled Peterson. "Pads, usually sewn inside the jersey, had a habit of shifting to areas other than those a player wanted protected. Football pants had bamboo sticks for thigh pads and some of the more expensive variety had soft pads for protection of kidneys and hips. A team would likely have a variety of battered helmets and if you took enough battering in the face, a rubber nose guard, held in place by your teeth, was in order."

"Kids back in my own high school days had to be loaded with a desire to play," he added. "Like carrying your equipment to and from school in an old flour sack every day. Like getting on a street car and riding four miles to a practice field every night after school. Like getting back on that street car or walking home after practice all sweaty, dirty and often battered and scratched. But it was fun."

Peterson went on to describe how newspaper reporters covered the game back in the day, without the modern amenities of a press box, or even a place to sit and write. "It's just as well, too, since I never had a desire to change an old habit of walking the sidelines to cover a game," he reminisced. "That's where the action is. Of course that's a place to get into trouble, too, and agility is sometimes a good substitute for lack of proper reasoning. There was once a game where ropes were drawn right up to the sidelines to keep spectators back. Proper position for a sports writer on the field would be behind the

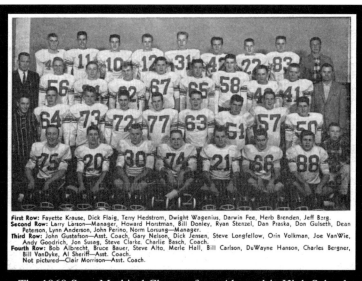

First Row: Fayette Krause, Dick Flaig, Terry Hedstrom, Dwight Wagenius, Darwin Fee, Herb Brenden, Jeff Berg.
Second Row: Larry Larson—Manager, Howard Horstman, Bill Donley, Ryan Stenzel, Dan Praska, Don Gulseth, Dean Peterson, Lynn Anderson, John Perino, Norm Lorsung—Manager.
Third Row: John Gustafson—Asst. Coach, Gary Nelson, Dick Jensen, Steve Longfellow, Orin Volkman, Joe VanWie, Andy Goodrich, Jon Sussg, Steve Clarke, Charlie Basch, Coach.
Fourth Row: Bob Albrecht, Bruce Bauer, Steve Alto, Merle Hall, Bill Carlson, DuWayne Hanson, Charles Bergner, Bill VanDyke, Al Sheriff—Asst. Coach.
Not pictured—Clair Morrison—Asst. Coach.

The 1960 State Mythical Champs from Alexandria High School

TOM MAHONEY

When former Gopher Tom Mahoney retired from coaching in 1990 he stood alone as the state's all-time winningest head coach. In 39 seasons at Lake City and Fairmont, Mahoney complied a record of 256-94-8, which, at the time, was No. 1.

His record 213th win came on Friday, Sept. 23, 1981, when his Fairmont Cardinals beat St. Peter. The big win moved him past the previous leader, Red Wilson, who had coached most of his career at Bemidji High School.

Aside from being an outstanding teacher and coach, Tom should also be recognized for his many contributions off the field as well. For decades he has been a member of nearly every committee of the MHSFCA and his commitment has continued since his retirement.

Tom has long been considered the "thinker" of the association, and many of the programs developed through the years have been from his brain-storming: including the All Star Game, the playoff system, the "Butch Nash" Award, the Distinguished Service Award, and many more. Fittingly, in 1990 he was inducted into the MHSFCA Hall of Fame.

Since he hung up the whistle for good, he has stayed active as MSHSL Region 2A Secretary. He has even finally found time for some golf. Tom and his wife of 45 years, Pat, live in Fairmont. They have seven children and many grandchildren.

KEEP YOUR DOBBER UP COACH!

line of scrimmage. This one accidentally got ahead of it though, and the result was running 35 yards and leading interference on a touchdown run into the end zone. It must have been legal because the officials didn't call it."

Through it all, Peterson fondly remembered the strong fatherly-figure of that of the high school football coach. "Emblazoned in memory is the picture of a coach on the sidelines holding the head of one of his players, who was never to compete again, in his lap," he said. "That coach was weeping unashamedly. It isn't the only time I've seen a coach weep, not in self pity, but because his kids deserved a better fate. Tears, sweat, toil, disappointment and a countering jubilation of pride all go into the makeup of a coach. And don't forget dedication and the fascination of having a hand in developing boys into stout-hearted men."

By 1972 the State High School League, behind years of lobbying from the Minnesota High School Football Coaches Association, decided to take over for Peterson and, for the first time, establish a long-overdue playoff system which would determine state champions for each of the newly designated five divisions: AA, A, B, C and 9-Man. (Class AA enrollment was 1,150 and above, Class A enrollment was 450-1,149, Class B enrollment was 200-449, Class C enrollment was under 200, and 9-Man was reserved for the discretion of the smallest schools.) Fully 477 of the 484 public high schools in Minnesota, or 98%, fielded football teams that year — involving over 40,000 boys. (That percentage figure was the highest of any state in the nation!) Finally, football, like hockey, basketball and baseball before them, would get a legitimate state champ. It was a long and arduous process that took some 20 years to come to fruition.

As far back as the early 1950's, representatives of high school football had routinely proposed a post-season format to the MSHSL, which included a single-game playoff using the "Pennsylvania Point" system. In 1964, a modest breakthrough came about when the MSHSL accepted the "10th game inter-conference playoff system." This led to the establishment of such popular attractions as the Suburban, Lake and Big-9 playoff games. In the Fall of 1971 there were 22 such inter-conference playoff games.

In the fall of 1970, an ad-hoc Citizens Advisory Committee was established by the Commissioner of Education to study and examine the structure and function of high school playoff games. After much debate, the committee's final report stated that a system of football playoffs should be established to determine a State Football Championship. The Board in turn asked the football coaches to draft a plan and submit their recommendations. A committee of high school football coaches then hammered out a playoff proposal. The committee was guided by certain fundamentals which included: (1) existing conferences and traditional rivalries must not be destroyed; (2) inter-conference games must be maintained; (3) a class plan was necessary as disproportionate school populations would create unfairness in determining a champion; (4) and for obvious reasons, the football season could not and should not be extended indefinitely. In March of 1972, ballots on the playoff proposal were sent to the superintendent, principal, athletic director, head football coach and school board representative in

Most Playoff Appearances:
(Playoffs Began in 1972)

No.	School
17	Stillwater
15	Mahnomen
13	Albany
13	Hutchinson
12	Deer River
11	Totino Grace
11	Moorhead
11	Burnsville
11	Cretin-DH
10	Litchfield
10	Apple Valley
10	St. Peter

State Championship Game Appearances

No.	School
10	Mahnomen
9	BOLD/Bird Is./LL
8	Stillwater
5	Burnsville
5	Cromwell
4	Detroit Lakes
4	Gaylord
4	Granite Falls
4	Minneota
4	Northfield
4	Silver Lake
4	St. Peter
4	Verndale

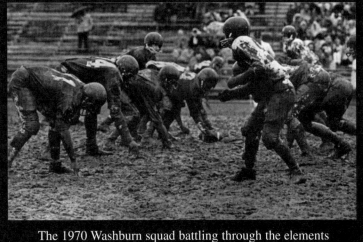

The 1970 Washburn squad battling through the elements

all school districts, with all five overwhelmingly accepting the proposal.

Schools were then ranked thanks to the advent of the computer, which now allowed teams to be tallied on a Rating Average. (The Rating Average equaled Total Points divided by the Number of Qualifying Games) The final Rating Average at the end of the season was also the basis for selecting teams for the playoffs. Teams with the four highest Rating Averages in each classification would then qualify for playoff berths. (For instance, the scoring system awarded 100 points for each win, provided the defeated team is in the same or higher classification.) So, with no further ado, I present to you summaries and synopsis of the high school playoffs from the first, in 1972, up to the new millennium.

1972 State High School Tournament

With the formalities out of the way, the first football playoffs of the Minnesota State High School League were held in the fall of 1972. Venues for the games ranged from Parade Stadium in Minneapolis, to local neutral sites throughout the state. Winners in the championship games for each class were as follows: Minneapolis Washburn beat Moorhead, 26-8, to claim the AA title. Burnsville spanked Sauk Centre, 46-19, for the Class A crown. Mountain Iron blasted Dassel-Cokato, 54-6, for the Class B championship, and in Class C action Gaylord upended Preston 26-6. Finally, Rothsay rolled over Cotton, 64-12, for the 9-Man title.

Hutchinson's Grady Rostberg

1973 State High School Tournament

Rochester John Marshall beat up on St. Paul Harding, 25-0, to take the Class AA title. Then, an amazing comeback was pulled off by the Eveleth Golden Bears, who trailed Willmar 18-0 and then rallied for a 28-18 victory for the Class A crown. New Prague outlasted Appleton, 13-7, for the Class B title, while Gaylord, who beat Holdingford, 29-6, won its second straight Class C championship. The 9-Man title game was a blowout as Lake Benton spanked Brandon by the final of 50-12.

Stillwater's George Thole

1974 State High School Tournament

Three school repeated as champions in 1974: Rochester John Marshall (Class AA), New Prague (Class B) and Lake Benton (9-Man). In AA action John Marshall crushed Bloomington Jefferson, 41-19, as fullback Kent Kitzmann ran for five touchdowns and caught a pass for another en route to gaining 195 yards on 40 carries. Alexandria took the Class A title with ease by beating Chaska 26-7. New Prague also rolled to a 41-12 win over Caledonia for the Class B crown, as fullback Harold Stevens scored three touchdowns, gained 142 yards rushing and caught two passes for 65 yards. Battle Lake, led by Brad Hustad's 10-yard pass to Jon Shorter in the second overtime, defeated Bird Island 34-26 for the Class C title. Finally, Lake Benton rolled to a 36-6 victory over Fisher for the 9-Man title as halfbacks Jeff Frey and Curt Weber combined to gain 244 yards rushing. (Adding to the state's football festivities in 1974 was the first annual North-South All-Star game played at the University of Minnesota's Memorial Stadium. Sponsors of the game were the three Shrine Temples along with the Minnesota State Football Coaches Association.)

1975 State High School Tournament

While each of the five 1975 championship schools completed their seasons with perfect 12-0 records, for the first time there wasn't a single repeat champion in the fourth annual tournament. Stillwater won an exciting 20-17 contest from previously unbeaten Richfield before 10,359 fans at Minneapolis' Parade Stadium for the Class AA title. Trailing by four points with just 18 seconds to go in the fourth quarter, the Ponies, faced with a 4th-and-goal situation from Richfield's six-yard line, were led to glory by Halfback Todd Butterfield. Taking the ball on a pitchout, he started to his left and then pulled up to hit Receiver Bob St. Aubin in the end-zone for the game-winning touchdown. St. Thomas Academy scored eight fourth quarter points to overcome a strong St. Peter club, 21-14 for the Class A championship at the University of St. Thomas. In Class B Gaylord won its third state title in four years by stopping a late rally to beat Onamia 14-13 at St. Cloud. Meanwhile in Class C action, Esko crushed Karlstad 62-0. Finally, in 9-Man, Ruthton rose to the top of the state's 65 9-Man teams by beating Audubon 42-20 in Cottonwood.

Cambridge's George Larson

1976 State High School Tournament

The 1976 state tournament once again featured five undefeated champions. In Class AA, White Bear Lake needed overtime to beat Cloquet by the final score of 14-13. St. Peter stomped on Mora, 56-12, to win the Class A title, and in Class B action Caledonia beat Sartell, 38-7. Class C saw New Richland-Hartland edge out Bird Island, 21-19, and Deer Creek beat up on Fergus Falls - Hillcrest Academy by the final score of 57-14 for the 9-Man championship.

1977 State High School Tournament

A record of nearly 9,000 fans were on hand at Minneapolis' Parade Stadium to witness Washburn blank Stillwater, 13-0, for the Class AA final. In Class A Fridley Grace topped Cold Spring Rocori 36-12, and in Class B action Granite Falls had little problem with Stewartville as they rolled to a 44-6 victory. Class C was a different story though, as Battle Lake needed overtime to barely edge out Henderson by the final of 21-20. Then, in 9-Man action, Deer Creek blanked Fergus Falls Hillcrest-Academy, 20-0, to repeat as state champs.

1978 State High School Tournament

The post-season format was changed for the 1978 season, as Classes A, B, C and 9-Man expanded from four schools to eight, with Class AA remaining at four. Under the new "quarterfinal-semifinal-final" system the 66 conference champions, instead of top computer-rated teams, would now advance to the playoffs. Edina West, after breezing through the playoffs undefeated and unscored upon, downed Fridley 21-0 for the Class AA crown. The only defending champion able to repeat in the seventh annual state tournament was

Richfield's Doug Kingsriter

Fridley Grace, which captured its second straight Class A championship on the strength of a field goal in the final quarter by Brian Swan to edge Apple Valley 17-14. New Richland-Hartland cruised to a 48-8 win over Barnesville for the Class B title, thanks to the running of Greg Rieck, who gained 118 yards on the ground, and Mark Dorn, who scored three touchdowns. In Class C action, Todd Jensen's late touchdown rallied Alden-Conger to a 15-14 upset victory over defending champion Battle Lake, who was seeking its second successive title and its third state championship in five years. Finally, in 9-Man play, Hoffman toppled Albrook 44-28 behind Halfback David Parks' four-touchdowns.

1979 State High School Tournament

Columbia Heights won the Class AA crown with an 8-3 win over Richfield, while Rochester Lourdes topped Apple Valley 27-6 in Class A. In Class B Gaylord downed Mahnomen 15-6 to win their fourth state championship in school history, and Bird Island-Lake Lillian posted a 34-6 win over Harmony in the Class C finals. And, last but not least, Russell topped Toivola-Meadowlands, 17-14, in 9-Man action.

1980 State High School Tournament

Burnsville downed Cambridge, 23-6, in the Class AA finals at Parade Stadium, and Crookston took the Class A hardware home by beating Pipestone 32-6. Mahnomen won the Class B title by blanking Austin Pacelli 34-0, while Bird Island-Lake Lillian repeated as Class C state champs by knocking off Mountain Lake, 20-7. Finally, Hoffman-Kensington out-dueled Toivola-Meadowlands, 18-14, for the 9-Man crown.

1981 State High School Tournament

Led by junior all-state quarterback Brett Sadek, who ran for one touchdown and passed for two more, Rosemount's Irish rallied from a 7-6 third-period deficit to cruise past Moorhead, 40-14, at Parade

Minneapolis West's Rolly Ring

So mean and nasty was Highland Park Guard Tony Lee, that he was banished from the game for life for once tearing an opponent's arms and legs off!

Stadium to win the Class AA title. In the Class A finals, St. Peter got a touchdown on a five-yard run in the fourth from Paul Maynard to edge out Hermantown, 18-14. Holdingford, who defeated defending champion Mahnomen in the semifinals, blitzed Pine Island 39-0 to win the Class B championship. The Huskers were led by the running of both Dan Stich (who scored three touchdowns) and Brian Reis (who added two of his own), who combined to rush for 454 yards. In the Class C finals Medford Quarterback Brian Wolfe led his team to a 19-0 lead in the first half over Clarkfield, only to choke off a late rally and hang on to a 33-28 victory. Then, in 9-Man competition, Argyle's Jay LaBine scored on a pair of 55-yard and 75-yard kickoff and punt returns, while his cousin, Mike LaBine, ran a kickoff back 77 yards for a touchdown to lead Argyle to a 31-19 victory over Starbuck.

MOST ALL-TIME TEAM VICTORIES					
School	Total	Wins	Losses	Ties	Dates
1. Cambridge	702	510	168	24	1910-99
2. Fairmont	713	491	200	22	1913-95
3. Mahnomen	650	480	161	9	1910-99
4. Stillwater	758	451	280	27	1915-99
5. Montevideo	679	406	246	25	1913-99
6. Redwood Falls	783	402	336	43	1899-99
7. Owatonna	740	400	310	30	1893-99
8. LeCenter	610	397	196	17	1928-99
9. LeSueur/LSH	627	391	219	17	1927-99
10. International Falls	683	388	263	32	1914-99
11. White Bear Lake	654	374	258	22	1913-99
12. Granite Falls	633	370	236	27	1926-99
13. Fergus Falls	658	369	274	15	1911-99
14. Mankato/West	767	366	365	36	1903-99
15. Albany	447	353	88	6	1955-99
16. Thief River Falls	667	351	294	22	1907-99
17. Mpls. Edison	508	350	142	16	1935 99
18. Jackson/ County	564	334	252	0	1928-99
19. Gaylord/Winthrop	429	316	105	8	1945-89
20. Verndale	459	312	138	9	1949-99

1982: PREP BOWL I

In 1982 the MSHSL took a huge leap forward when they announced that they had signed an agreement to play all five of their championship games at the newly constructed Hubert H. Humphrey Metrodome, in downtown Minneapolis. The new annual tournament, which would finally allow for all five games to be played on the same day and in the same location, would officially be called the "Prep Bowl." Other festivities of the day included a "massed band" consisting of more than 2,400 band members and 1,000 choir singers from around the state, as well as danceline and cheerleading performances. Nearly 43,000 fans turned out that November 20th for the inaugural day at the dome. (To put that in perspective, only 15,000 fans showed up at five different neutral sites around the state just the year before for the same games.) Teams could now find parity playing indoors, and the final Associated Press high school football rankings would now be for entertainment purposes only.

In the Class AA game Stillwater rallied late in the fourth to get over on Owatonna by the final score of 34-27. Owatonna's Bruce Bates opened the scoring in this one on a two-yard TD run midway through the first, only to see Stillwater's Matt Hasken, who rushed for 116 yards on the day, break loose on a 17-yard touchdown run to tie it up at 7-7. Owatonna came back in the second though, behind Bob Paal's eight-yard TD catch from Ken Kienholz. Stillwater answered with a touchdown run from quarterback Eric Thole, only to see Bates tally again on a one-yard plunge. Stillwater's Scott Clemons, who ran for 126 yards that afternoon, then tore loose for a 53 yard score late in the third. Thole ran another one-yarder in early in the fourth, only to see Owatonna come back on Bates' third touchdown run of the day to tie it up. Then, with just 4:50 left in the game, Stillwater's Terry Runk took a 54 yard pass from Thole to give the Ponies a 34-27 lead, and thus handing Owatonna its first loss in 18 games — a streak which extended back over two seasons.

Brooklyn Center downed East Grand Forks in the Class A title game, thanks in large part to the running of Kermit Klefsaas' four touchdowns. The Green Wave of East Grand Forks tried to mount a rally late in the fourth behind Steve Ristau's three-yard touchdown, but it was little too late as the Centaurs hung on for the title.

LeCenter started out strong and persevered to beat a very tough Mahnomen team for the Class B title. After a scoreless first half, Wildcats' receiver Tim Palmquist hauled in an 11-yard touchdown pass from quarterback Todd Anderson to make it 6-0. LeCenter then made it 12-0 at 11:53 of the fourth when Anderson hit Todd Traxier on a 42-yard bomb. The Indians mounted a rally late in the fourth behind Doug Liebl's four yard TD run, but came up short as LeCenter hung on for the 12-6 victory and a perfect 12-0 record.

Truman rallied in dramatic fashion to win the Class C championship on a last-second field goal over Belgrade. The Bluejays scored twice in the first thanks to both Pat Gunderson's four yard TD plunge (the extra point was blocked), and Bill Tainter's seven yard touchdown reception from Quarterback George Rosberg. Belgrade came back in the second behind Bruce Duevel's 46-yard run around the end, followed by Steve Buchholz's two-point conversion to make it 13-8. Duevel then scored again at 4:38 of the fourth to put his squad up 14-13. That's when Truman rallied behind Rosberg to get downfield in a hurry. Desperately getting into position with under a minute left, Bluejay's Kicker Ron Peterson walked out and calmly kicked a 29-yard field goal through the uprights to give Truman the dramatic 16-14 win.

In 9-Man action Westbrook upended Fergus Falls-Hillcrest Academy by the final of 34-12. Westbrook went up 21-0 into the third thanks to touchdowns from Lee Mischke, who hauled in a 62-yard bomb from Steve Elzenga, followed by a one-yard Elzenga plunge, and Dean Anderson's 38-yard run up the middle. The Comets then mounted a comeback, thanks to a fumble recovery in the end-zone late in the third to make it 20-6. Westbrook hung on to preserve their undefeated season though, thanks to a pair of late touchdowns from both Elzenga and Bruce Madson to ensure the 34-12 victory.

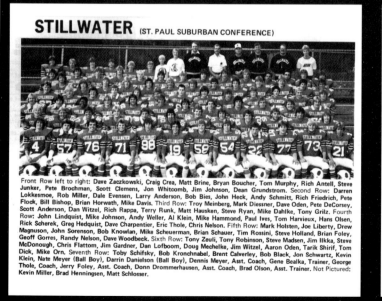

STILLWATER (ST. PAUL SUBURBAN CONFERENCE)

Front Row left to right: Dave Zaczkowski, Craig Crea, Matt Brine, Bryan Boucher, Tom Murphy, Rich Antell, Steve Junker, Pete Brochman, Scott Clemens, Jon Whitcomb, Jim Johnson, Dean Grundstrom. Second Row: Darren Lokkesmoe, Rob Miller, Dale Evensen, Larry Anderson, Bob Bies, John Heck, Andy Schmitt, Rich Friedrich, Pete Flock, Bill Bishop, Brian Horwath, Mike Davis. Third Row: Troy Meinberg, Mark Diessner, Dave Oden, Pete DeCorsey, Scott Anderson, Dan Witzel, Rich Rappa, Terry Runk, Matt Hausken, Steve Ryan, Mike Dahlke, Tony Grilz. Fourth Row: John Lindquist, Mike Johnson, Andy Weller, Al Klein, Mike Hammond, Paul Ives, Tom Harvieux, Hans Olsen, Rick Scherek, Greg Hedquist, Dave Charpentier, Eric Thole, Chris Nelson. Fifth Row: Mark Holsten, Joe Liberty, Drew Magnuson, John Sorenson, Bob Knowlan, Mike Scheuerman, Brian Schauer, Tim Rossini, Steve Holland, Brian Foley, Geoff Gorres, Randy Nelson, Dave Woodbeck. Sixth Row: Tony Zeuli, Tony Robinson, Steve Madsen, Jim Ilkka, Steve McDonough, Chris Flattom, Jim Gardner, Dan Lofboom, Doug Mechelke, Jim Witzel, Aaron Oden, Tarik Shirif, Tom Dick, Mike Orn. Seventh Row: Toby Schifsky, Bob Kronchnabel, Brent Calverley, Bob Black, Jon Schwartz, Kevin Klein, Nate Meyer (Ball Boy), Darrin Danielson (Ball Boy), Dennis Meyer, Asst. Coach, Gene Bealka, Trainer, George Thole, Coach, Jerry Foley, Asst. Coach, Donn Drommerhausen, Asst. Coach, Brad Olson, Asst. Trainer. Not Pictured: Kevin Miller, Brad Henningsen, Matt Schlosser.

BROOKLYN CENTER
(TRI-METRO CONFERENCE)

Front Row left to right: Craig Bergstrom, Sean Crute, Steve Sorensen, Ralph Rocha, Ken Tanji, Scott Bernardson, Steve Peterson, Kevin Smith, Brian Erickson. Second Row: Mike Edwards, John Giguere, Kevin Persons, Richard Jackson, Dave Contreras, Mgr. Duane Stern, Tom Worwa, Jim Laberda, Tom Hagel, Doug Jennrich. Third Row: Tom Tonneson, Bill Gallup, Kurt Schuman, Coach Bernie Wesloh, Coach Doug Darnell, Coach Warren Olson, Neil Neumann, Marty Bies, Bob Ford. Fourth Row: Ron Jennings, Phil Bernards, Mike Johnson, Joe Novak, Tracy Martin, Jim Galvin, Keith Schleeter, Kraig Leuthard, Kerm Klefsaas, Mark Pieper.

1982 Class AA Champs   1982 Class A Champs

LE CENTER
(MINNESOTA RIVER CONFERENCE)

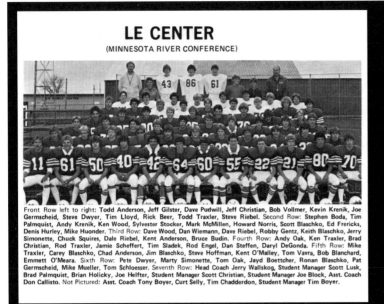

Front Row left to right: Todd Anderson, Jeff Gilster, Dave Pudwill, Jeff Christian, Bob Vollmer, Kevin Krenik, Joe Germscheid, Steve Dwyer, Tim Lloyd, Rick Beer, Todd Traxler, Steve Riebel. Second Row: Stephen Boda, Tim Palmquist, Andy Krenik, Ken Wood, Sylvester Stocker, Mark McMillen, Howard Norris, Scott Blaschko, Ed Frericks, Denis Hurley, Mike Huonder. Third Row: Dave Wood, Dan Wiemann, Dave Riebel, Robby Gentz, Keith Blaschko, Jerry Simonette, Chuck Squires, Dale Riebel, Kent Anderson, Bruce Budin. Fourth Row: Andy Oak, Ken Traxler, Brad Christian, Rod Traxler, Jamie Scheffert, Tim Sladek, Rod Engel, Dan Steffen, Daryl DeGonda. Fifth Row: Mike Traxler, Carey Blaschko, Chad Anderson, Jim Blaschko, Steve Hoffman, Kent O'Malley, Tom Vavra, Bob Blanchard, Emmett O'Meara. Sixth Row: Pete Dwyer, Marty Simonette, Tom Oak, Jayd Boettcher, Ronan Blaschko, Pat Germscheid, Mike Mueller, Tom Schloesser. Seventh Row: Head Coach Jerry Wallskog, Student Manager Scott Lusk, Brad Palmquist, Brian Holicky, Joe Helfter, Student Manager Scott Christian, Student Manager Joe Block, Asst. Coach Don Callisto. Not Pictured: Asst. Coach Tony Boyer, Curt Selly, Tim Chadderdon, Student Manager Tim Boyer.

1982 Class B Champs

TRUMAN
(MIDDLE 8 CONFERENCE)

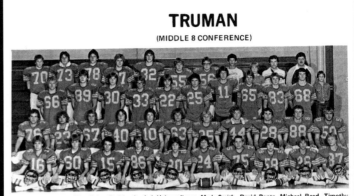

Front Row left to right: Brian Breitbarth, Jed Heimendinger, Mark Smith, David Bentz, Michael Reed, Timothy Kosbab, Timothy Henning, Wade Krenz, Wayne Wiederhoeft, Kent Williamson. Second Row: Patrick Atkinson, Dougla: Kneeland, Scott Sherman, Jeffrey Greiner, Ross Becker, James Lueth, James Bentz, Patrick Gunderson, Philip Jones, William Tainter, Jr., Darcy Drevlow. Third Row: Brian Tomford, Rick Mathwig, Kurt Cole, Joel Becker, Lee Firchau, Ronald Peterson, Jr., George Rosburg, Brian Dietz, Richard Wessel, Unidentified, Chad Stoddard, Student Manager. Fourth Row: Timothy Zehnder, Christopher Pierson, Bradley Vogt, Jeff Peterson, Kevin Metz, Unidentified, Jame: Voelker, Gerald Raddatz, Student Manager, Scott Lindaman, Student Manager, Randall Johnson, Asst. Coach, Hea: Coach Ronald Peterson.

1982 Class C Champs

WESTBROOK
(RED ROCK CONFERENCE)

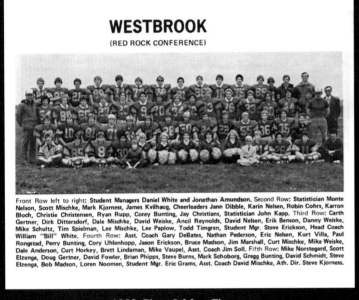

Front Row left to right: Student Managers Daniel White and Jonathan Amundson. Second Row: Statistician Monte Nelson, Scott Mischke, Mark Kjorness, James Kvilhaug, Cheerleaders Jann Dibble, Karin Nelsen, Robin Cohrs, Karron Bloch, Christie Christensen, Ryan Rupp, Corey Bunting, Jay Christians, Statistician John Kapp. Third Row: Carth Gertner, Dirk Dittersdorf, Dale Mischke, David Weiske, Ancil Reynolds, David Nelsen, Erik Benson, Danny Weiske, Mike Schultz, Tim Spielman, Lee Mischke, Lee Paplow, Todd Timgren, Student Mgr. Steve Erickson, Head Coach William "Bill" White. Fourth Row: Asst. Coach Gary DeBates, Nathan Pederson, Eric Nelsen, Kurt Villa, Paul Rongstad, Perry Bunting, Cory Uhlenhopp, Jason Erickson, Bruce Madson, Jim Marshall, Curt Mischke, Mike Weiske, Dale Anderson, Curt Horkey, Brett Lindaman, Mike Vaupel, Asst. Coach Jim Soll. Fifth Row: Mike Norstegard, Scott Elzenga, Doug Gertner, David Fowler, Brian Phipps, Steve Burns, Mark Schoborg, Gregg Bunting, David Schmidt, Steve Elzenga, Bob Madson, Loren Noomen, Student Mgr. Eric Grams, Asst. Coach David Mischke, Ath. Dir. Steve Kjorness.

1982 Class 9-Man Champs

1983: PREP BOWL II

Coon Rapids hung on in a nail-biter to beat a very tough Bloomington Jefferson squad for the Class AA state championship. The Jaguars opened the scoring on Shawn Day's 27-yard fumble recovery for a touchdown. The Cardinals answered back though, getting a pair of touchdown runs from both Brian Ploof and Bob Kelly late in the first. Jefferson then roared back for three straight scores. The first came in the second quarter when Pete Hill scored on a one yard TD, followed by a pair in the third from both Greg Nelson, who caught a 42-yard touchdown pass from Jay Anderson, and then a 25-yard Pat Beaty field goal. Rapids answered on a Ken Awalt TD pass from QB Chris McCartney, followed by a pair of one yard touchdown runs from both McCartney and Terry Heidgerken. Bloomington Receiver Dan Grant tallied on a six-yarder late in the fourth to get to within three, but when Awalt ran out of the end-zone with 25 seconds to go in the game, it was over. Coon Rapids had survived to earn the 34-31 win.

Hutchinson won the State A title by beating a very solid Park Rapids squad. The Tigers, led by fullback Paul Lenz's three touchdown runs in the first three quarters, went up 21-0. The Panthers rallied though, behind a pair of touchdowns from both Jeff Packer and Mitch Nelson in the third. Hutch Quarterback Andy Rostberg, son of the team's legendary coach Grady Rostberg, then took over. That's when the speedy quarterback ran in a pair of touchdowns during the fourth quarter to seal the 36-14 victory, and preserve the team's perfect record.

The Class B title game was a blowout, thanks to Jordan's gunslinging Quarterback Pete Dymit. Dymit heaved a pair of touchdown passes in this one, including a 73-yarder to Gary Fahrenkamp, and a 30-yarder to Dave Affolter. Mike Allar and John McFarland each also added short touchdown runs to seal the 27-0 win for Jordan. Jordan went unscored upon for the playoffs, and one of the biggest reasons for that was due to the outstanding play of defensive captain Lee Kes, who blocked two punts and recorded three sacks in the title game.

Southland posted a 28-0 spanking of Bird Island-Lake Lillian in the Class C finals to keep their record perfect for the year. The Rebels got a pair of third quarter scores on short runs from both Neal Kosberg and Todd Linaman. Southland added two more touchdowns in the fourth thanks to a couple of TD passes from Scott Retterath to both Brad Tompkins and Randy Smith.

Silver Lake started out strong and never looked back as they beat Norman County West/Climax for the 9-Man championship, 27-12. Silver Lake opened the scoring in the second quarter behind a pair of rushing touchdowns by both Jim Hemerick and Bruce Stifter. The Panthers answered back late in the second as Quarterback Darin Loe capped a six play drive by diving over his tackle for a two yard TD. Loe then hit Mike Kolness on a 22-yard scoring strike later in the third to make it 14-12 in favor of the Lakeites. Silver Lake took over from there though, as Hemerick and Bob Yurek each scored late in the fourth to put this one on ice.

COON RAPIDS (NORTH SUBURBAN CONFERENCE)

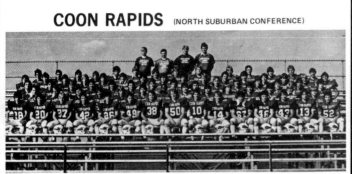

Front Row left to right: J. Hillyer, M. Black, M. Vikesland, R. Rosett, J. Zanotti, T. Burgos, R. Julkowski, Capt. A. Elliott, C. McCartney, P. Yelle, J. Fischer, T. Plankers, Brent Ploof, D. Haaf, B. Larson. Second Row: B. Napier, J. McCullough, M. Sundstrom, D. Dowling, J. Lero, J. Ruhl, P. Hamilton, B. Cook, V. Ruzynski, R. Sandstrom, J. Anzelc, P. Gorder, R. Kuzel, L. Pierce. Third Row: J. Johannsen, C. Colburn, K. Adams, D. Kessler, W. Parkin, B. Koenig, P. Gierl, T. Schroeder, T. Ohotto, T. Dolney, J. Lamkin, J. Haberman, R. Emerson, S. Zickermann. Fourth Row: S. McBride, Brian Ploof, B. Kelly, M. Limanen, R. Monroe, G. Borkowski, C. Johanns, K. Hansen, D. Isaacson, J. Dwyer, J. Goodmanson, R. Smith, R. Gunerius, C. Yunker, T. Heidgerken, D. Hemauer. Fifth Row: Mgr. R. Ringel, J. Boyce, J. Degnan, B. Funfar, M. Voss, K. Awalt, B. Sunnarborg, J. Scott, L. Plack, J. Knopik, J. Hetrick, L. Prescott, T. Copa, Mgr. C. Osburn. Sixth Row: Coaches Ron Scott, Jim Roback, Dan Dehnicke, Jeff Wolfe.

1983 Class AA Champs

HUTCHINSON (SUBURBAN WEST CONFERENCE)

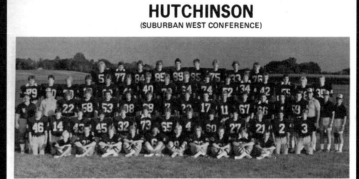

Front Row left to right: Josh Hoffman, Barry Watson, Chris Holy, Bryan Betker, Paul Moehring, Mark Wetterling, Dave Ladd, Steve Mogard, Bob Boune, Dana Watson. Second Row: Scott Walquist, Pat Mooney, Russ Jonas, Brad Altermatt, Mark Severson, Jay Hoffman, Jason Moehring, Jon Carlson, Randy Dostal, Pat Amiot, Jeff Bulau, Karl Viesselman, Jeff Jensen. Third Row: Coach Greg Pearce, Coach Bruce Rosenow, Rick Euerle, Larry Kramer, Eric Thovson, Brian Galles, Tim McGraw, Matt Larsen, Bill Field, Andy Rostberg, Kevin Heitz, Joel Raddatz, Chris Kirchoff, Paul Raddatz, Coach Denny Luke, Coach Grady Rostberg, Coach Jim Mills. Fourth Row: Tony Jahner, Paul Snyder, Tim Dobratz, Gene Ollrich, Scott Paulsen, Dan Johnson, Rob Pachan, Lance Swanke, Mark Koelln, Chuck Voight, Joe Thompson, Jeff Corl, Scott Sustacek, Mark Rubischko, Bob Hantge, Dean Ortloff. Fifth Row: Paul Lenz, Dave Kucera, Jon Valek, Todd Wrucke, Paul Briggs, Mark Benshoof, Pat Beatty, David Dietel, Scott Schlueter.

1983 Class A Champs

JORDAN (MINNESOTA RIVER)

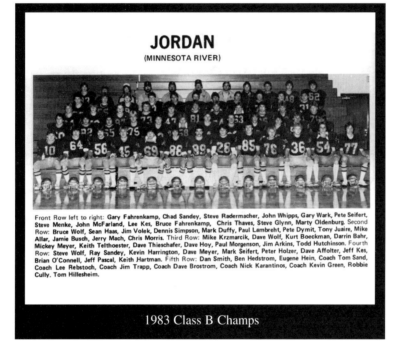

Front Row left to right: Gary Fahrenkamp, Chad Sandey, Steve Radermacher, John Whipps, Gary Wark, Pete Seifert, Steve Menke, John McFarland, Lee Kes, Bruce Fahrenkamp, Chris Thaves, Steve Glynn, Marty Oldenburg. Second Row: Bruce Wolf, Sean Haas, Jim Volek, Dennis Simpson, Mark Duffy, Paul Lambreht, Pete Dymit, Tony Juaire, Mike Allar, Jamie Busch, Jerry Mach, Chris Morris. Third Row: Mike Krzmarcik, Dave Wolf, Kurt Boeckman, Darrin Bahr, Mickey Meyer, Keith Telthoester, Dave Thieschafer, Dave Hoy, Paul Morgenson, Jim Arkins, Todd Hutchinson. Fourth Row: Steve Wolf, Ray Sandey, Kevin Harrington, Dave Meyer, Mark Seifert, Peter Holzer, Dave Affolter, Jeff Kes, Brian O'Connell, Jeff Pascal, Keith Hartman. Fifth Row: Dan Smith, Ben Hedstrom, Eugene Hein, Coach Tom Sand, Coach Lee Rebstoch, Coach Jim Trapp, Coach Dave Brostrom, Coach Nick Karantinos, Coach Kevin Green, Robbie Cully, Tom Hillesheim.

1983 Class B Champs

SOUTHLAND (WASIOJA CONFERENCE)

Front Row left to right: Ass't. Coaches Mike Johnson, Wayne Robertson, Todd Retterath, Scott Retterath, Tom Smith, Joe Price, Joe Kressin, Head Coach Richard Strand, Ass't. Coach Robert Bulger. Second Row: Jeff Lewison, Brian Landherr, Kyle Klaehn, Kenney Hammell, Ryan Smith, Doug Goergan, Randy Smith, Todd Linaman, Brian Bahr. Third Row: Bill Schmitz, David Schmitz, Eric Lee, Craig Hanson, Neal Kosberg, Steve Theobald, Jim Angell, Todd Anderson. Fourth Row: Gary Schneider, David Allen, Bob Bulger, Steve Hinz, Brian Reinartz, Brad Tompkins, Scott Tompkins, Mike Kilen, Brett Bergene.

1983 Class C Champs

SILVER LAKE (CIRCLE EIGHT CONFERENCE)

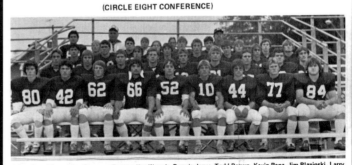

Front Row left to right: Duwayne Ranzau, Ken Wraspir, Durwin Jones, Todd Brown, Kevin Benz, Jim Blazinski, Larry Stifter, Mike Mickolichek, Bill Polchow. Second Row: Carl Cuhel, Bruce Stifter, Wade Stritesky, Jim Hemerick, Scott Tschimperle, Brian Blazinski, Jeff Mallak, Bob Yurek, Mike Ostlie. Third Row: Ervin Nowak, Tony Kadlec, Randy Zajicek, Todd Syvertson, Brad Blazinski, Mark Kosek, Dean Ruzicka, Bernie Koktan. Fourth Row: Bob Wraspir, Dave Hlavka, Todd Cuhel, Brian Wosmek, Brian Webb, Paul Stritesky, Brad Shamla, Craig Stibal. Fifth Row: Head Coach Buz Rumrill, Mgr. Randy Hatcher, Mgr. Gordy Chmielewski, Asst. Coach Dan Tschimperle.

1983 Class 9-Man Champs

Individual Record for Career Tackles (Solo & Assisted)

No.	Player	School	Year
587	Eric Stenzel	Mankato West	1996-99
579	Tim DeVlaeminck	Minneota	1986-89
553	Ted Greely	Kimball	1984-87

Individual Record for Sacks in a Career

No.	Player	School	Year
51	Nate Dwyer	Stillwater	1993-96
49	Steve Stauff	Cleveland	1995-97
34	Jarid Schoeck	Hancock	1990-91

1984: PREP BOWL III

George Thole's Stillwater Ponies claimed the Class AA title by scoring with less than two minutes left to stop Burnsville, 36-33. Stillwater's Jack Kindseth recovered a fumble in Burnsville's end-zone early in the first to put the Ponies up 6-0. The Braves answered just a few minutes later when Rob Boileson snagged a 20-yard pass from Kelly Ramswick to make it 6-6. Aaron Oden then ran in a one yarder, and later caught the two-point conversion to put Stillwater back up 14-6 early in the second. Burnsville's Fullback Jim Thornton added a one yarder of his own just two minutes after that, only to see Ponies' halfback Ken Dahlin run in a 12 yarder to get his squad back on top. Burnsville's Scott Branson answered less than three minutes later though, to make it 21-19 in favor of Stillwater. The Ponies scored the lone TD of the third quarter when Anderson scored on a two-yard plunge. The Braves once again responded in the crunch, this time taking the lead on a pair of fourth quarter rushing touchdowns by Ramswick and Scott Bloom. Down but not out, Stillwater rallied behind a bizarre safety with just 5:17 left in the game, followed by a dramatic one-yard touchdown run up the gut by Oden with just under a minute to go. Stillwater had made the improbable comeback, winning 36-33.

It was all Hutchinson in the Class A game, as the defending champions made quick work of the Centennial Chiefs. Andy Rostberg led the charge for the Tigers as he ran for one touchdown and threw two more to receiver Gene Ollrich. Running back Kyle Messner also added a pair of touchdown runs for good measure, as Hutch continued its amazing 27-game winning streak, which now extended over two years. (Rostberg was named as the state's co-player of the year, along with Cretin's quarterback Steve Walsh, who, after attending Miami, went on to star in the NFL with the Dallas Cowboys and Chicago Bears.)

Granite Falls upended Breckenridge in the Class B finals thanks to the running of Paul Bronson. Bronson first found the end-zone at 5:31 of the first quarter on a one yard plunge to put his squad up 7-0. Breckenridge tied the game at 7-7 after three, thanks to Doug Lorenz's 19-yard touchdown catch from quarterback Jay Ovsak. But Bronson iced it when he added his second score of the day with just 3:44 to play, this one a two yarder, as the Kilowatts held on for the 13-7 victory. It was Breckenridge's second runner-up finish in Class B in as many years.

The Harmony Cardinals beat the Glyndon-Felton Buffaloes for the Class C title in dramatic fashion. After a scoreless first, Harmony got touchdowns from both Mike Girolamo and Paul McKernan to go up 14-0. The Buffaloes answered right back in the third though, getting a pair of touchdowns from both John Dallman, a 19-yard scamper around end, and Brad Bolin, who took it in from the two. Then, with the score tied 14-14, QB Tim Burkholder hit a streaking Chris Martin on a 22-yard scoring strike midway through the final period to give the Cards the thrilling 20-14 victory.

In a rematch of the 1983 9-Man championship game, Norman County West held off a late rally from Silver Lake to bring home the hardware. Running back Brett Storsved scored two touchdowns in the first quarter to give his Panther's a quick 14-0 lead. Silver Lake answered when cornerback Todd Syvertson took a 27-yard fumble recovery into the back of the end-zone to make it 14-6. The Panthers pulled ahead in the third however, thanks to Jim Thompson's 38-yard TD pass from Darin Loe, followed by an untimely Silver Lake safety. Down, but not out, Silver Lake mounted a comeback highlighted by Tim Rumrill's 30-yard pass from Todd Chuhel, and another 15-yard TD pass by Thompson from Loe. But Storsved's third touchdown of the day, coupled with Brad Blazinski 15-yard pass from Scott Tschimperle with under two minutes to go, iced it for Norman County as they went on to beat Silver Lake, 37-20, thus ending the Lakeites' 26-game winning streak.

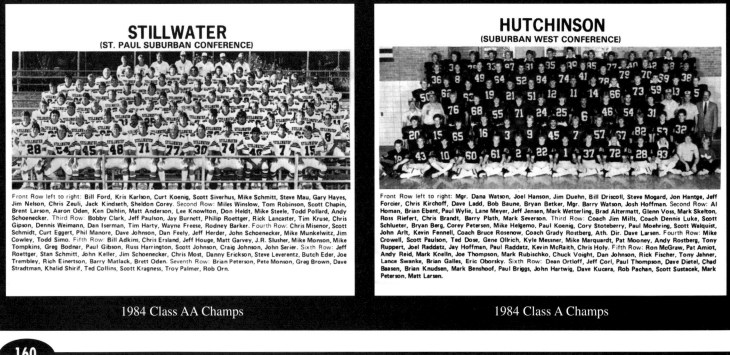

STILLWATER
(ST. PAUL SUBURBAN CONFERENCE)

Front Row left to right: Bill Ford, Kris Karlson, Curt Koenig, Scott Siverhus, Mike Schmitt, Steve Mau, Gary Hayes, Jim Nelson, Chris Zeuli, Jack Kindseth, Sheldon Corey. Second Row: Miles Winslow, Tom Robinson, Scott Chapin, Brent Larson, Aaron Oden, Ken Dahlin, Matt Anderson, Lee Knowlton, Don Heldt, Mike Steele, Todd Pollard, Andy Schoenecker. Third Row: Bobby Clark, Jeff Paulson, Jay Burnett, Philip Roettger, Rick Lancaster, Tim Kruse, Chris Gipson, Dennis Weimann, Dan Iserman, Tim Harty, Wayne Freese, Rodney Barker. Fourth Row: Chris Misenor, Scott Schmidt, Curt Eggert, Phil Manore, Dave Johnson, Dan Feely, Jeff Herder, John Schoenecker, Mike Munkelwitz, Jim Cowley, Todd Simo. Fifth Row: Bill Adkins, Chris Ersland, Jeff Houge, Matt Garvey, J.R. Slusher, Mike Monson, Mike Tompkins, Greg Bodnar, Paul Gibson, Russ Harrington, Scott Johnson, Craig Johnson, John Serier. Sixth Row: Jeff Roettger, Stan Schmitt, John Keller, Jim Schoenecker, Chris Most, Danny Erickson, Steve Leverentz, Butch Eder, Joe Trembley, Rich Einertson, Barry Matlack, Brett Oden. Seventh Row: Brian Peterson, Pete Monson, Greg Brown, Dave Stradtman, Khalid Shirif, Ted Collins, Scott Kragness, Troy Palmer, Rob Orn.

1984 Class AA Champs

HUTCHINSON
(SUBURBAN WEST CONFERENCE)

Front Row left to right: Mgr. Dana Watson, Joel Hanson, Jim Duehn, Bill Driscoll, Steve Mogard, Jon Hantge, Jeff Forcier, Chris Kirchoff, Dave Ladd, Bob Baune, Bryan Betker, Mgr. Barry Watson, Josh Hoffman. Second Row: Al Homan, Brian Ebent, Paul Wylie, Lane Meyer, Jeff Jensen, Mark Wetterling, Brad Altermatt, Glenn Voss, Mark Skelton, Ross Riefert, Chris Brandt, Barry Plath, Mark Severson. Third Row: Coach Jim Mills, Coach Dennis Luke, Scott Schlueter, Bryan Berg, Corey Petersen, Mike Helgemo, Paul Koenig, Cory Stoteberry, Paul Moehring, Scott Walquist, John Arlt, Kevin Fennell, Coach Bruce Rosenow, Coach Grady Rostberg, Ath. Dir. Dave Larsen. Fourth Row: Mike Crowell, Scott Paulson, Ted Dose, Gene Ollrich, Kyle Messner, Mike Marquardt, Pat Mooney, Andy Rostberg, Tony Ruppert, Joel Raddatz, Jay Hoffman, Paul Raddatz, Kevin McRaith, Chris Holy. Fifth Row: Ron McGraw, Pat Amiot, Andy Reid, Mark Koelln, Joe Thompson, Mark Rubischko, Chuck Voight, Dan Johnson, Rick Fischer, Tony Jahner, Lance Swanke, Brian Galles, Eric Oborsky. Sixth Row: Dean Ortloff, Jeff Corl, Paul Thompson, Dave Dietel, Chad Baasen, Brian Knudsen, Mark Benshoof, Paul Briggs, John Hartwig, Dave Kucera, Rob Pachan, Scott Sustacek, Mark Peterson, Matt Larsen.

1984 Class A Champs

GRANITE FALLS

Front Row left to right: Ass't. Coach Mike Flynn, Matt West, Paul Buchholz, John Berends, Jeff Patten, Derek Sebey, Don Geier, Bernie Torgerson, Eric Freitag, Knute Anderson, Kelly Timm, Mike Ashburn, Todd Tholkes, John Raney, Mgr. Chad Feldman, Mgr. Joshua Bakker. Second Row: David Hinz, Robbi Peterson, Paul Bronson, Karl Anderson, Bob Voller, Brian Livingood, Curt Markgraf, Tom Ladner, Bob Kulesa, Joe Gordon, Rick Enstad, Chris Steenson. Third Row: Head Coach Dave Brokke, Terry Fagen, Todd Rikke, Steve Rupp, John Wacholz, Troy Zieske, Dave McCoss, Mike O'Toole, Jeff Lalim, Dave Nielsen, Randy Lewison, Matt Baer, James Ross, Kurt Thorstad, Ass't. Coach Sid Long, Brad Odegard, Ass't. Coach Ryan Bremmer. Fourth Row: Ass't. Coach Dean Baldry, Todd Hoseck, Jon Tjosvold, Bob Lundin, Dean Smith, Jon Thoma, Chris Schuler, Dave Nordaune, Jim Stavne, Jeff Enstad, Keith Raney, Tom Benson, Ron Iverson, Brett Opdahl, Dave Bloomquist, Jeff Giese.

1984 Class B Champs

HARMONY

Front Row left to right: Casey Martin, Dave Garness, Rich Bigalk, Tom Roberts, Travis Wilford, Chris Pfremmer, Dean Johns, Jay Wangen, Jeff Nagel, Mgrs. Kory Bigalk, Jeff Gunderson, Beau Elston, Jake Hines. Second Row: Tom Young, Toby Jacobson, Scott Mandelko, Kevin Sikkink, Tom Dennstedt, Dan Miller, Dean Torgerson, Jeff Grebin, Tom Hutton, Terry Kraling, Tracie Erickson. Third Row: Chris Martin, Rob Lange, Kendall Bigalk, Mike Girolamo, Brian Funke, Paul McKernan, Matt Jarland, Mike Sikkink, Tim Burkholder, Bob Casterton, Troy Kraling, Craig Hanson.

1984 Class C Champs

1985: PREP BOWL IV

The undefeated Apple Valley Eagles got upset in the Class AA title game by the Burnsville Braves, thanks in large part to the performance of Braves quarterback Matt Larson, who passed for a pair of touchdowns and a Prep Bowl record of 250 yards. Burnsville's Rich Ingersoll opened the scoring when he capped off an 80-yard scoring drive by nabbing a 14-yard pass from Larson with just 14 seconds remaining in the first quarter. Apple Valley took the lead at 7-6 in the second thanks to Walter Davis' three yard run up the gut. Burnsville then regained the lead on Larson's second score of the day, an 11-yard TD around the right end. The fourth quarter was a wild one, as both teams exchanged touchdowns. Burnsville struck first behind Jim Thornton's one yard plunge, followed by Apple Valley's Chris San Agustin, who took an 87-yard reverse to pay dirt. The Braves responded though, this time with Tom Highley's nine yard pass from Matt Larson, only to see the Eagles rally behind San Agustin's one yard TD run late in the game. It was too little too late though as Burnsville held on to beat Apple Valley, 27-21.

NORMAN COUNTY WEST

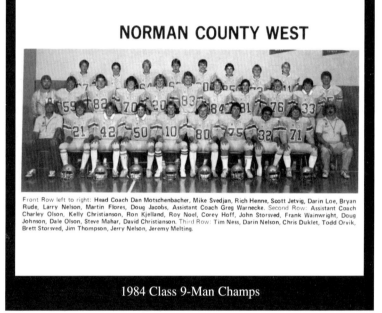

Front Row left to right: Head Coach Dan Motschenbacher, Mike Svedjan, Rich Henne, Scott Jetvig, Darin Loe, Bryan Rude, Larry Nelson, Martin Flores, Doug Jacobs, Assistant Coach Greg Warnecke. Second Row: Assistant Coach Charley Olson, Kelly Christianson, Roy Noel, Corey Hoff, John Storsved, Frank Wainwright, Doug Johnson, Dale Olson, Steve Mahar, David Christianson. Third Row: Tim Ness, Darin Nelson, Chris Duklet, Todd Orvik, Brett Storsved, Jim Thompson, Jerry Nelson, Jeremy Melting.

1984 Class 9-Man Champs

The Class A championship game was a dramatic affair between Mora and New Prague. The Trojans of New Prague got on the board first behind Eric Dorzinski's 17-yard run at 4:31 of the first. The Mustangs answered just a minute later behind Dave Epsen's five-yard pass from Chuck Masloski. Masloski then put his squad up 12-6 on a one yard sneak up the middle. New Prague rallied back though, first on a Steve Tupy 27-yard field goal early in the fourth, and then on Brad Biehn's electrifying 74-yard punt return with under a minute to go, as the Trojans won in style, 16-12. Said Biehn after the game: "It's made my whole life worthwhile..."

Jackson, despite turning the ball over five times, held off a late rally by Mahnomen to take the Class B title. The Indians got on the board first in this one thanks to Frank Burdick's 71-yard TD run. Jackson then scored a couple of quick ones in the second to go up 14-7. Leading the charge for the Blue Jays were Bruce Johnson, who tallied on a seven yard run, and Jeffrey Brown, who found the end zone from 18-yards out. Mahnomen's Jeff Large tied it back up on his three yard run, only to see Jackson go up for good on a pair of scores in the third. John Lilleberg took a 29-yard pass from future Minnesota Twins draftee Wade Wacker at 7:04 and then Jeffrey Brown added his second of the day with a 29-yard TD run off tackle. The Indians, who made it 26-20 after Jeff Large scored his second of the day from a yard out, threatened to score again late in the game but were stopped when Jackson intercepted a pass in the last minute to end it.

Glyndon-Felton, which fell to Harmony in the 1984 Prep Bowl title game, came back with a vengeance in 1985, this time waxing Zumbrota in the Class C finals. The Buffaloes erupted to score 18 points in the second quarter alone as they went on to claim the school's first-ever championship. Running back Tom Moll scored two touchdowns and set a Prep Bowl rushing record of 170 yards, while Quarterback Wayne LePard completed 10 of 16 passes, and scored one TD — an eight yarder to Brad Pake. For Pake, it was his third touchdown of the game, as the Bison rumbled to a 38-14 victory.

The 9-Man contest was also a blow-out as Westbrook pounded the defending champs from Norman County West by the final of 45-18. Norman County West took an early lead on Brett Storsved's two yard TD run, only to see the Wildcats roar back for 20-point second and 16-point third quarters. Leading the Wildcat charge was David Weiske, who scored four touchdowns on the afternoon and ran for more than 100 yards.

BURNSVILLE
(SECTION SIX CHAMPION)

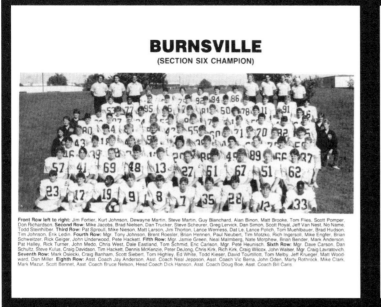

Front Row left to right: Jim Fortier, Kurt Johnson, Dewayne Martin, Steve Martin, Guy Blanchard, Alan Binon, Matt Brooke, Tom Flies, Scott Pomper, Don Richardson. **Second Row:** Mike Jacobs, Brad Nielsen, Dan Trucker, Steve Scheurer, Greg Lervick, Dan Simon, Scott Royal, Jeff Van Nest, No Name, Todd Steinhilber. **Third Row:** Pat Sproull, Mike Nieson, Matt Larson, Jim Thorton, Lance Werness, Dat Le, Lance Polich, Tom Muehlbauer, Brad Hudson, Tim Johnson, Erik Ledin. **Fourth Row:** Mgr. Tony Johnson, Brent Roesler, Brian Hennen, Paul Neubert, Tim Motzko, Rich Ingersoll, Mike Engfer, Brian Schweitzer, Rick Geiger, John Underwood, Pete Hackett. **Fifth Row:** Mgr. Jamie Green, Neal Malmberg, Nate Morphew, Brian Bender, Mark Anderson, Pat Halley, Rick Turner, John Medo, Chris West, Dale Eastland, Tom Schmid, Eric Carlson, Mgr. Pete Heunisch. **Sixth Row:** Mgr. Dave Carson, Dan Schultz, Steve Kulus, Craig Davidson, Tim Hackett, Dennis McKenzie, Peter DeJong, Chris Kirk, Rich Kirk, Craig Wilcox, John Walser, Mgr. Craig Lavratovich. **Seventh Row:** Mark Osiecki, Craig Banham, Scott Siebert, Tom Highley, Ed White, Todd Kieser, David Tourtillott, Tom Melby, Jeff Krueger, Matt Woodward, Dan Miller. **Eighth Row:** Asst. Coach Jay Anderson, Asst. Coach Neal Jeppson, Asst. Coach Vic Berra, John Oden, Marty Rothrock, Mike Clark, Mark Mazur, Scott Bennet, Asst. Coach Bruce Nelson, Head Coach Dick Hanson, Asst. Coach Doug Boe, Asst. Coach Bill Caris.

1985 Class AA Champs

NEW PRAGUE
(SECTION ONE CHAMPION)

Front Row left to right: Joel Edwards, Chris Becker, Keith Krouse, Troy Carlson, Curt Zweber, Dave Gregory, Dave Wann, John Nelson, Tim Carlson, Brian Bartzal, Dan Wermerskirchen, Mike Minar, Scott Jirik, Josh Howe, Craig Gregor, Dan Pint, Steve Schmitz, Al Pavek. **Second Row:** Dean Simon, Brad Biehn, Eric Dorzinski, Thom O'Neill, Jon Pesta, Jay Fredrich, DuWayne Bastyr, Craig Bartyzal, Nate Clyde, Sean O'Neill, Mark Bortnem, Phil Chromy, Jeff Chromy, Dan Pomye, Steve Tupy. **Third Row:** Stats - Angie Thomas, Michelle Chant, Tammy Jirek, Julie Novak, Tom Orr, Kevin Kallal, Dean Seymour, Paul Amundson, Matt Olson, Rob Schoenbauer. **Fourth Row:** Jeff Hennes, Mark Turek, Greg DeGross, Jeff Warmka, Steve Rau, Ken Turek, Asst. Coach Steve Lang, Asst. Coach Steve Collins, Head Coach Dan O'Brien, Asst. Coach Ron Gunderson, Dan Geisen, Rawlin Peulen, Darrel Wolf, Brad Bartyzl, Brian Frye, Dave Meger, Owen Sullivan Kurt Sticha.

1985 Class A Champs

JACKSON
(SECTION TWO CHAMPION)

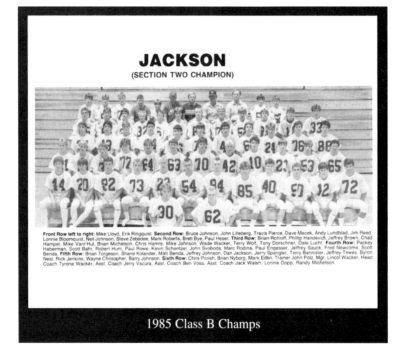

Front Row left to right: Mike Lloyd, Erik Ringquist. **Second Row:** Bruce Johnson, John Lilleberg, Travis Pierce, Dave Macek, Andy Lundblad, Jim Reed, Lonnie Bloomquist, Neil Johnson, Steve Zebedee, Mark Roberts, Brett Bye, Paul Heser. **Third Row:** Brian Rohloff, Phillip Handevidt, Jeffrey Brown, Chad Hampel, Mike Van't Hul, Brian Michelson, Chris Hamre, Mike Johnson, Wade Wacker, Terry Wolf, Tony Dorschner, Dale Lucht. **Fourth Row:** Packey Haberman, Scott Bahr, Robert Hunt, Paul Rowe, Kevin Schentzel, John Svoboda, Marc Rodina, Paul Engesser, Jeffrey Sauck, Fred Newcome, Scott Benda. **Fifth Row:** Brian Torgeson, Shane Kolander, Matt Benda, Jeffrey Johnson, Dan Jackson, Jerry Spangler, Terry Bannister, Jeffrey Tewes, Byron Neal, Rick Jenkins, Wayne Chrisopher, Barry Johnson. **Sixth Row:** Chris Porish, Brian Nyborg, Mark Edlin, Trainer John Polz, Mgr. Lincol Wacker, Head Coach Tyrone Wacker, Asst. Coach Jerry Vscura, Asst. Coach Ben Voss, Asst. Coach Jack Walsh, Lonnie Dopp, Randy Michelson.

1985 Class B Champs

GLYNDON-FELTON
(SECTION EIGHT CHAMPION)

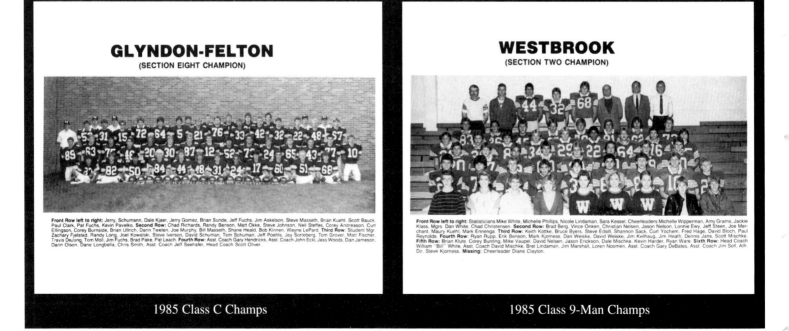

Front Row left to right: Jerry, Schumann, Dale Kjaer, Jerry Gomez, Brian Sunde, Jeff Fuchs, Jim Askelson, Steve Masseth, Brian Kuehl, Scott Bauck, Paul Clark, Pat Fuchs, Kevin Pavelko. **Second Row:** Chad Richards, Randy Benson, Matt Okke, Steve Johnson, Neil Stefles, Corey Andreason, Curt Ellingson, Corey Burnside, Brian Ullrich, Darin Tweten, Joe Murphy, Bill Masseth, Shane Heald, Bob Kinnen, Wayne LePard. **Third Row:** Student Mgr. Zachary Fjelstad, Randy Long, Joel Kowalski, Steve Iverson, David Schuman, Tom Schuman, Jeff Poehls, Jay Sorteberg, Tom Grover, Matt Fischer, Travis DeJong, Tom Moll, Jim Fuchs, Brad Pake, Pat Leach. **Fourth Row:** Asst. Coach Gary Hendricks, Asst. Coach John Eckl, Jess Woods, Dan Jameson, Darin Olson, Dane Longbella, Chris Smith, Asst. Coach Jeff Seehafer, Head Coach Scott Oliver.

1985 Class C Champs

WESTBROOK
(SECTION TWO CHAMPION)

Front Row left to right: Statisticians Mike White, Michelle Phillips, Nicole Lindaman, Sara Kessel, Cheerleaders Michelle Wipperman, Amy Grams, Jackie Klass, Mgrs. Dan White, Chad Christensen. **Second Row:** Brad Berg, Vince Onken, Christian Nelsen, Jason Nelson, Lonnie Ewy, Jeff Steen, Joe Merchant, Maury Kuehl, Mark Ennenga. **Third Row:** Keith Kottke, Bruce Byers, Steve Edsill, Shannon Sack, Curt Yochem, Fred Hage, David Bloch, Paul Reynolds. **Fourth Row:** Ryan Rupp, Erik Benson, Mark Kjorness, Dan Weiske, David Weiske, Jim Kvilhaug, Jim Heath, Dennis Jans, Scott Mischke. **Fifth Row:** Brian Klute, Corey Bunting, Mike Vaupel, David Nelsen, Jason Erickson, Dale Mischke, Kevin Harder, Ryan Ware. **Sixth Row:** Head Coach William "Bill" White, Asst. Coach David Mischke, Bret Lindaman, Jim Marshall, Loren Noomen, Asst. Coach Gary DeBates, Asst. Coach Jim Soll, Ath. Dir. Steve Kjorness. **Missing:** Cheerleader Diane Clayton.

1985 Class 9-Man Champs

1986: PREP BOWL V

The MSHSL once again changed the playoff format in 1986, going instead with a new expanded system that included 294 of the state's 423 programs. The new system was designed to give more teams throughout the state an opportunity to have a shot at making it into the post-season.

Apple Valley came out of the gates swinging in the Class AA title game, scoring the first three touchdowns of the day in the game's first 10 minutes. It got started when Jason Skapyak recovered a blocked punt in the end-zone, followed by a pair of 60+ yard touchdown runs by both Chris San Agustin and John Tetraull. Osseo got on the board late in the second thanks to Chad Mortenson's 61-yard pass from Quarterback Robb Lange, but that was all the firepower that the Orioles could muster. The Eagles added a couple more scores from Mark Perry, who caught a 28-yard pass from John Tetrault, and San Agustin, who tallied his second of the day by scoring from 58 yards out. The Eagles soared to a 35-6 victory.

Cambridge blanked Stewartville for the Class A title, 24-0, thanks to a trio of touchdowns from quarterback Wade Labatte. In addition to rushing one in from the one-yard-line, he also connected with Brett Tuma on a 32-yarder in the first, and then again to Jeremy Wicht on a five-yard slant in the fourth. (Wicht also ran for 153 yards on the day.) Peter Larkin added a 26-yard field goal for good measure, as the Blue Jackets rolled to victory.

Watertown-Mayer beat up on Granite Falls, 29-6, to capture the Class B title. Jason Hahn's 17-yard TD run in the first opened the scoring, while Darren Schuler's 57-yard pass from Bruce Wandersee at the 5:58 mark of the second made it 14-0. Rick Meyer's seven-yard TD in the third got Granite Falls close, but after Jim King's three-yard touchdown plunge, followed by Chris Brown's 66-yard pass interception return, this one was over.

Minneota buried Sherburn-Dunnell in the Class C title game, despite being up by only three points midway through the second quarter. Minneota Quarterback Chris Meidt, son of head coach Gerhard Meidt, passed for a record 259 yards and three touchdowns, and kicker Todd Swedzinske set a prep bowl record with a 38-yard field goal. Also figuring into the mix were Jim Strangman, who tallied three touchdown runs, and Bob DeSutter, who caught two TDs from Meidt. Jeff Jacobsen, Ryan Lunn and Nate Klima all scored for Sherburn, but it was too little too late as the Vikings went on to beat the Raiders, 42-19.

It was yet another blowout in the 9-Man finals as well, with Argyle taking out Silver Lake 32-7. Tom Durand scored three touchdowns that morning on runs of 31, 10, and 10 yards respectively. Silver Lake's lone score came on Dave Hlavka's 11-yard run in the first quarter. After Kelly Durand and Preston Stoltman each added a pair for good measure, it was all but over, as Argyle rolled to victory.

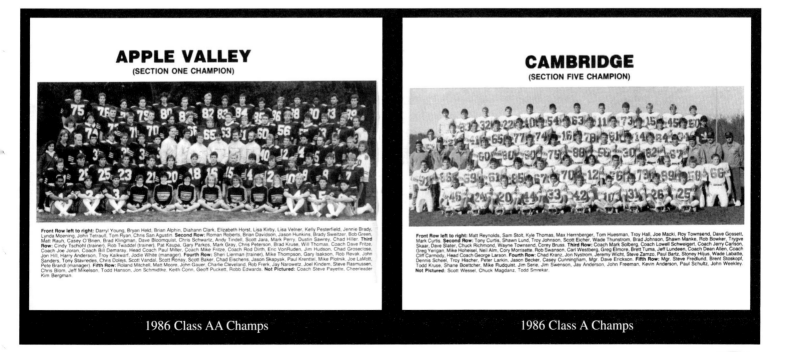

APPLE VALLEY
(SECTION ONE CHAMPION)

Front Row left to right: Darryl Young, Bryan Held, Brian Alphin, Diahann Clark, Elizabeth Horst, Lisa Kirby, Lisa Velner, Kelly Pesterfield, Jennie Brady, Lynda Moening, John Tetrault, Tom Ryan, Chris San Agustin. Second Row: Roman Roberts, Brian Davidson, Jason Hunkins, Brady Sweitzer, Bob Green, Matt Rauh, Casey O'Brien, Brad Klingman, Dave Bloomquist, Chris Schwartz, Andy Tindell, Scott Jara, Mark Perry, Dustin Sawrey, Chad Hiller. Third Row: Cindy Tschohl (trainer), Rob Twaddel (trainer), Pat Kaupa, Gary Parkos, Mark Gray, Chris Peterson, Brad Kruse, Will Thomas, Coach Dave Fritze, Coach Joe Joran, Coach Bill Demaray, Head Coach Paul Miller, Coach Mike Fritze, Coach Rod Dirth, Eric VonRuden, Jim Hudson, Chad Groseclose, Jon Hill, Harry Anderson, Troy Kalkwarf, Jodie White (manager). Fourth Row: Sheri Lierman (trainer), Mike Thompson, Gary Isakson, Rob Revak, John Sanders, Tony Stavredes, Chris Doleis, Scott Vandal, Scott Ronay, Scott Baker, Chad Eischens, Jason Skapyak, Paul Krentel, Mike Plotnik, Joe LaMott, Pete Brandl (manager). Fifth Row: Roland Mitchell, Matt Moore, John Gauer, Charlie Cleveland, Rob Frerk, Jay Narowetz, Joel Kindem, Steve Rasmussen, Chris Blom, Jeff Mikelson, Todd Hanson, Jon Schmidtke, Keith Conn, Geoff Puckett, Robb Edwards. Not Pictured: Coach Steve Payette, Cheerleader Kim Bergman.

1986 Class AA Champs

CAMBRIDGE
(SECTION FIVE CHAMPION)

Front Row left to right: Matt Reynolds, Sam Stolt, Kyle Thomas, Max Herrnberger, Tom Huesman, Troy Hall, Joe Macki, Roy Townsend, Dave Gossett, Mark Curtis. Second Row: Tony Curtis, Shawn Lund, Troy Johnson, Scott Eicher, Wade Thunstrom, Brad Johnson, Shawn Manke, Rob Bowker, Trygve Skaar, Dave Slater, Chuck Richmond, Wayne Townsend, Corey Bruss. Third Row: Coach Mark Solberg, Coach Lowell Schweigert, Coach Jerry Carlson, Greg Yerigan, Mike Hohensel, Neil Alm, Cory Morrisette, Rob Swanson, Carl Westberg, Greg Elmore, Brett Tuma, Jeff Lundeen, Coach Dean Allen, Coach Cliff Carmody, Head Coach George Larson. Fourth Row: Chad Kranz, Jon Nystrom, Jeremy Wicht, Steve Zamzo, Paul Bartz, Stoney Hiljus, Wade Labatte, Dennis Scheel, Troy Hischer, Peter Larkin, Jason Becker, Casey Cunningham, Mgr. Dave Erickson. Fifth Row: Mgr. Steve Fredlund, Brent Stoskopf, Todd Kruse, Shane Boettcher, Mike Rudquist, Jim Serie, Jim Swenson, Jay Anderson, John Freeman, Kevin Anderson, Paul Schultz, John Weekley. Not Pictured: Scott Wessel, Chuck Magdanz, Todd Smrekar.

1986 Class A Champs

WATERTOWN-MAYER
(SECTION FIVE CHAMPION)

Front Row left to right: Darren Olson, Jason Hahn, Joe Swartzer, Tony Seck, Jim King, Darren Schuler, Ron Stern, Rob Enos, Dan Helmbrecht, Chris Kadrie. Second Row: Jeff Berhow, Rick Crawford, Todd Jopp, Bruce Wandersee, Pat Daggett, Brent Theisen, Jason Thompson, Tim Schrupp, Pete Keizenberg, Tim McDonald. Third Row: Steve Ziermann, Chris Brown, Rick Stern, Russ Gatfon, Ben Schmit, Joel Clark, Jerry Hohn, Daryl Helmbrecht, Kevin Pollock, Neil Singleton. Fourth Row: Rick Schmidt, Shane Tietz, Brian Weege, Joe Janikula, Greg Kappes, Tim Schug, Todd Duske, Jon Lueck, Jason Widmer, David Younk. Fifth Row: Dan Gesinger, Jason Wandersee, Mike Myers, Steve Duske, Ben Kent, Jeff Thompson, Craig Guetzkow, Mike Burns, Darren Tesch, Scott Schmidt, Noah Mueller. Sixth Row: Coaches Dennis Baldus, Neal Roth, Phil Hanson, Jim Younk. Not Pictured: Mike O'Connell, Pat Burns, Charles Reineke, Mike Erickson, Todd Line.

1986 Class B Champs

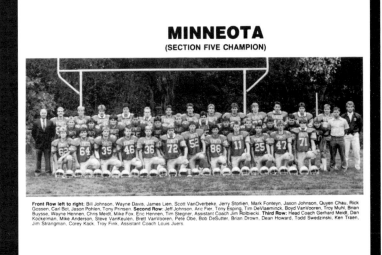

MINNEOTA
(SECTION FIVE CHAMPION)

Front Row left to right: Bill Johnson, Wayne Davis, James Lien, Scott VanOverbeke, Jerry Storlien, Mark Fonteyn, Jason Johnson, Quyen Chau, Rick Gossen, Carl Bot, Jason Pohlen, Tony Prinsen. Second Row: Jeff Johnson, Aric Fier, Tony Esping, Tim DeVlaeminck, Boyd VanVooren, Troy Muhl, Brian Buytsse, Wayne Hennen, Chris Meidt, Mike Fox, Eric Hennen, Tim Stegner, Assistant Coach Jim Rolbiecki. Third Row: Head Coach Gerhard Meidt, Dan Kockelman, Mike Anderson, Steve VanKeulen, Brett VanVooren, Pete Obe, Bob DeSutter, Brian Drown, Dean Howard, Todd Swedzinski, Ken Traen, Jim Strangman, Corey Kack, Troy Fink, Assistant Coach Louis Juers.

1986 Class C Champs

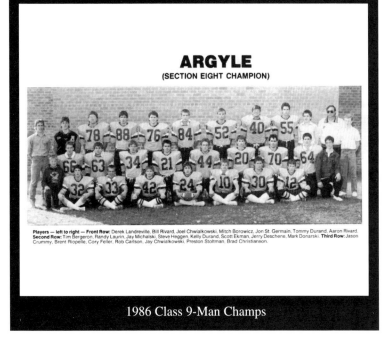

ARGYLE
(SECTION EIGHT CHAMPION)

Players — left to right — Front Row: Derek Landreville, Bill Rivard, Joel Chwialkowski, Mitch Borowicz, Jon St. Germain, Tommy Durand, Aaron Rivard. Second Row: Tim Bergeron, Randy Laurin, Jay Michalski, Steve Heggen, Kelly Durand, Scott Ekman, Jerry Deschene, Mark Donarski. Third Row: Jason Crummy, Brent Riopelle, Cory Feller, Rob Carlson, Jay Chwialkowski, Preston Stoltman, Brad Christianson.

1986 Class 9-Man Champs

1987: PREP BOWL VI

By 1987 there were 464 Minnesota high schools competing in football. Five of those entered the Prep Bowl with undefeated records, and for the first time since 1977, all five won championships.

Moorhead and Winona got together for the Class AA title clash, with the Spuds' defense being the difference. Moorhead Receiver Jay Cerise got the Spuds on the board first when he capped off a 91-yard scoring drive by nabbing a 45-yard pass from Rick Eidsness midway through the first. Winona answered with Paul Klinger's 10-yard run, only to see the Spud's defense take over — limiting Winona to just 39 total yards in the final two quarters. Moorhead kicker Greg Reinhiller then booted a pair of 35 and 32-yard field goals in the second half to preserve the 13-7 win.

Defending champion Cambridge fended off a late rally from Lakeville to win their second straight Class A crown. Kicker Peter Larkin got the Blue Jackets on the board first when he nailed a 20-yarder at the 6:14 mark of the first. John Nystrom then grabbed a 25-yard pass from QB Wade Labatte to make it 10-0 after one. After a Lakeville safety, a Casey Cunningham five yard touchdown run, and another Larkin field goal, Cambridge found themselves up 21-0 going into the fourth quarter. That's when the Panthers mounted their comeback. Lance Wolkow capped off a 70-yard scoring drive when he caught a 10-yard TD pass from Jay Johnson, followed by Todd Dwire's one yard plunge to make it 21-14 with two minutes to go. Lakeville then got the ball back and was driving deep when the bottom fell out. Cambridge's Jeremy Wicht, who ran for 110 yards on the day, intercepted a Jay Johnson pass and returned it 56 yards for a TD, as the Bluejackets posted their 26th successive victory.

Granite Falls completed their 14-0 campaign by defeating Ely, 43-20, in the Class B title tilt. All-state tight end Dave Anderson caught three touchdown passes from quarterback Tony Ladner and running back Rick Meyer added a pair of TD runs for the winning Kilowatts. Lance Ronn, Bill Muhvich and John Kastelic each tallied for the Ely Timberwolves, who came up short in the end.

Minneota defeated Grand Meadow, 27-7, to win their second straight Class C title behind the passing of Quarterback Chris Meidt. Meidt completed 26 of 41 passes for 262 yards and three touchdowns (to receivers Wayne Hennen, Mike Fox and Jeff Johnson), to complete his prep career as the nation's career record-holder in passing attempts (1,122) and completions (646), and even moved into second in all-time passing yards with 8,533. In addition, he became the first prep player in the US to throw 100 career touchdown passes. Ed Simes' two yard touchdown was Grand Meadow's only score on a day that belonged to the Vikings.

Silver Lake defeated Verndale, 30-14, for the 9-Man title to complete their perfect 14-0 season. Lakeites Quarterback Jeff Monahan passed for one touchdown and ran for another, while Tim Rumrill ran for one TD and recovered a fumble in the end-zone for another. Verndale got its two touchdowns from Scott Anderson, who found the back of the end-zone from both 55 and 32 yards out.

MOORHEAD
(SECTION SEVEN CHAMPION)

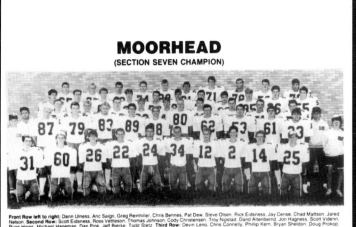

Front Row left to right: Darin Ulness, Aric Saign, Greg Reinhiller, Chris Bennes, Pat Dew, Steve Olsen, Rick Eidsness, Jay Cerise, Chad Mattson, Jared Nelson. Second Row: Scott Eidsness, Ross Vettleson, Thomas Johnson, Cody Christensen, Troy Nipstad, Dand Altenbernd, Jon Hagness, Scott Videnn, Ryan Hines, Michael Hageman, Dan Pink, Jeff Bjerke, Todd Stetz. Third Row: Devin Leno, Chris Connelly, Phillip Kern, Bryan Sheldon, Doug Prokop, Kyle Schiefert, Chad Sundem, Jeffrey Ohe, Reggie Carney, Scott Bradsteen. Fourth Row: Brett Mortenson, Scott Liebelt, Mark Mathiason, Steve Asheim, Scott Gauthier, Matt Gilbertson, Mario Dalen, Steve Nichols, Dave Suppes, Joey Nelson, Phil Larson. Fifth Row: Steve Collins, Chad Peterson, Gratn Harrington, Scott Glas, James Anderson, Jeff Bergman, Lance Larson, Chris Olson, Gary Sanden, Scott Bednarz.

1987 Class AA Champs

CAMBRIDGE
(SECTION FIVE CHAMPION)

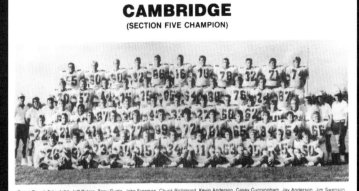

Front Row left to right: Jeff Peters, Tony Curtis, John Freeman, Chuck Richmond, Kevin Anderson, Casey Cunningham, Jay Anderson, Jim Swenson, Todd Kruse, Paul Schultz, John Weekley. Second Row: Shane Boettcher, Jon Nystrom, Jeremy Wicht, Pete Larkin, Paul Bartz, Stoney Hiljus, Chuck Magdanz, Troy Hischer, Steve Zamzo, Jason Becker, Jim Sene, Corey Bruss. Third Row: Coach Lowell Schweigert, Coach Mark Solberg, Coach Jerry Carlson, Mgr. Todd Peterson, Reynold Balicao, Dan Mettling, Gary Carlson, Matt Curtis, George Zajac, Brandt Lindgren, Jon Westover, Reed Wilmert. Fourth Row: Peter Theis, Marty Mix, Chris Lazarz, Jeremy Barry Bjergo, Mgr. Andy Palmquist, Coach Bob Salo, Coach Dean Allen, Coach George Larson, Fourth Row: Peter Theis, Marty Mix, Chris Lazarz, Jeremy Swenson, Eric Nystrom, Troy Leeb, Cory Melland, Scott Myren, Jim Hanson, Dan Linders, Ty Halgrimson. Fifth Row: Todd Smrekar, Tim Blakesley, Casey Laase, Bob Soderburg, Trent Brown, Wade Labatte, Loren Schroeder, Dennis Scheel, Tony Peterson, Bill Binger, Reed Hermanson.

1987 Class A Champs

GRANITE FALLS
(SECTION FOUR CHAMPION)

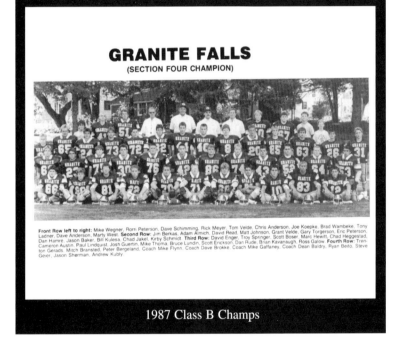

Front Row left to right: Mike Wegner, Rorri Peterson, Dave Schimming, Rick Meyer, Tom Velde, Chris Anderson, Joe Koepke, Brad Wambeke, Tony Ladner, Dave Anderson, Marty West. Second Row: Jim Berkas, Adam Almich, David Read, Matt Johnson, Grant Velde, Gary Torgerson, Eric Peterson, Dan Hamre, Jason Baker, Bill Kulesa, Chad Jakel, Kirby Schmidt. Third Row: David Enger, Troy Springer, Scott Boser, Marc Hewitt, Chad Heggestad, Cameron Austin, Paul Lindquist, Josh Guertin, Mike Thoma, Bruce Lundin, Scott Erickson, Dan Rude, Brian Kavanaugh, Ross Galow. Fourth Row: Trenton Gerads, Mitch Bransted, Peter Bergeland, Coach Mike Flynn, Coach Dave Brokke, Coach Mike Gaffaney, Coach Dean Baldry, Ryan Bello, Steve Geier, Jason Sherman, Andrew Kubly.

1987 Class B Champs

MINNEOTA
(SECTION FIVE CHAMPION)

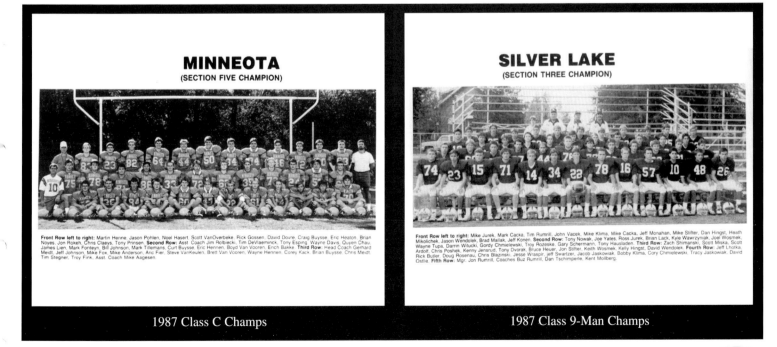

Front Row left to right: Martin Henne, Jason Pohlen, Noel Hasert, Scott VanOverbeke, Rick Gossen, David Dovre, Craig Buysse, Eric Heaton, Brian Noyes, Jon Rokeh, Chris Claeys, Tony Prinsen. Second Row: Asst. Coach Jim Rolbiecki, Tim DeVlaeminck, Tony Esping, Wayne Davis, Quyen Chau, James Lien, Mark Fonteyn, Bill Johnson, Mark Tillemans, Curt Buysse, Eric Hennen, Boyd Van Vooren, Erich Bakke. Third Row: Head Coach Gerhard Meidt, Jeff Johnson, Mike Fox, Mike Anderson, Aric Fier, Steve VanKeulen, Brett Van Vooren, Wayne Hennen, Corey Kack, Brian Buysse, Chris Meidt, Tim Stegner, Troy Fink, Asst. Coach Mike Aagesen.

1987 Class C Champs

SILVER LAKE
(SECTION THREE CHAMPION)

Front Row left to right: Mike Jurek, Mark Cacka, Tim Rumrill, John Vacek, Mike Klima, Mike Cacka, Jeff Monahan, Mike Stifter, Dan Hingst, Heath Mikolichek, Jason Wendolek, Brad Mallak, Jeff Konen. Second Row: Tony Nowak, Joe Yates, Ross Jurek, Brian Lack, Kyle Wawrzyniak, Joel Wosmek, Wayne Tupa, Darrin Witucki, Gordy Chmielewski, Troy Rozeske, Gary Schermann, Tony Hausladen. Third Row: Zach Shimanski, Scott Miska, Scott Ardolf, Chris Poshek, Kenny Jensrud, Tony Dvorak, Bruce Heuer, Jon Stifter, Keith Wosmek, Kelly Hingst, David Wendolek. Fourth Row: Jeff Lhotka, Rick Butler, Doug Rosenau, Chris Blazinski, Jesse Wrasplir, Jeff Swartzer, Jacob Jaskowiak, Bobby Klima, Cory Chmielewski, Tracy Jaskowiak, David Ostlie. Fifth Row: Mgr. Jon Rumrill, Coaches Buz Rumrill, Dan Tschimperle, Kent Mollberg.

1987 Class 9-Man Champs

1988: PREP BOWL VII

The most exciting game was saved for last at Prep Bowl VII, with Class AA Blaine hanging on to edge out Cretin-Derham Hall, 25-24, when it ran a dramatic two-point conversion with just two seconds left in the game. The Raiders took the opening drive 75-yards on 13 plays, and scored when Ted Johnson took a one yarder up the gut. Blaine then stormed back to tie it on Jason Wiehle's 8-yard TD around the right end. Cretin answered in style shortly thereafter when Weinke hit Johnson for a record 80-yard touchdown pass straight up the middle of the field. Blaine tied it on Wiehle's second TD run of the evening, an 11-yarder with 4:41 left in the half. Cretin's Jeff Rosga then nailed a 34-yard field goal to give his team the lead at half-time. Blaine responded behind kicker Noble Rainville, who tied it midway through the third on a 34-yard field goal. Weinke rallied the troops in the fourth, hitting Ted Johnson with a short screen up the middle for a 15-yard touchdown with 2:39 left in the game. That's when Blaine roared back behind the running of fullback John Buzick, who rushed for 94 yards on the day. Bengal quarterback Tom Newman's six-yard TD run around his left end capped of a thrilling 12-play, 73-yard fourth quarter drive. But in the end, Blaines Coach Dave Nelson went for the two-point conversion and the win, rather than tying it and having to out-duel Cretin's All-American Quarterback, Chris Weinke. (Following the victory, it was announced that Blaine was ranked 24th in the USA Today's final high school Super-25 rankings for 1988. In so doing, Blaine became the first-ever Minnesota high school team to be nationally rated. In addition, Weinke, who after playing professional baseball for six years, decided, at the tender age of 26, to go back to school in 1998 at Florida State University. In 1999 he led the Seminoles to the National Championship and in 2000 he is one of the leading Heisman Trophy candidates.)

Lakeville came out and avenged its 1987 Class A title game loss to Cambridge by beating Staples-Motley in a nail-biter. Lakeville Quarterback John Guentzel passed for a Prep Bowl record of 288 yards en route to tossing three touchdowns as the Panthers hung on to beat the Cardinals by the final score of 35-28. Chad Gilman was on the receiving end of two of those touchdown passes, while Lance Wolkow was the benefactor of the other — a 56-yarder late in the fourth. Staples-Motley scored first in this one, when Darren Gorder ran 38-yards for a touchdown. After Gilman's four-yard TD reception in the second, Gorder scored again, this time from two yards out. Lakeville's Todd Dwire and Chard Korba each scored rushing touchdowns midway through the second and third, only to see Staples-Motley rally behind a Arden Beachy one-yard touchdown plunge. That's when Guentzel hit Gilman and Wolkow on 55 and 34-yard TDs, respectively, to put it away. Beachy hit Loren Steinkraus on a 34-yarder late, but it was not nearly enough as Lakeville hung on for the 35-28 victory.

Trailing 7-0 after one quarter, the Breckenridge Cowboys rallied to defeat Morris, 21-7, for the Class B crown. Morris' Kent Moser got his squad on the board first, thanks to a 12-yard run which capped off a 77-yard drive early in the first. From there it was all Breckenridge though, as quarterback Jeff Vizenor took over and carried his team on his back. Vizenor hit Matt Hasbargen for a pair of touchdowns, and also returned an interception for another. Breckenridge overcame the "runner-up syndrome" with the victory, having lost the Class B title game in both 1983 and 1984.

Gerhard Meidt's Minneota Vikings made history by beating Rushford, 42-28, for the Class C crown, and in so doing became the first school to win three straight Prep Bowls. Minneota opened the scoring when Dave Dovre intercepted a ball early, which led to a Mark Tilleman's three yard touchdown run. From there it was back and forth. Rushford Quarterback Dana Grimsrud, who threw for 262 yards, hit Aaron Hungerholt early and often, as the receiver hauled in eight catches for 97 yards, and three touchdowns — including a 58-yarder. Minneota Fullback Mark Tillemans led the ground attack with 157 yards rushing and a trio of touchdowns. The game was tight late, but Minneota hung on. Cornerback and receiver Jim Lien caught his second TD of the afternoon, a 20-yarder from Boyd VanVooren, with 4:24 left in the game and then intercepted a key Trojan pass in the end-zone in the last two minutes of the game to ice it for the Vikings. Minnesota's winning streak now stood at 37 games and counting.

Hallock, trailing 18-14 at half-time, stormed back to defeat Stewart, 35-24, for the 9-Man title. Hallock's J.T. Anderson was the hero in this one, running for three touchdowns and gaining 168 yards on 25 carries. Stewart Quarterback Fritz Forcier scored one touchdown on the ground, and threw another to Corey Pagenkopf, while running back Russ Trettin led the Gophers' charge on the ground with 132 yards and a score. Hallock rallied behind the leadership of Anderson, and also from the running of Eric Isaacson, who ran for one touchdown and threw for another en route to gaining 104 yards on the ground.

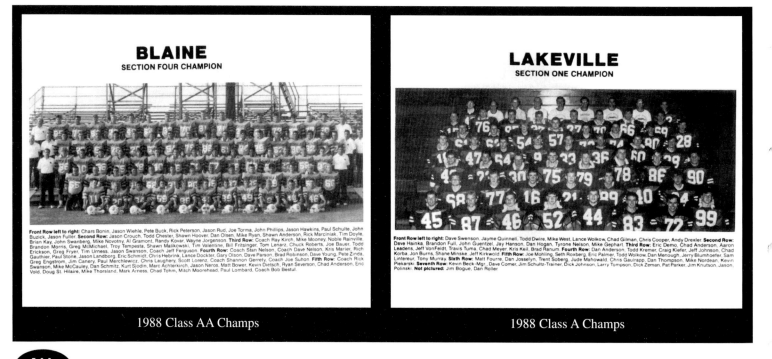

BLAINE
SECTION FOUR CHAMPION

Front Row left to right: Chars Bonin, Jason Wiehle, Pete Buck, Rick Peterson, Jason Rud, Joe Torma, John Phillips, Jason Hawkins, Paul Schulte, John Buzick, Jason Fuller. **Second Row:** Jason Crouch, Todd Chester, Shawn Hoover, Dan Olsen, Mike Ryan, Shawn Anderson, Rick Marciniak, Tim Doyle, Brian Kay, John Swanberg, Mike Novotny, Al Gramont, Randy Kovar, Wayne Jorgenson. **Third Row:** Coach Ray Kirch, Mike Mooney, Noble Rainville, Brandon Morris, Greg McMichael, Troy Tempesta, Shawn Malikowski, Tim Valentine, Bill Fritsinger, Tom Lenarz, Chuck Roberts, Joe Bauer, Todd Erickson, Greg Fryer, Tim Urness, Jason Swanson, Coach Jeff Ferguson. **Fourth Row:** Coach Stan Nelson, Coach Dave Nelson, Kris Marier, Rich Gauthier, Paul Stone, Jason Landborg, Eric Schmidt, Chris Hebrink, Lance Dockter, Gary Olson, Dave Parson, Brad Robinson, Dave Young, Pete Zinda, Greg Engstrom, Jim Canery, Paul Merchlewicz, Chris Laughery, Scott Lorenz, Coach Shannon Gerrely, Coach Joe Suhon. **Fifth Row:** Coach Rick Swanson, Mike McCauley, Dan Schmitz, Kurt Sjodin, Marc Achterkirch, Jason Neros, Matt Bower, Kevin Dietsch, Ryan Severson, Chad Anderson, Eric Vold, Doug St. Hilaire, Mike Thorsland, Mark Arness, Chad Tohm, Mitch Moorehead, Paul Lombard, Coach Bob Bestul.

LAKEVILLE
SECTION ONE CHAMPION

Front Row left to right: Dave Swenson, Jayme Quinnell, Todd Dwire, Mike West, Lance Wolkow, Chad Gilman, Chris Cooper, Andy Drexler. **Second Row:** Dave Hainka, Brandon Full, John Guentzel, Jay Hanson, Dan Hogan, Tyrone Nelson, Mike Gephart. **Third Row:** Eric Demo, Chad Anderson, Aaron Leadens, Jeff VonFeldt, Travis Tuma, Chad Meyer, Kris Keil, Brad Ranum. **Fourth Row:** Dan Anderson, Todd Kremer, Craig Kiefer, Jeff Johnson, Chad Korba, Jon Burns, Shane Minske, Jeff Kirkwold. **Fifth Row:** Joe Mohling, Seth Roxberg, Eric Palmer, Todd Wolkow, Dan Menough, Jerry Blumhoefer, Sam Linterceur, Tony Murray. **Sixth Row:** Matt Fourre, Dan Josselyn, Trent Soberg, Jude Mahowald, Chris Gaulrapp, Dan Thompson, Mike Nordean, Kevin Piekarski. **Seventh Row:** Kevin Beck-Mgr., Dave Comer, Jim Schultz-Trainer, Dick Johnson, Larry Tompson, Dick Zeman, Pat Parker, Jim Knutson, Jason Polinski. **Not pictured:** Jim Bogue, Dan Roller

1988 Class AA Champs

1988 Class A Champs

BRECKENRIDGE
SECTION EIGHT CHAMPION

Front Row: Amy Boldingh, Darcy Tillman, Tina Grenier, Amy Boll, Bill Hanson, Jennifer Hudson, Sara LeNoue, Caryn Randall and Lisa Herman. **Second Row:** Tris Kusnierek, Jeff Trauman, Bruce Yaggie, Jason Grawe, Paul Robertson, Jason Severson, Jason Ask, Mike Carlrud, Brad Abel and Ray McLaren. **Third Row:** Pat Casey, Gary Dohman, Jeff Vizenor, Corey Andeen, Peter Boldingh, Bruce Miller, Tom Larson, Matt Hasbargen, Monty Wiertzema, Tom Vad and Pat Beyer. **Fourth Row:** Stephen Engelmayer, Chad Dybdahl, Brad Wisneski, Mark Petersen, Scott Aamodt, Dan Aigner, Chad Albertson, Perry Langston, Corey Leinen and Scott Ferguson. **Fifth Row:** Mike Belseth, Bob Greeley, Ron Ekren, Jim Bock, John Wojtalewicz, Dennis Trydahl, Paul Sannes, Bill Mimnaugh, Mark Engebretson and Ron Thimjon. **Sixth Row:** Bill Paech, Alan Korth, Jeff Blowers, Jeff Snyder, Brad Terfehr, Pat Porter, Chris Betz, Trevor Hasse, Vance Johnson and Jeremy Ellingson. **Seventh Row:** Eric Aquila, Chad Stollenwerk, Chris Hansen, Bruce Harner, Steve Lawrence, Chris Amundson, Bill Korinek, Tracy Aarons, David Conzemius and Matt Johnson. **Eighth Row:** Travis Hasse, Jason Rurup, Greg Caspers, Chris Olson, Dustin Bruns, Brandon Chaffins, Mark Martin, Jeff Worner, Kyle Gowin, Carl Oltman and Mike McCullough.

1988 Class B Champs

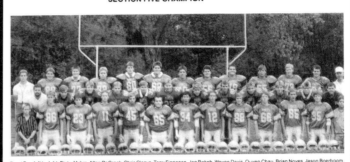

MINNEOTA
SECTION FIVE CHAMPION

Front Row left to right: Ricky Myhre, Allen DeCrock, Chris Claeys, Tony Finnegan, Jon Rokeh, Wayne Davis, Quyen Chau, Brian Noyes, Jason Boerboom, Scott Johnson, Jeff Sussner, Brian Schulte, Luke DePestel. **Second Row:** Assistant Coach Mike Aagesen, Tom Gislason, Stuart Smith, Jerry Storlien, James Lien, Mark Tillemans, David Dovre, Noel Hasert, Craig Buysse, Chad Stegner, Dave Stienessen, Assistant Coach Jim Folbiecki. **Third Row:** Assistant Coach Joel Skillings, Dennis Swedzinski, Brad Jeremiason, Mark Fonteyn, Rick Gossen, Tony Prinsen, Boyd VanVooren, Martin Hennen, Tony Esping, Tim DeVlaeminck, Curt Buysse, Eric Hennen and Head Coach Gerhard Meidt. **Absent from the photo are:** Chris Ahlschlager, Jason Pohlen, Marvin Prellwitz and Craig Schulte.

1988 Class C Champs

1989: PREP BOWL VIII

Burnsville's offense was in high gear during the Class AA title game against Stillwater, as they put together a well-rounded performance to take the crown, 21-7. Junior Quarterback Chad Emond was the Brave's catalyst, leading his team to a quick 21-0 lead before Stillwater could finally get on the board in the fourth quarter. Emond competed six passes for 108 yards and a touchdown, and rushed the ball 15 times for 46 yards and another score. Jake Kothe was on the receiving end of one of those touchdowns from Emond, as well as another from Running Back Dave Keenan. In addition, running backs Nate Wood and Ryan Williams, who had rushed for more than 2,000 yards during the season, combined for 89 yards that evening as well. The team's defense was the big story all year though, yielding just 5.2 points per game that season.

HALLOCK
SECTION EIGHT CHAMPION

Front Row left to right: James Satterlund, Chris Stokke, Chris Ingeman, Ryan Anderson-Mgr., Brian Olson, John Bergman. **Second Row:** Assistant Coach Kary Strandell, Peter Gudmundson, J.T. Anderson, Greg Kasprowicz, Fred Stockham, Eric Isaacson, Brad Anderson, Kent Waller, Chris Homstad. **Third Row:** Assistant Coach Todd Klein, Travis Giffen, Joel Anderson, Daryn Minske, Scott Nyegaard, Jason Nordling, Scott Hanson, Daniel Stockham, Jason Johnson, Erik Younggren, Head Coach Terry Ogorek.

1988 Class 9-Man Champs

The Class A game featured Albany defeating Totino-Grace by a final of 41-32. Albany set new Prep Bowl records for total yardage (510), and most yards rushing (362). Leading the charge for Totino-Grace was running back Ben Brunn, who racked up 139 yards on just seven carries, and scored three touch-downs. The game was a thrill-ride from start to finish in this one, which featured six lead changes. Totino-Grace's option touchdown run on the opening play electrified the Metrodome crowd as Eagle's QB Matt Vana flipped the biscuit to Ben Brunn, who then pranced in from 47 yards away to tally the first of his three touchdowns on the day. The Huskies then tied it on the next series on an 18-yard run by Brad Zenzen. The Eagles went up at the half thanks to all-state Receiver T. R. McDonald's 67-yard touchdown which made it 19-14. It was all Huskies from there on though, as Darryl Goebel took over. The speedy Halfback ran for 158 yards and scored three touchdowns in the second half, including a 47-yarder late in the fourth. Erik Wimmer, who rushed for 142 yards on the afternoon, iced it for Albany late in the game on a one-yard touchdown plunge to put the final nail in the coffin.

In the Class B finals, Perham's Charlie Nelson set a Prep Bowl record by returning the opening kickoff 91 yards for a touchdown. Gibbon-Fairfax-Winthrop scored twice in the second though, on runs by Jaymey Meyer and Jeff Deming. After a scoreless third, Deming scored again, only to see Nelson hit Jon Toester on a 90-yard bomb to get close. But G-F-W's Matt Miller scored on a 27-yarder late in the fourth to preserve the 27-15 victory.

The Class C contest was a nail-biter, as Waterville-Elysian hung on to beat Mahnomen, 14-7. Despite their seven turnovers, including five Mahnomen interceptions, the Buccaneers somehow managed to get the "W." Waterville-Elysian was down 7-0 at the half, thanks to Mahnomen Quarterback Jason Oakland's nine-yard touchdown pass to senior Tight End Dean Burdick. The Bucs came back in the second half though, behind a pair of Tauston Taylor touchdowns to seal the victory. The Indians, who also had five turnovers of their own, mounted a late rally but came up short.

The 9-Man game was a blow-out, with St. Clair crushing Albrook, 47-12. St. Clair's Sean Bezdicek was a one-man wrecking crew that afternoon. On offense Bezdicek scored on a 22-yard halfback pass from Brad Loeffler, he also caught a conversion pass and kicked an extra point. On defense he tallied three sacks, intercepted a pass, forced and recovered two fumbles — running one in for a 22-yard touchdown, made six tackles, and blocked a punt that was recovered in the end-zone by Loeffler, who, incidentally, tallied three touchdowns of his own.

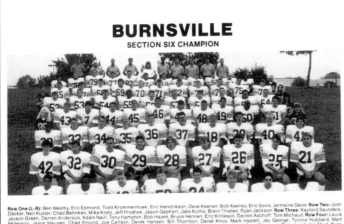

BURNSVILLE
SECTION SIX CHAMPION

Row One (L-R): Ben Westby, Eric Edmond, Todd Krommenhoek, Eric Hendrikson, Dave Keenan, Bob Keeney, Eric Sovis, Jermaine Davis. **Row Two:** Josh Decker, Neil Kuster, Chad Behnken, Mike Kretz, Jeff Proshek, Jason Gephart, Jake Kothe, Brent Thielen, Ryan Jackson. **Row Three:** Kaylord Saunders, Jayson Green, Darren Anderson, Adam Naill, Tony Hampton, Bob Hayes, Bruce Hennen, Eric Kittleson, Darren Aschoff, Tom Michaud. **Row Four:** Laura Pederson, Jason Haugen, Chad Emond, Joe Carlson, Derek Hansen, Bill Thornton, Derek Knox, Mark Hazlett, Jay George, Tyrone Hubbard, Matt Osiecki, Mindy Sebring. **Row Five:** Chris Nord, Tom Domres, Troy Coolidge, Jerry Ferguson, Mark Redetzke, Scott Sampson, Brian Lund, Joe Thull, Ryan Lake, Chad Mutzinger, Amy Beierle. **Row Six:** Shane Bennett, Adam Hanson, Mike Aldrich, Steve Sampson, Robb Thorstenson, Jason Welch, Brian Lentz, Bill Echloff, Kyle Kutz, Clay Cochran, Scott Hosier, Dan Shinn, Cortney Fox. **Row Seven:** Dennis Johnson, Brett Leschinsky, David Leach, Jason Beierle, Eric DeShon, Mike Donley, Rob Olson, Chris Lange, Stephen Schmid, Jay Brett, Dave Quast, Marcellus Evans, Rick Smith. **Row Eight:** Jay Anderson, Bill Caris, Doug Boe, Dick Hanson, Katy Call, Ben Roufs, Mark Griffin, Mick Schol, Don Leake, Neal Jeppson.

1989 Class AA Champs

ALBANY
SECTION SIX CHAMPION

Front Row kneeling: Adam Sand, Mike Kalthoff, Jerry Ostendorf, Darryl Trisko, Corey Scepaniak, Scott Gangl, Keith Studer, Ben Eiynk, Gary Schmitz, Manager. **Second Row:** Casey Junker, Curt Suchy, John Gilk, Bryan Smith, Jesse Johannes, Mark Woitalla, Duane Rausch, Coach Jim Mader. **Third Row:** Coach Mike Kleinschmidt, Keith Schloemer, Chris Kraus, Pete Carlson, Brennan Shay, Mark Witte, Allen Eiynk, Derrick Lenz, Darryl Goebel, Coach Bill Krogman. **Fourth Row:** Coach Dave Schorn, Willie Seiler, Erik Schwegler, Ted Nett, Steve Buttweiler, Kevin Havard, Karl Greig, Adam Borgerding, Mark Lucken, Ken Kierzek, Neal Suchy. **Fifth Row:** Todd Gerads, Erik Wimmer, Chris Theis, Dustin Pfipsen, Todd Rodenwald, Brent Schmitt, Stan Glass, Daryl Dirkes, Andy Richter, Chad Pundsack, John Court, John Schellinger, Charlie Gail, Jason Zwilling.

1989 Class A Champs

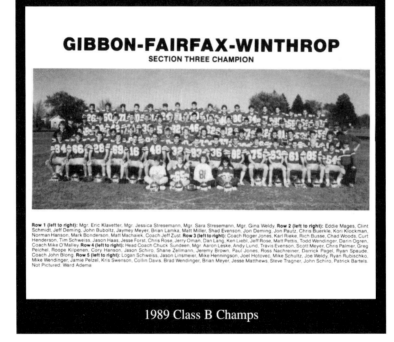

GIBBON-FAIRFAX-WINTHROP
SECTION THREE CHAMPION

Row 1 (left to right): Mgr. Eric Klavetter, Mgr. Jessica Stresemann, Mgr. Sara Stresemann, Mgr. Gina Weldy. **Row 2 (left to right):** Eddie Mages, Clint Schmidt, Jeff Deming, John Buboltz, Jaymey Meyer, Brian Lamka, Matt Miller, Shad Evenson, Jon Deming, Jon Pautz, Chris Buerkle, Kori Klockman, Norman Hanson, Mark Bonderson, Matt Machaiek, Coach Jeff Zust. **Row 3 (left to right):** Coach Roger Jones, Karl Rieke, Rich Busse, Chad Woods, Curt Henderson, Tim Schweiss, Jason Haas, Jesse Forst, Chris Rose, Jerry Oman, Dan Lang, Ken Liebl, Jeff Rose, Matt Pettis, Todd Weninger, Darin Ogren, Coach Mike O'Malley. **Row 4 (left to right):** Head Coach Chuck Sundeen, Mgr. Aaron Leske, Andy Lund, Travis Evenson, Scott Meyer, Chris Palmer, Greg Peichel, Roope Kilpenen, Cory Hanson, Jason Schiro, Shane Zellmann, Jeremy Brown, Paul Jones, Ross Nachreiner, Darrick Pagel, Ryan Spaude, Coach John Blong. **Row 5 (left to right):** Logan Schweiss, Jason Linsmeier, Mike Henningson, Joel Hotovec, Mike Schultz, Joe Weldy, Ryan Rubischko, Mike Wendinger, Jamie Pelzel, Kris Swenson, Collin Davis, Brad Wendinger, Brian Meyer, Jesse Matthews, Steve Tragner, John Schiro, Patrick Bartels. Not Pictured: Ward Adema.

1989 Class B Champs

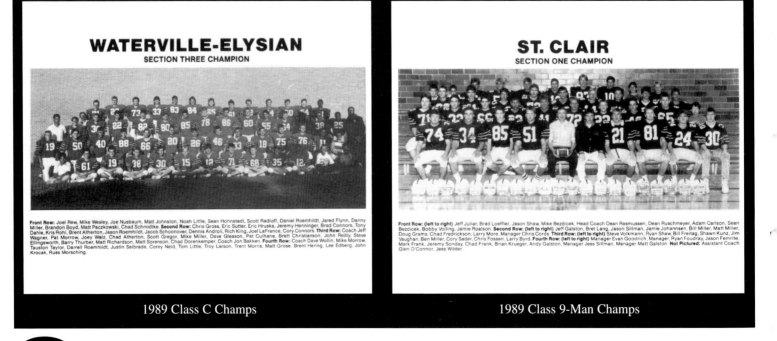

WATERVILLE-ELYSIAN
SECTION THREE CHAMPION

Front Row: Joel Rew, Mike Wesley, Joe Nusbaum, Matt Johnston, Noah Little, Sean Hohnstadt, Scott Radloff, Daniel Roemhildt, Jared Flynn, Danny Miller, Brandon Boyd, Matt Paczkowski, Chad Schmidtke. **Second Row:** Chris Gross, Eric Sutter, Eric Hruska, Jeremy Henninger, Brad Connors, Tony Dahle, Kris Rohl, Brent Atherton, Jason Roemhildt, Jacob Schoonover, Dennis Androli, Rich King, Joel LaFrance, Cory Connors. **Third Row:** Coach Jeff Wagner, Pat Morrow, Joey Walz, Chad Atherton, Scott Gregor, Mike Miller, Dave Gleason, Pat Culhane, Brett Christianson, John Reilly, Steve Ellingsworth, Barry Thurber, Matt Richardson, Matt Sorenson, Coach Jon Bakken. **Fourth Row:** Coach Dave Wollin, Mike Morrow, Tauston Taylor, Darrell Roemhildt, Justin Selbrade, Corey Neid, Tom Little, Troy Larson, Trent Morris, Matt Grose, Brent Hering, Lee Edberg, John Krocak, Russ Morsching.

1989 Class C Champs

ST. CLAIR
SECTION ONE CHAMPION

Front Row: (left to right) Jeff Juliar, Brad Loeffler, Jason Shaw, Mike Bezdicek, Head Coach Dean Rasmussen, Dean Ruschmeyer, Adam Carlson, Sean Bezdicek, Bobby Volling, Jamie Roalson. **Second Row: (left to right)** Jeff Galston, Bret Lang, Jason Sillman, Jamie Johannsen, Bill Miller, Matt Miller, Doug Grams, Chad Fredrickson, Larry More, Manager Chris Cords. **Third Row: (left to right)** Steve Volkmann, Ryan Shaw, Bill Freitag, Shawn Kunz, Jim Vaughan, Ben Miller, Cory Sader, Chris Fossen, Larry Byrd. **Fourth Row: (left to right)** Manager Evan Goodrich, Manager, Ryan Foudray, Jason Femrite, Mark Frank, Jeremy Sonday, Chad Frank, Brian Krueger, Andy Galston, Manager Jess Sillman, Manager Matt Galston. **Not Pictured:** Assistant Coach Glen O'Connor, Jess Wilder.

1989 Class 9-Man Champs

1990: PREP BOWL IX

Anoka hung on to beat Elk River, 19-14, in a classic title game for the Class AA title. Elk River drew first blood in this one, as Brian Reighard plunged in from the two midway through the first. Anoka, who found themselves trailing for just the second time that season, rallied behind QB Brook Parent's 67-yard pass to Jeremy Loretz, which led to a Mike Rudnick touchdown. Rudnick added another TD later that quarter as well. Then, early in the third, Parent hit Loretz on a 47-yard touchdown strike to give his squad a 20-7 lead. The Elks battled back though, as Scott Moe scored on a seven yard pass from Quarterback Matt Jones with just under six minutes to go. Then, after stopping Anoka, the Elks got the ball back for one last possession. That's when Pete Roback picked off his third interception of the evening, coming on the game's final drive to ice it for the Tornadoes.

Fridley rolled Sartell, 34-12, to claim the Class A championship. Fridley's balanced scoring attack was too much for Sartell as four different Tigers found the end-zone. Paul Sczepanski opened the scoring with a dramatic 72-yard touchdown run, while Mike Hermanson added a pair of TDs as well. Also getting in on the action were R.T. Taylor and Blane Tetreault, who also tallied. Adding insult to injury was Fridley's Jeff Swiatkewicz, who intercepted two passes in the game.

BOLD (Bird Island-Olivia-Lake Lillian), beat De La Salle, 15-14, in the Class B final, to finish their season with a perfect 14-0 record. In the title game, Jason Harrier scored on a one-yard plunge early in the first, only to see De La Salle score twice in the second on David Soukop's 68-yard run, followed by Jason Rudquist's 27-yard pass from Adam Kowles. Harrier tallied again late in the fourth to tie it. Then, with just seconds to go, BOLD faked the tying extra point and went for the win with Jamie Steffl catching a two-point pass from Tom Burkhart to give the team the dramatic victory.

Mahnomen, formerly a Class B powerhouse, took the Class C title by beating up on Waubun, Ogilvie, and Becker, 27-7 in the final. While quarterback Jeremy Oakland got the game's first touchdown, a one-yarder that followed his 33-yard punt return, this game was all Jason Miller. Miller, who rushed for 176 yards (2,055 yards on the season) had three TD runs for the Indians. Bulldog Quarterback Jamey Hussman capped off an 82-yard drive with a 16-yard TD late in the fourth, but it was way too little way too late.

Hills-Beaver Creek beat Argyle, 28-21 in the 9-Man title game, finishing the season with an unblemished 14-0 record. While Jon LaBine of Argyle had three rushing touchdowns, so too did Chad Miller of Hills-Beaver Creek, who also rushed for 217 yards on 26 carries. The Patriots hung on though, with Argyle pressing hard at the end to secure the win. Eagles sophomore Quarterback Nathan Lubarski drove the team 60-yards in the game's final moments to get to the four yard-line. There, with just 27 seconds on the clock, Lubarski tried and tried to get into the end-zone, first with a pitch to LaBine, then with a pass to Jason Yutrzenka — but to no avail. Finally, on the last play of the game he heaved up a Hail Mary, only to see it get knocked down. The Pat's had dodged the bullet.

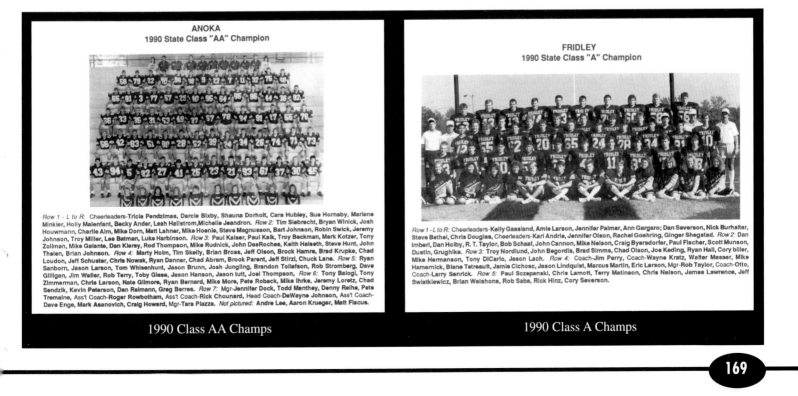

ANOKA
1990 State Class "AA" Champion

Row 1 - L to R: Cheerleaders-Tricia Pendzimas, Darcie Bixby, Shauna Dorholt, Cara Hubley, Sue Hornsby, Marlene Minkler, Holly Malenfant, Becky Ander, Leah Hallstrom, Michelle Jeandron. Row 2: Tim Siebrecht, Bryan Winick, Josh Houwmann, Charlie Alm, Mike Dorn, Matt Lahner, Mike Hoenie, Steve Magnusson, Bart Johnson, Robin Swick, Jeremy Johnson, Troy Miller, Lee Batman, Luke Harbinson. Row 3: Paul Kaiser, Paul Kalk, Troy Beckman, Mark Kotzer, Tony Zollman, Mike Galante, Dan Kiersy, Rod Thompson, Mike Rudnick, John DesRoches, Keith Halseth, Steve Hunt, John Thelen, Brian Johnson. Row 4: Marty Holm, Tim Skelly, Brian Bross, Jeff Olson, Brock Hamre, Brad Krupke, Chad Loudon, Jeff Schuster, Chris Nowak, Ryan Danner, Chad Abram, Brook Parent, Jeff Stirzl, Chuck Lane. Row 5: Ryan Sanborn, Jason Larson, Tom Whisenhunt, Jason Brunn, Josh Jungling, Brandon Tollefson, Rob Stromberg, Dave Gilligan, Jim Waller, Rob Terry, Toby Glose, Jason Hanson, Jason Iutt, Joel Thompson, Row 6: Tony Balogi, Tony Zimmerman, Chris Larson, Nate Gilmore, Ryan Bernard, Mike More, Pete Roback, Mike Ihrke, Jeremy Loretz, Chad Sendzik, Kevin Peterson, Dan Reimann, Greg Berres. Row 7: Mgr-Jennifer Dock, Todd Manthey, Denny Reihe, Pete Tremaine, Asst Coach-Roger Rowbotham, Asst Coach-Rick Chounard, Head Coach-DeWayne Johnson, Asst Coach-Dave Enge, Mark Asanovich, Craig Howard, Mgr-Tara Plazza. Not pictured: Andre Lee, Aaron Krueger, Matt Fiscus.

FRIDLEY
1990 State Class "A" Champion

Row 1 - L to R: Cheerleaders-Kelly Gaasland, Amie Larson, Jennifer Palmer, Ann Gargaro; Dan Severson, Nick Burhalter, Steve Bethel, Chris Douglas, Cheerleaders-Karl Andrie, Jennifer Olson, Rachel Goehring, Ginger Shegstad. Row 2: Dan Imberl, Dan Holby, R.T. Taylor, Bob Schaaf, John Cannon, Mike Nelson, Craig Byersdorfer, Paul Fischer, Scott Munson, Dustin, Grughke. Row 3: Troy Nordlund, John Begordis, Brad Simms, Chad Olson, Joe Keding, Ryan Hall, Cory biller, Mike Hermanson, Tony DiCarlo, Jason Lach. Row 4: Coach-Jim Perry, Coach-Wayne Kratz, Walter Messer, Mike Hamernick, Blane Tetreault, Jamie Cichosc, Jason Lindquist, Marcus Martin, Eric Larson, Mgr-Rob Taylor, Coach-Otto, Coach-Larry Senrick. Row 5: Paul Sczepanski, Chris Lamott, Terry Matinson, Chris Nelson, James Lawrence, Jeff Swiatkiewicz, Brian Welshons, Rob Saba, Rick Hinz, Cory Severson.

1990 Class AA Champs   1990 Class A Champs

B O L D (Bird Island-Olivia-Lake Lillian)
1990 State Class "B" Champion

Row 1 - L to R: Cheerleaders-April Elfering, Susan Meyers, Lisa Kopel, Lisa Plass, Jane Keltgen. *Row 2:* Head Coach-Steve Solem, Ass't Coach-Chuck Ross, Neil Herdina, Jason Zuhlsdorf, David Hotovec, Jamie Steffel, Ass't Coach- Jack Gomarko, Ass't Coach- Tangen. *Row 3:* Mgr-Bryon Metteer, Peter Kienholz, Maurice Schemmel, Raymond Boehme, Randy Paulsen, Ross Soukup, James Benson, Eric Keyser. *Row 4:* Jason Harrier, Chad Gomarko, Craig Boen, Joey Jensen, Brian Rodel, Jason Serbus, David Helder, Eric Dillon, Chad Herdina. *Row 5:* Shawn Kopel, Jason Stadther, Alan Kircher, Brian Wertish, L. Wayne Hoff, Thomas Burkhart, Kyle Kopacek, Guy Osterfeld, Matt Peris.

1990   Class B Champs

MAHNOMEN
1990 State Class "C" Champion

Row 1 - L to R: Captains-Keith Kirsch, Jeremy Oakland, Travis Kaste. *Row 2:* Dan McCollum, Dan Steinmetz, Bert Leslie, Jesse Struthers, David Johnson, Jason Hendrickson, Pat Noll, Dan Toso, Mike Thompson. *Row 3:* Cheerleader-Lana Wordon, Duane Liebl, Jeremy Refshaw, Chris Holmvik, Chris Newmann, Jason Paul, Steve Turner, Leo Kaiser, Mike Kramer, Mark Kahlbaugh, Cheerleader-Paula Otto. *Row 4:* Cheerleader-Kris Tommervik, Jason Miller, Jeremy Londo, Allen Jaeger, Brian Otto, Russell Sweep, Brandon Yost, Mike Halvorson, Chad Sweep, George Spaeth, Cheerleader-Jenny Yost. *Row 5:* Chad Leu, Grant Gunderson, Allen Houdek, Richard Halder, Jamie Trautner, Chad Flakne, Mike Luksik, Jeremy Seykora, David Markert, Cheerleader-Shella Busse. *Row 6:* Eric Bellanger, Roy Bjorge, Kyle Lacey, Chuck McNamee, Tony Athmann, Mike Kirsch, Tom Kahlbaugh, Ryan Refshaw. *Row 7:* Mgr-Ben Baumann, Ass't Coach-John Peterick, Head Coach-Ken Bauman, Ass't Coach-Ron Liebl, Mgr-Rob Tibbetts, Mgr-Doug Liebl.

1990 Class C Champs

HILLS-BEAVER CREEK
1990 State Class "9-MAN" Champion

Row 1 - L to R: Darin Knobloch, Wade Kellenberger, Blake Wysong, Jason Langford, Scott Ebert, Neil Bly, Stuart Moser, Jon Blomgren, Jason Bosch. *Row 2:* Greg Niessink, Tim Baker, Marc Brown, Jason Rauk, Brian Schoneman, Damon Knobloch, Robert Baatz, Chad Miller. *Row 3:* Chad Rauk, Brian Bennett, Rich Westphal, Randy Fick, David Dreesen, Kurt Bly, Tony Kellenberger, Stacen Burgers. *Row 4:* Stuart Soehl, Ass't Coach-Dan Ellingson, Ass't Coach-Steve Wiertzema, Head Coach-David Deragisch, Ass't Coach-Hugo Goehle, Shannon Tatge, Dallas Knobloch.

1990 Class 9-Man Champs

1991: PREP BOWL X

The 1991 Prep Bowl was thrown a huge curve ball thanks to mother nature. She decided to dump two to three feet of snow throughout much of the state just a few weeks prior to the state tournament, ultimately forcing the postponement of most of the section final games. Luckily though, they were later rescheduled and played inside the Metrodome, followed shortly thereafter by both the state tournament quarterfinals, semifinals and the Prep Bowl itself. The untimely snowfall even pummeled the Twin Cities area the day of the Prep Bowl, forcing Metrodome workers to scale the inflated roof and remove the heavy, wet snow which threatened to deflate it.

As far as the games were concerned, Burnsville went unfazed, winning their fourth Class AA football title with a 10-7 victory over Lakeville. The Panthers went up 7-0 in the first period on a one-yard run by Matt Hammond, only to see Burnsville tie the score in the second when Bob Keeney and Tony Deldotto combined on a 20-yard scoring strike. After Matt Johnson's 23-yard field goal in the third quarter put Burnsville up 10-7, it appeared that Lakeville, who was dominating the game's time of possession, was driving for the winning score late in the game. But, after marching 69 yards on 12 plays, the Panthers came up short by losing a crucial fumble in the game's final moments. Burnsville's John Doyle recovered the ball on his own 11-yard line as the Braves then simply ran out the clock to seal the win.

Spring Lake Park blanked Cold Spring Rocori, 20-0, for the Class A title behind the efforts of Joel Makala, who ran for 69 yards and scored two touchdowns, and Kicker Scott Muyres, who added a pair of 40 and 38 yard field goals to complete the team's scoring. The team's stellar defensive play included two pass interceptions in the end zone by Spring Lake Park cornerback Mark Smith. The Panthers were able to mount long, sustained drives and took advantage of several key Rocori mistakes in winning their first title.

The defending champs from BOLD shut-out Deer River, 14-0, to win the 1991 state Class B title. Special teams were the key to the Warriors victory as they scored on a 35-yard punt return by Chad Gomarko in the second, and then added an insurance touchdown in the third quarter when Defensive Back Jason Harrier intercepted a pass and returned it 30 yards for a TD. In addition, BOLD's Guy Osterfeld also brought the fans to their feet when he pranced 68 yards after fielding a Deer River punt. Tailback Jamie Steffel was the offensive leader for BOLD as he carried 17 times for 80 yards, ultimately finishing his senior season with 1,687 yards rushing.

Mahnomen senior Running Back Jason Miller finished his impressive high school gridiron career in style at the Class C title game. Miller, who set two new Prep Bowl rushing records, led his teammates to a 42-0 spanking of Mankato Loyola, thus giving the Indians their second straight championship. Miller's Prep Bowl records included Most Yards Rushing (252) and Most Touchdowns Rushing (4). In addition, the stingy Mahnomen defense allowed Mankato Loyola to post just 112 yards in total offense and limited them to just one first down in the second half.

In 9-Man action it all came down to a failed two-point conversion attempt, as Chokio-Alberta hung on for a 7-6 win over Grygla-Goodridge. Chokio-Alberta's Jon Hallman, who rushed for 92 yards in the game, scored on a two yard run in the second, and Eric Tomoson kicked what would prove to be the game-winner. Grygla-Goodridge rallied late though, and was able to score on an 11-yard touchdown run by Mitch Bernstein with 9:43 to play. Bernstein, however, was stopped short on the two-point conversion attempt, and the 7-6 score stood. The game was a defensive battle from there on out, as the two teams managed to gain just 374 yards in combined total offense. The Spartans hung tough in the end though and kept their undefeated record in tact with the victory.

BURNSVILLE
Section 6 Champion

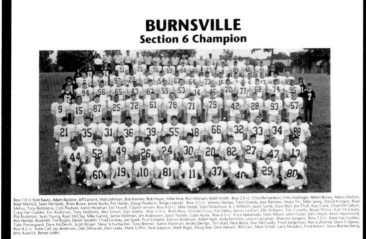

Row 1 (l-r): Kyle Kautz, Adam Rackow, Jeff Lansink, Matt Johnson, Bob Keeney, Bob Hayes, Mike Moe, Rich Moham, Keith Smith. Row 2 (l-r): Chris Richardson, Chris Naffziger, Albert Boney, Mario Shelton, Brad Minnick, Sean McNeely, Brian Busse, Jamie Bucks, Pat Harlan, Doug Hookum, Ringo Leipold. Row 3 (l-r): Jeremy Decker, Trent Goede, Jose Ramirez, Veary Yin, Mike Janey, David Kringen, Ryan Mehus, Tony Bottolene, Cory Plachon, Aaron Hickman, Eric Fryxell, Clayton Jensen. Row 4 (l-r): Mike Noble, Matt Dickenson, A. J. Wilhelm, Jason Sottle, Dave Bort, Joe Thull, Ajay Cook, Chad McCallum, Craig Van Guilder, Eric Anderson, Tony DelDotto, Alex Simon, Dan Stiehle. Row 5 (l-r): Brett Roos, Michael Gross, Pat Edens, Aaron Lenhart, Ellis Williams, Tom Costello, Bryan Prince, Kyle McCleary, Phil Anderson, Sean Young, Ryan McClay, Mike Caney, Jamie Wellman, Jim Andreasen, Jason Nordin, Gabe Ayala. Row 6 (l-r): Erica Nakahodo, Marc Meyer, John Foster, John Doyle, Kevin Hammond, Rick Hendel, Brad Hill, Tim Ripple, Derek Sendelir, Chad Lindsay, Joe Spark, Paul Schaefer, Darren Anderson, Adam Nazil, Andy Fernholz, Lance Carnahan, Shannon Jungens. Row 7 (l-r): Katie Van Guilder, Toby Prestegaard, Dave McDevitt, Scott Ringer, Steve Schumacher, Tony Bremer, Aaron Hartman, Andre Demps, Tim Watt, Nick Berra, Dan McCurdy, Trent Jorgenson, Rob Lurtsema, Dave Crepeau. Row 8 (l-r): Katie Call, Jay Anderson, Dan Donavan, Don Leake, Mark Griffin, Neal Jeppson, Mark Riggs, Doug Boe, Dick Hanson, Bill Caris, Mick Schol, Larry Meaders, Fred Kelsen, Steve Blankenberg, Jerry Kusnick, Renee Ledin.

1991 Class AA Champs

SPRING LAKE PARK
Section 5 Champion

Row 1 (l-r): Mark Jensen, Adam Blaido, Eric Stoner, Heather Relf, Shannon Blanchard, Daniel Snodgrass, Tina Mattson, Dawn Delaney, James Carney, Ryan Messer, Dan Grendahl. Row 2 (l-r): Chris Netland, Matt Hellenstein, Chris Roloff, Joel Makala, Brian Gronlund, Jeremiah Kalland, John Zgutowicz, John Stensrude, Mark Smith, Marty Gibson, Mike Vandervort. Row 3 (l-r): John Fosvick, Al Schlichting, Ass't Coach Gronert, Ass't Coach Welfe, Head Coach Jackson, Ass't Coach Copple, Ass't Coach Wabner, Ass't Coach Harnish, Jayme Anderson, Mike Ehlenfeldt, Doug Langewicz. Row 4 (l-r): Jason Medin, Matt Kurth, Doug Goodwin, Matt Herman, Tim Kocher, Jeff Tykeson, Travis Littlefield, Mark Monson, Brody Israelson, Kevin Byl. Row 5 (l-r): X, X, Brandon Ritter, Brett Littlefield, Chad Olson, Steve Kueppers, Scott Muyres, Josh Fulwider, Andy Scheck.

1991 Class A Champs

B O L D (Bird Island-Olivia-Lake Lillian)
1991 State Class "B" Champion

Row 1 - L to R: Cheerleaders-Shannon Engstrom, Jane Keltgen, Kristene Anderson, Laura Rau, April Beckman, Monica Hotovec. Row 2: Brian Rodel, Peter Kienholz, Kevin Mathiowetz, Guy Osterfeld, Jamie Steffel, Jason Zuhlsdorf, Jason Serbus, Shawn Kopel, Manager-Dan Torres. Row 3: Byron Metteer, Dean Rauenhorst, Melvin Maddock, Randy Paulsen, Maurice Schemmel, Kyle Kopacek, Jason Harrier, Chad Herdina, Greg Seidl. Row 4: Trainer-Kelli Hightshoe, Manager-Jeremy Kopel, Raymond Boehme, Dan Nissen, Troy Bohm, Jay Mahoney, Jon Kircher, Dan Amberg, Scott Hillemeier. Row 5: Chad Gomarko, Ross Soukup, Craig Boen, David Hackmann, Chad Elbert, Joey Jensen, Jay Helin. Row 6: Head Coach-Steve Solem, Assistant Coach-Jack Gomarko, Assistant Coach-Chuck Ross, Nathan Herdina, Brian Erickson, Jeremiah Jacobs, Jeff Zurn, Paul Mathiowetz, Michael McDowell.

1991 Class B Champs

MAHNOMEN
1991 State Class "C" Champion

Row 1 - L to R: Chris Neumann, Jason Miller, Chuck McNamee. Row 2: Brent Miller, Mike Halvorson, George Spaeth, Roy Bjorge, Erik Bellanger, Duane Liebl, Kyle Lacey, Mark Kahlbaugh, Russell Sweep, Jason Paul. Row 3: Chad Schouveiller, Scott Yost, Jeremy Gunderson, Tom Kahlbaugh, Jamie Traunter, Richard Haider, Stanley Dietz, Brandon Yost, David Markert, Ryan Refshaw, Allen Houdek. Row 4: Jason Strong, Andy Newmann, Jeremy Seykora, Matt Kraker, Reed Bjerk, Chad Rogers, Jason Francis, Grant Gunderson, Chad Sweep, Chad Flakne, Mike Luksik. Row 5: Josh Stone, Tim Neisen, John Littlewolf, Eric Handyside, Scott McCollum, Greg Gieseke, Pete Scheff, Andy Geray, Mike Kirsch, Tony Athmann. Row 6: Manager-Darren Rogers, Manager-Ben Baumann, Assistant Coach-John Peterick, Head Coach-Ken Baumann, Assistant Coach-Al Brusven, Assistant Coach-Ron Liebl, Manager-Derek Kochman, Manager-Doug Liebl. Row 7: Sheila Schoenborn, Sandy Eveslage, Jessica Asher, Lonna Worden, Jenny Yanish, Kari Johnson.

1991 Class C Champs

CHOKIO-ALBERTA
1991 State Class "9-MAN" Champion

Row 1 - L to R: Shaun Leuthard, Jon Hallman, Pat Kehoe, Kevin Spaulding, Eric Tomoson, Eric Gibson, Chad Marty, Jeremy Schmidgall. Row 2: Luke Monson, Wally Schmitz, Mike Schneider, Greg Fynboh, Dan Krueger, Tom Schott, Matt Raasch, Curtis Anderson, Carl Vogt. Row 3: Tim Schmidgall, Andy Ritter, Keith Vogt, Cory Fynboh, Jeff Klein, Mike Hettver, Bill Kehoe, Troy Bruer. Row 4: Shannon Pring, Lucas deNeui, Paul Mithun, Mark Berlinger, Jason Rilley, Dan DeCamp, Luke Jost, Scott Erickson, Kelly Backman. Row 5: Mark Gibson, James Raths, Charles Swanson, Matt Marlow, Dustin Tomoson, Kyle Anderson. Row 6: Coach-Neal Hofland, Manager-Niccole Hettver, Manager-Wendy Hawkenson, Assistant Coach-John Mithun.

1991 Class 9-Man Champs

LAKEVILLE
1992 State Class "AA" Champion

Row 1 - L to R: *Ken Klamm, Tim Gallagher, Craig Posch, Sean Herman, Bill Jensen, Mike Golecki, Tom Gallagher, Mike Kunkel, Ryan Lovelace, Eric Anderson, Phet Thammalangsy.* Row 2: *Steve Shade, Matt Zeidler, Mathan Maifeld, Kevin Kaesviharn, Tony House, Brian Thom, Nate Mohling, Brian Hanson, Tony Engel, Brian Sontag, Eric Jensen, Justin Hemann.* Row 3: *Seth Kranz, Don Benedict, Scott Sheridan, Chris Hornwak, Jason Albrecht, Aaron Maifeld, Chad Ubl, Jeremy Thornton, Mike Jansen, Andy Cannon, Derek Tharaldson, Chad Rice.* Row 4: *Nick Revak, Casey Erickson, David Zweber, Aaron Krukow, Jeff Brawley, Mike Doughty, Nate Rasmussen, Ryan Hopkins, Matt Henriksen, Jon Jellum, Ross Barnett, Ryan Khoury.* Row 5: *Tim Krebs, Adam Platt, Ryan Emmons, Jessie Barber, Troy Jensen, Corey Fox, Matt Hammond, Andy Zimmer, Dan Simpson, Scott Eugene, Marc Hollahan, Darren Campion.*

1992 Class AA Champs

DETROIT LAKES
1992 State Class "A" Champion

Row 1 - L to R: *Corey Johnson, Jaremy Kotta, Mike Engum, Chad Bauer, Brian King, Justin Schweigart, Jason Kelly, Mark Palm, Nate Huseby, Matt Friendshuh.* Row 2: *Brian Olson, Matt McKenzie, Matt Sullivan, Eric Gilbertson, Matt Horner, Toby Steinmetz, David Johnson, Nate Greenlaw, Corey Borah, Kenny Erickson, Ryan Manke.* Row 3: *Matt Anderson, Mark Rasmussen, Kregg Wolf, Isaac Inwards, Brent Wolf, Cory Manning, Steve Kath, Josh Beug, Kyle Schmit, Wayne Kading, Ryan Hermes, Chris Perry.* Row 4: *Jerod Coalwell, Brett Nansen, Travis Ballard, Travis Renney, Matt Wimmer, Bruce Retz, Erick Gunderson, Justin Guida, Kevin Brent.* Row 5: *Kevin Schlauderaff, Matt Schiller, Chris Hanson, Chad Rosell, Jason Selly, Tim Ramsey, Brian Porter, Brent Kuehne, Jason Upthegrove.* Row 6: *James Scherzer, Peter Edwards, Ardean Kellerhuis, Mike Miller, Joe Schweigert, Casey Jensen, Jason Maneval, Jason Ziegler, Jamie Pawlak, Dan Anderson.*

1992 Class A Champs

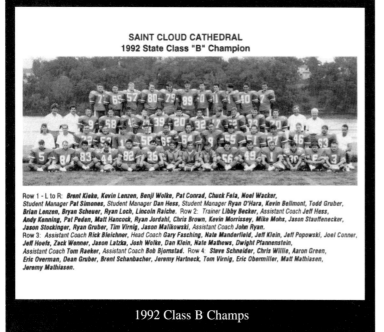

SAINT CLOUD CATHEDRAL
1992 State Class "B" Champion

Row 1 - L to R: *Brent Kieke, Kevin Lenzen, Benji Wolke, Pat Conrad, Chuck Fela, Noel Wacker, Student Manager Pat Simones, Student Manager Dan Hess, Student Manager Ryan O'Hara, Kevin Bellmont, Todd Gruber, Brian Lenzen, Bryan Scheuer, Ryan Loch, Lincoln Raiche.* Row 2: *Trainer Libby Becker, Assistant Coach Jeff Hess, Andy Kenning, Pat Peden, Matt Hancock, Ryan Jordahl, Chris Brown, Kevin Morrissey, Mike Mohs, Jason Stauffenecker, Jason Stockinger, Ryan Gruber, Tim Virnig, Jason Malikowski, Assistant Coach John Ryan.* Row 3: *Assistant Coach Rick Bleichner, Head Coach Gary Fasching, Nate Manderfield, Jeff Klein, Jeff Popowski, Joel Conner, Jeff Hoefs, Zack Wenner, Jason Latzka, Josh Wolke, Dan Klein, Nate Mathews, Dwight Pfannenstein, Assistant Coach Tom Raeker, Assistant Coach Bob Bjornstad.* Row 4: *Steve Schneider, Chris Willie, Aaron Green, Eric Overman, Dean Gruber, Brent Schanbacher, Jeremy Hartneck, Tom Virnig, Eric Obermiller, Matt Mathiasen, Jeremy Mathiasen.*

1992 Class B Champs

1992: PREP BOWL XI

Cretin-Derham Hall finished as the Class AA runner-up, losing to Lakeville by the final score of 19-7. The key to Lakeville's victory was their rock-solid defense, especially against future NFL Running Back Carl McCullough. McCullough, who gained 129 yards on the ground, was held out of the end-zone in this one. Conversely, Lakeville running back Matt Hammond rushed for 238 yards on 34 attempts and added a pair of touchdowns in the win.

After three trips to the Dome, Detroit Lakes was finally able to bring home the Class A championship trophy. The Lakers' stingy defense shut-out each of its three playoff opponents by the combined score of 72-0, concluding with a 21-0 victory over Farmington in the Prep Bowl title game. Detroit Lakes posted 290 yards of offense, intercepted five Farmington passes, and held the Tigers, who had averaged nearly 250 yards rushing per game, to just 47 yards on the ground.

St. Cloud Cathedral made the most of its first Prep Bowl appearance, winning the Class B title with a 7-6 victory of two-time defending champion BOLD (Bird Island-Olivia-Lake Lillian). After playing to a scoreless first half, BOLD Quarterback Chad Gomarko called his own number and scored a touchdown in the third quarter on a keeper. The extra point went wide though. Down but not out, Cathedral controlled the ball for nearly 11 minutes of the 12 minute fourth quarter, and tied it up on a five yard Nate Mandefeld pass to Running Back Jason Latzka out of the backfield. Latzka, who also doubles as the team's kicker, then put the final nail in the coffin by converting the extra point.

Mahnomen, making its 13th appearance since the football playoffs began in 1972, and seventh since the Prep Bowl was formed back in 1982, made it back-to-back-to-back Class C state championships in 1992. The Indians needed two overtime periods to beat Mankato Loyola in the finals, and in so doing, extended their winning streak to an amazing 39 games. After battling to a 6-6 tie during regulation, each team scored in the first extra session to make it 13-13. (Each team is given four downs to score from its opponent's 10-yard line in overtime.) Then, in the second overtime, after Mahnomen scored, Mankato Loyola quarterback Colin Rogness fumbled while rolling out to pass and Mahnomen recovered. Game over. The Indians held on to once again beat Mankato Loyola in the finals, this time by the final score of 20-13.

Finally, Stephen, a tiny northwestern Minnesota community with a school enrollment of just 60 students, rolled over Cromwell by the final of 36-20 in 9-Man action. Fully 28 of the school's 60 kids played on the undefeated team, which was making its first trip to the state tournament. Stephen dominated Cromwell in the first half, scoring 15 unanswered points, only to see Cromwell rally back in the second. Stephen hung tough though, led by their star Quarterback Bryce Lingen, who, in addition to passing for 356 yards and a touchdown, also rushed for a pair of TDs just for good measure. Stephen's defense was also a factor, however, holding two 1,000-yard+ Cromwell backs to a combined 113 yards.

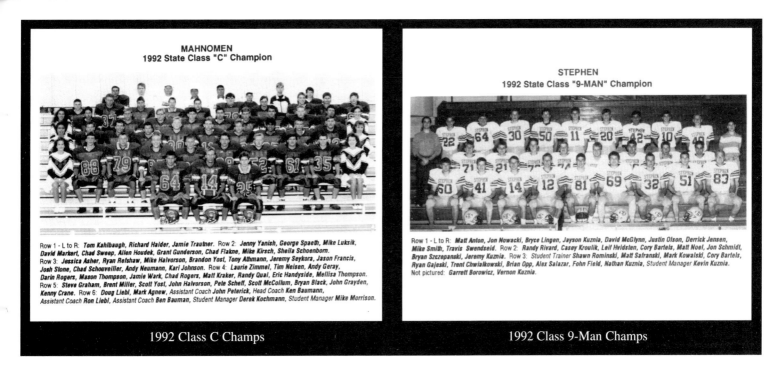

MAHNOMEN
1992 State Class "C" Champion

Row 1 - L to R: *Tom Kahlbaugh, Richard Haider, Jamie Trautner.* Row 2: *Jenny Yanish, George Spaeth, Mike Luksik, David Markert, Chad Sweep, Allen Houdek, Grant Gunderson, Chad Flakne, Mike Kirsch, Sheila Schoenborn.* Row 3: *Jessica Asher, Ryan Relshaw, Mike Halvorson, Brandon Yost, Tony Athmann, Jeremy Seykora, Jason Francis, Josh Stone, Chad Schouveiller, Andy Neumann, Karl Johnson.* Row 4: *Laurie Zimmel, Tim Neisen, Andy Geray, Darin Rogers, Mason Thompson, Jamie Wark, Chad Rogers, Matt Kraker, Randy Qual, Eric Handyside, Mellisa Thompson.* Row 5: *Steve Graham, Brent Miller, Scott Yost, John Halvorson, Pete Scheff, Scott McCollum, Bryan Black, John Grayden, Kenny Crane.* Row 6: *Doug Liebl, Mark Agnew, Assistant Coach John Peterick, Head Coach Ken Baumann, Assistant Coach Ron Liebl, Assistant Coach Ben Bauman, Student Manager Derek Kochmann, Student Manager Mike Morrison.*

STEPHEN
1992 State Class "9-MAN" Champion

Row 1 - L to R: *Matt Anton, Jon Nowacki, Bryce Lingen, Jayson Kuznia, David McGlynn, Justin Olson, Derrick Jensen, Mike Smith, Travis Swendseid.* Row 2: *Randy Rivard, Casey Kroulik, Leif Hvidsten, Cory Bartels, Matt Noel, Jon Schmidt, Bryan Szczepanski, Jeremy Kuznia.* Row 3: *Student Trainer Shawn Rominski, Matt Safranski, Mark Kowalski, Cory Bartels, Ryan Gajeski, Trent Chwialkowski, Brian Opp, Alex Salazar, Fohn Field, Nathan Kuznia, Student Manager Kevin Kuznia.* Not pictured: *Garrett Borowicz, Vernon Kuznia.*

1992 Class C Champs   **1992 Class 9-Man Champs**

1993: PREP BOWL XII

Quarterback Brian Rasmussen tied a Prep Bowl record by throwing three touchdown passes in leading Apple Valley to a 29-7 victory over Rochester John Marshall in the Class AA title game. On the receiving end of Rasmussen's 186-yard afternoon was Kevin Conn, who made four catches for 88 yards — two of which led to Eagle touchdowns. Brad DeFauw and Todd Martin also got into the scoring column when they hauled in TDs as well. John Marshall's only score of the game came on Running Back Jason Barbes eight yard touchdown scamper in the second quarter which put the team up 7-0. Apple Valley's defense shut out the Rockets from there though, intercepting JM's Quarterback Brent Solheim five times in the victory.

It was No. 1 vs. No. 2 in the Class A title game with the defending champs from Detroit Lakes coming to the Metrodome as the team to beat. The Lakers made a statement early, scoring on the first drive of the game with Matt Horner catching a Toby Steinmetz pass and taking it 36 yards for a touchdown. Northfield then answered with 1:26 left in the first half on a 26-yard pass from Sam Richardson to Jason Wefel. Turnovers killed the Raiders in the second half though, as DL scored on a 45-yard fumble recovery to put them ahead 14-7. Detroit Lakes led 21-7 in the fourth period and appeared on the way to its fourth TD of the game when Northfield forced a fumble and Scott LeRoy of the Raiders picked up the ball and ran it 88 yards to pay dirt. Steinmetz was the key though, leading his raiders with a game-high 94 yards rushing, and completing 6 of 11 passes for 100 yards and one touchdown. Steinmetz also intercepted a key pass from QB Sam Richardson with less than two minutes left in the game, to stop the Raiders' drive and secure the Lakers 21-14 victory. For DL, it was a fitting way to extended their winning streak to an impressive 27 games.

St. Cloud Cathedral came into the Class B finals dead set on making it back-to-back state titles. Standing in their way was Zumbrota-Mazeppa, who was led by future Gopher star, Parc Williams, who had rushed for 1,615 yards coming into the championship clash. Williams made a statement early, scoring on a 10-yard run to give his team a shot. But Cathedral, which led 7-6 at the half, scored two touchdowns in just over two minutes during the third to seal the deal. Leading the way was Mike Mohs, who scored twice and gained 125 yards rushing, Jeff Hoefs, who ran in a TD in the third, and Eric Overman, who caught a touchdown pass from Nate Manderfeld. The Crusaders defense took over from there as they hung on to defeat the Cougars, 28-6, and win their second straight championship.

Mahnomen made history by winning the Class C crown for a record fourth straight time — a feat never done before in Minnesota state football history. Ironically, the holder of the previous record of three straight titles, the Minneota Vikings, stood in their way. Mahnomen came out of the gates flying, as Running Back Brent Miller, who scored three TDs on 299 yards rushing in the game, scored on an 80-yard romp from the first play of scrimmage. Mahnomen Quarterback Jeremy Seykora threw only twice in the first half, with both tosses going for touchdowns, one to Jamie Wark and the other to Jason McArthur. Tony Athmann also got into the action, running for a TD as well. Vikings' quarterback Matt Myrvik played strong though, passing for one touchdown and running for two more in the losing cause. The winning Indians scored all of their points in the first half — 21 in the first quarter and 22 in the second — as they rolled, 43-23, to make history.

Senior Running Back Kyle Nietzel was the real deal in Chokio-Alberta's 35-0 pummeling of LeRoy-Ostrander in the Class 9-Man championship. The 175-pound spark-plug carried 30 times for 252 yards, scored three touchdowns, including a 77-yarder, and completed the season with 2,646 yards and 40 touchdowns. It was the second title in three years for the Spartans, whose defense held LeRoy-Ostrander's offense to just 139 yards.

Individual Record for Longest Field Goal		
Yards Player	School	Year
54 Mike Chalberg	Forest Lake	1990
54 Ken Johnson	Centennial	1995
53 Jim Gallery	Morton	1977
52 Dan Nystrom	Cooper	1998
52 Craig Lewis	Henry Sibley	1979

APPLE VALLEY
1993 State Class "AA" Champion

Photo caption not available.

1993 Class AA Champs

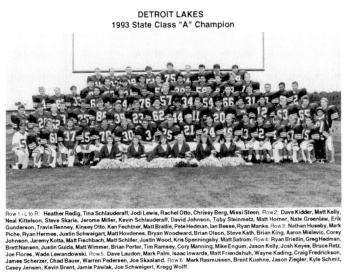

DETROIT LAKES
1993 State Class "A" Champion

Row 1 - L to R: Heather Redig, Tina Schlauderaff, Jodi Lewis, Rachel Otto, Chrissy Berg, Missi Steen. Row 2: Dave Kidder, Matt Kelly, Neal Kittelson, Steve Skarie, Jerome Miller, Kevin Schlauderaff, David Johnson, Toby Steinmetz, Matt Horner, Nate Greenlaw, Erik Gunderson, Travis Renney, Kinsey Otto, Ken Fechtner, Matt Bratlie, Pete Hedman, Ian Besse, Ryan Manke. Row 3: Nathan Huseby, Mark Piche, Ryan Hermes, Justin Schweigart, Matt Hovdenes, Bryan Woodward, Brian Olson, Steve Kath, Brian King, Aaron Mislevic, Corey Johnson, Jeremy Kotta, Matt Fischbach, Matt Schiller, Justin Wood, Kris Spenningsby, Matt Satrom. Row 4: Ryan Bristlin, Greg Hedman, Brett Nansen, Justin Guida, Matt Wimmer, Brian Porter, Tim Ramsey, Cory Manning, Mike Engum, Jason Kelly, Josh Keyes, Bruce Retz, Joe Flores, Wade Lewandoweki. Row 5: Dave Laudon, Mark Palm, Isaac Inwards, Matt Friendshuh, Wayne Kading, Craig Fredrickson, James Scherzer, Chad Bauer, Warren Pedersen, Joe Skaaland. Row 6: Mark Rasmussen, Brent Kuehne, Jason Ziegler, Kyle Schmit, Casey Jensen, Kevin Brent, Jamie Pawlak, Joe Schweigert, Kregg Wolff.

1993 Class A Champs

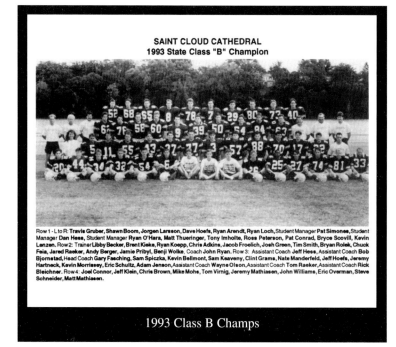

SAINT CLOUD CATHEDRAL
1993 State Class "B" Champion

Row 1 - L to R: Travis Gruber, Shawn Boom, Jorgen Larsson, Dave Hoefs, Ryan Arendt, Ryan Loch, Student Manager Pat Simones, Student Manager Dan Hess, Student Manager Ryan O'Hara, Matt Thueringer, Tony Imholte, Ross Peterson, Pat Conrad, Bryce Scovill, Kevin Lenzen. Row 2: Trainer Libby Becker, Brent Kieke, Ryan Koepp, Chris Adkins, Jacob Froelich, Josh Green, Tim Smith, Bryan Rolek, Chuck Feia, Jared Raeker, Andy Berger, Jamie Pribyl, Benji Wolke, Coach John Ryan. Row 3: Assistant Coach Jeff Hess, Assistant Coach Bob Bjornstad, Head Coach Gary Fasching, Sam Spiczka, Kevin Bellmont, Sam Keaveny, Clint Grams, Nate Manderfeld, Jeff Hoefs, Jeremy Hartneck, Kevin Morrissey, Eric Schultz, Adam Jenson, Assistant Coach Wayne Olson, Assistant Coach Tom Raeker, Assistant Coach Rick Bleichner. Row 4: Joel Connor, Jeff Klein, Chris Brown, Mike Mohs, Tom Virnig, Jeremy Mathiasen, John Williams, Eric Overman, Steve Schneider, Matt Mathiasen.

1993 Class B Champs

MAHNOMEN
1993 State Class "C" Champion

Row 1 - L to R: Brent Miller, Andy Neumann, Tony Athmann. Row 2: Jessica Asher, Jeremy Seykora, Scott McCollum, Reed Bjerk, Chad Rogers, Randy Qual, John Littlewolf, Chad Schouveiller, Scott Yost, Jason Francis, Josh Stone, Kari Johnson. Row 3: Chris Hillyer, Miqual Perez, Matt Kraker, Pete Scheff, Doug Liebl, John Grayden, Randy Winter, Kenny Crane, A. J. Goodwin, Mike Morrisson, John Halvorson, Connie Revier. Row 4: Laurie Zimmel, Kelly Simon, Greg Blue, Darren Rogers, Jamie Wark, Ryan Estey, Mason Thompson, Jason Darco, Steve Graham, Bryan Black, Melissa Thompson. Row 5: Eric Dahl, John Struthers, Zach Peterson, Jared Schafer, Jeff Geray, Shaun Ryan, Fred Specht, Gary Vik, Jason Luksik, Chad Habedank. Row 6: Brian Dahl, Jason McCarthur, Greg Simon, Assistant Coach Mark Agnew, Head Coach Ken Baumann, Assistant Coach John Peterick, Student Manager Derek Kochmann, James Sweep, Mike Haider.

1993 Class C Champs

CHOKIO-ALBERTA
1993 State Class "9-MAN" Champion

Row 1 - L to R: Kyle Anderson, Cory Fynboh, Luke Monson, Kyle Neitzel, Bill Kehoe, Mike Hettver, Keith Vogt, Andy Ritter. Row 2: Kelly Backman, Jason Rilley, James Raths, Dustin Tomoson, Mark Berlinger, Matt Marlow, Bryan Snortum, Mark Gibson, Troy Bruer. Row 3: Lucas deNeui, Paul Mithun, Shannon Pring, Scott Erickson, Luke Jost, Dan DeCamp, Tim Schmidgall. Row 4: Manager Shelly Backman, John Quackenbush, Chad Steuck, Nathan Burnett, Jacob Marty, Matt Staebler, Darren Nelson, Manager Jenny Marty. Row 5: Coach John Mithun, Peter Mithun, Tom Schneider, Mike Marty, Ed Picht, Jeff Johnson, Ritchie Giles, Coach Neal Hofland.

1993 Class 9-Man Champs

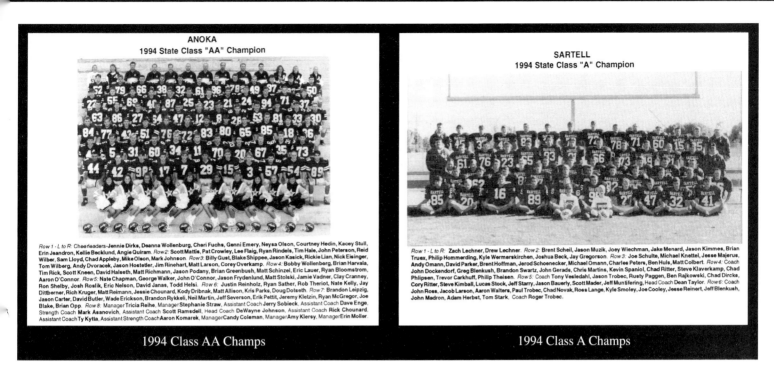

ANOKA
1994 State Class "AA" Champion

Row 1 - L to R: Cheerleaders-Jennie Dirks, Deanna Wollenburg, Cheri Fuchs, Genni Emery, Neysa Olson, Courtney Hedin, Kacey Stull, Erin Jeandron, Kellie Becklund, Angie Quiram. Row 2: Scott Mattis, Pat Crowley, Lee Flaig, Ryan Rindels, Tim Hale, John Peterson, Reid Wilber, Sam Lloyd, Chad Appleby, Mike Olson, Mark Johnson. Row 3: Billy Gust, Blake Shippee, Jason Kasick, Rickie Lian, Nick Eisinger, Tom Wilberg, Andy Dvoracek, Jason Hostetler, Jim Rinehart, Matt Larson, Corey Overkamp. Row 4: Bobby Wollenberg, Brian Harvala, Tim Rick, Scott Kneen, David Halseth, Matt Richmann, Jason Podany, Brian Greenbush, Matt Schinzel, Eric Lauer, Ryan Bloomstrom, Aaron O'Connor. Row 5: Nate Chapman, George Walker, John O'Connor, Jason Frydenlund, Matt Stolski, Jamie Vadner, Clay Cranney, Ron Shelby, Josh Roslik, Eric Nelson, David Janas, Todd Helsi. Row 6: Justin Reinholz, Ryan Sather, Rob Theriot, Nate Kelly, Jay Dittberner, Rich Kruger, Matt Reimann, Jessie Chounard, Kody Dribnak, Matt Allison, Kris Parks, Doug Dotseth. Row 7: Brandon Leipzig, Jason Carter, David Butler, Wade Erickson, Brandon Rykkeli, Neil Martin, Jeff Severson, Erik Pettit, Jeremy Kletzin, Ryan McGregor, Joe Blake, Brian Opp. Row 8: Manager Tricia Reihe, Manager Stephanie Straw, Assistant Coach Jerry Sobieck, Assistant Coach Dave Enge, Strength Coach Mark Asanovich, Assistant Coach Scott Ramsdell, Head Coach DeWayne Johnson, Assistant Coach Rick Chounard, Assistant Coach Ty Kytta, Assistant Strength Coach Aaron Komarek, Manager Candy Coleman, Manager Amy Klersy, Manager Erin Moller.

SARTELL
1994 State Class "A" Champion

Row 1 - L to R: Zach Lechner, Drew Lechner. Row 2: Brent Scheil, Jason Muzik, Joey Wiechman, Jake Menard, Jason Kimmes, Brian Truex, Philip Hommerding, Kyle Wermerskirchen, Joshua Beck, Jay Gregorson. Row 3: Joe Schulte, Michael Knettel, Jesse Majerus, Andy Omann, David Parker, Brent Hoffman, Jerod Schoenecker, Michael Omann, Charles Peters, Ben Huls, Matt Colbert. Row 4: Coach John Dockendorf, Greg Blenkush, Brandon Swartz, John Gerads, Chris Martins, Kevin Spaniol, Chad Ritter, Steve Klaverkamp, Chad Phlipsen, Trevor Carkhuff, Philip Theisen. Row 5: Coach Tony Vesledahl, Jason Trobec, Rusty Paggen, Ben Rajkowski, Chad Dircks, Cory Ritter, Steve Kimball, Lucas Stock, Jeff Starry, Jason Bauerly, Scott Mader, Jeff Muntifering, Head Coach Dean Taylor. Row 6: Coach John Ross, Jacob Larson, Aaron Walters, Paul Trobec, Chad Novak, Ross Lange, Kyle Smoley, Joe Cooley, Jesse Reinert, Jeff Blenkush, John Madron, Adam Herbst, Tom Stark, Coach Roger Trobec.

1994 Class AA Champs | **1994 Class A Champs**

1994: PREP BOWL XIII

The undefeated Anoka Tornadoes, who had won their regular season games by an average of 21 points that year, spanked the also unbeaten Alexandria Cardinals, 34-7, to take the Class AA state title. From the opening drive, the Tornadoes came out swinging. Anoka came right out of the gates and drove 62 yards on seven plays capped by a five-yard TD run from Justin Reinholz. Jason Podany then hit Jesse Chounard on a 47-yard touchdown pass to give Anoka a 14-0 half-time lead. The Cardinals' R.J. Nodland recovered a fourth-quarter fumble which later resulted in a Bill Zacher touchdown to give Alexandria their only points of the game. The Tornadoes' scored on their next possession though, giving them a 21-7 lead. Moments later an interception led to an eight-yard Reinholz touchdown, followed by Tom Walbert's quarterback sneak late in the game to give Anoka the victory. The Tornadoes were led by Reinholz, who scored two touchdowns and ran for 97 yards, and Richie Kruger, who racked up 104 yards as well.

The closest game of the day found the Sartell Sabres barely squeezing by the Northfield Raiders, 24-21, for the Class A championship. Northfield built a 14-0 half-time lead on an early interception which led to a one-yard Drew Wilson touchdown, followed by Jeff Otte's 35-yard touchdown catch just moments later. But less then eight minutes into the second half Sartell had tied it at 14-14, on touchdowns from Tom Stark and Adam Herbst, who caught a 66-yard pass. Stark later scored his second of the game from one yard out to give the Sabres the lead. Then, a dramatic fourth quarter 53-yard fake punt run by Northfield's Matt Petricka tied the game at 21-21. But with 13 seconds left on the clock, Sartell's Scott Mader, who had pinned Northfield deep in its own territory with a 55-yard punt just prior, kicked the game-winning field goal from 38 yards out to give his club the crown.

The 14-0 Triton Cobras, led by their star Quarterback and Defensive Back Kirk Midthun, triumphed over Becker, 40-21, in the Class B championship game. Midthun passed for 309 yards and threw for six touchdowns on the day. Four of them found their way to Judge Gisslen, who also posted 171 yards receiving, while the other two, a pair of 87 and 20 yarders, were hauled in by receiver Tim Busch. After a back and forth first quarter, Becker's Brandon Novak recovered a fumble and returned it 57 yards to give Becker a 13-12 lead at half-time. The game was a wild one from there on though, as Triton tallied 28 points in the final 24 minutes of the game to get the big "W."

In Class C action, Chatfield defeated Red Lake Falls, 34-14, to win their first ever championship. The Gophers were able to shutdown all-around athlete Blaise Larson, a 6-4, 201-pound junior, who entered the title game with 2,015 yards rushing and 28 touchdowns. Larson's 46 yards on this day were simply not enough to get it done however, as Chatfield rolled behind Halfback Nathan Maker's three touchdowns on 202 yards rushing. Also leading the charge for the Gophers was Shane McBroom, who threw a pair of touchdowns to Tight End Jesse Seegmiller. Red Lake Falls actually took a 14-8 lead on a pair of touchdowns by Jesse Barbot before Chatfield pulled ahead 15-14 at the half, and then outscored the Eagles 19-0 down the stretch.

Senior Mark Olsonawski was the difference in leading Kittson Central to a 36-16 victory over Verndale in the 9-Man championship. Olsonawski scored three touchdowns (on runs of 15, 12 and 40 yards), gained 132 yards on the ground, and intercepted three passes as the Wolfpack went on to roll the Pirates. Kittson Central was actually trailing 8-0 at the end of the opening quarter, but pulled ahead 12-8 at the half and then led 18-16 going into the final quarter when they posted 18 unanswered points.

MSHSCA Coach of the Year

1965	Bill Severin, Grand Meadow
1966	Stav Canakes, Edina
1967	Tom Mahoney, Fairmont
1968	Jerry Sullivan, Mpls. Roosevelt
1969	Art Hass, Austin, Region I
1970	Gary Gustafson, North St. Paul
1971	George Larson, Cambridge
1972	George Wemeier, Mpls. Washburn
1973	Dick Lawrence, Eveleth
1974	John Drews, Rochester J.M..
1975	Bob Swanson, Mountain Iron
1976	Lyle Eidsness, St. Peter
1977	Paul Benson, Granite Falls
1978	Jim Simser, New Richland-Hart.
1979	Ron Raveling, Columbia Heights
1980	L.E. Dreschel, Crookston
1981	Gary Roebuck, Holdingford
1982	George Thole, Stillwater
1983	Ron Scott, Coon Rapids
1984	Grady Rostberg, Hutchinson
1985	Norm Johnson, Mpls. Roosevelt
1986	George Larson, Cambridge
1987	Dave Brokke, Granite Falls
1988	Gehard Meidt, Minneota
1989	Jim Mader, Albany
1990	Ken Baumann, Mahnomen
1991	Neal Holland, Chokio-Alberta
1992	Larry Thompson, Lakeview
1993	Rick Manke, Detroit Lakes
1994	DeWayne Johnson, Anoka
1995	Ken Jacobson, Chatfield
1996	Clark Bergloff, Mora
1997	Bubba Sullivan, Northfield
1998	Keith Bergstedt, Cromwell
1999	Lyle Anderson, Cook County

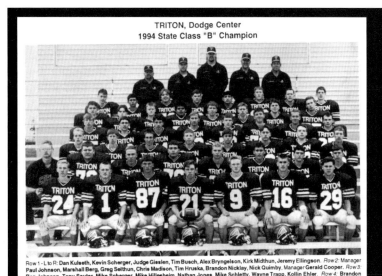

TRITON, Dodge Center
1994 State Class "B" Champion

Row 1 - L to R: Dan Kulseth, Kevin Scherger, Judge Gisslen, Tim Busch, Alex Bryngelson, Kirk Midthun, Jeremy Ellingson. Row 2: Manager Paul Johnson, Marshall Berg, Greg Selthun, Chris Madison, Tim Hruska, Brandon Nicklay, Nick Quimby, Manager Gerald Cooper. Row 3: Ben Johnson, Tony Sauter, Mike Scherger, Mike Hillesheim, Nathan Jones, Mike Schletty, Wayne Trapp, Kollin Ehler. Row 4: Brandon Vermilyea, Richie Kraemer, Luke Dobbs, Jaye Schmoll, Aaron Fredrickson, Brad Thornton, Jesse Winsell, Aaron Eldred. Row 5: Bill Organ, Niall McNeilus, David Roberts, Francisco Beltran, Chad Adams, Cory Mergen, Scott Pitzenberger, T. Jay Kleeberger. Row 6: Jason Twaddle, Eric Iverson, Tyler Twite, Kevin Brown, Genaro Menchaca, Jacob Kvam, Bryan Christianson, Hank Welch. Row 7: Assistant Coach Ralph Hanggi, Head Coach Don Hendeson, Assistant Coach Craig Schlichting, Assistant Coach Dennis Midthun, Assistant Coach Dominic Hillesheim.

1994 Class B Champs

CHATFIELD
1994 State Class "C" Champion

Row 1 - L to R: Managers Mark McMahon, Mike Urban, Mike Opat. Row 2: Assistant Coach Gary Hansen, Tim Stephas, Casey Patten, Brad LaPlante, Nathan Maker, Josh Goldsmith, Scott Tuohy, Trevor Niemeyer, Head Coach Ken Jacobson. Row 3: Assistant Coach Mike Walker, Aaron fohrman, Matt Johnson, Jason Irish, Rich Manahan, Josh Harmening, Jason Meyer, Tim McMahon, Matt McClellan, Assistant Coach Dan Hurley. Row 4: Matt Sogla, Justin Harmening, Jake Lane, Jason Worden, Jeremy Rabe, Jeremy Nelson, Peter Klema. Row 5: Chris Scrabeck, Shane McBroom, Jonathan Schroeder, Seth Allen, Wyatt Flies, Dan Conway, Mike Boelter. Row 6: Jeremy Wright, Matt Clemens, Jason Wright, Chris Jacobson, Chad Ferguson, Jesse Seegmiller, Darin Eisenman, Rob Goldsmith.

1994 Class C Champs

KITTSON CENTRAL, Hallock
1994 State Class "9-MAN" Champion

Row 1 - L to R: Bryce Derouin, Nathan Bowman, Kris Hokanson, Ryan Ingeman, Justin Johnson, Scott Erickson, Marc Gunnarson, Josh Deers. Row 2: Brian Olson, Courtney Moore, Tom Muis, Justin Soberaski, Josh Campbell, Greg Melin, Nathan Satterlund. Row 3: Taylor Sjostrand, Brett Niles, Brian Gatheridge, Brent Olsonawski, Bob Gunnarson, Andy Malm, Craig Backous. Row 4: Garrett Koop, Jeremy Peterson, Matt Campbell, Phil Pearson, Jeff Ryden, Joel Vagle, Kevin Balstad. Row 5: Drew Mortenson, Scott Younggren, Assistant Coach Jeff Keller, Head Coach Terry Ogorek, Assistant Coach Jeff Hart, Assistant Coach Brian Pastir, Mark Olsonawski, Ryan Johnson.

1994 Class 9-Man Champs

1995: PREP BOWL XIV

In their 16th trip to the state playoffs, the Stillwater Ponies defeated Rochester Mayo, 31-7, to win their fourth Class AA championship in six finals appearances. It even came on the 20th anniversary of their first championship back in 1975. Rochester Mayo threatened early, but Ponies' Corner Ryan Pletcher's interception led to an Aaron Runk two-yard touchdown just seven plays later. Down by 10 points, the Spartans planned to execute the old "Fumblerooski," a trick-play designed for Quarterback Steve Graber to slip the ball through center Ryan Finke's legs. But the ball bounced off Graber's shoulders though, and was picked up by Stillwater's Kory Johnson who returned it 20 yards into the end-zone to give the Ponies a 17-0 half-time lead. Rochester Mayo scored late in the fourth on a 31-yard fumble recovery for a touchdown, but it was too little too late. Runk led the Ponies that evening by scoring three touchdowns, giving him a school record of 55 over his career.

In their sixth consecutive playoff appearance, the undefeated Detroit Lakes Lakers defeated St. Peter, 39-15, for their third Class A title in four years. Detroit Lakes jumped out to a quick 14-0 lead before the game was even two minutes old. The Lakers' Craig Fredrickson took the opening kickoff 93-yards for touchdown to set the early tone. St. Peter then fumbled on the next play and the Lakers capitalized with a Todd Steinmetz touchdown. St. Peter did mount a rally to come within two points at the end of the third quarter, but the fourth quarter was all Lakers as Josh Keyes' rushing touchdown along with his 13 yard TD interception return capped the DL victory.

The Kingsland Knights, with a combined record of just five wins and 36 losses between 1990 and 1994, were the Cinderella story of the 1995 Prep Bowl. Their 22-3 victory against Breckenridge capped a perfect 14-0 turn-around season, and the school's first Class C title. Trenton Hyland led the Knights running for one touchdown and then returning an interception 36 yards for another in the second half. The Cowboys had three takeaways in the first quarter alone, but Breckenridge failed to cash in and was forced to punt. They even got the ball to within the 35 yard-line three times — but were able to score only three points. The Knights were a team of destiny, as they went on to win their inaugural title in their first-ever playoff appearance in school history.

The defending champion Chatfield Gophers' 12-6 upset victory of the top ranked Hawley Nuggets was the lowest-scoring Class C final in Prep Bowl history. After a scoreless first half, Chatfield took a 12-0 lead midway through the third quarter thanks to a pair of Luke Thieke touchdowns. Casey Marshall's one-yard TD run brought Hawley to within six in the fourth quarter, as they tried to mount a late comeback. The Nuggets had one final chance with 10 seconds on the clock, but the Gophers' Justin Harmening and Chris Scrabeck sacked quarterback Mike Olson to end the game.

In the 9-Man game, Cromwell defeated LeRoy-Ostrander, 26-18, handing the Cardinals their second runner-up finish in three years. After a back and forth first half, Dean Nyberg hit James Anderson for a two-point conversion pass that gave Cromwell a 20-18 lead that they were able to hold for the final six minutes of the game. The favored Cardinals came from behind in the fourth quarter though when Brian Granholm made a huge play. Granholm forced a LeRoy-Ostrander fumble and returned it deep into enemy territory to give Cromwell possession of the football with just a few minutes to go. Tyler Homstad then scored the winning touchdown on a four-yard run to give Cromwell the dramatic victory. Incidentally, the title was the first for a Northwestern team since Esko won the Class C division back in 1975.

STILLWATER AREA
1995 State Class AA Champion

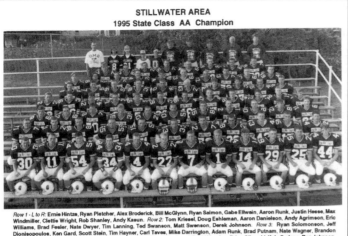

Row 1 - L to R: Ernie Hintze, Ryan Pletcher, Alex Broderick, Bill McGlynn, Ryan Salmon, Gabe Ellwein, Aaron Runk, Justin Heese, Max Windmiller, Clettie Wright, Rob Shanley, Andy Kasun. *Row 2:* Tom Kriesel, Doug Eshleman, Aaron Danielson, Andy Agrimson, Eric Williams, Brad Fesler, Nate Dwyer, Tim Lanning, Ted Swanson, Matt Swenson, Derek Johnson. *Row 3:* Ryan Solomonson, Jeff Dionisopoulos, Ken Gard, Scott Stein, Tim Hayner, Carl Taves, Mike Darrington, Adam Runk, Brad Putnam, Nate Wagner, Brandon Gorder. *Row 4:* Kroy Johnson, Brant Ireland, Eric Hering, Tony Marchand, David Horning, Brian Gilewski, Kyle Carlson, Ben Johnson, Joe Gould, Nick Siljendahl, Mitch Ellingson, Dave Eichten. *Row 5:* Ryan Eskierka, Matt MacDonald, Dan Nord, Sean Frasier, Jeff Hoppe, Tim Safe, Chris Fisher, Erich Wolff, Shawn Seibert, Ben Gerde. *Row 6:* Zach Boardman, Peter Dahdah, Mike Coleman, Rich Hooley, Adam Larson, Joe Matel, Adam Kramer, Tony Raboin, Kevin Mathews, Paul Diercks. *Row 7:* Adam Stafne, Brian Dobson, Greg Coleman, Ben Beaudet, Ryan Polzin, Dan Hanson, Brock Stoltzmann, Chris Schmoeckel. *Row 8:* Student Managers Scott Drommerhausen, Andrea Reber, Tiffany Forster, Hans Larson, Ross Halverson, Head Coach George Thole, Assistant Coach Jerry Foley, Assistant Coach Dick Klein, Assistant Coach Gary Gustafson, Assistant Coach Scott Hoffman.

1995 Class AA Champs

DETROIT LAKES
1995 State Class A Champion

Row 1 - L to R: Cheerleaders Heidi Kilde, Melissa Olson, Chrystal Chamberlain, Keely Bueckers, Anita McKeown, Kristen Allrich, Joy Mertes. *Row 2:* Rory Manke, Zach Zirbel, Justin Wood, Matt Hovdenes, Steve Skarie, Neal Kittelson, Josh Keyes, Pete Hedman, Matt Brattie, Kris Spenningsby, Jamie Schweigert. *Row 3:* Quinn Dallmann, Nate Haspel, Tim Sundby, Wade Lewandowski, Dave Laudon, Craig Fredrickson, Joe Skaaland, Bryan Woodward, Dan Josephson, Anthony Schiller, Brian Redig. *Row 4:* Kenny Blattenbauer, Craig Hinson, Charlie Haggart, Brian Flanagan, Nick Bowers, Mark Potvin, Ronnie Sprafka, Jon Pratt, Ryan Wickum, Ryan Kotta, Kent Gronvold. *Row 5:* Ben Bergman, Richard Whiting, Wayne Schneider, Shawn Rehm, Mark Porter, Mike Steffl, Brady Peterson, Matt Behr, Paul Okeson, Reid Whitworth, Jeff Olmstead, Nate Pierson. *Row 6:* Doug Muzik, J.J. Larson, Troy Fingalson, Aaron Bratten, Adam Schneider, Joey Fingalson, Todd Steinmetz, Nick Hagedorn, Andy Reiffenberger.

1995 Class A Champs

KINGSLAND, Spring Valley
1995 State Class B Champion

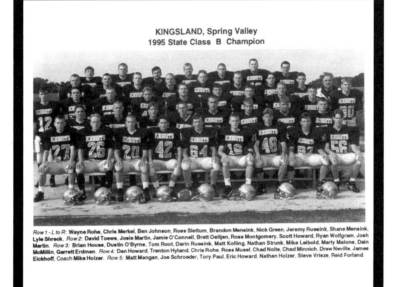

Row 1 - L to R: Wayne Rohe, Chris Merkel, Ben Johnson, Ross Slettum, Brandon Mensink, Nick Green, Jeremy Ruesink, Shane Mensink, Lyle Shreck. *Row 2:* David Toews, Josie Martin, Jamie O'Connell, Brett Oeltjen, Ross Montgomery, Scott Howard, Ryan Wolfgram, Josh Martin. *Row 3:* Brian House, Dustin O'Byrne, Tom Root, Darin Ruesink, Matt Kolling, Nathan Strunk, Mike Leibold, Marty Malone, Dain McMillin, Garrett Erdman. *Row 4:* Dan Howard, Trenton Hyland, Chris Rohe, Ross Musel, Chad Nolte, Chad Minnich, Drew Neville, James Eickhoff, Coach Mike Holzer. *Row 5:* Matt Mangan, Joe Schroeder, Tory Paul, Eric Howard, Nathan Holzer, Steve Vrieze, Reid Forland.

1995 Class B Champs

CHATFIELD
1995 State Class C Champion

Row 1 - L to R: Cheerleaders Jackie McCabe, Susan Wright, Heather Timm, Kari Baker, Amy Patten, Kristi Hamann, April Copeman, Becky Hylland. *Row 2:* Matt Sogla, Eric Rain, Jon Sutherland, Tim Walker, Jeremy Rabe, Josh Goldsmith, Seth Allen, Scott Tuohy. *Row 3:* Peter Kiema, Justin Harmening, Matt Rabe, Jason Bothun, Tony Kiema, Dan Conway, Tom Hahn, Ryan Hawkins. *Row 4:* Student Manager Steve Opat, Assistant Coach Mike Walker, Assistant Coach Gary Hansen, Head Coach Ken Jacobson, Assistant Coach Dan Hurley, Assistant Coach Brent Rauk, Student Manager Mark McMahon. *Row 5:* Troy Proper, Matt Hinckley, Jared Borst, Jason Worden, Noloan Schild, Andy Hamann. *Row 6:* Matt McClellan, Chris Scrabeck, Wyatt Flies, Trever Niemeyer, Luke Thieke, Shane McBroom, Brian Bicknese, Casey Borgen, Matt McCabe, Matt Johnson. *Row 7:* Darin Eisenman, Aaron Fohrman, Mike Boelter, Jake Lane, Jeremy Wright, Dan Schellhammer, Jason Meyer, Chris Jacobeon, Rob Goldsmith, Tim McMahon.

1995 Class C Champs

CROMWELL
1995 State Class 9-MAN Champion

Row 1 - L to R: Student Manager Rusty French, Student Manager Tony Homstad, Eric Waldemarsen, Craig Freiermuth, Mason Hansen, Michael Johnson, Mike Olesiak, Rick Hanhela, Student Manager Justin Goranson. *Row 2:* Nick Axtell, Shayne Korpela, Carl Switzer, Darin Smith, Tom Gervais, Dean Goranson. *Row 3:* Matthew Martin, Matthew Hakala, Jeff Anderson, Seth Koivisto, Brian Lind, James Anderson. *Row 4:* Jason Graff, Daniel Dahl, Brandon Suhonen, Troy Bridge, Seth Aho, Tyler Homstad. *Row 5:* Ryan Mattson, Travis Homstad, Pete Eggert, Cory Schleret, Cory Aho, Jon Graff. *Row 6:* Coach Keith Bergstedt, Mark Ponce, Dean Nyberg, Brian Granholm, Gabe Aho, LeAlan Shelton, Ryan Olesiak, Coach Dan Holgate.

1995 Class 9-Man Champs

1996: PREP BOWL XV

The Class AA finals featured five lead changes, including two in the final three minutes, before Eden Prairie was able to eke out a 23-22 victory over Blaine. This game had it all: a 42-yard field goal, a 60-yard deflected TD pass, a flea-flicker on the winning drive, and a game-deciding two-point conversion attempt at the buzzer. The Bengals, whose defense hadn't allowed any points in 18 previous quarters of play, and had shut-out their last four opponents, found themselves down 15-9 after a 24-yard TD run by Eden Prairie's Grant Sentz late in the third quarter. The Bengals then drove 80 yards on 10 plays to regain a 16-15 advantage. The Eagles roared right back though with a 75-yard scoring drive that ended with a 25-yard pass from Ricky Fritz to Ryan Iverson. Fritz then scored the two-point conversion on a keeper to give his squad a seven-point lead with just over a minute to go. Blaine brought the game to within one point after a 60-yard, six-play drive capped by Jason Albrecht's second TD toss of the game, but gambled and came up short on the two-point conversion that would've given them the win.

In a battle of great defense, unranked Mora took the Class A championship by defeating Northfield, 7-3. Mora's Travis Lagasse scored a touchdown late in the second quarter, capping a 32-yard drive following a short Northfield punt. Mora's 200-pound Running Back Nate Kirschner caught four passes for 79 yards and made a key fumble recovery in the last minutes to ice the game for the Mustangs. Ironically, Northfield edged Mora with 211 total offensive yards compared to Mora's 165, but was unable to get into the end-zone.

Golden Valley's Breck School defeated Windom Area, 24-7, for the Class B state title. Breck's defense was the key in this one, led by a Prep Bowl record six interceptions, including two by Eric Anderson which led to scores. In addition, Breck recovered two fumbles, one of which also set up a touchdown. (One of the stars of the Breck team was Regis Eller, son of Vikings' great Carl Eller.) Windom Area scored its only points in the final minutes of the second quarter, and came up short in the end.

In a bizarre mirror finish of the 1995 Class C Prep Bowl final, Chatfield defeated No.1-ranked Hawley by an identical 12-6 margin to take the crown. Chatfield jumped out to a quick 12-0 lead midway through the third quarter on Justin Harmening's one-yard touchdown run. Hawley got on the board early in the fourth quarter when Travis Olson hit Sheridan Johnson for a touchdown, capping a nine-play, 69-yard drive. Then, with about three minutes remaining, Hawley had a controversial touchdown taken away from then when the officials called the Nuggets for an illegal procedure penalty. Chatfield's defense played huge, recording five sacks in the game to earn the team its third consecutive state title and extend its winning streak to 24 games.

Defending champion Cromwell nearly blew a 38-18 lead, but held on to win its second straight 9-Man championship and extend its impressive winning streak to 26 games. Both offenses were big in this one, with Cromwell accumulating 412 yards of fire-power and Verndale recording 315. Senior Tyler Homstad was one of Cromwell's heroes, rushing for 142 yards on 32 carries. So too was Michael Olesiak, who's 64-yard touchdown run gave the Cardinals a 38-18 lead early in the third. Verndale then attempted an amazing second-half comeback, scoring five of the game's next six touchdowns. Leading the charge was Mike Kricher, whose two touchdown receptions made it a 38-24 game. Late in the third, Cromwell recovered a fumble for a TD to make the score 46-30. But, with 9:04 remaining, Quarterback Allan Gades pulled Verndale back to within a touchdown with a 15-yard pass and two-point passing conversion, followed by Joe Kerns' dramatic three yard touchdown run three minutes later to make it 46-44. Verndale went for the tie, but a failed two-point conversion led to Cromwell running out the remainder of the clock to seal the deal.

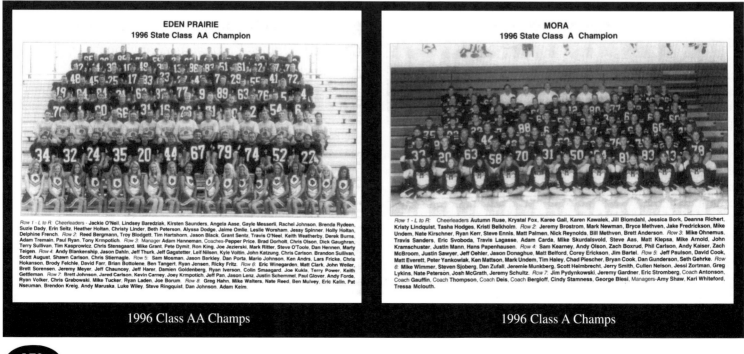

1996 Class AA Champs

1996 Class A Champs

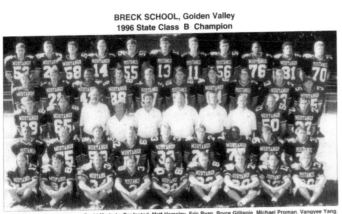

BRECK SCHOOL, Golden Valley
1996 State Class B Champion

Row 1 - L to R: Mark Andersen, David Moriarty, Tor Instad, Matt Hemsley, Eric Ryan, Bryce Gillispie, Michael Proman, Vangyee Yang, Mike McKeon. *Row 2:* Kee Lockhart, Anders Reinertsen, George May, Tom Richardson, Andrew Christopherson, Jeff Kemnitz, Seth Barnes, Karl Dedolph, Jesse Doheny. *Row 3:* John Beane, Mike Boosalis, Assistant Coach Rich Joseph, Assistant Coach Dan Doheny, Head Coach John Thiel, Assistant Coach Brian Schauer, Assistant Coach Brett Bergene, Assistant Coach Rick Thurston, Drew Johnson, Jon Simmons. *Row 4:* David O'Hagen, Eric Anderson, Paris Johnson, Smith Wilkenson, Greg Robinson, Anders Seeland, John Fraser, Eli Kramer, Ed Dunn, Chris Dale. *Row 5:* Ross Hussey, Bowen Osborn, Peter Prudden, Adam Drill, Carl Nelson, Gavin Hoffman, Colin Brooks, Pat Varecka, Jason Keene, Regis Eller, Chris Johnson.

1996 Class B Champs

CHATFIELD
1996 State Class C Champion

Row 1 - L to R: Cheerleaders - Roxi Rabe, Teresa Swanson, Jenny Hammell, April Copeman, Becky Hylland, Tisha Greenslade, Meghan Thieke, Jodi Giehtbrock. *Row 2:* Student Manager Steve Opat, Assistant Coach Dan Hurley, Assistant Coach Mike Walker, Head Coach Ken Jacobson, Assistant Coach Gary Hansen, Assistant Coach Travis Armstrong, Student Manager Mark McMahon. *Row 3:* Kevin Donahoe, Mark Paynic, Jason Drogemuller, Ryan Hawkins, Josh Eisenman, Tony Klema, Noloan Schild. *Row 4:* James Kozinski, Adam Smith, Casey Borgen, Dustin Rich, Chris Priebe, Joe Boelter, Mike Manahan, Mike Opat. *Row 5:* Justin Harmening, Matt Sogla, Adam Daniels, Matt Hinckley, John Copeman, Jon Sutherland, Matt McCabe. *Row 6:* Chris Scrabeck, Trever Niemeyer, Luke Thieke, Jared Borst, Tim Walker, Dan Conway, Brian Bicknese, Troy Proper, Andy Hamann, Matt Davidson. *Row 7:* Darin Eisenman, Mike Boelter, Jeremy Wright, Dan Schellhammer, Aaron Fohrman, Tom Hahn.

1996 Class C Champs

1997: PREP BOWL XVI

Prep Bowl XVI was the first to feature the state's new six-class (A-through-AAAAA) football system. The Bengals of Blaine wanted to avenge their 1996 Class AA championship loss to Eden Prairie, but came up four points short in the Class AAAAA championship, losing to the Eagles, 32-28. Blaine Running Back Marvin Spencer was quiet during the first half but awoke in the third quarter with a 54-yard touchdown scamper to give the Bengals a 15-point lead. Eden Prairie drew within two points soon thereafter, first with a 17-yard Ricky Fritz to Chris Stiernagle touchdown pass in the third, and then again just 13 seconds into the fourth on a two-yard run by James Thomas. Stiernagle scored his second touchdown of the game on a four-yard pass from Ryan Iverson, but for the second time in the quarter, the Eagles two-point conversion attempt failed. Then, less than a minute later, Blaine's Tony Roller hit Reondo Davis flying down the left sideline for an 83-yard touchdown pass. The Eagle's answered, however, with a 47-yard touchdown pass of their own from Fritz to Iverson, thus cementing the second consecutive "big school" championship for Eden Prairie.

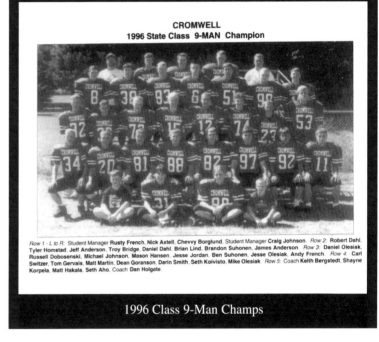

CROMWELL
1996 State Class 9-MAN Champion

Row 1 - L to R: Student Manager Rusty French, Nick Axtell, Chevvy Borglund, Student Manager Craig Johnson. *Row 2:* Robert Dahl, Tyler Homstad, Jeff Anderson, Troy Bridge, Daniel Dahl, Brian Lind, Brandon Suhonen, James Anderson. *Row 3:* Daniel Olesiak, Russell Dobosenski, Michael Johnson, Mason Hansen, Jesse Jordan, Ben Suhonen, Jesse Olesiak, Andy French. *Row 4:* Carl Switzer, Tom Gervais, Matt Martin, Dean Goranson, Darin Smith, Seth Koivisto, Mike Olesiak. *Row 5:* Coach Keith Bergstedt, Shayne Korpela, Matt Hakala, Seth Aho. Coach Dan Holgate.

1996 Class 9-Man Champs

The Northfield Raiders pounded on Detroit Lakes, 28-0, to take the inaugural Class AAAA championship. It was finally meant to be for the Raiders, who won their first state title in five appearances. Northfield's Matt Geiger was the hero, rushing for 93 yards and three of the team's four touchdowns. The fourth touchdown came on a 39-yard fumble recovery by Matt Faust in the third quarter. On paper, the game should have been much closer. The Raiders actually generated fewer yards than the Lakers (209 to 239), and Northfield only had the ball for 17:35 compared to Detroit Lakes' possession time of 30:25. Detroit Lakes' offense was led by Corey Brogren who rushed for 115 yards, while Quarterback Ryan Kotta was six of 18 passing for 53 yards.

It was an all-Huskies mush-fest for the Class AAA title tilt, with the Huskies of Albany beating up on the Huskies of Jackson County Central by the final of 55-7. Down 7-0, Jackson County Central tied it up on Rob Brown's second quarter touchdown. But, after going into the lockerroom deadlocked at 7-7, Albany came out smoking in the second half and erupted for 42 points. Troy Hoffarth led Albany's rushing attack, churning out 120 yards on 12 carries that included three touchdowns. Hoffarth also caught two passes for 33 yards and returned an interception 39 yards.

Despite being held scoreless during the entire second half, the Pelican Rapids Vikings hung on to defeat the Buccaneers of Waterville-Elysian-Morristown, 34-32, for the Class AA championship. Amazingly, Pelican Rapids scored all of its 34 points while having possession of the ball for just 10 minutes and 16 seconds of the first half. Conversely, the Vikings only had possession for an additional one minute and 43 seconds in the entire second half. Vikings Running Back Terry Motz carried the load, rushing for 135 yards and a pair of touchdowns. Quarterback Matt Soberg opened the scoring for Pelican Rapids with a six-yard TD run around the right end in the first quarter, and later threw a touchdown pass to Ryan Sjostrum midway through the second. Sjostrum also returned a kickoff 81 yards for another touchdown in the second as well. Waterville-Elysian-Morristown's Tony Stoering led the rushing attack with 113 yards and a TD. Quarterback Cory Hackett also ran in a two-yard TD, as well as throwing for 174 yards and an additional three TDs to the likes of Gabe Hauer, Jason Geiser, and Justin Miller. It was not enough though, as the Buccaneers' came up two points short.

The Vikings of Cook County held on to a one-point first-half lead to win the Class A championship, 13-12, over Adrian. Cook County drew blood in the first quarter on the first of Barry Pederson's two touchdown runs. Adrian rallied to put together a pair of scoring drives, but missed both two-point conversion attempts — a mistake that would ultimately cost them in the end. The Dragons' scoring came from Bryan

Metz, who had 97 yards on 23 carries, and from Matt Konz, who tallied 97 yards on 15 carries. Both teams had plenty of opportunities to put points on the board throughout the second half, but turnovers killed most of their scoring threats. Adrian finally got its fans on their feet late in the fourth when it appeared that they had taken the lead on a 91-yard touchdown pass. But, an illegal procedure penalty nullified the play. The Dragons stayed alive though and drove down to the Cook County 30-yard line with under a minute to go in the game. There, after a couple of good shots, they came up short when Quarterback Matt Konz threw an interception to end the game.

The Verndale Pirates ended Cromwell's incredible 38-game winning streak in the 9-Man championship game, defeating the Cardinals by the final of 18-12. The Cardinals dominated the first half of play behind the rushing of Running Backs Mike Olesiak and Tom Gervais, who ran for a combined 70 yards. Quarterback Dean Goranson also rushed for 41 yards and a touchdown, and added a 40-yard TD pass to Carl Switzer. Verndale's only first-half score came on a 16-yard run by Joe Kern. Kern would add another though, finishing with 102 rushing yards on 26 attempts. Jared Forcier added a seven-yard TD run for the Pirates as well. The turning point in what had been an evenly matched contest came late in the fourth quarter. Deadlocked at 12 apiece, Cromwell's Carl Sitzer fumbled and Verndale's Jeremy Elfstrum recovered. The Pirates were unable to score though, as Kicker Mitch Carr went wide left with a 28-yard field goal attempt. Cromwell took possession, but a fumble on a pass attempt by Dean Goranson was recovered by Verndale's Zach Hinckle on the 18-yard line. From there, Kern's two-yard dive into the end zone made it 18-12. The two-point conversion failed. Cromwell then took the ensuing kickoff down to Verndale's 39, but Dean Goranson threw an interception with just 1:08 left. Verndale then simply took a knee and ran out the clock to avenge its loss to Cromwell the year before.

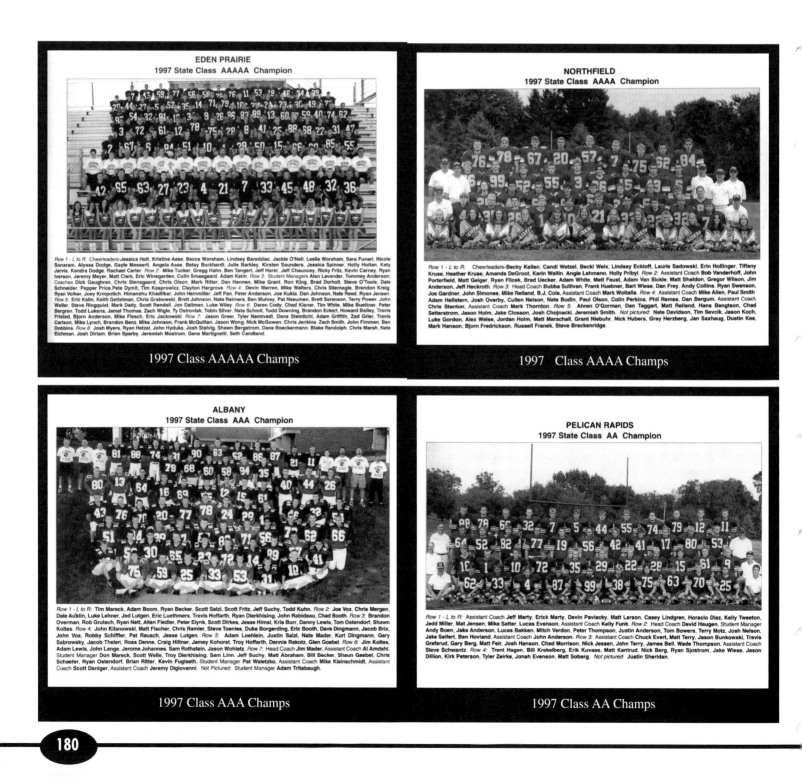

EDEN PRAIRIE
1997 State Class AAAAA Champion

Row 1 - L to R: Cheerleaders-Jessica Holt, Kristine Aase, Becca Worsham, Lindsey Baredziac, Jackie O'Nell, Leslie Worsham, Sara Funari, Nicole Sonaram, Alyssa Dodge, Gayle Messerli, Angela Aase, Betsy Burkhardt, Julie Barkley, Kirsten Saunders, Jessica Spinner, Holly Holtan, Katy Jarvis, Kendra Dodge, Rachael Carter. Row 2: Mike Tucker, Gregg Hahn, Ben Tangert, Jeff Harer, Jeff Chauncey, Ricky Fritz, Kevin Carney, Ryan Iverson, Jeremy Meyer, Matt Clark, Eric Winegarden, Colin Smaagaard, Adam Keim. Row 3: Student Managers Alan Lavender, Tommey Anderson; Coaches Dick Gaughran, Chris Stensgaard, Chris Olson, Mark Ritter, Dan Hennen, Mike Grant, Ron King, Brad Dorholt, Steve O'Toole, Dale Schneider, Pepper Price,Pete Dymit, Tim Kasprowicz, Clayton Hargrove. Row 4: Devin Warren, Mike Walters, Chris Stiernagle, Brendon Kreig, Ryan Volker, Joey Krmpotich, Himanshu Khadilkar, John Heinmiller, Jeff Pan, Peter Anderson, Joe Kukla, Dan Johnson, Nate Reed, Ryan Jensen. Row 5: Eric Kalin, Keith Getteiman, Chris Grabowski, Brett Johnson, Nate Reimers, Ben Mulvey, Pat Nseumen, Brett Sorenson, Terry Power, John Weiler, Steve Ringquist, Mark Dady, Scott Rendall, Jon Dallman, Luke Wiley. Row 6: Daren Cody, Chad Kisner, Tim White, Mike Buettner, Peter Bergren, Todd Lukens, Jamel Thomas, Zach Wigle, Ty Ostrovlak, Tobin Silver, Nate Schmit, Todd Downing, Brandon Eckert, Howard Bailey, Travis Fristed, Bjorn Anderson, Mike Flesch, Eric Jackowski. Row 7: Jason Greer, Tyler Namtvedt, Dane Steinlicht, Adam Griffith, Zed Grler, Travis Carlson, Mike Lynch, Brandon Benz, Mike Johnson, Frank McQuillan, Jason Wong, Nick McGowan, Chris Jenkins, Zach Smith, John Fimmen, Ben Dobbins. Row 8: Josh Myers, Ryan Hetzel, John Hyduke, Josh Stalvig, Shawn Bergstrom, Dane Boeckermann, Blake Randolph, Chris Marsh, Nate Elchman, Josh Dirlam, Brian Sparby, Jeremiah Mostrom, Gene Martignetti, Seth Candland.

1997 Class AAAAA Champs

NORTHFIELD
1997 State Class AAAA Champion

Row 1 - L to R: Cheerleaders-Becky Keilen, Candi Wetzel, Becki Weix, Lindsay Eckloff, Laurie Sadowski, Erin Hollinger, Tiffany Kruse, Heather Kruse, Amanda DeGroot, Karin Wallin, Angie Lehmann, Holly Pribyl. Row 2: Assistant Coach Bob Vanderhoff, John Porterfield, Matt Geiger, Ryan Flicek, Brad Uecker, Adam White, Matt Faust, Adam Van Sickle, Matt Sheldon, Gregor Wilson, Jim Anderson, Jeff Heckroth. Row 3: Head Coach Bubba Sullivan, Frank Huebner, Bart Wiese, Dan Frey, Andy Collins, Ryan Swenson, Joe Gardner, John Simones, Mike Relland, B.J. Cole, Assistant Coach Mark Wottalla. Row 4: Assistant Coach Mike Allen, Paul Smith, Adam Hellstern, Josh Overby, Cullen Nelson, Nate Budin, Paul Olson, Colin Perkins, Phil Remes, Dan Bergum, Assistant Coach Chris Stanton, Assistant Coach Mark Thornton. Row 5: Ahren O'Gorman, Dan Taggart, Matt Reiland, Hans Bengtson, Chad Setterstrom, Jason Holm, Jake Closson, Josh Chojnacki, Jeremiah Smith. Not pictured: Nate Davidson, Tim Sevcik, Jason Koch, Luke Gordon, Alex Weise, Jordan Holm, Matt Marschall, Grant Niebuhr, Nick Hubers, Gray Herzberg, Jan Saxhaug, Dustin Kes, Mark Hanson, Bjorn Fredrickson, Russell Franek, Steve Breckenridge.

1997 Class AAAA Champs

ALBANY
1997 State Class AAA Champion

Row 1 - L to R: Tim Mareck, Adam Boom, Ryan Becker, Scott Salzl, Scott Fritz, Jeff Suchy, Todd Kuhn. Row 2: Joe Vox, Chris Mergen, Dale Austin, Luke Lehner, Jed Lutgen, Eric Luethmers, Travis Hoffarth, Ryan Dierkhising, John Rabideau, Chad Booth. Row 3: Brandon Overman, Rob Grutsch, Ryan Nett, Allen Fiedler, Peter Eiynk, Scott Dirkes, Jesse Himsl, Kris Burr, Danny Lewis, Tom Ostendorf, Shawn Koltes. Row 4: John Kilanowski, Matt Fischer, Chris Ramler, Steve Toenies, Duke Borgerding, Eric Booth, Dave Dingmann, Jacob Brix, John Vos, Robby Schiffler, Pat Rausch, Jesse Lutgen. Row 5: Adam Loehlein, Justin Salzl, Nate Mader, Kurt Dingmann, Gary Sabrowsky, Jacob Thelen, Ross Denne, Craig Hiltner, Jamey Kohorst, Troy Hoffarth, Dennis Rakotz, Glen Goebel. Row 6: Jim Koltes, Adam Lewis, John Lange, Jerome Johannes, Sam Rothstein, Jason Wohletz. Row 7: Head Coach Jim Mader, Assistant Coach Al Amdahl, Student Manager Don Mareck, Scott Welle, Troy Dierkhising, Sam Linn, Jeff Suchy, Matt Abraham, Bill Becker, Shaun Gaebel, Chris Schaefer, Ryan Ostendorf, Brian Ritter, Kevin Fugleseth, Student Manager Pat Waletzko, Assistant Coach Mike Kleinschmidt, Assistant Coach Scott Daniger, Assistant Coach Jeremy Digiovanni. Not Pictured: Student Manager Adam Tritabaugh.

1997 Class AAA Champs

PELICAN RAPIDS
1997 State Class AA Champion

Row 1 - L to R: Assistant Coach Jeff Marty, Erick Marty, Devin Pavlacky, Matt Larson, Casey Lindgren, Horacio Diaz, Kelly Tweeton, Jedd Miller, Mat Jensen, Mike Satter, Lucas Evenson, Assistant Coach Kelly Funk. Row 2: Head Coach David Haugen, Student Manager Andy Boen, Jake Anderson, Lucas Bakken, Mitch Verdon, Peter Thompson, Justin Anderson, Tom Bowers, Terry Motz, Josh Nelson, Jake Seifert, Ben Hovland, Assistant Coach John Anderson. Row 3: Assistant Coach Chuck Evert, Matt Terry, Jason Bunkowski, Travis Grefsrud, Gary Berg, Matt Feir, Josh Hanson, Chad Morrison, Nick Jessen, John Terry, James Bell, Wade Thompson, Assistant Coach Steve Schwantz. Row 4: Trent Hagen, Bill Krekelberg, Erik Kuvaas, Matt Kantrud, Nick Berg, Ryan Sjostrom, Jake Wiese, Jason Dillion, Kirk Peterson, Tyler Zeirke, Jonah Evenson, Matt Soberg. Not pictured: Justin Sheridan.

1997 Class AA Champs

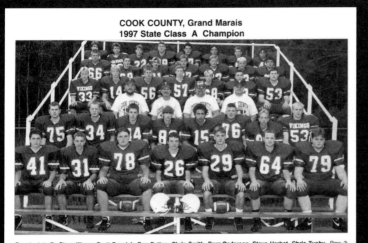

COOK COUNTY, Grand Marais
1997 State Class A Champion

Row 1 - L to R: Steve Waver, Brett Barwick, Ben Patten, Chris Smith, BarryPederson, Steve Herbst, Chris Tuohy. *Row 2:* Shawn Starkey, Jared Smith, Mike Wirt, Nathan Wallerstedt, Joe Deschampe, Craig Horak, Tryg Watterhouse, Glen Hedstrom. *Row 3:* Assistant Coach Mark Patten, Head Coach Lyle Anderson, Assistant Coach Dale Bockovich, Assistant Coach Mike Boomer. *Row 4:* Ben Brandt, Woody Seim, Troy Berneking, Brian Kubes, Travis Van Doren, Rick Tavernier, Jeff Mattson. *Row 5:* Trever Berneking, Jesse Kimball, Brian Weitz, Jake Hammond, Erik Anderson, Todd Gervais, Richard Bohnen. *Row 6:* Ben Rude, Sean Riley, Matt Gwash, Ryan Petz, Cory Pederson, Charlie Trovall, Joey Pederson. *Not pictured:* Noah Waterhouse, Dustin Nelson, Brandon Marxen, Robert James, Jake Moritz, Jason Moritz.

1997 Class A Champs

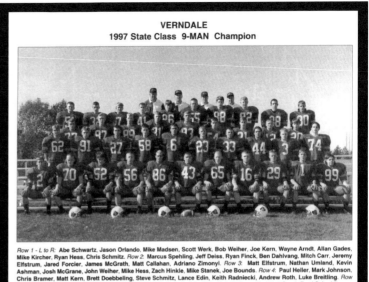

VERNDALE
1997 State Class 9-MAN Champion

Row 1 - L to R: Abe Schwartz, Jason Orlando, Mike Madsen, Scott Werk, Bob Weiher, Joe Kern, Wayne Arndt, Allan Gades, Mike Kircher, Ryan Hess, Chris Schmitz. *Row 2:* Marcus Spehling, Jeff Deiss, Ryan Finck, Ben Dahlvang, Mitch Carr, Jeremy Elfstrum, Jared Forcier, James McGrath, Matt Callahan, Adriano Zimonyi. *Row 3:* Matt Elfstrum, Nathan Umland, Kevin Ashman, Josh McGrane, John Weiher, Mike Hess, Zach Hinkle, Mike Stanek, Joe Bounds. *Row 4:* Paul Heller, Mark Johnson, Chris Bramer, Matt Kern, Brett Doebbeling, Steve Schmitz, Lance Edin, Keith Radniecki, Andrew Roth, Luke Breitling. *Row 5:* Assistant Coach Tim Seaton, Head Coach Michael Mahlen, Assistant Coach Jeff Moore, Assistant Coach Brad Schmidt.

1997 Class 9-Man Champs

1998: PREP BOWL XVII

It was a battle of first-time qualifiers in the Class 5-A title game when Woodbury took to the turf against Champlin Park. After beating defending champion Eden Prairie, 32-22, in the semifinals, the Woodbury Royals pounded the Champlin Park Rebels, 28-7, to win their first Prep Bowl championship. After going up 7-0 in the first quarter on Bobby Grandas' short touchdown pass to Matt Swansson, the Royals went to their ground attack in the second. Louis Ayeni, who had 179 yards rushing on the day, ran an 11-yarder in to put the Royals ahead by 13 points. Then, seven minutes later, Grandas ran one in to make it 21-0. Grandas then completed his second touchdown pass of the day to Swansson, this one coming with 19 seconds remaining in the first half to make it 28-0. After a scoreless third, the Rebels scored their only touchdown of the game when Paul Rumsey caught a 10-yard pass from Cavan Scheer. It was too little to late though as Woodbury held on for the 28-7 victory.

After losing in the semifinals of the 1997 tournament, the undefeated Hutchinson Tigers won their first state title since 1984 by defeating Owatonna in a nail-biter, 21-20. Hutchinson was led by Running Back Chris Davis, who ran for 112 yards on 21 carries and two touchdowns, while Owatonna was led by Quarterback Tim Nierengarten, who threw for 96 yards, rushed for 20 yards and added a pair of touchdowns. Down by two points at the end of the first half, the Huskies rallied in the second on a 15-play 75-yard drive that ended with Matt Skala's one-yard TD run. Nierengarten ran the ball into the end zone to complete the two-point conversion and the Huskies suddenly found themselves ahead 20-14. The Tigers came back in the fourth behind Kirchoff, who dropped back and hit Tim Thode with a 14-yard TD pass to go ahead 21-20. Owatonna came back hard though and had a chance to win it with a field goal in the final minutes. But, when Rob Donohue's 39-yard chip-shot attempt fell short of the uprights, this 4-A final was over.

Foley, in their first-ever appearance in the state tournament, handed the Huskies of Jackson County Central their second consecutive runner-up title, en route to claiming the Class 3-A championship. The Huskies got on the board first when Jesse Voss scored on a three-yard run in the first quarter. But the Falcons went ahead when Jon David caught an 89-yard pass from Quarterback Mike Kieffer, followed by Jon Miller's two-point conversion. Foley blew it open when David caught his second TD pass from Kieffer late in the second quarter, followed by Greg Garceau's 26-yard touchdown run up the middle to give the Falcons their 21-7 final score.

In their 15th overall appearance in the state playoffs, the Mahnomen Indians hung on to defeat BOLD of Olivia, 27-26, in the Class 2-A championship game. After a 14-14 tie following the first half, Mahnomen pushed ahead to lead by one point at the end of the third, 21-20. Then, in the fourth, the Indians scored on quarterback Ben Baumann's seven-yard pass to Adam Simon in the back of the end-zone. The Warriors rallied behind Cam Bailey's Quarterback sneak late in the fourth quarter to make it 27-26 in favor of the Indians. The Warriors then gambled on going for the win, but their two-point conversion attempt on a run failed, and Mahnomen went home with its fifth state title. The Indians running backs were the difference, with DeVries rushing for 205 yards and a touchdown, and Teeman gaining 84 yards and a score of his own. The Warriors were led by Bailey, who rushed for two touchdowns, and passed for 141 yards and another touchdown.

In a bit of deja vu of the 1997 Class 1-A title game, the Vikings of Cook County once again defeated the Dragons of Adrian. The Dragons pushed the Vikings into two overtimes this time before ultimately losing, 38-32. After a scoreless first, Adrian Quarterback Matt Konz, who ran for 253 yards in the game, took over, rushing for 112 yards and scoring twice in the second quarter alone. Vikings Quarterback Erik Anderson answered with a touchdown of his own with 17 seconds remaining in the first half to make the score 16-6 at half-time. Cook County then went up when Richard Bohnen scored on a 43-yard TD, followed by Anderson hooking up with Receiver Troy Berneking on a 62-yard scoring strike to make it 18-16. Adrian rallied in the fourth, driving the ball 88 yards in seven plays and scoring on a 21-yard pass from Konz to Mark Kroon. But the Vikings answered and tied it at 24 on their next possession when Bohnen busted loose for a 44 yard TD run. Cook County's Travis Lange blocked the kick though, leaving both teams tied at the end of regulation. The Vikings won the coin toss in the opening overtime and elected to play defense. Adrian scored two plays later as Konz completed a seven-yard run, followed by a two-point conversion pass to Ben Kroon. But, the Vikings also scored, as Todd Gervais completed a 10-yard run and Anderson converted on a run to tie the score at 38 points and send the game into a second OT. Adrian won the coin toss in the second overtime and elected to defend. Bohnen made them pay for that decision, rushing for his third touchdown of the day and giving his Vikings the lead. The Dragons then came up short on their final possession of the game, as Vikings' lineman Troy Berkening stopped Bryan Metz on Cook County's one-yard line to end it with a dramatic finish.

For the third time in four years, Cromwell won the 9-man championship. After losing the championship to Verndale in 1997, the undefeated Cardinals came back to beat Hillcrest Lutheran Academy of Fergus Falls, 40-22. The Cards exploded out of the gates to take a 28-0 lead

Individual Record for Passing Yards in a Career

Yds	Player	School	Year
8533	Chris Meidt	Minneota	1984-87
7482	Ryan Keating	Minnetonka	1994-97
7186	Kirk Midthun	Triton	1992-95
6038	JJ Korman	Bethlehem Academy	1990-93
6038	Cory Hackett	Waterville EM	1996-99

Individual Record for Passing TDs in a Career

No.	Player	School	Year
101	Chris Meidt	Minneota	1984-87
83	Ryan Keating	Minnetonka	1994-97
81	Kris Beuckens	Hoffman/Kensington	1985-88
81	Kirk Midthun	Triton	1992-95
77	Cory Hackett	Waterville EM	1996-99

in this one before the Comets could get on the board early in the third quarter. Cromwell's Mason Hansen scored on a two-yarder and Danny Nyberg completed the two-point conversion to put the Cardinals up 8-0 at the end of the first. Cromwell then picked off three of Hillcrest Lutheran Academy quarterback Dan Scheid's passes in the second quarter. The Comets finally tallied early in the third when Nick Hansen caught a pass from Scheid and ran it 10 yards for the TD. The Comets then got it to 28-16 when Scheid scored on a Quarterback sneak. Cromwell finally put it away in the fourth though, when Dan Olesiak rushed for two more touchdowns — ultimately finishing the day with 144 yards on the ground. In addition, Hansen also tied the record for pass interceptions in a game with three.

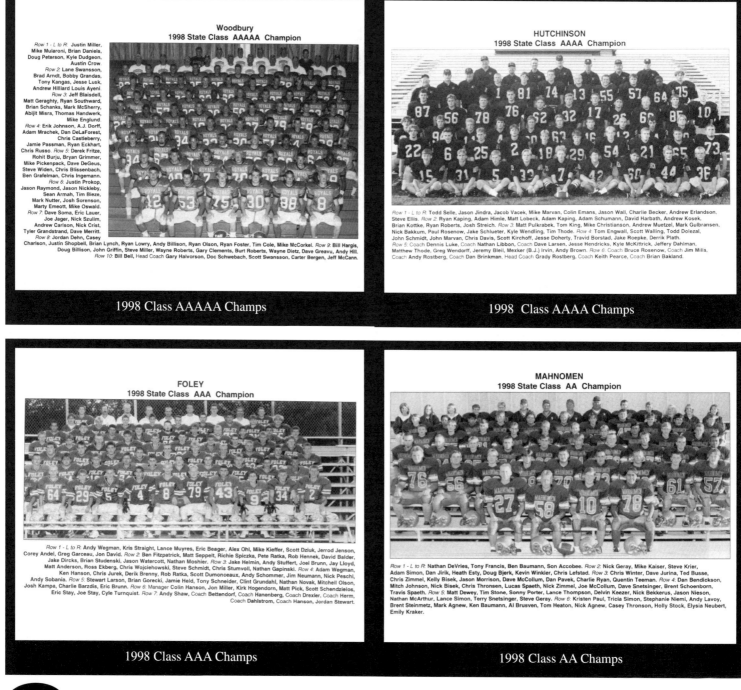

Woodbury
1998 State Class AAAAA Champion

Row 1 - L. to R: Justin Miller, Mike Mularoni, Brian Daniels, Doug Peterson, Kyle Dudgeon, Austin Crow. *Row 2:* Lane Swansson, Brad Arndt, Bobby Grandas, Tony Kangas, Jesse Lusk, Andrew Hilliard Louis Ayeni. *Row 3:* Jeff Blaisdell, Matt Geraghty, Ryan Southward, Brian Schanks, Mark McSherry, Abijit Misra, Thomas Handwerk, Mike Englund. *Row 4:* Erik Johnson, A.J. Dorff, Adam Mrachek, Dan DeLaForest, Chris Castleberry, Jamie Passman, Ryan Eckhart, Chris Russo. *Row 5:* Derek Fritze, Rohit Burju, Bryan Grimmer, Mike Pickenpack, Dave DeGeus, Steve Widen, Chris Blissenbach, Ben Grafelman, Chris Ingemann. *Row 6:* Justin Prokop, Jason Raymond, Jason Nickleby, Sean Armah, Tim Bieze, Mark Nutter, Josh Sorenson, Marty Emeott, Mike Oswald. *Row 7:* Dave Soma, Eric Lauer, Joe Jager, Nick Szulim, Andrew Carlson, Nick Crist, Tyler Grandstrand, Dave Merritt. *Row 8:* Jordan Dehn, Casey Charlson, Justin Shopbell, Brian Lynch, Ryan Lowry, Andy Billison, Ryan Olson, Ryan Foster, Tim Cole, Mike McCorkel. *Row 9:* Bill Hargis, Doug Billison, John Griffin, Steve Miller, Wayne Roberts, Gary Clements, Burt Roberts, Wayne Dietz, Dave Greavu, Andy Hill. *Row 10:* Bill Bell, Head Coach Gary Halvorson, Doc Schwebach, Scott Swansson, Carter Bergen, Jeff McCann.

1998 Class AAAAA Champs

HUTCHINSON
1998 State Class AAAA Champion

Row 1 - L. to R: Todd Selle, Jason Jindra, Jacob Vacek, Mike Marvan, Colin Emans, Jason Wall, Charlie Becker, Andrew Erlandson, Steve Ellis. *Row 2:* Ryan Kaping, Adam Himle, Matt Lobeck, Adam Kaping, Adam Schumann, David Harbath, Andrew Kosek, Brian Kottke, Ryan Roberts, Josh Streich. *Row 3:* Matt Pulkrabek, Tom King, Mike Christianson, Andrew Muetzel, Mark Gulbransen, Nick Bakkum, Paul Rosenow, Jake Schlueter, Kyle Wendling, Tim Thode. *Row 4:* Tom Engwall, Scott Walling, Todd Dolezal, John Schmidt, John Marvan, Chris Davis, Scott Kirchoff, Jesse Doherty, Travid Borstad, Jake Roepke, Derrik Plath. *Row 5:* Coach Dennis Luke, Coach Nathan Libbon, Coach Dave Larsen, Jesse Hendricks, Kyle McKittrick, Jeffery Dahlman, Matthew Thode, Greg Wendorff, Jeremy Bleil, Mexker (B.J.) Irvin, Andy Brown. *Row 6:* Coach Bruce Rosenow, Coach Jim Mills, Coach Andy Rostberg, Coach Dan Brinkman, Head Coach Grady Rostberg, Coach Keith Pearce, Coach Brian Bakland.

1998 Class AAAA Champs

FOLEY
1998 State Class AAA Champion

Row 1 - L. to R: Andy Wegman, Kris Straight, Lance Muyres, Eric Beager, Alex Ohl, Mike Kieffer, Scott Dziuk, Jerrod Jenson, Corey Andel, Greg Garceau, Jon David. *Row 2:* Ben Fitzpatrick, Matt Seppelt, Richie Spiczka, Pete Ratka, Rob Hennek, David Balder, Jake Dircks, Brian Studenski, Jason Watercott, Nathan Moshier. *Row 3:* Jake Helmin, Andy Stuffert, Joel Brunn, Jay Lloyd, Matt Anderson, Ross Ekberg, Chris Wojciehowski, Steve Schmidt, Chris Stumvoll, Nathan Gapinski. *Row 4:* Adam Wegman, Ken Hanson, Chris Jurek, Derik Brenny, Rob Ratka, Scott Dumonceaux, Andy Schommer, Jim Neumann, Nick Peschl, Andy Sobania. *Row 5:* Stewart Larson, Brian Gorecki, Jamie Held, Tony Schneider, Clint Grundahl, Nathan Novak, Mitchell Olson, Josh Kampa, Charlie Barzdis, Eric Brunn. *Row 6:* Manager Colin Hanson, Jon Miller, Kirk Hogendorn, Matt Pick, Scott Schendzielos, Eric Stay, Joe Stay, Cyle Turnquist. *Row 7:* Andy Shaw, Coach Bettendorf, Coach Hanenberg, Coach Drexler, Coach Herm, Coach Dahlstrom, Coach Hanson, Jordan Stewart.

1998 Class AAA Champs

MAHNOMEN
1998 State Class AA Champion

Row 1 - L. to R: Nathan DeVries, Tony Francis, Ben Baumann, Son Accobee. *Row 2:* Nick Geray, Mike Kaiser, Steve Krier, Adam Simon, Dan Jirik, Heath Esty, Doug Bjerk, Kevin Winkler, Chris Lefstad. *Row 3:* Chris Winter, Dave Jurina, Ted Busse, Chris Zimmel, Kelly Bisek, Jason Morrison, Dave McCollum, Dan Pavek, Charlie Ryan, Quentin Teeman. *Row 4:* Dan Bendickson, Mitch Johnson, Nick Bisek, Chris Thronsen, Lucas Spaeth, Nick Zimmel, Joe McCollum, Dave Snetsinger, Brent Schoenborn, Travis Spaeth. *Row 5:* Matt Dewey, Tim Stone, Sonny Porter, Lance Thompson, Delvin Keezer, Nick Bekkerus, Jason Nieson, Nathan McArthur, Lance Simon, Terry Snetsinger, Steve Geray. *Row 6:* Kristen Paul, Tricia Simon, Stephanie Niemi, Andy Lavoy, Brent Steinmetz, Mark Agnew, Ken Baumann, Al Brusven, Tom Heaton, Nick Agnew, Casey Thronson, Holly Stock, Elysia Neubert, Emily Kraker.

1998 Class AA Champs

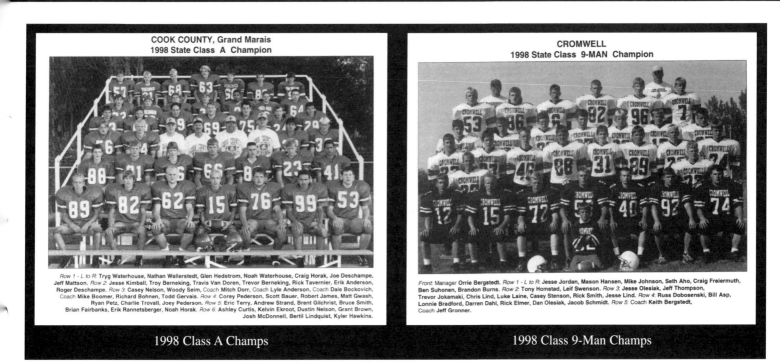

COOK COUNTY, Grand Marais
1998 State Class A Champion

CROMWELL
1998 State Class 9-MAN Champion

Row 1 - L to R: Tryg Waterhouse, Nathan Wallerstedt, Glen Hedstrom, Noah Waterhouse, Craig Horak, Joe Deschampe, Jeff Mattson. *Row 2:* Jesse Kimball, Troy Berneking, Travis Van Doren, Trevor Berneking, Rick Tavernier, Erik Anderson, Roger Deschampe. *Row 3:* Casey Nelson, Woody Seim, Coach Mitch Dorr, Coach Lyle Anderson, Coach Dale Bockovich, Coach Mike Boomer, Richard Bohnen, Todd Gervais. *Row 4:* Corey Pederson, Scott Bauer, Robert James, Matt Gwash, Ryan Petz, Charlie Trovall, Joey Pederson. *Row 5:* Eric Terry, Andrew Strand, Brent Gilchrist, Bruce Smith, Brian Fairbanks, Erik Rannetsberger, Noah Horak. *Row 6:* Ashley Curtis, Kelvin Ekroot, Dustin Nelson, Grant Brown, Josh McDonnell, Bertil Lindquist, Kyler Hawkins.

Front: Manager Orrie Bergstedt. *Row 1 - L to R:* Jesse Jordan, Mason Hansen, Mike Johnson, Seth Aho, Craig Freiermuth, Ben Suhonen, Brandon Burns. *Row 2:* Tony Homstad, Leif Swenson. *Row 3:* Jesse Olesiak, Jeff Thompson, Trevor Jokamaki, Chris Lind, Luke Laine, Casey Stenson, Rick Smith, Jesse Lind. *Row 4:* Russ Dobosenski, Bill Asp, Lonnie Bradford, Darren Dahl, Rick Elmer, Dan Olesiak, Jacob Schmidt. *Row 5:* Coach Keith Bergstedt, Coach Jeff Gronner.

1998 Class A Champs

1998 Class 9-Man Champs

1999: PREP BOWL XVIII

Cretin, led by the amazing performances of Receiver Walter Bowser and Quarterback Joe Mauer, went on to beat Hastings, 42-21, in the Class 5-A final. Mauer completed 15 of 22 passes for 306 yards and tossed four touchdowns, while Bowser had six catches for 164 yards and three touchdowns in helping the Raiders win their first state title in football. Cretin took a 7-0 lead in the game's opening series when Kim Sarin scored on a 7-yard run. The Raiders then made it 14-0 when Marcus Freeman scooped up a Dan Voigt fumble in the Hastings backfield and took it 24 yards for the score. Hastings came back to tie it though, first with Quarterback Greg Begnaud's 65-yard TD, followed by a Prep Bowl record 99-yard, six-play drive that ended with Voigt finding the end-zone to make it 14-apiece in the second. Cretin then exploded for three touchdowns in the final two minutes of the half, capitalizing on three Hastings turnovers, to jump out to a 35-14 half-time lead. After a Rob Reiling interception, Mauer hit Sarin on a 56-yard TD for the first one, followed by a pair of 70 and 10 yard touchdown bombs from Mauer to Bowser to complete the surge. Then in the fourth, Mauer and Bowser hooked up yet again, this time on an 18-yard scoring strike to put it out of reach. Josh McLay added one with under a minute to go for Hastings, but by then this one was over. (Incidentally, Joe Mauer also starred for the USA as a catcher in the 2000 World Junior Baseball Championships, and will be a sure No. 1 major league draft pick as well.)

Mankato West beat Cambridge-Isanti, 35-28, in the state 4-A championships, thanks to the efforts of Chris Boyer, who ran for 200 yards and three TDs. The Scarlets got on the board first in this one, thanks to Boyer's first score of the day — a one yard plunge to make it 7-0. Cambridge rallied to tie it on Greg Ziebarth's four yard touchdown at 3:49 of the first. Mankato then went ahead 21-7 on Jay Nessler's seven yard run up the middle, followed by Boyer's second score of the day which was also a seven yarder. The Bluejackets rallied behind fullback Jeff Lenzen's one yarder, only to see Scarlet's wide receiver Calen Wilson return a punt 93-yards down the left sideline for the score. Down but not out, Cambridge came back with a pair of touchdowns from Preston Treichel and Ziebarth to tie it at the end of three. Both teams battled in the fourth, but Boyer's third short TD of the day proved to be the difference as the Scarlet's defense hung on to preserve the 35-28 victory.

The Class 3-A title game featured the state's premier player, De La Salle's Dominique Sims. Sims, a quarterback and safety, had an interception, ran for 106 yards and a pair of touchdowns, had 47 receiving yards and passed for another 31 yards, en route to leading his Islanders to a 28-7 victory over St. Michael-Albertville. After a scoreless first, Sims made it 7-0 on his first TD of the afternoon, a one-yard plunge over the middle. From there the Islanders just kept on rolling, thanks toRunning Back Rod Malone, who scored a pair of 43 and 10-yard touchdowns in the second and third quarters. Sims then added another one-yarder midway through the fourth to all but seal the deal. Shane McLaughlin made sure his team didn't get shut-out by catching a meaningless 13-yard TD pass from Derek Brant with under a minute to go for good measure. (Incidentally, three stars from De La Salle's team went on to play Division One football that next Fall. Sims, who, after being recruited by most every major college in the country, opted to play ball for the Golden Gophers. Derreck Robinson chose to attend Iowa while running back/linebacker Jarod Newberry went to Stanford.)

The undefeated Waterville E-M Buccaneers spanked West Central Area, 34-0, to capture the 2-A crown. Quarterback Cory Hackett was the real deal in this game, scoring a pair of rushing touchdowns while throwing for three more. Two of them, a couple of 21-yarders, went to Wide Receiver Jesse Appel, while the third found Gabe Hauer for a 76-yard bomb. The Buccaneers defense was also a huge factor, virtually shutting down the Knights offense throughout the better part of the game.

The undefeated Cook County Vikings proved to once again be the team of destiny at Prep Bowl XVIII, hanging on to beat LeCenter, 14-6. The LeCenter Wildcats got on the board first in this one, when Eric Closser hauled in a 23 yard touchdown pass from quarterback Andy Schmidt at 6:57 of the first. The Vikings rallied to take a 7-6 lead though, when Erik Anderson scored over the middle on a one yard plunge. The defense hung tough from there on out, as the Vikes added some insurance late in the fourth when Woody Seim caught a 24-yard touchdown strike from Anderson at the 11:11 mark to seal the deal.

A very impressive 12-0 Stephen-Argyle Central team started out strong and hung on down the stretch to beat Nicollet by the final score of 18-8 to win the 9-Man title. The Storm drew first blood in this contest courtesy of running back Brett Stoltman's three yard burst around the end at the 5:03 mark of the first. Quarterback Andy Aarke then made it 12-0 when he scored from two yards out early in the second. Midway through the third Aarke increased his team's lead to 18-0 when he found Reece Setterholm on a 37-yard slant pass over the middle. The Raiders tried to mount a rally late in the fourth when Nate Wenner capped off a nice drive by catching a seven-yard pass from Ryan Hulke at the 9:26 mark. But in the end it was too little too late, as the Storm persevered to take the 18-8 victory.

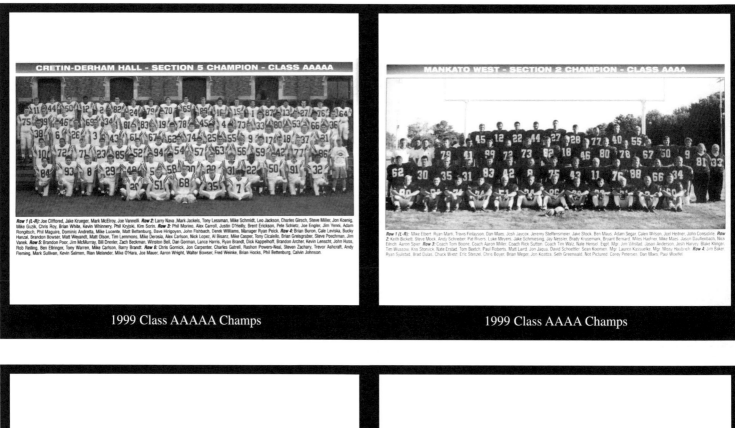

CRETIN-DERHAM HALL - SECTION 5 CHAMPION - CLASS AAAAA

Row 1 (L-R): Joe Clifford, Jake Krueger, Mark McElroy, Joe Vannelli. Row 2: Larry Nava, Mark Jackels, Tony Lessman, Mike Schmidt, Leo Jackson, Charles Girsch, Steve Miller, Jon Koenig, Mike Guzik, Chris Roy, Brian White, Kevin Whinnery, Phil Kryjski, Kim Sorin. Row 3: Phil Morino, Alex Carroll, Justin O'Reilly, Brent Erickson, Pete Schletz, Joe Engler, Jim Yenni, Adam Rongitsch, Phil Maguire, Dominic Andretta, Mike Lucente, Matt Bettenburg, Dave Hirigoyen, John Fishbach, Derek Williams, Manager Ryan Peick. Row 4: Brian Buron, Cale Leviska, Bucky Hanzal, Brandon Bowser, Matt Weyandt, Matt Olson, Tim Lemmons, Mike Derosia, Alex Carlson, Nick Lopez, Al Bisanz, Mike Casper, Tony Dicalello, Brian Greisgraber, Steve Poechman, Jim Vanek. Row 5: Brandon Poor, Jim McMurray, Bill Drexler, Zach Beckman, Winston Bell, Dan German, Lance Harris, Ryan Brandt, Dick Kappelhoff, Brandon Archer, Kevin Lenscht, John Huss, Rob Reiling, Ben Eltringer, Tony Warren, Mike Carlson, Barry Brandt. Row 6: Chris Gornick, Jon Carpenter, Charles Gatrell, Rashon Powers-Neal, Steven Zachary, Trevor Ashcraft, Andy Fleming, Mark Sullivan, Kevin Salmen, Rian Melander, Mike O'Hara, Joe Mauer, Aaron Wright, Walter Bowser, Fred Weinke, Brian Hocks, Phil Bettenburg, Calvin Johnson.

MANKATO WEST - SECTION 2 CHAMPION - CLASS AAAA

Row 1 (L-R): Mike Elbert, Ryan Marti, Travis Finlayson, Dan Maes, Josh Jaycox, Jeremy Steffensmeier, Jake Stock, Ben Maus, Adam Segar, Calen Wilson, Joel Hedner, John Considine. Row 2: Keith Bickett, Steve Mock, Andy Schreiber, Pat Rivers, Luke Meyers, Jake Schmiesing, Jay Nessler, Brady Krusemark, Bryant Bernard, Miles Haefner, Mike Maes, Jason Dauffenbach, Nick Eirich, Aaron Spier. Row 3: Coach Tom Boone, Coach Aaron Miller, Coach Rick Sutton, Coach Tim Walz, Nate Hensel, Eqpt. Mgr. Jim Vifnstad, Jason Anderson, Josh Harvey, Blake Klinger, Tim Wussow, Kris Storvick, Nate Erstad, Tom Beetch, Paul Roberts, Matt Laird, Jon Jagua, David Schoettler, Sean Koomen, Mgr. Lauren Kassuelke, Mgr. Missy Haubrich. Row 4: Jim Baker, Ryan Sjolstad, Brad Dulas, Chuck West, Eric Stenzel, Chris Boyer, Brian Meger, Jon Kozitza, Seth Greenwald. Not Pictured: Corey Petersen, Dan Maes, Paul Woelfel.

1999 Class AAAAA Champs

1999 Class AAAA Champs

DeLaSALLE, MINNEAPOLIS - SECTION 4 CHAMPION - CLASS AAA

Row 1 (L-R): Sam Erickson, Arthur Gardner, Jeff Kaczmarczyk, Mitch Nelson, Raymond Jones, Matt Mahmoodi, Brian Morris, Rod Malone. Row 2: Cheo Smith, Kellen Reeves, Nick Thomas, Lucas Kaster, Jared Newberry, Derreck Robinson, Dominique Sims, Justin Baylor, Kris Miller, Mandla Nkiwane. Row 3: Coach Nick Grue, Brian Carruthers, Nathan Witt, Justin Lentz, Andy Schneider, Josh Fors, Zach Babington-Johnson, Chris Connery, Lansine Toure, Water Girl Jessica Holton. Row 4: Coach Zac Lerner, Isaac Stone, Kyle McLean, Tommie Hill, Aaron Robinson, C.J. Hallman, Brian Moore, Tyler Pivec, Ryan Virden, Andy Aubert, Coach Ben Williamson. Row 5: Head Coach Tony Johnson, Joe Zierden, Santino Craven, Brad Amelsberg, Alan Anderson, Cory Huggar, David Coyle, Jay Lambert, Matt Horejsi, Coach Ray Holton. Not pictured: Justin Soderberg, Marcu Whitlock, Robin Bell, Natan Rayman, Philip Baebenroth.

WATERVILLE-ELYSIAN-MORRISTOWN - SECTION 2 CHAMPION - CLASS AA

Photo caption not available.

1999 Class AAA Champs

1999 Class AA Champs

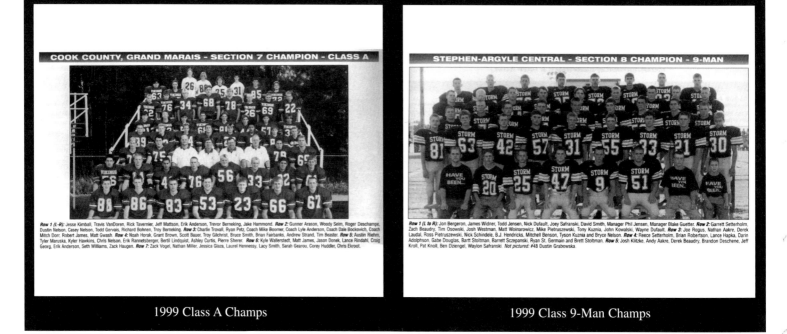

COOK COUNTY, GRAND MARAIS - SECTION 7 CHAMPION - CLASS A

Row 1 (L-R): Jesse Kimball, Travis VanDoren, Rick Tavernier, Jeff Mattson, Erik Anderson, Trevor Berneking, Jake Hammond. Row 2: Gunner Arason, Woody Selim, Roger Deschampe, Dustin Nelson, Casey Nelson, Todd Gervais, Richard Bohnen, Troy Berneking. Row 3: Charlie Trovall, Ryan Petz, Coach Mike Boomer, Coach Lyle Anderson, Coach Dale Bockovich, Coach Mitch Dorr, Robert James, Matt Gwash. Row 4: Noah Horak, Grant Brown, Scott Bauer, Troy Gilchrist, Bruce Smith, Brian Fairbanks, Andrew Strand, Tim Beaster. Row 5: Austin Riehm, Tyler Maruska, Kyler Hawkins, Chris Nelson, Erik Rannetsberger, Bertil Lindquist, Ashley Curtis, Pierre Sherer. Row 6: Kyle Wallerstedt, Matt James, Jason Donek, Lance Rindahl, Craig Georg, Erik Anderson, Seth Williams, Zack Haugen. Row 7: Zack Vogel, Nathan Miller, Jessica Glaza, Laurel Hennessy, Lacy Smith, Sarah Gearou, Corey Huddler, Chris Ekroot.

STEPHEN-ARGYLE CENTRAL - SECTION 8 CHAMPION - 9-MAN

Row 1 (L to R): Jon Bergeron, James Widner, Todd Jensen, Nick Dufault, Joey Safranski, David Smith, Manager Phil Jensen, Manager Blake Guetter. Row 2: Garrett Setterholm, Zach Beaudry, Tim Osowski, Josh Westman, Matt Woinarowicz, Mike Pietruszewski, Tony Kuzmia, John Kowalski, Wayne Dufault. Row 3: Joe Rogus, Nathan Aakre, Derek Laudal, Ross Pietruszewski, Nick Schindele, B.J. Hendricks, Mitchell Benson, Tyson Kuznia and Bryce Nelson. Row 4: Reece Setterholm, Brian Robertson, Lance Hapka, Darin Adolphson, Gabe Douglas, Bartt Stoltman, Barrett Sczepanski, Ryan St. Germain and Brett Stoltman. Row 5: Josh Klitzke, Andy Aakre, Derek Beaudry, Brandon Deschene, Jeff Kroll, Pat Knoll, Ben Dziengel, Waylon Safranski. Not pictured: #48 Dustin Grabowska.

1999 Class A Champs

1999 Class 9-Man Champs

184

The State of the State:

The future of Minnesota high school football looks brighter than ever. The numbers are up and the quality of play is too. More and more kids are getting opportunities to play college football at both the Division I as well as at Division II and III levels today. The tournament has come a long way since the first playoffs back in 1972. That year the paid attendance for all playoff games was $39,751 while in 1999, nearly $110,000 in revenue was generated during the playoffs leading up to Prep Bowl XVIII. Numbers-wise there is another interesting trend. In 1980 there were 495 high school football teams in Minnesota, with nearly 23,000 kids playing the sport. In 1998 there were just 384 teams — with the difference being that in 1998, the number of kids playing the game skyrocketed all the way to 32,000. (Much of the reason for this decline in team numbers was due to school consolidation in small communities.)

Additionally, in 1980 the average team size was 45 players per roster, while in 1998 that number jumped to 84 (with J.V.'s). Another interesting phenomenon occurred in 1997, when an additional 6,500 kids signed up to play high school football in Minnesota. The reason why? Probably because the Vikings made the playoffs and started to show signs of promise, and the Gophers looked like they were finally ready to turn the corner. Kids see this and want to be a part of it. Football has done a good job of marketing itself to kids, and it is surely no coincidence that the Major League Baseball strike around that time also influenced a lot of them to try something new. All in all the state of the state of high school football in Minnesota is good, and will only get better. For all of the folks that hate the Dome, they sure do love it come November when they can watch all six playoff games in one day and under one roof. Oh yeah, and in a balmy 70 degree temperature too!

Most Career Coaching Victories (200-Win Club Through 1999)

Wins	Losses	Ties	Coach	School	Years	Games Coached
296	63	6	George Larson	Cambridge	38	365
285	69	2	George Thole-R	Stillwater	31	356
281	62	2	Ken Baumann	Mahnomen	30	345
277	89	2	Grady Rostberg- R	Hutchinson	34	368
265	122	11	George Smith- R	Mahtomedi	43	398
259	102	9	Les Dreschel	R. L. Falls/Crookston	40	370
256	94	8	Tom Mahoney- R	Fairmont	38	358
252	105	3	Jim Roforth	Osakis	39	360
248	117	5	Ron Stolski	Brainerd	37	370
247	119	3	Buzz Rummrill- R	Glencoe/Silver Lake	36	369
242	91	13	John Hansen-R	Osseo	37	346
236	79	0	Gerhard Meidt- R	Rothsay/Minneota	32	315
233	73	3	Mike Mahlen	Verndale	31	309
232	70	2	Neal Holland	Chokio-Alberta	30	304
224	87	0	Dane Nigon	Totino Grace	28	311
223	99	2	Stuart Nordquist	International Falls	33	324
223	91	1	Jim Simser	Fairmont/New Richland	31	315
217	121	1	Don Stueve-R	Fergus Falls	37	339
216	130	6	Billy Beck-R	Lac Qui Parle Valley	39	352
214	95	1	Jerry Wallskog	LeCenter/(BDRSH)	32	310
213	63	0	Clark Bergloff	Mora	26	276
212	83	8	Ken "Red" Wilson	Bemidji	34	303
209	107	1	Roger Lipelt-R	Wayzata	34	317
203	102	2	DeWayne Johnson	Anoka	30	307
203	66	1	Stav Canakes	Edina	27	270
202	106	13	Bruce Frank-R	Le Sueur	37	321
201	85	0	Ron Johnson	Clearbrook/Gonvick	30	286
200	120	2	Con Natvig	Swanville	33	322
200	89	0	Ken Mauer-R	St. Paul Harding	32	289

R= Retired

Individual Record for Receptions in a Career

No.	Player	School	Year
189	Paul Martin	Elk River	1996-99
174	Cary Miller	Minneota	1982-84
155	Tim Busch	Triton	1991-94
141	Rob LaRue	Minnetonka	1994-96
128	Kyle Loven	Swanville	1983-84

Individual Record for Receiving Yards in a Career

Yards	Player	School	Year
3009	Paul Martin	Elk River	1996-99
2694	Tim Busch	Triton	1991-94
2311	Kyle Loven	Swanville	1983-84
2250	Gabe Hauer	Waterville EM	1997-99
2152	Rob LaRue	Minnetonka	1994-96

Individual Record for Receiving TDs in a Career

No.	Player	School	Year
35	Joel Hassert	Minneota	1988-90
31	Paul Martin	Elk River	1996-99
31	Gabe Hauer	Waterville EM	1997-99
30	Mike Kicher	Verndale	1995-97
26	Tim Stegner	Minneota	1985-87

Individual Record for All-Purpose Yards in a Career
(Rushing, Passing, Receiving & Returns)

Yards	Player	School	Year
8334	Kirk Midthun	Triton	1992-95
6892	Matt Konz	Adrian	1996-99
5964	Frank Burdick	Mahnomen	1984-87
5953	Todd Linaman	Southland	1981-83
5888	Brian Metz	Adrian	1995-98

Individual Record for Most Points Scored in a Career

No.	Player	School	Year
492	Stacey Beyer	Hoffman/Kensington	1986-88
491	Brian Metz	Adrian	1995-98
474	Rick Meyer	Granite Falls	1984-87
451	Jason Miller	Mahnomen	1988-91
75	Jeff Frey	Lake Benton	1972-74

Individual Record for Rushing in a Career

Yards	Player	School	Year
5395	Jason Miller	Mahnomen	1988-91
5336	Brad Loeffler	St. Clair	1986-69
5086	Mike Baird	Winsted Holy Trinity	1994-97
5081	Steve Rosin	Nicollet	1990-93
4742	Stacey Beyer	Hoffman/Kensington	1986-88

Individual Football Record for
Most yards gained Rushing in a Single Game

Yards	Player	School	Year	Opponent
461	Brian Day	Brainerd	1996	St. Cloud Apollo
431	Bill Barrett	Harmony	1966	Wykoff
419	Tim Weninger	Simley	1975	Farmington
409	David Price	Braham	1997	Hinkley-Finlaysan
385	Thomas Tapeh	St. Paul Johnson	1997	Highland Park

Individual Record for Rushing TDs in a Career

No.	Player	School	Year
82	Stacey Beyer	Hoffman/Kensington	1986-88
81	Brad Loeffler	St. Clair	1986-69
77	Rick Meyer	Granite Falls	1984-87
75	Jeff Frey	Lake Benton	1972-74
71	Blaise Larson	Red Lake Falls	1993-95

MOST STATE CHAMPIONSHIPS

No.	School	Years	Class
6	Mahnomen	1980, 90, 91, 92, 93, 98	B, C, C, C, C, 2A
5	Burnsville	1972, 80, 85, 89, 91	A, AA, AA, AA, AA
4	Gaylord	1972, 73, 75, 79	C, C, B, B
4	BOLD/Bird Is./LL	1979, 80, 90, 91	C, C, B, B
4	Stillwater	1975,82.84, 95	AA, AA, AA, AA
3	New Prague	1973, 74, 85	B, B, A
3	Detroit Lakes	1992, 93, 95	A, A, A
3	Granite Falls	1977, 84, 87	B, B, B
3	Minneota	1986, 87, 88	C, C, C
3	Chattfield	1994, 95, 96	C, C, C
3	Cromwell	1995, 98, 98	9M, 9M, 9M
3	Hutchinson	1983, 84, 98	A, A, 4A
3	Cook County	1997, 98, 99	C, 1A, 1A

(Note: Before the playoff system began in 1972 several news publications designated teams as "state champion." For example, Austin was so designated in 1947, 50, 51, and 61.)

Northern Minnesota Football Champions

(*As Selected by Bemidji Pioneer Sports Editor, Jim Carrington)

Year Team	Record	3-A—2A—A	9-MAN
1962 - Bemidji	8-0		
1963 - Moorhead	8-0		
1964 - St. Cloud Tech	8-0		
1965 - Bemidji	8-0		
1966 - Moorhead	7-1		
1967 - Cloquet	9-0		
1968 - Moorhead	8-1		
1969 - Moorhead	7-0		
1970 - Duluth Morgan Park	9-0		
1971 - Moorhead	10-0		
1972 - Moorhead	10-0		
1973 - Eveleth	8-1		
1974 - Duluth Denfeld	9-1		
1975 - Hibbing	10-0		
1976 - Cloquet	10-0		
1977 - Fergus Falls	8-1		
1978 - Hibbing	9-1		
1979 - Duluth Denfeld	8-2		
1980 - Crookston	10-0		
1981 - Moorhead	10-2		
1982 - Duluth Denfeld	8-2		
1983 - Park Rapids	12-1	1983 - Mahnomen	x
1984 - Park Rapids	11-1	1984 - Mahnomen	1984 - NCW
1985 - Moorhead & Little Falls	10-3 / 9-3	1985 - Mahnomen	1985 - NCW
1986 - Moorhead	9-3	1986 - Esko	1986 - Argyle
1987 - Moorhead	14-0	1987 - Ely	1987 - Verndale
1988 - Moorhead	10-2	1988 - Deer River	1988 - Hallock
1989 - Moorhead	9-3	1989 - Mahnomen	1989 - Albrook
1990 - Brainerd	11-2	1990 - Mahnomen	1990 - Argyle
1991 - Brainerd	9-2	1991 - Mahnomen	1991 - Goodridge/Grygla
1992 - Detroit Lakes	13-0	1992 - Mahnomen	1992 - Stephen
1993 - Detroit Lakes	13-0	1993 - Mahnomen	1993 - Cherry
1994 - Alexandria	13-1	1994 - Red Lake Falls	1994 - Kittson Central
1995 - Detroit Lakes	14-0	1995 - Hawley	1995 - Cromwell
1996 - Detroit Lakes	13-0	1996 - Hawley	1996 - Cromwell
1997 - Detroit Lakes	11-0	1997 - Pelican Rapids	1997 - Verndale
1998 - Alexandria	11-1	1998 - Mahnomen	1998 - Cromwell
1999 - Alexandria	11-1	1999 - Cook County	1999 - Stephen- Argyle

Year	Class	Champions	Runners-Up	Score
1972	Class	Champions	Runners-Up	Score
	AA	Mpls. Washburn	Moorhead	26-6
	A	Burnsville	Sauk Centre	46-19
	B	Mountain Iron	Dassel-Cokato	54-6
	C	Garylord	Preston	26-6
	9-Man	Rothsay	Cotton	64-12
1973	Class	Champions	Runners-Up	Score
	AA	Rochester- JM	St. Paul Harding	25-0
	A	Eveleth	Willmar	28-18
	B	New Prague	Appleton	13-7
	C	Garylord	Holdingford	29-6
	9-Man	Lake Benton	Brandon	50-12
1974	Class	Champions	Runners-Up	Score
	AA	Rochester JM	Bloom. Jefferson	41-19
	A	Alexandria	Chaska	26-7
	B	New Prague	Caledonia	41-12
	C	Battle Lake	Bird Island	34-26 (2 OT)
	9-Man	Lake Benton	Fisher	36-6
1975	Class	Champions	Runners-Up	Score
	AA	Stillwater	Richfield	20-17
	A	St. Thomas Acd.	St. Peter	21-14
	B	Gaylord	Onamia	14-13
	C	Esko	Karlstad	62-0
	9-Man	Ruthton	Audubon	42-20
1976	Class	Champions	Runners-Up	Score
	AA	White Bear Lake	Cloquet	14-36 (OT)
	A	St. Peter	Mora	56-12
	B	Caledonia	Sartell	38-7
	C	New Richland--Hartland	Bird Island	21-19
	9-Man	Deer Creek	Fergus Falls-Hillcrest Luth. Acd.	57-14
1977	Class	Champions	Runners-Up	Score
	AA	Mpls. Washburn	Stillwater	13-0
	A	Fridley Grace	Cold Spring-Rocori	36-12
	B	Granite Falls	Stewartville	44-6
	C	Battle Lake	Henderson	22-20 (OT)
	9-Man	Deer Creek	Fergus Falls-Hillcrest Luth. Acd.	20-0
1978	Class	Champions	Runners-Up	Score
	AA	Edina West	Fridley	21-0
	A	Fridley Grace	Apple Valley	17-14
	B	New Richland-Hartland	Barnesville	48-8
	C	Alden-Conger	Battle Lake	15-14
	9-Man	Hoffman	Albrook	44-28
1979	Class	Champions	Runners-Up	Score
	AA	Columbia Heights	Richfield	8-3
	A	Rochester Lourdes	Apple Valley	22-6
	B	Gaylord	Mahnomen	15-6
	C	Bird Island-LL	Harmony	34-6
	9-Man	Russell	Toivola-Meadowlands	17-14
1980	Class	Champions	Runners-Up	Score
	AA	Burnsville	Cambridge	23-6
	A	Crookston	Pipestone	32-6
	B	Mahnomen	Austin Pacelli	34-0
	C	Bird Island-Lake Lillian	Mountain Lake	20-7
	9-Man	Hoffman-Kensington	Toivola--Meadowlands	18-14
1981	Class	Champions	Runners-Up	Score
	AA	Rosemount	Moorhead	40-14
	A	St. Peter	Hermantown	18-14
	B	Holdingford	Pine Island	39-0
	C	Medford	Clarkfield	33-28
	9-Man	Argyle	Starbuck	31-19
1982	Class	Champions	Runners-Up	Score
	AA	Stillwater	Owatonna	34-27
	A	Brooklyn Center	E. Grand Forks	30-8
	B	LeCenter	Mahnomen	12-6
	C	Truman	Belgrade	16-14
	9-Man	Westbrook	Hillcrest Luth.-Fergus Falls	34-12
1983	Class	Champions	Runners-Up	Score
	AA	Coon Rapids	Bloom Jefferson	34-31
	A	Hutchinson	Park Rapids	36-14
	B	Jordan	Breckenridge	27-0
	C	Southland (Adams)	Bird Island-Lake Lillian	28-0
	9-Man	Silver Lake	Norman Cty West Climax	27-12
1984	Class	Champions	Runners-Up	Score
	AA	Stillwater	Burnsville	36-33
	A	Hutchinson	Centennial	32-7
	B	Granite Falls	Breckenridge	13-7
	C	Harmony	Glyndon-Felton	20-14
	9-Man	Norman Co. West	Silver Lake	37-20
1985	Class	Champions	Runners-Up	Score
	AA	Burnsville	Apple Valley	27-21
	A	New Prague	Mora	16-12
	B	Jackson	Mahnomen	26-20
	C	Glyndon-Felton	Zumbrota	38-14
	9-Man	Westbrook	Norman Co. West	45-18

Year	Class	Champions	Runners-Up	Score
1986	Class	Champions	Runners-Up	Score
	AA	Apple Valley	Osseo	35-6
	A	Cambridge	Stewartville	24-0
	B	Watertown-Mayer	Granite Falls	29-6
	C	Minneota	Sherburn-Dunnell	52-19
	9-Man	Argyle	Silver Lake	32-7
1987	Class	Champions	Runners-Up	Score
	AA	Moorhead	Winona	13-7
	A	Cambridge	Lakeville	28-14
	B	Granite Falls	Ely	43-20
	C	Minneota	Grand Meadow	27-7
	9-Man	Silver Lake	Verndale	30-14
1988	Class	Champions	Runners-Up	Score
	AA	Blaine	Cretin-Derham Hall	25-24
	A	Lakeville	Staples-Motley	35-28
	B	Breckenridge	Morris	21-7
	C	Minneota	Rushford	42-28
	9-Man	Hallock	Stewart	35-24
1989	Class	Champions	Runners-Up	Score
	AA	Burnsville	Stillwater	21-7
	A	Albany	Totino Grace	41-32
	B	Gibbon-Fairfax-Win.	Perham	27-15
	C	Waterville-Elysian	Mahnomen	14-7
	9-Man	St. Clair	Albrook	47-12
1990	Class	Champions	Runners-Up	Score
	AA	Anoka	Elk River	14-0
	A	Fridley	Sartell	34-12
	B	BOLD	De La Salle	15-14
	C	Mahnomen	Becker	27-7
	9-Man	Hills-Beaver Creek	Argyle	28-21
1991	Class	Champions	Runners-Up	Score
	AA	Burnsville	Lakeville	10-7
	A	Spring Lake Park	Rocori	20-0
	B	BOLD	Deer River	14-0
	C	Mahnomen	Mankato Loyola	42-0
	9-Man	Chokio-Alberta	Gyrgla/Goodridge	7-6
1992	Class	Champions	Runners-Up	Score
	AA	Lakeville	Cretin-Durham Hall	19-7
	A	Detroit Lakes	Farmington	21-0
	B	St. Cloud Cath.	BOLD	7-6
	C	Mahnomen	Mankato Loyola	20-13
	9-Man	Stephen	Cromwell	36-20
1993	Class	Champions	Runners-Up	Score
	AA	Apple Valley	Rochester J.M.	29-7
	A	Detroit Lakes	Northfield	21-14
	B	St. Cloud Cath.	Zumbrota-Mazeppa	28-6
	C	Mahnomen	Minneota	43-23
	9-Man	Chokio-Alberta	LeRoy-Ostrander	35-0
1994	Class	Champions	Runners-Up	Score
	AA	Anoka	Alexandria	34-7
	A	Sartell	Northfield	24-21
	B	Triton	Becker	40-21
	C	Chatfield	Red Lake Falls	34-14
	9-Man	Kittson Central	Verndale	36-16
1995	Class	Champions	Runners-Up	Score
	AA	Stillwater Area	Rochester Mayo	31-7
	A	Detroit Lakes	Saint Peter	30 15
	B	Kingsland, Spring Valley	Breckenridge	22-3
	C	Chatfield	Hawley	12-6
	9-Man	Cromwell	LeRoy-Ostrander	26-18
1996	Class	Champions	Runners-Up	Score
	AA	Eden Prairie	Blaine	23-22
	A	Mora	Northfield	7-3
	B	Breck School	Windom Area	24-7
	C	Chatfield	Hawley	12-7
	9-Man	Cromwell	Verndale	46-44
1997	Class	Champions	Runners-Up	Score
	5-A	Eden Prairie	Blaine	32-29
	4-A	Northfield	Detroit Lakes	28-0
	3-A	Albany	Jackson Cty Central	55-7
	2-A	Pelican Rapids	Waterville E-M	34-32
	A	Cook County	Adrian	13-12
	9-Man	Verndale	Cromwell	18 12
1998	Class	Champions	Runners-Up	Score
	5-A	Woodbury	Champlin Park	28-7
	4-A	Hutchinson	Owatonna	21-20
	3-A	Foley	Jackson Cty Central	21-7
	2-A	Mahnomen	BOLD, Olivia	27-26
	A	Cook County	Adrian	15-8
	9-Man	Cromwell	Hillcrest Luth.-Fergus Falls	40-22
1999	Class	Champions	Runners-Up	Score
	5-A	Cretin	Hastings	42-21
	4-A	Mankato West	Cambridge-Isanti	35-28
	3-A	De La Salle	St. Michael Albertville	28-7
	2-A	Waterville E-M	West Central Area	34-0
	A	Cook County	LeCenter	14-6
	9-Man	Stephen-Argyle	Nicollet	18-8

Afterword by John Randle

John Randle has become synonymous with the Minnesota Vikings. Like Alan Page, Jim Marshall, Carl Eller, and the legendary "Purple People Eaters" before him, Randle has aspired from very humble beginnings to become one of the NFL's preeminent defensive linemen. Today, the undrafted "walk-on" from tiny Texas A&I University is a seven-time Pro-Bowl starter. Did I mention that his 105 sacks over the past decade are the most in the NFL? He is also the epitome of durability and hard work, having never missed a game in his 11-year career. A tireless and tenacious competitor who constantly draws double and triple-teams, he has become a quarterback's worst nightmare. In 1998 John showed the fans of Minnesota just how much he loved it here, by turning down less money from several other teams to remain a Viking. Sure, his $32.5 million deal wasn't chump-change, in fact, it made him the highest-paid defensive player in league history, but hey, let's get real....this future Hall of Famer has been worth every penny!

Nothing has come easy for this kid, and he deeply appreciates everything he has gotten from the fans who have treated him like "family." Having grown up in a one-bedroom, tin-roofed shack — with an outhouse out back, John has a deep respect and appreciation for the game and the people who have truly changed his life. That's why the fire burns so bright in him — he knows where he came from, and will never forget how hard he has worked and sacrificed to get to where he is today.

With his trademark war-paint and intense Tasmanian Devil-like attitude out on the field, this bundle of high-octane turbo energy has become the heart and soul of the Vikings' defense. A chiseled physical specimen and world-class trash-talker to boot, there is a soft-side to this giant of a man, who, at times, is also just a big teddy bear. So, with that, who better than to talk about the "state of the state" and the next 100 years of Minnesota football, than one of the Purple's all-time fan favorites — the top dog "alpha-male," Johnny Randle.

"I am truly honored to be a part of Minnesota's amazing football tradition. I never knew about the heritage of football here, what with the Vikings, Gophers and even the old Duluth Eskimos, but now I know that it is big. Real big. I mean having come from Texas, where football is like religion, I have really come to respect the fans here, and how much they love and appreciate the game. So for me to be asked to be a part of a book about Minnesota's football history was truly an honor."

"This is a great time for football in Minnesota right now. The Vikings have been strong and will continue to only get better, and the Gophers have also turned the corner. They made it to a bowl game last season and will be very tough in the Big Ten again this year as well. It's even great to see how many people come out for the "Prep Bowl." I guess I never knew how big high school football was up here, but people really take it seriously. Now that I am a Minnesotan, I root for all of the Minnesota teams, whether it's the Vikings, Gophers, Timberwolves, Twins or even the Lynx. Hey, I even miss the North Stars! I just think that when the Minnesota teams do well, everybody in the sports world up here benefits from that. So I would love nothing better than to see everyone bring home a championship, but especially the Vikings — something that will definitely happen sooner than later."

"Overall, I think that the fans in Minnesota are special. It's a very intimate relationship that I have been lucky enough to foster with them and I really cherish that. People up here can't wait to say hello to you and come up to meet you. Whether I am pumping gas or grocery shopping, people just want to come up and shake your hand. That's unique I think. It's like everyone knows everyone here, and that is so nice to be around. Even though this is a big city, it has a small town feel to it, and that is very important to me. I grew up in a small town, so I enjoy that mentality. It's just really nice having so many great people behind us on Sundays at the Dome. It gets so loud and crazy in there and I love it. The fans really get into it and all you can see is a purple haze. Sometimes it's intoxicating being in there because it's like another world. As soon as they start playing the song "Welcome to the Jungle," when Mitch Berger kicks off, I just completely transform into another person on the football field. From that moment on, it's go-time!"

"I can honestly say that I love it here and that this will always be my second home. When I first started out here as a rookie, I couldn't wait to get out of town as soon as the season was over, but slowly I began to enjoy the winters here too. I gave it a shot, and found out that there is a lot of great stuff to do here during the off-season as well. It has grown on me, and now with golf and hunting I look forward to being up here in the outdoors as much as possible."

"If I could, I would call every Viking's fan on the phone one at a time and personally say 'thank you' for letting me come into their homes and letting me be a part of their lives. I want to thank them for taking a kid who was a million miles from home, who knew nothing about Minnesota, and took him in, put their arms around him and treated him like he was their son. Thanks for showing me what life was about, how to treat and respect people, and for making me into the man that I am today. Whether we won or lost, the fans have always treated me with such respect. Losing to Atlanta back in 1998 was such a heart-breaking time for me, and I felt responsible to the fans for letting them down. So, until I am finished playing this game, I am going to give it all I've got — not so much for me, but for them."

"When it's all said and done, I just want to be remembered as a guy who played as hard as he could on every snap and never quit. I want to be remembered as a winner, and someone who wasn't afraid to mix it up to help his teammates get to the top. With free agency today, there aren't too many guys who are able to stay with one team throughout their careers. So, I'm extremely lucky and feel very honored to have played my entire career here. To be fortunate enough to play this game, which is what I truly love, and to make a living at it is incredible — so I count my blessings every day for what I have."

"As far as the future of this team goes, I think it looks awesome. Things have changed in the league right now, and the salary cap has made for a lot more parody than in years past. Teams have shorter windows of opportunity now and they need to step up and take their shot while they can. But hey, I like what we're doing now. The offense is rock solid and I really like what we did with the defense during the off-season. Sure we lost a couple of guys to free agency, but we added some great talent and still have a tremendous football team that can win it all. Never, ever, count out the purple. This is a tremendous organization, a great football community, and I am just proud to be a part of it all. Go Purple!"

INDEX

List of Works Cited:

1. Ross Bernstein: Interviews from over 50 Minnesota sports personalities and celebrities
2. "Fifty Years • Fifty Heroes" A Celebration of Minnesota Sports, by Ross Bernstein, Mpls, MN, 1997.
3. "Frozen Memories: Celebrating a Century of Minnesota Hockey," by Ross Bernstein, Mpls, MN, 1999.
4. "Hubert H. Humphrey Metrodome Souvenir Book": compiled by Dave Mona. MSP Pub.
5. "Football Beginnings in Minnesota," By Charles H. Alden, University of Minn., Ex. '89.
6. "Gold Glory," by Richard Rainbolt, Ralph Turtinen Publishing, Minneapolis, 1972.
7. "The History of Minnesota Football," The General Alumni Assoc. of Minn., 1928.
8. "Glory days," by Mark Craig, Star Trib, Dec. 26, 1999.
9. "Remember Bronko, Bernie, Bud and Bruce?," by Jay Walljasper, Minnesota Mag, Sept. 1979.
10. "The Minnesota Huddle," by Stan Carlson, Huddle Publishing Co., Minneapolis, 1937.
11. "Fifty Years At Memorial Stadium," by Dave Shanna, Alumni News, September 1974.
12. "Big Ten Football," by Gregory Richards and Mellissa Larson, Crescent, NY, 1987.
13. Years of Gopher Football: A Decade-by-Decade Analysis," by Charles Johnson
14. Years of Golden Gopher Football," Edited by Ralph Turtinen, Published by the U of M Men's Athletic Dept., 1981.
15. Rashad, Ahmad, with Peter Bodo, Rashad: "Vikes, Mikes and Something on the Backside," Viking 1988.
16. Tarkenton, Fran, and Jim Klobucher, "Tarkenton," Harper & Row, 1976.
17. "Minnesota professional football: The Super Bowls." by Tim Klobuchar and Michael Rand, Star Tribune, January 24, 1999.
18. "The Minnesota Vikings," by Richard Rainbolt, Nodin Press, 1975.
19. "Winter was a pioneer, not a founding father," Bruce Bennett, Duluth News 7-30-96.
20. years ago, the NFL met Duluth," by Bruce Bennett, Duluth News Tribune, 9-15-96.
21. "Purple Hearts and Golden Memories," by Jim Klobuchar: Quality Sports Pubs, 1995.
22. "Ten Years of Indoor Wars - The History of Arena Football," by Sheller and Kotar.
23. "Levine extends football career with Fighting Pike," by Todd Zolecki, MN Daily, May 10, 1996.
24. "A Football Family," by Pete Mollica, Youngstown Vindicator, July/August 1998.
25. "Football Facts and Figures," by Dr. L. Baker, Rinehart & Co. Pub., New York, 1945.
26. "Family Fued: St. Thomas vs. St. John's," By Gene McGivern, St. Thomas Mag, Fall '99.
27. "A History of St. Thomas Football," by Mike E. Minor (1981), St. Thomas Media G., 1999.
28. "Augsburg Football History," by Don Stoner, SID, Augsburg, 1999.
29. "Ed Widseth, an All-America Gopher tackle, dies at 86," John Millea, Star Trib, 12-5-98.
30. "Golden Boy of the Golden Gophers," by William Johnson, Sports Ill., Dec. 19, 1991.
31. "The Legend of Bronko Nagurski," by Bob Hammel, Football Letter, 1998.
32. "A football legend," by Brian Wicker, Star Tribune, 10-24-99.
33. "Bronko Nagurski," by Bob Carroll, The Coffin Corner, Volume IV, 1982.
34. "Pro Football's All-Time Greats," by George Sullivan, Putnam Publishing, NY, 1968.
35. "Nagurski comes out of hibernation," by Sid Hartman, Star Tribune, Jan. 20, 1984.
36. Jim Souhan and Kent Youngblood, "Blocked kick hurt," Star Tribune, September 20, 1999.
37. "Pug Lund, Minnesota star halfback in '30s, reaches new goal in his 80s," by Doug Grow, Star Tribune, June 18, 1993.
38. "Joesting: NFL Redjacket Days Tough, Too," by Bob Beebe, Mpls Star, Aug. 4, 1961.
39. "Marines Triumph," Mpls Star, 10-15-23.
40. "A man of many jackets," by Jim Patterson, "The Coffin Corner," Volume XV, 1993.
41. "Marines surprise touted Racine grid stars with 13-6 victory," Mpls. Tribune, Nov. 5, 1923.
42. Jim Souhan, "A look at a long rivalry," Star Tribune, September 25, 1999.
43. "The Husky Tradition: A History of Men's Athletics at St. Cloud State," by John Kasper.
44. "Mythical Northwest Title at state at Athletic Park," Mpls. Tribune, Nov. 26, 1927.
45. "From raw talent to football greatness, the U of M changed Aaron Brown's life," by Len Levine, Sportsnews, Sept. 1994.
46. Don Banks, "Vikes show bit of '98 stardom in first quarter," Pioneer Press, October 3, 1999.
47. "A Team Named Ernie?," by Bob Carroll, "The Coffin Corner," Volume IV, 1982.
48. "This was Football," by W.W. Pudge Heffelfinger, A.S. Barnes & Co., NY, 1954.
49. "When the game had characters," by Mickey Herskowitz, Pro Magazine, July 31, 1976.
50. "Eskimos forged a lasting legacy," by Tom Larson, Duluth News-Tribune, April 1, 2000.
51. "Greatest athlete is a personal choice," by John Gilbert, Budgeteer News, Dec. 28, 1999.
52. "Lumberjacks take to the turf in search of a winning plan," Jayson Hron, Budgeteer, 1999.
53. "The Duluth Connection," by David Neft, The Coffin Corner, Volume IX, 1987.
54. "Dear Cal," The Coffin Corner, Vol. X, '88.
55. "70 Years Ago, NFL Met Duluth," Duluth News-Tribune, Sept. 15, 1996.
56. "Nevers' Eskimos start training at Two Harbors today," Duluth News Trib., 9-7-26.
57. "Pro Football's All-Time Greats," by George Sullivan, Putnam Publishing, NY, 1968.
58. "The Pro Football Chronicle," by Dan Daly and Bob O'Donnell, Collier Books, NY, 1990.
59. "Drew Pearson's catch still etched in memories," by John Millea, Star Trib., Jan. 8, 2000.
60. "Rookie Kramer shows great poise in leading comeback," Sid Hartman, StarTrib, 12-5-77.
61. "Winter sells share in Vikings," by Sid Hartman &Bob Sansevere, Star Trib, 10-14-85.
62. "Paul Krause: Defender," by Joe Zagorski, The Coffin Corner, Volume IX, 1987.
63. "Thanks you honor," by Steve Rushin, Sports Illustrated, Aug. 2000.
64. "Home Free," by Peter King, Sports Illustrated, March 2, 1998
65. "When it comes to the Vikings, there are two things you can count on happening this season," by Bob Sansevere, August 10, 2000.
66. "Vikings' fourth Super Bowl loss appears to hurt the most," by Sid Hartman, Trib, 1-10-77.
67. "True Hearts & Purple Heads," by Jim Klobuchar, Ross & Haines, Inc. Mpls., 1970.
68. "Van Predicted Win Over Bears in July," by Sid Hartman, Mpls. Trib, September 18, 1961.
69. "Grant says Chiefs are team without a weakness," by Sid Hartman, Mpls. Trib, 1-12-70.
70. "The Super Bowls," by Tim Klobuchar and Michael Rand, Star Tribune, January 24, 1999.
71. "Csonka takes it to Vikings," by Sid Hartman, Mpls. Tribune, January 14, 1974.
72. "Finks resigns from Vikings; ownership desire called reason," by Sid Hartman, Star Trib, 5/20/74.
73. "Minnesota's Vikings: The Scrambler and the Purple Gang" by Bob Rubin, Prentice Hall, Englewood Cliffs, NJ, 1973.
74. "Stalwart Gophers Rout Grange in 1924 Classic," by Fred Just, The MN Huddle, 1940.
75. "Oh, How They Played the Game," by Allison Danzig, MacMillan Pub., NY, 1971.
76. "Giants relate Tarkenton to Vikings," by Sid Hartman, Star Tribune, February 28, 1972.
77. "Grant says Chiefs are team without a weakness," by Sid Hartman, Mpls.Trib, 1-12-70.
78. "The Complete Story of the NFL," by Turner Publishing, Atlanta, 1994.
79. "The Game that Was," by Myron Cope, Thomas Y. Crowell Publishing, NY. 1974.
80. "The Pro Football Chronicle," by Dan Daly and Bob O'Donnell, Collier Books, NY, 1990.
81. "Big Ten Football," by Mervyn Hyman & Gordon White Jr., MacMillan Pub., NY, 1977.
82. "Pro Football's Great Moments," by Jack Clary, Bonanza Books, NY, 1982.
83. "Super Season: The Vikings' Unforgettable Year," by Roland Lazenby, Benchmark Press, Chicago, 1998.
84. "ESPN's Ultimate Pro Football Guide," by Baxter & Hassan, Hyperion Books, NY, 1998.
85. "The Minnesota Vikings," by Julian May, Creative Education Pub., Mankato, MN, 1980.
86. "ESPN Outtakes," by Dan Patrick, Hyperion Books, NY, 2000.
87. "Golden Gophers Sing Sad Refrain," by Sid Hartman, Minneapolis Tribune, January 3, 1961.
88. "Big Ten Football," by Gregory Richards and Mellissa Larson, Crescent Books, NY, '87.
89. "Pro Football's All-Time Greats," by George Sullivan, Putnam Publishing, NY, 1968.
90. "Joesting: NFL Redjacket Days Tough, Too," by Bob Beebe, Mpls. Star, Aug. 4, 1961.
91. "Marines Triumph," Mpls. Star, 10-15-23.
92. "Marines surprise touted Racine grid stars with 13-6 victory," Mpls Tribune, Nov. 5, 1923.
93. "Nevers' Eskimos start training workouts at Two Harbors today," Duluth News Trib., 9-7-26.
94. "When the game had characters," by Mickey Herskowitz, Pro Magazine, July 31, 1976.
95. "On the road again and again...In 117 day's during 1926-27 Duluth played 29 games — 27 away," Ralph Hickok, Sports Ill, Sept. 9, 1987.
96. "Boom Boom began razing Met long ago," by Jim Klobuchar, Star, Dec. 18, 1981.
97. "From raw talent to football greatness, the U of M changed Aaron Brown's life," by Len Levine, Sportsnews, Sept. 1994.
98. "What is the future of Gopher football?," by Sid Hartman, Mpls. Trib., Nov. 25, 1955.
99. "Pug Lund, Minn star halfback in '30s, reaches new goal in his 80s," by Doug Grow, Star Tribune, 6-18-93.
100. "A football legend," by Brian Wicker, Star Tribune, 10-24-99.
101. "The Legend of Bronko Nagurski," by Bob Hammel, Football Letter, 1998.
102. "Football Beginnings in Minnesota," by Charles H. Alden, University of Minn., Ex. '89.
103. "Football: 70's and 80s," by Nuba M. Pletcher - Chairman Emeritus - History Dept.
104. "Remember Bronko, Bernie, Bud and Bruce?," by Jay Walljasper, MN Mag, Sept. '79.
105. "Fifty Years At Memorial Stadium," by Dave Shanna, Alumni News, September 1974.
106. "Family Fued: St. Thomas vs. St. John's," By Gene McGivern, St. Thomas Mag, Fall '99.
107. "A History of St. Thomas Football," by Mike E. Minor, St. Thomas Media Guide, 1999.
108. "http://www.footballresearch.com" — Pro Football Researchers Association.
109. "Pro Football: Its Ups and Downs," by Dr. Henry March, J.B. Lyon Co. NY, 1934
110. "The Fireside Book of Pro Football," by Richard Whitingham, Fireside Pub., NY, 1989.
111. "The Other Side of the Glacier," Bud Grant.
112. "A Football Family," by Pete Mollica, Youngstown Vindicator, The Extra Point, July/August 1998.
113. "Gustavus Athletics," by Lloyd Hollingsworth, Gustavus Adolphus Press, St. Peter, MN., 1984.
114. "Carleton moves confidently into its second century," by Merrill Jarchow, 1992.
115. "Carleton: the first century," by Leal Headley and Merrill Jarchow, Carelton, 1992.
116. Tarkenton, Fran, and Jim Klobucher, "Tarkenton," Harper & Row, 1976.
117. "40 Years of State Football Recalled," by Ted Peterson, "Minn. Football Journal," 1969.
118. "Sun Burned," by Mark Craig, Star Tribune, Jan. 1, 2000.
119. "The History of Women's Professional Football," by Stuart Kantor, WPFL web-site.
120. "A grand illusion: Women's pro football players put their lives in the hands of two sports hustlers," by George Dohrmann and Jim Caple.
121. "Sid!" by Sid Hartman & Patrick Reusse - Voyager Press, 1997.
122. "Minnesota Trivia," by Laurel Winter: Rutledge Hill Press, Nashville, TN, 1990
123. "NCAA Championships": The Official National Collegiate Champs & Records, by the NCAA. 1996.
124. The Star Tribune Minnesota Sports Hall of Fame insert publication
125. "Can You Name That Team?" David Biesel
126. "Scoreboard," by Dunstan Tucker & Martin Schirber, St. John's Press, 1979.
127. "Awesome Almanac Minnesota," by Jean Blashfield, B&B Pub., Fontana, WI, 1993.
128. "The Encyclopedia of Sports," by Frank Menke, AC Barnes Pub., Cranbury, NJ, 1975.
129. "My lifetime in sports," by George Barton, Stan Carlson Pub., Minneapolis, 1957.
130. "Professional Sports Teams Histories," by Michael LaBlanc, Gale Pub., Detroit, MI, 1994.
131. "The Encyclopedia of North American Sports History," by Ralph Hickock, 1992.
132. "Minnesota State Fair: The history and heritage of 100 years," Argus Publishing, 1964.
133. "Concordia Sports - The First 100 Years" by Vernon Finn Grinaker, Concordia Website.
134. "Sports Leagues & Teams," by Mark Pollak, McFarland Pub., Jefferson, NC, 1996.
135. "Rashad," by Ahmad Rashad with Peter Bodo: Viking Press, 1988
136. "The Vikings, the First 15 Years," by Jim Klobuchar, Minn. Vikings Publications, 1975.
137. Minnesota Almanacs - (various 1970s)
138. "Season Review": ESPN Sports Almanac by Jerry Trecker, Total Sports Pubs., 1983.
139. "NFL Football" (Official Fans Guide) by Ron Smith, Collins Pub., NFL Properties, 1995.
140. "Gagliardi of St. John's": The Coach, the Man, the Legend: by Don Riley and John Gagliardi: R. Turtinen Publishing
141. "Before the Dome," by David Anderson: Nodin Press, 1993.
142. "On to Nicollet," by Stew Thornley, Nodin Press, 1988.
143. "Gopher Sketchbook," by Al Papas, Jr.: Nodin Press, 1990.
144. Tribune: Vikings article, Jan. 13, 1976.
145. Sports Illustrated, Fran Tarkenton article, Jan 5, 1976.
146. Ambassador Mag: "Leveling the Playing Field," by Curt Brown, July, 1996.
147. Minnesota Monthly Mag: "Bent but Not Broken," by Paul Levy, August 1996.
148. Star Tribune: article on Alan Page - "Mindworks" by Misti Snow, May 25, 1993.
149. Minneapolis Star: "Twice Down for Nine Count - St. John's Rallied" - Dec. 16, 1963.
150. St. Cloud Times: John Gagliardi article - Nov. 4, 1963.
151. "Gold Glory": by Richard Rainbolt: Ralph Turtinen Publishing, 1972.
152. "No Time for Losing," by Fran Tarkenton: Revell Publishing, 1967.
153. "In on a Win and a Prayer," Sports Illustrated, Jan. 5, 1976.
154. "Minnesota Vikings"- Professional Team Histories, NY Press.
155. Roland Lazenby, Super Season: The Vikings' Unforgettable Year, (Banockburn, IL, HS Media Inc., 1998).
156. John Rosengren, "Catcher on the fly," Spike Magazine, Winter 1999.
157. Jim Souhan, "Veteran Vikings may not have many more chances to be champs," Sept. 12, 1999, Star Tribune.
158. Kent Youngblood, "Lethal weapon 2," Star Tribune, September 5, 1999.
159. David Scott, "Moss hysteria," Sport Magazine, August 1999.
160. Denne H. Freeman, "Slippery Moss eludes Cowboys," State Journal Reg., Nov. 26, 1998.
161. Kent Youngblood, "Bitter loss keeps Vikings motivated," Star Trib., August 2, 1999.
162. Jim Souhan, "Healthy Moss has teammates eager to watch him," Star Trib., Aug. 23, 1999.
163. Jim Souhan, "Moss takes aim at Woodson," Star Tribune, September 16, 1999.
164. Jim Souhan, "Favre upends Vikings 23-20," Star Tribune, September 27, 1999..
165. Associated Press, "Moss is MVP in NFC's Pro Bowl victory," February 7, 2000.
166. Jim Souhan, "Moss more concerned with winning," Star Tribune, October 18, 1999.
167. Jim Souhan, "Moss vs. Sanders: a treat to behold," Star Tribune, November 5, 1999.
168. Don Banks, "George, Moss lead way back from special-team mistakes," Pioneer Press, Dec. 21, 1999.
169. Jim Souhan, "Vikings hurdle Lions 24-17," Star Tribune, January 3, 2000.
170. MSHSL Media Guides (various 1950-2000)
171. Minnesota Vikings Media Guides (various)
172. 191.University of Minnesota Men's Athletics Media Guides (various 1900-2000)
173. Media Guides: Bemidji State, Moorhead State, UM-Duluth, Minnesota State, Mankato, St. Cloud State, Augsburg, Bethel, Carlton, Concordia, Hamline, Macalester, St. John's, St. Mary's, St. Olaf, St. Thomas, Southwest State and other related media guides and web-sites.
173. Various MSFCA Yearbooks from 1960-99.